A New History of Kentucky

This book was published with generous support from
James Graham Brown Foundation
Mary and Barry Bingham, Sr., Fund
The Filson Club Historical Society
and
The National Endowment for the Humanities

A New History of Kentucky

Lowell H. Harrison and James C. Klotter

Copyright © 1997 by The University Press of Kentucky

Scholarly publisher for the Commonwealth, serving Bellarmine College, Berea College, Centre College of Kentucky, Eastern Kentucky University, The Filson Club Historical Society, Georgetown College, Kentucky Historical Society, Kentucky State University, Morehead State University, Murray State University, Northern Kentucky University, Transylvania University, University of Kentucky, University of Louisville, and Western Kentucky University.

Editorial and Sales Offices: The University Press of Kentucky
663 South Limestone Street, Lexington, Kentucky 40508-4008

02 01 00 99 98 97 6 5 4 3 2 1

Library of Congress Cataloging-in-Publication Data

Harrison, Lowell Hayes, 1922-
    A new history of Kentucky / Lowell H. Harrison and James C. Klotter.
      p. cm.
    Includes bibliographical references and index.
    ISBN 0-8131-2008-X (cloth : alk. paper)
    1. Kentucky—History.   I. Klotter, James C.   II. Title.
F451.H315   1997
976.9—dc20   96-35904

To Thomas D. Clark

Contents

Illustrations

Tables

Preface

Kentucky has a rich history. The goal of this book is to present that history in a clear and comprehensive fashion so readers can discover how Kentuckians lived throughout recorded time. Undertaking such a task is a challenge, for the resulting story is one of change and complexity, of continuity and the commonplace; there are many stories to be told, each one important.

Readers of a history of the commonwealth must understand that the state has been many things to many people at different times in its past. It was the First West, the initial state west of the mountains; it was a border state between the North and South and was represented with a star in the flags of both the Confederate States and the United States; it was a place whose residents came to think of themselves as southern—with a few exceptions—and it is usually included in that region when divisions are made. In short, Kentucky blends many parts of the American experience, and studying its history helps us to understand the heritage of the United States.

Yet states are different, and only in understanding those differences can a national history be fashioned. For citizens in the Commonwealth of Kentucky, an awareness of the lives of the people of the past and of the actions they took is crucial to knowing the influences that affect the state even yet. What Kentucky is results from what the state has been. Without an understanding of the state's past, present-day actions cannot be accurately judged. Moreover, by comprehending the actions of people of different times and backgrounds, modern-day citizens can better know those around them in the present. Looking through the glasses of history offers clearer images, and, ultimately, better understanding, of the people of the state, region, nation, and world.

Presenting the history of one state is a difficult task, for such an account should not only be readable but should also cover all the relevant historical points. It should show internal interactions and external relationships. Some will read such histories for the story, some for reference, some for understanding. All those audiences must be addressed. A history of the state must also cover all parts of the commonwealth and all of its people—not just the great and near-great but also the often voiceless and forgotten. It is their story too. Such accounts should be broad-based as well, focusing not only on the more traditional government-and-politics approach but also on the environment and conservation, economic history (agriculture, business, transportation, labor), social structures and life, ethnicity, education, religion, social reforms, literature and the arts, agrarianism and urbanization, and, simply, the mind and spirit of Kentucky. Groups whose history has been more ignored in previous works, particularly women and blacks, must receive recognition in any new historical account. Those who inhabit the various regions of the state must have their history told as well, so that the work is not predominantly that of one geographic area. The fact that many major resource collections and the chief newspapers are in one region, and that other areas have often not had their past told carefully in historical works, makes that regional bias harder to overcome, but all the state's people must have their place on the pages of history.

To tell the state's story, each author has taken a portion of that past in which he has specialized and written on it. Lowell H. Harrison prepared the section covering the period to 1865 (chapters 1-14), while James C. Klotter wrote the material addressing the state's history since 1865 (chapters 15-25). Both depended heavily on those who have written interpretative accounts before, and the Acknowledgments section herein only recognizes a few of those to whom a great debt is owed. But the authors have also used the words of people living at the times they are exploring, the contemporary expressions, the primary sources, whether in letters, diaries, newspapers, interviews, or other forms. Readers who wish to learn more about some aspect of the state's past should return to those sources of yesteryear to understand the forces at work in each era. Much of the state's history remains unwritten, and many people and events await historical interpretation as future writers revise history.

This, then, is the story of how one state's people over the ages loved and hated, how they failed and triumphed, how they acted and reacted, how they lived and died. It is an account of both noble and ignoble actions, of heroes and fools, of courage and cowardice. It is Kentucky's story.

A New History of Kentucky

Part I

Kentucky before 1820

1

A Place Called Kentucke

A Newfound Paradise

"What a buzzel is amongst people about Kentucke?" inquired a minister in 1775. "To hear people speak of it one would think that it was a new found paradise." When words failed Lewis Craig as he tried to describe the beauty of heaven during a sermon, he exclaimed that "it is a mere Kentucky of a place." Despite the dangers of the trip to Kentucky and the uncertainty of life once there, men, women, and children poured westward to populate the virgin land. A gentleman making a leisurely overland trip in 1792 reported passing 221 Kentucky-bound zealots in a day's ride of thirty miles: "They seemed absolutely infatuated by something like the old crusading spirit to the holy land." Another observer also noted the crusading spirit of the migrants. "Ask these Pilgrims what they expect when they git to Kentucke. The Answer is land. Have you any? No, but I expect I can get it. Have you anything to pay for land? No. Did you Ever see the Country? No, but Every Body says it is good land."

According to explorers, the land teemed with game waiting to be killed, the clear streams were filled with delectable fish eager to be caught, and the countless turkeys and other fowls longed to be eaten. Charles Scott (1739-1813), a future governor of the state, returned from his first visit to Kentucky with glowing descriptions of great forests. The trees, he said, were eight to fifteen feet in diameter, and they grew so close together that a man could barely squeeze between them. When he told of a giant elk whose horns measured ten feet from tip to tip, a skeptic asked how the elk got through the forests. "That was their business and not mine," Scott replied, unabashed. He persisted in touting the marvels of the new land, to which he soon moved. Once in Kentucky he continued to be amazed by its wonders. During corn plant-ing time he stuck his walking stick in the ground and forgot to retrieve it. At harvest, he reported, every stalk of corn in the field had two ears, and even the walking stick had a nubbin growing at the top.

Such tales of fertility were not un-common. When pioneer C.L. Rootes tried to persuade an eastern friend to join him in Ken-tucky, he asserted that "female Animals of every sort are very profilick, it[']s frequent for ewes to bear 3 lambs at a time, & women and cows to have Twins at a time."

The exact meaning of the word *Kentucky* is not known. The term may have been a Wyan-dot word meaning "land of tomorrow" or an Iroquoian word that could be translated as "place of meadows." It does not mean "dark and bloody ground." That legend probably came from remarks made by Cherokee chiefs Dragging Canoe and Oconostota at Syca-more Shoals when Richard Henderson bought what rights the Cherokee had to a large part of Kentucky. "There is a dark cloud over that Country," Dragging Canoe reportedly warned, and Oconostota said to Daniel Boone as they parted, "Brother, we have given you a fine land, but I believe you will have much trouble set-tling it." Both chiefs spoke truly, as the next twenty years of Kentucky's history testified.

The Kentuckians Called Indians

The first European explorers in the seventeenth and early eighteenth centuries found some Indians living in the area that would become known as Kentucke. Evidence remained at the time to indicate that more Indians had lived there at an earlier period. Especially interest-ing were the large mounds, often located in areas where Indians were no longer living. Eu-ropeans often assumed that the construction of such structures was beyond the abilities of the Indians with whom they came in contact, and

they concluded that a white-based civilization had once existed in Kentucky. Speculation dif-fered concerning its origin. Were these people the lost tribes of Israel? Prince Murdoc and his Welsh followers? survivors of lost Atlantis? What had happened to the vanished people?

Since the development of the study of archaeology, more has been learned about the people who enjoyed the beauties of Kentucky long before Europeans arrived. Scientists have generally agreed that the misnamed Indians of North and South America descended from northwestern Asians who crossed a land bridge between Siberia and Alaska some eleven to twelve thousand years ago, then spread across the two continents of the Western Hemisphere. But recent discoveries of sites on both conti-nents that can be reliably dated twelve to fifteen thousand years ago have raised doubts about that chronology. Nomadic tribes could hardly have spread over such great distances in a pe-riod of a few centuries, and some archaeologists now suggest that the initial immigration may have occurred as long ago as thirty to fifty thou-sand years. *Indian* is obviously a misnomer, but *Native American* is as well. The Indians were also immigrants; they just arrived long before the Europeans did.

Archaeologists now divide Kentucky's settlement by humans into five broad eras. The Paleo-Indian period extends from about 10,500 B.C. to 8000 B.C., and the dates may well be pushed back into the past as more is learned about the first comers. Humans at the time lived just south of the great glaciers in a climate that was cooler than Kentucky has ex-perienced in modern times. These early settlers were hunters and gatherers. Game was available to them that would later be exterminated, and they gathered edible items from plants and trees; it is unlikely that they cultivated crops. They probably lived in small nomadic groups that could range over a broad area in search of food. They made well-crafted flint weapons.

During the Archaic period (ca. 8000 B.C. to 1000 B.C.), Indian life became more com-

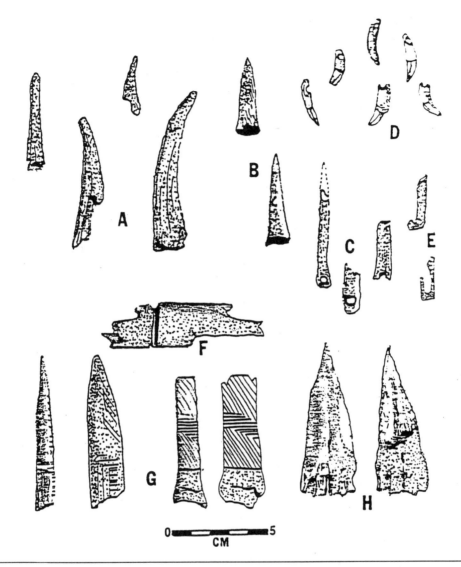

Bone and antler artifacts from the Paleo-Indian and Archaic periods from a site in southern Jefferson County; a, antler tine flakers; b, antler projectile points; c, bone needles; d, drilled canid canines; e, bone fishhooks; f, cut antler; g, engraved bone implements; h, bone condyular awls or beams (courtesy of Dr. Joseph E. Granger)

plex. Hunting continued to be vital for survival, but people placed more emphasis on the gathering of food from wild plants and nut-bearing trees. Toward the end of the Archaic period a form of squash may have been cultivated, and dogs had been domesticated. Excavations of camp sites show that considerable trade occurred over great distances. Kentucky sites have revealed copper from the Great Lakes region and shell from the Gulf of Mexico. Stone weapons were improved during the Archaic period, but the bow and arrow was still unknown. Conditions improved, and the population grew slowly.

The Woodland period, extending from about 1000 B.C. to A.D. 1000, saw the development of a more complex society. The economy was still based on hunting and gathering, but agriculture gradually became more important, although plants that were cultivated still consisted largely of squash, gourds, and native weed plants such as sunflowers. Weapons and tools became more sophisticated, and the development of ceramics led to pottery. The dominant Woodland culture in the Ohio Valley above present-day Louisville and in the Bluegrass and northern Kentucky areas was called the Adena. Beginning around 450 B.C. these people began to construct burial mounds, some of them quite large, as well as extensive earthworks enclosing ceremonial areas. Both sexes were buried in the gradually growing mounds, but priority was probably given to the chiefs and others who held the highest social status in the culture. The size and number of the mounds amazed the European explorers and settlers and validated Indian claims to longtime occupation of the region. Rituals concerning death became increasingly complex during the Woodland period, demonstrating a concern for the afterlife.

The Late Prehistoric era (A. D. 1000 to 1750) was an eventful time in the story of the people who inhabited Kentucky. Corn was introduced, perhaps from South America via Mexico, around the beginning of this era, and it soon became the ideal wilderness crop, easy to raise, gather, and store. Beans were also introduced from Mexico, and the hoe became a common tool. The introduction of corn, beans, and other crops increased the demand for arable land, and villages were more likely to become permanent than in previous eras. Tribes and chieftains became more significant, and the people often built stockades for protection. Hunting continued to be important, with deer as the main source of meat, and the use of practical bows and arrows made hunting easier. A Mississippian culture developed in western Kentucky and the surrounding area, while a Fort Ancient culture dominated in the eastern portion of what became Kentucky. While the two cultures displayed a number of similarities,

the temple mounds and chiefs' houses common in the Mississippian culture were lacking in the Fort Ancient.

The most striking and far-reaching change in the Late Prehistoric period occurred with the first contacts between the people of the interior and the Europeans who had founded colonies along the Atlantic coast. The European impact drastically and permanently altered the cultural patterns of the Indians. An increasingly complex society that in many respects was still in the Stone Age was unable to compete successfully with the technology and luxuries of European civilization that enterprising traders brought to the Ohio Valley. European diseases proved deadly to the forest dwellers, who had no immunity against them. By 1750 the Indian population had declined sharply, partly because of deadly epidemics, partly because of numerous wars as the cultures clashed. The Shawnee, who struggled with the Kentucky settlers more than any other tribe, probably numbered no more than three or four thousand by 1750. Pushed by the aggressive Iroquois, the Shawnee had moved over much of the southeastern United States before the first permanent white settlements were established in Kentucky.

Both the Indians and the Europeans prized the Kentucky land. A clash over its ownership was inevitable, for the two parties differed widely on the way it should be used. The European colonists believed in individual ownership, complete with legal documents testifying to that status, and in fences that would define their ownership and warn off intruders. The Indians viewed the land as being held in common and used for the good of all. They were horrified and alarmed when the pioneers claimed individual ownership and began to build cabins, erect fences, and plow the land. If the whites were successful, the traditional communal use of the land would be gone forever.

Treaties did not have the same meaning to the two parties either. To the Indian, having permission to use a territory was not the same as possessing it. In the 1768 Treaty of Fort

This mound in Montgomery County was approximately 9.5 meters high and 55 meters in diameter before excavation in the 1930s. It was a distinguishing feature of the Adena area of the Woodland period (William S. Webb Museum of Anthropology).

Stanwix the Six Nations agreed that the Ohio River from Fort Pitt to the Tennessee River would be a part of their boundary. As the whites interpreted this agreement, the treaty meant that the Indian title to Kentucky had been extinguished except for the area west of the Tennessee River. That belief was not shared by several tribes. The Cherokee made several treaties, notably the Treaty of Hard Labor (1768) and the Treaty of Lochaber (1770), which pushed the boundary of Virginia westward to the Kentucky River and southward to Pound Gap. Some of the Kentucky land had been sold twice.

The Late Prehistoric era was eventful for people who inhabited the Kentucky region. The last known Indian town in Kentucky, Eskippakithiki in present-day Clark County, had a population that reached a peak of eight hundred to one thousand. The town was protected by a stout stockade some two hundred yards in diameter, and it was surrounded by thirty-five hundred acres of land that had been cleared for crops before trader John Findley visited the Shawnee stronghold in 1752. For reasons that remain obscure, the town was abandoned soon afterward. When European explorers and then pioneers began to appear in greater numbers, the area that became Kentucky had no permanent Indian settlements, with one or two possible minor exceptions. A number of tribes continued to use the land, however, sometimes setting up hunting camps that might remain fixed for months at a time, sometimes hunting in the area for shorter periods, sometimes wag-

ing tribal warfare, sometimes using the land as a passageway between northern and southern tribes. The early white settlers encountered members of at least a dozen tribes, but the ones that gave the most resistance to the settlement of Kentucky were the Shawnee from north of the Ohio River, the Cherokee from the southeast, and the Chickasaw from the southwest.

The Algonquian-speaking ancestors of the Shawnee had apparently lived in Kentucky, usually in villages of a few hundred inhabitants, for a considerable period. After being pushed out of Kentucky about 1690 as a result of the Iroquois fur wars, the Shawnee moved to the Pennsylvania area. They came back to the Ohio Valley region toward the midpoint of the eighteenth century, but their claims to Kentucky were jeopardized by land agreements made with the whites by both the Iroquois and the Cherokee. Although the Shawnee probably numbered fewer than four thousand individuals when the white settlement of Kentucky began, they fought valiantly against the aggressive settlers. They constituted a formidable threat to the whites in Kentucky until 1795. Many a pioneer housewife cautioned a crying child, "Hush or the Shawnee will get you."

Two Women in Kentucky

Mary Draper Ingles (1732-1815) was apparently the first colonial woman to visit Kentucky, although her visit was involuntary. Seventeen-year-old Mary married William Ingles in 1749 or 1750, and the couple settled in Drapers

Meadow in Montgomery County, Virginia. In quick succession Mary gave birth to two boys, and she was again pregnant on July 8, 1755, when about two dozen Shawnee suddenly attacked the homestead. Most of the male settlers were busy with the wheat crop and did not have their guns at hand. William, unable to reach his family, escaped death or capture by hiding behind a log. The Indians took horses, household goods, Mary Ingles, her sons, and her sister-in-law. Although wounded, Mrs. Draper carried the youngest child so that Mary could carry the other boy. Mary pretended indifference to her captivity, and she won praise from the Shawnee for her cooking skills. On the third night she gave birth to a girl; the march was resumed the next morning. When pursuit did not develop, the Shawnee chose to make a leisurely twenty-nine-day trip to Indiantown at the mouth of the Scioto River. Mary's sons and sister-in-law were sent elsewhere, and Mary was adopted as a daughter of the chief.

In early autumn Mary was included in a party sent to Big Bone Lick to procure salt. Although she had to leave her baby behind, Mary decided to escape, and she persuaded an older Dutchwoman from Pennsylvania, who was also a captive, to go with her. Lightly armed and without a supply of food, the women tried to follow the Ohio River upstream. When they encountered large tributaries, they had to go upstream until they found a crossing, and then return to the Ohio. Hunger was their constant partner, and they feared the human and animal dangers of the wilderness. The Dutchwoman became partially insane and tried to kill Mary, convinced that Mary was the cause of all her troubles. Reluctantly, Mary had to slip away from her companion.

At last Mary reached the Kanawha River and followed it upstream toward her home. After forty harrowing days of hunger, danger, and terror, Mary Ingles met a man she had known for years. He did not at first recognize her. After three days of partial recovery, he took her on horseback to her home. Tormented with fear of being captured again, Mary insisted that

the family move back east of the Blue Ridge Mountains. The Dutchwoman also survived and made her way back to Pennsylvania. One of Mary's sons died in captivity, but the other was reunited with his family in 1768.

Tall, black-haired Virginia Sellards Wiley endured a similar ordeal several years later. Born in Pennsylvania about 1760, she married Thomas Wiley in 1779. In 1789 they were living in what is now Bland County, Virginia. On October 1, Tom was away when a band of eleven Indians from four tribes attacked the cabin and killed Jenny's youthful brother and three of her children. Claimed by a Shawnee chief, she was taken captive. Her baby was killed a few days later when it slowed her progress, and a son born prematurely was also killed. The Indians spent the next several months in camps in Kentucky, in present-day Carter, Lawrence, and Johnson Counties. Jenny was forced to do camp work and to plant a corn crop in the spring. Tied up when the band went on a hunt, she got her rawhide bonds wet in a rain and escaped. She reached Harmon's Station on John's Creek just ahead of her pursuers, about nine months after her capture. In 1800 Jenny and Tom brought their five children to Johnson County, where she died in 1831.

Kentucky's pioneer women faced the same dangers and hardships that the men did, although they received little of the attention lavished on some of the men. These incidents and many others proved that women could cope with the rigors of frontier life.

The Long Hunters in Kentucky

Nothing could check for long the exploration and subsequent settlement of Kentucky. Hunters were the key figures in the explorations that prepared the way for settlers. In that era of slow travel, *Long Hunters* was the general term applied to hunters who disappeared into the wilderness for an extended period to hunt deer, beaver, and other fur-bearing animals. At least one good hunting season was needed to return a profit on a trip, and many hunters stayed longer. After hunting in the area that would become Tennessee, Elisha Walden led a dozen men into Kentucky through Cumberland Gap in 1763. In June 1769 some twenty Virginia and North Carolina Long Hunters entered through Cumberland Gap. They worked their way west as far as modern Wayne County, then turned north to the Dix and Laurel Rivers. A member of the party, Abraham Bledsoe, reported one of the dangers the hunters encountered when he carved on a poplar tree: "2300 deer skins lost. Ruination by God." The party's cache of skins had fallen victim to Indians and animals. Both northern and southern Indians who used Kentucky as a favorite hunting ground saw the Long Hunters as intruders who killed just to obtain the skins and let most of the meat go to waste. The Indians ordered such violators to leave, minus their deerskins but often unharmed.

James Knox was one of the best known of these often anonymous figures. One of many Scotch-Irish frontiersmen, he came to Kentucky in 1769 with a party of Long Hunters. An adept woodsman, he led other groups in 1770 and 1771 to the largely unexplored Green River region. Knox returned east to fight in the Revolution, and afterward he came back to Kentucky to live. Held in high regard by his contemporaries, he served in the Virginia legislature in 1788 and in the Kentucky Senate from 1795 to 1800. A close friend of early settler Benjamin Logan, Knox married Logan's widow in 1805.

The large parties of Long Hunters followed a general pattern. They came through Cumberland Gap into southeastern Kentucky, then scattered to find good hunting. The actual hunting was done in small parties of not more than three or four men. As the game was killed off or scared away, these hunters had to travel greater distances. Hastily constructed half-shelters served as base camps where supplies were stored and where the skins and furs were processed for travel to markets back east. Old or disabled men might remain in camp to take care of the processing. When the catch was

all that the packhorses could carry, the men broke camp and began the return journey. Benjamin Cutbird was an exception to this pattern. In 1766 he and his party followed an obscure Indian trail through the Appalachian Mountains instead of using Cumberland Gap. Then they hunted westward along what would become the Kentucky-Tennessee boundary, all the way to the Mississippi. They carried their catch to New Orleans, where they persuaded the Spanish authorities to let them sell the skins and furs. This feat was repeated by Hancock Taylor in 1769, but anyone who attempted such a route was at considerable risk from the Spanish authorities.

Daniel Boone Is Enthralled with Kentucky

Best known of the Long Hunters was Daniel Boone (1734-1820), who became the symbol of the frontier, both for his contemporaries and for later generations. He was depicted as the "natural man," one who preferred the wilderness to the artificiality of civilization, one who had the same affinity for nature as the Indians with whom he contended. Although Boone was often praised for his Indian fighting, he told a son that he was sure of having killed just one warrior during his long career on the frontier. Yet the Boone who loved the solitude of the wilderness and enjoyed the life of a Shawnee warrior was in the employment of a large land company when he led the first settlers to Boonesborough. He speculated in land, and he frequently sought positions of trust and profit on his frontier. The paradox that was Daniel Boone reflected the paradox of the frontier itself.

On November 2, 1734, the Scotch-Irish Boone was born in Berks County, Pennsylvania, to Quaker parents. After his father, Squire Boone, moved the family to the Yadkin Valley in North Carolina in 1751 or 1752, young Daniel chose to hone his hunting skills in preference to farming. He and John Findley, Boone's senior by a dozen years, took jobs as wagon drivers with the ill-fated campaign of

Chester Harding's portrait of Daniel Boone at age eighty-five. Harding was the only artist who painted Boone from life (courtesy of The Filson Club Historical Society).

General Edward Braddock when he failed to take Fort Duquesne in 1755. Findley had been in Kentucky on a trading venture that was terminated by a French and Indian attack, and during the drivers' slow progress toward the French fort he told Boone about the beauty of Kentucky, its wealth of game, and the fertile land just waiting to be claimed. More than a decade passed before Boone was able to explore the earthly paradise that Findley had described, but Kentucky remained firmly fixed as Boone's goal.

Meanwhile Daniel courted and married Rebecca Bryan (1739-1813) in 1756. The couple moved a few miles to Sugar Tree Creek, North Carolina, where they remained for ten years except for an interval in 1758-60 when Indian attacks forced a retreat into Virginia. The scarcity of game brought about short moves toward the frontier in 1766 and 1768 and whetted Daniel's desire to see Kentucky. Becky was the quintessential frontier wife in an era when women had few rights. She apparently never learned to read or write, but she had ten children between 1757 and 1781, and during Daniel's long absences she carried much of the burden of caring for the family and doing the

essential farming. Rebecca was the solid foundation on which the family depended.

Boone made a trip to Florida in 1765, but he was not impressed with the new British possession. Two years later he, brother Squire, and a third man reached eastern Kentucky on a long hunting expedition, but he did not find there the marvelous land that John Findley had described in vivid terms. Then in early 1769 Findley, whom Boone had not seen for nearly fourteen years, appeared on his doorstep peddling household wares. Findley's gift for colorful exaggeration and his fascination for Kentucky had not diminished. On May 1, 1769, Boone, Findley, Boone's brother-in-law John Stuart (also spelled Stewart), and three men hired to do the camp work departed from the Upper Yadkin for Kentucky. Before reaching Cumberland Gap, they were surprised to find Joseph Martin and a crew of twenty men clearing land, building cabins, and planting crops at a site nearly one hundred miles beyond the last known station in Holston Valley. Martin's Station would become an important point on the road to Kentucky later followed by so many pioneers. Some supplies could be obtained there, and small parties could await the arrival of larger numbers to ensure a safer passage through the wilderness. It was also the point at which the realities of travel forced the abandonment of cherished pieces of furniture and other possessions that packhorses could not carry through Cumberland Gap.

Crossing through the Gap, Boone and his five companions made camp at Station Camp, near the future site of Irvine. While the others worked on the camp, Boone and Findley explored northward to locate the Shawnee town at which Findley had traded seventeen years earlier. The lush bluegrass they found growing there was not native to Kentucky. It may have been introduced to Kentucky by Findley and other wilderness traders, who used grass to protect their more delicate wares. From a high point (later called Pilot Knob), Daniel Boone got his first look at the rolling hills and fields of central Kentucky. The land was teeming with game, including herds of several hundred buffalo. Deerskins had a ready market in the East, and Boone, Findley, and Stuart kept the campkeepers busy preparing the skins they brought in from their hunts. For six months the piles of compressed skins grew steadily.

Then on December 23, 1769, Boone and Stuart were captured by a Shawnee hunting party led by "Captain Will," who spoke some English. The Shawnee, who had not accepted the Iroquois sale of lands south of the Ohio to the whites, had already driven off some hunters who had encroached on their favorite hunting grounds. Warned by the noise Boone and Stuart made as they were forced to lead the way to their camp, the other members of the hunting party fled. Taking the large collection of skins and the horses of the hunters, the Indians admonished their captives not to return to Kentucky. Captain Will left Boone and Stuart a few supplies to enable them to get home safely.

Furious over the loss of their skins and horses, Boone and Stuart followed the Indian trail and that night quietly recovered their horses. But they were overtaken by the Shaw-

nee the next morning when they stopped to rest their mounts, and this time they were carried off by their captors. Seven days later, when the group reached the Ohio River, Boone and Stuart escaped. Beyond Station Camp they caught up with their four companions, who had started home. When they met Squire Boone and Alexander Neeley, who were bringing out additional horses and supplies, Daniel Boone and John Stuart decided to remain. The four men shifted the camp closer to the abandoned site of the Shawnee town and resumed hunting and trapping. Stuart disappeared during the winter of 1770. Five years later a skeleton and a powder horn bearing his initials were found in a hollow tree. Neeley became discouraged and departed, but the Boone brothers remained. In the spring of 1770 Squire took their catch back east and returned with more supplies and horses; in the fall he repeated the dangerous journey. Daniel was left alone for months, but these times were among the happiest of his life. Boone enjoyed reading, and he usually had a book or two with him: *Gulliver's Travels* was a particular favorite. He loved the wilderness and felt at home in it. In 1770 some Long Hunters heard a peculiar sound. When they cautiously investigated, rifles at the ready, they found Daniel Boone lying on his back in a meadow and singing at the top of his voice for sheer joy.

The brothers started home in March 1771, their horses laden with a valuable catch of beaver pelts as well as deerskins. They were in Powell's Valley when a party of Indian warriors, probably Cherokee, overpowered them and took their horses and cargo. The Boones were allowed to depart. Despite the two trips Squire had made with their catch the previous year, the brothers had probably lost money on this long hunt. By then Daniel Boone probably knew Kentucky more thoroughly than any other white man, and he decided to take his family there as soon as possible.

When he saw how rapidly the Holston Valley was being settled, he realized that soon the rising tide of population would spill over into Kentucky. If he wanted to obtain the best land, if he wanted to enjoy Kentucky while it was still in its pristine state, he could not afford a long delay. Captain William Russell, a prominent trader, farmer, landowner, and local Virginia official, was also anxious to relocate. He would lead the party, and Boone would guide it.

In the summer of 1773 Boone, his family, and other relatives who chose to make the move said good-bye to the ones who remained behind. It was a poignant parting, for there was a strong possibility that they were separating for the last time. By mid-August the Boone party had met the Russell group at Castle's Wood. Wagons could not then pass through Cumberland Gap, and all that could be taken was loaded on packhorses. Infants and chickens, heads bobbing as the trek got under way, were loaded in baskets slung across horses' backs. The extra horses, cattle, and hogs were driven in the rear of the procession. Prepara-

tions completed, the party of some fifty persons started for Kentucky on September 25, 1773.

On October 9 a group of eight men and youths carrying additional supplies camped three miles behind Boone's party. Several miles behind them was Russell, with the remainder of the expedition. About daybreak the middle camp was attacked by nearly twenty Indians, most of whom were Delaware. Only one of the eight escaped unharmed. James Boone and Henry Russell, sons of the expedition's leaders, were wounded and then tortured until they pleaded for death. The other two parties were not molested, but after considerable discussion they decided to turn back. Some of them went all the way back to the North Carolina homes they had so recently left. Boone would not abandon his hopes of living in Kentucky, and his family retreated only to a cabin in Clinch Valley. The first effort to establish a settlement in Kentucky had failed, but the pressure for opening the region continued.

2

Exploring the Western Waters

The Early Explorations

No one can name with certainty the first man of European descent who explored in Kentucky. He may have been one of the anonymous, far-ranging French *coureurs du bois,* or one of the Jesuit priests who ventured into so many remote areas of the West. The explorations of such intrepid Frenchmen as Jacques Marquette, Louis Joliet, and René-Robert Cavelier, Sieur de La Salle, gave France a claim to much of the Ohio and Mississippi River Valleys and alerted the French government to the strategic importance of the great waterways. In 1749 Pierre-Joseph Céloron de Bienville led a sizable expedition to claim the Ohio Valley. In the Big Sandy area this force buried a number of lead plates to lay claim to the region. France wanted to connect its holdings in Canada with the port of New Orleans and the lower Louisiana settlements, and well before 1775 such French settlements as Detroit, Kaskaskia, Vincennes, and Cahokia were firmly established.

As early as 1642 the Virginia General Assembly authorized a few men to explore the West and establish a trade with the Indians they found there. But "West" then meant the region east of the mountain barrier; the time was not ripe for transmontane ventures. In 1669 the Assembly gave general permission for western exploration, and two years later Colonel Abram Woods dispatched an expedition to discover the rivers that flowed into the South Sea. Thomas Batts and Robert Fallon crossed the Blue Ridge Mountains and found the New River, which did flow westward. In 1673 James Needham led another Woods-sponsored expedition that was charged with opening direct trade with Indian tribes in the West. Young Gabriel Arthur, a member of Needham's party, was left with a friendly tribe, known as the Tomahittan, on the Hiwassee River to learn their language. During the winter of 1673-74 he crossed Kentucky with a war party that attacked the Shawnee in Ohio. Arthur was wounded and captured, but he was saved from burning by an Indian who was sympathetic to him. Arthur finally escaped, and in 1678 he surprised friends and relatives by appearing in Virginia. His accounts of both the land and the tribes who inhabited it supplied the first detailed information about Kentucky. Traders became increasingly interested in the fur and skin trade with the Indians, who were developing a desire for European goods of many kinds. Both France and Great Britain encouraged such trade, for they hoped to win the allegiance of the Indian tribes—or at least their neutrality—during the series of intercolonial wars, which lasted from 1689 to 1763.

Both generals and diplomats focused their attention on the Forks of the Ohio, one of the strategic spots in North America. In 1753 a young Virginian named George Washington was sent to warn the French away from the fort they had established at Duquesne in the disputed region. Despite such setbacks as General Edward Braddock's defeat in 1755, the British won the struggle, and in 1763 the Treaty of Paris gave Canada and all French claims east of the Mississippi, with the exception of New Orleans, to the British. Spain received the French claims to the trans-Mississippi and to the city of New Orleans. Possession of the West became a British concern, and Virginia was in the forefront of the race for westward expansion.

While the population east of the mountains slowly occupied the prime acres in the eastern portion of the Old Dominion, a surprisingly large number of explorers were expanding the knowledge of the transmontane. In 1742 John Howard led a party of five onto the western slopes of the mountains. He may have left the first record of deposits of coal, a resource that would much later become so im-

portant to the Kentucky economy. Howard and his companions went down the Kanawha River to the Ohio. They constructed a bullboat and continued in it down the Ohio and the Mississippi. Suspicious French authorities arrested them and later sent Howard and some others to France for trial. John Peter Salling escaped while in New Orleans and succeeded in making his way back to Virginia. Through their lengthy journey, Howard's party supplied considerable information about the future boundaries of Kentucky, and the group's treatment by the French revealed the determination with which a nation that owned the mouth of the Mississippi would try to monopolize the use of the great river system.

George Croghan of Pennsylvania was one of the most successful of the early traders and explorers, thanks to his ability to win the confidence of a number of western tribes and to gain concessions from them. While he focused most of his efforts north of the Ohio River, his men traded with the Indians at Eskippakithiki, near present-day Winchester. Croghan successfully secured Indian assistance, or at least neutrality, during the inconclusive King George's War (1744-48). His incomparable knowledge of the West and its inhabitants provided great assistance to such early explorers as Christopher Gist, who covered parts of northern Kentucky in 1751.

The Role of the Land Companies

On this trip Gist was an agent for the Ohio Land Company, which had been formed in 1747 by Thomas Lee. Its members included such prominent Virginians as Governor Robert Dinwiddie, Augustine Washington, George Mason, and Robert Carter. Their royal grant of two hundred thousand acres between the Monongahela and Yadkin Rivers reaffirmed the Virginia claim to that region. Gist's 1750-51 proposed trek to the Falls of the Ohio, begun in the company of a young slave, was aborted when friendly Indians reported that Indians who supported France were camped at the Falls. In 1753 Gist guided George Washington and probably saved his life during the trip to warn the French away from the Forks of the Ohio. The scout continued to be active in the French and Indian War until his untimely death from smallpox in 1759.

If the Ohio Company settled one hundred families on its grant within seven years, it would qualify for an additional three hundred thousand acres. Despite substantial investments and later expansions of its grant, the company was unable to make a solid land claim in Kentucky until 1775, when Hancock Lee did some surveying on a tract of two hundred thousand acres that the company claimed in the valley of the South Fork of the Licking River. The company had received its grant from the British government, and with the coming of the American Revolution it fell out of favor with the new Virginia state government. The Ohio Company perished in the 1790s, having accomplished little in the way of actual settlement.

The Loyal Company, also based in Virginia and chartered in 1749, sought to participate in the bonanza the West was believed to offer. Speaker of the Virginia House John Robinson, Joshua Fry, Edmund Randolph, and Jack Lewis were among the influential men who secured a grant of eight hundred thousand acres from the governor in what is now southwestern Virginia and southeastern Kentucky. To locate good sites for settlements and to promote land sales as quickly as possible, the company employed a thirty-five-year-old physician, Dr. Thomas Walker (1715-94), who had a greater interest in exploring and surveying than in the practice of his profession. Accompanied by five men, Walker left his home near Charlottesville, Virginia, on March 6, 1750. Mounted on horseback and carrying supplies on two packhorses, the small party passed through Cave Gap (later called Cumberland Gap) into Kentucky. Walker named a large river they crossed after the duke of Cumberland. The men endured severe hardships in the wilderness. They built a eight-by-twelve-foot cabin near present-day Barbourville as a base, and there they planted some corn and peach

stones. They got within a day or two of the Bluegrass, but when Walker climbed a tree he saw only more rugged terrain ahead. Thus the party failed to reach the Bluegrass, where they would have found the good land they sought. They turned eastward and finally reached home four months after their departure. The company was disappointed in the results, but Walker's detailed account of his journey supplied helpful information for those who came after him.

Walker became director of the Loyal Company in 1753 and later became its agent, a position he retained until his death in 1794. He made a number of other scouting and surveying expeditions, but he enshrined his name in Kentucky's history by running the deviant survey of the southern boundary in 1779-80; the boundary became known as Walker's Line. Most of the activities of the Loyal Company concentrated in the valleys of the Holston and Clinch Rivers.

While the Ohio and Loyal Land Companies added to the growing body of knowledge about Kentucky, neither of them attained the success envisioned by their entrepreneurial owners. Individuals and small independent parties accomplished more in exploring Kentucky and opening it to settlement than these two companies did. A surprising number of British colonists saw parts of Kentucky before the first permanent settlements were established in 1775.

Official Interest in the West

Mary Ingles's publicized ordeal as a captive of the Shawnee prompted Virginia governor Robert Dinwiddie to dispatch Major Andrew Lewis and about 340 men, including several score Cherokee warriors, against the Shawnee. The expedition encountered bad weather along the Big Sandy, supplies gave out, and men deserted. This 1756 expedition was an embarrassing failure. In 1758 the British forced the French to abandon Fort Duquesne, and Fort Pitt took its place. The 1763 Treaty of Paris later confirmed the British control of the Ohio Valley.

The results of the lengthy conflict between the British and the French renewed the interest of British colonists in the land beyond the mountains. Elimination of the French presence made settlement there less dangerous, and Virginia, as usual short of cash, had promised to pay its soldiers in land grants. The best acres east of the mountains had been claimed. The more that people heard of Kentucky, the more attractive it became. The increasing population was exerting pressure against the mountain barrier.

Colonists protested vehemently when King George III issued the Proclamation of 1763. It prohibited settlements west of the crest of the Appalachian Mountains and ordered anyone who had settled beyond this line to withdraw to the east. Private purchases of land from the Indians were declared illegal. The detested proclamation was not intended to represent permanent practice; the British government simply wanted time in which to decide on a western policy. Would the claims of Virginia and several other colonies be recognized, or would new colonies be chartered to fill the vast area to the west? Time was needed to move Indians out of the way, regardless of the land decision. Surely it would do no harm to hold up settlement west of the mountains until such issues were settled. To officials in London, the Proclamation Line made good sense.

The line and the policy looked different from Virginia. The land was Virginia's by a 1609 charter from English king James I, and it was needed at once to honor obligations to men who had fought for king and empire. The Indians could be bought off or brushed aside, and the French no longer represented a danger to settlers. The time was ripe for settlement of the West, and Kentucky was the place to begin.

Pontiac's Rebellion (1763-65) appeared to justify the Crown's position. Pontiac, an Ottawa chief, decided to roll back the British expansion into the Indian lands by striking at the British posts in the Northwest before the Redcoats had recovered from their long war with the French. Detroit held out, but the Indians captured a number of other forts. Fort Pitt was threatened, but despite heavy losses Colonel Henry Bouquet defeated the Indians at Bushy Run in early August 1763 and relieved the fort. This uprising may have delayed British expansion into Kentucky, but the victory at Bushy Run, breaking the hold of the Indians in the Upper Ohio Valley, opened one of the major routes used by immigrants to Kentucky during the next several decades.

On the Eve of Settlement

Dozens of Long Hunters, surveyors, and prospective settlers were in Kentucky during the years just before the outbreak of the American Revolution. In December 1772, with the approval of Virginia governor Lord Dunmore, Thomas Bullitt (1730-78) advertised his intention of going to Kentucky the next year to make surveys for military land warrants. When he left Pittsburgh on May 11, 1773, Bullitt had a company of more than thirty men, including James Harrod and Hubbard Taylor. Harrod, who had been in Kentucky as early as 1767, was probably Bullitt's guide. At the mouth of the Kanawha they were joined by the McAfee brothers (James, Robert, and George) and two other men. Another group of seven caught up with them, so that the party numbered forty or more. In an effort to avoid problems with the Indians, Bullitt and six others visited the Shawnee town of Chillicothe. Bullitt promised the Shawnee that Governor Dunmore would come soon to pay them for the land south of the Ohio, where the Shawnee would be welcome to continue hunting; the Indians promised not to harm the surveyors. Soon surveying was under way at such spots as Salt Lick Run (near present-day Vanceburg) and Big Bone Lick. As the group broke up, the McAfees and some others, including Hubbard Taylor and his assistants, surveyed numerous tracts, including some near the future site of Frankfort.

Bullitt led others to the Falls of the Ohio, where they did extensive surveying for a number of persons who held warrants. James Harrod may have left the party then, perhaps in the company of Hubbard Taylor. The two appear to have investigated the future site of Harrods-burg, for Harrod seemed to have that location in mind when he tried to establish a station in 1774.

By the end of the summer of 1773 the surveyors had completed most of the work they had come west to do, and they began to return home. When Bullitt and others tried to register their surveys, they encountered trouble from Colonel William Preston, the surveyor for recently created Fincastle County, which included all of Kentucky and portions of what would later be West Virginia and western Virginia. The surveyors had not met his requirements, Preston complained, but Governor Dunmore ordered him to register the Falls of the Ohio surveys in the Fincastle records. In December 1773 Dunmore authorized military warrants to be located anywhere in Virginia territory.

In the spring of 1774 Colonel Preston sent deputy John Floyd (1750-83) west with a surveying party. Floyd had the help of Hubbard Taylor and some others who had been with Bullitt the previous year. Other men joined the party on the way down the Ohio, and then some left at the mouth of the Kentucky River to go in search of Harrod, who was said to be building "a kind of Town" somewhere in the interior. Floyd took the others to the Falls of the Ohio, where they did considerable surveying. Small parties split off in different directions, and scattered surveys were made on choice tracts in northern and central Kentucky. The group had been warned of Indian unrest and dissatisfaction at the outset of the trek, and several whites were killed before the end of the summer. Dunmore, foreseeing a general Indian war, ordered that the surveyors be warned of the danger in Kentucky. William Russell sent Daniel Boone and Michael Stoner to warn the dozens of men in the western country. The messengers were to follow the Kentucky River to the Ohio, go down it to the Falls, and then return by way of the Cumberland. The surveyors had already become alarmed, and most of them were gone or were preparing to depart when Boone and Stoner arrived.

The Shawnee and other tribes north of the Ohio had become alarmed about the pressure the whites were exerting against Kentucky and other western areas. The deadly guns of the Long Hunters were killing off much of the game, and an influx of surveyors usually signaled that settlers would soon arrive. The Shawnee were especially angered because their claims to Kentucky and other parts of the Ohio Valley had been ignored in the Treaties of Hard Labor (1768) and Fort Stanwix (1768) by both the whites and the Cherokee and Iroquois, respectively. Then Governor Dunmore visited Fort Pitt and checked Pennsylvania expansion into the region by extending Virginia's authority to include it. Indians began to take action against white intruders, and the casualties increased. John Connolly, appointed the Virginia agent at Fort Pitt (now called Fort Dunmore, although the original name was restored at the time of the Revolution), was a brash administrator who made little effort to accommodate the Indians. Incidents continued to multiply. Several Indians were murdered by whites, and the tribes demanded retaliation.

Dunmore decided to break Indian power in the Upper Ohio Valley before the Indian threat became too acute. He proposed to lead a thousand men down the Ohio from Fort Dunmore into Indian territory north of the river. Andrew Lewis would bring militia down the Kanawha River from the frontier counties of Virginia and join him. Westerners who were eager to open Indian lands to settlement flocked to join the expedition. Isaac Shelby, William Russell, William Fleming, William Preston, Samuel McDowell, William Christian, James Harrod, George Rogers Clark— these were a few of the men important in Kentucky's early history who joined the expedition.

Lewis raised a force of thirteen hundred that advanced in three groups. When Lewis arrived at Point Pleasant at the mouth of the Kanawha, he was attacked by Cornstalk, the capable principal chief of the Shawnee, on October 10, 1774. The warriors, estimated at three hundred to eleven hundred—those who fought them usually selected the higher figure—waged a determined, skillful battle against the larger white army. They inflicted some two hundred casualties, but Indian losses were also heavy. The Shawnee decided to make peace rather than wage a devastating war. In the preliminary Treaty of Camp Charlotte, the Indians promised to return captives, slaves, horses, and valuable goods that they had seized and to cease hunting south of the Ohio River. As a pledge of good faith, they supplied a number of hostages. In return, the colonists were to remain south of the Ohio. Some of the Indians refused to accept these terms, and the chiefs were not always able to control the dissenters.

For the moment, however, the Indian question in the Upper Ohio Valley appeared settled. During the next two decades or more the Ohio River would become a major route for western migration. Prospective white settlers were poised to make the move to Kentucky, and permanent settlement soon began.

The Boundaries of Kentucky

Kentucky's boundaries evolved over a long period of time. The Virginia Company's revised royal charter from King James I in 1609 extended the struggling colony's boundaries to two hundred miles north and south of Old Point Comfort, inland "from Sea to Sea, West and Northwest," and one hundred miles out to sea on each coast. The kingly grant was open to various interpretations, but based on it Virginia claimed a large part of the North American continent. In 1763 the Treaty of Paris that ended the French and Indian War curtailed this generous claim. Great Britain acquired Canada, and Spain was left in possession of the territory west of the Mississippi River. The British Proclamation Line of 1763 prohibited settlements beyond the crest of the mountains, but Virginians were soon testing that line. In fact, the colonists were not quite ready to flood across the mountains to the "Western Waters." The restriction on westward settlement was ended, however, by the colonists' declaration of independence

and their subsequent victory in the Revolutionary War.

At the start of the American Revolution, Virginia extended as far west as the Mississippi River and also into a good part of the lands north of the Ohio River that became known as the Northwest Territory. In 1781, in an effort to provide the emerging Articles of Confederation government an independent source of income, Virginia joined other states with western land claims in ceding to the central government its interest in most of the Northwest Territory. Excluded was enough land near the Ohio River to provide promised grants to George Rogers Clark and the men who had accompanied him on his famous 1778-79 military expedition against the British.

When Kentucky separated from the Old Dominion and became a state on June 1, 1792, the agreement required the boundaries of the new state to remain the same as the boundaries of the District of Kentucky before separation. These boundaries, however, had been vague at several key points, and adjustments had to be made. In 1776 Virginia had set the eastern boundary. From the low-water mark on the Ohio River opposite the mouth of the Big Sandy River, the line followed the Big Sandy to its junction with Tug Fork. From there the boundary ran along Laurel Ridge of Cumberland Mountain to a spot called "seven pines and two black oaks," where it crossed the Virginia-North Carolina line. Agreement had to be reached later concerning which Tug Fork was part of the boundary line.

Establishing the southern boundary required several surveys and nearly three-quarters of a century. Walker's Line, surveyed by a joint commission in 1779-80, ran westward to the Tennessee River. This commission also indicated a point on the Mississippi River in Indian territory where the line would have reached had it been extended. Where it intersected the Tennessee River, however, the boundary was some twelve miles north of the 36°30' parallel it should have followed. In 1818 Andrew Jackson of Tennessee and Isaac Shelby of Kentucky negotiated for the United States a treaty with the Chickasaw Indians. For three hundred thousand dollars, payable over fifteen years, the Indians ceded the Jackson Purchase west of the Tennessee River to the United States. Kentucky gained approximately two thousand square miles of land. The meandering Mississippi created an unusual situation at New Madrid Bend, where a sector of Missouri separated a piece of Kentucky from the rest of the state. To augment the confusion, the Mississippi actually flowed north for a short distance. The Munsell Line divided the Jackson Purchase along the 36°30' line, from which the Walker survey had deviated.

Another survey in 1821 closed a gap left by the Walker survey. In 1830 another joint effort to establish a definite boundary left an intriguing violation in Simpson County. According to one explanation, wealthy resident Sanford Duncan was dismayed when he realized that the approaching surveyors would pass north of his home and make him a Tennessean. In an inspired moment he informed the wilderness-weary crew that food and a barrel of fine Kentucky whiskey awaited them if he remained a Kentuckian. Thirst apparently overcame professional scruples, for an irregular wedge still penetrates Tennessee at that point.

In 1859 Kentucky and Tennessee made a last effort to resolve all their boundary questions. Starting this time on the Mississippi at a point called Compromise, the surveyors worked eastward, erecting stone markers every five miles. The easternmost marker was placed a short distance south of the point where the old Wilderness Road passed through Cumberland Gap. Perhaps tired of the long controversy, both states accepted this version of the boundary, including the straying Walker survey. Kentucky thus lost considerable land that lay north of the 36°30' line.

Controversy over the Ohio River boundary lasted even longer than the dispute about Kentucky's boundary with Tennessee. Despite some disagreements at the time, the usual assumption in the early nineteenth century was that Kentucky owned the river to its low-water mark on the north bank of the river, an assumption accepted by the U.S. Supreme Court in 1820. Chief Justice John Marshall pointed out that since Virginia had ceded its claims to the lands northwest of the Ohio River, the Old Dominion had retained ownership of the river, although its use and navigation were to be "free and common to the citizens of the United States." Other states also became involved in the boundary question. Virginia and Ohio clashed in 1845 when some men who helped fugitive slaves escape from western Virginia (later West Virginia) were caught as they climbed the riverbank on the Ohio side. Which state had jurisdiction there? The controversy also affected fishing in the river, the building of bridges to span it, and the validity of a marriage performed in midstream by an Ohio justice of the peace.

Similar disagreements involved Indiana and Illinois after they became states. The most celebrated dispute hinged on the ownership of Green River Island, a tract of some two thousand acres opposite the mouth of the Green River. In 1792 the Ohio had flowed north of the island, but in time the channel had shifted southward and the island had become part of the mainland, attached to Indiana. The Supreme Court upheld Kentucky ownership in 1890 because the island had belonged to Kentucky in 1792. Various disputes continued until March 1993, when Kentucky and Illinois finally reached an agreement that Ohio and Indiana had previously accepted. The Kentucky boundary is the 1792 low-water mark on the north bank of the river, and each state holds a minimum of one hundred feet of the river from the accepted boundary line. The sudden appearance of casino riverboats escalated the stakes involved. A continuing problem is that few if any markers indicate the location of the low-water mark in 1792.

The much shorter Mississippi River boundary presented fewer problems. The British-French treaty of 1763 set the boundary at midpoint as the river ran at that time. Subse-

Kentucky Counties and Geographic Regions

quent changes in the channel were declared to have no effect. Most of the disputes over this boundary concerned the ownership of islands, notably Wolf Island in the river below Columbus. In 1871 the Supreme Court awarded the island to Kentucky; the shifting of the channel did not alter an established boundary.

The Physiographic Regions

Kentucky's configuration presents problems in providing geographic locations. How does one explain a state that has no northwest? The state has been described as a one-humped camel, as a lion with its mane in the mountains and its tail lashing the Mississippi, and as a wedge opening a way into the transmontane West. Although the area can be divided and subdivided into an endless number of regions (such as the Inner Outer Bluegrass), the most commonly accepted pattern describes the state as having five physiographic regions. These regions seldom have sharply defined boundaries, and it is often difficult to tell just where one gives way to another. Geographer P. P. Karan observed that "few if

any states have such enormous diversity within such small compass."

The Eastern Coalfield contains about 10,500 square miles and includes all or part of thirty-five counties. The easternmost portion, sometimes called the Mountain and Creek Bottom subregion, has little level land and was usually bypassed by the early settlers. Cumberland Gap, a notch nearly one thousand feet deep in Cumberland Mountain, was the early passageway into both the mountainous region and much of the Bluegrass. Rich in coal and timber, the region became known in the twentieth century for its human poverty and for the success of absentee owners and companies at draining much of the wealth from the commonwealth. This area still has diverse timber, and both hard and soft woods are intermingled. The Eastern Coalfield is bounded on the west by the Pottsville Escarpment, a high rock wall that is noted for its waterfalls, particularly the Cumberland Falls, which boasts the only moonbow in the Western Hemisphere. The Knobs, a row of conical hills sometimes listed as a separate region, comprises leftover bits of the escarpment that marks the boundary with the Bluegrass.

To many persons in and out of the state, the Bluegrass *is* Kentucky, and this idea has often annoyed or infuriated people who live in other parts of the state. Containing about eight thousand square miles, the region comprises roughly one-fifth of the state. It is often subdivided into the Inner Bluegrass, the Eden Shale Belt, and the Outer Bluegrass. Lexington is at the heart of the region. The Bluegrass extends to the Ohio River and contains nearly half the state's population as well as its highest-priced agricultural land. Dominant during the pioneering era, the region has never lost that position. While it has considerable forest land, the savannah-type topography of open plains with occasional trees is more common. The pioneer population was concentrated in this area. The early settlers found natural pastures and land that could be easily cleared for cultivation. Visitors from Daniel Boone's time to the present have marveled at the parklike appearance of the rolling hills. Early Kentucky tax laws declared that first-class land was land equal to Fayette County land; second-rate land was any that was inferior to the Fayette acres.

The Pennyroyal (or Pennyrile), named for a plant of the mint family, consists of about twelve thousand square miles. It sweeps across much of the central part of the state and encloses the Western Coalfield. The region is sometimes subdivided into three main areas: the Eastern Pennyroyal, which has the highest elevation of the three; the Central Pennyroyal, which features gently rolling karst plains with numerous caves and sinkholes, including Mammoth Cave, the world's longest known cave system; and the Clifty area, which includes the Western Pottsville Escarpment and the Dripping Springs Escarpment. These two escarpments mark the division between the Pennyroyal and the Western Coalfield. While the Green, Barren, and Rough Rivers flow through the Pennyroyal, much of the area's drainage is underground. This region has few surface streams compared with the rest of the state.

The Western Coalfield lies north of the Pennyroyal, inside its great arc, and includes all or part of twenty counties. Containing more than forty-six hundred square miles, it has become noted in the twentieth century for its strip mining of coal. It also continues to be one of the state's major agricultural regions.

The Jackson Purchase, comprising almost twenty-four hundred square miles, is nearly surrounded by major rivers. Much of the land in its eight complete counties is good bottomland. The Purchase was systematically surveyed, and thus its residents avoided many of the land disputes that plagued other parts of the state.

Kentucky pioneers were not fully aware of these major physiographic divisions, but from their arrival they distinguished among the different classes of land across the state. In the early days, most of them had the Bluegrass as their goal.

3

Settling a New Land

Harrodsburg, the First Permanent Settlement

The first permanent settlements in Kentucky date from 1775, but they represented only the faint beginnings of a massive flow of population that would make statehood possible as early as 1792. Much of the activity in Kentucky in 1775 still centered around surveyors who were preparing the way for settlers and, accompanying settlement, the endless lawsuits over land that continued well into the nineteenth century. The continued scramble for good claims involved both individuals and companies. Unlike the system common in New England, where land was surveyed and boundaries were established before settlers were allowed to occupy it, the Virginia land system allowed claims to be selected and occupied before official surveying was done. The Virginia system brought money into the state treasury quickly, but it led to many shingled (overlapping) claims, endless boundary disputes, and frequent outbursts of violence among rival claimants.

The Ohio Company sent Hancock Lee and a party of surveyors into central Kentucky in the summer of 1775 to locate a two-hundred-thousand-acre tract. Most of their work was done on the North Fork of Elkhorn Creek and the South Fork of Licking River. Leestown was laid off near the future site of Frankfort. Lee and his associates also claimed numerous acres for themselves and others for whom they held warrants. But the Loyal Company was able to block the validation of the Ohio Company claims, and the Ohio Company entries were opened to others after the passage of the land act of 1779. Some surveyors were inexperienced, and some spent little time looking for indications of previous surveys when they found good land. Claims inevitably conflicted, and within a few years much of Kentucky would be shingled with overlapping and disputed claims. The rapid growth of the legal profession owes much to this situation. Only the land in the Jackson Purchase received the systematic survey that characterized the settlement of the Northwest Territory.

Harrodsburg is credited with being Kentucky's first permanent settlement, although scattered cabins and half-camps had been built in eastern and central Kentucky well before 1775. James Harrod (ca. 1746-92) was a Pennsylvanian who saw much Indian warfare during his childhood and early youth. He matured into a slender man, an inch over six feet tall, with black hair and a black beard. He became an excellent woodsman and a crack shot. After participating in the late stages of the French and Indian War, Harrod became interested in the Illinois country. Gifted with a knack for languages, he learned French and several Indian tongues. Then he turned his attention southward and explored in Kentucky and Tennessee, where he became acquainted with Daniel Boone. Harrod was also bewitched by the charms of Kentucky, and he decided to settle there. Note specially ambitious, he found himself pushed into positions of leadership because his abilities were obvious to those who knew him.

In the spring of 1774 Harrod was elected to lead thirty-one men who had assembled at Fort Redstone, Pennsylvania, on their way to Kentucky. They descended the Ohio River in canoes, then paddled up the Kentucky River to present-day Mercer County. They went overland a few miles, and then on June 16, 1774, they began laying out Harrodsburg (originally Harrodstown) on a site Harrod had previously selected. The men surveyed and marked claims, laid off town parcels, and drew lots to establish an order for selection. Then they started constructing cabins and clearing land for a late corn crop. Harrod established a claim at Boiling

Springs, a few miles away, where he intended to live. But Lord Dunmore's War was brewing, and after some Indian attacks, the group decided to flee for their lives. Harrod and most of his settlers arrived at Point Pleasant on the evening after the battle had occurred there.

The stipulations of the postbattle treaty encouraged Harrod to return to Harrodsburg in 1775. He led a somewhat larger party of forty-two to fifty men to the cabins abandoned the previous year. As the group neared the location, they discovered that others were working in the area. The McAfee brothers and their company claimed that Harrod's group had ignored the 1773 claims marked by the McAfees, who had not returned to the site in 1774. Fortunately, most of the McAfee claims lay north of the Harrod ones, although there was some overlapping. A peaceful settlement was worked out that avoided conflict. (Later lawsuits, however, would continue for generations.) On the Kentucky frontier the most compelling claims were those that boasted the construction of cabins and the planting of corn, and in these respects the Harrod claims were superior.

Boonesborough, Boone, and Henderson

Boonesborough was another early settlement and probably the most famous one in the state, largely because of the presence of Daniel Boone. When it was founded, Boone was in the employment of Judge Richard Henderson and the Transylvania Company. Henderson (1735-85) was born in Virginia, but his family moved to North Carolina when he was a child. As a young man he read law, was admitted to the bar, and in 1768-73 served as an associate justice of the colony's superior court. Able and ambitious, Henderson suffered financial losses during the Regulators' Rebellion in 1770-71, and he turned his attention to the West, where he thought he might recoup his losses. Henderson dreamed of an empire, not merely a big estate, and for such a project he needed more money than he had. He started with a group called Henderson and Company, but on

August 27, 1774, he enlarged it into the Louisa Company, backed by such investors as Thomas and Nathaniel Hart and John Williams. As Henderson's plans developed, the company was again reorganized and enlarged on January 6, 1775, into the Transylvania Company. Although other attempts to secure a royal charter for a western colony had failed, Henderson believed that he could succeed. Ignoring Virginia and North Carolina laws that prohibited the purchase of Indian land by private individuals and disregarding as well the Proclamation of 1763, he opened talks with some Cherokee chiefs about buying a vast tract from them. Since the Shawnee had renounced claims south of the Ohio, the Cherokee appeared to offer Henderson the best chance to claim the land he wanted by purchase. He envisioned an area south of the Ohio River, west of the Kanawha, and north of the Tennessee.

Henderson may have had some earlier connections with Daniel Boone; he may, for example, have extended credit to Boone in return for information about Kentucky. Their first recorded contact, however, resulted from Henderson's persistent efforts to collect on debts owed by Boone. In the spring of 1770 he had a warrant issued for Boone's arrest for nonpayment. But Henderson and his associates knew Boone's reputation, and when they needed an experienced frontiersman who knew Kentucky, they employed him. After Henderson and Nathaniel Hart reached a preliminary agreement with some Cherokee chiefs to purchase Indian land for ten thousand pounds' worth of trade goods, Boone spent part of the 1774-75 winter urging the Indians to attend a meeting to ratify the decision at Sycamore Shoals, on the Watagua River in what is now eastern Tennessee. Boone was to help with the negotiations and to assist in determining boundaries. Then he was to mark a road into Kentucky and fortify a site for the company's initial settlement. In return, he was to receive two thousand acres of prime land from the Transylvania Company. The men Boone recruited for the job were to receive ten pounds each for a month or so of hard and

probably dangerous work, and they would be among the first to get a chance to select good land. Several of his recruits were well known to Boone: Michael Stoner, William Bush, and David Gass had hunted with him. Young William Hays married fourteen-year-old Susannah Boone in early March 1775, just before Daniel rode off to Sycamore Shoals. As usual Boone was in debt, and an annoyed creditor got an order for his arrest. The sheriff wrote across the back of the warrant: "Gone to Kentucky." A number of future Kentuckians had a similar economic motive for going west.

Extensive and expensive preparations had been made to feed the thousand or more Cherokee Indians who assembled at the Shoals while Henderson and his associates bargained with Little Carpenter, Dragging Canoe, Oconostota, and the other chiefs. Boone was consulted frequently, for he probably knew Kentucky better than any man there, red or white. Disagreements flared up among the Indians, although most of them acknowledged that they had no valid claim to the land they were selling. In reality, the company was getting a quitclaim to territory that it had no right to purchase and the Indians had no right to sell. Dissatisfaction later increased among the Indians, when they discovered how little came to each individual from what had seemed to be a mountain of trade goods. Dragging Canoe foresaw the relentless advance of the land-hungry whites, and he argued that the Indians should never give up claims to any land west of the mountains. He is reputed to have warned Henderson that the land south of the Kentucky River was a "bloody ground" that "would be dark and difficult to settle."

Henderson modified his original request and accepted somewhat vague boundaries for a broad area bounded by the Cumberland, Kentucky, and Ohio Rivers as well as for a passageway through the southwestern Virginia mountains to Cumberland Gap.

Before the Treaty of Sycamore Shoals was signed on March 17, 1775, Boone had departed to begin his difficult task of opening a road into Kentucky. He had thirty to thirty-five men, and Susannah, the recent bride, and a slave woman went along to do the cooking. They, and not Rebecca Boone and some of her other daughters, were the first women at Boonesborough. Boone selected the route to be followed and did much of the hunting for the party. The men managed to improve the Warriors' Path so that wagons might, with some difficulty, travel it until they reached Cumberland Gap. At that point they had to admit that construction of even a rough road was beyond their resources. Through the Gap and farther west, they strove to clear a trail that packhorses could use. They sometimes followed buffalo trails as Boone sought the easiest route through difficult terrain. The men hacked their way through dead brush and heavy stands of cane, and at last on March 22 they could see the rolling land that was their goal. Their spirits soared. The end was in sight.

On April 1 Boone wrote Henderson a letter and sent it by a special messenger. Just before daybreak on March 25 Indians had fired on the camp, mortally wounding Captain William Twetty, killing his slave Sam, and seriously wounding Felix Walker. Three days later the Indians attacked an isolated hunting party and killed and scalped two men. Boone had called in all the detached parties; they were to meet at the mouth of Otter Creek. Boone wrote that his party would start for Otter Creek at once, and he would construct a fort there. "My advice to you Sir, is, to come or send as soon as possible. Your company is desired greatly, for the people are very uneasy, but are willing to stay and venture their lives with you, and now is the time to flusterate the intentions of the Indians, and keep the country whilst we are in it. If we give way to them now, it will ever be the case." Some of the men panicked and departed for the settlements they had left. Others hastily built a log shelter in which Walker began to recover and Twetty died. Boone took a few men and cut a trace to the site on the south bank of the Kentucky River that he had selected for their settlement.

Henderson's larger party was at Martin's Station when Boone's letter was delivered on April 7. In addition to forty laden packhorses, Henderson had several wagons loaded with food, ammunition, seed corn, garden seeds, and merchandise to meet frontier needs. A sizable herd of horses and cattle had been driven behind the procession. Wagons could go no farther, and much of their loads had to be stored at the station; the packhorses' loads were redistributed. Boone's news sent some of Henderson's party scurrying for the safety of the settlements. Henderson pushed the others into an advance. He was not about to abandon his dream of building an empire in the West. On the way Henderson met others fleeing from the dangers in Kentucky; he feared that he might meet Boone and the rest of his party at any turn of the trail. Henderson's prospects depended upon Boone's ability to hold out until help arrived. Henderson's tearful pleas and the promise of ten thousand acres of company land persuaded Captain William Cocke to make a dangerous solitary ride to let Boone know that help was coming. When Cocke arrived on April 14, Boone immediately sent Michael Stoner to guide the Henderson party to Fort Boone. They arrived on April 20, to find a calm camp. Another man had been killed on April 4, but since then the Indians had vanished. Henderson acknowledged his debt to Boone: "It was owing to Boone's confidence in us, and the people's in him, that a stand was even attempted." In his joy Henderson promised Boone five thousand prime acres. The name of Fort Boone was changed to Boonesborough.

Boone had selected a spot on a floodplain by the river near a good spring, just downstream from the mouth of Otter Creek. Henderson moved the location up to a meadow that was less likely to be flooded, and he drew plans for a large rectangular fort with two-story blockhouses at each corner. Each of the long sides would contain a central gate and eight cabins, whose outer walls would form the stockade. The two short sides would each have five cabins; the outer walls of these cabins would

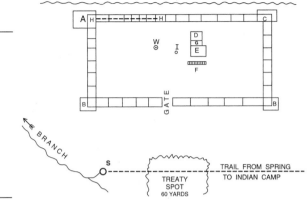

KENTUCKY RIVER BANK

Sketch of Boonesborough by
Moses Boone, son of Squire
Boone. A, Henderson's Kitchen;
B, two-story bastion; C, Phelp's
house; D, Squire Boone's house;
F, ball battery; G, Boone's gun
shop; H, ditch or countermine;
I, flagstaff; W, well; S, sulphur
spring and fresh water (courtesy
of Neal O. Hammon)

make up most of the short walls. Boone agreed to construct the fort, but he had little success in getting men to work on it. The road contract had expired, and the men were eager to locate their land, start clearing it, plant some crops, and build their own cabins. Some of the men even refused to stand their turns on guard duty, and Boone failed to get a militia company organized. The Indians seemed to have vanished, and no further danger was anticipated. Henderson wrote that he almost wished that the Indians would do his enterprise a favor: if they scalped a man a week, the others would keep working.

A food shortage soon developed, a common situation at early stations. When Boone's party arrived, the area had an abundance of game, including hundreds of buffalo, an animal many of the men had never seen. Hunting was indiscriminate and wasteful, with only the choice cuts of meat being used. Hunters soon found that the game had been killed or frightened away. They had to go fifteen or twenty miles to find meat, and such long ventures left them more exposed to Indian attacks. The packhorses could bring in only limited supplies of food, and as early as April 25 William Calk wrote: "This day we Begin to live with out Bread." The supply of salt was soon nearly exhausted. Men labored to clear ground and plant crops, but at best it would be months before a harvest could be expected. Disappointed at

their first taste of Paradise, men left the settlement until no more than twenty remained. Eighty had been there after Henderson's party arrived.

On June 13 Daniel Boone left, taking with him some young men, to get the salt that had been stored at Martin's Station. Boone was committed to living in Kentucky, and he returned to the settlements to bring his family and other recruits to Boonesborough. He was accompanied part way by Richard Callaway (1722-80), who was on a similar mission. Callaway had joined the Henderson enterprise about the time Boone did, and he had been responsible for getting the trade goods to Sycamore Shoals. His Virginia family enjoyed an economic and social position well above that of the Boones, and Callaway was twelve years older than Boone and held a higher militia rank. It irked him to be under Boone's command on the road-building job, and he would welcome an opportunity to remove Boone from his position of trust.

When Boone reached Clinch Valley, Rebecca was in the ninth month of a difficult pregnancy. The child was not delivered until late July, and young William soon died. Rebecca could not travel for several weeks, but the young men who had come for the salt refused to return to Boonesborough without their leader. While waiting for his wife to recover, Boone recruited a number of single men to go west with him, but only three families were in the party when it started for Kentucky in mid-August. About half of these recruits, including the families, turned off the trail and went to Harrodsburg. Boone, his family, and the riflemen reached an anxious Henderson on September 8. Later that month Callaway brought in several dozen settlers, including his own and three other families. Squire Boone followed with his family and some unattached men, and the population of Boonesborough regained the numbers it had had in the spring. With Boone's return, Henderson was free to hurry back to North Carolina to try to deal with the company's complex affairs.

Benjamin Logan and St. Asaph

Another of the leading early settlers was Benjamin Logan (1743-1802), who was born in Orange County, Virginia. Logan had little formal education, but he became adept in forest lore, and even as a young man he displayed leadership qualities. He bought land in the Holston region, and in 1772 he married Ann Montgomery. In his frontier location Logan came in contact with many of the Long Hunters, and he also caught the Kentucky fever. He went to Kentucky in the spring of 1775. Records do not indicate clearly whether he went part way with Henderson's party on its way to Boone's assistance or whether he made the trip with John Floyd's party. Floyd, a deputy surveyor of Fincastle County, had worked in Kentucky (then a part of far-flung Fincastle) in 1774 and was returning with a party of thirty men. In either case, Logan did not join the people at Boonesborough. If he was with Henderson, legend has it that they quarreled at Hazel Patch and Logan turned aside to establish his own station at St. Asaph, named by a Welshman to honor the date of the canonization of a Welsh monk.

Floyd was the first leader at St. Asaph, but he was often away on surveying duties. Logan's leadership abilities were so evident that he was soon recognized as the settlement's leader, and the locale was usually called Logan's Station

or Logan's Fort. Logan was an imposing figure: just over six feet tall, he weighed nearly 180 pounds, and he was very strong. Usually quiet and prudent, Logan was one of the best rough-and-tumble fighters in Kentucky. Some people who disagreed with him thought that he was arbitrary and overbearing, but most thought that Logan's way was usually the best way.

Life in the Forts

In the years between the founding of the first settlements in Kentucky and the battle of Fallen Timbers, fought in 1794 near present-day Toledo, Ohio, effectively ending the Indian danger in Kentucky, numerous stations sprang up, as immigrants poured into the region. One modern study located 187 stations in an area of the Bluegrass now comprising twelve counties, and that count probably underrepresents the extent of settlement. Of course, all of these stations were not constructed on the scale of Boonesborough or Harrodsburg. A station was a defensible residential structure designed to protect its occupants from Indian attacks. A fortified one-family cabin could qualify as a station, but two or more families commonly lived in close proximity for mutual defense. Their homes might simply be sited so that they could provide covering fire for each other, or their cabins might be connected by a stockade. Such stations were often hastily constructed and were vacated as soon as possible.

Forts, much less numerous than the stations, were normally much larger and better prepared for defense, with blockhouses and stockades. A well-constructed fort, defended with determination, was almost impregnable to arrows and rifles. The only forts captured in Kentucky, Martin's and Ruddle's, were taken in 1780 when British captain Henry Bird led a force of 150 whites and nearly a thousand warriors against them. The decisive difference then was that the invaders had some small cannon that the stockades could not withstand.

One common weakness of forts was their dependence upon an outside source of water.

29

At Logan's Fort a cabin was built over a spring outside the stockade. Then a ditch was dug to connect the two and was covered over with logs and a layer of dirt. In case of siege, the defenders had a protected passageway to the spring.

The distinction between forts and stations was often blurred. Forts frequently housed a number of persons. New immigrants often started their Kentucky stay at a fort, taking advantage of this convenient way of becoming acquainted with the country and its prospects. They resided at the fort temporarily, for they wanted to get on their own land as quickly as possible. In times of Indian troubles, families often fled from their individual stations to the safety of the forts, taking what possessions, including animals, they could with them. When the danger abated and families ventured to return to their holdings, they often found their cabins burned and their crops destroyed. The forts sometimes had a small permanent population, perhaps including a storekeeper or a blacksmith who needed a central, protected location in the growing community.

Life in a crowded fort, where little privacy was possible, often proved difficult even in peaceful times. Colonel William Fleming, a member of the land commission, visited Harrodsburg in 1780 and left a harrowing description of what he saw:

> The Spring at this place is below the Fort and fed by ponds above the Fort so that the whole dirt and filth of the Fort, putrified flesh, dead dogs, horse, cow, hog excrements and human odour all wash into the spring which with the Ashes and sweepings of filthy Cabbins, the dirtiness of the people, steeping skins to dress and washing every sort of dirty rags and cloths in the spring perfectly poisons the water and makes the most filthy nauscous potation of the water imaginable and will certainly contribute to render the inhabitants of the place sickly.

When David Trabue visited Boonesborough two years earlier he remarked that "the people in the fort was remarkable kind and hospitable to us with what they had. But I thought it was hard times—no bred, no salt, no vegetables, no fruit of any kind, no Ardent sperrets, indeed nothing but meet." Another visitor to Boonesborough in the spring of 1778 had found "a poor distressed ½ naked, ½ starved people, daily surrounded by the savages, which made it so dangerous, the hunters were afraid to go out to get Buffalo Meat." During the "Hard Winter" of 1779-80 food was so scarce at Strode's Station that the people called turkey "bread" and bear flesh "meat." After brief exposure to fort and station life, some immigrants returned to more settled communities. Early Kentucky, with all of its promise for the future, was no place for the faint of heart.

The overwhelming advantage of the forts and the large stations was the degree of safety that they offered. And despite its disadvantages, life in the crowded forts did offer the companionship that was so often missed on individual homesteads, where loneliness was a common complaint, especially among the women, who were tied to the home more closely than the men. In 1779, when George Rogers Clark returned to the Falls of the Ohio from the Illinois country, he brought a good supply of rum and sugar from the French towns. The christening of a new fort on the south bank of the Ohio River afforded an excuse for a party, and invitations were carried to the interior forts. The partygoers from Logan's Station spent a night at Harrodsburg, then started the next morning in a joint party of twenty-six men and women. Indian signs forced a return to Harrod's fort, and when the trip resumed the following day, only fifteen men and three women made the journey. They arrived safely, the women put on their finest clothes, and the Harrods opened the ball by dancing the first jig to the violin playing of a French musician. The abundant toddies kept the party going for several days.

A Government for Kentucky

Richard Henderson's plans for the Transylvania colony included a government. In May 1775 Kentucky's pioneer population may have approached three hundred persons, most of whom were hostile to the aspirations of Henderson and his company. Disputes over landownership could easily lead to outright hostilities, and Henderson saw a need for a civil government. He called for each of the four settlements— Boiling Springs, Boonesborough, Harrodsburg, and Logan's Station—to send delegates to Boonesborough on May 23 to provide for a temporary government. The host fort was allocated six delegates; the others each had four. The men met under a spreading elm tree and heard Henderson orate on the rights of the company, its plans for the colony, and the policies that were to be followed. The company was to remain in firm control of the territory, and land would be sold at company prices. Twelve elected delegates would make up the lower house of a legislature, but the proprietors would constitute the upper house. Henderson would provide executive leadership, and the company would collect feudal-type quitrents of two shillings per hundred acres.

The delegates passed a number of measures that most of them agreed were needed. They provided for courts, a militia, the collection of debts, and the punishment of criminals. Daniel Boone got bills accepted to preserve the game and provide for better breeding of horses; Squire Boone proposed a measure to protect and preserve rangeland. Daniel Boone, James Harrod, and William Cocke were appointed as a committee to consult with Henderson about the sale of land and to request that grants be made only to actual settlers. The delegates were supposed to meet again in the fall, but they never did. In September the Transylvania Company angered potential purchasers by doubling the price of land. At the same time favored friends were allowed bargain prices, and the proprietors reserved for themselves the choice acres at the Falls of the Ohio.

These high-handed actions lost the company the popular support without which it had no chance of making good its claim to a large portion of Kentucky. Such pioneer leaders as James Harrod, James McAfee, John Floyd, and Benjamin Logan had contested the

company claims from the beginning. Now the number of protesters increased. Lord Dunmore, the last royal governor of Virginia, had issued a proclamation to halt the efforts of "one Richard Henderson and other disorderly persons" to purchase Indian lands and to establish a government in the West. After the American Revolution began, Henderson sought recognition of the scheme from the governments of the new states of North Carolina and Virginia. Sharply rebuffed by their governors, Henderson appealed to the First Continental Congress that was trying to provide a national government and coordinate the war effort. Attorney James Hogg and other company officials went to Philadelphia in October 1775 to lobby on behalf of the company, but they were unsuccessful.

A tall, slender redheaded newcomer to Kentucky was instrumental in ending the company's lingering hopes. After surveying in central Kentucky in 1775, George Rogers Clark (1752-1818) decided that Kentucky would be his home. "A richer and more beautiful country than this, I believe has never been seen in America yet," he wrote a brother. In 1776 he resolved to take an active role in determining the region's future. Clark's plan was to have an assembly in Kentucky elect delegates to negotiate with Virginia for Kentucky's future. If terms were satisfactory, Kentucky would be a part of the Old Dominion. If an agreement could not be reached, Kentucky would establish an independent government, supported by the fertile land. Harrod also wanted to call an assembly, but he thought that it should elect delegates to Virginia's General Assembly.

Clark called an assembly at Harrodsburg for June 6, 1776, but he did not arrive until that evening. In his absence, those attending selected him and attorney John Gabriel Jones to go east and seek Kentucky's creation as a separate county. The petition to the legislature suggested that it was foolish to fight the British while allowing "such a respectable body of prime riflemen to remain in a state of neutrality." Clark and Jones arrived in

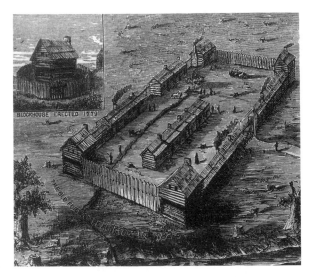

The Lexington blockhouse in 1779 and the old fort in 1782 (from George W. Ranck, *History of Lexington, Kentucky* [1872])

Williamsburg after the adjournment of the convention that had been trying to convert the colony of Virginia into a state. After an initial rejection, Clark persuaded the members of the Executive Council to donate five hundred pounds of desperately needed gunpowder to their "Friends in Distress" in Kentucky, by suggesting that "if a country was not worth protecting, it was not worth claiming." The donation of gunpowder was in itself a de facto recognition of Virginia's claim to Kentucky, but the claim was made definite on December 31, 1776, when Virginia's Montgomery, Washington, and Kentucky Counties were created from Fincastle. With the exception of the future Jackson Purchase, the boundaries of Kentucky County enclosed approximately the same land as the state would have in 1792.

On June 24, 1776, the Virginia General Assembly passed a resolution: "*Resolved,* That no purchase of Lands within the chartered limits of *Virginia* shall be made, under any pretense whatever, from any *Indian* tribe or nation,

without the approbation of the *Virginia* Legislature." Then on November 4, 1778, the General Assembly specifically declared Richard Henderson's "purchase" void but added that he and the Transylvania Company deserved some compensation for their efforts to settle Kentucky. Ultimately, a grant of two hundred thousand acres was made between the Green and Ohio Rivers. North Carolina also gave a grant of land, but these acreages constituted a tract far smaller than the empire of which Henderson had dreamed.

As a Virginia county, Kentucky acquired the usual form of county government and representation in the General Assembly. The land laws of the state applied to Kentucky County, and the Transylvania claims were opened to settlement. Kentucky's troubles continued, however. The American Revolution was well under way, its outcome was uncertain, and Kentucky's survival remained in doubt.

4

The Years of the American Revolution

Settlements under Attack

Fighting a war and trying to establish a nation absorbed the attention of seaboard patriots during the American Revolution. Little attention and less help could be devoted to the pioneers who had settled on the Western Waters. Even after Virginia extended its jurisdiction to the Kentucky settlements, its assistance to their residents was limited and sporadic. The war in the West was fought on a minute scale, but it was fought for survival. Historian Stephen Aron has calculated that an inhabitant of Kentucky was seven times as likely to be killed as were the eastern Americans. The West had no civilian population; women, children, and noncombatant men were as likely to fall victim to Indian raids as were the fighting men. If the Kentuckians were defeated, they faced death, captivity, or flight back east.

Some chose flight without waiting for defeat. By late spring 1776 the pioneer population of Kentucky was estimated to be no more than 200, and most of these people were in forts at Boonesborough, Harrodsburg, and Logan's Station (St. Asaph). The area north of the Kentucky River had been almost abandoned. John Floyd reported to William Preston on July 21, 1776: "I think more than 300 men have left the country since I came out, and not one has arrived—except a few down the Ohio." By early 1778 Kentucky had by one count only 121 able-bodied riflemen (84 at Harrodsburg, 22 at Boonesborough, and 15 at Logan's Station) in a total population of about 280.

Life was dangerous even near the forts. On a Sunday afternoon, July 14, 1776, thirteen-year-old Jemima Boone and Elizabeth and Frances Callaway, ages sixteen and fourteen, disobeyed orders and went canoeing on the Kentucky River. Seized on the north shore by a small band of Cherokee and Shawnee warriors, they were hurried northward. The girls made every effort to delay their progress and to leave signs of their passage. The pursuers found the trail hard to follow, and Daniel Boone feared that they were losing ground. Gambling on his woodcraft and his knowledge of Indians, Boone cut across the country and intercepted the trail where he had thought it would be. On the third day, overconfident as they neared the Licking River, the Indians halted to cook meat from a buffalo calf. Boone's party crept up stealthily, but a premature shot allowed the Indians to escape. Two who were wounded, however, were later reported to have died. This spectacular rescue became a part of the legend of pioneer Kentucky. Elizabeth Callaway soon married Samuel Henderson, who had rushed half-shaven to join in the pursuit. The following spring the other girls also married young men who had helped rescue them. Their ages tell much about marriage on the Kentucky frontier.

The pace of attacks increased. Nathaniel Hart's cabin, less than a mile from the fort, and his crops were destroyed during the rescue of the girls. Other attacks drove isolated settlers to the safety of the forts or to the greater safety of the settlements east of the frontier. In October 1775 John McClelland had built one of the first stations north of the Kentucky River at Royal Spring, in modern Georgetown. An attack on nearby Leestown in April 1776 alarmed the people and spurred their construction of fortifications. But McClelland was killed in December of that year, and the survivors moved to Harrodsburg. Benjamin Logan pushed the completion of a stockade at St. Asaph, although the other two forts, Boonesborough and Harrodsburg, afforded some protection against raids from the north.

Shawnee chief Cornstalk tried to preserve peace, but in a warrior culture it was essential for a young man to attain full status through warfare. The whites, who were intruding into

traditional tribal lands, offered a prime target. Outrages committed by some whites demanded retaliation, and the presence of the whites afforded opportunities for the Indians to acquire horses and other plunder. When Cornstalk, a son, and some other Indians were killed at Point Pleasant by a group of frontiersmen in 1777, Cornstalk's successor, Black Fish, as well as others who wanted war, had the proof they needed. The whites could not be trusted, and they must be driven out of the land.

During the early days of the Revolution the British made little use of the western Indians. Lieutenant Governor Henry Hamilton at Detroit advised his government that "Parties of Indians conducted by proper Leaders" should be sent against the American frontier settlements. In June 1777 he received an order to employ as many Indians as possible in "making a Diversion and exciting an alarm on the frontiers of Virginia and Pennsylvania." These Indians were to be properly led to "restrain them from committing violence on the well affected and inoffensive Inhabitants." Within a month Hamilton had sent out fifteen war parties, each of which numbered, on average, nineteen warriors and two whites. Six months later Hamilton had received 72 prisoners and 129 scalps. Although he did not actually purchase scalps, Hamilton became known and hated in Kentucky as the Hair Buyer. This policy may have been a serious British mistake, for it united the frontier as nothing else could have done. During the Revolution a number of Tories came to Kentucky, often to escape Patriot persecution along the seaboard. William Clinkenbeard claimed that when he came through the wilderness during the winter of 1778-79 the travelers he overtook were "all grand Tories, pretty nigh." War parties did not question possible victims to ascertain political views, and the Kentucky Tories generally shared the same aversion to Indians as did the other settlers.

The proliferation of raids made it dangerous for settlers to venture outside the walls of a fort, but horses and cattle had to be taken to graze, crops had to be tended, and hunting had to be done. Simon Kenton (1755-1836) proved invaluable to the people at Boonesborough. He would slip out at night, go miles away to make a kill, and then slip back into the fort under cover of darkness the next night. He also carried messages from fort to fort when such travel was extremely hazardous. Born in Fauquier County, Virginia, Kenton had refused to attend school and could never do more than scrawl his name, but he mastered forestlore. He fled to Kentucky because he thought he had killed a rival in a fight over a girl; he dropped his alias, Simon Butler, when he learned that his rival had only been knocked unconscious. Kenton and Thomas Williams entered Kentucky in 1775 at Limestone Creek. Then they went inland a few miles to clear land and plant what was probably the first corn crop north of the Kentucky River. Standing an inch over six feet and weighing about 190 pounds, Kenton was immensely strong yet swift on foot. His slow, soft speech sometimes left an impression of mildness to persons who had never witnessed him in action. A bailiff told to collect a small debt in 1786 wrote his excuse for failure on the back of the note: "Too dangerous to go where Kenton is." Kenton moved with his eyes on the ground, with quick glances around to detect hostile signs. He was Boone's equal as a woodsman. It was said that one day in the forest Boone sensed the presence of another person. He took evasive cover, and for hours he and his unseen adversary each maneuvered unsuccessfully to get a clear glimpse of the other. Finally Boone stepped into the clearing and called, "That you, Simon?" Kenton stepped out and grinned. "Howdy, Boone."

The besieged forts had few such woodsmen. Most of the men were farmers who fought only to protect themselves, their families, and their property. Some farming had to be done despite the danger, and men worked in common fields near the stockades while half their number stood guard. It was not a satisfactory solution to their problems.

County status brought the appointment of Colonel John Bowman as commander of the militia. Until Bowman came west, George Rogers Clark was the ranking officer, with Boone, Harrod, Logan, and John Todd as captains. The first militia muster was held at the forts on March 5, 1777. Two scouts were chosen from each fort to give some warning of war parties coming from the north; Simon Kenton was an obvious choice for this assignment.

Daniel Boone and Chief Black Fish

The raids assumed a new dimension when Black Fish led two hundred or more Shawnee across the Ohio River and established a base camp near the crossing of the Licking. From there he sent out small parties to do what damage they could. On March 7, 1777, a male slave was killed and his master wounded as they worked in a field at Boonesborough. At about the same time some settlers who were making maple sugar were attacked near Harrodsburg. Hugh McGary, in the search party to see why the sugar makers were late, found the mutilated body of his stepson. Later, when Indians began to burn the cabins outside the stockade, McGary was in the party that rushed outside to drive them off. When a warrior wearing the shirt of his stepson was killed, McGary, insane with rage, hacked the body into bits and fed the pieces to his dogs.

The Shawnee attacked Boonesborough on the morning of April 24 and killed a man who had gone outside the gate. Kenton, standing by the gate, shot the Indian who waved the bloody scalp. Boone, Michael Stoner, and a dozen or so others rushed out in pursuit of the retreating warriors. Stoner fired and hit an Indian, but he was himself wounded twice. Several dozen Shawnee cut between their pursuers and the fort, and Boone yelled for the settlers to fight their way back to the fort. In the wild melee a bullet smashed Boone's ankle, and he fell to the ground, barely conscious. Kenton shot the warrior about to scalp Boone, then smashed the skull of another with a rifle butt. He scooped up Boone and ran with him to the safety of the stockade. Later, from his bed, Boone paid Kenton a well-earned accolade:

35

"Simon, you have behaved like a man today. Indeed, you are a fine fellow."

The attacks continued. On May 30 a milking party of men and women was fired on outside Logan's Station. One man was killed, and Ben Harrison was left for dead outside the fort. Later he was seen to make a small movement. Rifles could protect him during the day, but he was sure to be killed at night. Toward dusk, Benjamin Logan, rolling a large bale of wool for cover, crawled to Harrison, hoisted the wounded man to his shoulder, and sprinted for the gate without being hit in the uncertain light. Harrison died of his wounds in less than two weeks. Logan, possibly in the company of James Harrod and a few others, made a hurried trip to the Holston settlements in search of aid. Nothing was forthcoming from that source, but Colonel John Bowman, responding to earlier pleas, had raised a hundred militiamen from Botetourt and Montgomery Counties in Virginia, and he reached Boonesborough on August 1. If Kentucky could be held, the militia was to remain there; if it could not be held, then the militiamen would conduct the settlers to safety. Indian attacks along the Upper Ohio River, particularly in the vicinity of Wheeling, made it difficult to send more reinforcements to Kentucky.

Henry Hamilton had offered inducements for settlers to come to British forts, and he promised generous treatment for men who would fight for His Majesty King George III. Among those who joined the British were Matthew Elliott, Alexander McKee, and Simon Girty. Captured by the Seneca Indians in 1756, Girty (1741-1818) was adopted into the tribe and lived with the Seneca for three years. After going over to the British in 1778, Girty worked as a scout and interpreter, participating in numerous raids. "The Great Renegade" was one of the mildest epithets Kentuckians applied to him. Girty was supposed to have watched with approval the torturing of prisoners, particularly the prolonged death of Colonel William Crawford at the stake in 1782. On the other hand,

Girty occasionally saved prisoners from death, including Simon Kenton, with whom he had served in Lord Dunmore's War.

The continued Indian incursions made it difficult for the Kentucky settlers to raise crops and to bring supplies into the settlements. Shortages developed, and salt to preserve meat was desperately needed. Benjamin Logan suggested that the salt springs be made public property if their owners did not produce the salt needed. In early January 1778 Daniel Boone led thirty men to Lower Blue Licks to make salt in the large iron kettles that Colonel Bowman had brought with him. Working hard, the men were able to produce about ten bushels a day, and supplies were soon rushed to the settlements. While hunting on a cold, snowy February 7, Boone was captured by several Shawnee, part of a 120-man war party led by Chief Black Fish. The Shawnee would kill the salt makers, Black Fish told Boone, and then they would go on to wipe out his fort.

Fearing that the Indians would succeed, Boone quickly devised a plan to save Boonesborough. His men would kill many warriors before they fell, Boone warned, but if they were promised good treatment he could persuade them to surrender. The people at the fort were about ready to join the British, he said, but the women and children would not survive a long winter march to the Shawnee towns. In the spring he would lead the Indians back to Boonesborough and get the fort's inhabitants to surrender. Black Fish accepted the plan, but Boone had difficulty in getting the salt makers to surrender. When Boone was allowed to present his plan to a council of all the Shawnee warriors, it was accepted by a vote of 61-59.

That night Boone was forced to run the gauntlet, for he had argued to protect his men but, as Black Fish reminded him, "You made no bargin for yourself." Running at full speed between two lines of warriors and veering from side to side to avoid some of the blows, Boone neared the end of the ordeal when an Indian warrior stepped into his way to deliver a punishing blow. Boone butted the warrior in the chest, knocked him down, and completed his run to the cheers of both the salt makers and most of the Indians. In the Indian towns as the prisoners were dispersed, Boone was adopted as a son of Black Fish and his wife. He was named Big Turtle. Hamilton ransomed some of the Americans at twenty pounds each, and a few did enter British service. Within a year or two most of the others managed to return home. Boone enjoyed the Indian way of life, but he made a carefully planned escape on June 16, 1778, to warn Kentucky settlers of an impending invasion. Boone rode a horse until it collapsed, and then he continued on foot, trying to conceal his trail without losing too much time. He was pursued, but the trackers lost trace of him. He covered 160 miles in four days, and on June 20 he arrived at Boonesborough. Except for daughter Jemima and her husband, Flanders Callaway, his family had left, believing him to be dead.

A number of people at Boonesborough viewed Boone with suspicion. Some of the salt makers who had returned believed that he had come back to secure the surrender of the fort. Richard Callaway, jealous of Boone's reputation and position, was willing to believe the worst. Boone explained what he had done and warned that a major Shawnee attack would occur within a few days. Under his direction, repairs and additions were made to the fort's defenses. A few men came from other forts to help, but even after male slaves and half-grown boys were armed, Boonesborough had only sixty riflemen, plus a dozen women and about twenty children.

As weeks passed without a sign of the attack, Boone's loyalties were in even greater doubt. He regained some credibility at the end of August by leading eighteen men on a raid of a Shawnee town a short distance north of the Ohio River. On the way back they discovered that Black Fish, with four hundred warriors from several tribes, and a company of British militiamen under the command of a Captain

de Quinde were ahead of them. Boone's party bypassed their foes and reached Boonesborough safely on September 6.

The longest siege of any Kentucky fort began the next day. Boone met Black Fish outside the fort. The chief chided his "son" for running away and reminded him of his promise to surrender the fort. Hamilton had sent a letter promising a pardon and safe conduct to Detroit to those who accepted British allegiance. Boone replied that he would have to consult with other leaders in the fort. Some of these besieged people apparently wanted to accept the offer, but Callaway declared that he would kill the first person who proposed surrender, and Squire Boone said that he would fight to the death. The vote to resist was then unanimous. Since reinforcements were expected from Virginia, Boone was instructed to play for time. Black Fish accepted a truce to give the settlers time to consider the offer. The women used the time by going to the spring outside the stockade and filling every container in the fort with water. Men resumed digging a well inside the stockade.

When Boone informed Black Fish that the fort would not surrender, the two men agreed to a parley the next day that would involve all the chiefs and the leaders of the fort. After considerable discussion, the parties signed a treaty by which they apparently accepted the Ohio River as a boundary. After a waiting period, both sides could hunt and trade in the territory of the other. The Americans appeared to have agreed to give allegiance to the British king, but they were still playing for time. They had no authority to make a treaty or to dispose of land claimed by Virginia.

The meeting ended in a general melee when two Indians approached each of the settlers: Did they intend to take them hostage or merely to shake hands to seal the treaty? Daniel Boone received a cut on the back, and Squire, who had a knack for getting wounded, took a bullet in the shoulder, but all the settlers fought their way back into the fort. Rifle fire drove

George Rogers Clark may have saved the Kentucky settlements during the American Revolution. Portrait attributed to John Westey Jarvis (courtesy of The Filson Club Historical Society)

away the Indians who tried to break through the gate.

The besieged fort drew plunging fire from the hill across the river, and passageways had to be cut through the walls of the cabins. Jemima was hit by a spent ball that did no damage. Elizabeth Callaway took a broom to a man she found hiding under a bed. "I am not made for fighting," he protested, as she flogged him. Several horses and cattle were killed in the stockade. When the Indians tried to burn the cabins, inventive Squire Boone made squirt guns from old musket barrels so the defenders did not have to go onto the roofs to put out the flames. The siege was pushed with unusual determination, and signs soon indicated that the Indians were digging a tunnel from the riverbank. They meant this tunnel to pass under the walls of the fort. The settlers sank a countertrench, but a heavy rain that helped extinguish the fires also caused part of the Indians' tunnel to collapse. Much of the mutual taunting involved Pompey, a black interpreter for Black Fish, who was finally shot when he revealed himself to deliver another taunt.

The Indians' last major attack was beaten off on the night of September 17, and although some firing continued the next morning, the besiegers' camp was broken up. Daniel Boone believed that the Indians had thirty-seven killed; there was no estimate of the wounded. In the fort two were killed, and a few were wounded, including Daniel, who had a slight injury. Long-awaited reinforcements from Virginia arrived a few days after the siege was lifted.

Not long afterward, Richard Callaway and Benjamin Logan filed charges of treason against Boone. The trial took place at Logan's Station before Kentucky militia officers. The crux of the matter concerned Boone's intentions: Was he planning treason, or was he misleading the enemy to gain time? Boone explained that he had the salt makers surrender to prevent an attack on Boonesborough that could have been made at that time. Thereafter he misled the British and the Indians; what happened at the siege spoke for itself. The court agreed with Boone, found him innocent of the charges, and promoted him to major. Callaway was among those who never agreed with that verdict.

Black Fish broke up his party into small bands that inflicted more damage than the large party had done in the siege. The war of attrition seemed to have no end, and it was taking a toll in both material losses and morale. Unless conditions changed, the Americans might decide to quit the endless struggle and either accept British sovereignty or retreat from the land that had lured them westward.

George Rogers Clark and the Illinois Campaign

Recognizing this danger, George Rogers Clark decided to do something to combat it. Kentucky could be saved only if the Virginians took the offensive against the Indians in their homeland, not by waging defensive warfare. Clark wanted to force the British out of their posts north of the Ohio River and either defeat or neutralize the Indian tribes in that region. Detroit was his goal, but he planned to approach it by way of the French towns in the Illinois country. After that—well, something might be done in the Spanish southwest to open the Mississippi River to American trade.

Governor Patrick Henry and his key advisers approved the plan, and the Virginia legislature appropriated twelve hundred pounds in depreciated currency. Clark could enlist seven companies of fifty men each and keep them for three months after they reached Kentucky. Most legislators assumed that the purpose of the expedition was to defend the Kentucky settlements, but the governor's secret instructions gave Clark wide latitude for offensive action.

Clark was able to enlist only 150 men before departing for Kentucky. He hoped to get more from the Holston settlements, but he realized that the situation in Kentucky was so serious that he could not strip many men from the undermanned forts there. "I knew our case was desperate," Clark wrote later, "but the more I reflected on my weakness, the more I was pleased with the enterprise." His small army,

accompanied by several families, landed on Corn Island, near the Falls of the Ohio, on May 27, 1778. A fort was constructed, cabins were built, a corn crop was planted, and the soldiers drilled. When Clark finally revealed his plans, most of Company A deserted.

Clark left Corn Island on June 24 with about 175 men and landed at deserted Fort Massac, a few miles down the Ohio from the mouth of the Tennessee River. The force marched to Kaskaskia and took it by surprise on the night of July 4. A master of psychological warfare, Clark won over most of the French inhabitants, and some of them helped secure the surrenders of Cahokia, Prairie du Rocher, Vincennes, and several smaller communities. Clark established good relations with Fernando de Leyba, the Spanish commander at St. Louis, who provided some help with the acute supply problem. (There is no proof that Clark fell in love with de Leyba's beautiful sister.)

Something had to be arranged with the Indian tribes in the region, for they outnumbered the Americans several times over. Clark's approach was to tell them to stand aside; his goal was Detroit, not their land. But if they wanted to fight the Long Knives, he hoped that they would do so like men so he would not be embarrassed. Clark later explained that in dealing with the Indians he "gave Harsh language to supply the want of Men; well knowing that it was a mistaken notion in many that soft speeches were best for Indians." His approach was effective, and Clark soon won the support, or at least the neutrality, of a number of tribes who had previously sided with the British. He was one of the most effective Indian negotiators of his generation.

Some of his men returned home as their enlistments expired, and Clark enlisted French volunteers to keep his numbers intact. His supply problem was critical, for the French towns could provide only some of his needs, and he had to use his own credit to buy what was needed. The problem would have been worse but for the efforts of Oliver Pollock, the fiscal agent for both Virginia and the Continental Congress in New Orleans. Pollock pledged his own credit and later went into bankruptcy, but somehow he kept a trickle of essential supplies moving up the Mississippi to Clark. Then on January 29, 1779, Francis Vigo, a Spanish merchant from St. Louis, informed Clark that Colonel Hamilton, moving rapidly after he learned of the American invasion of Illinois, had captured Vincennes on December 17 without firing a shot. Winter was well advanced, and Hamilton had decided to wait until spring to complete the conquest of the Illinois towns. Most of his Indian warriors and many of the French troops had gone home; they would return for the spring campaign.

If Clark awaited Hamilton's attack in the spring, he would be defeated by overwhelming numbers. If he retreated to Kentucky, Hamilton would follow and destroy his small force there. Clark and his officers agreed that their only chance was to surprise Hamilton, 180 wilderness miles distant, with a winter campaign. A riverboat, renamed the *Willing*, was armed with some artillery, outfitted as a galley, and sent under the command of Captain John Rogers to make a circuitous voyage on the Kaskaskia, Mississippi, Ohio, and Wabash Rivers to a point south of Vincennes, where it could lend support to the overland expedition and cut off possible escape in that direction. The galley departed on February 5, and the overland march began the next day.

Much of the land was flooded, and the packhorses had to be abandoned. The food supply was soon exhausted, and it was unfortunate that the horses had been left behind, for they could have been eaten. Clark was everywhere along the line of sodden men, lifting spirits with jokes and songs. At one critical moment when some of the men seemed on the verge of rebellion, he smeared his face with gunpowder, gave a war whoop, and plunged into the water ahead. The men followed. But Clark also took the precaution of stationing dependable Captain Joseph Bowman and twenty-

five trusted men at the rear of the line with orders to shoot anyone who refused to wade. A drummer boy who sang comic songs while floating on his drum did a great deal to help morale. The strong helped the weak, and somehow they got to Vincennes. There was no sign of the *Willing*.

The French in the town were told to remain in their homes unless they wanted to fight for the British. They did not tell Hamilton of Clark's presence. Hamilton, however, put his seventy-nine-man garrison on alert after some of his scouts reported strangers in the area. Riflemen inflicted several casualties on the garrison and made using Fort Sackville's cannon a dangerous prospect. One or two Americans were wounded, and they had the distinction of being the first battle casualties since the expedition had left the Falls of the Ohio. On the morning of February 24 Clark demanded an unconditional surrender, for he learned that a large party of reinforcements might arrive soon, and it was possible that Indians might come to Hamilton's aid. As the leaders conferred near the town church, a French-Indian raiding party returned, and its members were killed or captured. Four warriors were tomahawked and their bodies tossed in the river. Hamilton was visibly shaken by the atrocity, as Clark had hoped he would be, but the American also wanted to demonstrate to the Indians that the British could not give them the protection that had been promised.

Hamilton surrendered Vincennes on February 25, becoming another victim of Clark's psychological warfare. Clark's men captured several boatloads of supplies and trade goods nearing the town, and they obtained some welcome clothing and food. On March 8 Hamilton and twenty-six other Britishers started under guard on a long trip that would end in a Virginia prison. They spent several days at Harrodsburg while passing through Kentucky, and Hamilton was apprehensive about their reception. The settlement was braced for a possible Indian attack; it would have been ironic had Hamilton come under fire from a raiding party he had sent out. In fact, the prisoners received a poorer reception at Logan's Station. Logan and his wife were civil and hospitable, although Logan was favoring a broken arm acquired during a recent fight with Indians. On the other hand, Hamilton reported, "We were accosted by the females especially in pretty coarse terms."

When the *Willing* finally arrived at Vincennes on February 27 it brought a message from Virginia governor Patrick Henry. Illinois County had been created, and John Todd would take over its civil administration. The legislature had voted thanks for the campaign, and Clark had been promoted to colonel. John Montgomery would bring enough troops in the spring to ensure the taking of Detroit, so Clark gave up the tempting idea of taking it at once. He moved back to Kaskaskia and began preparations for a Detroit expedition beginning about June 20, 1779. The money he spent in preparing for it was never repaid by Virginia, and many of Clark's later financial problems dated from this period in his career.

The Detroit hopes faded with the coming of spring. Montgomery brought 150 Virginia riflemen instead of the 500 promised. John Bowman had been expected to bring 300 from the Kentucky settlements; Hugh McGary arrived with 30. Bowman had conducted his own largely ineffective raid on the Shawnee town at Chillicothe. Virginia had not provided adequate funding, and Clark had exhausted his credit with the Illinois merchants. Bitterly disappointed with the shattering of his dream of capturing Detroit, Clark left Montgomery in charge in Illinois and returned to the Falls of the Ohio. Fourteen months had passed since he left there on his audacious campaign.

Continued Indian Activity

Since Clark's departure, Kentucky's population had increased, and some new stations had been established. More settlers were daring to leave the forts and work on their own land, but the Indian danger was not at an end. In October 1779 a large band of warriors, accompanied by Simon Girty and other renegades, surprised some cargo boats going up the Ohio at a spot a few miles above the mouth of the Licking River. Captain David Rogers and most of his seventy men were killed. Small parties of Indians continued to harass Kentuckians, but the "Hard Winter" of 1779-80 brought peace for a few months. Bitter cold blanketed Kentucky from late November until late February. Ink froze inside cabins, wild animals and domestic cattle died, maple trees exploded as their sap froze, ice was two feet thick on the Kentucky River, and some smaller streams froze solid. Survival became the main concern, and warfare almost ceased until the spring thaws.

George Rogers Clark began to have problems with such Kentucky military leaders as Boone, Harrod, and Logan when the British made a coordinated effort to retake the West in 1780. Expeditions would sweep north and south along the Mississippi River, and another would recover the Illinois towns. Captain Henry Bird, employing both Indian and white troops, would move south from Detroit, take Fort Nelson at the Falls of the Ohio, and then capture the stations and forts in the interior. Clark was responsible for the defense of both Illinois and Kentucky, and the Falls was the logical place for his headquarters. But the commanders of the interior forts wanted him to move his base to them so they would have better protection. He was criticized when he spent time and effort constructing Fort Jefferson on the Mississippi River about five miles south of the mouth of the Ohio, although Governor Thomas Jefferson had ordered it. The county militia leaders could block Clark's plans by refusing him the manpower he needed. Clark was one of the few in the West who had an overall view of the military needs of that extensive theater. He was hampered by courageous, well-meaning men who were parochial in their outlook.

Clark hurried northward and reached Cahokia on May 25, 1780, a day before the British arrived. He defeated them, then hastened southward to Fort Jefferson. Clark ordered all available men to go by boat to the assistance of Fort Nelson at the Falls, while he and two companions made a hurried and hazardous trip across the country. Captain Bird, with an army of nearly a thousand men, including Simon Girty, Alexander McKee, and some other whites, brought some cannon through the wilderness. Ruddle's Station surrendered after a few shots on June 24. The settlers were promised that they would be taken to Detroit as British prisoners, but Bird could not control the Indians. A number of prisoners were killed, and a great deal of property was destroyed. Martin's Station also surrendered, as did some other small settlements in the area. Indiscriminate slaughter of cattle soon created a supply problem for the invaders and their 350 prisoners. Bird had wanted to capture Fort Nelson first, but the Indians had refused to go there because of a rumor that Clark was there. They were satisfied with their success, they still feared Clark, and Bird was forced to leave Kentucky. About 200 of the captives were retained by the tribes who had participated in the campaign; Bird had about 150 when he arrived at Detroit on August 4. At least thirteen of the men volunteered for service with the British rangers.

While Bird was still on the way to Detroit, Clark began planning a retaliatory strike to show the Indians that they could no longer raid in Kentucky and return to their homes with impunity. When he found men more interested in land speculation than in volunteering for the expedition, he allegedly closed the land office on his own authority, then stationed guards to stop those who might try to flee through Cumberland Gap. By the end of July nearly a thousand men, the largest force raised in Kentucky to that date, had assembled at the mouth of the Licking River. Although Clark confiscated a boatload of provisions going to the Falls of the Ohio, food was scarce. When his army crossed the Ohio on August 1, Clark moved cautiously to avoid an ambush. The Shawnee at Chillicothe fled before the Americans arrived, but buildings were burned, and crops were destroyed. The Indians put up a stiff fight at Piqua, but cannon fire drove them out of their fortifications. Benjamin Logan's flanking movement was not completed in time to trap the Indians, and most of them escaped. The Kentuckians had fourteen killed and thirteen wounded; Clark estimated the enemy losses at double those figures. When the expedition recrossed the Ohio, its members had covered 480 miles in thirty-one days.

Meanwhile, Fort Jefferson had been attacked in July, and both the soldiers and the civilians who had sought refuge there were near starvation. Clark returned east in the autumn of 1780 to seek support for a 1781 expedition that would at last capture Detroit. General Washington agreed to let Clark borrow military supplies, including artillery and entrenching tools, from Fort Pitt. The items were to be returned or replaced later. Governor Jefferson instructed Clark to lead an expedition from the Falls on March 15, 1781. With ample supplies and 2,000 men, Clark, promoted to brigadier general in the Virginia army, was to move against the Indian tribes if he decided that taking Detroit was not feasible. But by 1781 Virginia had become the major theater of the Revolution, and the men, supplies, and funds promised Clark could not be found. Virginia's decision to give its claims north of the Ohio River to the general government weakened support for a Virginia expedition, and men from other states were slow to enlist. In June 1781, when legislator Patrick Henry secured passage of a resolution ordering the Detroit project halted, it began to fall apart. When Clark left Fort Pitt in early August, he had only 400 men, and some of them deserted on the way down the Ohio. Colonel Archibald Lochry, following with a smaller group of Pennsylvanians, was ambushed near the mouth of the Miami River and had 107 men killed or captured.

Clark called a meeting in early September to enlist the aid of the county lieutenants. "I wait, as a spectator," he told them, "to see what a country is determined to do for itself when reduced to a state of desperation." The colonels and the Virginia officers could not agree on a plan of action except to assert that forts should be constructed at the mouths of the Kentucky and Miami Rivers and Virginia should be asked to sponsor a major expedition against Detroit in 1782. When Colonels Logan and John Todd did not supply the help that they had promised for building the forts, Clark was blamed for not completing them. New governor Benjamin Harrison told Clark that he could have only 304 men to protect the frontier and to garrison the forts on the Ohio River. He would do the best he could, Clark responded, but "my chain appears to have run out." Insulted by those "who have for several years past been in a continual dread of me," he tried to resign, but Harrison persuaded him to stay on. Clark then urged the construction of armed boats to patrol the Ohio River and to discourage invasions.

Defeat at Lower Blue Licks

The major fighting of the American Revolution ended when General Charles Cornwallis surrendered at Yorktown, Virginia, in October 1781. Kentuckians greeted the news with acclaim, but the end of the war had little immediate effect in the West. The British occupied forts in the West for several more years, and from these outposts they continued to encourage the Indians. In Kentucky, 1782 became known as the Year of Blood. At an intertribal council held in June 1782, the Indians decided to eliminate the Kentucky settlements while British help was still available. Kentuckians redoubled their pleas for help, but Governor Harrison responded: "The Executive therefore recommends to the citizens on our frontiers to use every means in their power for preserving a good understanding with the savage tribes, and to strike no blow unless compelled by necessity."

Kentucky's population was large enough by 1782 to provide an adequate defense if a concerted effort was made. But petty quarrels and personality conflicts emerged, the growing population gave most settlers a sense of security, and Clark still lacked authority to direct the militia. By early July he and Colonel John Floyd managed to construct and arm a seventy-three-foot riverboat rowed with forty-six oars and carrying a one-hundred-man crew and several cannon. Stationed near the mouth of the Licking River, the boat did deter Indians from crossing the Ohio at that point. The Indians still feared Clark, and rumors that he was at last leading a force against Detroit kept many of the Indians, particularly the Shawnee, north of the Ohio.

In March 1782 some Wyandot warriors struck Strode's Station about twenty miles from Boonesborough, killed two settlers, wounded another, and carried off several slaves. The war party was pursued by Captain James Estill and twenty-five men, some of them from Logan's Station. On March 22 Estill caught up with the raiders at Little Mountain, near the future site of Mount Sterling. Almost evenly matched, the opponents fought one of the most vicious battles in the history of Kentucky's Indian warfare. Estill was encouraged by shouts from Monk, one of the captured slaves. Estill was killed after suffering at least three wounds, and thirteen of his men were killed or seriously wounded. The Wyandot Indians had equally heavy losses, but they remained in control of the battlefield, and the engagement was considered to be an Indian victory. Monk escaped during the battle. A powerful five-foot-five-inch man weighing two hundred pounds, he carried one of the seriously wounded settlers nearly twenty-five miles to Estill's Station. Estill's son freed Monk, who may have been the first slave freed in Kentucky. Monk, already known for maintaining an apple nursery at Boonesborough, later manufactured gunpowder for some of the stations. Still later, he became a Baptist preacher and lived in Shelbyville.

The main Indian invasion was delayed for several months until it was certain that Clark was not advancing on Detroit. Alexander McKee and Simon Girty crossed the Ohio River accompanied by fifty rangers and about three hundred Indians; they had expected to have a thousand. Scouting was so lax that they penetrated nearly a hundred miles into Kentucky before their presence was known. On August 12, 1782, they defeated a party of eighteen settlers at Upper Blue Licks, then moved on to Bryan's (Bryant's) Station, about five miles northeast of Lexington. Four Bryan brothers, relatives of Rebecca Boone, had built the station in 1779. One of the largest in the region, it had forty-four cabins and blockhouses at each corner of the stockade. The Indians hoped to draw the defenders outside by having a hundred men stage an attack, then withdraw as if in flight. This diversion failed on August 16, as cautious heads in the fort sensed a trap. A cherished legend is that the twenty-six women and girls in the fort went to the outside spring to replenish the supply of water, gambling that the concealed Indians would not hinder them. A relief party from Lexington managed to get seventeen of its members into the fort, attacks were beaten off, and the rangers and Indians started withdrawing on August 17, after killing cattle, burning buildings, and damaging crops outside the stockade.

By the morning of August 18 relief forces numbering about 182 men had arrived from nearby stations. Led by John Todd, they started in pursuit without waiting for Benjamin Logan, who was coming with a large reinforcement. The retreating Indians and rangers made no effort to conceal their tracks, and such experienced woodsmen as Daniel Boone became suspicious of what might lie ahead. The settlers caught up with the raiders at the Lower Blue Licks crossing of the Licking River on August 19. Boone feared an ambush on the other side of the river, but Hugh McGary had been chided for timidity the previous morning when he had advised waiting for Logan's arrival, and he was still smarting from that taunt. While Boone was suggesting a division of their force to develop a pincers movement, McGary declared that Boone was cowardly. Then McGary charged across the river, shouting for everyone who wasn't a coward to follow him. A rush

ensued, and even cautious men saw no choice but to join in the crossing. "Come on," Boone said to his militiamen, "we are all slaughtered now."

The rangers and Indians waiting in ambush opened a devastating fire on the rash Kentuckians. Stephen Trigg commanded on the right of the American advance, John Todd in the center, and Boone on the left. This division, however, implies more organization than existed by that time. After a few minutes of fighting, Boone's men were advancing. They discovered that Trigg's group had been shattered in a minute or so, and the Indians were pouring in behind the center and the left. Forty Americans were probably killed in the first five minutes, and others were dying in hand-to-hand fighting as the Indians attacked with knives and tomahawks. The settlers had made no provision to protect their horses when most of them dismounted after crossing the river, and the Indians were threatening to seize the mounts.

Boone held most of his men together. He told them to retreat to the river through the forest on their left, which would provide some protection while he and a few others covered the retreat. His son Israel refused to leave him and was killed almost at once. The massacre continued as the men struggled to get back across the ford. Benjamin Netherland rallied a few men who had the courage to halt on the south shore and give covering fire to their comrades splashing through the blood-stained water. The survivors, many of them on foot, fled for the safety of Bryan's Station. The Indians gave up the pursuit after a mile or two and returned to plunder the battlefield and scalp and mutilate the bodies of the dead Kentuckians. The raiders had about ten men killed and fourteen wounded; some sixty settlers were killed, and a few were captured. It was Kentucky's worst defeat of the Indian war. Boone was said to have wept in later years whenever he talked about the disaster. One can imagine the family's grief when he told Rebecca that they had lost another son. Logan and nearly five hundred men met the fleeing survivors on the trail out of Bryan's Station. They helped bury the dead in a common grave on August 24.

Defeat demands scapegoats, and Hugh McGary was damned by many. He blamed the commanding officers who had sought to win a victory without waiting for Logan to arrive. George Rogers Clark also criticized "extremely reprehensible leadership" that had not done adequate scouting. Although he had not been near the battle, Clark was blamed by some of the militia officers. In a report to the governor, Logan distorted and omitted facts to charge Clark with having neglected the defense of Kentucky; he did not mention his failure to give Clark the help that had been promised. When Boone urged that five hundred men be sent to defend Kentucky, he asked that they be placed under the command of the county lieutenants. "If you put them under the Direction of Genl. Clarke," Boone said, "they will be Little or no Service to our Settlement, as he lies 100 miles west of us, and the Indians northeast, and our men are often called to the Falls to guard them."

The militia leaders still viewed the Kentucky situation with parochial vision, and they refused to admit that they had given Clark inadequate support. In addition, they ignored the fact that the Falls area was also receiving Indian attacks. Kincheloe's Station, for example, was surprised on September 2, and thirty-seven settlers were captured. Clark's enemies worked assiduously to undermine his position. Rumors soon circulated that he had become a drunkard who was incapable of directing military affairs. Governor Harrison accepted such stories uncritically.

Still, Clark was asked to lead a retaliatory raid without waiting for the state's permission to take offensive action. He worked carefully with the 1,050 men who gathered at the mouth of the Licking River by November 1, to make sure that each knew what to do in any foreseeable contingency. When the men advanced, he made sure that they were not ambushed. The Indians avoided battle, and from New Chil-

licothe (Piqua), Clark sent out small raiding parties to do as much damage as possible over the largest possible area. The Kentuckians had one man killed and one wounded; Clark reported Indian losses as ten killed and seven captured. By November 17 the expedition reached the Ohio River, and the men were released there. While the Indian strength was hardly touched by this raid, the shortage of food delayed raids for several months.

On the last day of March 1782 Clark received a letter that told him how effectively his enemies had reached the governor's ear. Blamed for numerous failures, including the debacle at Blue Licks, Clark was warned to consult with the commissioners of western accounts about his financial affairs. Clark wrote a spirited but moderate reply, although it must have been painful for him to display such restraint. The governor had been misled, Clark suggested, by persons "who keep your government in confusion." In a milder letter dated December 19, Harrison gave Clark permission to retire and come east to settle his tangled accounts. It was the spring of 1783 before Clark rode to the Virginia capital, so destitute and threadbare that he requested an advance on what he was owed in order to buy some decent clothes. He had been careless in bookkeeping, and some of his receipts had disappeared into the bureaucratic maw and were not found until the twentieth century. At last Clark received a letter dated July 2, 1783, in which Governor Harrison accepted his resignation and thanked him graciously "for the very great and singular services you have rendered your country in wresting so great and valuable a territory out of the hands of the British enemy, repelling the attacks of their savage allies, and carrying on a successful war in the heart of their country." The praise was merited. No man did more to save Kentucky during its most perilous days than did Clark.

The Treaty of Paris, 1783

Before Clark's resignation, Kentuckians had learned of the preliminary peace treaty drafted

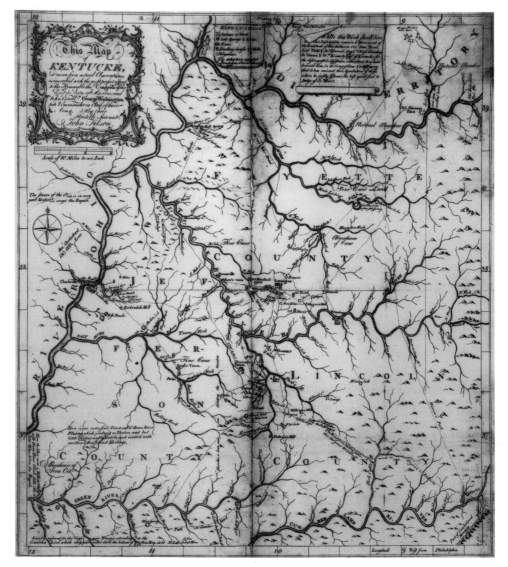

John Filson's *Map of Kentucke*, 1784, was sold both separately and along with his book *The Discovery, Settlement, and Present State of Kentucke* (1784) (courtesy of The Filson Club Historical Society).

by the American and British delegations. As Americans they were concerned in some measure with all provisions of the Treaty of Paris, but some terms had particular application to the people in the West. The western boundary would be the midchannel of the Mississippi River, and the British promised to withdraw their troops from within the boundaries of the United States "with all convenient speed."

Spain had entered the war against Great Britain in 1779 as a co-belligerent, not as an ally of the United States, and when peace was made with Great Britain, Spain regained Florida, including a strip along the Gulf Coast. Spain also had possession of the territory south of Canada and west of the Mississippi River. Its control of the mouth of the Mississippi would become of great concern to Kentuckians as they began producing surplus crops, for the Mississippi was their only practical outlet.

Contrary to what was long believed, there is no proof that Clark's success in the Old Northwest resulted in the U.S. acquisition of that territory. Benjamin Franklin argued that if the British kept it, they would have troublesome neighbors in the American frontiersmen. In American possession and inhabited largely by Indians, the territory would be a buffer zone between Canada and the American frontier settlements. Also, Franklin added, a generous settlement in the treaty would encourage good relations between Great Britain and its former colonies. The British, however, would not have relinquished their claims to the Northwest so readily had they still been in firm possession of it. Clark's influence should not be overemphasized, but it should also not be ignored.

During most of the war years survival had been the primary concern of the men and women who were Kentucky's pioneers. But even as the struggle continued, other changes and events were occurring in the West that put Kentucky on the road to statehood.

5

The Road to Statehood

Traveling to Kentucky

Despite the dangers from Indians that at times threatened to eliminate the early Kentucky settlements, the population of settlers increased substantially during the years of the American Revolution. In the late spring of 1775 the total number of settlers was probably no more than 150, including two women at Boonesborough. The first real surge of settlers came after Clark's campaign of 1778-79 seemed to promise greater security for the Kentucky stations. So many persons left the Fort Pitt vicinity for Kentucky that an officer stationed there feared that the area would be depopulated. In the spring of 1780 John Floyd wrote from the Falls of the Ohio that "near 300 large boats have arrived this spring at the Falls with families." He estimated that the stations on or near Beargrass Creek contained at least 600 men.

The surge subsided about 1781 but resumed in 1784. Virginia paid its soldiers with military land warrants, with the amount of land awarded depending upon a soldier's rank and length of service. Discharged soldiers and their families thus increased the ranks of immigrants into Kentucky. Some observers believed that the population may have doubled in 1784, the first year in which Kentucky farmers produced large surplus crops. A British agent put the 1788 population at 62,000, and the census of 1790 reported 73,077 persons. By 1800 Kentucky had 220,955 inhabitants, a gain of more than 200 percent since 1790. That rate of growth could not be sustained, but by 1810 an 84 percent increase from 1800 brought the population to 406,509.

Virginia supplied most of the immigrants, and substantial numbers also came from Pennsylvania and North Carolina. A few newcomers had been born abroad, but the great majority of the population in 1790 were native-born. Most of Kentucky's settlers came in search of greater economic opportunities, and that meant the acquisition of land. Blacks were the major exception. In 1790 Kentucky had 11,830 blacks who were slaves and only 114 who were free. Few slaves had any choice about moving to Kentucky; they did as their masters ordered. A modern study concludes that 51.6 percent of the white population in 1790 were of English descent, 24.8 percent were Scots and Scotch-Irish, 9.0 percent were Irish, 6.7 percent were Welsh, 4.9 percent were German, 1.6 percent were French, 1.2 percent were Dutch, and 0.2 percent were Swedish.

Some historians have detected a decline in the quality as well as a change in the number of immigrants about 1784. A striking change in leadership occurred about then. Most of the prominent leaders of the early years—Boone, Harrod, Clark, Kenton—had little part in the movement that led to statehood in 1792. Benjamin Logan was the main exception. One of the outstanding pioneer leaders, Logan was narrowly defeated for the governorship of the state as late as 1796.

Immigrants usually followed two main routes into Kentucky. Until near the turn of the nineteenth century, more newcomers came through Cumberland Gap than made the voyage down the Ohio River, although wheeled vehicles were not able to pass through the Gap until 1796. Efforts to improve the trail by private subscriptions were not successful, and in 1795 Governor Isaac Shelby (1750-1826) commissioned James Knox and Joseph Crockett to improve it at a cost of two thousand pounds, an average of twenty pounds per mile. The road was not paved, and heavy rains made it impassable. But on October 15, 1796, the *Kentucky Gazette* announced that "waggons loaded with a ton freight, may pass with ease, with four

good horses." The use of wagons made travel easier and somewhat reduced the cost of bringing in goods overland.

Two of the main sites on this road were Martin's Station south of the Cumberland Gap and Crab Orchard inside Kentucky. Boone's Trace into Boonesborough was little used after the first few years; Scagg's Trace through Flat Rock to Crab Orchard was much more heavily traveled. Martin's Station and Crab Orchard were the main assembly points for people going through the Gap. The narrowness of the passage through the mountains made it easy for Indian raiding parties to find potential victims, but frontier civilization advanced so rapidly that soon bands of white outlaws were also preying upon unwary travelers. An occasional rash individual or small party would risk running the passage, but most travelers preferred to go in large parties, even if they had to wait for enough people to assemble. When John Breckinridge (1760-1806) was in Kentucky in 1789 looking for a site for a future home, he received a letter from Polly, his anxious wife: "Pray my Dear Mr. Breckinridge be very caucious in comeing home especially in comeing through the wilderness. As my whole happiness or Misery as to this life depands on your return I would wish you to have a large company." When groups formed, they customarily elected a leader whom the others promised to obey until the dangerous miles were passed. Occasionally a group even went so far as to draw up formal written articles that spelled out the duties and responsibilities of each person.

Some of the people who wanted to get a new start in Kentucky could not afford the horses that made travel overland more comfortable and quicker. Methodist bishop Francis Asbury (1745-1816) wrote in 1803 of seeing "men, women, and children, almost naked, paddling bare-foot and bare-legged along, or labouring up the rocky hills, whilst those who are best off have only a horse for two or three children to ride at once." Yet he also must have met the numerous wagons and herds of cattle

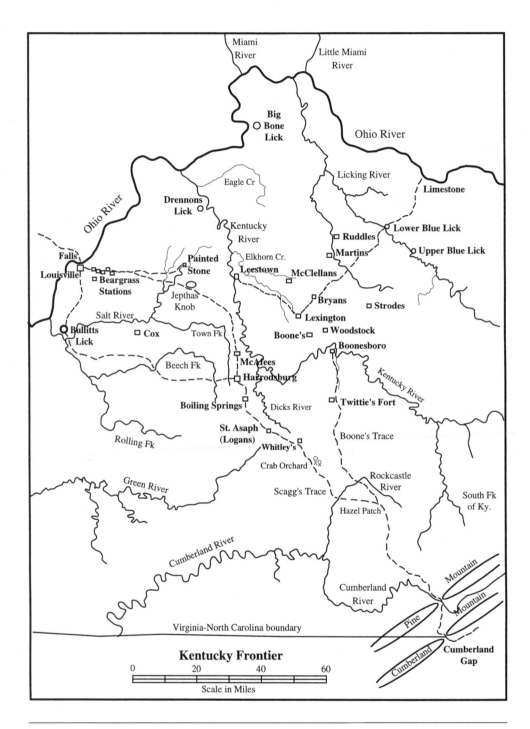

Miami
River

Little Miami
River

Big
Bone
Lick

Ohio River

Licking River

Limestone

Ohio River

Eagle Cr

Drennons
Lick

Kentucky
River

Lower Blue Lick

Ruddles

Upper Blue Lick

Painted
Stone

Elkhorn Cr.

Martins

Falls

Leestown

McClellans

Louisville

Beargrass
Stations

Jepthas
Knob

Bryans

Strodes

Salt River

Lexington

Bullitts
Lick

Cox

Town Fk

Boone's

Woodstock

Beech Fk

McAfees

Boonesboro

Harrodsburg

Kentucky River

Boiling Springs

Dicks River

Twittie's Fort

St. Asaph
(Logans)

Rolling Fk

Whitley's

Boone's Trace

Crab Orchard

Green River

Scagg's Trace

Rockcastle
River

Hazel Patch

South Fk
of Ky.

Cumberland River

Mountain

Cumberland
River

Mountain

Virginia-North Carolina boundary

Pine

Cumberland
Gap

Cumberland

Kentucky Frontier

0   20   40   60

Scale in Miles

and horses of wealthy planters, whose removal was made easy by the efforts of slaves. The allure of Kentucky affected persons of every socioeconomic status, and by the tens of thousands they passed through Cumberland Gap into what they hoped was the land of promise.

The Ohio River was the other main passageway into Kentucky. Pittsburgh was the point from which distances were measured. An early and somewhat inaccurate source informed travelers on the river that 500 miles would take them to Limestone (Maysville); 626 to the Kentucky River; 703 to the Falls of the Ohio; 922 to the Green River; and 1,183 to the Mississippi River. Many of those who used the water route started well above Pittsburgh, on the Allegheny or the Monongahela or on one of their navigable tributaries. Getting to the launching point sometimes involved traveling several hundred miles over difficult terrain.

The immigrants used several types of crafts. Indian-type canoes ranged widely in size. Some carried one or two people and a small amount of property, and others were as much as thirty-six feet long, with room for a dozen people and several thousand pounds of freight. Canoes were fragile, though, and they were most often used by daring individuals who had to make a rapid trip downstream. The dugout, sturdier than the canoe, also varied a great deal in size. When Daniel Boone prepared to move to Spanish Missouri in 1799, he and his son Nathan cut down a huge poplar tree and made a dugout some fifty or sixty feet long and five feet wide. The labor-intensive task of burning and cutting out a dugout discouraged the widespread use of this craft.

Keelboats were used most often during the days before the steamboat for upstream trips or downstream ones when speed was important. The early keelboats ranged from about forty to one hundred feet in length and seven to twenty feet in width. Larger vessels were built later, to carry passengers in some degree of comfort as well as to haul freight. The pointed ends and the keel, a beam running the length of the hull, made the boat relatively easy to steer

and allowed it to go upstream with a reasonable expenditure of effort. Some boats on the larger rivers were outfitted with sails, but travel usually depended upon rowing or poling. Although the hard, tedious work required a large crew, a keelboat could carry goods cheaper than could a wagon over the poor roads available at the time.

Most of the Kentucky settlers who came down the Ohio, however, made the journey on various kinds of flatboats, which should not be confused with rafts. Flatboats were rectangular, flat-bottomed wooden boats that only went downstream. Thus the boats provided a ready supply of cheap timber at their destinations. A small flatboat might measure twelve by twenty feet. Boats twenty-five by fifty feet were common, and some were considerably larger. The sides were usually built up two or three feet above the bottom. Most flatboats had a cabin for the passengers and the crew, often with a fireplace providing warmth in cold weather and the opportunity for cooking without having to risk going ashore. A pen or stable was often provided for the livestock. A long rear oar and two or four shorter oars on the sides allowed some degree of steering. A traveler could build his own boat, but that took more time than many impatient settlers were willing to spend. At several key points completed boats could be purchased or ordered built to specifications. An industrious group of Germans at Redstone on the Monongahela River constructed flatboats almost on an assembly line basis. While costs varied, a boat twelve feet wide might sell for about a dollar per foot of length.

Flatboats usually tied up at a shore overnight and in bad weather, but some travelers risked the danger from snags and other water hazards in order to make better time. A good day's journey was reckoned at fifty to a hundred miles. A forty-foot boat needed at least three hands for navigation; it was better to have more. Even small boats could carry eight or ten tons, and some of the large ones could handle seventy or eighty tons. This load capacity meant that downstream freight rates were relatively

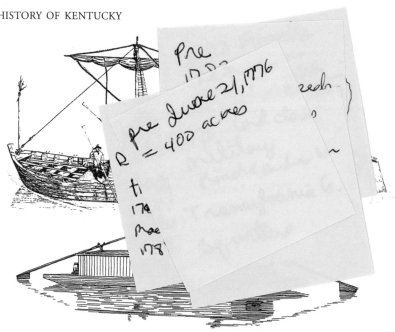

The keelboat and the flatboat were especially important before the advent of the steamboat.

cheap. Carrying an order of goods the sixty-three miles overland from Limestone to a Lexington store usually cost more than transporting the goods from Pittsburgh to Limestone on the river. When James Wilkinson bought a four-wheeled carriage in the East and brought it to Lexington in 1788, a flatboat was the only method of conveyance available to him. When the South Union Shakers dispatched their first load of animals and goods to New Orleans in 1824, their fifteen-by-sixty-foot flatboat carried 100 sheep and 250 hogs in addition to barrels of kraut, garden seed, and other items. Kentucky's major ports for flatboats during this period were Limestone (Maysville) and the Falls of the Ohio (Louisville).

River travelers encountered numerous dangers and problems. The loaded flatboats were tempting targets for Indians who sought plunder and scalps, and white outlaws also soon preyed upon the would-be settlers. The outlaws at Cave-in-Rock on the Illinois side of the Ohio River opposite present-day Crittenden County and the infamous Harpe brothers, Micaja and Wiley, were feared throughout the region.

White prisoners were sometimes used to lure boats to the northern shore, where they could be attacked; midstream assaults by canoe were rare but did occur. The river itself was often inhospitable, although many travelers wrote of the beauty of the Ohio in its pristine state. The heavy flatboats drew considerable water, steering was a slow process with the clumsy crafts, and passengers and crew often found themselves trying to get the boat off a sandbar or replacing a stove-in plank. Low water might immobilize a boat for weeks or months at a time; wise travelers planned a trip during the seasons when waters were high and currents swift. Winter ice could also cause exasperating delays. The river was littered with snags, free floating trees, and other hazards that endangered even a carefully handled boat. None of the myriad problems, however, could halt the flood of future Kentuckians who made the river journey.

Land Claims in Kentucky

The rapid growth of population brought about several political and administrative changes during the years of the Revolution. Virginia as a colony and then as a state had considerable experience in dealing with expanding frontiers. The usual practice was to create an enormous county that encompassed areas just being explored; as its population grew, the big county was divided into more compact units. From 1772 Kentucky was a part of Fincastle County, Virginia; by the end of 1776 Fincastle was divided into Kentucky, Montgomery, and Washington Counties, the latter two of which remained in Virginia when the Kentucky separation occurred in 1792. By 1780 the growth of Kentucky County justified a division into Fayette, Jefferson, and Lincoln Counties. These three counties continued to be referred to collectively as Kentucky, and in March 1783 the Virginia General Assembly created the District of Kentucky as a judicial region. Many legal cases that previously could be heard only in Richmond could henceforward be tried in the District, although appeals from the Kentucky courts had to be taken east, at great expense in money and time. The District's Supreme Court met for the first time at Harrodsburg on March 3, 1783, with John Floyd and Samuel McDowell presiding. George Muter joined them on the bench in 1785.

Before Kentucky achieved statehood, six additional counties had been created: Nelson (1784), Bourbon, Madison, and Mercer (1785), and Woodford and Mason (1788). Each county sent two representatives to the Virginia House of Representatives, where the Kentucky delegates were greatly outnumbered by those from the eastern part of the state. With the creation of a county came the establishment of county and quarter session courts and the appointment of court clerks and justices of the peace. Local government created opportunities for lawyers, and their ranks grew rapidly. Better educated than most of their contemporaries, trained in speaking and writing, and usually young and ambitious, lawyers played an important role in the acquisition of statehood and the development of the new state.

The appearance of attorneys in growing numbers was not always greeted with acclaim.

Kentuckians knew the bitter joke, probably as old as the profession, that while a community might be too small to support one attorney, two or more could thrive there. Lawyers were necessary in a litigious society, however, and well before statehood Kentuckians were noted for their cantankerousness over land issues.

The Jackson Purchase was the only area in Kentucky that was systematically surveyed. In most of the state surveying was done haphazardly, often by surveyors who were inexperienced, sometimes nearly illiterate, and too often unscrupulous. Reference points were often natural features that could change over time—such as "three oak trees" or "a sharp bend in the creek." These kinds of markers could lead to atrocious controversies and feuds. Honest men might well miss the marks by which someone had made a claim; less honest individuals might deliberately file an overlapping claim and scurry to get title to it before the original claimant completed the process. Daniel Boone and Simon Kenton were the best known of the pioneers who shed their own blood to win Kentucky but lost all the acres they had claimed. Ill equipped to deal with the practices and the morals of the civilization that replaced the frontier they loved, both men left the state to which they had contributed so much.

In 1776 three types of land claims existed in Kentucky: military claims based on service in the French and Indian War, claims purchased from the Transylvania Company, and squatters' claims that had no legal basis but could hardly be ignored. Although the Transylvania claims were invalid, Virginia decided to accept them as having been purchased in good faith. In 1776 the Virginia Convention gave preference to the pioneers who were actually settling the western lands. Anyone who had been in Kentucky for a year before June 24, 1776, or had raised a corn crop was entitled to four hundred acres. This hastily conceived act and a somewhat similar one in 1777 were replaced by the Land Act of 1779. Those persons who held a claim and had raised a corn crop before January 1, 1778, were entitled to four hundred acres at $2.25 per

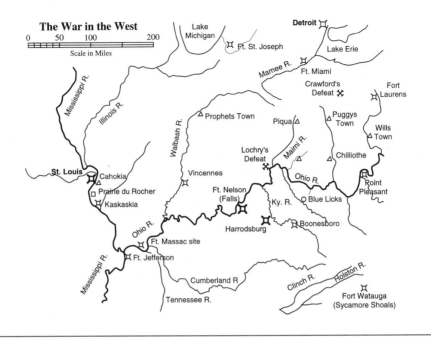

The War in the West

0   50   100   200

Scale in Miles

Lake Michigan

Detroit

Ft. St. Joseph

Lake Erie

Mamee R.

Ft. Miami

Crawford's Defeat ✗

Fort Laurens

Mississippi R.

Illinois R.

Walbash R.

Prophets Town

Piqua

Puggys Town

Wills Town

Lochry's Defeat

Maimi R.

Chilliothe

St. Louis   Cahokia

Vincennes

Ohio R.

Point Pleasant

Prairie du Rocher

Ft. Nelson (Falls)

Ky. R.

Blue Licks

Kaskaskia

Ohio R.

Harrodsburg

Boonesboro

Ft. Massac site

Ft. Jefferson

Mississippi R.

Cumberland R

Clinch R.

Holston R.

Tennessee R.

Fort Watauga (Sycamore Shoals)

The War in the West (courtesy of Neal O. Hammon)

hundred acres and could preempt one thousand acres at $40.00 per hundred acres. A cabin or hut had to be constructed on the property for the claimant to qualify for the preemption. Virginia accepted its depreciated currency in payment, so the actual cost was not high.

A purchaser had to go through four steps to obtain a title to the land—until and unless the title was challenged. One disgruntled Kentuckian complained, "Who buys land there, buys a lawsuit."

First, the purchaser had to obtain a land warrant. Military warrants, based on rank and length of service, were numerous, and the land south of the Green River was reserved for these claimants. Treasury warrants could be purchased at prices that changed from time to time. An individual who had brought immigrants to Kentucky could apply for special "importation rights," and those eligible for the 1779 preemption rights could apply for them. Warrants were often bought and sold, and the system was so lax that warrants were issued for more acres than Kentucky had.

Second, the warrant holder had to file an entry with the county surveyor, listing the number of acres claimed and locating the land generally by reference to natural landmarks or buildings if they existed in that area. Many controversies arose from this requirement, for claims could easily overlap.

Third, the county surveyor had to conduct an actual survey, something that many were not qualified to do accurately. Differences between the entry and the survey were common, and money could be made by hunting for the odd bits of land that had been left unclaimed by surveys.

Fourth, after the survey had been completed, the plat and field notes were supposed to be turned in at the land office within a year. (A land office was opened at Harrodsburg in 1779, eliminating the necessity of making a trip to the office in Richmond.) That office would then issue a patent as proof of ownership. The land office did not have comprehensive maps for most of Kentucky, and it often granted shingled claims.

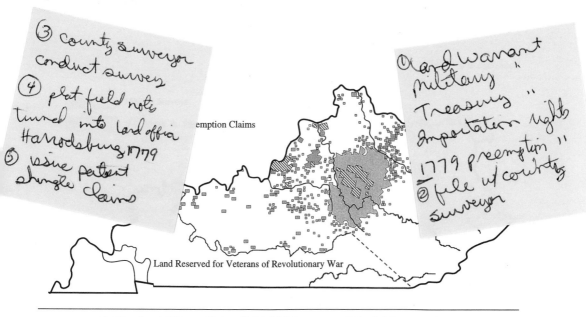

Settlers' and Military Claims, 1774-1780 (courtesy of Neal O. Hammon)

The four-step procedure was cumbersome and often entailed considerable travel, and many Kentucky pioneers did not bother to go through all the steps. Mann Butler, one of the state's first historians, wrote: "Here commenced that scramble for land, which has distressed and isolated society in Kentucky almost as calamitously, as pestilence or famine. . . . The breaking up of favorite homes, improved at the hazard of the owner's life, and fondly looked to as a support for declining age; and a reward for affectionate children, swept away by refinements above popular comprehension, produced most widespread discontent and distress; promoted a litigious spirit, and, in some instances, a disregard of legal rights in general, which had presented itself in such odious and afflicting aspects."

Aware of serious problems, the lawmakers of 1779 set up a court of land commissioners to settle the disputed claims as quickly as possible. The four commissioners—William Fleming, James Barbour, Samuel Lyne, and James Steptoe—held their first session at Logan's Station on October 13, 1779. The court then moved to several other locations before ending its work in April 1780. During that six-month period the court settled 1,328 claims covering more than 1.3 million acres. Inevitably, the court left as many persons displeased

with its rulings as those who were happy with them, and new conflicts and disputes arose all the time.

An act of May 1781 allowed county courts to have surveys done for people who could not pay for them. A family could then get four hundred acres for only twenty shillings per hundred acres, and that price was reduced to thirteen shillings in 1783 when the two years' lifetime of the act was extended by six months. This limited effort was one of the few indications that Kentucky was a "poor man's frontier." In truth, Kentucky never fit this description, except perhaps briefly in the Green River area. The possibility of getting fourteen hundred acres under the terms of the 1779 act encouraged speculators and dishonest practices. Land jobbers who had no intention of becoming farmers hurried about the District acquiring claims by using the names of friends. At least twenty-one individuals and companies acquired grants in excess of one hundred thousand acres. In 1792, only seventeen years after settlement began, approximately two-thirds of adult white males in Kentucky did not own land.

Background to Separation from Virginia

The Virginia Constitution of 1776 provided an orderly procedure by which an area could separate from the state, and most Virginians probably expected Kentucky to take advantage of this provision some time in the future. George Rogers Clark had considered the possibilities of independence in 1776, and four years later a petition signed by more than six hundred inhabitants of Kentucky and Illinois asked the Continental Congress to form a new state along the Ohio Valley. Some discontented petitioners sought Clark's leadership in this undertaking, but he rejected their approaches. In 1780 Thomas Paine made a case for separation with another of his famous pamphlets: in *The Public Good* Paine argued that because of the Proclamation Line of 1763, the transmontane had reverted to the Crown and was no longer a part of Virginia. Anyway, he continued, the differences between Virginia and Kentucky were so great that the two would be better off apart. A petition to Congress in 1782 followed this reasoning, but to no avail. Two years later two Pennsylvania agitators, Joseph Galloway and George Pomeroy, upset some Kentucky landowners by asserting that Virginia titles were invalid. Quick trials and guilty convictions under an obscure colonial law forced the two troublemakers into hasty departures from Kentucky.

The grievances against the Virginia government centered arou
Many Kentuckians b
would never pay seriou
problem. Most irksom
that offensive action c
the District of Kentuc
sion from Richmond
tuckians protested; t
did but got almost r
tax of five shillings
sury warrants for tra

hundred acres incensed large landowners and prospective land speculators. The West had been so neglected that even the postal service had not been extended to it. Months might pass before Kentuckians learned of new laws or administrative decisions. Even after lower courts were established in Kentucky, the time and money required to go back east to conduct appeals

proved so burdensome that Kentuckians were effectively denied justice. The District was also hurt economically by an unfavorable balance of trade that drained money to the East and hampered business. Nearly all Kentuckians complained that neither the state nor the central government, which after 1781 operated under the Articles of Confederation, was sufficiently concerned about the unrestricted use of the Mississippi River. The river was the only practical outlet for surplus products from Kentucky. In 1784 substantial surpluses were produced for several crops, and on June 26 Spanish authorities closed the river and New Orleans to American use. The national government responded with an attempt by John Jay, the secretary for foreign affairs, to negotiate a treaty by which the United States would give up the right to use the river for twenty-five or thirty years in return for a commercial treaty that would benefit East Coast merchants. The southern states blocked that proposal, but even Virginia was not doing anything to guarantee free use of the river and the right of deposit at New Orleans to its citizens in the District of Kentucky.

Some contemporary observers noted the uncanny resemblance that many of the grievances of Kentuckians bore to those of the American colonists before the Revolution. The only difference, one Kentuckian complained, was that Kentucky was represented in the Virginia General Assembly (although outvoted by delegates from the East), while Americans had not been represented in the British Parliament. The question implied in such reasoning was clear: Was it time for Kentucky to separate from Virginia? At least some people wondered whether Kentucky would not be better off separated from the United States as well.

Starting toward Statehood

An Indian scare started Kentucky on the long and confusing road to statehood. In the late autumn of 1784 Benjamin Logan, colonel of the Lincoln County militia, heard rumors of Indian attacks. The district court was meeting in Danville, and the meeting that Logan called to consider what should be done was well attended. Some of those present wanted to strike the Indians in their homelands, but Caleb Wallace, George Muter, and others protested that such a response was illegal. Ebenezer Brooks suggested that separating from Virginia would result in what was best for Kentucky. His motion was not seconded, but the idea was in the open. By the second day Logan learned that the rumors of Indian attacks were just rumors, but the men decided to call a meeting in Danville for December 27, 1784, to decide what should be done concerning separation. Each militia company in the District of Kentucky was asked to send a delegate to what became the first statehood convention.

Throughout the ten conventions that discussed separation from Virginia, politically aware Kentuckians fell into three loosely associated factions: the partisans, the planters, and the court party. These groups had no formal organization, no declared platform, and no system for making nominations and raising money. They were not political parties in the modern sense. Thus it is dangerous to try to trace too close a connection between them and the parties that did develop in the 1790s.

The partisans were generally the landless men for whom Kentucky had not been a land of opportunity. They wanted to break up the large estates and redistribute the land. Since Virginia would obviously not do that, the partisans looked toward the national government for help. After Congress agreed to honor the Virginia grants, some of the partisans dreamed of separation from the United States. If statehood was won, they hoped to control the new state government through democratic processes that seemed radical to their opponents. Ebenezer Brooks, Samuel Taylor, and John Campbell were among the leading partisans, but they could not match the leadership of the other factions.

The gentry, a small minority of the total population, worked to assure the voters that political power was in their own hands but also to persuade them to select natural aristocrats as

their leaders. During this critical period the gentry split into two factions, divided more by personal and family differences than by principles.

Members of the country faction, also called the planters or surveyors, were likely to be the large landowners and slaveholders who were determined to hold on to what they had acquired. A strong central government would help ensure a stable economic system. Colonel Thomas Marshall, father of John Marshall, the Chief Justice of the United States from 1801 to 1835, led this faction; his nephew Humphrey Marshall (1760-1841) was its most controversial member. Humphrey had a knack for infuriating opponents, and his long career was marked by duels and fights. He often had the last word, for he wrote the first comprehensive history of Kentucky in 1812, and in it and in the revised and enlarged 1824 edition he lambasted his opponents. Among the other country faction leaders were Robert Bullitt, Robert Breckinridge, John Edwards, and Joseph Crockett. As a group, the country faction sought separation from Virginia on mutually agreeable terms, followed by admission into the Union.

As its name implied, the court party was dominated by lawyers and judges, although it had other members as well. Most of these people had arrived too late to acquire large tracts of land. Landownership was a badge of gentility, however, and most of them aspired to that status. They were much interested in the political system of which they were a part. Trained in delivering speeches and drafting documents, they were active in most of the ten statehood conventions. They were also interested in economic development, manufacturing as well as agriculture and commerce. Some of them wondered if Kentucky's future would be best served by membership in the Union. Should Kentucky look for greater opportunities elsewhere? James Wilkinson (1757-1825), who was not a lawyer, became the major advocate of this approach. Among the other notable leaders were John Fowler, Benjamin Sebastian

57

(1745-1834), John Brown (1757-1837), Harry Innes (1752-1816), Caleb Wallace (1742-1814), and Samuel McDowell (1735-1817). George Muter became an apostate when he switched to the country faction.

Nine Conventions but Not a State

The road to statehood required ten conventions and nearly as many years. Some continuity was provided by Samuel McDowell, who presided over all except the first and ninth conventions, and Thomas Todd (1765-1826), who was the clerk of all except the first one. Some of the journals have disappeared, and the surviving ones contain no information about the debates and discussions. Two decisions indicated the democratic frontier spirit of the early Kentuckians. In calling for the second convention, the delegates to the first one ignored the Virginia requirement of equal county representation and assigned delegates according to estimated population. Virginia soon blocked that approach. The fifth convention decided to abandon all religious and property qualifications and to allow free white males of age to vote.

Few Virginians opposed separation if the rights of Virginians in Kentucky were protected. Indeed, before statehood was achieved, many persons in the Old Dominion were probably eager to get rid of the troublesome people beyond the mountains. Several reasons explain why the process took so long. One was the laudable desire to make sure that the delegates did represent the wishes of "the good people of Kentucky." Ascertaining that desire meant the calling of another convention, with separation as the issue before the voters. The fourth convention could not make a quorum in September 1786 because many of the delegates were engaged in one of two expeditions fighting the Indians. By the time the group convened in January 1787, the Virginia legislature had called for another convention. Statehood seemed near in the summer of 1788, but at the last moment the Articles of Confederation Congress decided that granting permission to enter the Union should be done by the Con-

gress that would be formed under the new Constitution of the United States. The Third Enabling Act passed by the Virginia General Assembly was not acceptable to the Kentuckians, whose demand for revisions meant that yet another convention would have to be held.

Several of the delegates waiting for the meeting of the fourth convention passed time by discussing and debating issues at the Danville Political Club, organized in December 1786. The club's membership included Harry Innes, Christopher Greenup, Thomas Todd, George Muter, Peyton Short, Benjamin Sebastian, and Samuel McDowell. A state historian called it "a training school for the future statesmen of Kentucky." The debaters considered such topics as separation from Virginia, the best composition for a legislature, the use of the Mississippi River, and the essential elements of a constitution. They also conducted a four-meeting analysis of the federal constitution. Nonpolitical topics included the feasibility of not raising tobacco and intermarriage with Indians. Discussions were usually spirited and sometimes heated. An army officer passing through Danville in April 1787 complained in his diary: "Very much disturbed by a Political Club which met in the next room where we slept and kept us awake until 12 or 1 o'clock." The club continued until at least 1790, and a number of its members discussed some of the club's topics again during the conventions.

The new federal constitution that was debated in the Danville Political Club was viewed with considerable suspicion by most Kentuckians. The vote in the Virginia ratifying convention was expected to be so close that the fourteen Kentuckians might decide the issue. Proponents of the Constitution, led by James Madison, John Marshall, and George Nicholas (1743-99), made an able defense of the document and pointed out that its amending process allowed changes to be made as needed. Nicholas told the Kentucky delegates that they had nothing to fear from it. He was preparing to move to Kentucky himself, and he would not do anything to harm his future home. The con-

James Wilkinson lived a life of intrigue. No superior was safe from his machinations. Portrait by John Wesley Jarvis (courtesy of The Filson Club Historical Society)

vention ratified the Constitution on June 25, 1788, by a vote of 89-79, with ten of the fourteen Kentucky delegates voting in the negative. Humphrey Marshall, Robert Breckinridge, and Rice Bullock favored acceptance; for some reason, delegate Notley Conn did not vote.

Another complication on the road to Kentucky's statehood was that at some stages in the lengthy process some Kentuckians wanted to separate unilaterally from the United States as well as Virginia and possibly forge a relationship with Spain. James Wilkinson was the leader in this scheme. Born in Maryland in 1757, Wilkinson rose to the rank of brigadier general during the Revolution, despite a penchant for intrigue that brought him into conflict with George Washington, Benedict Arnold, and Horatio Gates. No superior was ever safe from Wilkinson's machinations. His lavish lifestyle required more income than the East provided, and he moved to Kentucky in 1784, opened a store in Lexington, and speculated in land. He acquired a following of young men who were attracted by his generosity with

food and drink and his air of sophistication. Fluent with tongue and pen, Wilkinson made an excellent first impression.

Beset by financial problems, Wilkinson made an audacious journey to New Orleans in 1787. He convinced Governor Esteban Rodríguez Miró that Kentucky was near separation from the United States and that he could determine what course was taken. He could direct American immigration into Spanish territory, he could prevent an invasion of westerners to open the use of the Mississippi River by force, and he could bring Kentucky into the Spanish orbit. In return, he wanted a trade monopoly, a royal pension, and a suitable rank and position if Kentucky became associated with Spain. Miró had to refer the requests to Spain, but he gave the Kentuckian permission to sell as much as thirty-seven thousand dollars' worth of produce in New Orleans. For the moment Wilkinson was the only New Orleans outlet for Kentucky products.

Wilkinson sailed from New Orleans to the East Coast, then traveled home in style, with a four-wheeled carriage pulled by a perfectly matched team and with black servants as outriders. Kentucky had seen nothing to compare with it. Neither Wilkinson's contemporaries nor later historians have ever agreed on his goals in what became known as the Spanish Conspiracy. Did he hope to move an independent Kentucky into an association with Spain, perhaps as a province that he would govern? Or did he finesse the gullible Spaniards into granting the trade concession while he had no intention of entering into any political association, even if he could have brought it about? Throughout his long and checkered career James Wilkinson had a knack for survival that depended upon keeping all of his options open until he could see what would be the best course for him. He was never found guilty of any of the many charges brought against him. It may be that in the Spanish Conspiracy he had no clear goal in mind exc_____ acquire money and position.

Prices soared as _____ed goods until Miró begge_' _____ especially of tobacco_ _____ state during thi_ _____ almost certain' _____ Yet even du_____ _____ men quest_____ _____ intrigue clung _____ he did not answe___ _____ to take Kentucky ou_ _____ best chance came in the _____ in November 1788. The dele_____ ___us because in July Congress had re_ ____rmission for Kentucky to enter the Union, _nd some of them wanted to declare separation unilaterally and immediately. Kentucky *must* have the free use of the Mississippi River, Wilkinson told the delegates, and since Spain would not grant it to the United States, Kentucky must act alone. He proposed that they draft a constitution, declare independence from Virginia, and organize a government. If terms were satisfactory, then Kentucky might join the Union; if terms were unsatisfactory, then Kentucky would have to look elsewhere.

Then Wilkinson turned toward John Brown and remarked that a gentleman was present who had important information about the Mississippi. Brown, one of Wilkinson's faithful henchmen, had been a member of the Virginia delegation to Congress. In several conversations with Spanish minister Don Gardoqui, Brown had been told that Kentucky could secure rights that would never be granted to the United States. Wilkinson apparently hoped that Brown's account of those talks would sweep the delegates into taking the action he had suggested. But Brown had drifted away from Wilkinson's position, and his lukewarm remarks foiled Wilkinson's hopes of securing precipitate action.

Economy was not in Wilkinson's vocabulary, and in 1789 he made another trip to New Orleans in a desperate attempt to shore up his perilous financial condition. During this trip he wrote a memorial in which he listed a number of prominent Kentuckians and indicated the amount of money that would be required to suborn them. When that list became known, some Kentuckians whose names appeared on it _ere embarrassed. Miró provided some expense ___ey, and Wilkinson continued to try to con_____ __anish officials that he could determine ___ _ of the American West. Questions ___ _is activities were increasing, however, _ere his debts. In 1791, when he managed _ get a commission in the regular army, this exotic Kentuckian left the state. Assigned to the Northwest Territory, he began at once to undermine the position of General "Mad Anthony" Wayne.

The Virginia Compact

The Fourth Enabling Act, passed on December 18, 1789, met Kentucky's objections to the Third Enabling Act. Better known as the Virginia Compact, it set forth the conditions of separation under which Kentucky finally obtained statehood. It called for the ninth convention to meet in late July 1790. If that convention accepted the terms of the compact, then the ninth convention could provide for the calling of the tenth one, provided that

Congress agreed to the separation before November 1, 1791, and released Virginia from all federal obligations in regard to Kentucky. The boundaries of the state would be the same as existed for the District of Kentucky; Kentucky would assume "a just proportion" of the debt of the United States and would pay the costs of its expeditions against the Indians since January 1, 1785; Virginia land grants would remain valid and secure; the land rights of nonresident owners would be protected; Virginia land warrants located on or before September 1, 1791, would be valid; Virginia military warrants could be located in Kentucky until May 1, 1792; use of the Ohio River was to be free and common to all citizens of the United States; and a joint commission of six members would settle disputes arising under the compact. The convention would determine what laws would be in force until the new state legislature took action.

The ninth convention voted 24-18 to accept the terms of the Fourth Enabling Act, and it arranged for the constitutional convention to meet in Danville on the first Monday in April 1792. Vermont's request for statehood was moving through Congress, and its presence alleviated the concern over the admission of a new southern state. On February 4, 1791, Congress completed passage of the bill admitting Kentucky to the Union. The formal date of admission would be June 1, 1792. Kentucky would be the Union's fifteenth state.

Drafting the 1792 Constitution

Some skeptics in Kentucky and elsewhere wondered whether the District had men who were capable of framing a constitution and implementing a state government. Kentucky lacked the infrastructure of institutions and experience that Virginia enjoyed. John Brown expressed a concern that has been pertinent to state politics for more than two centuries: "It would be a circumstance truly humiliating, if at this day when the subject of Government is so fully understood, Kentucky actuated by motives of niggardly economy, should adopt a bad form of Government rather than incur the necessary

expense of a good one." Several Kentuckians tried to get James Madison to draft a constitution for the state, but he refused to go beyond a statement of general principles.

Fortunately, George Nicholas had moved to Kentucky and was its leading attorney. Bald and rotund—a friend described him as a "plum pudding with legs"—Nicholas appeared older than his years. He swore when he left Virginia after the bitter battle over ratification of the federal constitution that his political days were ended. But he was concerned about Kentucky's future, and he wrote his friend James Madison in May 1789 that the general government must act to meet the legitimate complaints of the westerners. If disappointed by the inaction of the government, Nicholas warned, "I shall be ready to join in any other Modes for obtaining our rights." Madison should recall, he added, that after failing to put down the Revolution, Great Britain would have eagerly agreed to the terms that the colonists had requested but been denied: "Reasonable terms when once rejected will not give satisfaction." Nicholas came out of his brief political retirement to become a member of the tenth statehood convention and to earn the sobriquet Father of the First Kentucky Constitution.

The delegates received a great deal of advice about what they should do. Members of the partisan faction favored more direct democracy than did most of their opponents, and they tried to influence the convention by forming county committees to instruct the delegates. Such committees were formed in at least five counties—Bourbon, Fayette, Madison, Mason, and Mercer—and may have existed elsewhere. The Bourbon group was the most active, and the *Kentucky Gazette* made its proposals well known. These groups represented a minority of the population, however, and their views were considered radical or visionary by most voters. Harry Innes was one of many elite citizens who scorned the pretensions of the "peasantry." Such pretensions, he believed, gave "a very serious alarm to every thinking man." The partisans did stir up considerable controversy, and

This replica of the Mercer County Courthouse, in which most of the ten statehood conventions met, stands on Constitution Square in Danville (courtesy of the Kentucky Department of Parks).

they may have had some influence in keeping the constitution from being a quite conservative document.

One of the most unusual letters to the *Gazette* came from "A Medler" who identified herself as a woman. If this was true, then this letter may well have represented the first entry of a woman into political discussions in Kentucky. Few Kentuckians of that period dreamed of women's being allowed to vote, and women simply did not participate in political debates. The "meddler" echoed the partisans' objection to having "great men" draft the constitution and direct the government. She observed that the most solid wisdom was "among those who live above poverty and yet below affluence."

The animosity that many citizens felt toward lawyers was stated by "Salamander," who asserted that "the fewer Lawyers and Pick pockets there are in a country, the better the chance honest people have to keep their own." This sentiment was so strong that only two attorneys were elected to the constitutional convention, and a serious but unsuccessful effort was made to exclude them from the legislature.

"Phillip Philips," a newcomer to Mercer County, predicting the ultimate end of slavery, angered some readers by asserting that if blacks received as much education as whites, it would be apparent that the mental capacities of the two races were almost identical. He drew quick rebuttals, but "Brutus Senior" wrote that having slaves was the same as having stolen property. If slaves lacked such traits as honesty

and honor, it was because of the effect that the institution had upon those held in bondage.

The efforts of the county committees and the realization that the convention would have far-reaching effects on the state resulted in a spirited election. The forty-five delegates were nearly all men of some wealth. Two-thirds of them owned at least five slaves, and nearly all had considerable property in land, horses, cattle, and household goods. The seven ministers—three Presbyterians, three Baptists, and one Methodist—all held views that were somewhat antislavery. As a group the delegates had limited public experience; Nicholas did much to fill that void.

The convention opened on Monday, April 2, 1792. One of the most controversial issues concerned the judiciary and Nicholas's effort to expedite the settlement of land cases. He proposed that the state's supreme court should have original and final jurisdiction in land cases. Nicholas suddenly resigned his seat on Saturday, April 7, possibly because he had not discussed that issue with the voters during the campaign. He was too valuable to lose. A special election was hurriedly scheduled for the following Monday, and the Mercer County voters reelected him. The convention did not meet on Monday because of inclement weather, and Nicholas was back in his seat on Tuesday.

The Reverend David Rice (1733-1816), a Presbyterian minister better known as Father Rice, led the attack on slavery. When he came west in 1783 he was not favorably impressed by Kentucky. Hundreds who had heard him preach begged him to remain, though, and he consented to do so. Few antislavery advocates in Kentucky were abolitionists who demanded immediate, uncompensated freedom for the slaves; they were emancipationists who were willing to take time to end the institution. But they believed that a start must be made, and the state's first constitution was the point at which to begin. Rice attacked slavery as being immoral, unjust, and harmful to the community, and he urged his fellow delegates to include the principle of emancipation in the constitution and to prevent the importation of slaves into the state.

Nicholas was the major defender of slavery. The arguments he employed continued to be used until the institution ended in December 1865, with ratification of the Thirteenth Amendment to the U.S. Constitution. He cited the Bible and history to prove that slavery had always existed, and he insisted that the Virginia Compact prevented any interference with property rights. Kentucky could not afford the cost of buying and freeing slaves. Individuals should be able to free slaves at their own expense, but Nicholas warned that mass emancipation would result in miscegenation and racial debasement. The key vote on a motion to delete the proslavery article 9 of the state constitution was a surprisingly close 16-26 defeat. The history of Kentucky might have been far different had the decision been reversed. Disappointed by the outcome, Rice resigned from the convention. All seven ministers had voted against slavery, and that fact helps explain why ministers were prohibited from serving in the Kentucky legislature.

On Friday, April 13, James Garrard (1749-1822) reported twenty-two resolutions from the Committee of the Whole. These became the basis for the writing of the constitution during the next few days. Nicholas chaired a select committee of ten that drafted a docu-

ment. Each county had a representative on the committee; Jefferson County had two, Benjamin Sebastian and Alexander S. Bullitt. The committee worked over a long weekend, and Nicholas presented a draft constitution on Tuesday, April 17. Changes to the document were made in the Committee of the Whole, and when Samuel McDowell wrote a friend on Wednesday, he predicted that the delegates would finish the next day. "And I think," he said, "we will have a tolerable good Constitution." Several changes were made on Wednesday, and the document received a final reading and approval on Thursday morning. McDowell signed the journal, and Todd attested his signature. No one else signed, and the constitution was not submitted to the voters for approval. The convention had done its work in thirteen working days, over a span of eighteen days total.

The 1792 Constitution

Most of the delegates believed that experience was the best guide to constitution making, and they drew heavily upon the 1790 Pennsylvania Constitution, a reworking of the more radical constitution of 1776. They were not trying to create a utopian political structure. One careful study concluded that 75 of the 107 sections were based directly on the Pennsylvania model; others came from the constitutions of Maryland, the United States, and South Carolina. Twenty sections were original with the tenth convention. Article 11 provided for another convention as early as 1799 if experience showed that changes were needed; no provision was made for individual amendments. While the document referred to both "state" and "commonwealth," Commonwealth of Kentucky became the state's official name.[1]

The founders feared tyranny, so separation of powers was emphasized. But the constitution also included a system of checks and balances, to prevent any branch of the government from becoming too strong. Considerable

---

1. Kentucky chose the term *commonwealth* because it was used by Virginia and the people were accustomed to it. Virginia probably adopted the designation because it was used during the brief period in the mid–seventeenth century when England was a republic. The Anglo-Saxon word *wela* is said to mean "sound and prosperous state."

attention was given to a bicameral (two-house) legislature. Representatives were elected annually, with voting based on population, not on county equality. A state census was to be taken every four years; Kentucky was growing too rapidly to wait ten years for the federal count. In contrast to the members of the House of Representatives, elected by direct popular vote, senators were elected by a body of electors for four-year terms. Each county had a state senator; other senators were to be elected from across the state. Since Kentucky's population was younger than the national average, the age limits were twenty-four for the House and twenty-seven for the Senate. Members of the first Kentucky General Assembly were exempted from the requirement that a legislator could not accept a created position or one for which the pay had been increased during his term until a year after the end of his term. The new administration would have to draw some of its members from the legislature. Each house could expel a member by a two-thirds vote. Since a member could not be expelled twice for the same reason, however, an expelled member could secure political vindication by being reelected to the body that had discarded him.

The governor was given more power than was customary in the early postrevolutionary era. Elected by the electors for a four-year term, he could succeed himself. No provision was made for a lieutenant governor. In case of a vacancy, the Speaker of the Senate acted as governor until a new governor qualified. The governor appointed the attorney general and the secretary of state, as well as numerous local officials. Sheriffs and coroners, however, were elected. In popular elections, ballot voting was required; since a ballot could be seen by the sheriff, though, it was not a true secret ballot.

In establishing a court system, the convention followed the example of the federal constitution. Kentucky was to have a supreme court, known as the Court of Appeals, and such inferior courts as the legislature established. The most controversial aspect of the judiciary article was the Nicholas-sponsored provision that the Court of Appeals should have original and final jurisdiction in land cases. Judges could be removed by impeachment or by address of a two-thirds majority of both houses of the legislature.

Nicholas later said that article 9, concerning slavery, might not have been included had the antislavery advocates not been so persistent. The legislature was prohibited from freeing a slave without the consent of the owner and full payment of the value of the slave. Immigrants must be allowed to bring their slaves into the state, but importation of slaves for commercial use could be forbidden. The legislature was directed to provide ways for masters to free their own slaves and to require humane treatment.

The glaring omission in the 1792 constitution was any statement on public education. Some delegates may have believed that the few private schools were sufficient, others may not have seen any need for education, and some may have believed that providing educational opportunities was not a proper function of the state. The delegates had provided for the most liberal suffrage requirements in the nation in 1792, but they did not admit a connection between general education and informed voting. This early neglect of a vital function of government set a pattern that the commonwealth has followed all too often during the past two centuries.

The constitution represented reasonable compromises among different points of view. While considered quite liberal in some respects, it was moderate enough to reassure conservatives who had feared even worse. Most important, it had brought to a close the apparently endless struggle for statehood. The road to statehood had been long and sometimes difficult, but it had been traversed with an admirable regard for constitutional procedures and frequent consultation with the voters. Now the new state faced a challenge: Could Kentuckians implement their constitution by creating a viable government?

6

From Constitution to Constitution, 1792-1799

Starting the Government

"And politics—the damnedest / In Kentucky": Kentucky has not earned this reputation by favoring nonpartisan elections.[1] The 1792 elections held to implement the new constitution may have been the most nonpartisan ones in the state's history. Without organized political parties and with many possible candidates reluctant to accept office, the election was low-key, with little of the partisanship that later became synonymous with Kentucky politics.

Little time remained between April 19, 1792, when the tenth statehood convention adjourned, and June 1, when statehood became official. Voters elected electors, representatives, sheriffs, and coroners at their county courthouses on May 1. Two weeks later the forty electors met in Lexington and elected the governor, Isaac Shelby, and eleven senators. One senator was elected from each of the nine counties; Alexander Bullitt (Jefferson Co.) and Peyton Short (Fayette Co.) were elected at large. The governor and eight of the senators had been electors. Although statehood became a fact on June 1, Shelby did not take the oath of office until June 4, and the legislature did not meet until that day.

Born in Maryland in 1750, Shelby received limited formal education. He moved with his family to the vicinity of modern Bristol, Tennessee, near the North Carolina-Virginia line, in 1772. Shelby won distinction in Lord Dunmore's War, then spent several years surveying and locating land in the western parts of Virginia and North Carolina, sometimes for himself, sometimes for the Transylvania Com-

---

1. John Wilson Townsend, *"In Kentucky" and Its Author "Jim" Mulligan* (1935), 8-9.

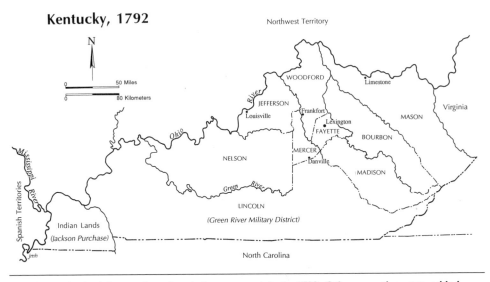

Kentucky, 1792

N

0   50 Miles
0   80 Kilometers

Northwest Territory

Spanish Territories

Mississippi River

Ohio

Green River

Indian Lands
(Jackson Purchase)

NELSON

LINCOLN
(Green River Military District)

WOODFORD

JEFFERSON
Louisville

Frankfort
Lexington
FAYETTE

MERCER
Danville

Limestone

MASON

BOURBON

MADISON

Virginia

North Carolina

jmh

Kentucky had 9 counties when it became a state in 1792. Other counties were added through 1912, resulting in a present total of 120.

pany. Elected to the Virginia legislature in 1779, he could not serve because his home was discovered to be in North Carolina. Shelby saw considerable action during the American Revolution as a colonel in the North Carolina militia; his chief claim to fame came from the annihilation of British major Patrick Ferguson's raiding party of some eleven hundred men at King's Mountain on October 7, 1780. In late 1783 Shelby and his bride, Susannah Hart Shelby, moved to Lincoln County. They soon built an imposing stone house they called Traveler's Rest. Shelby was more interested in farming than in politics, but his reputation for sound, mature judgment sent him to several of the statehood conventions. He must have realized that he would receive consideration as the state's first governor, but in his autobiography he wrote that he hesitated for several days before accepting the election. His sense of duty and the realization that time was short helped overcome his belief that his experience did not qualify him for the position. After his accep-

tance, he spent a night in Danville, then was escorted to Lexington, where he took the oath of office on June 4. His administration as the state's first governor in some ways resembled that of George Washington as first president of the United States. Neither possessed the most brilliant intellect available, neither was a great writer or spellbinding orator, and neither was a political philosopher. Both were known for sound judgment and integrity; they were good judges of character; they had a sense of duty and responsibility; they had the courage to pursue a firm course once they had decided on it. Each had the confidence of a large majority of the people he had been called upon to govern.

The legislature met in a large two-story log structure that the town of Lexington had erected as a marketplace. Alexander Bullitt was elected Speaker of the Senate; Robert Breckinridge became the first Speaker of the House. The General Assembly met in joint session on June 6 to hear the governor's first message. In his brief remarks Shelby expressed hopes for the

Isaac Shelby was Kentucky's first governor (1792-96). He came out of retirement to serve again from 1812 to 1816, during the War of 1812. Portrait by Matthew Jouett, the state's best known portrait painter (courtesy of The Filson Club Historical Society)

success of their political venture and suggested some topics that needed to be considered. He did not propose detailed bills; legislators of that era were jealous of their prerogatives. The first session of the first General Assembly lasted twenty-three working days, but a great deal was accomplished, as the governor and legislators worked in harmony. Numerous appointments were made. George Nicholas became attorney general; Benjamin Logan and Charles Scott (1739-1813) were made major generals in charge of the militia, with the Kentucky River as the dividing line; Harry Innes, Benjamin Sebastian, and Caleb Wallace were appointed to the Court of Appeals; George Muter, Samuel McDowell, and Christopher Greenup were placed on the Court of Oyer and Terminer when it was created. As expected, several legislators accepted administrative or judicial positions, and special elections had to be arranged.

The revenue bill was a vital piece of legislation. One provision indicated that Kentucky was emerging from the frontier stage: all revenue had to be paid in specie; tobacco and tobacco certificates had been a common substitute. A tax on land, slaves, and livestock was the principal source of revenue. The annual tax on one hundred acres was two shillings, or about thirty-three cents. Slaves were also taxed at two shillings per year, except for the elderly and crippled, who could be exempted by the county court. Horses, mares, colts, and mules were taxed at eight pence each, while a stud's tax was the same as the covering fee. Cattle were taxed at three pence each. Vehicles, except for exempted ones used for agricultural production, were taxed at four or six shillings per wheel. An ordinary (a tavern) was licensed at ten pounds annually, as were retail stores. Billiard tables received a "sin tax" of ten pounds each. Ignoring the colonial opposition to stamp duties, the legislators placed fees on legal papers ranging from three to twelve shillings. Since revenue would be collected slowly, the treasurer was authorized to borrow two thousand pounds at 5 percent interest to cover the costs of government for much of the first year. A confusing aspect of Kentucky's finances was that British money continued to be used, along with the recently adopted American dollar system.[2]

The legislature had to create a court system, except for the mandated Court of Appeals. Counties received eight to sixteen justices of the peace, depending upon population estimates. Any three of these justices constituted a county court, but all or most of them sat on important cases. Their decision could be appealed to the quarter sessions court if the value of the suit exceeded fifty shillings or five hundred pounds of tobacco. The justices of the peace who sat on the quarter sessions court could not also sit on the county court. In a violation of the doctrine of separation of powers, the county court had a number of administrative functions. Because of poor transportation—the legislature decreed that twenty-five miles made a full day's journey—citizens came in contact with their county government much more frequently than they did with either the state or federal governments.

The quarter sessions courts heard the most important civil cases and the criminal cases in which possible sentences extended to loss of life or limb. The three-judge Court of Oyer and Terminer met twice a year to try the more serious criminal cases. Its decisions could not be appealed.

During its first session the General Assembly dealt with a variety of issues. The office of state auditor was created; the militia was organized; surveyors were provided for each county; tax commissioners were authorized; payment was provided for the members and employees of the constitutional convention and the members and employees of the General Assembly. (A legislator received one dollar per day during the session; the Speakers got three dollars.) Four new counties were created; districts were established for the election of representatives to Congress; some towns were chartered; regulations were issued concerning stray animals. Numerous private requests and petitions

were received, but most of them were ignored. Members of the General Assembly learned legislative skills quickly; several problems were simply postponed to the next session. On June 18, 1792, a joint session elected John Brown and John Edwards to the U.S. Senate and John Logan as state treasurer.

On that busy day the House began the complicated procedure formulated by the constitutional convention for the selection of a site for the state capital. The House elected twenty-one persons whose names would be placed on a list of prospective committee members. Two days later the representatives from Fayette and Mercer Counties alternately struck names from the list until five remained as the Site Election Committee. The committee frankly indicated that a primary factor would be the inducements offered by communities that sought the status of state capital. The members received several bids, inspected them, and on December 5, 1792, recommended Frankfort. Andrew Holmes, a wealthy businessman, had purchased most of James Wilkinson's Frankfort property, including his large house, and he led the Frankfort drive to secure the position of Kentucky's capital. His offer included rent-free use of the house for seven years, a number of choice building lots, fifteen hundred pounds of nails, ten boxes of ten-by-twelve-inch glass, and other assorted building materials, in addition to three thousand dollars in specie. Boonesborough made a strong bid in land and specie, but Frankfort had the advantage of a more central location. Frankfort was selected because of its offer and its location. It was not a compromise between the proposals of Lexington and Louisville. When the second session of the General Assembly adjourned on December 22, it was "to hold its next session in the house of Andrew Holmes, at Frankfort on the Kentucky River."

The New Land Policy

The continued growth of population after 1792 led to changes in Kentucky's land laws. Consid-

---

2. A British pound was then equal to about $3.33. A shilling was worth 16⅔ cents.

erable acreage was unclaimed, and while most of it was not in choice locations, it still represented a valuable asset. Of particular interest was the region south of the Green River that had been reserved for holders of Virginia military warrants. Farmers were discovering that the Barrens were not as barren as the name implied, and few veterans still held their warrants. Should unclaimed land be sold or rented to provide revenue for the state? If sold, should the state favor individual landholders or dispose of the land to large speculators? Of the several offers from speculators, the most ambitious came from a five-man Philadelphia company. Its agent, Elisha I. Hall, tried in 1795-97 to purchase all of the estimated four to six million acres of undistributed land. To improve his chances, he involved such prominent Kentuckians as John Brown, Harry Innes, George Nicholas, and John Breckinridge in the enterprise. Hall's offer of $260,000, payable over six years, would have resulted in a price of 4.3 to 6.5 cents per acre. Hall's lobbying secured passage in the state Senate, but the House rejected the deal.

Pressure increased from settlers who had exercised squatters' rights and wanted to secure a clear title at a low cost. In 1795 a family already on the land was allowed a preemption right to purchase two hundred acres at thirty dollars per hundred acres. Latecomers clamored for the same right, and in February 1797 the General Assembly passed another land act. A settler in the Green River region before July 1798 could preempt one or two hundred acres at a price of sixty dollars per hundred acres of first-class land or forty dollars per hundred acres of second-class land. (All of the land in the region was classified as second class.) While the price was higher than in the 1795 act, a year was allowed for payment, and a grace period was allowed at 5 percent interest to those who had paid under the earlier acts. A political fight ensued between the Bluegrass residents who wanted to dispose of the Green River land at a high price, without credit, and the growing number of Green River residents who wanted

relief in the form of low prices, credit, and a longer period in which to pay. John Breckinridge expressed typical Bluegrass scorn for opponents when he wrote in 1796 that the Green River region was "filled with nothing but hunters, horse-thieves & savages, . . . where wretchedness, poverty & sickness will always reign." But counties were being created rapidly in the Green River country, and under increased pressure the legislature gradually lowered prices and extended more generous terms for credit. As a result, by 1800 the Green River counties had a higher percentage of householders who owned land than did any other region in the state. For the state as a whole, only 49.2 percent of the householders owned land; of the eleven Green River counties, only one fell below that average. In eight of the Green River counties, the percentage ranged from 54.3 to 67.0. Skeptics of easy credit were proved correct in their doubts: two-thirds of the credit purchases were soon in arrears.

By the beginning of 1800 the nine counties present at statehood in 1792 had increased to forty-two, and the rapid rate of formation continued on into the nineteenth century. The petitions for creating new counties usually stressed convenience more than population growth. Creation of some counties with small populations raised questions about representation in the legislature. The usual practice in the 1790s was to require a specified number of free male inhabitants over twenty-one years of age for a county to send a representative to the legislature but to grant one representative even if that requirement was not met. An act in 1795 allowed a new county a representative before the next apportionment was made only if the parent county gave up a seat. Some of the nasty political battles of the period involved county creation and representation and the location of the county seat. Some counties lost heavily in seats and political clout. Fayette County had nine seats in the House in 1792, but only four in 1800; Nelson County's representation dropped from six to three. Counties grew so rapidly that some of the new ones had difficulty

The first permanent capitol building was constructed of stone in Frankfort in 1793-94. It burned in 1813 (courtesy of the Kentucky Historical Society).

finding well-qualified men to fill local government positions.

Indian Problems in the Northwest Territory

Indians, especially those north of the Ohio River, continued to resist white settlement. Large-scale raids had ceased, but small bands continued to infiltrate the state. Harry Innes, who had become a federal district judge in 1789, estimated that fifteen hundred persons had been killed or captured and twenty thousand horses had been stolen in Kentucky between 1783 and 1790. The losses continued to mount. Kentuckians were convinced that the federal government was as negligent in dealing with the problem as Virginia had been. In truth, the new national government was constrained by a small army and inadequate finances.

A federal effort to take action in 1790 had turned into a disaster. When General Josiah Harmar, an Indian agent for the government, and General Arthur St. Clair, governor of the Northwest Territory, decided to attack the homelands of the tribes that had broken earlier peace treaties, they had to depend largely upon untrained militiamen from Kentucky and Pennsylvania. Colonel John Hardin commanded the Kentucky troops, and neither he

nor Harmar was equal to the task. They could not control the undisciplined troops, and Hardin suffered two humiliating defeats in the fall of 1790 at the hands of the tribes along the Miami River, endangering the entire command. Both Harmar and Hardin were court-martialed but were found not guilty. A smaller expedition against the Wabash River tribes also failed.

In January 1791 President Washington set up a five-man board of advisers in Kentucky. Charles Scott, Harry Innes, John Brown, Benjamin Logan, and Isaac Shelby recommended that an army of regular soldiers and western recruits should take the offensive against the Indians in the Northwest. Despite protests from Kentuckians, General St. Clair was given command. Ill with gout, St. Clair had to be lifted on and off his horse, and he sometimes commanded from a litter. The Kentuckians, who made up two-thirds of the force, were led by Generals Charles Scott and James Wilkinson. Two preliminary raids met some success. In May 1791 Scott led some 700 mounted volunteers against Ouiatanon, a village of the Miami tribe. Scott's men killed or captured about 73 Indians, burned the town, and destroyed crops. In August 1791 Wilkinson, with a force of 523 men, duplicated that success in a raid along the upper Wabash River.

The main expedition under St. Clair, however, repeated the Harmar fiasco. St. Clair started with nearly two thousand regulars, but he was so disliked that the draft had to be used in Kentucky to raise one thousand men. The expedition left Fort Washington (now Cincinnati) on October 1, 1791, but its ranks dwindled from desertions and illness, and St. Clair was unable to mold his troops into a disciplined fighting force. On November 3 the army camped on a small tributary of the Wabash that St. Clair thought was the St. Mary's River. He planned to construct some protective works the next day, but the Indians and some Canadians attacked before sunrise on November 4. The militiamen gave way almost at once, and in their mad flight they disrupted the ranks of the regulars. The Indians had seldom fought with such determination, and what started as a fighting retreat for the Americans became a panic-stricken rout. In addition to six hundred casualties, St. Clair lost some of his artillery and much of his supplies. This defeat occurred despite the fact that the Indian force was probably smaller than the American army. The defeat was one of the worst that the United States ever had in a battle with Indians.

President Washington chose General "Mad Anthony" Wayne to settle the matter. Wayne's nickname belied the caution with which he approached the task, for he spent nearly two years in careful preparation. In the meantime Indians continued to do damage in Kentucky, and Shelby frequently called out small detachments of militia to scout or to guard particular points. Forty men and two officers, for example, were assigned to give some protection to those using the Wilderness Road. A deadly little battle occurred near Rolling Fork of the Salt River in August 1792, when a band of sixteen warriors was caught by an equal number of pursuers. Three whites and fifteen Indians were reported killed. Daniel Drake (1785-1852) recalled in his recollections of life near May's Lick that as late as 1794 the family's ax and scythe were kept under the bed to supple-

ment the rifle in case of attack by Indians. Children were warned to go to sleep quickly, "or the Shawnees will catch you." The first morning chore, he said, was to climb into the loft and peep through the cracks to be sure that Indians were not lurking outside the door, waiting for it to be opened.

Wayne's careful preparations restored some faith in regular army officers, and when he advanced in July 1794 he had some fifteen hundred mounted Kentucky riflemen. Commanded by Generals Charles Scott and Thomas Barbee, they supplemented Wayne's thousand or so regulars. About thirteen hundred Indians from several tribes, reinforced by some Canadians, had assembled near Fort Miami on the Maumee River, near present-day Toledo, Ohio. The British had constructed Fort Miami on American soil in defiance of the peace treaty of 1783. The Indians, strongly positioned in a tangle of fallen timbers (hence the name of the battle), were attacked by the regulars in a bayonet charge, while the Kentuckians were sent on flanking movements. The Indians were decisively defeated in less than an hour, and when they sought refuge in the fort, the British refused them admittance. Their defeat and betrayal by the British induced the tribes to accept the Treaty of Fort Greenville in 1795, which opened the Northwest Territory to settlers. Many Kentuckians who had not obtained the land they wanted in Kentucky took advantage of the provisions of this treaty. The Indian danger in the state ended except for a few isolated incidents. In Jay's Treaty of 1795 the British agreed to withdraw from the forts on American soil by June 1, 1796.

Slavery Remains an Issue

The future of slavery continued to be an issue in Kentucky in the 1790s. During the decade the number of slaves increased by 241 percent, representing a much greater growth than that of the population as a whole. The percentage of householders owning slaves increased slightly, from 23.2 to 25.2 percent, but there were wide variations among counties. Jessamine led, with 40.7 percent; Knox County had only 9.0 percent. The average slaveholder in Kentucky in 1800 held 4.39 slaves. The Bluegrass continued to be the center of the state's slaveholding, but the institution became stronger in all parts of the state during the last decade of the eighteenth century. The increased demand for slaves presented a problem, for the 1792 constitution allowed the General Assembly to prohibit the importation of slaves for commercial purposes. Such a law was not enacted in Kentucky during this period, but the Virginia act of 1782 to that effect remained in force in the state. Planters and would-be slaveholders wanted the prohibition repealed, for the natural increase of slaves did not meet the demand, and the shortage kept prices high. The opponents of slavery saw an absolute prohibition against bringing in slaves as a first step toward the ultimate end of the institution.

When the General Assembly took action in 1794, the Virginia regulations were relaxed in two important ways. First, masters who were convicted of bringing in slaves illegally were fined three hundred dollars, but the slaves themselves were not freed. Second, a Kentucky citizen or an immigrant to the state could bring, or cause to be brought, slaves into the state for the owner's own use. That provision was difficult or impossible to enforce, and it provided a ready loophole with which one could circumvent the intent of the act. The 1794 act did ease the Virginia requirements for the manumission of slaves. The owner was relieved of the legal requirement for the support of the freed person, and some of the harsh laws regulating the life of a freed slave were abolished. Manumission was left as a choice for an individual slave owner to make.

Antislavery advocates remained active after their defeat in the 1792 constitutional convention. Much of their strength came from religious groups. Presbyterian minister David Rice remained active in the cause and in 1794 tried unsuccessfully to start an abolition society in the state. When it became apparent that another constitutional convention might soon be called, antislavery advocates looked toward it as a means of attacking the evil institution.

Political Parties and the Democratic Society

Political parties with a definite form began to develop during President George Washington's first administration. Some of the differences concerned such issues as Alexander Hamilton's financial program; others involved foreign relations, particularly relations with Great Britain and France, as the French Revolution developed into a general war. At the heart of the disputes that led to the organization of parties were philosophical questions: What is the purpose of government? What role should it have in economic development? From what groups must it obtain support? What position should the people occupy? In time individuals and groups who coalesced around such leaders as James Madison and Thomas Jefferson became known as Democratic Republicans, then later as Jeffersonian Republicans. Their opponents were best known as Federalists. One of the Federalists' chief problems was the sharp differences among their leaders. Alexander Hamilton and John Adams disagreed on many points, some of them concerning issues, some of them based on personal animosities. During the same period Kentuckians turned from the amorphous factions of the prestatehood era and embraced the emerging Federalist and Democratic Republican parties. Historians and political scientists have disagreed about the origins of these political parties. Did the rise of national parties lead to local parties in the states? Or did the development of state parties lead to the formation of national parties? Perhaps they developed more or less simultaneously, each reinforcing the other.

Given the frontier conditions in Kentucky, the state's association with Virginia, and the contacts many Kentuckians had with Madison and Jefferson, it was inevitable that most Kentuckians would be Democratic Republicans. This group included most of the state's leaders, for their economic and political status was not challenged by the Jeffersonian concept of a natural aristocracy that would usually provide leadership.

George Nicholas was the leading Democratic Republican in the state until his untimely death in 1799. His main rival as a politician and lawyer was John Breckinridge, who moved to the state in 1793, after serving in the Virginia General Assembly and being elected to the U.S. House of Representatives. Breckinridge decided not to raise tobacco at Cabell's Dale, his sixteen-hundred-acre plantation a few miles outside Lexington, for fear the crop would ravage the soil there as he had seen it do in Virginia. Instead, he concentrated on developing a great horse farm. Thirty-two years old when he became a Kentuckian, Breckinridge was a tall, slender man with reddish brown hair and a zest for politics. Within months after his arrival in Lexington, he was deeply involved in current problems.

The issue of the Mississippi River had flared up again, reviving questions about the Spanish Conspiracy. The growth of Kentucky's agricultural production had made use of the river and its main seaport of vital importance to Kentuckians. But negotiations with Spain were moving at a glacial pace, as Spain played for time. Some concerned Kentuckians decided that pressure must be exerted on the national government to push for an immediate solution. The instrument they used was a democratic society modeled after one that had been organized in Philadelphia in the spring. A preliminary meeting was held on August 22, 1793. Four days later the society was organized, with John Breckinridge as chairman and John Bradford and Robert Todd as vice chairmen. A committee of correspondence was established, and monthly meetings were scheduled. Other societies were established at Paris and Georgetown, but the Lexington group dominated. While its membership probably never exceeded fifty, its influence was out of proportion to its size. Many community leaders were members, and most Kentuckians approved of its aims.

Spain was then allied with Great Britain, and the Democratic Society also supported the French Revolution and the government that emerged from it. Especially in its early stages, the French Revolution had the support of many Americans, and members of the Democratic Society were not the only ones who planted liberty poles, wore the French tricolor, and addressed each other as "Citizen." France had come to the aid of the United States during its revolution. Was it not time to repay the debt?

During the autumn of 1793 the Lexington Democratic Society focused on the Spanish question. The group asserted "that the free and unrestricted use and navigation of the river Mississippi is the NATURAL RIGHT of the Citizens of this Commonwealth" and demanded that the federal government secure that right. Breckinridge drafted the *Remonstrance of the Citizens West of the Mountains to the President and Congress of the United States,* and he may have penned *To the Inhabitants of the United States West of the Allegany and Apalachian Mountains.* These tracts hinted at direct action if the national government did not soon secure the westerners' natural rights to the use of the river. When he read his copies of these documents, President Washington wrote Secretary of State Edmund Randolph in alarm: "What if the government of Kentucky should force us either to support them in their hostilities against Spain or disavow and renounce them? War at this moment with Spain would not be war with Spain alone. The lopping off of Kentucky from the Union is dreadful to contemplate, even if it should not attach itself to some other power." The president fumed at the activities "of those who are aiming at nothing short of the subversion of the government of their state."

The danger was complicated by bitter, disillusioned George Rogers Clark, who offered to raise and lead a French legion of fifteen hundred men against the Spanish settlements in Louisiana. His offer was happily accepted by Citizen Edmond-Charles Genet, the envoy of revolutionary France to the United States. Clark received a commission and many promises of support. Four more French agents were sent to Kentucky to assist André Michaux, a French botanist and secret agent who was looking for a number of specimens in the state. Although sympathetic to Clark's proposal, the Lexington Democratic Society did not openly endorse it. Genet's rash efforts to use the United States as a base of operations against Great Britain brought about his dismissal in February 1794, and in March Washington issued a proclamation forbidding Clark's expedition. The president got little support from Isaac Shelby when he warned the governor of the proposed scheme. Shelby replied that he doubted his legal right to halt the expedition. Citizens had the right to leave the state and to bear arms, and he could not see how intentions could be perceived and punished. Shelby confessed years later that he knew that Clark's expedition was already dead because of insufficient funds; he was simply putting more pressure on the federal government. The Lexington Democratic Society became so bellicose that friends warned Breckinridge the group was going too far. Judge Harry Innes stayed away from the meetings so he would not have to disqualify himself if a trial resulted.

The Bourbon County Democratic Society was guided by some of the partisan leaders of the prestatehood days. In addition to protesting the Mississippi issue, they advocated a more democratic society in which power would come from the people and not from the members of the elite. The Scott County Democratic Society was more moderate than either of the others, although it did consider a motion, later withdrawn, to outfit an armed vessel and send it down the Mississippi River to challenge Spanish control.

The federal government was already attempting to resolve the problem. Jay's Treaty with Great Britain, so reviled in America, was misinterpreted by Spain as being a possible step toward an Anglo-American alliance. Thomas Pinckney, special envoy to Spain, had found it difficult to get even an audience with Spanish officials; suddenly he found himself courted by diplomats anxious to sign a treaty with their American friends. The Pinckney Treaty, ratified on March 3, 1796, guaranteed freedom of navigation of the Mississippi River and the right of deposit of goods at New Orleans or some other convenient spot. While the Spanish did not admit to having stirred up the Indians in the Southwest, they promised to provide restraint in the future. For the time being, the issue of the Mississippi River was resolved.

Although the details were not publicly known for another decade, the Spanish Conspiracy flared up again. Before Pinckney's Treaty was made, Hector Baron de Carondelet, the Spanish governor in Louisiana, sent word to Judge Benjamin Sebastian by one Thomas Powers. Spain was willing to open the Mississippi to the West but not to the United States. Sebastian, who had been a close associate of James Wilkinson, was asked to send representatives to New Madrid to meet with Colonel Don Manuel Gayoso de Lemos. Sebastian consulted with George Nicholas, Harry Innes, and William Murray, who advised him to go and see what was being proposed. News of the Pinckney Treaty appeared to end the matter, but in 1797 Spanish officials again made overtures to Sebastian. Powers was hustled out of American jurisdiction by Wilkinson before too much was known. In 1806 Humphrey Marshall revealed the affair, and Sebastian was forced from office when it was learned that he had been receiving a Spanish pension of two thousand dollars a year. Innes was implicated, but neither the Kentucky General Assembly nor the U.S. House of Representatives pressed charges against him. He was perhaps saved because on the second approach to Sebastian, Innes and Nicholas drafted a reply to the Spanish officials: "We declare unequivocally that we will not be concerned either directly or indirectly in any attempt that may be made to separate the Western Country from the United States."

A Few Good Federalists

The Kentucky Federalists constituted a minute percentage of the population. Their best-known leaders, Humphrey Marshall and William Murray, the latter a prominent and successful lawyer, were targets of mobs and the subjects of many petitions and remonstrances. On one occasion when a Frankfort mob had carried him to the Kentucky River for a dunking, Marshall, a noted infidel, appealed to Baptists in the crowd. "Now allow me to say that according to Baptist rules it is irregular to administer baptism before the receiver gives his experience. If you are determined to proceed, let the exercise be performed in decent order. Let me give my experience first." The concept was so ludicrous that the mob dissolved in laughter. Marshall won a surprising political victory in 1794 when he defeated John Breckinridge for election to the U.S. Senate. On the first ballot Marshall had 18 votes, Breckinridge 16, John Fowler 8, and John Edwards 7. The second vote, limited to the top two candidates, saw Marshall win 28-22. Marshall's membership in the Kentucky House may have contributed to his victory, but the basic reason was the surge of Federalist support following the successful Indian campaign and the easing of the Mississippi issue. Such Federalist wins in Kentucky were rare.

Moving toward a New Constitution

Shelby believed in a strict interpretation of executive power, and he cooperated with the legislature to do what seemed best for the state. By the end of his administration the Indian danger was over, use of the Mississippi River had been achieved, the state government was functioning smoothly, and some of the troublesome land claims had been resolved. He must have felt a glow of self-satisfaction as he retired to Traveler's Rest, his public duty fulfilled, his public service ended.

Shelby's departure in 1796 led to one of Kentucky's many disputed elections. James Garrard, a Virginian by birth, had come to Kentucky in 1783. As a planter, he opposed slavery; as an active Baptist minister who founded several churches, he favored religious tolerance and was suspected of entertaining heretical Unitarian ideas; as a member of the aristocracy, he

sought democratic reforms. Garrard had served in five of the statehood conventions and had helped write the constitution. When the electors voted for Shelby's successor in May 1796, Garrard received 17 votes, Benjamin Logan 21, Thomas Todd 14, and John Brown 1. The constitution did not say whether a majority or a plurality was required for election, but the electors decided to vote again on the top two candidates. Most of the Todd votes went to Garrard, who was declared elected. Logan's supporters appealed to attorney general John Breckinridge, who refused to render an official opinion because neither the law nor the constitution authorized him to do so. Breckinridge declared, however, that as an attorney and a private citizen, he believed that Logan was elected. Logan appealed to the state Senate, which had the power to settle disputed gubernatorial elections, but the senators decided that the law giving them that authority was unconstitutional because it did not promote "the peace and welfare" of the commonwealth. By then Garrard had been in office for five months, and Logan abandoned the quest.

This dispute offered another indication that the constitution needed some changes. Criticisms were numerous and diverse. One objection was the undemocratic nature of the constitution, with its use of electors and the appointment rather than the election of many officials. The Senate was too aristocratic, the court system was hostile to ordinary people, and the county governments were oppressive and unconstitutional because justices of the peace were allowed to sit in the legislature. Many citizens opposed extended or life terms for any official, including judges. Others opposed slavery and wanted the state to provide a way to emancipation. Some voters opposed the exclusion of ministers from the General Assembly. Year by year the protests continued. Some of the pressure could have been relieved by specific amendments, but the constitution did not offer a method for its amending.

George Nicholas had wanted to initiate general revision after two or three years of experience with the constitution, but the convention had called for a referendum in 1797. If a majority of those voting for representatives in 1797 and in 1798 also voted for a constitutional convention, then the next legislature would call for such a convention. Otherwise, a convention could be called only by a two-thirds majority of both houses of the legislature. The General Assembly received petitions for a convention as early as 1793. House bills calling a convention passed in 1793 and 1794, but the Senate killed them. A 1795 joint committee agreed that changes were needed, but 1797 was so close by then that nothing more was done.

In February 1797 the General Assembly passed a bill calling for a constitutional referendum to be taken at the May elections. The referendum was published once in the *Kentucky Gazette,* and sheriffs were directed to post copies on courthouse doors and to read the measure aloud at the opening of each day's voting. The results were so confusing as to cast doubt upon the entire process. Several counties made no return on the referendum. A preliminary count of 9,814 votes for representatives showed that 5,446 favored the convention, 440 opposed it, and 3,928 had ignored the issue.

The General Assembly wrangled over the results in its January 1798 session. Should sheriffs who had not responded be asked to make an estimate? What attention should be given to the "silent" vote? Was the required majority a majority of all the votes cast for representatives or only a majority of those voting on the referendum? The session ended with a deadlock between the houses and no decision. As the debate continued in the press and public meetings, Breckinridge led the antirevisionists. The bellowing for a convention, he charged, came from envious idlers whose time was spent "sauntering in the street, hanging around billiard tables, scampering through race fields, and mid-night carousing." He suggested that if slave property could be taken, then land might be taken next. Nicholas and other "aristocrats" who felt threatened were also active in the fight. So were their opponents, and these were more numerous.

A newcomer to the state, young Henry Clay (1777-1852) jeopardized his Kentucky future by writing an antislavery article under the pen name of "Scaevola." He backed away from the issue when he realized that his stand might adversely affect his political prospects.

Despite the absence of a sanctioning act, the 1798 election went ahead with the second referendum vote. The revisionists achieved a clear victory. Of 16,388 voters, 9,188 voted for a convention, and the revisionists also won a majority of seats in the House. When the fall session opened, priority was given to the Kentucky Resolutions, but on November 21 the House voted 36-15 for a convention in 1799. The Senate finally agreed, and the convention was set for July 22, 1799, in Frankfort. Members were to be elected at the May elections on the same basis and in the same number as members of the House.

If the "aristocrats" had lost a campaign, they had not necessarily lost the war. They could still be victorious if the right people were elected to the convention. The fight that conservatives such as Nicholas and Breckinridge had made against the Alien and Sedition Acts had restored some of their popularity (see chapter 7), and they campaigned vigorously to influence the May election of delegates. Part of their campaign in Fayette County was a large public meeting held at Bryan's Station on January 26, 1799. Nicholas delivered the major address, and plans were made for another meeting there in March. A slate of proposed delegates to the convention was drawn up, and in May all six of them were easily elected, with four of them also being elected to the House. Similar programs and planning took place elsewhere. Between the May elections and the convening of the convention, conservatives exchanged ideas on what the convention should do. Nicholas refused to stand for a convention seat, but he was active in directing the preconvention conservative campaign. He died suddenly on July 25, three days after the convention opened.

Only ten of the fifty-eight delegates had served in the first constitutional convention. Alexander Bullitt was elected president, and other organizational matters were quickly completed. Sessions were usually held in the mornings and late afternoons, and as in 1792, much of the work was done in the Committee of the Whole. All the members were men of some wealth. Only Patrick Brown of Hardin County was not a slaveholder; he had been until becoming an antislavery advocate. Twenty-eight members owned ten or more slaves. The 1799 delegates had much more experience in office-holding than the 1792 delegates. Only three ministers were at the convention, down from seven in 1792, but the number of lawyers had increased sharply, from two to nine. No one dominated this convention the way Nicholas had in 1792. He, John Breckinridge, and Caleb Wallace had drafted a series of resolutions, which Breckinridge introduced and defended. The convention journal recorded only official actions, but twenty-six recorded votes occurred, far more than in the first convention. Breckinridge kept some scribbled notes for his own use during the discussions, but these were far from being a record of the debates.

Breckinridge and Caleb Wallace were the principal speakers for their faction. They were most often challenged by Samuel Taylor and John Bailey, but Alexander Bullitt, Robert Johnson, and Philemon Thomas differed with their conservative colleagues on the principle of separation of powers in the government when they favored legislative supremacy. Green Clay, a wealthy planter, was the gadfly of the convention, never happier than when he had others upset or angry. He outraged most of the delegates by defending the Alien and Sedition Acts and asserting that all real governmental power belonged to the national government. Yet he chaired the committee appointed to draft the constitution from the resolutions adopted by the convention. Other well-known delegates included Harry Innes, Thomas Marshall, Benjamin Logan, and John Adair. Younger members active in the deliberations included William Logan, William Bledsoe, Felix Grundy, and John Rowan, all attorneys.

After a careful statistical analysis of the twenty-six roll call votes at the 1799 convention, historian Joan Wells Coward found four groups that voted together enough to be called voting blocs, although none of them were totally consistent. The largest and most cohesive group consisted of eighteen conservatives who generally agreed with the Bryan's Station platform. Fearful for their property rights, they wanted to eliminate some of the democratic features of the 1792 constitution. A second bloc, smaller and more diverse, consisted of some of the Bryan's Station people and a small group of planters, including Green Clay and Robert Johnson, who strongly opposed any constraints on the legislature. A third group, centered on John Adair and several young lawyers, also wanted legislative supremacy, but they were not fully insiders, and they opposed measures that might place limits on where ambition could take them in an open political system. Smallest and most poorly defined of the four blocs was the most democratic group. John Bailey was its chief spokesman.

On many issues, however, a delegate might vote independent of the bloc with which he was usually identified. No sharp cleavages occurred between aristocrats and democrats. Varied in their beliefs and goals and without adherence to an ideological platform, the delegates hammered out a constitution based on pragmatic factors more than philosophical beliefs. While a number of changes were made in the 1792 constitution, much of the first document was retained.

Kentucky's Second Constitution, 1799

Despite all the discussion of slavery, the 1792 article concerning the subject was readopted with almost no changes. A motion to give the legislature full power to halt the importation of slaves at some future date was defeated 14-37. The suffrage requirements specifically excluded free blacks, mulattoes, and Indians. The 1792 constitution had not been that clear.

Some of the governor's extensive appointing power was transferred to the county courts. They could appoint minor officials, and each county court presented the governor with lists of two names for each office. From these lists he was to select justices of the peace, sheriffs, and coroners. Ranking militia officers were allowed to appoint subordinates on their staffs; the lower-ranking officers were to be elected by their men.

The ballot method of voting had been blamed for considerable fraud, and the second constitution reverted to voice voting. Proponents claimed that the poor man could thus be sure that he was not being robbed of his vote. Of course, he could be exposed to great pressure when he publicly announced his vote.

Representation caused extended debate. The Nicholas-Breckinridge group wanted representation to be based on population, for fear that the growing number of Green River counties would exert too much influence. Other delegates were sure that county representation would be more equitable. After several changes, the convention agreed to allow counties that did not have enough people to justify a representative to group together in order to send a representative, and to allow similar groupings when adjacent counties had a surplus population large enough to add a representative. While the county was continued as a unit, the adjustments came close to the practice of allocating seats by population.

The electors were discarded, and the governor, the new lieutenant governor, and the senators were to be elected by direct popular vote. A new seat would be added to the Senate whenever three new seats were added to the House. Efforts failed to add property holding as a Senate requirement, and the proposal that a senator must be either married or a widower was also defeated.

Breckinridge, Innes, and Wallace all favored direct election of the governor. The electors were obviously going to be discarded, and they did not want the executive to be dependent upon the legislature. The veto power

was weakened; a veto could be overridden by a majority of all members of both houses instead of the two-thirds voting that had been required. Garrard, a more active governor than Shelby, had clashed with the legislature on several occasions, and some of the restrictive changes directed at the governorship may have been aimed at him. The decision to make a minister ineligible for the office of governor was a clear snub to Garrard. The governor was also now ineligible for reelection for seven years after the end of his term.

Issues concerning the judiciary were hotly debated. Critics believed that it was too centralized and too independent. Part of the opposition stemmed from the Court of Appeals decision in *Kenton v. McConnell* in 1794, which had cast doubts on many of the Virginia land titles. The judges had refused to appear when summoned by the House, and when censured by the General Assembly, they had denounced the legislature generally and some of its members specifically in a widely read pamphlet. Alexander Bullitt wanted the legislature to review the judges' opinions and to have the power to remove those who rendered erroneous opinions. A number of delegates experienced in government believed that separation of powers was not desirable and was impossible in practice. They wanted clear legislative supremacy. After John Breckinridge defended the court system, a proposal to establish circuit courts lost 23-30. (In 1802 circuit courts did replace district and quarter sessions courts.) The legislature was left with the power to determine what courts should exist in addition to the Court of Appeals.

Breckinridge, fearing frequent efforts to alter the constitution, proposed an amending process that made changes possible but difficult. Once again, no provision was made for individual amendments. Within the first twenty days of the beginning of a regular session, a majority of all the members of both houses would have to pass a law providing for a referendum on calling a convention. Then the convention had to be approved by a majority of all the citizens who were eligible to vote for representatives. If that majority was obtained, another vote would be taken the next year. If the vote was again favorable, the legislature would provide for a convention.

Popular ratification was not considered necessary. After the constitution was approved and signed by the members of the convention, it went into effect on June 1, 1800. Had it been voted on, it would probably have been approved by a large majority. While no delegate would have called it perfect, the constitution reflected the adjustments that had been worked out since 1792, including the changes most desired by a majority of the voters. The new constitution was somewhat more democratic, there was some decentralization in favor of the coun-

ties, and most citizens probably agreed that the legislature should have more power than the other branches. Conservatives were relieved that potential damage had been contained within reasonable limits, and their property rights remained secure. This revision remained in effect for fifty years, in part because of general satisfaction with it, in part because of the difficulty of changing it.

The duly enrolled constitution was adopted on the morning of August 17, 1799, by a vote of 53-3. Thomas Clay of Madison County created some excitement when he scribbled after his name, "I protest against it." His declaration was erased, and he was persuaded to confine his remarks to the convention journal.

7

Kentucky in the New Nation, 1792-1815

The Kentucky Resolutions

The move toward constitutional revision was delayed briefly by a national issue on which most Kentuckians were agreed. As party warfare intensified on the national scene, the Federalists found themselves under severe attack by the Democratic Republicans, despite their success in electing John Adams to succeed George Washington as president. The election of Thomas Jefferson, leader of the Democratic Republicans, as vice president said something about the confused political situation.

A surge of anti-French sentiment developed after the XYZ Affair, in which French representatives demanded bribes before Americans could begin negotiations for a bilateral treaty, and an undeclared naval war started in 1798. Despite warnings from members of their own party, some Federalists pushed the Alien and Sedition Acts through Congress in 1798. These ill-conceived measures were designed to repress critics of Federalist policies and politicians. The Naturalization Act increased from five to fourteen years the time required for naturalization of a foreigner. The Alien Friends Act authorized the president in time of peace to imprison or deport any alien whose presence he considered dangerous to the nation; the Alien Enemies Act extended those presidential powers to wartime. The Sedition Act made it a high misdemeanor to assemble with the intent to oppose the legal measures of the government or to interfere with their execution, and it defined as a misdemeanor the publication of false or malicious writing about the president or Congress. Guilty parties faced fines up to five thousand dollars and imprisonment up to five years. Twenty-five individuals were prosecuted under the Sedition Act, and ten of them were found guilty. They were Democratic Republican editors and printers who were condemned for being critical of the administration. Was political opposition to be illegal? Did the Federalists violate civil rights? Were the acts unconstitutional?

Protests were intense in Kentucky. Most Kentuckians disliked and distrusted the Federalist Party and the Adams administration. Kentuckians had been vocal in their objections to the whiskey tax that had brought on a "Whiskey Rebellion" in Pennsylvania, the administration's pro-British, anti-French foreign policy, and the government's dalliance with the Mississippi question and the Indian problem. Was the administration looking for a pretext to send in an army, as Isaac Shelby later wrote, "to quell a disorderly spirit which had been represented to exist in our citizens"? Kentucky's reaction to the acts was swift, negative, and almost unanimous. Farmers neglected their crops to attend the mass meetings that protested the Federalist legislation.

The Clark County meeting on July 24, 1798, may have been the first one in the state, and its resolutions of protest were typical of those framed elsewhere. One called the bills affecting aliens "unconstitutional, impolitic, unjust and disgraceful to the American character." The Sedition Act was "the most abominable that was ever attempted to be imposed upon a nation of free men." Then the meeting passed a resolution: "Resolved, That there is sufficient reason to believe, and we do believe, that our liberties are in danger; and we pledge ourselves to each other and to our country, that we will defend them against all unconstitutional attacks that are made upon them."

The Lexington protest meeting on August 13 drew a crowd considerably larger than the town's population. Scheduled for the Presbyterian church, it had to be moved outdoors. George Nicholas was the featured speaker, and his long address brought frequent applause. It repeated most of the arguments he had used in

his article "Political Creed" that the *Kentucky Gazette* had published on July 30. After describing the acts as unconstitutional, Nicholas called for them to be tested in the courts. Kentuckians of that day had an endless capacity for oratory, and when Old Nick completed his extended remarks, a cry went up for Henry Clay. Clay climbed onto the wagon bed that served as a platform and delivered an extemporaneous speech that caught the fancy of the crowd and made Clay a well-known public figure. A contemporary wrote that it "would be impossible to give an adequate idea of the effect produced." Two Federalists who demanded a chance to reply were in some danger until Nicholas and Clay intervened on their behalf.

A writer in the *Kentucky Gazette* of August 22 suggested that the state legislature take action to express the sentiments of Kentuckians. Governor Garrard was known to be highly incensed over the Federalist legislation. Some protest was almost certain to come from the next session of the General Assembly.

The ill-advised legislation gave the Democratic Republicans an ideal issue for the 1800 presidential election. They could appeal to the voters as the defenders of their civil liberties against a party that was trying to deprive them of those rights. To avoid prosecution, Jefferson as vice president in the Adams administration had to mask his opposition. A state legislature could not be charged with sedition, so James Madison wrote resolutions for the Virginia legislature, and Jefferson prepared a stronger set for North Carolina. But the fall elections did not go as well for the Democratic Republicans in North Carolina as they had hoped. The Kentucky outrage, on the other hand, was well known.

John Breckinridge went to Virginia in late August for his health and to visit family and friends. While there, Breckinridge wrote Caleb Wallace, suggesting that Wallace draft some resolutions for the fall session of the Kentucky General Assembly. When Breckinridge returned to Kentucky just in time for the session, he brought with him Jefferson's resolutions. Pledged to keep Jefferson's authorship secret, Breckinridge quietly accepted both the praise and the blame as the supposed author. Garrard in his message to the legislature on November 7, 1798, denounced the Alien and Sedition Acts and suggested that the legislature declare its views fully. The next day Breckinridge introduced Jefferson's resolutions. The first seven were as Jefferson had written them; some changes had been made in the last two. Jefferson's reference to nullification as a remedy was deleted; emphasis was placed on having Kentucky's members of Congress press for repeal. Some minor changes were made in the House during extended debate. Federalist William Murray insisted in vain that only the courts could declare an act of Congress unconstitutional. While the acts may have been impolitic, he deplored the heat and haste with which the House had considered them.

In reply, Breckinridge stressed the compact theory to explain the nature of the Union. The states and the people possessed all the powers that had not been granted to the federal government. Since that government was an agent of the states, the states could determine whether it had exceeded its just powers and, if it had, could declare unconstitutional acts null and void. If Congress refused to repeal such acts upon the request of a majority of the states, Breckinridge continued, "I hesitate not to declare it as my opinion that it is then the right and duty of the several states to nullify those acts, and to protect their citizens from their operations." The House made a few minor changes on Saturday, November 10, and then accepted the Kentucky Resolutions. Murray voted against all nine provisions, but on at least five votes his was the only negative. John Pope led the efforts in the Senate to make some modifications, but the House rejected the Senate's changes, the upper house capitulated, and Governor Garrard signed the resolutions.

The resolutions asserted that each member state of the federal compact had "an equal right to judge for itself, as well as of infractions as of the mode and measure of redress." The Alien and Sedition Acts were "void and of no force." But instead of nullifying the acts, the Kentucky Resolutions called for the other states to join Kentucky's members of Congress in pressing for their repeal.

Kentucky opinion overwhelmingly favored the resolutions, and Breckinridge's political stock soared. Dispatched to the various states, the Kentucky Resolutions attracted national attention. The Federalists had control of every state legislature north of the Potomac River, and several negative replies were received. Vermont sent one of the best-reasoned responses. The people had formed the government, and no state had the right to judge the actions of the national government.

Had no answer been made to the negative replies, Kentucky might have been seen as abandoning its position. The General Assembly in November 1799 adopted a Kentucky Resolution, a long restatement of what had been said the previous year. The most significant change was the statement in 1799 that nullification by the states of unauthorized federal acts was the rightful remedy. Such nullification was not then used, however, and after Jefferson's victory in "the Revolution of 1800," the Federalist acts expired or were repealed. But the Kentucky Resolutions of 1798 and 1799 stated the states' rights philosophy that justified nullification of a federal act by a state. Carried to an extreme, the doctrine would later be used to justify secession if a state decided it could not protect its rights any other way. Pandora's box was cracked in the 1790s, even if it was not fully opened.

The authorship of the 1799 resolution is still in doubt. Two respected historians, Adrienne Koch and Harry Ammon, concluded that after Madison softened Jefferson's draft, the resolution was transmitted to Breckinridge through Wilson Cary Nicholas, who was going to Kentucky to help settle his brother's estate. Koch and Ammon decided that Breckinridge was probably not the author, because the nullification provision that was deleted in 1798 was reintroduced in 1799. But Breckinridge had used the term *nullification* during the 1798 House debate, and he may have deleted it then in order to get the largest possible vote. On December 13, 1799, Breckinridge wrote Jefferson after sending him a copy of the resolution. "It was at the opening of the session concluded on to make no reply," the Kentuckian explained, "but on further reflection lest no improper conclusion might be drawn from our silence, we hastily drew up the paper which I enclosed you."

A New Penal Code

One of the most forward-looking changes made in Kentucky during the early years of statehood was a reform of the barbarous penal code. Inherited from Virginia, it was based on the English system that still imposed the death penalty for more than two hundred crimes, including stealing a fish. Thomas Jefferson's bill to revise the Virginia penal code had failed to pass in that state, but John Breckinridge pressed for reform in Kentucky. He persuaded the Lexington Democratic Society to study the issue, and in November 1793 it called for reforms that would make punishment proportionate to the offense. Breckinridge wrote the petition to the state legislature, and by 1796 he was drafting a more humane code. As a member of the House in January 1798, he introduced the measure.

Punishment that exceeded the injury, he said, was a violation of a person's natural rights. Murder should be punished by death, for there was no other equivalent punishment, but the death penalty for all other crimes should be abolished. His proposed changes were based upon four principles: to reform and save the offenders, to make reparations to the injured parties, to repay the public for the cost of prosecution, and to make an example that might deter others. Confinement and hard labor should bring the most hardened character to reflect on his crime and repent of it. A prisoner should be taught an honest trade that he could use upon reentering society. Pennsylvania had already started such a program; it was time for

Kentucky to act. "Let us remember that those unfortunate wretches are our fellow citizens," Breckinridge concluded, " . . . that to err is the lot of humanity, & that in punishing offenses, large, very large allowances ought to be made for the frailties of Human nature."

The new penal code adopted in February 1798 abolished the death penalty except for first-degree murder. Provision was made for the construction of a thirty-inmate penitentiary, the first one west of the Allegheny Mountains. Prisoners were not coddled. Their workday, shortened to eight hours during the three winter months, was filled with hard and servile tasks such as stonecutting and making nails, shoes, chairs, and tinware. Rations consisted of bread, Indian meal, or other inferior dishes, with two portions of coarse meat a week. The new code and the penitentiary were later judged to be inhumane and harsh, but in their day they represented a considerable advance. In this area Kentucky did not lag behind most of the other states.

The Louisiana Purchase

Most Kentuckians were delighted with the election of Thomas Jefferson as president, although exasperated when the outcome had to be decided in the House of Representatives because each Democratic Republican elector voted for both Jefferson and Aaron Burr, and there was no way to distinguish which vote was for president and which for vice president. Also in 1800, Governor Garrard was elected for a second term, and John Breckinridge was sent to the U.S. Senate, where he became one of Jefferson's floor leaders. Much of the Federalist legislation either expired or was repealed. As the president liked to say, the Republican ship of state took a new tack. Hubbard Taylor spoke for most Kentuckians when he wrote James Madison: "I cannot but express my heart felt joy to find so general a satisfaction pervade this country I live in, at the election of Mr. Jefferson."

Then another crisis developed. On October 16, 1802, Spanish intendant Don Juan

Ventura Morales, over the protests of the governor, withdrew the right of deposit of goods at New Orleans without designating an alternate place as the Pinckney Treaty required. The situation was more serious at the time than it had been in the late eighteenth century, for Kentucky now had much more produce to export. Furthermore, powerful France was also involved. American authorities had learned that in the secret Treaty of San Ildefonso (1800), Napoleon Bonaparte, who dreamed of reestablishing the French empire in America, had forced Spain to cede the entire Louisiana province to France. The transfer had not been made, but the treaty was a cause for concern nevertheless. Jefferson knew how vital the matter was for the westerners, and the American minister to France, Robert Livingston, was instructed to try to purchase New Orleans and Florida or some other area that might be used as a port. "The day that France takes possession of New Orleans, we must marry ourselves to the British fleet and nation," Jefferson wrote.

Kentuckians were outraged by the reopening of the issue they thought had been settled. The General Assembly pledged support for any measures that might be necessary for a solution. Citizens were convinced that Kentucky alone could send thirty thousand troops to New Orleans, and many of them wanted the state to take unilateral action to solve the Mississippi question permanently. Federalists, seeing a chance to drive a wedge between eastern and western Democratic Republicans, adopted a bellicose attitude toward protecting the rights of the westerners. Jefferson urged restraint, and the resolutions that Breckinridge introduced in the U.S. Senate provided men and money to take action but left their use to presidential discretion. Jefferson also attempted to ease tension by sending James Monroe of Virginia to France as a special envoy. Monroe might not accomplish anything that Livingston could not do equally well, but he was popular in the western part of the country.

Before Monroe arrived in Paris, the French suddenly offered to sell all of Louisiana

to the United States for approximately fifteen million dollars. Livingston and Monroe had no authority to commit their country to such a bargain, but they could not wait months for authorization from Washington. Napoleon had suddenly decided to abandon his American dream; he could as suddenly change his mind again.

News of the purchase astounded and delighted Kentucky. Public celebrations were organized, and countless toasts were drunk to everyone who might have played a part in the solution to the problem. A hitch developed when the Spanish minister to the United States protested that France had not carried out promises it had made in 1800, so the province still belonged to Spain. Jefferson rejected that argument and made preparations to take Louisiana by force if necessary. The Kentucky governor was requested to have four thousand troops ready by December 20, 1803, to descend on New Orleans. The General Assembly voted to give 150 acres to each man who volunteered for the mission, and the state's quota was soon filled as war fever raged. Then word arrived that Spain had turned Louisiana over to France, and two months later the territory came under American jurisdiction.

Jefferson still had a Louisiana problem. A few years earlier he had argued that the Constitution did not authorize creation of Alexander Hamilton's first national bank; implied powers could not be used. But nothing in the Constitution said that the United States could purchase Louisiana from France; indeed, the Constitution did not provide for the purchase of territory at all. Yet he could not reject this solution to one of the nation's most troublesome problems. Jefferson turned to Breckinridge for help. In a letter dated August 12, 1803, he discussed the future of the West. He doubted that a new confederation would be founded on the banks of the Mississippi, "for the West will be settled by our Sons," but if the West ever wanted to separate, it should be allowed to do so. Upper Louisiana could be used for Indian lands until the territory east of the Mississippi was filled. He assumed that Congress would approve the purchase treaty, but he thought the constitutional issue should be resolved by an amendment. He scribbled down the amendment he proposed: "Louisiana, as ceded by France to the U.S., is made a part of the U.S."

Breckinridge ignored the amendment request. He was delighted with the acquisition, he would be in Washington promptly to help pass the measures necessary for the purchase and the government of the territory, and he had already been in touch with other western senators to enlist their support. He said nothing about the amendment. The solution to a major problem was more important than a strict construction of the Constitution. President Jefferson had to swallow his constitutional scruples.

The Burr Conspiracy

By the time he left the vice presidency in March 1805, Aaron Burr (1756-1836) seemed to have finished his political career. Both parties were displeased with his role in the 1800 election, when he neither allied himself with the Federalists to defeat Jefferson nor declared himself interested only in being Jefferson's vice president. Then in a duel on July 11, 1804, he mortally wounded Alexander Hamilton and was indicted for murder. Brilliant, ambitious, charming, not yet fifty years old, Burr turned to the West for new opportunities. Precisely what he had in mind is still questioned. He conferred several times with James Wilkinson, and he also apparently approached Robert Murray, British minister to the United States, to see what assistance might be provided to help detach the West from the United States.

"In New York I am to be disfranchised, in New Jersey, hanged," Burr wrote. "Having substantial objections to both, I shall not . . . hazard either, but shall seek another country." He reached Frankfort, Kentucky, on May 25, 1805, and stayed with John Brown. He appears to have talked with John Adair (1757-1840) and perhaps others about the possibility of taking Mexico in case the United States went to war with Spain. Then Colonel Burr went to

Tennessee, where he visited with Andrew Jackson and other leaders. Burr met Wilkinson at Fort Massac, then visited New Orleans before returning to Kentucky in August. He had a conspirator's ability to tailor his remarks to what he sensed the other party wanted to hear, and he was a master of statements that could be interpreted different ways. Without definite proof of wrongdoing, the *Kentucky Gazette* issued a warning on November 3, 1805, against a man whose career "was fraught with a degree of duplicity which can never be satisfactorily defended."

Burr got some financial backing from Herman Blennerhassett, an exotic and gullible Irishman who was trying to create an eden on an island in the Ohio River. He seems to have accepted Burr's explanation that his purpose was to colonize a large land grant west of the Mississippi. Burr also hinted at the possibility of invading Mexico or forming a new government in the Mississippi River Valley. Burr caught the attention of Joseph Hamilton Daveiss (1774-1811), the federal district attorney in Kentucky. Suspecting a conspiracy, Daveiss wrote the first of several warning letters to Jefferson in January 1806. The president only asked for additional information.

Later in the year Burr acquired another relentless foe in a new Frankfort newspaper, the *Western World.* It began publication in July 1806 under the editorship of John Wood and Joseph M. Street, who had walked from Virginia to Kentucky the previous year. The two may have been backed by Daveiss and Humphrey Marshall, although this charge was denied. A series of articles on the old Spanish Conspiracy attracted readers, and the editors were subjected to lawsuits, threats, and duels because of the paper's contents. The most obvious result was that Judge Benjamin Sebastian was found guilty by the House of Representatives of accepting a two-thousand-dollar annual pension from Spain. No charges were pushed after he resigned his position. Federal district judge Harry Innes filed suit against the paper and won his case. By the time Wood and Street published their fourth issue, they charged that another conspiracy was being hatched to take Kentucky out of the Union and that the traitor Aaron Burr was heading it. Jefferson at last sent John Graham, secretary of the Territory of Orleans, to investigate.

Burr traveled west again in the summer of 1806. He halted at Blennerhassett's Island to see about the construction of fifteen boats that could carry five hundred men. When he reached Lexington in October he managed to get a loan of twenty-five thousand dollars from the Kentucky Insurance Company, which acted as a bank. Daveiss created a sensation on November 3, when he appeared before Judge Innes and moved that Burr be compelled to appear and answer charges that he was preparing an expedition against Mexico, the possession of a friendly power. Innes delayed a ruling for several days, possibly because he was not sure of the pertinent law, possibly because he wanted to confer with others who had been associated with James Wilkinson in earlier days. Daveiss hoped that an inquiry would uncover enough information for an indictment. Innes dismissed the motion a few minutes before Burr entered the courtroom, accompanied by several advisers, including Henry Clay, one of his attorneys.

Dignified and calm, Burr defended himself in a well-received speech to the court and the spectators who had crowded in. He was blameless, he assured his listeners, but the wild charges were interfering with his private plans. If a trial was needed to free him from such outrages, he would appreciate having a speedy one. Agreement was reached for a trial on November 11.

Daveiss was embarrassed on November 11 when he had to ask for a postponement; Davis Floyd of Jeffersonville, Indiana, one of his key witnesses, was attending the Indiana legislature and could not be present. Burr seized the opportunity to deliver another well-received speech. Magnanimously, he agreed to postpone his private business, no matter how inconvenient that might be, in order to prove

his innocence in open court. Judge Innes set the trial for December 2, and Daveiss scurried off to round up witnesses.

Henry Clay, concerned about rumors of unsavory plotting by his client, asked Burr for a written statement, which Clay received on December 1. Burr gave Clay a categorical denial that he was in any way involved in action against the United States. "My views have been explained to, and approved by several of the principal officers of the government," he declared, "and, I believe are well understood by the administration, and seen by it with complacency."

Temporarily satisfied by Burr's elaborate disclaimer, Clay continued to represent him. On December 2 Daveiss confessed that John Adair, another important witness, was not in court. He asked for another postponement, but Clay argued that his client was entitled to immediate action on the charges. Daveiss presented an indictment to the grand jury the next day, but his charge against John Adair as a co-conspirator with Burr was rejected as "not a true bill." Two days later the same verdict was returned on the charges against Burr, and the jury stated that it had heard nothing that would in the slightest degree incriminate either man. That evening a grand ball and reception were held to honor the vindicated former vice president.

The crushing blow to Burr's plans came from James Wilkinson. The general's instinct for survival was still working, and when he decided that Burr's scheme would fail, he disassociated himself by denouncing Burr in a self-serving letter to the president. When Graham arrived in Ohio to investigate what had happened, he asked that Burr's expedition be halted, and the militia seized several boats. On November 27 Jefferson issued a proclamation ordering the expedition stopped. When Burr joined his followers near the mouth of the Cumberland River, fewer than one hundred persons were there, including some women and children.

John Adair arrived in New Orleans and was arrested on Wilkinson's orders, and some suspected Burr adherents were sent east for trial. Burr agreed to surrender to civilian authorities at Natchez. When a grand jury there returned a verdict of "no true bill" on the charges against him but officials tried to hold him anyway, Burr fled, hoping to escape to Spanish Florida or to a British vessel along the Gulf Coast. He was caught and sent to Virginia to be tried in the U.S. circuit court over which Chief Justice John Marshall presided. The trial became a classic struggle between the judicial and executive branches of the federal government. The administration was unable to get Burr convicted of treason or plotting against a friendly government, but he lived in exile in Europe for many years. Kentucky was blamed for being disloyal during the Burr and Spanish Conspiracies. A Lexington mass meeting in January 1807 tried to dispel that canard by resolving "that all charges & insinuations against the people of this State, of dissatisfaction to the Union or the Government of the United States, are gross misapprehensions and without foundation." Clay decided that Burr was guilty and had deliberately misled him. John Adair sued Wilkinson for false arrest and won an apology and a twenty-five-hundred-dollar award. Adair was elected governor in 1820.

The most damaging piece of evidence against Burr was a letter in cipher that he was accused of writing. In recent years research has indicated that the letter may have been penned by Senator Jonathan Dayton of New Jersey. If true, Burr's guilt is less certain. Dayton was indicted in 1807 for complicity in Burr's scheme, but the indictment was quashed after Burr's acquittal.

Some hopeful Kentucky militiamen who had been called out during the scare over the Burr expedition requested land grants because of this service. They were denied; the Burr affair was not a war.

Continued Problems with Europe and the Indians

For a state so far removed from an ocean, Kentucky displayed a surprising interest in foreign affairs during the early years of the nineteenth century. Some of Kentucky's exports found their way to European markets, and many of the manufactured goods and luxury items that Kentuckians purchased were imported from Europe. But much of the interest stemmed from Kentuckians' spirit of nationalism. They resented, deeply and vocally, what they saw as snubs of the United States by despotic European governments. Much of the anger was directed against Great Britain, particularly against British naval policies. The crowning of Napoleon as emperor had destroyed some of the affection for revolutionary France, but Kentuckians were more hostile toward Great Britain than France. Many Kentuckians were willing to fight to defend American rights and to win the respect owed the young republic.

Another aspect of international relations involved a flare-up of the Indian problem. Kentucky was no longer subject to raids, but many Kentuckians were interested in the Northwest Territory, and former Kentuckians were swelling the population of that region. Part of the lure was the systematic system of township survey; land claims were less likely to be challenged there than in Kentucky. Since land hunger can apparently never be satisfied, some of the state's citizens were looking toward Canada, especially the area known as Upper Canada, for future expansion.

After the Treaty of Greenville, Indian problems in the Northwest declined for several years. The tribes were gradually compressed into a smaller area as the flood of settlers pushed them westward. Then a Shawnee chief named Tecumseh undertook to rally the tribes and halt the whites' advance. He argued that no land sale or cession was legal unless it was agreed to by all of the tribes, since they owned the land in common. He traveled extensively in an effort to unite the tribes in a great confederation strong enough to stop further encroachment upon tribal lands. Tecumseh hoped that in time the Indians would adjust to European civilization. He received covert encouragement from British officials in Canada, who hoped that an Indian buffer state would block American expansion in the Northwest.

Tecumseh and his half-brother The Prophet soon clashed with William Henry Harrison (1773-1841), a Virginian who had served with General Wayne and had remained in the Northwest Territory to build a career. Appointed governor of the Territory of Indiana in 1800, Harrison was instructed to persuade the Indians to cede land but to win their confidence and protect them from the relentless pressure of white settlers. Those instructions were irreconcilable, and he found an able opponent in Tecumseh. In 1809, after Harrison secured the cession of 2.5 million acres along the Wabash River, Tecumseh warned that he would oppose the occupation of that area. A large force of warriors assembled at a village where Tippecanoe Creek entered the Wabash. When Tecumseh went south to enlist tribes for his confederation, he believed he had Harrison's promise that nothing would be done until his return. But Harrison, under rising pressure to open the ceded lands, advanced his army, which included many Kentuckians. On the night of November 6, 1811, he camped about a mile from the Indian village. The warriors attacked on the morning of November 7, two hours before dawn. Both sides endured heavy casualties. In Harrison's army, 62 were killed and 126 wounded, representing a casualty rate of just over 20 percent. Probably about 200 Indians were lost. Among the American dead was Major Joseph Hamilton Daveiss, who had been so active in the Burr affair. After daybreak the Kentucky mounted riflemen were able to outflank their stubborn foes and force them to retreat. Abandoned Prophetstown was burned, but it was reoccupied when the Americans retired to Vincennes.

The battle of Tippecanoe convinced Tecumseh that the Americans could not be trusted, and it encouraged him to turn to the British for assistance. It also encouraged the British to give it. The battle convinced western Americans, including those in Kentucky, that peaceful expansion of the frontier would not be possible as long as the British exerted strong influence with the Indian tribes. The battle of Tippecanoe has often been called the opening battle of the War of 1812.

In Defense of Neutral Rights

The rights of a neutral during wartime are defined from widely different perspectives, depending on whether the definer is a neutral or a participant. As a neutral, the United States stood to profit handsomely from the wars between France and Great Britain if the basic American definition of the rights of neutrality was accepted. Trade that had been closed by economic regulations might be opened. But neither belligerent would accept the American contention that free ships meant free goods, and each imposed restrictions that would handicap its foe. Since Great Britain had much the larger navy, most of the American problems were with John Bull. Problems had arisen in the 1790s, but an uneasy truce that prevailed between 1801 and 1803 eased the tensions. When war was resumed in 1803, President Jefferson and Secretary of State Madison were determined to preserve the nation's neutrality while trying to promote the American right to trade freely. The country's military forces had been sharply reduced, and the United States was poorly prepared for any type of war. Incidents were inevitable. Few Kentuckians could have given a precise definition of such terms as *impressment* and *visit and search,* but most of them were convinced that the British more than the French were violating American rights. They became seriously concerned after June 22, 1807, when the British ship *Leopard* fired upon the unprepared U.S. frigate *Chesapeake* and forced its surrender.

Most Kentuckians demanded retaliation. Some were convinced that Great Britain was using the war as an excuse to curb American trade and to make the United States an economic vassal. Several attempts to win concessions through economic coercion between 1807 and 1812 failed. Jefferson's embargo nearly ruined American commerce and seri-

William Henry Harrison during the War of 1812. Although he was not a Kentuckian, Harrison was the state's favorite commander in the Northwest (courtesy of the Library of Congress).

ously affected farmers who lost their export market. Neither the Non-Intercourse Act (1809) nor Macon's Bill No. 2 (1810) had much success. Kentucky remained strongly Democratic Republican—or Jeffersonian Republican, as the party was then being called—but Jefferson and Madison were criticized for delaying so long when it was obvious that only war promised a solution.

Henry Clay, the War Hawk

Henry Clay was the rising figure in Kentucky politics after death removed George Nicholas in 1799 and John Breckinridge in 1806. After reaching Kentucky in 1797 with little wealth, Clay had quickly established himself. As he once admitted to a son, "I never studied half enough. I always relied too much upon the resources of my genius." But he was a dramatic, emotional, and popular speaker who was highly successful as a trial lawyer. His wit and sharp tongue sometimes got him in trouble but delighted those who agreed with him. Nearly six feet tall, lanky, with an expressive face and an exceptionally wide mouth, Clay was a strik-

ing if not handsome man. He was congenial by nature and a delightful conversationalist. His love of drink and gambling endeared him to many Kentuckians. John C. Calhoun, one of Clay's longtime political foes, was reported to have said, "I don't like Henry Clay. He is a bad man, an imposter, a creature of wicked schemes. I wouldn't speak to him, but, by God, I love the man." Except to a strict Puritan, there was something appealing about the man who near the end of a convivial evening leaped upon the banquet table and danced down its sixty-foot length, accompanied by the sound of breaking glass and china. The next day he cheerfully settled the bill for $120.00.

One of Clay's greatest strokes of good fortune was his 1799 marriage to Lucretia Hart, four years his junior. She gave him connections with some of the most prominent families in the state. Dark-eyed and dark-haired, Lucretia was a plain woman who disliked the Washington society in which Henry flourished. She bore eleven children, two of whom died as infants. Her amiable disposition and concern for others endeared her to many friends. Fortunately for Henry, she was a good businesswoman and manager, and during his long absences she was largely responsible for the management of Ashland, their estate near Lexington. Upon his return home, she delighted in handing him the large check that he had left with her for expenses; she had had no need to use it. Almost unnoticed, she provided the support that helped sustain Henry Clay during his long and controversial career.

Clay served in the Kentucky House in 1803-6, then completed the term of John Adair in the U.S. Senate in 1806-7. Elected again to the state House, he became its Speaker in January 1808. He had a notable clash in 1809 with Humphrey Marshall, one of the few Federalists in the state. To encourage local manufacturing and to take a hit at British imports, Clay introduced a resolution to require all members of the General Assembly to wear homespun clothes. Of course Marshall immediately embraced the finest imported broadcloth. The two men traded insults on the floor, and only the intervention of colleagues prevented a fight there. Instead, they fought a duel in Indiana on January 19, 1809, in which each received a slight wound. Clay filled another unexpired U.S. Senate term in 1810-11, then was elected to the U.S. House of Representatives in 1811. He was a leader of the large group of young, aggressive "War Hawks" who demanded that Madison ask for war with Great Britain. They pressured Madison into being the war candidate in order to get their support in the presidential election of 1812. As Speaker of the House, Clay had an important role in directing the war effort.

Two other members of the Kentucky delegation in the House, Joseph Desha (1768-1842) and Richard M. Johnson (1781-1850), helped Clay in his efforts to increase the army and navy and make other belated efforts to prepare the nation for the impending conflict. As the months passed without a declaration of war, Kentucky's dissatisfaction with the national administration increased. Newspaper editorials thundered for war, and mass meetings demanded action to vindicate national honor. The die was finally cast on June 1, 1812, when President Madison sent a war message to Congress. The House voted for war 79-49 on June 4; the Senate did so 19-13 on June 18. The delay in the vote and the size of the minority indicated significant opposition to the conflict, most of it in the Northeast. The only Kentuckian in Congress who opposed the declaration of war was John Pope. Elected to the Senate in 1807 as a Democratic Republican, Pope opposed the declaration because it was not also directed against France. Opponents accused him of being a Federalist, and his popularity suffered for several years.

The War of 1812 in the Northwest

Kentuckians had an important part in the western theater of operations during the War of 1812, for they supplied many of the troops for the western armies. The American plan was to attack Canada simultaneously from several points, conquer it quickly, and use it to win concessions from Great Britain. Expectations of a swift victory faded rapidly. Elderly and timid, General William Hull surrendered the key post of Detroit in August 1812, and the other assaults were checked.

Before the end of 1812 Kentuckians had made up two and a half regiments in the expanding regular army. The Seventh and Seventeenth Infantry Regiments and half of the Nineteenth comprised about twenty-two hundred men and officers. Nearly nine thousand other Kentuckians served in volunteer and militia units that were involved in the war before the end of the year. Recruitment was less successful for units likely to be used outside the Northwest; this would be obvious in the New Orleans campaign of 1814. Good leadership was vital, for nonregular troops were usually poorly trained, poorly disciplined, and poorly equipped. Since these men enlisted for periods seldom longer than six months, they could rarely be turned into an effective fighting force.

The state, like the national government, had done little to prepare for war. One exception was the election of Isaac Shelby in 1812 for a second term as governor. As the nation moved closer to war, demands increased that Kentucky's Cincinnatus be called from his fields to direct the commonwealth's military operations. Shelby saw the interruption of retirement as a duty to be accepted, and he was easily elected.

Influential Kentuckians lobbied the national administration for immediate use of the state volunteers while patriotic ardor was high. Unfortunately, when two thousand of the militiamen were ordered to reinforce General Hull at Detroit, they were placed under the command of Brigadier General James Winchester of Tennessee. Not only was he unpopular, but he soon became the laughingstock of his troops. As one of his privates reported in his diary, some soldiers "killed a porcupine and skinned it and stretched the Skin over a pole that he used for a particular purpose in the night, and he went and sat down on it, and it liked to have ruined him." Henry Clay, Governor Scott, and others urged the appointment of William Henry Harrison to the western command. On his last day in office, Scott consulted with Shelby, Henry Clay, and other leaders on what should be done. They decided to increase the War Department's request for two thousand men to thirty-four hundred and to put Harrison in command by making him a brevet major general in the Kentucky militia. While it was probably illegal, Harrison's selection was acclaimed across the state. Soon after assuming the governorship Shelby suggested the formation of a board of westerners who would direct the war in the West instead of the War Department. His suggestion was rejected, but Harrison was given command of the entire army in the Northwest.

Shelby supported Harrison's advance toward Detroit by sending one thousand mounted volunteers under the command of Major General Samuel Hopkins on a raid against the Indian tribes in Indiana and Illinois. This raid was designed to divert attention from Harrison's expedition, but so many of the men deserted that Hopkins was forced to return to Kentucky.

Harrison's army, divided into three columns, bogged down in the wilderness as the supply problem became critical. Then in January 1813, by using sleds on the frozen Maumee River, General Winchester got his 1,300 Kentuckians to the Rapids of the Maumee, where the three columns were to meet before the final march to Detroit. Learning that some Indians and Canadians were guarding supplies at Frenchtown on the Raisin River some thirty-five miles away, Winchester sent 650 men to capture the supplies. Led by Lieutenant Colonels William Lewis and John Allen, the Kentuckians captured the small village on the afternoon of January 18. With the addition of some reinforcements, the group numbered about 1,000 men when it was attacked before dawn on January 22 by a somewhat larger force of Canadians and Indians commanded by General Henry Proctor and Wyandot chief Roundhead. Proctor's three small cannon proved decisive. The Kentucky riflemen who were sheltered behind a picket fence fought off assaults, but the Seventeenth Infantry Regiment was battered by the cannon fire. The members of this regiment and some militiamen sent to help them dissolved in a panic-stricken rout. Allen was killed trying to rally his men, and Winchester and Lewis were both captured.

Major George Madison, commanding the militia inside the picket fence, refused to surrender until told to do so by Winchester and until being promised that his men would be protected. Despite the promise, some of the prisoners were killed, and many of the eighty wounded left behind to await transportation were slaughtered by the Indians. At least four hundred Kentuckians were killed in the battle and its bloody aftermath, and "Remember the Raisin" became the Kentucky battle cry for the rest of the war.

Hopes for a swift victory were dispelled, and some Kentuckians were discouraged by the defeat. News from the other fronts was also bad, and Kentuckians tended to blame President Madison and his administration for inept leadership. Recruitment slowed in the state, and demands were heard for an enlarged regular army that would assume more of the military burden. When volunteers failed to fill the three-thousand-man command the General Assembly authorized after the Raisin River debacle, Shelby had to use a draft to complete the ranks. Many of the recruits were inferior specimens who had been hired as substitutes. Shelby informed Harrison and the Madison administration that little could be expected from Kentucky until naval control was secured on Lake Erie and enough regular troops were made available in the Northwest to assure success. More Kentuckians began to view a negotiated peace with favor.

Harrison's army had dwindled to about 2,000 by the spring of 1813, and about half of them were at Fort Meigs on the Maumee River. The fort held out when Proctor attacked on May 1 with nearly 2,400 soldiers and warriors. A messenger arrived on May 4 to report that General Green Clay was bringing 1,200 men by boat to relieve the garrison. Clay sent Lieutenant Colonel William Dudley with 700 men to spike the British cannon and then to join the rest of the Americans on the other bank. But some of Dudley's men rashly attacked the British camp. Dudley was killed, and 650 members of his force were killed or captured. Prisoners were being slaughtered until Tecumseh arrived and halted the killing. Proctor had to lift the siege on May 9 after many of the Indians and Canadians deserted. Morale dropped again in Kentucky when news of Dudley's defeat arrived. A second attack on Fort Meigs failed in late July, and twenty-one-year-old Major George Croghan became a state hero when his 160 regulars of the Seventeenth Infantry held Fort Stephenson against Proctor's army of some 1,400 men.

Shelby left Newport at the beginning of September 1813 with 3,500 riflemen to reinforce Harrison. A few days later, Oliver Hazard Perry defeated the British fleet on Lake Erie, and an American invasion of Upper Canada could proceed without the danger of having its supply line cut. When Harrison gathered his scattered detachments on the shore of Lake Erie, he had some 5,000 men, most of them Kentuckians, to oppose Proctor's 1,000 British regulars and Tecumseh's 3,000-3,500 warriors. Fearful of being cut off, Proctor abandoned Detroit and retreated up the River Thames. Harrison followed on October 2 with about 3,000 men, including Richard M. Johnson's mounted riflemen, some of Shelby's troops, and 125 army regulars. The Americans caught up with the retreating enemy on October 5.

Johnson's regiment, divided in two sections, rode through the British regulars and routed them in a matter of minutes. When the half regiment led by Johnson encountered heavy fire from Indians who were concealed in the heavy growth of a swamp, Johnson dismounted his men to fight on foot. To draw the Indians' fire, he called for a twenty-man "Forlorn Hope." Fifteen were killed at once, and four were wounded. Among the dead was a sixty-three-year-old Lincoln County pioneer, William Whitley, who became one of the state's war heroes. Johnson took two wounds but continued fighting, receiving three more. Shelby sent reinforcements forward, and the Indians were rousted out of their swamp. Tecumseh was killed, and with his death went the collapse of the confederation he had tried to form. At least in popular legend, Johnson was hailed as the one who killed Tecumseh, and that claim helped him secure the vice presidency of the United States in 1836.

The battle of the Thames was the last major action for Kentuckians in the Northwest. It did much to erase the memory of earlier defeats, and it strengthened the state's desire for Upper Canada. Didn't it belong to Kentucky by conquest? The months following that battle were the brightest of the war for Kentuckians. Spirits ran so high that there was considerable opposition to Madison's acceptance of the British offer to open direct negotiations. But at least Henry Clay would be one

Tecumseh saving prisoners at the battle of Fort Meigs (courtesy of the Indiana Historical Society Library)

of the American negotiators. Yet there were setbacks in the east, and Kentuckians learned with dismay that Napoleon had abdicated. The end of the war in Europe meant that the victorious British army could be sent against the Americans. The capture of Washington, D.C., and the burning of its public buildings pointed up the inadequacy of American preparations. Still, the attack of gloom was lightened by the successful defense of Baltimore and the naval victory of Thomas MacDonough on Lake Champlain, which thwarted an advance of a major British army from Canada.

Believing that their part of the war was over, Kentuckians were reluctant to volunteer for more military service. The annual total of state recruits declined from 11,114 in 1812 to 4,156 in 1814. Governor Shelby protested a call for 1,000 men to strengthen the Detroit garrison; Ohio could meet the need. In any case, Shelby added, no Kentucky volunteers would leave the state until the United States guaranteed their pay. Too many earlier volunteers had never been paid.

The Battle of New Orleans

Still, a number of Kentuckians were involved in the last battle of the war. Learning of a probable British attack on New Orleans and other areas along the Gulf Coast, both the Louisiana governor and the War Department asked for Kentucky's help. Three regiments were raised, but neither the national nor state government made adequate preparations for outfitting and transporting them. James Taylor, quartermaster of the state militia, raised the money for boats by taking out a six-thousand-dollar mortgage on his land. General Andrew Jackson was amazed at the poor condition of the Kentucky units when they arrived at New Orleans on January 4, 1815: "I have never seen a Kentuckian without a gun and a pack of cards and a bottle of whiskey in my life." The Louisiana legislature and private citizens did what they could to remedy the shortages, but time was limited.

General Sir Edward Pakenham with nine thousand troops was preparing to assault Jackson's motley force of five thousand that had the advantage of a good defensive position. Brigadier General John Adair found weapons for about one thousand Kentuckians, who backed up the center of the American line. They contributed to the slaughter of two thousand British soldiers, including Pakenham, who were attempting to break the American line.

Four to five hundred Kentuckians commanded by Colonel John Davis had been ordered to reinforce 450 Louisiana militiamen on the west bank of the Mississippi River, opposite the site of the major battle. Davis had been able to get miscellaneous arms for only half of his men, and when the Americans were attacked by some 1,200 British troops, the defense collapsed. The overall British losses had been so heavy that the victors did not follow up their success.

In his official report Jackson underestimated the number and the contributions of the Kentuckians who fought on his main front, and he blamed the Kentuckians for the debacle across the river. Kentuckians were incensed by his comments, and Adair demanded an apology, which Old Hickory refused to give. The two had an acrimonious exchange of public letters during the next two years, and Jackson finally admitted that he had not had full information when he wrote his report. A court-martial cleared Colonel Davis of any conduct deserving censure.

Kentuckians were still celebrating the victories at the Thames and New Orleans when news came that the peace treaty had been signed in Ghent on December 14, 1814. It had

been signed before Jackson repelled the southern invasion, but coming when it did, the news of the treaty only added to the celebration in the state. While the treaty brought peace, it ignored most of the differences that had helped bring on the war. The bits of conquered territory were returned to their prewar owners, and the end of the European war made it possible to ignore the issue of neutral rights when no agreement could be reached. The defeat of the British in the Northwest and the death of Tecumseh effectively ended the Indian question in that area, and the tribes continued to be pushed aside for white settlers. The peace did make possible a number of agreements within the next few years, in particular the Rush-Bagot Agreement of 1818, which provided for the almost complete disarmament of the U.S.-Canada border.

Even if they remembered the early defeats, Kentuckians could take pride in their part in the war. About 67 percent of the white men who were qualified by age and health to participate in the war did so, and most of them saw field service. Some 25,705 Kentucky men served as regulars, volunteers, and militia. Of the 1,876 Americans killed during the War of 1812, approximately 1,200 (64 percent) were Kentuckians, despite the fact that the state was never invaded. Kentucky's fighting men emerged from the war with an enhanced reputation.

Noah Ludlow expressed the legend of the fighting Kentuckian and helped it grow in May 1822, when he sang "The Hunters of Kentucky" to a cheering, foot-stomping audience in New Orleans.[1] Its eight verses recounted Kentucky's role in the battle of New Orleans, with no mention of the retreat on the west bank. The second verse caught the flavor of the legend:

> We are a hardy, free-born race,
> Each man to fear a stranger,

---

1. B.A. Botkin, ed., *A Treasury of the American Folklore* (1944), 3, 9-12.

Whate'er the game, we join in chase,
    Despising toil and danger;
And if a daring foe annoys,
    Whate'er his strength and forces,
We'll show him that Kentucky boys

Are "alligator horses."
Oh! Kentucky, the hunters of Kentucky,
    The hunters of Kentucky.

8

Kentucky after Fifty Years of Settlement

The Immediate Postwar Years

The War of 1812 has often been called the Second War of American Independence. At home and abroad, there had been doubt that the young republic would survive. By 1815 little doubt remained. The United States was a vigorous nation, steadily increasing in strength, that had fought the foremost power in Europe to a draw. The Federalists had committed political suicide through the Hartford Convention. The party planned to take advantage of the war to present an ultimatum to the national government for terms that would allow it to block many of the actions of the majority party. The implication was that if the demands were not accepted, the New England states might withdraw from the Union. Most Kentuckians condemned this approach as near treason; they ignored the Kentucky appeal to states' rights in 1798 and 1799. States' rights was a defense for a state in the minority, and Kentucky was no longer in that status. As the Federalists disappeared, the state and nation entered a period when there was only one viable political party. Of course differences did exist within the Democratic Republican Party, and it had a number of would-be presidents within its ranks. Among them was Henry Clay, clearly Kentucky's leading politician until the mid-nineteenth century and one of the nation's outstanding statesmen.

A wave of nationalism swept the country after the war ended. Economic progress, including new systems of transportation and communication, appeared to bind the sections more closely into one. The federal government embarked upon a nationalist program that would have been rejected a few years earlier. The Tariff of 1816 was intended in part to protect and promote American industry; the Second Bank of the United States was three and a half times as large as the bank that had been allowed to expire in 1811; the judicial decisions of the U.S. Supreme Court under John Marshall emphasized nationalism; the foreign policy of the Monroe administration reflected a nation with much more confidence in itself. One of the strongest bonds of nationalism was the sharing of common sentiments, ideals, and memories by most of the country's citizens— what President Abraham Lincoln would call in his First Inaugural Address the "mystic chords of memory." The national flag was more often displayed; Uncle Sam began to be used as a national symbol. Henry Clay was evolving a broad program called the American System or the American Plan. It was designed to appeal to all sections of the nation—and to elect Clay president. The United States was changing rapidly, and so was Kentucky.

The state enjoyed a brief economic boom after the end of the war. Pent-up European demands had to be met, and two poor crop years in Great Britain increased the need for American produce. Prices were good for a couple of years, then dropped back to normal levels. Many Kentuckians were lured into speculative investments in land, and many of them were overextended when prices fell. The war had provided protection for the start of a number of manufacturing enterprises, such as iron furnaces and textile mills, and much of that expansion had been based on credit. Such businesses were hurt when Great Britain made a determined effort to recover its markets in the United States. The Kentucky Insurance Company, chartered in 1802, was essentially a bank, and in 1806 it was joined by the Bank of Kentucky, which established a number of branches. Then in 1818 the General Assembly catered to the cry for easy credit by chartering forty-six banks, sometimes called the Forty Thieves, so that almost every town of any size had a bank. The Second Bank of the United States estab-

lished branches in Louisville and Lexington, but it soon aroused opposition because of a kind of fiscal policing of the state banks. A state that a few years earlier had to rely heavily on barter because of the lack of currency was suddenly almost awash in banknotes. This easy credit accelerated the speculative boom.

The boom was short-lived, both for Kentucky and for the nation as a whole. By 1819 the country was well into the Panic of 1819. This depression lasted for several years and was the worst that the new nation had experienced. Debtors with reduced incomes could not make the payments to which they were committed. Many of them, faced with ruin, began to cry for relief. Robert B. McAfee later recalled that "the Country was immensely in debt and the Price of all produce was lower than ever known in Kentucky, indeed very little of the Products could ever be sold at any price." He remarked that "those causes seemed to retard business of every description." In the town of Hartford in Ohio County, only one store remained open. Some destitute farmers were reportedly selling milk cows for as little as $1.25 each. Combating depressions was not then seen as a function of government, as it would be in the next century, but the economic situation became so serious that a growing number of citizens demanded help.

The Missouri Compromise

During the nationalist period, sometimes called the Era of Good Feelings, the controversy over the admission of Missouri into the Union reminded thinking citizens that sectionalism could endanger the future of the republic. Sectionalism was not new. It had contributed to Kentucky's delay in obtaining statehood, and it had played a part in several other issues. It had never been as open or as intense, however, as it was at the time of Missouri's request for admission to the Union in 1819. The ensuing controversy revealed that slavery had become an important issue for many persons in the country, and that many of them were determined to stop its further

97

spread. Jefferson in retirement at Monticello said that the dispute "like a fire bell in the night, awakened and filled me with terror." As a border slave state, Kentucky was caught up in the controversy.

In February 1819 Representative James Tallmadge of New York had introduced a resolution providing that importation of slaves into Missouri would be halted and that children born of slave parents would be free but could be held in bondage to age twenty-five. By the end of 1819 there were eleven free and eleven slave states, and southerners believed that equality in the Senate must be maintained. The compromise that was finally reached in March 1820 admitted the state of Missouri without the passing of the Tallmadge Amendment but also admitted Maine as a free state. To avoid a similar dispute each time a territory applied for admission, Senator Jesse B. Thomas of Illinois got approval of the 36°30' North latitude as the dividing line between slave and free in the rest of the Louisiana Purchase. Then Kentucky's Henry Clay helped work out an illogical compromise on another point. Missouri was admitted although a clause in its constitution— prohibiting free blacks and mulattoes from entering the state—violated the U.S. Constitution, but the state promised that the provision would not be used to deprive any citizen of the United States of his or her rights. A third and less important compromise involved the presidential vote of 1820. Missourians chose three electors, who cast their votes, but was Missouri actually admitted in time for the vote to be legal? The solution was to announce that James Monroe had been reelected president by a vote of either 228-1 or 231-1, depending on whether the Missouri votes were counted. The outcome was not affected.

The Kentuckians of the 1820s

James Harrod disappeared in 1792 and was presumed dead. Benjamin Logan died in 1802, George Rogers Clark in 1818 after being an invalid for years, Daniel Boone in Missouri in

1820, Isaac Shelby in 1826. The departure of these heroes of the pioneer era and the deaths of former presidents Thomas Jefferson and John Adams on July 4, 1826, emphasized to many Kentuckians that a new generation was managing state and national affairs. Old men and women still lived who could recall from personal experience the dangers of the critical early years and the vicissitudes of the push for Kentucky's statehood. But they were now living in a Kentucky that was much different from the wilderness that had lured them westward.

The population had increased enormously from the estimated 150 persons in 1775 to 564,135 in 1820. In the decade of the 1790s, the population had more than tripled. Such a growth rate could not be sustained, for so much of Kentucky's good lands had been claimed that the state no longer promised the opportunities that it once had. Indeed, after the 1820s more people left the state than came to it, so that future growth of population would depend upon natural increase. As a consequence, Kentucky's growth rate would be less than that of the nation as a whole. While the state population continued to grow in absolute numbers, its relative size began to decrease. Between 1790 and 1830 the black population grew faster than did the white. Blacks reached their peak in the state's population in 1830 at 24.7 percent, of which 0.7 percent were free blacks. Thereafter the proportion of the black population declined slowly, until in 1860 slaves made up 19.5 percent of the total population and free blacks 0.9 percent. Most of Kentucky's agriculture did not require large numbers of workers, the Nonimportation Act of 1833 curtailed the importation of slaves for sixteen years, and Kentucky became an important source of slaves for the Lower South.

In 1790 the composition of Kentucky's population resembled that of North Carolina more closely than any other state; by 1820 it most closely resembled that of Virginia. Between those dates the percentage of Kentuckians of English heritage increased from 51.6 to 56.6. The Welsh and German elements also increased, while the Scottish and Irish elements declined significantly. The great majority of Kentuckians, however, had been born in the United States. In 1860, even after the considerable influx of German and Irish immigrants in the 1840s and 1850s, only 5.2 percent of Kentucky's people were European-born. Most of the state's population between 1820 and 1860 consisted of the descendants of people who had settled in Kentucky before 1820.

Some Kentuckians were concerned about immigration long before the relative decline in the state's population became evident. As early as 1797, Mason County had a Washington Emigration Society, which published promotional literature to attract people to that county. The Lexington Emigrant Society tried to attract settlers and, before Louisiana was purchased, to refute charges that people were leaving Kentucky to settle in Spanish territory. After the purchase the society continued to tout the advantages of Kentucky as a land of promise.

The Rise of the Cities

Most Kentuckians in the 1820s lived on farms, but the number of town dwellers had increased,

and urban areas were playing an increasingly important role in the economic, political, and social development of the state.

The census of 1790 listed only five towns in the District of Kentucky: Lexington, with a population of 834; Washington, 462; Bardstown, 216; Louisville, 200; and Danville, 150. Both the number and the size of the towns increased as the state's population soared during the next three decades, but Lexington remained the commonwealth's largest town until nearly 1830, when Louisville replaced it.

Lexington was unique among the important towns in the West of this period, since it was not located on a navigable stream. This was a handicap, but the town was at a crossroads for commerce and immigration, and it was at the center of an exceptionally fertile area. Some hunters were reportedly camped at a spring in central Kentucky in June 1775 when they learned of the battle of Lexington that had been fought in Massachusetts in April. Hence the name was set, but a settlement was not established until April 1779, when Robert Patterson and his company built a fort. The Virginia General Assembly entrusted power to a board of five trustees in 1782, and the town grew rapidly. By 1800 it had 1,795 inhabitants and was a flourishing trade center with many stores

Table 8.1
Population of Kentucky, 1790-1860

Year	Whites		Slaves		Free blacks		Total
	N	%	N	%	N	%	
1790	61,133	83.7	11,830	16.2	114	0.2	73,077
1800	179,871	81.4	40,343	18.3	741	0.3	220,955
1810	324,237	79.8	80,561	19.8	1,711	0.4	406,509
1820	434,644	77.0	126,732	22.5	2,759	0.5	564,135
1830	517,787	75.3	165,213	24.0	4,917	0.7	687,917
1840	590,253	75.7	182,258	23.4	7,317	0.9	779,828
1850	761,413	77.5	210,981	21.5	10,011	1.0	982,405
1860	919,517	79.6	225,483	19.5	10,684	0.9	1,155,684

Source: U.S. Census

and shops, some of them quite specialized. The region was well suited for growing hemp, and the increasing southern demand for bagging and rope promoted the growth of textile factories and ropewalks. Other manufacturing followed, and the area produced a large surplus of agricultural products for export. Wealthy families supported a surprising number of private schools and academies, several bookstores and printing houses, a public subscription library with two thousand volumes before the War of 1812, and Transylvania University. Lexington was often called the Athens of the West. When the first city directory was published in 1806, it listed fifty different occupations. John Wesley Hunt, who made a fortune from trade, rope manufacturing, horse breeding, and banking, built a splendid townhouse to display his success. The city's amenities were also well supported by the owners of the estates being developed in the Bluegrass. The people at such county estates as Ashland and Cabell's Dale contributed much to the city's development. For several decades Lexington was the cultural center of Kentucky and, arguably, of the West.

Table 8.2
Ethnic Origin of Kentucky's Population, 1790 and 1820

Ethnicity	1790	1820
English	51.6	56.6
Scotch-Irish and Scots	24.8	18.2
Irish	9.0	8.2
Welsh	6.7	8.7
German	4.9	5.6
French	1.6	1.5
Dutch	1.2	1.0
Swedish	0.2	0.2

Source: Thomas L. Purvis, "The Ethnic Descent of Kentucky's Early Population: A Statistical Investigation of European and American Sources of Emigration, 1790-1820," *Register of the Kentucky Historical Society* 80 (1982): 263

As the town grew, the trustees moved to curb or eliminate the rowdiness of the early days. Horse races and stray stock were ordered off the streets, and a jail was constructed, with a painted line indicating the extended limits for the inmates whose crime was being in debt. Wooden chimneys were prohibited in 1791, and by 1800 some streets were paved. In 1812 the trustees voted to erect twenty street lamps, and the next year they promised free oil to householders who would provide and maintain their own street lamps. The town had three fire engines in 1815, and a start had been made toward a police force. Most visitors to Kentucky visited Lexington, and most of them complimented the town and its citizens. James Flint wrote of an 1818 visit that "Lexington is still considered the capital of fashion in Kentucky. There are here many genteel families, a few of whom keep coaches. The town, on the whole, exhibits a well-dressed population."

The Falls of the Ohio actually constituted a rocky rapids that over a distance of about two miles dropped the level of the river more than twenty feet. While the Falls could be navigated by boats at periods of high water, it was the only barrier of its kind between Pittsburgh and New Orleans. When the water level was too low for boats to pass the rapids safely, passengers and goods had to be transported around the obstacle. The potential value of the location was apparent to anyone who saw the importance of water transportation, and some of the first Kentucky land claims were surveyed near the Falls. Much of the land was low, with stagnant ponds that were suspected of causing fevers and other diseases. Since the area was on Kentucky's northern boundary, it was more exposed to Indian raids than were the forts in the interior.

Speculator John Connolly received a two-thousand-acre grant at the Falls for his services during the French and Indian War, and in 1773 he sent Captain Thomas Bullitt and a small party to survey the

Lexington's Main Street in the early 1850s was unpaved. The buildings shown here were among the largest and tallest in the town, which boasted a population of some nine thousand people (from J. Winston Coleman Photgraphic Collection, Transylvania University Library).

Boats needed high waters to turn these falls into rapids. The Falls of the Ohio was the only such barrier to river traffic between Pittsburgh and New Orleans (courtesy of The Filson Club Historical Society).

claim and to lay out a town, which Connolly planned to develop. John Campbell, another land speculator, became Connolly's partner, and in 1774 they advertised town lots for sale as if the town already existed. Indian unrest and the outbreak of the American Revolution blocked their enterprise.

The first settlement was made on Corn Island in 1778 by the families that came down the Ohio with George Rogers Clark. During the winter of 1778-79 and the spring of 1779 they moved to another stockade on the Kentucky shore. In 1779 John Floyd, who had done much of the surveying in the area, built a house on Beargrass Creek. Eleven squatters also

built on his tract, and other stations were constructed in the vicinity of the creek. The settlement was named Louisville in 1779 in honor of King Louis XVI of France, who had made a treaty of alliance with the nascent United States. The next year the Virginia General Assembly chartered the town. Growth was slow, and the Indian danger remained serious for several years, even after Clark made his headquarters there. Floyd complained in April 1782 that "we are all obliged to live in our forts in this country, and notwithstanding all the caution we use, forty-seven . . . have been killed or taken prisoners by the savages, besides a number wounded, since January." Floyd became the colonel of the county militia after Jefferson County was created in 1780, and the responsibilities he assumed for the county's defense left him "greatly distressed and perplexed" about its future: "I really am doubtful we shall not yet fall a prey to the savages." Some settlers were fleeing to the supposed safety of the forts in the interior. The county would be deserted, Floyd commented wryly, except for "the inability of the settlers to remove, having lost most of their horses, and the Ohio runs only one way."

Yet people continued to arrive, and Floyd became more optimistic about Louisville's prospects. The settlers would soon be able to move out of the forts, he predicted, and he began planning a larger house with suitable furnishings. Then in early April 1783 Floyd and a small party were riding for Bullitt's Lick when they were ambushed by Indians and Floyd was mortally wounded.

As the Indian danger lessened, many of the new arrivals moved to communities outside the town. As late as 1800 Louisville was listed as having only 359 inhabitants. Its site near the Falls of the Ohio had not proved as beneficial as some speculators had anticipated; the Spanish decision to close the Mississippi to American trade had been a serious blow to growth. Then Pinckney's Treaty had eased that problem, and the Louisiana Purchase had solved it. General Wayne's victory at Fallen Timbers had ended the Indian threat. An era of new growth began on October 28, 1811, when the steamboat *New Orleans* arrived in Louisville on its maiden voyage from Pittsburgh to New Orleans. In 1807 an estimated two thousand flatboats loaded with produce had arrived at Louisville for the downstream markets. But the difficult and expensive upstream traffic was perhaps one-tenth as large. The steamboat made two-way traffic profitable and extensive, and Louisville's growth accelerated. Flour, cotton bagging and ropes, tobacco, bacon, and lard were the major exports, but apples and Kentucky bourbon also found ready markets in the Lower South. Later in the nineteenth century slaves would become prominent in the

southern trade. Passenger traffic was also important. The steamboats made a major contribution to the speed and comfort of travelers. Some of the later boats provided palatial accommodations for those who could afford them; deck passengers did not fare as well.

By 1820 Louisville's population had increased to 4,012. Ten years later it had soared to 11,345, including nearby Portland and Shippingport. In 1828 the legislature classified Louisville as the first city in the commonwealth. By then a considerable amount of manufacturing was being done there. Paul Skidmore began the production of steam engines in 1812; a six-story Merchant Manufacturing Mill for flour production opened in 1815, as did the Hope Distillery Company, one of the largest distilleries in the country. Other business enterprises included ropewalks, soap factories, tobacco plants, and a growing number of smaller enterprises. Commission houses and wholesale merchants carried on extensive business over an expanding area, the carriers of goods and passengers around the Falls prospered, and more lawyers plied their profession in the growing community.

Louisville sometimes gave the impression of being two quite separate communities. One was the sedate, respectable Louisville that conducted most of the business, patronized the multiplying shops, and built the comfortable homes and mansions that impressed visitors to the city. Literary societies, theatrical performances, and dancing schools testified to this community's wealth and sophistication. The river Louisville attracted a rowdy element that became famous along the great river network. The rivermen were more interested in waterfront taverns, cheap brothels, and gambling dens than in the other Louisville's cultural activities. Grand juries were appalled at the vice and crime along the waterfront, but the area continued to flourish. The waterfront became known for its vicious no-holds-barred fights in which eyes were gouged out and noses and ears were bitten off. Thomas Ashe left the impression that he did not get far from the waterfront in 1806, for he made a blanket indictment: "The inhabitants are universally addicted to gambling and drinking. The billiards rooms are crowded from morning to night, and often all night through." The legendary keelboatsman Mike Fink became the symbol of the bragging, swaggering, hard-drinking boatmen who poured through the Louisville riverfront. His boast that he was "half horse, half alligator" and could "out-run, out-jump, out-shoot, out-drink, drag out and lick any man in the country" was exaggerated, but the tales of his supposed exploits contained enough truth to make him one of the best-known figures in the West. He died of a gunshot to the heart in 1823.

Shippers complained about the expense and inconvenience of transferring goods and passengers around the Falls of the Ohio, and the possibilities of a canal received early attention. The Ohio Canal Company got a Kentucky charter in 1804 to construct a canal on the Indiana side of the river. Its location was later shifted to the Kentucky side, and the commonwealth invested fifty thousand dollars in company stock, but the company was not able to construct the waterway. The Louisville and Portland Canal was not completed until 1830, at a cost of approximately three-quarters of a million dollars. It came too soon, though, for the draymen who had benefited from the rapids.

Louisville during the first half of the nineteenth century found itself in sometimes bitter competition with two other cities. Lexington, reluctant to relinquish its dominant position, was the major in-state rival. Since it could not compete for river traffic, Lexington turned to railroads as soon as possible. Cincinnati was the major out-of-state rival to both Louisville and Lexington. Cincinnati and Louisville would fight for river supremacy, then Lexington would join in the railroad wars. St. Louis was also a rival, but it was not considered to pose the threat that Cincinnati presented.

Louisville and Lexington were not the only urban centers in the state, but they were the most important before the Civil War. Covington and Newport were among the largest towns after Louisville, but they were considered satellites of Cincinnati. Frankfort was important because it was the state capital. (Its name apparently resulted from a 1780 Indian raid that killed one Stephen Frank at a ford on the Kentucky River.) In 1800 its 628 inhabitants placed it second only to Lexington as a population center. It had bad luck with the early state capitols. A three-story structure completed in 1794 burned in 1813, and its successor, completed in 1816, was likewise destroyed by fire in November 1824. The Greek Revival structure designed by Gideon Shryock and completed in 1830 still stands as one of the state's loveliest public buildings. Frankfort developed some manufacturing, and it was one of the important ports on the Kentucky River, but its growth was outpaced by that of several other towns. Its 1860 population was 3,702. The highlight of each year was the meeting of the legislature.

Eight towns other than Louisville and Lexington were listed as having more than a thousand inhabitants in 1830: Paris, Georgetown, and Harrodsburg from the early Bluegrass settlements; Shelbyville and Bardstown to the west; Maysville as the immigrant port of entrance for the Bluegrass; and Hopkinsville and Russellville for the Green River country. Even smaller towns were important economic, political, and social centers, and some of them would soon outstrip several of the 1830 leaders. By 1860 Bowling Green was considerably larger than Russellville and about the size of Hopkinsville. Bardstown and Shelbyville both had smaller populations in 1860 than in 1830.

Some interesting towns of the late eighteenth century never got beyond the planning stage. Lystra and Franklinville were to have been located near the Rolling Fork of Salt River in Nelson County. Lystra's plat showed large squares with a park in the center of each one and a great central park surrounded by avenues one hundred feet wide. Spaces were reserved for churches, the town hall, a college, and places

103

of amusement. Ohiopiomingo was to have been built on the Ohio River about thirty miles below Louisville. Its ambitious plan called for more than one thousand homes, each sited on a one-hundred-by-three-hundred-foot lot. Each settler was to get five hundred acres on a ninety-nine-year lease. No rent was due for the first three years if a house and barn were constructed and at least twenty acres were put under cultivation. Hygeia, to be located on the Ohio River opposite Cincinnati, was the most elaborate dream town of the nineteenth century. None of these towns were built. Speculators, though, could think of complete towns instead of acres of wilderness.

Characteristics of Kentuckians

Few foreign visitors to Kentucky were able to resist writing about its people, and numerous observations are available for this period of the state's history. Great differences existed among the state's inhabitants, however, and statements made about one group might not be true of other groups. A traveler who visited a series of wealthy planters who owned thousands of fertile acres and benefited from the labor of dozens of slaves saw a quite different Kentucky from the visitor who came in contact with landless families living in crowded one-room cabins with little prospect of ever improving their condition. Table manners were different if one dined at a table where the host always dressed for dinner and employed a skilled cook than if one ate at a common table in a dirty tavern. In between such extremes existed an almost infinite gradation of economic and social differences, which make generalizations dangerous. Yet some characteristics of early nineteenth-century Kentuckians were repeated so often that they must have some validity.

Travelers were often struck by the physical appearance of the Kentuckians they encountered. "In the persons they are large and generally handsome," an Englishman wrote in 1818, "but are too much inclined to corpulency." They had the reputation, he added, of being the best warriors in the United States.

That rumor might be true if only their courage was considered, but he recalled that the Kentuckians often lacked discipline, and at times during the recent war their soldiers had fallen into panic. Yet these were the men who had fought and won the land from the Indians, and they had won the Northwest from Great Britain. Another visitor made a comment that has often been repeated in the state: "Kentucky has the most beautiful women and the finest horses in America."

Few travelers failed to comment upon the hospitality displayed by Kentuckians. One gentleman commented that "they will stop you on the road, and oblige you to go to their houses, if they have ever seen you in respectable society." Another gentleman remarked that the Kentuckians he met shared what they had and would have been offended by any offer to pay. An English traveler found that Kentuckians had strong anti-England sentiments but were very hospitable to the individual Englishman visiting among them.

Perhaps connected with the trait of hospitality was curiosity, a characteristic frequently mentioned. People who lived in a somewhat isolated region were often hungry for news of almost every kind. Travelers reported that they were bombarded with questions: What's your name? Where are you from? Where are you going? How much did that horse cost? What do you make? Are you married? What do you do? The Kentuckians who fired such a barrage of questions were willing to respond to similar inquiries. Some outsiders found their hosts garrulous, with horses and lawsuits their most common subjects. But they were also generally proud of their world, and they were eager to expound upon its wonders: the beauty of Kentucky, the charm of their particular locality, the superiority of the United States, the speed of Kentucky horses. Kentuckians were often described as being honorable and truthful, friendly and generous, independent-minded but always willing to join in a cooperative undertaking. Nearly all Kentuckians were convinced that a democratic society was the ideal.

They might be impressed by visitors' titles, but they did not want such titles in Kentucky.

Of course there were some less flattering descriptions of the "unique people" called Kentuckians. Their friendliness could become wearing; they might be too gregarious for a weary traveler who longed for a bit of solitude. Kentuckians were sometimes seen as unable to control their passions or to submit to the group discipline needed in a harmonious society. They were sometimes too sensitive and too irascible, so that supposed slights degenerated into fights or duels. At least one visitor found his hosts "cruel and implacable," a people who seldom or never forgave a wrong or insult. He blamed these undesirable traits on the pioneer period, when the Kentuckians had fought the Indians for survival. A number of travelers also saw Kentuckians as too addicted to gambling. They may have heard of the famous Henry Clay–John Bradford episode. After a stretch of bad cards, Bradford owed Clay forty thousand dollars, more than the value of his entire estate. When he approached Clay to see what could be done to discharge his debt, Clay said, "Give me a note for $500 and forget the rest." Soon afterward, luck turned, and after an especially bad night Clay owed Bradford eighty thousand dollars that he could not pay. Bradford had a solution: "Just give me back my note for $500 and we're even."

A few personal traits or habits elicited unfavorable comment from some visitors. Kentucky men were said to keep their hands busy by whittling on a piece of wood and would use a chair if other wood was not handy. The haste with which food was attacked in taverns and other places with common tables appalled some foreigners accustomed to more leisurely dining. It also left some of them hungry, as the food disappeared before they summoned enough courage to enter the scramble. Excessive swearing was often criticized. So was spitting, especially when done by those who were chewing tobacco or dipping snuff. Any number of bespattered travelers concluded that the famous Kentucky skill with the long rifle did not carry over into accuracy in spitting.

Part II

Kentucky, 1820-1865

9

Politics and Politicians, 1820-1859

The Critical Court Struggle

By 1820 Kentucky was essentially a one-party state, since the Federalists had almost disappeared, but during the next few years the commonwealth came close to civil war as the result of some of the most vicious politicking that Kentucky has ever endured. As the Panic of 1819 worsened, many Kentuckians found themselves hopelessly in debt. Demands for help crescendoed. The critical court struggle—also called the Old Court–New Court Controversy—was fought between people who wanted relief for debtors and continuation of the cheap-money Bank of the Commonwealth and the proponents of sound banking and the sanctity of contracts as they were written. This struggle became a contest between the relief and the antirelief advocates.

Governor Gabriel Slaughter (1767-1830), who served from 1816 to 1820, often at odds with the legislature, agreed to a repeal of the 1818 act creating forty-six banks and to the abandonment of damages allowed on protested bills of exchange. On February 11, 1820, the legislature allowed a delay in the payment of some debts by passing a replevin bill, which provided a legal means of recovering property, said to have been wrongly taken, if the parties agreed to accept a court's decision on the dispute. When a state court issued an execution order, a twelve months' delay was granted if the plaintiff (creditor) endorsed the bill with the statement "Notes of the Bank of Kentucky or its branches will be accepted in discharge of this judgment or decree." If the plaintiff would not so endorse the paper, the debtor could postpone the debt for two years. The creditors were being pressured to accept at face value the depreciated notes of the bank.

John Adair (1757-1840), popular because of his dispute with Andrew Jackson, won the governorship in 1820 in a tight four-man race. While he called for reforms in education and the penitentiary system and the improvement of Ohio River navigation, he also emphasized the urgent need to help debtors who were near bankruptcy. A majority of the legislators elected that year also favored relief, and over strong objections they chartered the Bank of the Commonwealth on November 29, 1820, as a cheap-money relief measure. Its capital stock of two million dollars was entirely owned by the state, and the bank could issue three million dollars in banknotes. The notes soon declined in value, but that circumstance was expected to ease the burden of debts. A gentleman who paid a five-dollar debt with a ten-dollar bill from a sound Virginia bank was surprised to receive in change three five-dollar notes of the Bank of the Commonwealth. The replevin act was modified in December 1820 to reflect the value of the banknotes issued by the two state banks. The execution of a judgment could be delayed two years if the plaintiff would not accept the notes of either bank; it could be delayed one year if the plaintiff accepted only Bank of Kentucky notes; and the delay was three months if the creditor accepted only Bank of the Commonwealth money. The Bank of Kentucky angered the Relief Party with its sound money policies, and its charter, which in 1819 had been extended to 1841, was revoked in December 1822. The items exempted from a forced sale indicated what was then considered the minimum equipment for making a living: a horse, a plow, a hoe, and an ax.

Creditors protested that the replevin acts were unconstitutional, that they repudiated the validity of contracts. Reliefers asked, Why have a government if it doesn't help its people? Inevitably, cases went to the courts. Circuit court judge James Clark heard *Williams v. Blair* and ruled that the replevin law violated both the state and federal constitutions. He defended his ruling against a legislative attack, and by a 59-35 vote the House failed to get the two-thirds majority needed to remove him by address of the two houses. Circuit court judge Francis Preston Blair rendered a similar decision in Fayette County in *Lapsley v. Brashear*. Both decisions went to the Court of Appeals. After heated hearings, Chief Justice John Boyle and Associate Justices William Owsley and Benjamin Mills ruled in October 1823 that the stay law and all related efforts to alter contract performance were unconstitutional. They arrived at that conclusion by different routes, but the verdicts were unanimous.

The justices were denounced in resolutions and petitions, but the legislature could not muster the two-thirds majorities needed to remove them. The state divided sharply on the issue, but there were more debtors than creditors. Antireliefer George Robertson (1790-1874) wrote that "no popular controversy, waged without bloodshed, was ever more absorbing and acrimonious than that which raged, like a hurricane, over Kentucky for about three years." Some persons feared that civil war might break out, that the very organization of society was in danger. John Rowan, George Bibb, William T. Barry, Amos Kendall, John Adair, and Joseph Desha were among the Relief Party leaders. Their principal antirelief opponents included George Robertson, Ben Hardin, John Pope, John J. Crittenden, and Robert Wickliffe.

The Relief Party turned to the voters for a solution. They had concluded that the legislature was the dominant branch of government; it should be able to bring the judges to heel. In 1824 the Relief Party backed Joseph Desha (1768-1842) for governor. When he defeated Christopher Tompkins by a vote of 38,378-22,499, the reliefers had their mandate to proceed. A proposal to cut the salaries of the judicial offenders to twenty-five cents per year was discarded.

On December 9, 1824, however, the Kentucky Senate voted to abolish the Court of

Appeals. The House engaged in a lengthy and sometimes almost violent debate on December 23, during which Governor Desha lobbied on the floor in a flagrant violation of House rules. The next day the representatives voted 54-43 to repeal the act that had organized the Court of Appeals and to replace the court with a new Court of Appeals of four members. William T. Barry was made chief justice of the New Court, with James Haggin, John Trimble, and B.W. Patton (later replaced by R.H. Davidge) as the associate justices. Achilles Sneed, clerk of the Old Court, was ordered to turn the court's records over to Francis Preston Blair, clerk of the New Court.

The state was flooded with speeches, petitions, letters to the editor, and pamphlets discussing the issues involved. George Robertson penned such a masterful defense of the Old Court's position that the Relief majority in the Senate, fearing that the defense would "blow us sky-high," refused to print it in the *Senate Journal.* The Old Court party consisted largely of persons who belonged to the creditor class, but it gained support from citizens of less wealth who were concerned by the threat to the constitution and the concept of the balance of power. The New Court people talked of legislative supremacy and the people's will. They reminded their opponents that Thomas Jefferson had eliminated the federal circuit courts and their judges after he became president. (The elderly Jefferson declined to get involved in the Kentucky controversy.) When Sneed refused to turn over the Old Court records, Blair led an assault. The attackers broke into the room where the records were kept and took the papers they could find. Sneed was fined ten pounds for contempt of court for not relinquishing the papers. The Old Court then met in a Frankfort church, but it could do little without the case records. Kentucky had two supreme courts, neither of which recognized the other. The controversy could easily have changed into armed warfare. The *Louisville Morning Post* was then being published by Albert G. Hodges and William Tanner, who

disagreed on the legality of the courts. So Tanner filled two pages of the paper with pro-New Court materials, while Hodges loaded the other two pages with praise for the Old Court. At last they flipped a coin to see who would buy out the other, and Tanner became the sole editor.

The Old Court supporters rallied and won control of the House in 1825, and on November 24 the House voted to repeal the New Court law. But after the 1825 election the New Court-Old Court partisans were numerically tied in the Senate, and Lieutenant Governor Robert B. McAfee killed the repeal bill with his vote.

In 1826 a legislator proposed a draconian solution: Accept the resignations of all New Court and Old Court judges, all members of the General Assembly, and the governor and lieutenant governor, and let the state start all over. The bill passed the House but was killed in the Senate. Instead, in December 1826 the legislature passed an act that declared all the New Court legislation illegal and restored the Old Court. Desha's veto was overridden, and on January 1, 1827, Blair delivered the court records in his possession. When John Boyle resigned to accept a federal judgeship, George Bibb was made chief justice. To clarify a tangled situation, Old Court justices Mills and Owsley resigned and were immediately reappointed. The Senate refused to confirm them, and Joseph R. Underwood and George Robertson were appointed and confirmed. Robertson became chief justice when Bibb resigned to go to the U.S. Senate. In April 1829 the Court of Appeals declared in *Hildreth's Heirs v. McIntire's Devisees* that all of the actions and decisions of the New Court had been void.

By then prosperity had returned, and the clamor for debtor relief had subsided to a normal level. The Kentucky controversy had attracted national attention and derision, and the state's reputation suffered. The Bluegrass State seemed less attractive after this dispute, and its progress was probably slowed. It was in the decade of the 1820s that the number of people leaving the state began to exceed the number entering it. Still, a dangerous situation had been resolved without resort to the civil war that many Kentuckians had feared would come. Desha's reputation was damaged by his extremely partisan participation in the controversy. He was also condemned for pardoning his son Isaac, who was found guilty of murder and sentenced to death by two juries. Desha's role in forcing the departure of Transylvania University president Horace Holley antagonized many Kentuckians who favored education. A visitor to the state in 1825 remarked of the governor: "He is said by some to possess talents; I have never been furnished with the evidence." By 1828 many Kentuckians would have agreed with that assessment.

The Second Party System

In the 1820s a new party alignment was developing in both the state and the nation. The first party system had pitted the Federalists against the Democratic Republicans. The Federalists had more success nationally than they enjoyed in Kentucky, but in 1816 they supplied their last presidential contestant, and for several years the United States had one political party. But a monolithic party is sure to develop differences, some of them coming from disagreement on principles, some of them emerging from personality clashes. It oversimplifies the emergence of the second party system in Kentucky to assume that the Old Court adherents became the Whigs of the 1830s. Many of them did make that shift; many of them did not. The new party differences were based partly upon national issues, partly upon state and even local issues. By the 1830s Henry Clay was one of the prominent politicians in the country, and his national endeavors were reflected in the political situation in the state.

The emerging political affiliations could not be determined just by reference to economic and social backgrounds. One might venture cautiously that a Kentuckian with some wealth was more likely to vote Whig than Democrat, but there were many wealthy Democrats and poor Whigs. Both Democrat and Whig leaders came from the same elite class; slaveholding was common among the leaders of both parties. The Kentucky Whigs had their greatest strength in the center of the state; the Democrats were strongest on the periphery. The Jackson Purchase was strongly Democratic, but the Whigs had pockets of support in the mountains. Faith in Henry Clay may have been the main unifying factor among the Kentucky Whigs. A Democratic Republican from his entrance into politics, Clay became a National Republican in the 1820s as the new parties emerged. Then he became a Whig as that party coalesced in opposition to Andrew Jackson and the Democrats. Clay had a national vision of what the country could become, and he inspired others to support that vision. In his American System, westerners supported a protective tariff in return for federal aid for internal improvements. The envisioned result would be sectional interdependence with everyone working to promote a stronger and most prosperous nation. Clay's scheme also included an enlarged national bank to provide fiscal stability and investment funds. While he disliked slavery in theory, he was a slaveholder who tolerated the institution as a practical matter. A pragmatic politician, Clay earned his reputation as the Great Compromiser.

The dominant figure in the Democratic Party was General Andrew Jackson, who was aided by a corps of able assistants. While the Democrats, like the Whigs, had partisans of quite different opinions, they tended to be suspicious of large business enterprises and monopolies such as the Second Bank of the United States. They favored freedom of economic opportunity, unhampered by governmental restrictions, and they believed in political freedom, including universal suffrage for white men. As he proved during the South Carolina nullification crisis, Jackson believed in the supremacy of the national government while opposing extended national authority.

The Whig Ascendancy

Governor Thomas Metcalfe (1780-1855) was elected by the National Republicans in 1828 after being Kentucky's first gubernatorial candidate nominated by a party convention. A stonemason who had helped construct some of the state's public buildings, Old Stonehammer defeated Democrat William T. Barry in an extremely close race, 38,930-38,231. Democrat John Breathitt was elected lieutenant governor over Joseph R. Underwood. Metcalfe was especially interested in promoting internal improvements, and some progress was made during his administration. He was not successful in establishing an adequate system of public schools. He favored the high tariff of 1828 and opposed South Carolina's nullification of the tariff as being unconstitutional.

John Breathitt (1786-1834) used his 1828 victory as a springboard to the governorship in 1832 over a weak National Republican candidate, Richard A. Buckner of Green County. Again the vote was close, 40,715-39,473. In an inspiring example of participatory democracy, Oldham County had a 162.9 percent turnout of its eligible voters. This record has never been exceeded in Kentucky, although several efforts

have been made. Since the National Republicans won control of the General Assembly, Breathitt was unable to get much important legislation passed before his death on February 21, 1834. The 1832 election had repeated the 1828 split between the governor and the lieutenant governor, and National Republican James T. Morehead (1797-1854) of Warren County served the remainder of Breathitt's term, from 1834 to 1836.

Morehead was the first governor born in the state of Kentucky. After the August 1834 elections, the Whigs, as the National Republicans were being called, had majorities in both houses of the General Assembly. Democrat James Guthrie (1792-1869) was ousted as president of the Senate and replaced by Whig James Clark (1779-1839). Morehead favored internal improvements, as did most Kentuckians of that era, but he was essentially a caretaker governor. The use of "Whig" as a party label began in the spring of 1834, and the first great Whig Party convention was held in the state on July 4, 1834. The Whigs' attempt to fasten a Tory label on the Democrats did not succeed.

As a circuit court judge in 1822 James Clark had declared the stay laws unconstitutional. He was a strong Clay supporter, a staunch Whig, and a bitter opponent of Andrew Jackson. In 1836 he defeated Democrat Matthew Flournoy for the governorship by a comfortable margin, 38,587-30,491. As governor from 1836 to 1839 Clark sought better fiscal accounting, changes in the criminal code to combat a perceived rise in crime, and the creation of a common school system. The legislature established a framework for public schools but did not supply funds to put it into operation. When Clark asked for a law to prevent the distribution of abolitionist materials in the state, the General Assembly refused on the grounds that such a measure would interfere with freedom of speech. The Panic of 1837, which lasted for several years and may have been more severe than the Panic of 1819, created fiscal problems for the state, but it did not lead to another critical court struggle. Clark died in office on August 27, 1839.

Charles Anderson Wickliffe (1788-1869), brother of wealthy slaveholder Robert Wickliffe, was an independent Whig who had supported Jackson in 1825, when the House of Representatives elected the president, and he had often opposed Clay's policies. He stayed in the Whig Party because he hated the Jackson Democrats even more. His margin of victory for lieutenant governor in 1836 was less than half that of Clark's margin for the governorship. The Panic of 1837 was well under way when Wickliffe became governor on September 5, 1839. Since the state had ended the previous fiscal year with a deficit of forty-two thousand dollars, he urged the passage of a small tax increase. The General Assembly, however, would only authorize the borrowing of funds. Historians have been grateful to Wickliffe for his interest in protecting the state archives. Wickland, the home that he and his wife, Margaret, built in Bardstown later became known as the Home of Three Governors: Wickliffe himself lived there, son Robert C. became governor of Louisiana, and grandson J.C.W. Beckham was governor of Kentucky from 1900 to 1907.

One of the most entertaining of the Whig governors was Robert Perkins Letcher (1788-1861), who served from 1840 to 1844. He was better known as Black Bob. Dark-complexioned and corpulent, Letcher was a gregarious man who made lasting friendships and was a masterful stump speaker. He could hold a crowd enthralled for hours, then distract his opponent's listeners by playing rousing tunes on his fiddle. Letcher had won thirteen elections before beating Democrat Richard French in 1840 by a margin of 15,720 votes in a poll of 95,020. His main concern was to preserve Kentucky's solvency despite the loss of revenue because of the depression. His solution was to reduce expenditures, and work on roads and rivers was reduced sharply. Letcher successfully resisted major relief bills, but he did accept some minor relief measures. He prided himself on having small annual surpluses and on the resumption of specie payments by state banks in 1842.

William Owsley (1782-1862) was one of the best of the rather mediocre Whig governors. Tall and slender, he had practiced law and served several terms in the General Assembly, but he was best known as one of the Old Court judges. In 1834-36 he had been secretary of state in Governor Morehead's administration. In the 1844 election Owsley won over a strong Democratic candidate, General William O. Butler, in a close race, 59,680-55,056. He was able to pay off some of the state debt, but he urged the legislature to fund the system of public education that existed largely on paper. The legislators did little, but Owsley appointed an irascible Presbyterian minister, Robert J. Breckinridge (1800-1871), as superintendent of public instruction. During his 1847-53 tenure Breckinridge prodded Kentucky into making its first real progress toward providing education for its white children.

Although Owsley opposed war with Mexico, once the Mexican War started he participated actively in providing for the state volunteers. His reputation was tarnished by several actions in which he appeared blind to political consequences. He pardoned Delia Ann Webster of Vermont, who had been found guilty of helping fugitive slaves escape from Kentucky, and he engaged in a bitter intraparty wrangle with Ben Hardin. After supporting Owsley in 1844, Hardin was appointed secretary of state. The two became estranged when Hardin was given little voice in the making of patronage appointments. Owsley removed Hardin on September 1, 1846, but the Senate and later the Court of Appeals upheld Hardin's refusal to vacate the office. His position vindicated, Hardin then resigned. Owsley also attracted adverse attention by excessive nepotism in placing family members in office. Weary of quarrels and criticism, he told the General Assembly that the approach of the end of his administration "excites in my breast no emotions of regret."

Owsley was followed by John J. Crittenden (1786-1863), second only to Henry Clay among Kentucky's Whigs. Born in Woodford County, Crittenden later moved to Russellville to practice law. An aide-de-camp to Governor Shelby during the War of 1812, Crittenden later became noted as the state's foremost defense attorney in murder cases. In April 1854 he won acquittal for Matthews Flournoy Ward with an eloquent appeal for mercy in one of the state's most notorious murder trials. Ward had killed William H.G. Butler, principal of Louisville High School, who had punished one of Ward's younger brothers. Several witnesses had seen the shooting, but the jury accepted Crittenden's appeal. An angry mob then set fire to the Wards' home. Crittenden had an alert eye for advancement, and he resigned from numerous positions to accept other posts. Before 1848 he had served several terms in the General Assembly, had been Kentucky's secretary of state, had been in the U.S. Senate several times, and had been the nation's attorney general.

A loyal supporter of Henry Clay for most of his political life, Crittenden switched to Zachary Taylor in 1848 because he thought Clay could not be elected. After actively campaigning for Taylor and for himself, Crittenden defeated Lazarus W. Powell for governor by a vote of 66,860-57,397. As governor, Crittenden urged the legislature to call the constitutional convention that the voters had demanded and to use wisely the property tax that the voters had approved for public schools (two cents per one hundred dollars in property valuation). He requested funding for a comprehensive geological survey of the state and the rebuilding of the state penitentiary, which had burned. He also wanted a sinking fund that would pay the interest on the state debt and gradually eliminate the debt. The legislature gave him most of what he requested for education, and he showed promise of being one of the best pre-Civil War governors. But in his typical fashion, Crittenden resigned the governorship in July 1850 to become attorney general in President Millard Fillmore's cabinet.

John L. Helm (1802-67), the last of the succession of Whig governors, was a successful attorney and Whig politician who had extensive service in the General Assembly before his election as lieutenant governor in 1848. He was especially interested in election reform and railroad development, and he opposed the transfer of money from the sinking fund to the school fund to meet a shortage in the latter. Helm had little more than a year to serve after Crittenden's resignation in 1850, and he was primarily a caretaking chief executive.

The Mexican War

Militant Kentucky men who longed for military glory had their chance in the war with Mexico (1846-48). A number of Kentuckians had migrated to Texas and participated in the Texas revolution and the formation of the Lone Star Republic. The United States recognized the independence of Texas but did not then annex it. Mexico did not admit or accept the loss of that huge province. By the mid-1840s the question of the annexation of Texas had become part of the growing controversy over the expansion of slavery in the United States. A number of Americans, with both proslavery and antislavery views, had become convinced that slavery would expand or would ultimately die, like a grass fire that consumes itself when not allowed to spread. The slave South, outnumbered in the House of Representatives, hoped to protect its interests by maintaining state equality in the Senate. Texas, which might be divided into several slave states, appeared ideally suited for the expansion of slavery. Aside from the slavery issue, the concept of manifest destiny called for the addition of more territory, and Texas fell within what some expansionists saw as the natural boundaries of the United States. When James K. Polk won the presidential election of 1844 over Henry Clay, war became almost certain. Mexico and the United States had a number of problems, such as unpaid debts and border raids, but the excuse for war came after Texas was annexed to the United States in 1845. Mexico recognized neither the annexation nor the American claim that the Rio Grande was the boundary. After Polk sent troops into the disputed territory, the inevitable clash occurred, and the president declared that American blood had been shed on American soil. War was declared despite considerable opposition from the Northeast generally and proponents of antislavery wherever they were.

Most Kentuckians welcomed the war. When the War Department asked Kentucky for two infantry regiments and one of cavalry, 105 companies, some of them not fully organized, volunteered their services. Owsley accepted 30 of them to meet the state's quota and refused the other 75. Most of the ones selected were from the Bluegrass and some urban areas along the Ohio River, and howls of outrage came from other parts of the state. As usual, finances were a problem. Governor Owsley decided to take care of the state volunteers without waiting for authorized funds. The Bank of Kentucky loaned $250,000, and a group of Louisville merchants advanced $54,000. By the time the General Assembly met in 1847, these lenders had been reimbursed. The governor also had problems with the appointment of officers, for in Kentucky such service was often

seen as necessary for a political career. Owsley usually selected good Whigs, but he could not take care of everyone, and President Polk appointed Democrats William O. Butler and Thomas F. Marshall to the top positions.

As letters came from the men on active duty or as those who had been discharged returned with stories of hardships, the volunteering frenzy diminished. In the second call for volunteers in August 1847, Kentucky's quota was two infantry regiments to serve for the duration of the war. Owsley tried to select from the areas neglected the previous year. His task was easier this time, and he took twenty of the thirty-two companies that volunteered. The *Western Citizen,* published in Paris, the seat of Bourbon County, had boasted in June 1846 that "there is something in the very air of Kentucky which makes a man a soldier." That claim was less true in 1847.

Kentuckians fought in both of the major armies that invaded Mexico, but the First Kentucky Mounted Regiment and the Second Kentucky Foot Regiment that fought with Zachary Taylor in the northern part of that country received the most attention. The regiments did well at the battle of Buena Vista on February 22-23, 1847. When some of those who died there were buried in the Frankfort Cemetery, Theodore O'Hara, who had served in Mexico, read his "Bivouac of the Dead," one of the best-known poems written by a Kentuckian in the nineteenth century.

Some 5,113 Kentuckians volunteered for service in the Mexican War. Of this number, 77 (1.5 percent) were killed in action, 509 (10.0 percent) died from disease or accident, 792 (15.5 percent) were discharged, often for physical reasons, and 161 (3.1 percent) deserted.

The Treaty of Guadalupe Hidalgo (1848) gave the United States the Rio Grande border for Texas and the sprawling Mexican Cession. In return the United States paid $15 million and assumed claims of $3.25 million. The 1848 discovery of gold in California soon resulted in another sectional struggle over the future of slavery in the new territories, to which the Missouri Compromise did not apply.

The 1850 Constitution

Many citizens were dissatisfied with the second Kentucky constitution, and several attempts were made to call another convention. A bill to ascertain the sense of the electorate passed the General Assembly in 1837, but fewer than 27 percent of the voters favored holding a convention. The continuing criticisms were varied. Many critics wanted more democratic control of the government, which usually meant elected officials in place of appointed ones. Others wanted to curb what they saw as the irresponsible fiscal policies of the legislature and its concentration on private bills. The *Kentucky Yeoman* of March 10, 1848, charged that not half a dozen of the six hundred bills passed in the previous session "will probably be of the least public utility to the country. . . . if there had been no Legislature this winter, the country would have been one hundred thousand dollars better off." The growing debt of the state concerned many citizens. The opponents of slavery wanted a constitution that would at least provide a way to eliminate the "peculiar institution" in the future. And at last a growing number of Kentuckians believed that a public school system should be a constitutional function of the state. Had the constitution provided for individual amendments, some of the discontent could have been relieved; as it was, the accumulation of complaints could be addressed only through the cumbersome convention process.

In January 1847 a convention bill received approval in the House by a vote of 81-17 and in the Senate by 20-8. Most Democrats were for it, but so were many Whigs, and to some extent the drive for a constitutional convention was a nonpartisan movement. In the August 1847 election the convention measure received 92,639 favorable votes and 44,672 negative ones. The 1848 vote showed a shift in favor of the convention; it was approved 101,828-32,792. The legislature then provided

for a convention of one hundred members to meet in Frankfort on October 1, 1849.

The parties ran candidates, and the Democrats gained a narrow majority of the seats (52-48) and elected James Guthrie president. The two largest groups by occupation were lawyers (forty-two) and farmers (thirty-six). The delegates also included nine physicians, four merchants, three clerks, two ministers, one hotelkeeper, one mechanic, and two unclassified individuals. The delegates differed a great deal in ability and participation. As George D. Prentice (1802-70) observed of the convention in the *Louisville Journal*, "It contained men remarkable for their information, and others remarkable for the want of it." Charles A. Wickliffe, Garrett Davis, William Preston, John W. Stevenson, Squire Turner, Archibald Dixon, Ben Hardin, James Guthrie, and Beverly L. Clarke were probably the most valuable members of the body. The most prominent speakers were Wickliffe, Hardin, Turner, Clarke, and David Meriwether. Several members apparently never spoke except to vote. Some outstanding Kentuckians were not there. Henry Clay and John J. Crittenden refused to seek seats; George Robertson, Robert J. Breckinridge, Charles Slaughter Morehead, and Thomas F. Marshall were defeated in their quest for election. For the first time in the state's constitutional conventions, a record was kept of the debates: a 1,129-page *Report* was printed.

The persistence of the antislavery advocates prompted the proslavery majority to make the ownership of slaves an absolute property right. Garrett Davis was the primary author of the slavery article, which declared that "the right of property is before and higher than any constitutional sanction, and the right of the owner of a slave to such slave and its increase is the same and as inviolable as the right of any property whatsoever." Elsewhere the constitution stated that even the largest majority did not possess absolute, arbitrary power over the "lives, liberty and property of freemen." The General Assembly was directed to enact legislation ordering any free negro or mulatto coming into Kentucky or any slave afterward emancipated to leave the state or suffer penitentiary confinement. Efforts to put into the constitution the provisions of the recently repealed Nonimportation Act of 1833, which prohibited the importation of slaves for commercial purposes, were defeated. A number of ministers held antislavery views, and that fact helps explain why only two were delegates and why ministers continued to be excluded from the General Assembly. The slavery debate in the convention indicated that a large majority of Kentuckians in 1849 at least condoned slavery and that under existing conditions there was no chance in the foreseeable future to end slavery in the state. Ben Hardin chortled near the end of the convention that "we promised to fix the constitution so that a majority could not oppress a minority, and we have done so."

The proposal to include a provision for public schools in the constitution drew considerable opposition. Ben Hardin asserted that "they are generally under the management of a miserable set of humbug teachers at best," and he deplored the waste of money from the property tax that the legislature had recently enacted. But for the first time a Kentucky constitution made provision, however inadequate, for a common school system and a school fund that was believed to be protected from legislative raids. The education article gave constitutional sanction to the efforts at educational reforms that were under way.

In the move toward more democratic control of the government, most of the state and local offices that had been appointive were made elective. Elections were, however, limited to one day, an indication that travel had become easier since 1799. Voting continued to be by voice. The elective principle was also applied to judges, who were to be elected for fixed terms.

The legislature received considerable attention. All members of the House were elected at the same time for two-year terms; half of the senators were elected each two years. The growing cities were given more representation in the General Assembly, and a census was mandated each eight years so changes in representation could be made frequently. The legislature, which had been seen as the very heart of government, was now perceived as needing to be checked. Most of its time-consuming special legislation, such as granting divorces and making name changes, was turned over to the courts. The General Assembly was forbidden to make use of the sinking fund for any purpose other than paying the interest and principal of the state debt until that debt was paid in full. The legislature could not contract debts in excess of five hundred thousand dollars except "to repel invasion, suppress insurrections, or, if hostilities are threatened, provide for the common defense." With few exceptions, debts had to carry provisions for taxes that would pay the interest and extinguish the debt within a thirty-year period. The vote to borrow also had to receive a majority of the popular votes cast on that issue. Any appropriation of more than one hundred dollars had to be passed by a majority of the total membership of each house on a recorded vote. Sessions of the General Assembly were limited to sixty days unless two-thirds of both houses decided on an extension. The constitution makers of 1849 were obviously disenchanted with the legislature. Their solution was to curb it, not to increase the powers of the executive to offset it.

The constitution clarified the term of a replacement when a governor died in office or resigned, an event that had happened three times in the first half of the century. If a vacancy occurred before two years of a term had been completed, the person holding the post was required to call a special election to fill the remainder of the term. The governor could not succeed himself during the four years following his term; the previous constitution had a seven-year prohibition.

Dueling, as distinguished from plain fighting, had been confined to upper-class males, although the practice was outlawed by a series of laws beginning in 1799. A gentleman might horsewhip an inferior or shoot him down, but he did not sully the dueling etiquette by engaging an inferior in an affair of honor. Most of the state's leaders came from the upper social class, and many persons feared that the genteel practice would get out of hand. An 1811 law that required a nondueling oath for office-holders had not been effective, so a constitutional oath was inserted in 1849 for all members of the legislature, state officers, and members of the bar. People were disqualified from holding those positions if, after the adoption of the constitution, they participated in a duel in any capacity. After five years, however, the governor could grant a pardon that removed all restrictions.[1]

The amending process remained essentially unchanged. No provision was made for individual amendments, and the requirement for voter approval in two successive elections in order to hold a convention was retained.

The convention adopted its work on December 21, 1849. Unlike its predecessors, this constitution required approval by the voters at an election on the first Monday and Tuesday in May 1850. The convention would then reassemble on the first Monday in June. If the voters approved, the new constitution would be declared in effect. If the voters rejected the new constitution, the convention would readopt the 1799 constitution.

Most of the opposition to ratification came from Whigs, who saw the constitution as a Democratic product. Former chief justice Robertson was not alone in objecting to an elected judiciary, and he also complained because the amending process remained so difficult. Advocates of legislative independence objected to the restraints placed on the General Assembly, including the specification of the length of annual sessions. Some bemoaned the removal of the governor's appointive power; some objected to voice voting; some opposed the inclusion of education in the constitution; a few could not accept the strong proslavery article. Garrett Davis, John L. Helm, and

Thomas F. Marshall authored a lengthy condemnation of the constitution and distributed five thousand copies across the state. Calling themselves Friends of Constitutional Liberty, they tried to establish branches of their group in each county.

The ratification vote showed that the Friends of Constitutional Liberty were out of touch with most of their fellow citizens. Adoption of the new constitution won overwhelming approval, with a vote of 71,635-20,302. The convention reassembled on June 3, swore in four new members to fill vacancies, and then spent several days making minor changes. On June 11, 1850, the delegates proclaimed the new constitution to be in effect, and all signed the revised version. The late changes were not submitted to the voters for approval.

Once again Kentucky had made some modifications in its government without instituting radical changes. The constitution of 1850 was an essentially conservative document incorporating a few changes that most voters considered desirable. The endorsement given to education and the emphasis placed upon the election of officials were perhaps the two most far-reaching modifications.

Henry Clay for President

Pride in Henry Clay helps explain why many Kentuckians had an intense interest in national politics during the first half of the nineteenth century. Although he never became president, Clay was a leading political figure in the nation for at least three decades. He was a more capable statesman and certainly a more interesting person than a number of the presidents during that era. To Abraham Lincoln, Clay was "my beau ideal of a statesman, the man for whom I fought all my humble life." Charismatic, a dramatic and emotional speaker, a witty conversationalist, a pragmatic politician, a devout nationalist, Clay had strong support from a devoted band of supporters. But he had strong opponents as well. Many Americans disagreed

---

1. Repeated in the fourth constitution, this anchorism seems destined to accompany the state into the twenty-first century.

with his American System, which featured a high tariff, heavy expenditures for internal improvements, and a powerful national bank. Some voters believed that his skill as a compromiser indicated a willingness to sacrifice principle for expediency. His devastating wit created enemies among those who were victims of it. His ability to "drink, carouse, swear and gamble with the best of them" endeared him to many persons; it alienated others, who saw a lack of character and sound judgment. As a politician he had the disadvantage of having a strong rival in his own section of the country; Andrew Jackson, next door in Tennessee, was an implacable foe. Historian Clement Eaton once wrote that "Clay had one serious defect that disqualified him from being a consummate master of the political art; he talked too much and wrote too many letters." But he could bring his Senate audience to tears when speaking about the plight of Indians.

Clay entered the 1824 presidential race as a strong contender in the one-party contest. Andrew Jackson drew 99 electoral votes, John Quincy Adams 84, William H. Crawford 41, and Clay 37. Since the House of Representatives selected from among the top three, Clay was eliminated, but he had great influence in that body. Crawford's serious illness disqualified him, and Adams's nationalistic program was much closer to Clay's ideas than was Jackson's program. Adams did not like the Kentuckian, but Clay was a party leader who had a strong claim to a place in the administration. After talking to Adams at some length, Clay accepted the post of secretary of state. The Jacksonians immediately raised the cry of "corrupt bargain" that haunted Clay for the rest of his life. The charge that he sold his influence in the House in return for the cabinet position appears to be false, but it did not disappear.

Clay's next bid for the presidency came in 1832. Elected to the Senate in 1831, he led the opposition to the Jackson administration. Nominated by the Kentucky legislature and those of some other states, Clay lost to Jackson by 219-49 electoral votes. Clay's support of the high tariff and his efforts to secure the recharter of the Second National Bank gave Old Hickory some winning issues.

Thanks largely to the skillful management of New York politician and journalist Thurlow Weed, the 1840 Whig convention nominated William Henry Harrison, whose military reputation helped him win the presidency. After Harrison's death a month into his term, Clay expected to dominate the John Tyler administration. But Tyler was actually an anti-Jackson Democrat, and he refused to accept Clay's program and advice.

By the 1840s slavery and its possible expansion had become a major national issue. Clay was a large slaveholder who believed that slavery was morally wrong but constitutional and deeply embedded in southern life. He had a long association with the American Colonization Society, but its best efforts barely affected the problem. Before the 1844 campaign, Clay and Martin Van Buren, who was assumed to be the Democratic candidate, apparently agreed to ignore the slavery issue in their campaigns. But James K. Polk, a Tennessee expansionist, took the nomination from Van Buren and shrewdly called for "the re-annexation of Texas and the re-occupation of Oregon." Clay hastily responded with a series of letters that left confusion about just where he stood on the issue. After a colorful campaign Polk got a popular majority of just 38,000 in a vote of 2.7 million but won the electoral vote by a wide margin, 170-105.

A former Kentuckian who ran on the Liberty Party ticket may have cost Clay the presidency. Once a wealthy slaveholder, James G. Birney (1792-1857) had become an abolitionist. He received only 62,000 votes nationally, but 16,000 of them were in New York, mostly in the western part of the state, which was normally Whig. Polk carried New York by a margin of only 5,000 votes. Had Clay won New York, he would have been elected by a slim margin of 141-134 electoral votes.

Once again Clay retired from public life. He was nearly sixty-eight years old, he had suffered several tragedies in his family, he was heavily in debt with a large mortgage on his beloved Ashland, his health was not good, his energies were flagging, and his estate demanded his attention. It was imperative that he spend his last years putting his affairs in order. The lure of politics was too strong to ignore, though, and he had the fatal political affliction of optimism. Clay let party leaders know that he was available to lead the ticket in 1848. But the Whigs were desperate for a victory, and even such a devoted disciple as Crittenden had decided that Clay could not be elected. They had won in 1840 with a military hero; now they turned to General Zachary Taylor. As one Clay deserter explained, "I have voted for Mr. Clay all the time, have *bet* on him, and lost, until I am *tired,* and have finally concluded that Mr. Clay is *too pure a patriot* to win in these demagoguery times."

Bitterly disappointed at being discarded and increasingly concerned about the developing national crisis, an ill and aged Clay returned to the Senate in 1849 to wage his last battle for moderate compromise and the preservation of the Union. His proposals were introduced in an omnibus bill, which he thought could be passed as a unit. On July 22, 1850, Clay held the stage for three hours, explaining his proposals, answering questions, and appealing to the spirit of patriotism and nationalism to secure passage of his bill. It could not be passed intact, and the exhausted Clay went to Newport for most of August to rest. Stephen A. Douglas of Illinois did much of the work in getting the Compromise of 1850 passed in five separate bills. Clay accepted the changes upon his return and worked for the acceptance of the measures.

When he reached Lexington on the evening of October 2 he was greeted by a huge crowd. Clay spoke for several minutes, then asked to be excused, "for, strange as it may seem, there is an old woman at Ashland whom I would rather see than the all of you." During the time remaining to him Clay labored to preserve the Compromise of 1850 and the nation. When he made his last will in July 1851 he pro-

vided that slave children born after January 1, 1850, would be freed, the males at twenty-eight, the females at twenty-five, and then colonized. "Harry of the West" returned to Washington in the summer of 1851 but could attend only the opening session of the Senate. Too ill to go back to Ashland, Clay died in his room at the National Hotel on June 29, 1852. Thirty thousand mourners welcomed him home to Kentucky.

Since Kentucky supported Clay in his losing efforts, the state did not have a good record in electing presidents during this period. The state lost with Clay in 1824, 1832, and 1844. It also lost with William Henry Harrison in 1836 and Winfield Scott in 1852. The commonwealth was on the winning side with Jackson in 1828, Harrison in 1840, Taylor in 1848, and James Buchanan in 1856. Kentuckians voted overwhelmingly against Lincoln in both 1860 and 1864. Thus, in the eleven presidential elections from 1824 through 1864, Kentucky backed the winner only four times.

Parties in Turmoil

As the sectional struggle intensified, the national political parties were one of the bonds holding the country together. With supporters on both sides of the Mason-Dixon Line, a party had to find a moderate position if it expected to remain intact. Two of the most significant political developments of the turbulent 1850s were the disintegration of the Whig Party and the rise of the sectional Republican Party. Racked by internal dissent, the Democrats managed to hold together until 1860. The political story in Kentucky was somewhat different. The state Whigs showed more vitality than did the national party, and the Republicans did not become a major factor in Kentucky before the Civil War.

The Democratic Party in the state was developing some able leaders by midcentury. Linn Boyd from the Jackson Purchase, James Guthrie from Louisville, Lazarus Powell (1812-67) from Henderson, and John C. Breckin-

This daguerreotype of Henry and Lucretia Clay was probably taken on the couple's fiftieth wedding anniversary, April 11, 1849. The Whigs had abandoned Henry Clay by 1848, and he knew that he would never become president (courtesy of The Filson Club Historical Society).

ridge (1821-75) from Lexington gave the party the strongest leadership it had enjoyed for many years. The Democrats had been seen as the party most responsible for the popular new constitution, and Powell used that advantage to defeat his friend and onetime law partner, Archibald Dixon, for the governorship in 1851. The race was extremely close, 54,613-53,763, but Powell became the first Democrat to be elected governor since 1832. The Whigs retained control of the General Assembly and were able to block most of his proposals. They did agree upon a comprehensive geological survey, on which David Dale Owen did an excellent job. Powell backed Superintendent of Public Instruction Robert J. Breckinridge in his educational reforms, and the two got the school tax increased from two to five cents per one hundred dollars in property valuation.

The state Whigs were in difficulty. Their national party disappeared when many of the northern Whigs refused to accept the proslavery provisions of the Compromise of 1850. The death of Henry Clay in 1852 was a serious blow, for he had done much to unify the party. While some Whigs continued to cling to their party label, others saw no future in the state party when the national party was breaking up. Many of them joined the new Ameri-

can Party, otherwise known as the Know-Nothings.

Nativism is the policy of advancing the interests of the native-born citizen by excluding the foreign-born from the same rights and privileges. It had existed from the beginning of the nation, but the first Native American Party convention was held in Philadelphia on July 4, 1845. A month later a meeting was held in Kentucky. In the late 1840s and early 1850s the Great Potato Famine in Ireland and the 1848 revolutionary unrest in Europe brought an increased number of immigrants to the United States. The 1850 census reported that only 4 percent of Kentuckians were foreign-born, with the Irish and Germans as the largest groups. Nearly half of the state's total foreign-born lived in Louisville. Nativist enmity also extended to Catholics, although they had been among Kentucky's pioneers. The first teacher at Harrodsburg, Jane Coomes, was a Catholic. The state's 35,000 Catholics in 1850 made up about 4 percent of the population, and the 48 Catholic churches were dwarfed by the 803 Baptist, 530 Methodist, and 224 Presbyterian churches. Some of Henry Clay's supporters blamed his 1844 presidential defeat upon nonnative voting, and the recent increase of immigrants frightened others. During the 1849 constitutional convention Garrett Davis proposed to restrict the rights of foreign-born citizens to vote and hold office. He objected to Catholics because that church was a "religious-politico institution." William Preston and Charles Wickliffe led the rebuttal, and Davis's resolution lost on a vote of 6-80.

A number of the newcomers to Louisville who had been active reformers in their previous countries shifted their attention to needed American reforms, including the end of slavery. The three German-language newspapers in Louisville gave publicity to these efforts. The confused political situation in the traditional parties opened the way for a party that catered to nativism. The *Covington Journal* of July 22, 1854, commented that "old political ties and associations seem to be broken up, and the uncertainty as to how far the 'Know-Nothing' movement may affect the result, destroys the basis of all competition." George Prentice, the influential editor of the *Louisville Journal,* helped promote the growth of the Know-Nothings with attacks on the foreign-born and Catholics. "The general issue is between Americanism and foreignism," he asserted in his July 8, 1855, issue.

The Know-Nothings won some city elections in Louisville, Covington, and Lexington, and in February 1855 the state party nominated William V. Loving of Bowling Green for governor. When he withdrew because of ill health, he was replaced by Charles Slaughter Morehead (1802-68), who had served several terms in the legislature and two terms in the U.S. House of Representatives as a Whig. The Democrats finally selected Beverly L. Clarke of Simpson County as their candidate. In a campaign that featured the nativist concepts, Morehead won, 69,816-65,413, and the new party captured both houses of the General Assembly. Some of the Know-Nothings were not anti-Catholic, antiforeign bigots; they were voters without a party who hoped that this one would push the slavery issue into the background and help preserve the Union, which they believed to be in danger. They were over-

shadowed by the rowdy element that was responsible for the "Bloody Monday" riots in Louisville on election day, August 6, 1855. Starting with efforts to keep the "undesirables" from voting, the riots saw at least twenty-two persons killed, more wounded, and great property damage resulting from fire and pillage. The losses would have been greater had not such citizens as Mayor John Barbee, who was a Know-Nothing, intervened to protect individuals and property. The outrages contributed to the decline of the party; by 1857 the Louisville party headquarters had become a German theater.

Governor Morehead in his inaugural address called for "perfect equality" for all naturalized citizens. Because of the recent improvements in the public schools, Kentucky faced a serious shortage of qualified teachers. The General Assembly accepted Morehead's proposal that Transylvania University be reorganized as a state school with a teacher training college. Opponents argued that public school funds could not be used for higher education, and in 1858 the Assembly repealed the legislation. The militia system had been effectively killed in 1854, when a law called for a muster only every six years, and Morehead was unable to get legislation to reorganize it. He did get the Kentucky State Agricultural Society chartered in 1856 and funds provided for an annual state fair to promote agricultural production. He also oversaw a long-overdue expansion and improvement of the state penitentiary at Frankfort, although the convict leasing system, from which the warden was expected to make a profit, was open to abuse.

By 1853 the revitalized Democratic Party was almost equal to its rival after years of Whig ascendancy. The parties split the Kentucky representatives in Congress evenly, 5-5. The Whig Party did not die in the state quite as rapidly as did the national party, although a number of Whigs joined the American Party as an alternative to becoming Democrats or throwing away votes on the tiny Temperance Party. In the 1855 election the Know-Nothings captured six of the ten House seats in Congress and sixty of the seats in the Kentucky House. Only twenty-five Whigs attended an April 1856 state meeting in Lexington.

The Democrats won control of the Kentucky House in 1857 and gained eight of the ten House seats in Washington. By the next year the American Party was effectively dead. Some Kentucky members united with the Douglas Democrats as that party began to splinter or in 1859 united with what remained of the Whig Party in a coalition called simply the Opposition. This group nominated Joshua Bell for governor. The Democrats selected Beriah Magoffin (1815-85) from among four major contenders. During the campaign Bell and Magoffin engaged in face-to-face debates, much as Abraham Lincoln and Stephen A. Douglas had done in Illinois the previous year. The Opposition put its opponents on the defensive by blaming them for all of the nation's recent problems, especially the question of slavery in the territories. Magoffin won, but the 8,904-vote margin was less than had been expected. The Democrats were showing signs of the disruption that the party would face in 1860.

10

Economic Development

Transportation by Land and Water

Adequate transportation is perhaps the most important single factor in the economic development of an area. Other factors mean little unless materials and people can be brought together where needed for production and then products can be distributed to those who require them. In long-settled areas, adequate transportation facilities are built over an extended period. Isolated Kentucky grew so rapidly from its first days of settlement that its transportation needs were magnified. In the pre–Civil War years the cry for "internal improvements" was almost incessant.

When the early explorers reached Kentucky, they found a few Indian trails, notably the Warriors' Path that crossed the region from the Cumberland Gap to the Ohio River, and any number of game trails. The woods bison had a good eye for terrain, and many of the early pioneer roads followed the paths engineered by this large mammal. Daniel Boone opened the famous packhorse trail to Boonesborough, and other trails were soon developed that led to new stations and forts. Virginia's few efforts to improve communications with the West were more successful on paper than on the ground. Kentucky's General Assembly in 1797 gave the county courts authority to oversee road construction and repair. Costs were held down by use of corvée, unpaid labor required from "all male laboring persons" over sixteen years of age for a certain number of days. Most local roads in Kentucky were built and maintained under this system until 1849, and traces of it lingered into the twentieth century in some counties. Practically all of these roads were dirt and were almost impassable in bad weather.

As early as 1793 the state assumed some responsibility for the main traveled roads. One of the first projects was to make the Wilderness Road passable for wagons and carriages. In 1797 the legislature erected a tollgate at Cumberland Ford and leased it to Robert Craig, the highest bidder. Both the upkeep of the road and Craig's profits were to come from the tolls collected. Post riders, as well as women and children under sixteen, were exempt from paying, and in 1798 so were immigrants who were bringing their families to Kentucky. A man, horse, mule, or mare paid nine pence, three pence was charged for each head of cattle going eastward, and carriages were charged three or six pence, depending on whether they had two or four wheels. The legislature changed the tolls from time to time. As early as 1803 some stagecoach travel was available between population centers.

In 1810 the General Assembly authorized a five-thousand-dollar lottery to improve the road between Maysville and nearby Washington. Continued demands for roads led to more lotteries and more tollgates. Salaried gatekeepers were employed in 1815, and thus the state had a chance to make money if traffic was heavy. "Internal improvements" became a battle cry after the War of 1812 and was an integral part of Henry Clay's American System. Charters for the Lexington and Louisville Turnpike Road Company and the Louisville and Maysville Turnpike Road Company in 1817 set a pattern for better roads that would be generally followed for several decades. The companies were capitalized at $350,000 each, and the state could purchase five hundred shares if it wished. Stockholders elected officers annually. Once a road was satisfactorily completed, a toll could be collected each five miles, except that no tollgate could be located within a mile of a town. Dividends were supposed to be between 6 and 12 percent. The list of those exempt from tolls was growing. Persons going to church, to a funeral, to vote, and to a militia muster were passed through. An effort to avoid payment

could result in a fifteen-dollar fine, but this penalty did not end the bypassing of tollgates whenever possible. After twenty years the state could take over a road by purchasing the private stock.

The Panic of 1819 discouraged state participation and made the raising of funds by private companies more difficult. The return of prosperity increased the pressure for better roads, for the costs of land transportation were almost prohibitive. In 1824 Governor Desha proposed that hard-surfaced roads be constructed by the state with the net profits "forever sacredly devoted to the interests of education," but little was done. Some Kentuckians, including Henry Clay, wanted the national government to help. Thomas Metcalfe, then in the U.S. House of Representatives, proposed a federal appropriation for a Maysville to Lexington road that would be part of a branch of the National Road (running from Cumberland, Maryland, to Vandalia, Illinois) that would connect Zanesville, Ohio, and New Orleans. That plan came to an end when President Jackson vetoed the bill.

An important breakthrough did occur in 1830, when a four-mile macadamized road was completed between Maysville and Washington. A prototype for more extensive endeavors, it represented the best road construction in the state before the Civil War. Scrapers were not being used then, and the work was done with plows, picks, shovels, and rock hammers. Such roads were usually thirty to fifty feet wide, including the drainage ditches. They had a somewhat convex shape for better drainage: an area about ten feet wide in the center of the road was covered with stones and topped with a ten-inch layer of packed small cracked rocks and gravel. Travel was possible on a macadamized road in almost any weather, and the cost of freighting decreased, as a team could haul a much heavier load than when pulling on dirt roads. Such roads cost between five thousand and eight thousand dollars per mile.

The success of the short road between Maysville and Washington encouraged both

These advertisements appeared in the *Spirit of the Times,* published in Bowling Green in 1826 and 1827 (courtesy of the Kentucky Library, Western Kentucky University).

the state and private companies, and considerable construction on other roads was done before the Panic of 1837 halted work. A state Board of Internal Improvements provided some direction for the growing number of projects. By 1837 the state had invested some $2.5 million in private companies; private investment amounted to about $2 million. Approximately 343 miles of stone-surfaced roads had been completed, and 236 miles were under construction. Thirty miles had been built without state participation. The better roads resulted in a sharp increase in stagecoach travel, as new routes were opened. The standard Concord stage used in Kentucky carried six passengers inside and one who sat outside with the driver. Baggage was lashed to the top or the back of the coach. Teams of four or six horses were changed about every ten miles. Allowing for stops during the day, coaches tried to average about eight miles per hour. In 1834 the 180-mile trip from Louisville to Nashville could be covered in two days if the traveler started at 5:00 A.M. and kept going until 9:00 P.M. each day. The coach made an overnight stop at Bell's Tavern near Glasgow Junc-

127

United States Mail Line,

From Louisville, Ky. through to Washington City, Baltimore, Md. and Richmond, Va.

The MAIL PACKETS leave Louisville daily, at 10 o'clock, A. M. for Cincinnati, and thence, four times a week to Guyandotte, viz.: on Mondays, Wednesdays, Thursdays, and Saturdays, at 5 o'-clock, P. M., where they connect with a DAILY LINE OF POST COACHES, to Washington City, Baltimore, and Richmond, Va. Passing the White Sulphur, Hot, and Warm Springs, travelling only by day-light.

☞ Passengers by the MAIL PACKETS will have a preference for seats in the STAGES from Guyandotte.

J. C. Buckles, AGENT.

Traveling in the 1830s might involve the use of both steamboats and stagecoaches. "Travelling only by day-light" was a luxury that not everyone could afford (from *The Louisville Directory, 1832,* courtesy of the Kentucky Library, Western Kentucky University).

tion, and the one-way cost was twelve dollars per passenger.

Road construction resumed in the 1840s as the depression ended, but concern was growing over the involvement of the state in such enterprises. By 1849 Kentucky had invested $2.7 million in eighteen hard-surfaced roads that would total 962 miles when completed; 775 miles were then available for use. The company charters did not allow the state to establish uniform rates, but representatives of the companies met in 1847 and drew up a detailed list of tolls that most of them followed. The typical charges on a five-mile segment were five cents for each horse or mule and rider; one cent for each head of cattle; twenty cents for a two-horse wagon carrying three thousand pounds, with an additional ten cents for each excess thousand pounds; and thirty cents for a four-horse carriage. Travel on the good roads was expensive, and considerable use was made of

"shun roads" to bypass the tollgates. Most of the gates were left open from 10:30 P.M. to 5:30 A.M., and that situation promoted night travel. Gatekeepers had to be alert to prevent solemn-looking travelers from joining funeral processions to avoid the tolls.

By the end of the 1840s the railroads were adding to the competition that the steamboats had given the roads, and the turnpike companies' returns on investment were often less than they had anticipated. The state investments became a political issue, with the Democrats charging the Whigs with extravagance. The 1850 state constitution placed such severe limits on state debt that Kentucky's participation in turnpike enterprises was effectively ended. Towns and counties, however, often continued to make such investments.

During the Civil War the turnpike companies agreed to charge the Union armies only half price. The federal government suspended payment before the end of 1862, however, on the not unreasonable grounds that the troops were defending Kentucky and should not have to pay any tolls. No tolls were collected from John Hunt Morgan on his Kentucky raids on behalf of the Confederate States of America.

Kentucky's roads in 1860 left much to be desired. The macadamized ones were good for their day, but most of the state's roads were still dirt. People who had to use them suffered from a serious economic handicap. At least one improved road served most of the larger towns; Maysville, Lexington, and Louisville were the major centers. Overall, the road improvements had provided the state with substantial economic benefits.

Kentucky has the most miles of navigable streams of any of the contiguous states, and the rivers and creeks were of course in place when the first explorers arrived. Using some crafts, travelers could navigate the waterways as they were, and a variety of boats provided much of Kentucky's early transportation. Flatboats and keelboats became the most important. Even the keelboat made slow, difficult, and expensive progress going upstream, however, and the greatest use of water transportation came after the development of the steamboat. The appearance of steam power on the rivers was the most important change in transportation in Kentucky during the first half of the nineteenth century.

Although Robert Fulton is usually credited with the invention of the steamboat, John Fitch may have had an equally good claim. Fitch came to Kentucky in 1780 and located three tracts of land in what is now Nelson County. Back east in the 1780s, he built and successfully operated steamboat models. Congress granted him a patent in 1791, but he lacked funds for the further development of his boats. While he had experimented with a horse-powered boat, he decided that the steam engine was the best source of power. Fitch returned to Kentucky and continued work on his boats, but he never secured the financial back-

ing that would have enabled him to make a success of it. Disappointed, he died in Bardstown in 1798, probably from an overdose of opium and whiskey, possibly as a result of suicide. That same year Edward West, a Lexington watchmaker, demonstrated a model steamboat on Elkhorn Creek.

The early river steamboats resembled small oceangoing vessels. The *New Orleans,* which reached Louisville on October 28, 1811, had the deep hull needed for ocean travel and carried two masts for sails. The *New Orleans* could not pass the Falls of the Ohio until a rise in the waters occurred in December. The potential of the river steamboats was realized when builders decided that flatbottomed sidewheelers were suitable for the rivers. Machinery was moved up from the hull to the first deck, with an engine for each paddlewheel. Some of the boats drew less than a foot of water, and they opened traffic to localities that had been deemed impossible to reach by boat. One venturesome captain boasted that he could take his boat anywhere that had had a heavy dew. Sometimes a crew member waded ahead of the boat in shallow water to find the best channel. Of course such ventures often resulted in a boat's being stranded on a sandbar with the captain praying for a heavy rain upstream. The *Sylph* made an unexpected stop near Frankfort in the fall of 1829 when it encountered a yoke of oxen pulling a wagon across a ford in the Kentucky River. A departure time might be listed in a newspaper as "on the first rise of water."

The biggest and most famous boats were the ones on the Ohio and Mississippi Rivers. They did not at once wipe out the flatboat traffic because that mode of transport was so cheap if time was not important, but they quickly ended much of the upstream keelboat travel. Boat races that became famous, especially when run paddlewheel to paddlewheel, occurred on the major streams. The most stirring runs from New Orleans to Louisville came in 1853. In May the *A.L. Shotwell* made the run in four days, twenty-one hours, and thirty minutes. A few days later the *Eclipse* set out to break that record. Firewood was taken aboard from towed flatboats and another steamboat while the *Eclipse* kept steaming upstream. A six-minute passenger stop at Memphis resulted in a new groom's getting aboard while his bride was left on the dock. The new record was four days, nine hours, and thirty minutes. It stood less than a week, for the *A.L. Shotwell* then made the trip in a disputed time of four days, nine hours, and twenty-nine minutes. Such races resulted in many accidents and fires. One of the river traditions was that a captain stayed with his boat until it touched shore and passengers had a chance to escape. The lifetime of a steamboat on the Western Waters was less than five years.

Louisville boomed as a commercial center, with the steamboats pouring goods in and out of the city as freight costs dropped. By 1850 boats totaling 14,820 tons were registered at the Falls City. Steamboats had been built there since the *General Shelby* was constructed in 1815. The Falls of the Ohio continued to be a serious barrier much of the year, though. The problem was eased when the Louisville and Portland Canal opened in 1830, but it could not handle the larger boats, and agitation for a larger canal continued. Kentucky avoided most of the national canal craze that sent Indiana into bankruptcy.

The steamboats may have had an even greater impact on some of the interior towns, which acquired an important means of transportation for the first time. Bowling Green was an example. Located on the Barren River some 30 miles from the point at which it emptied into the Green and 175 river miles from Henderson, where the Green flowed into the Ohio, the town seemed unlikely to receive steamboat traffic. The rivers to it were narrow and winding, and many tree and rock obstacles littered the channel. With a drop of more than one hundred feet along its length, the Green had a series of obstacles similar to the Falls of the Ohio. The Green and Barren Rivers were usable only at intervals and were extremely hazardous. In 1808 and 1811 the General Assembly provided some assistance by allowing local authorities to require men who lived within five miles of the rivers to do three days of work in the waters each year to keep the channels as clear as possible.

The major figure in pushing for improved traffic on the rivers was James Rumsey Skiles of Bowling Green, appropriately named after James Rumsey, a steamboat developer. Fascinated with the possibilities of improving traffic conditions on the Green and the Barren, Skiles was soon the acknowledged expert in the Green River country. As a young man, he preached the need for locks and canals to provide adequate slackwater navigation. A daring little boat, the *United States,* managed to reach Bowling Green in January 1828, but Skiles realized that a more reliable waterway was needed. A local Green and Barren River Navigation Company was formed in 1830, but investors were wary of such a risky proposition. Skiles was in the state House in 1825-28, and he became a skilled lobbyist. In 1833 the legislature provided $526 for an engineer to do a feasibility study. Abner Lacock reported that the construction of five locks and dams at a cost of $99,000 would permit boats to reach Bowling Green in relative safety. Misled by estimates that the work would average $733 a mile, the General Assembly voted $30,000 in 1834 for the two lower locks and dams. Skiles was made head of a Board of Commissioners to oversee the project.

The undertaking took longer and cost more than was estimated. A state Board of Internal Improvements provided some assistance after 1835. In anticipation of the completion of the project, Skiles constructed wharf and warehouse facilities at Bowling Green and organized a narrow-gauge Portage Railroad to run about a mile and a half from the boat landing to the center of town. He went to Pennsylvania and employed Alonzo Livermore, an expert engineer whose enthusiasm for improving rivers

A steamboat waits at the boat landing on the Barren River at Bowling Green. For nearly a
century steamboats carried passengers and goods between Bowling Green and Evansville
(courtesy of the Kentucky Library, Western Kentucky University).

rivaled that of Skiles. Livermore contended
that with another dozen locks and dams he
could extend navigation all the way to Greensburg, 275 miles from the Ohio. Then from the
upper Barren River, at a modest additional cost,
he could construct a canal that would connect
the Green River system with the Cumberland
River. Even the less ambitious plan proved
more difficult and expensive than anticipated,
and the Panic of 1837 curtailed the sources of
funds. Supervision was shifted to the Kentucky
Board of Internal Improvements, and in 1839
Skiles was left off this board. He was sloppy in
his record keeping, and being a staunch Democrat did not help his cause with Whig administrations.

The project was declared completed
in October 1842, although some work remained. The total cost was listed in 1847 as
$859,126.79, an average of nearly $5,000 per
mile. Traffic routes were soon established with

Louisville and New Orleans, but Evansville
was the key center for most of the traffic. Much
of it was irregular; only two or three boats made
regular weekly trips between Bowling Green
and Evansville. Tolls were relatively cheap when
compared with turnpike prices. In 1847 an
adult passenger paid eighty-eight cents to pass
through all five locks; a horse went for fifty-two
cents, a cow for thirty-five cents; and a ton of
salt cost sixty-five cents. The tolls often failed to
cover repairs and never paid the interest on the
state loans. Skiles ruined his health and lost
most of his personal fortune in his labors.

Traffic was sharply curtailed by the Civil
War. During the early months after the end of
Kentucky's neutrality, the Green River Valley
became a sort of no-man's-land as the opponents began to learn something about fighting
a war. Damage to the locks and dams would
have been extensive except that Confederate
general Simon Bolivar Buckner (1823-1914),

whose home was near Munfordville, jammed Lock No. 3 with logs instead of blowing it up.

The Green and Barren Rivers story was repeated on most Kentucky streams, as communities fought for a share in the steamboat bonanza. The construction on the Kentucky River, where five locks and dams opened ninety-five miles of slackwater navigation in December 1842, may have been the most successful.

Even as the steamboat era in Kentucky reached its peak in the 1850s, the railroads were beginning to pose a serious challenge. The Baltimore and Ohio was considered the nation's first railroad when construction started on July 4, 1828. Kentucky railroads were not far behind. Lexington, anxious to overcome its disadvantage of not being on a river, got a charter in 1830 to build a rail line to some undesignated point on the Ohio River. Louisville was selected as the destination, Henry Clay became chairman of the board, and work started in October 1831. On January 31, 1834, the line reached Frankfort. The descent into the town was so steep that passengers could ride the train free of charge or for twenty-five cents be carried down in a hack. Horse-drawn cars were used first, then replaced by a steam engine. A serious wreck was blamed by some concerned citizens on Sunday travel. Louisville opponents who charged that the railroad would alter the life of the city delayed construction on that end of the line by carrying their fight all the way to the Kentucky Court of Appeals. They lost, and the Lexington-Louisville line was completed in 1851.

In a very ambitious six-million-dollar scheme, investors sought to establish a line that would connect Louisville, Cincinnati, and Charleston, South Carolina, and would have several branches. The *Kentucky Gazette* of August 30, 1838, predicted that the railroad would "strengthen the bonds of union between the South and the West, and . . . make Kentucky what the God of her creation designed— the finest portion of the habitable globe." The Panic of 1837 intruded, and that line was never

built. Several other ambitious projects received charters before the Civil War, but most of them failed to attain their promise. Work began on a Lexington and Big Sandy Railroad in November 1853, but the line got only to Mount Sterling before construction was suspended. The Kentucky Central Railroad had more success in connecting Lexington with Cincinnati and some Bluegrass towns such as Paris. A Henderson and Nashville Company was organized in 1852, but the people in the western part of Kentucky were more interested in the Mobile and Ohio Railroad that reached Columbus, on the Mississippi, in early 1861. They hoped to build a line from Paducah through Mayfield to connect with the Mobile and Ohio Railroad at Columbus.

Kentucky's most successful railroad of the era was the Louisville and Nashville, chartered in 1850. Towns and counties along its route provided much of the $3.8 million for working capital. Two routes were feasible in the southern portion of the state. Bowling Green secured the railroad by raising $1 million in Warren County, then getting a charter to construct its own railroad to Nashville. The L&N quickly agreed to build through Bowling Green. Completed in 1859, the L&N cost $7,221,000 but was profitable from almost the moment it opened. Passenger trains covered the 185 miles in ten hours, about one-third of the time taken by a stagecoach. The L&N's success was aided by two outstanding railroad men. When James Guthrie left office as secretary of the U.S. Treasury in 1857, he became a vice president of the line, then served as president from 1860 to 1868. Albert Fink, born and trained as an engineer in Germany, came to the United States in 1849 and had a highly successful career with the B&O. Lured away by the L&N in 1857, Fink supervised construction of some of the most difficult segments on the Kentucky line. His bridge over the Green River near Munfordville received national attention as the second-longest iron bridge in the country. Fink became the railroad's chief engineer in 1859 and did an outstanding job of keeping it

repaired during the Civil War. The L&N was a vital supply line for the Union armies as they fought their way into the South.

By 1860 Kentucky had about 597 miles of working track, and the railroad had proved itself superior to the steamboat in several respects. The state had provided little assistance in the construction, for the debt limits in the 1850 constitution had restricted what could be done. Most of the direct governmental aid came from local governments.

Agriculture

From the pioneer days through the Civil War, agriculture was the primary economic activity in Kentucky. Subsistence farming was the first step in the development of agriculture in Kentucky, and corn was the ideal crop for that purpose. It could be planted in unplowed ground, it could be used in a variety of ways as food for both persons and livestock, and it was easier to gather and store than small grains. When the ground was prepared, crops such as beans, pumpkins, and melons could be grown among the corn. While the first corn crop was growing, the farmer had to start the laborious task of clearing the land. Settlers in the Barrens or the savannah sections of the Bluegrass had an advantage over those who lived in heavily wooded areas. While the forests provided many things for the early settlers, they were also a major problem. A good hand with an ax might clear three acres during a winter. He probably girdled a tree "Kentucky style" and left it to die.

Sunlight was let in to the crops as soon as the dead leaves fell. As the branches fell, they were piled against the trunk and burned. Roots had to be cut and grubbed out, and at some future day the tree stumps had to be dug, pulled, or blasted out. The poor agricultural practices of the day meant that soil fertility was soon exhausted. For many farmers, clearing land was a lifelong job.

As more acres became available, the farmer added other crops, perhaps wheat and oats. A vegetable garden, often part of a woman's domain, was an early addition. A money crop was needed as soon as possible, and that usually meant hemp or tobacco. The need for clothing brought on flax and some sheep. A horse was a necessity, and a cow was almost as urgently needed. As the game disappeared, hogs and chickens were added. Fruit trees were set out as soon as possible; apple and peach were the usual choices.

A barn was required for protection against both the weather and wolves, and fences had to be built, usually of rails, to keep animals out of the crops and livestock at home. Hogs were often allowed to run wild in the forests; a supply of salt would help keep other animals close to home. All of the urgent improvements required much labor. Few hired hands were available, and few farmers could afford to pay them. A landless man was more likely to work as a tenant than as a hired hand. A great deal of heavy labor was done by cooperative effort—log rolling, house and barn

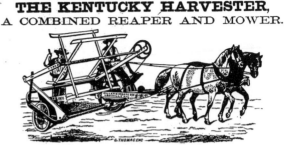

THE KENTUCKY HARVESTER,
A COMBINED REAPER AND MOWER.

THE GREAT POPULARITY OF THIS REAPER THROUGHOUT THE WEST AND SOUTH, where it is more generally known and used than any other, makes it unnecessary to do more than state, for the information of those unacquainted with it, a few of its most prominent advantages:

This Machine, in every essential part, is constructed of Wrought Iron and Steel.

It has no equal in lightness of draft, durability, strength, and simplicity.

It can be changed from a Reaper to a Mower in five minutes. The cutters can be raised or lowered at pleasure by the driver while in motion, without stopping his team.

It will cut as low as *one inch or as high as twenty two inches*.

Every Machine is put together at the Factory, and operated with the cutters in by steam, which insures their perfect working when put together in the harvest field.

OVER ONE THOUSAND of these Harvesters were sold and used last harvest, and in no instance has a failure occurred or a Machine been returned.

Two Thousand now Building for the Harvest of 1859!

WE WARRANT EVERY MACHINE.

☞ All orders and letters promptly responded to.

☞ For further particulars and recommendations we refer to our Reaper Circular, which will be forwarded on application to us or any of our Agents.

Price of Complete Machine, at Louisville, Ky., $150.

April, 1859—3t.   MILLER, WINGATE & CO., Manufacturers, Louisville, Kentucky.

Most Kentucky farms in 1859 were too small to justify the purchase of such expensive farm machinery (from *The Kentucky Farmer*, courtesy of the Kentucky Library, Western Kentucky University).

raising, corn husking. Work got done, and the occasion provided a welcome opportunity for a social affair to relieve the tedium and boredom of life on an isolated farm. Other than pioneer wives in some of the German families, women in early Kentucky seldom worked in the fields except in cases of emergency, but they found an endless number of chores in the houses and gardens. Children were an economic asset on the farms. Girls assisted their mother while learning household skills they would require when they became homemakers. Having more men than women was characteristic of a frontier, and most of the girls married at a young age. Sons provided vital help to their father as they learned the skills that they would need later on their own farms. Many Kentuckians of that period believed that the sons were bound to the family farm until they were twenty-one years old. Slaveholding families had a labor advantage over the nonslaveholders, but they were always a minority of the population, and as late as 1860 the average slaveholder in the state owned just over five slaves. The more

slaves, the more that had to be raised to support them.

As a farm became more productive, it began to produce surplus products that could be sold or bartered for goods not produced on the farm. Tobacco, hemp, cloth, maple sugar, bacon, hams, eggs, butter, lard, hides, apples, and whiskey were among the most common surplus items. Salt and tools were some of the items often sought off the farm. The common tools for a farm were an ax, hoe, sickle, scythe, and plow. The essentials for the homemaker were a large iron pot, skillet, churn, spinning wheel, needles, and scissors. Both men and women had many other wishes to be satisfied as soon as goods could be afforded.

The large farms and plantations varied a great deal from the smaller acreages on which most Kentuckians lived. Jacob Hughes, for example, was a wealthy banker-farmer-cattleman who had some eighteen hundred acres on the Winchester Road outside Lexington. He worked his land with ten hands, since much of it was devoted to cattle and hogs. He averaged feeding and selling three hundred cattle a year in the eastern markets, and he sent two hundred hogs a year to Cincinnati. He also raised two hundred acres of corn, one hundred acres of wheat and rye, and twenty acres of grass for hay. His profit in 1835 was $9,945; it increased to $10,475 in 1836.

Hemp, grown from early pioneer days, required extensive labor, but its fibers were in demand for rope, sailcloth, rough bagging, and floor coverings. Lexington and Fayette County became the center of both hemp growing and manufacturing. In 1838 the eighteen rope and bagging factories there employed one thousand workers. Prepared for the market, the fibers brought $70-112 a ton, and an acre might yield close to nine hundred pounds of fiber. The demand increased in the 1840s with the growth of cotton production, and in 1841 Congress directed the navy to use American-produced rope. Hemp production declined in the 1860s, as Manila fibers from the Philippines began to capture the world market for rope. By then tobacco had become an important cash crop.

Indians had cultivated tobacco in Kentucky long before the arrival of the first Europeans. Most of the pioneers had raised tobacco in the East, and they started patches in Kentucky as soon as possible. High-priced in proportion to its bulk, tobacco was often used as a medium of exchange before the coming of a money economy. Tobacco was the most valuable commodity Wilkinson carried to New Orleans in 1787, and that year Virginia licensed tobacco inspection warehouses to ensure the quality of the crop sold. In 1859 Kentucky produced 108,126,840 pounds, a quarter of the nation's total production. During the Civil War Kentucky took over first place from war-ravaged Virginia. Most of the crop was exported from the state in hogsheads weighing one thousand to thirteen hundred pounds. Tobacco manufacturing was comparatively simple, and before 1860 Louisville was producing large amounts of chewing tobacco, snuff, cigars, and

pipe tobacco. Cigarettes became popular after the war.

One of the most exotic agricultural endeavors in the state was silkworm production. It attracted considerable attention in the late 1830s and early 1840s, when people in several parts of the state decided that Kentucky's climate was ideal for the enterprise. The Kentucky Silk Manufacturing Company secured a state charter in January 1838 and planned to open a silk-producing community at Tallmadge, about twelve miles east of Henderson. Acres of white mulberry trees were planted, and a small amount of silk was actually produced. The worms were less taken with the state's climate than had been forecast, and the cost of labor in Kentucky was much higher than in the silk-producing countries of Asia. The Shakers at South Union and Pleasant Hill also experimented with silk, as did some Kentuckians in Lexington and other parts of the state. Garden seed was also produced and packaged by the Shakers and sold widely across the nation. By the early 1860s the eighty-acre Downer Nursery located near Fairview was shipping several hundred thousand fruit trees each year, in addition to strawberries and other plants.

Some of the explorers of Kentucky recognized its potential for raising cattle, and the early pioneers brought horses, cattle, hogs, and sheep with them. Most of the first cattle were scrubs, but within a few years some individuals began efforts to improve the herds. Matthew Patton of the Potomac area of Virginia had an improved herd, and when members of his family came to Kentucky in 1785 they brought some Patton cattle with them. Matthew moved to the Nicholasville area in 1790, bringing along his bull Mars and a fine cow named Venus. Within a few years individuals or small groups began to import blooded cattle from England. In 1817 Lewis Sanders imported ten head of choice English cattle. When Henry Clay was in England in 1815 after helping negotiate the Treaty of Ghent, he was much impressed by the Herefords, and two years later he had four head shipped to Ashland.

Robert W. Scott became one of Kentucky's best farmers and cattlemen after he abandoned a legal practice for farming in the 1830s. He converted some worn-out and poorly managed land in Franklin and Woodford Counties into Locust Hill Plantation, a model farm. His Durham shorthorns attracted attention for their ability to gain weight rapidly, and his improved hogs and sheep sold well for breeding stock. His grassland was so lush that he grazed cattle on it for two dollars per head per month. A tireless agitator for scientific agriculture, Scott sponsored several pieces of legislation and tried to get an agricultural college established.

Dr. Samuel Martin organized the Fayette County Importing Company in 1839, and it soon brought in seven bulls and twenty-one cows. The Northern Kentucky Importing Company, started in 1853, proved that imports were profitable. Twenty-five head purchased in England for $11,780 sold in Kentucky for $47,860. Brutus Clay was so anxious to improve the state's herds that when he held a cattle auction, he sold only to Kentuckians who promised not to take the animals out of the state for at least a year. Bourbon County was the first area in the state to get some of the famous shorthorns from the English Bates herd. Most of the cattlemen who worked to improve the stock lived in the Bluegrass region, and the improvements were first noticeable there. Cattle raising was important, however, in almost every part of the commonwealth. A common description of a thin woman tells something about cattle in another part of the state: "She's as bony as the hips of a Green River cow."

Some cattle were being driven to Virginia as early as 1793, and the numbers increased after 1800. Most of the herds passed through Cumberland Gap, but some went to markets by other routes. Drives usually started between mid-February and mid-June and took

up to two months, averaging seven to nine miles a day. Even so, a 1,000-pound animal would probably lose up to 150 pounds on the trip. Herds usually numbered from one hundred to two hundred head, but some comprised as many as a thousand. The average weight of cattle for butchering increased from 450-500 pounds in 1793 to 900-1,000 pounds in 1836. Efforts to improve the stock did meet some success.

Horses were a necessity in early Kentucky, both for mobility and for tending the soil. Ninety-two percent of the taxpayers in 1800 owned a horse; the average owner had 3.2 animals. With about 4 percent of the nation's white population, Kentucky had 12 percent of the country's horses. Timothy Flint commented on Kentucky's horse industry in the early 1830s: "Horses are raised in great numbers, and of the noblest kinds. A handsome horse is the highest pride of a Kentuckian; and common farmers own from ten to fifty. Great numbers are carried over the mountains to the Atlantic states; and the principal supply of saddle and carriage horses in the lower country is drawn from Kentucky, or the other western states."

The happy combination of well-drained fertile land, good water, soil rich in calcium and phosphorus, and a horse-loving people gave Kentucky a preeminent position in raising fine horses. One of the first laws passed at Boonesborough under the spreading elm was designed to improve the breeding of horses. Lexington was still a small town when it had to forbid races in the streets. One of the main grievances against the Indians was their fondness for stealing horses. Some horsemen began to develop breeds for particular purposes, one of which was speed.

As in the case of cattle, much dependence was placed on the importation of English-bred horses. In 1797 a horse named Blaze was apparently the first English-bred horse brought to the state. The English started their *General Stud Book* in 1791; the United States did not

The racehorse Lexington was foaled at the establishment of Dr. Elisha Warfield Jr. in 1850. After winning six of seven races, Lexington led the sire list for sixteen years, longer than any other stallion. Edward Troye painted this portrait in 1868 (from J. Winston Coleman Photographic Collection, Transylvania University Library).

have such documentation of bloodlines until 1893. Before then such knowledgeable and reputable horsemen as Dr. Elisha Warfield Jr. were trusted to know the bloodlines. He received a just reward for his efforts in 1850 when one of his foals was Darley, later known as Lexington. The winner of six of seven races and the sire of six hundred offspring, a third of them track winners, Lexington was one of the most famous thoroughbreds of all time. In an era when endurance and speed were both important, his best time for a four-mile heat was seven minutes, nineteen and three-quarter seconds. John Wesley Hunt purchased Royalist, a thoroughbred racehorse, from the Prince of Wales (later King George IV), made him available as a sire in Lexington in 1804-5, then sold him in 1806 to Nashville associates of Andrew Jackson.

The Kentucky Jockey Club, organized in Lexington in 1797, sponsored four-mile heat races and established rules that were generally adopted at other state tracks. The sport became so popular that Swiss-born artist Edward Troye made a living from painting portraits of purebred horses and cattle for proud owners. Many of his works were done of Kentucky animals.

Harness horses did not receive the early attention lavished on the runners. James B. Clay, son of Henry Clay, brought Mambrino Chief to Ashland in 1854 from New York. The Chief became Kentucky's most famous

trotter of the pre-Civil War era. After Robert A. Alexander inherited Woodburn Farm from his father, he made it one of the nation's foremost breeding establishments for both runners and harness horses.

One of the state's first horse farms was sixteen-hundred-acre Cabell's Dale, six miles outside Lexington. From the time John Breckinridge moved to Kentucky in 1793, raising horses was his goal. In 1801 he arranged with Captain George Banks for the services of his English-bred stud, Speculator. The arrangement was continued through 1804, when Breckinridge got another stud. When Breckinridge died in 1806, he had at least 125 horses at Cabell's Dale, and he was beginning to generate the product that he valued the most.

Mules became an important part of the state's livestock industry after 1830. John Breckinridge had started raising them on his horse farm in 1804, and in the fall of 1805 he had purchased a Spanish jack named Bonaparte. Breckinridge's death the following year ended the experiment, but Henry Clay revived interest in the breeding of mules in the 1830s, and prices rose rapidly. A mule named Warrior brought five thousand dollars in Lexington in 1837. Most of the jacks were imported from Spain, Malta, and southern France. Within a few generations the Kentucky-bred jacks were two or three hands taller than their European contemporaries (a *hand* is a hand's breadth, fixed at four inches). Mules were notorious for being stubborn and having violent tempers, but they outlived horses, adapted better to a hot climate, and required less food. Kentucky mules were in great demand in the cotton-growing South, and prices were so good that on some Kentucky farms, mules were the most profitable agricultural product.

Kentuckians raised more hogs than any other animal. Most of them were turned loose to thrive on forest mast, but they were also good scavengers in cornfields where cattle had eaten. The hogs supplied a major part of a family's diet as large game disappeared, and cured hams and bacon could be sold or bartered. Hogs were sometimes driven as far as Charleston, South Carolina, to market. Efforts were made to improve the breeds, and reports of pen-fed animals that reached one thousand pounds indicate that some success was achieved. By mid-century the Berkshire, Bedford, and Irish were the most popular breeds in the state.

Sheep were also important, although they were not raised in as large a number as hogs or admired as much as horses. In addition to mutton, the sheep supplied the wool that provided constant labor for many Kentucky women. Sheep required much more attention than hogs. They were easy prey for wolves and wild dogs, and Kentucky's obsession with sheep-killing dogs started early in the state's history and contributed to several feuds. The Merino breed was favored in the 1820s and early 1830s. Then came the Bakewells, Saxons, Southdowns, and New Leicesters before the Cotswolds became the favorites in the 1850s.

In 1816 Lewis Sanders organized and held outside Lexington the first livestock show in the state. In an inspired moment he offered silver julep cups as prizes. The excellent response resulted in the creation of the short-lived Kentucky Society for Promoting Agriculture in 1816, with Isaac Shelby as president, as well as the opening of a number of other fairs. In 1838 the Kentucky Agricultural Society was formed. The fairs soon broadened their scope for wider appeal. Field crops, fruits, and vegetables were added attractions, followed by preserved foods and cooked dishes. Textile divisions were opened, and before 1860 some of the larger fairs featured mechanical exhibits of new farm equipment such as mowers, reapers, and threshers. Fairs also became social events. Many families that came from a distance brought bedding and food to last as long as the fair did. In time, some of the fairs added carnival-type attractions and numerous contests for which prizes could be won. A few of the fairs grew so large before the Civil War that they could almost be classified as state fairs.

In 1860 Kentucky had 83,689 farms. Only 1,244 of them comprised more than five hundred acres, more than 58,000 consisted of fewer than a hundred acres, and more than 34,000 had fewer than fifty acres. The 1850s were a period of rapid agricultural growth. Improved farmland increased by 1,675,938 acres during the decade, and the cash value of the state's farms rose from $155 million in 1850 to $291 million in 1860. Among the fifteen slave states in the Union in 1859, Kentucky ranked first in the production of rye, barley, horses, and mules; second in hemp, tobacco, corn, wheat, and sheep; third in hogs; and fourth in cattle. Kentucky's agricultural production enhanced the importance of the state during the Civil War.

Manufacturing

If *manufacturing* means "the transformation of raw materials into goods for use," then every pioneer household was a small factory, with most of its output consumed within the family. In the traditional division of labor, the males worked with crops; tanned leather; made shoes, harnesses, and saddles; turned out furniture, barrels, piggins, and noggins; and perhaps operated a small still or gristmill. A rifleman molded his bullets and made much of his other equipment. The females in the family spun, wove, and knitted cloth from wool, buffalo fur, nettle fibers, and flax and made the family clothing. They manufactured soap, candles, and maple sugar in addition to their regular chores.

Barter often secured the "store-boughten" items not manufactured at home.

Kentucky manufacturing was more limited if the term is defined in commercial terms as "the transformation of raw materials into products for sale to consumers." Yet some manufacturing of this nature was done early in the pioneer era, and the amount had increased a great deal before the Civil War.

Some of the first industrial activity involved the grinding of grain and the sawing of lumber. Horse- or water-powered mills were more efficient than many hand operations in individual families. Even with the construction of dams, waterpower was unpredictable on many streams, and disputes flared over the dams' interference with boats and rafts of logs. A miller usually took his pay as a portion of the product, perhaps one-eighth of the output.

Salt was also in constant demand, and since most families did not own a salt spring or well, salt manufacturing constituted another early industry. The salinity of water varied, but usually several hundred gallons of brine had to be evaporated to obtain a bushel of salt. Cutting wood and hauling it to the insatiable fires at a saltworks required heavy labor. Bullitt's Lick was probably Kentucky's first commercial saltworks, but it was followed by dozens of others. Hugh White had extensive works in Clay County in the early years of the nineteenth century. Elated when he dug a successful well on Lockard's Creek, he announced, "I had promised God that if I was successful at Lockard's Creek, I would never drink another drop." His doctor advised him to taper off alcohol gradually; a sudden cessation might be dangerous. White warned his friends that "no friend of General White will ask him to take a drink," and with his friends' help he kept his promise.

Saltwater was potentially very valuable. One of the more profitable operations was the Henley Haddix Salt Lick in Perry County. The well was 240 feet deep, but it was reputed to produce a bushel of salt from only one hundred gallons of water. In 1838 it was making

ten bushels a day. Salt making declined in Kentucky toward midcentury after salt mines were found in other parts of the nation.

Gunpowder was so essential on the frontier that its manufacture started early. Saltpeter—potassium nitrate—was scraped from the floors of caves, refined and powdered, then combined with charcoal and sulfur to produce black powder. By 1800 twenty-eight caves had produced more than a hundred thousand pounds of gunpowder. In 1810 Lexington alone had six powder mills. The War of 1812 sent the 1810 price of seventeen cents per pound to one dollar, and cave hunting became a mania. Mammoth Cave, located by settlers in the late 1700s—reputedly when a hunter followed a wounded bear into it—became a major producer of saltpeter, with as many as seventy persons working inside the cave. The demand slackened after the war, and other sources of saltpeter were found outside the state.

Distilleries provided a way to get bulky grain to market in a more portable (and potable) form. This manufacturing started with the early settlers, but the process for making bourbon whiskey came about 1789. Elijah Craig, a Baptist preacher in Scott County, is most often credited with perfecting the process, but several others also had claims. The standard that was later adopted decrees that bourbon must be produced from mash that contains at least 51 percent corn, be distilled at no more than 160 proof, and be aged in charred oak barrels that cannot be used again for that purpose. On many early farms the still was as essential as a plow. The first known advertisement for bourbon whiskey was published in the *Western Citizen* on June 26, 1821; by the 1840s the product was known across the country. As early as the 1790s Kentuckians displayed a reluctance to pay a federal whiskey tax, and the bootlegger symbolized the state to many outsiders.

Iron ore was found in many parts of the state, and iron products were in steady demand. In 1791 Jacob Myers constructed a small furnace on Slate Creek in what is now Bath County. A few months later he sold three-quarters of the company, and it became the Bourbon Iron Works Company. Early furnaces were usually built of stone, about twenty-five feet square at the base and twenty-five to forty feet high. They were placed against a small hill whenever possible so the ore, limestone, and charcoal could be loaded from the top. At the Bourbon Iron Works, Salt Creek supplied power for the blast when the water was high enough. Full production was about three tons of pig iron a day. Eight or ten men were required to produce the charcoal, and several others worked at the furnace. By 1792 the Bourbon Company was advertising a range of products such as kettles, plowshares, and dog irons. The company was reorganized in 1795 when prominent politicians George Nicholas, John Breckinridge, and Christopher Greenup became partners.

By cutting off British products, the economic war with Great Britain and the War of 1812 stimulated the Kentucky iron industry. In 1816 Joseph Bruen opened his Iron Foundry and Machine Shop in Lexington; it produced a great deal of decorative ironwork, often custom-made, for citizens in the Bluegrass. Among other well-known ironworks were the Aetna Furnace in Hart County, the Bush Creek Iron Furnace near Greensburg, and Raccoon Furnace in Greenup County. In 1837 the eleven businesses in Greenup County produced more iron than the rest of the state, and Kentucky ranked third in iron production nationally. The Panic of 1837 closed many of the enterprises, and Kentucky's iron production declined. Muhlenberg County emerged in the 1850s as one of the new leaders in the state. Robert S.C.A. Alexander, the Kentucky-born member of a wealthy Scots family, tried to develop an ideal facility at his Airdrie Furnace with the aid of experienced workers from Scotland. After spending three hundred thousand dollars without producing any salable iron, Alexander abandoned the project and went on to a much more successful career as an agriculturalist.

As new ore deposits were found, other furnaces were built in Trigg, Lyon, and Livingston Counties. In 1851 Lyon County resident William C. Kelly discovered how to make steel by blasting cold air through molten iron to burn out the impurities. Englishman Henry Bessemer discovered the process at about the same time and took out an American patent in 1856. The U.S. Patent Office later recognized Kelly as the original inventor, but the process had already become known as the Bessemer process. Seventeen furnaces were still operating in Kentucky in 1860, when they produced 42,500 tons of pig iron. The peak had already passed, and most of the remaining Kentucky furnaces could not meet the postwar competition from other parts of the country.

The textile industry flourished for a time in the state, with much of the activity centered in Louisville and Lexington. Cotton was imported from the South to supplement wool and other local fibers. "Kentucky jeans," known as a durable cloth for work clothing, was worn on many Deep South plantations. The state's slaughterhouses supplied hides as well as hams, bacon, and other meat products. Until nearly midcentury, most shoemakers did not distinguish between left and right feet, and work shoes continued to be interchangeable until well after the Civil War. Hats were being manufactured in Kentucky before 1793, when a firm in Lexington employed two dozen hands. Daniel Boone, who detested coonskin caps, may have known that a good beaver felt could be bought there for about three pounds. Gunsmiths made weapons, especially the noted Kentucky rifle. David Weller, who came to Kentucky about 1795 and settled in Nelson County, made rifles for a time with Jacob Rizer. Weller moved to Elizabethtown and lived and worked there from 1826 to 1847. His products were prized, and at his death he was one of the wealthiest men in Hardin County.

Papermaking started in Lincoln County in 1787 with Jacob Myers, a German immigrant. The timing was fortunate, for the *Ken-*

tucky Gazette began printing in 1787, and in the 1790s it was joined by several other publications. One of the frequent problems for the papermakers was the shortage of good rags.

Some efforts were made to promote manufacturing even before statehood, but the War of 1812 probably did more to encourage such activity than any deliberate efforts. After the war Congress enacted tariff bills that made the encouragement and protection of infant industries a matter of national policy. Additional support came from the Kentucky Society for the Encouragement of Domestic Manufactures, organized in Lexington in 1817. The advocates of industrial growth faced several problems: insufficient capital and inexperienced capitalists, greater potential profits in land speculation and commerce, the scarcity and high costs of skilled workers, economic depressions, the lack of a sound currency, and the absence of an industrial tradition.

Kentucky's most rapid growth in manufacturing before 1860 came after the recovery from the Panic of 1837. In 1840 the state had $5,945,000 invested in manufacturing; in 1860 the figure was $20,256,000. The value of industrial output in 1850 was $21,710,000; in 1860 it was $37,931,000, and Kentucky ranked fourth among the slave states. In 1860 Kentucky had 3,450 manufacturing establishments, which employed 19,587 males and 1,671 females, with total wages of $6,021,082.

As manufacturing increased, the growing white population supplied most of the workers. A considerable number of blacks, however, also worked in industry. In 1801 Peter January rented six slaves from John Breckinridge to work in his Lexington ropewalk. This eased a surplus slave problem for Breckinridge, who would not sell a slave but whose horse farm did not require as many hands as tobacco or hemp farms did. Textile mills and hemp factories used considerable numbers of slaves, and an occasional skilled black worker might be found in almost any type of operation. The German immigrants around midcentury supplied

a number of skilled workers in several fields. Apprenticeship was the traditional method of learning a skilled trade, such as silversmithing or gunsmithing. The medieval aspects of apprenticeship were disappearing, but the method continued to be used.

The Extractive Industries

Most of Kentucky was covered with virgin timber when the first settlers began destroying it. The typical pioneer saw the forest as both an asset and a problem, and he attacked it as if the forests were inexhaustible. Countless millions of board feet were burned just to get rid of them, although a goodly amount was used for houses, barns, fences, boats, fuel for homes and manufacturing, and scores of other uses. Gradually, wastefully, the great stands of timber fell before the ax, until only remnants remained to tantalize future Kentuckians with glimpses of what the area had once been.

Some of the emerging industries did make use of the timber resources. Furniture makers used cherry and walnut for some of their finest pieces and poplar and pine for everyday items. Many log cabins were covered with planks, and new houses and barns were likely to be constructed with boards. Flatboats and steamboats were built in Kentucky, requiring wood. Some lumbering was done for sale, but the great commercial depletion came after the Civil War.

The early explorers and settlers recognized various mineral deposits. Thomas Walker and Christopher Gist both noted coal deposits on their explorations. Those who sought minerals hoped to locate precious metals; gold was preferable, silver acceptable. This frontier longing gave birth to one of Kentucky's most persistent legends—the lost John Swift silver mines. A John Swift of Virginia traded and sometimes lived with western Indians in the 1750s and 1760s. The Indians had supposedly extracted silver from a Kentucky mine to buy European goods. From the mining or from pirate loot, Swift was reputed to have acquired a hoard of silver, most of which had to be left behind when he returned to the East. He became blind and could not go back to his cache, and others, armed with his descriptions and vague maps, failed to locate the cache or the mine. Hopeful people have continued the search to this day.

Coal was found in numerous places; it must have been known to the Indians for many years. The easy accessibility of wood slowed the use of coal, although its use increased in the nineteenth century. It began to be used for home heating in the towns as the timber supply became scarcer, and it had some industrial use. Alney McLean and his son William are often credited with beginning the use of the coalfield in the western part of the state on their Green River farm. By 1830 William was taking coal to Evansville by barge. Oxen were hauling supplies of coal to Russellville from the Mud River Mine. By the late 1850s coal was being carried on the Green and Barren Rivers to Bowling Green as well as to Evansville for wider distribution, and several small surface mines had been opened in Henderson County. The state's thirty-three coal mines listed in the 1860 census employed 757 men and produced 285,760 tons of coal. Union County was then the top producer. The geological survey of David Dale Owen in the 1850s revealed how widespread coal deposits were in the state.

The search for saltwater resulted in the first discoveries of oil in Kentucky. In 1819 digger Martin Beatty of Virginia was drilling a salt well on the South Fork of the Cumberland River in what is now McCreary County when he struck oil at 536 feet. The oil ruined that well, and it became a nuisance when it flowed into the river and caught fire. Ten years later Beatty was drilling a well on a farm near Burkesville. "I will strike salt or strike hell," he boasted, but on March 11, 1829, his drill broke through a limestone layer into a pocket of oil and gas that became Kentucky's first gusher. An eyewitness reported four days later that the stream was still at least fifteen feet high and that

the escaped oil had burned on the Cumberland River for a mile: "It burns well in a lamp and is said to paint and oil leather and I have no doubt it will be a good medicine for many complaints particularly the Rumatick pain. The whole atmospheir is perfumed with it. It is a compleat Phenominon." Some of the oil was bottled and sold for internal or external use, by humans or animals, for almost any ailment. Other strikes were made, and before the Civil War someone discovered that paraffin oil (kerosene) could be derived from the product more easily than from any other source. Its exploitation would come later.

Commerce

Kentucky engaged in limited commercial activities from the early days of settlement, but commerce was hampered by the slow and difficult contacts with the outside world. The solution to the vexing Mississippi River question and the transportation improvements in the nineteenth century led to a rapid commercial expansion. For many years Philadelphia and New Orleans were the cities with which Kentucky had the closest commercial ties. The trade that developed depended heavily upon credit. State farmers received most of their money when their cash crop was sold; they needed credit from the local stores until that time. The storekeepers, in turn, had to buy much of their stock on credit extended by their suppliers, who probably had bank credit. For much of the pre-Civil War period commerce was hampered by an inadequate supply of money as well as banks of dubious stability.

Most of Kentucky's exports consisted of livestock and agricultural produce. From the early 1800s bourbon whiskey and hemp products found ready markets. Ginseng and whiskey were the only crops that could return a profit if sent overland to Philadelphia; livestock that provided their own transportation could also return a profit. Except for the animals walking to market, the availability of transportation determined the direction of commerce. Until the advent of the steamboat, most commerce flowed with the rivers. Most imported goods came down the river from Pittsburgh on flatboats to Kentucky merchants and consumers; most of the state's exports went down various streams to the Ohio, then down the Mississippi to New Orleans. There they were loaded on oceangoing ships and carried to the East Coast ports or, in smaller quantities, to Europe or other markets. Kentucky merchants who could afford to do so made one or two trips a year back east to place orders and renew their credit with suppliers. Wagons carried goods to Pittsburgh or to ports on some of the tributaries of the Ohio. Because of transportation and credit costs, prices in Lexington were as much as 60 percent higher than Philadelphia prices. The steamboat and railroad reduced this differential but did not eliminate it.

In the nineteenth century the exportation of slaves became a conspicuous part of the state's commerce. The breaking up of families and the kidnapping of free blacks made exportation one of the most hated aspects of slavery. Some slaveholders became "slave poor" rather than sell any of their slaves, and to some slaveholders the slave trader was an abomination to be shunned. As the frontier ended in the state and the need for slaves declined while their number increased, the cotton, sugar, and rice plantations developing in the Lower South had a growing demand for workers. Prices for slaves varied a great deal, depending upon age, health, and gender and upon general economic conditions. Overall, prices rose during the 1790-1860 period, and profits could be made by selling Kentucky slaves "down the river." Yet Lewis C. Robards, a well-known Lexington dealer, overextended and failed in his business. The best estimate is that in the 1830s Kentucky exported approximately twenty-three hundred slaves annually. The number declined to about two thousand in the 1840s, then rose to thirty-four hundred in the 1850s. The total was about seventy-seven thousand for the three decades. Most of the slaves sold never saw

Kentucky again or the loved ones from whom they were separated.

To most Kentuckians, however, *commerce* probably meant the transactions at the local country store. Most small-scale merchants accepted produce in exchange for goods, and most of them extended credit to their trusted customers. In a bad crop year or in a falling market for produce, it was easy for a storekeeper to go broke, and many did. Yet most Kentuckians would probably have agreed with former governor Lazarus W. Powell in 1857, when he gave an optimistic analysis of the state's commerce: "Kentucky occupies a central position in this Union; one that enables her to supply the cotton, sugar and rice growing States of the South with corn, hemp, hogs, meat, cattle, mules and horses, of which she grows a large surplus; and also sufficiently near to supply the large cities and manufacturing towns of the North with her surplus products." Kentucky's trade with the North grew rapidly after the development of railroads.

Banks and Money

Banking in the state started with the Kentucky Insurance Company of Lexington, chartered in 1802 to insure boats engaged in the New Orleans trade. Its charter also authorized banking, giving the company the right to issue currency, and the Kentucky Insurance Company soon concentrated on that aspect of its business. The Bank of Kentucky, partly state-owned, was chartered in 1806. It opened a number of branches but was criticized for not meeting the needs of the people. In 1818, the year the Kentucky Insurance Company failed, the legislature created forty-six new banks so that even a small town had one. The Second National Bank established branches in Lexington and Louisville and acted as an unwanted watchdog over the state banks. Kentucky made unsuccessful efforts to tax the national bank branches so they would have to close down. In January 1820 the stockholders of the Bank of Kentucky voted to suspend specie payments and to issue more paper money, which soon declined in value. Relief legislation was designed to force creditors to accept the depreciated notes for payment of debts. The independent bank bill was repealed in February 1820, leaving only the thirteen branches of the Bank of Kentucky and the two branches of the Second National Bank, but in March the General Assembly created the state-owned Bank of the Commonwealth, with numerous branches. The new bank could issue as much as twenty-six million dollars in banknotes. The charters of the Bank of Kentucky and the Bank of the Commonwealth were both repealed in 1822.

After the relief controversy subsided, a demand arose for more banks of a conservative nature. The Louisville Bank of Kentucky was chartered in 1834 and authorized to establish six branches; the Northern Bank of Kentucky, located in Lexington, was chartered in 1835 and was allowed four branches. The Panic of 1837 found the state's banks in better condition than in 1819, and they were able to resume specie payments in June 1842. From then until the Civil War, they were generally in a stable condition.

The lack of a sound currency hampered commerce and forced the use of substitutes. Barter was cumbersome but workable. In 1788 John Bradford offered subscriptions to the *Kentucky Gazette* for "Beef, Pork, Flour, Wheat, Rye, Barley, Oats, Indian Corn, Cotton, Wool, Hackled Flax or Hemp, Linen or Good Whiskey." In 1780 John Sanders made his boat at Louisville a sort of bank. He traded for furs and skins, for which he issued paper receipts that circulated locally as money. After selling his cargo in New Orleans, he returned to Louisville with Spanish dollars and redeemed his receipts. A few years later James Wilkinson issued tobacco receipts in much the same way.

The Virginia notes became almost worthless, and in the 1790s the U.S. Treasury issued only coins. With Kentucky's unfavorable balance of trade, few of the coins remained very long in the state. Thanks to the intermittent Mississippi trade, Spanish dollars were more common in Kentucky than American coins. To get change, the silver dollars were cut up into bits, with the smallest piece being worth six and one-quarter cents. The use of "cut money" led to frequent cheating, with a dollar often containing five quarters. Occasionally a business would issue pieces of paper known as "shinplasters" that could be redeemed at the business. Some British money remained in circulation, and until about the War of 1812 many Kentuckians quoted prices in either pounds or dollars—and often both.

As banks were created they issued their own notes, which varied a great deal in value and were easy to counterfeit. Many communities had a "money judge" with a keen eye for detecting anything wrong with a bill. Some businesses subscribed to *The Detector,* a semimonthly publication that described and evaluated banks and their banknotes. John Marshall had said in *McCulloch v. Maryland* (1819) that "the power to tax involves the power to destroy," and in March 1865 Congress imposed a tax of 10 percent on state banknotes, beginning in July 1866. This put an end to such notes.

Revenue and Taxation

State taxes were first largely property taxes applied at specific rates, such as thirty-four cents per hundred acres of first-class land. Property tax was placed on an ad valorem basis in 1814. In the year November 11, 1798, to November 7, 1799, the revenue was £15,364.8.¾, including £4,125.0.2 in the treasury at the start of that fiscal year. The total expenditures for the year were £15,364.3.3. The largest costs were for the General Assembly, the jail and penitentiary, criminal prosecutions, salaries of officials, and the constitutional convention. The state also bought the governor a ream of paper for £1.10.0.

The main sources of revenue and expenditures were much the same in 1850, except that by midcentury the state was spending some small amounts for education, mental health care, and the deaf and dumb and the blind. A considerably larger sum (15.46 percent of the expenditures) was also being spent for internal improvements.

The total revenue received in the first year of statehood was approximately 27¢ for each white inhabitant. By the 1850 fiscal year the revenue had risen to $598,602, with the per capita contribution for each white resident being 64.6¢. The burden of state taxation before the Civil War was remarkably light, both in the amounts paid and in the assessed valuation of property. The trend toward larger expenditures for internal improvements was checked by the 1850 constitution, and the expenditures for public schools did not become large until much later.

A sampling of Kentucky tax records concluded that the average adult free male was worth between nine hundred and twelve hundred dollars in 1800. Adjusting the figures to 1800 dollars, this study asserted that the wealth of the average free male increased about 2.4 percent a year from 1800 to 1840 and about 2.8 percent annually from 1840 to 1860.

A lottery has been described as a way of raising money when the people and the legislature are not willing to increase taxes. In the period from December 1792 to the Civil War, the legislature authorized more than eighty lotteries, most of them before 1823, ranging in value from five hundred dollars to one hundred thousand dollars. Schools and internal improvements were the most common targets for the lottery revenue, but libraries, a fire engine, a linen factory, and a bridge were also funded with these proceeds. Some restrictions were placed on lotteries as opposition to the concept increased, and in 1852 the legislature ordered them halted within three years. That act was declared unconstitutional by the state courts, and in 1862 Kentucky was one of the three states in the Union still using a lottery. English journalist Edward Dicey wrote of an 1862 trip to Kentucky: "Kentucky is the first state in the Union where I saw lottery offices in every street, and where the old notices in the shop windows . . . caught my eye, requesting passersby to tempt fortune, and to win five thousand dollars at the risk of one." Most of these lotteries were less successful than the sponsors anticipated, and they did not come close to meeting the needs of the state in the areas they touched.

11

Social and Cultural Changes

The Status of Women

In "Captain Stormfield's Visit to Heaven" Mark Twain described a heaven whose inhabitants are judged by their potential, not by what they accomplished on earth. For example, the ranking military commander is a little bricklayer from back of Boston who had been rejected when he volunteered during the American Revolution, but had he been given the opportunity he would have been the earth's greatest military genius.

It would be interesting to see how Kentucky women from the pre-Civil War era would fare in Captain Stormfield's heaven, for they certainly did not have an opportunity to realize their potentials. The professions were closed to them, they could not vote in a supposedly democratic society, they could not make a will of their own, and their property became their husband's if they married. In the eyes of the law, they were bound to their husband almost as a slave was bound to a master. They had little opportunity to get an education beyond the elementary level; if they did go to a more advanced school, it was probably a finishing school that prepared them for the life of a genteel lady. Slaves were about the only persons in the state who had fewer rights than white women; the truly unfortunate person was the female slave. The great majority of Kentucky's women lived and died in obscurity, remembered in census records and on tombstones as "The loving wife of . . ." Most of the women mentioned in histories of the state for the pre–Civil War era are there because of their association with a man or men. Still, a few women won recognition in the male-dominated world of early Kentucky.

Mary Draper Ingles and Virginia Sellards Wiley were not the only women who became famous because of Indian attacks. The Neville family was living in Nelson County in the summer of 1787 when rifle fire broke Mr. Neville's arm and leg as he opened the door to see why the dog was barking. Mrs. Neville barred the door, but the Indians chopped a hole in it. She seized an ax and killed or seriously wounded the four who tried to enter. When sounds on the roof indicated that others were going to try the chimney, she ripped open a feather bed and threw the feathers on the fire. When two half-choked and half-blinded warriors tumbled to the hearth, she dispatched them with her ax, then wounded the last invader as he attempted the door. This doughty Amazon became famous among both whites and Indians. Many other frontier women, however, died during the Indian wars; many who survived lost members of their families.

In 1809 Jane Todd Crawford rode horseback sixty-four miles to Danville, supporting an ovarian tumor weighing more than twenty pounds.[1] Dr. Ephraim McDowell warned her that eminent European surgeons had declared such an operation hopeless, but she decided to proceed. Anesthesia was not available at the time, and little was known of aseptic practices. Twenty-five days later Crawford was well and ready to return home.

Delia Ann Webster won the admiration of the few Kentucky abolitionists. This native of Vermont visited Kentucky in 1843 and with two friends remained to establish the Lexington Female Academy. In September 1844 she and Calvin Fairbanks helped three slaves escape across the Ohio River. Sentenced to two years in the penitentiary, she so impressed Governor William Owsley that he soon pardoned her. She left the state, then returned in 1854 to a Trimble County farm on the Ohio River that

became a stop on the Underground Railroad. When authorities became suspicious of her activities, she fled to Indiana to avoid arrest. Animosity toward her continued after the Civil War, and arsonists burned her Kentucky property so often that she was again forced to leave the state.

Hannah Dunn became a local celebrity in the Henderson area. She and her husband, Captain John Dunn, opened a log store on the Ohio River bank in 1792 and a few years later added a tavern with "the best food and liquor to be found between Fort Pitt and New Orleans" and "featherbeds for all guests." In 1796 they also opened a gristmill that offered "grinding and packing." Hannah, a tall, powerful woman, did the packing—the delivery of flour and meal to customers. She also worked in the tavern as bartender and bouncer and in her spare time chopped cordwood. She was fond of hunting, and she frequently returned from these ventures with a dead bear draped across her shoulders. Not many rivermen dared test her will or strength.

Catherine Spalding's family moved to Nelson County about 1795, when she was two years old. In 1813 she and two other women started the Roman Catholic Sisters of Charity of Nazareth near Bardstown. Spalding was chosen general superior and served in that position a total of twenty-five years. An exceptional administrator, she opened academies in Union County, Lexington, and Louisville. She also established St. Vincent's Orphanage and St. Joseph's Infirmary in Louisville. Spalding University in Louisville is named for her, honoring her contributions to education, health care, and social services.

Few Kentucky women appeared interested in the antebellum women's rights movement that was making slow progress in some parts of the nation. Two leaders of the movement, however, did visit Louisville. Frances Wright spoke there in 1828 to urge equal edu-

---

1. A twenty-pound cyst has the bulk of about three and a half gallons of water.

cation for women. Men were degraded by the restrictions they placed on women, she told a predominantly male audience. Lucy Stone did a series of four lectures in Mozart Hall in November 1853. Editor George D. Prentice admitted that "public speaking is generally regarded as implying bold presumption in a woman," but he was assured that she was "modest and unassuming." Fears were expressed that Stone's ideas would have a harmful effect upon Louisville women, and few husbands allowed their wives and daughters to attend the lectures. Few Kentucky women appeared to have much awareness of the movement until after the Civil War, when a number became actively involved. Some Kentucky women won a minor victory in 1838, when the General Assembly allowed widows who lived in rural school districts and had school-age children to vote in elections for school trustees.

The lifestyles of antebellum Kentucky women ranged widely. The mistress of a large plantation might have a dozen slaves to do housework, while a much larger group of women lived in small cabins. Ann Biddle Wilkinson offered evidence of the socioeconomic gulf that existed when she wrote her Philadelphia family in 1788 about the ordeal of living in Lexington among people "that has been brought up so differently from myself." Most of the travelers who described the Kentuckians they met apparently spent much of their time among the social elite. Elias P. Fordham wrote of his 1817-18 trip, "From the little I have seen, and the much I have heard, I judge they [Kentucky women] are the most spirited women in the world. They are exceedingly fond of dress, and are generally very handsome." *Niles' Register* had commented in 1814 that the equality of the frontier (itself a myth) was disappearing in Lexington. "Society is polished and polite. They have a theatre; and their balls and assemblies are conducted with as much grace and ease as they are anywhere else, and the dresses of the parties are as tasty and elegant." Frances Trollope was perceptive enough to be aware of the contrasts: "It is rare to see a woman in this [low

economic] station who has reached the age of thirty, without losing every trace of youth and beauty."

A daughter of one of the top social families had access to the fashionable finishing schools for young ladies, to a comfortable home life, to exciting balls and parties, to visits to the best watering places, to marriage to a young man rising in his profession or the owner of a large property, and to a married life relieved of household drudgery. The daughter of a lower-class white family could look forward to little education, to hard work helping her mother, to little travel beyond an occasional visit to the county seat, to marriage with a man who was trying to earn a living on a hardscrabble farm, and to bearing a child every year or two, only to see several of her offspring die in early childhood. Women at both social extremes had duties and responsibilities, both had moments of happiness and despair, but the worlds in which they lived represented two quite different Kentuckys.

Motherhood was one common bond, and legal submission to the husband was another. If a marriage became intolerable, divorce was difficult, even after the courts took over its jurisdiction from the legislature. The burden of proof was on the woman, whose duty was to endure and obey. That concept was difficult to overcome, as was the stigma usually attached to a divorcée.

Too few pre–Civil War Kentucky women left accounts of their lives, and so they remain somewhat vague figures in the background of the period. They were indispensable to the development of the state, although they seldom appear in its public records.

Public Education

Schools got an early start in Kentucky, then were neglected for many years. Jane Coomes taught a dame school in Harrodsburg in 1776, and some attempt at education was soon made at the other stations. John ("Wildcat") McKinney became famous in 1783 when he had a life-and-death struggle with a wildcat that attacked him in his Lexington classroom. Early schools, often housed in log cabins, had little in the way of books or other equipment. Support depended upon tuition paid by the parents of the students attending. Teachers were poorly paid, and instruction at "blab schools" depended upon rote memorization.

Academies, privately owned and operated with the intention of making a profit, were often boarding schools for students from a distance. An academy's students were usually taught by one person, and so the level of instruction depended on that person's knowledge; in some schools Latin and Greek were part of the curriculum. Since many of the proprietors were ministers who needed a second source of income, religion was often stressed. Few academies were coeducational, but several were founded for girls and young women. In 1805 Mary Beck, a Frenchwoman, opened an academy in Lexington. Its ambitious seven-year program featured music, dance, drama, and painting in addition to English, mathematics, and history. Beck was also a talented artist.

Some citizens agitated for better schools, and in 1794 the General Assembly chartered Kentucky Academy at Pisgah. Others soon followed, as practically every county tried to have at least one school. The legislature provided grants of six thousand acres of unclaimed land to each academy, but much of this land was of poor quality and gave little support. The mortality rate among academies was high. Salem Academy in Bardstown was one of the best when James Priestly, a Presbyterian minister, was in charge.

Too many Kentuckians saw no need for more than the rudiments of reading, writing, and arithmetic. Others saw education as a private matter of no concern to either the local or the state government. Some who objected to governmental support of education were fearful of the cost; others believed that schooling was a luxury in the frontier days when the children were needed to work. Neither of the first two state constitutions mentioned education,

and the incomplete convention records do not indicate that the topic was even discussed.

Gabriel Slaughter was the first governor who made a real effort to establish a system of public education. "Every child born in the state," he told an unresponsive legislature in 1816, "should be considered a child of the republic, and educated at the public expense, when the parents are unable to do it." Education was the foundation of republican government, he asserted, and he returned the next year with a detailed plan for an educational system, including the creation of a school fund to finance it. His successor, John Adair, more interested in making Transylvania into a great university, did not push Slaughter's concept. In 1821 the legislature did create a commission headed by Lieutenant Governor William T. Barry and Secretary of State John Pope to gather information from other states. A questionnaire drew enthusiastic responses from such national figures as John Adams, Thomas Jefferson, and James Madison. The report, submitted in December 1822 and written by Amos Kendall, editor of the *Frankfort Argus,* recommended a comprehensive system that would encompass elementary education through a great state university. This report was printed and distributed but not adopted. In 1821 the General Assembly had created a literary fund, chiefly derived from half of the clear profits of the Bank of the Commonwealth, for the support of education, but little of the money got to the county schools. When the state ran short of money it "borrowed" from the literary fund, and internal improvements had a higher priority than education.

In a typical legislative approach to a problem it did not want to face, the General Assembly in 1829 ordered another study. Thomas Alva Wood, president of Transylvania University, and Benjamin O. Peers, a professor there, outlined a public school system; their able report was largely ignored. Governor Thomas ("Old Stonehammer") Metcalfe acknowledged that he had "experienced all the disadvantages of a neglected education," but he emphasized spending for transportation projects rather than for schools. In 1830 the legislature did authorize county courts to establish school districts and to levy taxes to support them. Participation was optional, and few counties were willing to carry the burden. Little was done.

A survey conducted in 1832 revealed that of 140,000 children studied between ages five and fifteen, only 31,834 attended any school. Russell County had just one school. Teachers were paid between one hundred and four hundred dollars annually. Spurred by such dismal statistics, the Kentucky Association of Professional Teachers (1833) and the Kentucky Common School Society (1834) organized to educate the public about the need for an educational system. Some money became available when the national government began to distribute much of the embarrassing surplus in the U.S. Treasury to the states as loans. In February 1838 the state legislature established a Board of Education, provided for an appointed superintendent of public instruction, allocated the distribution of money from the school fund, and decreed that each school district of thirty to fifty pupils would have a five-member Board of Trustees with a five-member county Board of Commissioners. Each district could levy a tax equal to the money received from the state. Again, little was done to implement the scheme, as county voters could reject it. In 1840 the state treasurer refused to release any money for education because the state had a deficit. By 1843 only $2,504.00 had gone to the districts; $125,884.25 was available. In the ten-year period 1838-47, seven men, all Protestant ministers, were superintendent. As the *Frankfort Commonwealth* declared on December 7, 1847, "The Common School System of Kentucky is a mockery."

Most counties did not even report their educational statistics. Teachers were usually certified and employed by the county commissioners and the district trustees. Appointments were more likely to depend upon family and political connections than upon knowledge and pedagogical skills. One cautious applicant, asked if he taught "a round world or a flat world," was reported to have replied that while he was a little uncertain on the subject, he would teach whichever one the trustees wanted.

Then in 1847 Governor Owsley appointed the Reverend Robert J. Breckinridge, son of John Breckinridge, as superintendent of public instruction. He was so obsessed with education that his conduct sometimes bordered on intolerance. A tireless advocate of his cause, Breckinridge preached the gospel of education across the state, and the *Louisville Morning Courier* proclaimed, "Kentucky has . . . her Horace Mann." Breckinridge persuaded the legislature to replace the money borrowed from the school fund and to add other revenue sources to it, and the voters approved a school tax of two cents per one hundred dollars of property valuation by a two-to-one margin. The 1850 constitution recognized support of public education as an essential function of government, despite some bitter opposition. The office of state superintendent was made elective, and Breckinridge was elected to the post. In a battle of wills, he bested Governor John Helm in an 1851 struggle over the handling of interest on the school fund.

Breckinridge did not win all his battles, though. He opposed the removal of all tuition because of the shortage of funds, and he objected to having the state board select textbooks. But between 1847 and 1853, when Breckinridge resigned, enrollment increased from 20,402 to 201,223; average attendance in the elementary schools rose from 10,220 to 72,010; and the school fund grew from $991,000 to $1,400,270.01, although the expenditures for schools increased from $6,268.30 to $137,347.70. By 1853 only North Carolina among the slave states could match Kentucky's educational progress.

Progress continued to be made until the system was disrupted by the Civil War. One promising venture in 1856 was the reorganization of Transylvania University to include a normal school for training teachers. Two years later that decision was reversed, and teacher training, like so many other needed reforms, had to await the postwar years. The schools lacked many of the ingredients considered necessary for a good system. But there were some exceptional teachers and students eager to learn, and when they came together the results were sometimes better than the state had any right to expect. A school was often the focal point that gave some sense of unity to a community and provided the citizens with welcome social activities. School districts, however, were often torn by divisive clashes among contesting groups.

Kentucky did not outlaw the teaching of slaves, but little was done to make them literate. Some owners feared that literacy would make it easier for a slave to run away. Some slaves received limited education at church schools, which were most common in the cities and towns. The Reverend Henry Adams was teaching in Louisville as early as 1829; his school grew until it employed four teachers. William H. Gibson Sr. started teaching in Louisville in 1847 and was so successful that he established grammar schools in Frankfort and Lexington. Bowling Green, Maysville, and Richmond also had schools for blacks at least part of the time, and in 1850 sixteen counties reported that some blacks were in school.

Kentucky had a few unusual schools in this period. As early as 1799 Jacob E. Leare taught an evening school in Lexington that was a predecessor of business colleges. His classes included double-entry bookkeeping and merchants' accounts. By the 1825 Treaty of Washington, the Choctaw Indians received six thousand dollars annually for twenty years to educate tribal youths. Richard M. Johnson, a strong advocate of education, got the Choctaw Academy established in Scott County near his home. The tribe wanted the boys educated so that they would fit into American society, and they were given American names. Among those enrolled at the academy were boys named John C. Calhoun, Henry Clay, and Thomas Hart Benton. The Baptist Church conducted the school and reported to the federal Office

of Indian Affairs. In 1835 enrollment reached a peak of 188. Later enrollment declined as the tribe became concerned that the youths were losing too much of their Indian heritage, and the school closed in 1842.

In December 1822 the legislature established an Asylum for the Deaf and Dumb in Danville, with an annual appropriation of three thousand dollars. A Virginia visitor in 1825 was impressed by the ability and knowledge of the twenty-five or so students who studied in the coeducational classes. The state purchased Lexington's Fayette Hospital in 1824 and established one of the nation's first state-supported mental hospitals. In 1842 the Kentucky Institution for the Education of the Blind opened in Louisville with some private money, ten thousand dollars from the public school fund, and tuition from those who could afford it. By 1850 forty-three students aged six to fifteen were enrolled. One of the outstanding teachers was Joseph B. Smith, a Harvard graduate, who was the first blind person to graduate from an American college.

Higher Education

Without accrediting associations to restrict them, schools of the era could call themselves whatever they wished. Many Kentucky towns still have a College Street, named for some long-ago educational institution. Most of these schools were actually no more than academies, and most had short lives. The level of education on a frontier often declined with the rise of the first native-born generation. The pioneers brought their education with them; their offspring seldom had educational facilities readily available. One solution was for young Kentuckians to study at William and Mary College or some other seaboard school. Yet the first steps were taken toward establishing a college in Kentucky even before statehood was achieved.

In 1780 and 1783 the Virginia legislature chartered "a public school or Seminary of Learning" in the District of Kentucky and gave it twenty thousand acres of land. The trustees

started a grammar school near Danville with David Rice as teacher in early 1785, then moved it to Lexington in 1789. In 1799 the school was combined with Kentucky Academy, a Presbyterian school, and named Transylvania University with James Moore as president. Law and medical departments, the first in the West, were added to the liberal arts department. Transylvania was dominated by Presbyterians after 1802, until a liberal element on the board staged a revolt and brought in Unitarian Horace Holley as president in 1818. The school flourished under Holley's leadership and soon became one of the best and largest colleges in the country. In 1820, when Thomas Jefferson was trying to found the University of Virginia, he declared that unless something was done "we must send our children for education to Kentucky or Cambridge." He feared that the students who went to Kentucky would never return to Virginia. The medical college at Transylvania became especially well known. Holley's able faculty in the medical college included Constantine Rafinesque (at Transylvania from 1819 to 1826), a brilliant if eccentric naturalist; Daniel Drake (1817-18, 1823-27); and Charles Caldwell (1819-37). William T. Barry (1818-21) and Jesse Bledsoe (1822-25) taught in the law school. In 1837 Caldwell led half the medical faculty to Louisville, where they founded the Louisville Medical Institute.

Presbyterians charged Holley with being a "warm advocate" of "the Theatre, Ballroom, and Card Tables." Governor Joseph Desha asserted that Holley had created an elitist institution, and the General Assembly cut off state support. Holley's resignation in 1827 ended the university's most glorious period of achievement. In his last report to the board, Holley remarked that during his tenure at Transylvania, the university had awarded 644 degrees, compared with 22 in the previous nineteen years. "We are satisfied with the contrast," said Holley. "Are they?"

The school enjoyed an academic revival in 1842-49 under the leadership of an able Methodist minister, Henry B. Bascom. When the Methodist Church split in the 1840s, the southern Methodists withdrew their support for the institution because they did not have complete control. By the Civil War Transylvania was little more than a high school. Its buildings were used as a Union hospital during the war.

After the Presbyterians lost Kentucky Academy in the merger that created Transylvania, they secured a state charter in 1819 for a school at Danville. The state did not fulfill its obligations, and in 1824 the school was turned over to the Presbyterians with the provision that it could not be a church seminary. John C. Young, a twenty-seven-year-old minister, became president of Centre College in 1830 and served until 1857. The Danville Theological Seminary was created in 1853 to serve those who wanted to become ministers. Only seven students graduated from Centre in

1863, but the school managed to remain open during the Civil War.

The University of Louisville began in 1837, when the city council created the Louisville Medical Institute and the Louisville Collegiate Institute. The legislature combined the two institutes in 1846 and added a law department to form the University of Louisville. The units were financially separate until 1851, and a court decision in 1854 restored their autonomy. The academic department languished until the twentieth century.

So many denominational colleges were started in Kentucky after the War of 1812 that in 1847 the state was said to have more colleges than any other state in the Union. Among the longest lasting were St. Joseph's (1819, Catholic), St. Mary's (1821, Catholic), Augusta (1822, Methodist), Cumberland (1826, Methodist), and Georgetown (1829, Baptist). Few of the denominational colleges had an adequate income, and much of the work they did was below the college level. Augusta College was forced to close in 1849 because the community could not tolerate the antislavery views propounded there.

A number of schools were opened for women. Logan Female College in Russellville started in 1846 as a school for boys and girls, but a decade later it became the Female College, sponsored by the Methodist Church. A new charter in 1860 changed the name to Russellville Collegiate Institute and authorized the school to issue degrees. Baptists in Hopkinsville secured a charter in 1854 for a high school for young women. The school opened in 1856 but two years later was rechartered as Bethel Female College. Its buildings were used by Confederate troops during the Civil War, and in 1863 the work of the institution was suspended for a year.

The prewar years also saw the beginnings of Berea College. The Reverend John G. Fee believed that Kentucky needed a college "which would be to Kentucky what Oberlin is to Ohio, anti-slavery, anti-caste, anti-rum, anti-sin." Fee opened a common-level school at Berea in 1855, but he and John A.R. Rogers, who joined him, saw the need for more advanced work. Before they could put their dream into operation, Fee and his colleagues were forced to leave because of their antislavery views. Berea College did not get started until after the Civil War.

The remote origins of the University of Kentucky can also be traced to the antebellum years. Some dissident faculty members left Georgetown College and founded Bacon College in the same town in 1837. The new school moved to Harrodsburg in 1839 on the promise of more financial aid, which did not materialize. College work at Bacon College ceased in 1850, but John B. Bowman later succeeded in raising money and securing a charter for Kentucky University in 1858. The Christian Church of Kentucky was to have two-thirds of the seats on the governing board. The institution opened in 1859, but it was hurt severely by the Civil War. In 1865 the trustees accepted an offer from Transylvania University to move Kentucky University to Lexington. Then began the complicated changes that led to the creation of the University of Kentucky in 1916.

Religion

One of Harrodsburg's delegates to the Boonesborough legislative meeting in May 1775 was the Reverend John Lyth, an Anglican minister. On Sunday, May 28, he conducted what may have been the first public worship service held in Kentucky. The Anglican Church in America became a casualty of the Revolution, and the Episcopal Church came later to Kentucky than did several other denominations and had a smaller number of adherents. James Moore, dismissed by the Presbyterian synod, was ordained as an Episcopal minister and returned to Lexington in 1794. Two years later an Episcopal church was organized there, and Moore later became the first president of Transylvania University.

The Baptists, largest of the Kentucky denominations, were present in Kentucky from the first days of settlement. Squire Boone was credited with preaching the first sermon in what became Louisville and also with conducting the first marriage in Kentucky on August 7, 1776. The Baptists received a major addition to their numbers in early December 1781, when Lewis and Elijah Craig and Captain William Ellis led the Traveling Church, a congregation of five hundred to six hundred members, from Virginia to the region near present-day Lancaster. Lewis Craig compared the journey to the trek of Moses and the Israelites to the Promised Land. This large group founded several other congregations. In 1807 David Barrow started the Baptist Licking-Locust Association, Friends of Humanity, one of the first antislavery groups in the state. A feature of the self-governing Baptist congregations was a strict watch over members' conduct, based on "rules of decorum" that all in the church were supposed to obey. The most frequent causes for hearings were drinking, swearing, dancing, fornication, adultery, and fighting. Baptist minister James Garrard was the state's second governor.

Francis Asbury was the leading Methodist in the United States. Born in England in 1745, he came to North America as a missionary in 1771. The next year John Wesley appointed him superintendent of missionary work in America. Asbury first came to Kentucky in 1790; before his death in 1816 he had returned to the state eighteen times. Some preachers may have ridden circuit earlier, but in 1786 Bishop Asbury appointed James Haw and Benjamin Ogden to that role in the District of Kentucky. Four visits a year to a church was to be the maximum; one visit was often more common.

David Rice was the best known of the early Presbyterian ministers in Kentucky. A graduate of the College of New Jersey (Princeton), he came to Kentucky in 1783 in response to a petition from some three hundred pioneers in the Danville area. A great organizer, he established several congregations, the Transylvania Presbytery, and the Synod of Kentucky.

He sought unsuccessfully to place in the 1792 constitution some provision for the gradual elimination of slavery. A firm believer in education, he began teaching classes in his cabin near Danville in February 1785. The Presbyterians emphasized the importance of an educated clergy more than did most of the major frontier denominations.

By 1792 Catholics were numerous in several Kentucky communities, most of them in the Bardstown region, although the first Catholic church was not built in that town until 1798. Bishop John Carroll of Baltimore sent French-born Father Stephen Badin to Kentucky in 1793; Father Charles Nerinckx, a Belgian, was sent to assist Badin in 1805. During his nineteen years in Kentucky, Nerinckx worked tirelessly to build churches, often doing much of the physical labor himself, and he directed the organization of the Sisters of Loretto in 1812. Nerinckx described the labors: "Early rising, hard work, and late meals, tell on us all, and we are so lean that we will soon be able to worry through the narrow gate of heaven." Bardstown was one of the four new dioceses created in the United States in 1808. The Right Reverend Benedict Joseph Flaget came to Kentucky in 1811 as bishop for the western country. The bishop's residence was moved to Louisville in 1841. Nativism was a lurking problem for Catholics in the United States most of the time; it became more serious in Kentucky in the late 1840s and 1850s with the rise of the American Party, or the Know-Nothings.

Several other denominations also had churches in the state but had relatively few adherents. Among the more important were the Cumberland Presbyterians, the Christian Church, the Disciples of Christ, Lutherans, and Unitarians. Jewish synagogues had been built in Louisville and Lexington by 1850.

One of the smallest but most unusual groups was the United Society of Believers in Christ's Second Appearing, commonly called the Shakers. Founded by Mother Ann Lee,

The Centre House was constructed at the Shaker community of South Union around 1825. South Union never recovered from the effects of the Civil War, and the Shakers sold their land and buildings there in 1922 (courtesy of the Shaker Museum at South Union).

Shakerism developed out of the English Quaker movement. The main tenets of the Shakers included a belief in the possibility of direct communication between Christ and Christians, millennialism, celibacy, perfectibility, and communal living. Mother Ann led a small group to America in 1774, and by the 1830s nineteen Shaker communities existed, two of them in Kentucky. The one at Pleasant Hill, near Harrodsburg, was founded in December 1806. The village ultimately had some 500 residents and about 250 buildings of every kind. The Shakers at Pleasant Hill used four thousand acres of land and were noted for their excellent farming. Shaker celibacy meant an absence of natural increase of adherents, and the Civil War resulted in extensive damage to the community. By 1910 only a dozen members remained. The community at South Union, about twelve miles from Bowling Green, was started in 1807. At its peak South Union had about six thousand acres of land and 350 workers. The Shakers at South Union also sold goods widely; their garden seed was highly praised. This community suffered the same decline as Pleasant Hill, and the last of the South Union property was sold in 1922.

Despite the dedicated efforts of the pioneer clergy, religion had a rather low status in Kentucky at the end of the eighteenth century. Many settlers had moved beyond the ready reach of a church, and they were preoccupied with the difficulties involved in winning a new land. The deist thought of Thomas Paine and the French Revolution had also exerted considerable influence. A young man who was reading law with John Breckinridge believed "that a person could not be religious and a Lawyer at the same Time." People seemed more interested in gaining material wealth than in spiritual salvation. "All the conversation is of corn and tobacco, or land and stock," complained Presbyterian minister James McGready. "But for them the name of Jesus has no charm, and it is rarely mentioned unless to be profaned." Dissatisfaction with the moral climate was increasing, and the Great Revival exploded in Kentucky, then spread rapidly through most of the South.

McGready came to Logan County in late 1796. Deeply influenced by revivals in North Carolina, he hoped to instill the same spirit in the churches he served in the region of the Red, Gasper, and Mud Rivers. People responded to his preaching, and he began to hold prolonged services that ran from Friday evening to Sunday night. In June 1800 two visiting ministers, John and William McGee, asked to be allowed to participate at the Red River meeting, although John was a Methodist. Excitement developed that evening as John McGee's shouts and exhortations drew a spontaneous outburst from members of the congregation. In July a meeting held at Gasper River was the spark for which many had prayed, and enthusiasm spread like wildfire. One of the largest of the camp meetings took place at Cane Ridge in Bourbon County in August 1801. Presbyterian Barton W. Stone sponsored it, but with thousands in attendance, several preachers held forth at the same time. Some worshipers were seized by the "holy jerks," their arms and legs and heads being thrown around in violent motions so that long hair cracked like a whip being snapped. Others bounded around the camp, bouncing off trees, wagons, and people as if they were rubber balls. Still others went into trances and were laid out in silent rows as if they were dead.

Such bizarre behavior alienated some people who saw no manifestation of the Holy Spirit in such irrational, emotional conduct. Some denominations had remained aloof from the beginning, the Presbyterians as a group soon dissociated themselves, and many Baptists withdrew from what seemed more and more to be a Methodist phenomenon. By the time the Great Revival had run its course about 1805, evangelical churches had become an important and lasting influence in the South. Evangelicalism concentrated on the conversion of the individual and paid little heed to broader socioeconomic issues. But it affected the lives of thousands, and the morality it taught and the code of conduct it espoused helped shape the attitudes of Kentuckians.

Skeptics wondered how long the influence would last as campers went home to normal conditions. Some returned quickly to their sinful ways, but other men and women had undergone lifetime changes. Some backsliders were reported to have changed direction again in 1811-12, when great earthquakes repeatedly rocked the eastern half of the nation. With their epicenter at New Madrid, Missouri, the quakes lasted for several months and resulted in some significant geographic changes. A bright comet appeared during that period,

and many frightened Kentuckians viewed it and the quakes as signs that the world was coming to an end. The *Bedford (Pa.) Gazette* reported that the people in Louisville did not have a church until the first major quake shook the town; the next day one thousand dollars was raised to build a place of worship. After the next quake, another thousand was contributed. A third quake produced a similar result. Then the earthquakes ceased, and Louisvillians raised seven thousand dollars to construct a theater.

The Presbyterian Church had differences over doctrine as well as slavery, and in 1836-38 it split into Old School and New School factions. Most Kentucky Presbyterians remained with the Old School, which was more conservative on both doctrine and slavery. Then in the mid-1840s the Baptists and Methodists divided into northern and southern branches, largely over slavery issues. In the case of the Baptists, the question was whether slaveholders could do missionary work; the Methodists argued over whether a slaveholder could be a bishop. Most of the churches in Kentucky went with the southern branches, but there were many exceptions. These divisions dissolved some of the bonds of union that had helped combat the rising spirit of sectionalism.

One of the standard defenses of slavery was that it brought Christianity to the slave. Wasn't service on earth a small price to pay for the hope of life eternal? Some masters were sincerely concerned about this issue, and slaves were members of many Kentucky congregations, usually on a segregated basis. Blacks were sometimes allowed to worship separately if a few whites were present to guard against plotting. Ministers often preached on such texts as "Servants, obey your masters," and most slaves must have been conscious of the extreme inequities in their lives. In time some of them were able to secure their own churches and ministers. Such churches became a vital part of the black subculture that was developing with few whites aware of it. One of the noted black preachers was "Old Captain" Peter Duerett, who came to Kentucky with the Traveling Church. He may have been self-ordained, but the First African Baptist Church of Lexington, which he founded, grew to 300 members under his leadership. He was followed by London Ferrill, who built the church to 1,828 members. It was the largest congregation in the state, white or black. Then Frederick Braxton, who obtained his freedom, had 2,223 members before the church divided in 1861. Henry Adams, a free black, led the separation movement in Louisville after coming to that city in 1829 as the black minister at the First Baptist Church. The black members, half of the congregation, separated in 1842. For the next thirty years Adams was the city's leading black minister. Most Kentucky towns of any size had black churches, with some degree of independence, by the Civil War.

Anthropologists disagree about the extent to which African culture influenced the religious services and the lives of black Christians. What is certain is that the black churches were extremely important in the lives of their members. In addition to the spiritual aspects, the churches provided centers for social, cultural, and educational activities. They provided a reasonably safe avenue for expressing opinion, and they gave practical training in business affairs and leadership techniques. To some extent, the black churches helped prepare their members for freedom.

Literature

The decades before the Civil War have been called the golden age of American literature. Such a statement could not be made about Kentucky. While a body of writing had been done in the state, much of this output would have difficulty qualifying as literature. It is little read today except for its historical interest.

Gilbert Imlay came to Kentucky about 1783 and remained at least two years and perhaps longer. His *Topographical Description of the Western Territory of North America* (1792) is still used by students of the period. In 1793 he published *The Emigrants; or, The History of an Expatriated Family.* Considered to be the first Kentucky novel, *The Emigrants* relates in the form of letters the romantic adventures of an English family that came to Louisville. In it Imlay made an unusual plea for women's rights. Imlay disappeared from records about 1796, but he may have lived as late as 1828.

John Alexander McClung, a native Kentuckian, wrote some historical sketches and *Camden* (1830), a novel about the American Revolution in the South. Robert Montgomery Bird spent considerable time in Kentucky but may never have considered himself a Kentuckian. *Nick of the Woods; or, The Jibbenainosey: A Tale of Kentucky* (1837) told of Indian warfare around 1782. In the story, a man kills Indians in revenge for the deaths of his wife and children. An Owensboro lawyer and businessman, James Weir, wrote of outlaws in western Kentucky in *Lonz Powers; or, The Regulators* (1850), his best novel. Charles Wilkins Webber of Russellville did a popular collection of short stories called *The Hunter-Naturalist; or, Wild Scenes and Wild Hunters* (1852). A New Yorker who lived in Kentucky for several years, Mary Jane Holmes discovered the idealized Bluegrass world. Before 1865 she wrote five novels based on Kentucky, including *Tempest and Sunshine; or, Life in Kentucky* (1854) and *Lena Rivers* (1856). The best-known novel written about Kentucky by an outsider was the antislavery propaganda novel of Harriet Beecher Stowe, *Uncle Tom's Cabin,* published in book form in 1853. William Wells Brown, born a slave although his father was white, is considered the state's first black novelist. His best-known work was *Clotel; or, The President's Daughter: A Narrative of Slave Life in the United States* (1853). Brown accused Thomas Jefferson of fathering two children by his black housekeeper. The book was published in England when no American publisher would touch it. Elizabeth Bryant Johnston, born in Mason County, wrote in *Christmas in Kentucky* (1862) about an admirable slaveholder enmeshed in a system he disliked but could not escape. Sallie Rochester Ford in *Raids and Romance of Morgan and His*

Men (1864) depicted Kentucky cavalryman John Hunt Morgan as a gallant cavalier.

Kentucky had many would-be poets during the prewar years; unfortunately, the state's newspapers gave too many of them an outlet. Thomas Johnson Jr., known as the Drunken Poet of Danville, published a thin volume of poetry in 1789 called *The Kentucky Miscellany*. Among the best poetic works in the state were William Littell's *Festoons of Fancy* (1816), which also included some prose, and William Orlando Butler's book *The Boatman's Horn and Other Poems* (1821), whose title piece was the state's first popular poem. Two other poets were known largely for single poems that caught the public's fancy: Theodore O'Hara for "The Bivouac of the Dead" (1847) and Mary E.W. Betts for "A Kentuckian Kneels to None but God" (1851). Betts's poem was based on the proud reply of Colonel William Logan Crittenden as he was executed by Spanish authorities in Cuba. Amelia B. Welby, a sentimental writer, was the most popular poet in the state around midcentury. Many of her efforts were published in the *Louisville Journal* by George D. Prentice, who wrote quite a bit of poetry himself. Welby's *Poems by Amelia* (1845) went into at least seventeen editions. The newspaper editor's verse was published later as *The Poems of George D. Prentice* (1878). Prentice was famous for his short, pithy editorial comments. When he learned that someone was planning to collect and publish them, he issued his own selection, called *Prenticeana; or, Wit and Humor in Paragraphs* (1860).

A number of Kentuckians wrote autobiographical accounts of the events they witnessed that are still very useful. Especially good are Daniel Drake's *Pioneer Life in Kentucky* (1870) and George Robertson's *Scrap Book on Law and Politics, Men and Times* (1855). The interest in the state's early years led to the 1836 formation of the Kentucky State Historical Society. John Rowan became president in 1838 after a reorganization. The group was dormant from 1852 until 1878, when it was revived in Frankfort.

Several general histories of the state were written in the pre-Civil War period. Although usually called Kentucky's first history, John Filson's book *The Discovery, Settlement, and Present State of Kentucke* (1784) was more of a promotional travel account than a history. William Littell was hired by some of the men accused of being in the Spanish Conspiracy to vindicate their actions. He did so in *Political Transactions in and concerning Kentucky* (1806) and *A Narrative of the Settlement of Kentucky* (1806). Littell was answered by Humphrey Marshall in his *History of Kentucky*, first published in 1812, and in the revised and enlarged edition of 1824. While quite partisan, Marshall used documents that later disappeared, and his account was malicious enough to make interesting reading. In his old age John Bradford called upon his memory and the files of the *Kentucky Gazette* to write a series of sixty-six articles called "Notes on Kentucky," which appeared in the *Gazette* in 1826-29. They were never reprinted in their entirety until 1993, when Thomas D. Clark edited *The Voice of the Frontier: John Bradford's Notes on Kentucky*. Mann Butler, one of the foremost educators of his day, did a good nonpartisan job in his *History of the Commonwealth of Kentucky* (1834). Lewis Collins used articles from a number of contributors in *Historical Sketches of Kentucky* (1847), and the book's "Annals of Kentucky" contained many nuggets of fascinating lore. Collins's son Richard H. Collins revised and enlarged his father's work to two volumes, aided by even more contributors. The *History of Kentucky* appeared in 1874 and has been reprinted several times.

Newspapers

Newspaper editing and writing was a hazardous occupation in pre-Civil War Kentucky. Papers were strongly partisan, and editors, direct and personal in their comments, received frequent invitations to be horsewhipped or to fight a duel. Charles Wickliffe killed editor Thomas R. Benning in 1829 when he would not reveal the authorship of a letter in the paper. A few months later Wickliffe was killed in a duel with editor James Trotter. Most of the early papers came out once a week, were only four pages long, and had a limited circulation. They included little or no local news; their readers would know about local events before the paper appeared. The news was more likely to be a long account of a debate in Congress or a description of Napoleon's latest campaign. More could be learned about the community by going to the advertisements than to the news columns. Since few papers made a profit, editors published pamphlets, almanacs, and books in addition to doing job printing and hoping to become the state printer. Most of the papers carried poems, essays, and historical sketches of individuals and events. The mortality rate for newspapers was very high.

Bradford's *Kentucky Gazette* was not challenged until James H. Stewart started the *Kentucky Herald* in Lexington about 1793-95. Louisville got its first paper, the *Farmer's Library*, in 1801, with Samuel Vail as editor. John Ward and Joseph M. Street attracted attention to the *Western World* by their attacks on the Spanish Conspirators. The *Lexington Observer and Reporter* (1807) and the *Frankfort Yeoman* (1840) were two of the best newspapers in central Kentucky. William W. Worley, editor of the *Observer and Reporter,* displayed great initiative in getting news from the East, publishing it quickly, and distributing his papers before his rivals got started. In 1826 Shadrach Penn turned the *Louisville Public Advertiser* into the first daily paper west of the mountains. George D. Prentice came to the state to write a campaign biography of Henry Clay, but after he started editing the *Louisville Journal* in 1830, he and Penn fought for dominance. Penn could not match his rival's wit, and in 1841 he moved to St. Louis. In one of his famous paragraphs, Prentice wrote: "Some newspaper establishments are operated by steam. In others, horse or ass power is employed. Should our neighbor obtain, as he promises, a steam press, he will have a combination of advantages—a paper printed by steam and edited by an ass."

He once duped Penn by sending him a well-preserved, carefully pressed copy of a year-old New Orleans paper that had a spectacular murder story on the front page. It was timed to arrive as Penn started his press run. Excited by his monopoly of the story, Penn redid his paper to include it without ever noticing the date. Prentice frequently reminded him of this blunder. W. N. Halderman became a rival of Prentice in 1844, when he established the *Louisville Courier.* In 1849 Halderman pioneered in state journalism by sending a reporter to Frankfort to cover the work of the constitutional convention.

Two state papers gained fame for their antislavery views. By 1845 Cassius Marcellus Clay (1810-1903) was having difficulty getting his antislavery letters and articles published in the newspapers. On June 3, 1845, he began publishing the *True American* in Lexington. Although Clay's appeal was for gradual emancipation, his well-known reputation for violent encounters belied the mildness of his views. In August, while he was recovering from typhoid fever, a Committee of Sixty removed his press and shipped it to Cincinnati. Clay abandoned the enterprise the next year to ride off to the Mexican War. In 1850 mechanic William Shreve Bailey began publication of the abolitionist *Newport News* (later called the *Free South*). A mob burned Bailey's building in 1851, advertisers boycotted him, and he was sued frequently and threatened constantly. With the assistance of ten children who could set type, he kept the paper going until he went to England in 1860 to raise funds for the antislavery movement.

Medicine

The frontier had many diseases and few adequate treatments for them. Scarlet fever, measles, mumps, whooping cough, diphtheria, dysentery, influenza, cholera, smallpox, typhoid fever, yellow fever, various diarrheal ailments, pneumonia, pleurisy, venereal diseases, and milksickness were among the most common ones. Smallpox vaccination was known but not universally practiced. One of the most common complaints was ague. Kentuckians at the time often used the term to denote any sort of general ailment, much as their descendants would later blame almost anything on a virus. The prevailing medical theory was that illnesses were caused by invading foreign matter that could be eliminated by bleeding, sweating, and purging. Patients were bled who in later years would have been given a transfusion. Bleeding was also sometimes done as a preventive measure to ward off illness. Home remedies were sometimes as effective as anything the doctors had to offer. A measles patient was told to drink a tea made from sheep dung to cause the measles to break out; birth pangs were supposedly reduced by concealing a knife between the straw tick and the feather bed of the woman in labor.

Physicians who performed surgery were handicapped by a lack of knowledge concerning infection and also by the absence of anesthetics. George Rogers Clark listened to martial music while a leg was being amputated, and Jane Todd Crawford repeated psalms during her ovariotomy. Some doctors observed that patients were more likely to survive a clean amputation than a dirty treated wound, and amputations were performed to prevent infections. Several Kentucky doctors won renown for their surgery. Ephraim McDowell performed the first successful ovariotomy in 1809, and Walter Brashear succeeded in amputating a leg at the hip joint in 1806. Benjamin W. Dudley, who studied in Paris and London for four years after graduating from the medical college at the University of Pennsylvania, specialized in lithotomy, the removal of bladder stones, and had only three deaths in 225 operations. Daniel Drake helped organize several medical schools and started the *Western Medical and Physical Journal.* His major medical publication was the two-volume *Principal Diseases of the Interior Valley of North America* (1850).

Kentucky was a national leader in the training of doctors before the Civil War. The Transylvania University Department of Medicine, one of the best and largest in the country, graduated 1,881 doctors through 1859, when it closed. Professional disagreements and personality conflicts caused dissension among its distinguished faculty; in 1818 Dr. Dudley seriously wounded Dr. William H. Richardson in a duel. About half the faculty left and went to Louisville in 1837. The Louisville Medical Institute, which opened that year and became the medical department of the University of Louisville in 1846, graduated 1,500 doctors by 1861. A Kentucky School of Medicine was established in Louisville in 1850.

The state was hard hit by two Asiatic cholera epidemics in 1832-35 and 1848-54. Physicians did not know that the dread disease was caused by food and water that had been contaminated by the fecal discharges of its victims. Since the disease was usually fatal, people often fled when cases were reported in a community, thus spreading the illness to the havens they sought. In the first epidemic, Russellville and Lexington were estimated to have lost 10 percent of their populations. Some heroic individuals stayed to ease the suffering of the dying and to bury the dead. William ("King") Solomon, an alcoholic who had been declared a vagrant without visible means of support, became a Lexington hero by laboring to dig graves. The epidemics did convince a number of towns that something had to be done to make them cleaner.

Amusements

During the pioneer days, log rollings, house or barn raisings, cornhuskings, and any work that brought people together provided social opportunities for the neighborhood. A lavish meal was set out, a jug or two was made available, and the fiddles were brought out for a dance afterward. Square dancing was popular, but it was contested in the towns by more formal dances. Court days, militia days, pest hunts—any occasion that brought people together helped relieve the monotony of everyday life. Added attractions were shooting matches (per-

When the Oakland Race Course opened in 1832, it brought Louisville into national prominence in racing circles. This painting was done about 1840 (courtesy of the J.B. Speed Art Museum).

haps for a quarter of beef), gander pulling, bear fights, cockfighting, coon fighting, or battles between local champions with no holds barred except that weapons were not allowed. Less bloody were foot and horse races, as well as tomahawk and knife throwing. Women were more likely to engage in such activities as quilting parties and apple peelings. At one shooting match, however, Mrs. William Whitley outshot the men.

Horse races, popular from very early days, were a showcase for the improved breeds, both running and harness. Betting was certain to accompany argument as to the best horse. Card playing was popular among those who did not see it as a mortal sin, and large stakes were often involved.

As the frontier days receded, other amusements became more common, although some of the early leisure activities lingered in isolated areas for generations to come. Towns on the main rivers had a decided advantage in attracting circuses and traveling shows. Exotic animals were always a major attraction. Panoramas, minstrel shows, plays, and farces drew well and were suited to the showboats that began to ply the rivers. As the agricultural fairs expanded to include more attractions, they brought in carnival-type acts and exhibits. Horse races were also a feature of the fairs.

Weddings were a favorite excuse for happy gatherings, especially during the frontier days, when erecting a house or a barn for the newlyweds was often a part of the fun. The shivaree was both dreaded and anticipated by the newlyweds, for the noisy, prolonged harassment before the couple was finally bedded was a tribute to their popularity. Courtships were often brief, as were periods of mourning for widows, for the family was an essential social and economic unit on the frontier. A circuit minister might preach a funeral sermon, then perform a wedding ceremony for the surviving spouse before riding on to his next meeting.

As the towns grew, local drama and musical groups were formed, along with literary societies and debate clubs. Professional performers began to find it profitable to make swings into Kentucky. Ole Bull (Bornemann), a Norwegian violinist, played in Louisville in 1845, and Jenny Lind, the Swedish Nightingale, created intense excitement in the Falls City with a series of three concerts in the new Mozart Hall in April 1851. Tickets reportedly sold for as much as $175. Popular songs, published as sheet music, also sold well. Two of the most popular songs about Kentucky were written by non-Kentuckians. Samuel Woodworth of Massachusetts wrote "The Hunters of Kentucky" (1815), and Pennsylvanian Stephen Collins Foster penned "My Old Kentucky Home, Good Night" (1853). There is no proof that Foster was inspired by a visit to Federal Hill in Bardstown, now known as My Old Kentucky Home.

161

Lexington was the early musical center in the state. A vocal teacher, a music academy, and a singing school were all advertised before 1800, and Joseph Green was building pianos there in 1805. Some musical training was considered desirable for young ladies, and those who attended academies and finishing schools found a possible outlet for their creative urges. Available records show at least fifty-six concerts in Lexington between 1805 and 1840, but one of the charges against Transylvania president Horace Holley was that he had instrumental musical parties at his home on Sunday evenings. Mary Austin Holley was herself an accomplished musician. Innkeepers discovered that profits could be made from plays and concerts held in their meeting rooms, and they often rented space to music and dance teachers. On March 12, 1817, Sanford Keen's Tavern presented a concert that opened with part of Beethoven's First Symphony; this was only the third time that Beethoven had been performed in the United States. Wilhelm Iucho, who came to Lexington in 1834, did more for music in the town than anyone in the antebellum years, as performer, teacher, and composer. William Ratel organized musical groups in Georgetown, Danville, and Lancaster in addition to his work in Lexington. Four musical societies were established in Lexington before 1840: the Kentucky Musical Society, the Handel and Haydn Society, the Harmonic Society, and the Musical Amateurs. Among the many noted visiting performers were Charles Edward Horn, Henry Russell, and Madame Feron.

Music was one of the attractions at the state's springs, where many who could afford to do so took both the waters and vacations. Most of these places had a resident band for dances and brought performers in for concerts. Guests were encouraged to participate in musical programs staged by the management.

In 1828 comedian Thomas D. Rice was appearing at Drake's Theatre in Louisville when he chanced to see an elderly, crippled black man who worked at Crow's livery stable

singing an improvised song. Each verse ended with "Jump, Jim Crow" and a comic dance step. Rice's role in The Rifle was that of a "Kentucky Cornfield Negro," and he added a song and dance called "Jump Jim Crow" that stopped the show for encore after encore. Soon a nationally popular song, at the time it had nothing to do with segregation.

The first theatrical performance in Kentucky was probably two plays performed by Transylvania students on April 10, 1790. Luke Usher opened the commercial New Theatre in Lexington on October 12, 1808. Two years later he also had theaters in Louisville and Frankfort. His nephew Noble Luke Usher brought Samuel Drake, a theater manager in Albany, New York, to Kentucky about 1815 to manage the chain of houses. For the next twenty years Drake was the key figure in theater in the state. In the 1820s he moved to Louisville and concentrated on productions in the City Theatre. Between 1814 and 1843, when the City Theatre burned, 1,024 plays were performed there. In 1830 it could seat about seven hundred patrons, including some in expensive boxes. The gallery was "regarded as a rendezvous for the women of the streets and a convenient place to ply their trade." A fifty-foot saloon bar did a brisk business; coffee was also available.

Casts were small to reduce costs, and that sometimes caused problems. In one performance a character played by Samuel Drake Jr. was killed in the last act. Drake had to fall offstage so that he could grab his violin and play as the curtain fell. In another play he had to provide music while still delivering lines. He managed that by playing behind the curtain, then sticking his head through the curtain to make his speeches. The play Pizarro required the dramatic entrance of several white robed and veiled virgins. The half dozen people in the procession included an elderly woman, a girl of fourteen, an Irishwoman who cleaned the dressing rooms, and the property man. The audience was silent on opening night until

Graham's Springs in Mercer County was promoted by Dr. Christopher C. Graham. After the four-story hotel was completed in 1842, the owner boasted that his resort could accommodate a thousand guests at an inclusive rate of twenty dollars per month (from J. Winston Coleman Photographic Collection, Transylvania Library).

the property man and the cleaning woman appeared. Then someone groaned, "Oh, such virgins!" The audience exploded in laughter, joined by the members of the cast.

Theatrical offerings were varied to suit as many tastes as possible. Shakespeare was offered frequently, but so were farces. Drake staged a number of musical programs that would not have been available otherwise. For example, he displayed Anthony Philip Heinrich, sometimes called America's First Composer, one of whose works was "The Dawning of Music in Kentucky; or, The Pleasure of Harmony in Solitude." Theater in Louisville added a new dimension at midcentury with the beginning of the German theater. During his brief stay in the Falls City, Xavier Strasser was the key figure. The Apollo Hall became the home of the German performers.

Daniel Boone was not the only Kentuckian who enjoyed reading; for many, that was a favorite amusement. Many families brought some books to Kentucky with them. John Breckinridge's careful preparations for moving to the Bluegrass included ordering a trunkful of volumes from England. Within a few years of Lexington's founding, stores in the town were offering a selection of titles. Joseph Charles often left his Lexington store to peddle books as far away as Nashville and the Indiana Territory. In 1805 Lexington hosted a professional meeting of Booksellers and Printers of the Western Country; John Bradford was the group's

president. In 1795 Harry Toulmin, James Brown, John Breckinridge, and John Bradford led the formation of a subscription library that was to serve both the subscribers and Transylvania University. Within a year four hundred volumes had been obtained. It became the Lexington Library in 1800 when it moved off campus. A group of boys formed the Lexington Juvenile Library, which by 1816 had 1,135 volumes. In 1816 it merged with the adult library to create a holding of four thousand volumes.

Subscription libraries were started in a number of other communities before the Civil War. Charters were usually obtained from the state, and the participants bought shares in the library, usually in five-dollar increments. A shareholder could often select books to be purchased to the extent of his or her investment. Some libraries got permission from the General Assembly to hold lotteries for making more purchases. As many as sixty-one social libraries were organized between 1801 and 1856, but many of them had disappeared before 1856.

Some organizations established libraries to satisfy the interests of their members. Among them were medical, legal, scientific, and agricultural societies. Two of the largest belonged to the medical schools in Lexington and Louisville. The Mercantile Library in Louisville was started in 1842 to help young clerks improve themselves. All of the colleges that were started before the war had libraries, many of them insufficient for their students. Presidents Horace

Holley of Transylvania and Howard Malcolm of Georgetown were especially active in building the holdings at their institutions, which compared favorably with those of most eastern colleges. Libraries were usually open for brief periods, sometimes daily, sometimes weekly, and funds were normally scarce, but David R. Sayre of Lexington gave Centre College five thousand dollars to erect a library building, which was occupied in 1862. The state provided some assistance to the medical schools in Lexington and Louisville, and after about 1838 it distributed state documents to college libraries. The federal government also distributed some government documents. College literary societies often had their own libraries separate from those of the college. By 1860 the total volumes on the Transylvania campus numbered close to fourteen thousand, with half of them in the medical department; Georgetown and Centre each had about seven thousand books. The collection at St. Joseph's College numbered five thousand volumes, half of them in foreign languages, chiefly French and Latin. In some cases townspeople were allowed to use the college libraries.

The Kentucky State Library, organized about 1820, was confined largely to legal publications until the Civil War. A state librarian was authorized in 1833 and allocated five hundred dollars a year for five years to make purchases. George A. Robertson, a nephew of the judge, served for seventeen years, then later returned for another six. By 1852 the salary of the librarian had climbed to four hundred dollars per year. In 1860 the library had more than ten thousand volumes. The library started by the Kentucky Historical Society grew slowly because the organization was inactive for many years, but the collection was protected and preserved by other organizations.

Even as libraries, plays, musical programs, and other cultural activities became available to more Kentuckians, many of them still found pleasure in hunting and fishing. By midcentury such big game animals as bison, elk, and bear had disappeared or could be found only in remote areas. But the forage available on farmland may have resulted in an increase in the number of deer, and small game abounded in most of the state. Fish were plentiful in the numerous streams and lakes and the growing number of farm ponds. Although some Kentuckians still acquired basic food through hunting and fishing, these activities were no longer as important for supplying food as they had been in earlier days. They had become more important as forms of leisure. Some of the hunters and fishers probably cherished the tie that those activities made with the not-so-distant past.

As one looks back at the amusements of Kentuckians during the pre-Civil War era, the most surprising omission from today's perspective is the absence of organized and professional sports. The most popular modern sports had either not been invented (basketball) or were still in such a rudimentary stage of development that they bore little relationship to the present game (football, baseball). Few teams were found even in large cities, and those that did exist usually comprised amateur participants. If men's teams were rare, women's teams were almost nonexistent. Competition on the college level was limited to clashes between teams representing academic classes or literary societies. Horse racing may have resembled its modern form more closely than any other sport found in antebellum Kentucky.

Architecture

The first structures erected in Kentucky were the log buildings of a type common in the states from which the pioneers came. Some cabins went to two stories, sometimes with two large rooms on each floor. The development of sawmills soon made lumber available for building, and many of the log cabins were then enclosed in larger structures. Nails were being manufactured in Kentucky by 1788, and their availability encouraged the use of lumber. After the end of Indian dangers, kitchens were frequently detached from the rest of the house for fire safety and comfort in summer.

Stone and brick were soon being used for more elaborate houses as well as public buildings, such as the first statehouse and several county courthouses. William Whitley's home, Sportsman Hill, probably completed in the 1780s, may have been the first brick house west of the mountains. A fine example of an early brick house was Locust Grove, built near Louisville about 1790. It featured an upstairs ballroom measuring nineteen by thirty-one feet.

Many of the early mansions followed a Georgian-Federal style popular in the eastern states. John Brown's home in Frankfort, Liberty Hall, was a good example. Thomas Jefferson, however, favored Roman and Renaissance classical forms, sometimes called the Monumental Classical, and this style was used for a number of public buildings, including St. Joseph Proto-Cathedral in Bardstown and the second state capitol. Matthew Kennedy, the architect for the second capitol, favored the Monumental Classical style. It was challenged by the Greek Revival style, for which Gideon Shryock was the major advocate in Kentucky. Born in Lexington in 1802, Shryock worked with his father, a building contractor, then went to Philadelphia to work and study with William Strickland, one of the nation's most renowned architects. Shryock was only twenty-five when he won the competition to design the third state capitol.[2] Among his other works were the Franklin County Courthouse, the main building at Transylvania University, and the Orlando Brown home in Frankfort. The Greek Revival style, best suited for large buildings, was most popular during 1830-50.

The Gothic style, which became prominent about the same time as the Greek Revival, was a sort of romantic challenge to the Greek style, but a number of architects moved freely between the two. John McMurtry came to Kentucky from Maryland in 1833 and for the next half century was one of Kentucky's most versatile builders, moving easily among various styles.

The Italianate style became popular in Kentucky in the 1850s, due in part to the influence of Isaiah Rogers, who came to the state in 1852. Among his major works were Frankfort's Capital Hotel, the Louisville Hotel, and the Newcomb and Alexander Buildings in Louisville. The Newcomb and Alexander Buildings were the first five-story buildings erected in the state. Another innovation in the 1850s was the appearance of buildings with cast-iron fronts.

Of course, the construction of a great majority of houses and other structures in Kentucky during this period did not involve an architect who followed prevailing styles. In many instances, a local builder just put up what he and the owner agreed upon. They might well consult some of the plan books that showed a number of houses of relatively simple design.

Art and Artists

Portraiture was the most important type of art in Kentucky before the Civil War. It was the only way to preserve a likeness until the arrival of photography. Daguerreotypists were in the state as early as 1841, and John Hewitt had a studio in Louisville in 1842. Until near the end of the nineteenth century, however, the painter had a clear advantage. The best known of a large group of artists was Matthew Harris Jouett. Born near Harrodsburg in 1787 or 1788, he graduated from Transylvania University in 1808 and began to study law. After the War of 1812, in which he served as a captain, Jouett turned to art. In 1816 he studied with Gilbert Stuart for a few months and was able to double his price for a portrait to fifty dollars. Between then and his death in 1827 he is believed to have done at least 334 portraits and miniatures; he did not sign his pictures, and that made attribution difficult. He painted many Kentuckians, but he often spent the winter months painting in the Lower Mississippi states. Among the other portrait painters,

2. This is the old capitol building in Frankfort, now standing in restored form.

Joseph H. Bush, Oliver Frazer, and Samuel Woodson Price were best known.

Two artists associated with Kentucky were noted for their animal portraits. When John James Audubon came to Louisville in 1807 with Ferdinand Rozier to open a store, he had already started painting the birds of America. In 1810 the partners moved the store to Henderson. After Rozier left the state, Audubon, in debt and grieved by family misfortunes, returned to Louisville, where he gave art lessons and painted portraits to support his family until they left Kentucky in 1819. His masterpiece, *Birds of America,* was published in four volumes between 1827 and 1838. *Quadrupeds of America* appeared in five volumes in 1842-45. Edward Troye was a noted painter of horses and cattle, many of them in Kentucky. For Kentuckians, his most famous painting was of the thoroughbred Lexington in 1854.

Few Kentucky artists of the pre-Civil War period displayed much interest in landscapes or any subject other than portraits. The reason must have been primarily economic; portraits were more likely to sell than anything else.

Joel Tanner Hart was the only Kentucky sculptor of note during the antebellum years. Born in Clark County in 1810, he demonstrated talent carving headstones and monuments in Lexington. A marble bust of Cassius M. Clay was his first important work, and he did a number of other Kentucky likenesses. Hart moved to Italy in 1849 but made several trips back to the United States. His best-known works, *Morning Glory* (1869) and *Woman Triumphant* (begun 1875, completed by George Saul), were done in the postwar years. Hart believed that his poetry was as important as his sculptures, but critics did not agree with him.

Kentucky was blessed with a number of craftsmen who were artists in their fields.

Silversmiths were important until near the mid-nineteenth century, when mass production techniques almost ended their craft. They worked mainly with Spanish silver dollars and American coins. The simple flatware of the early days gave way to much more elaborate work in the nineteenth century. Asa Blanchard, usually conceded to be the best craftsman, worked in Lexington from 1808 until his death in 1838. John Kitts was the best known of Louisville's silversmiths. James S. Sharrard was known not only for his skills but also for his mobility. He had shops in at least half a dozen Kentucky towns in the western part of the state, including Henderson, Owensboro, and Paducah.

Some excellent work was also done by furniture makers. Most of the early skilled ones came from Virginia, Maryland, and Pennsylvania, but several were from Great Britain. Because imported wood was expensive, they made extensive use of native cherry and walnut; several other woods were also frequently used. Sideboards were among the most prized and expensive items, but dining tables and chairs were also in great demand. Corner cupboards and chests of drawers were less elaborate. The lovely simplicity of the Shaker furniture is better appreciated today than it was while the Shaker artisans were making it.

Few of the Kentucky immigrants came west to escape the culture of their previous homes. On the contrary, most of them wanted to establish a similar culture as soon as possible in their new homes, or even to improve upon what they had known elsewhere. They were not always as successful as they wished, and progress was uneven across the commonwealth. By the Civil War, however, much had been accomplished in many fields.

12

Slavery and Antislavery

The Black Population

Slavery existed in Virginia from the early years of the colony, and Kentucky inherited the institution without much dissent. Blacks helped explore Kentucky, and they shared the hardships and dangers of the white pioneers without having the prospects for advancement that the whites believed Kentucky offered. A census taken at Fort Harrod in the spring of 1777 counted 19 slaves, 7 of them children under ten years of age, in a total population of 198. Monk Estill gained his freedom as a reward for his heroic actions at the battle of Little Mountain in 1782, but the number of free blacks was very small.

Conquering a frontier required extensive labor, and slaves helped meet that need. In 1790 slaves constituted 16.2 percent of the population; free blacks were only 0.2 percent. From 1790 through 1830, the black population increased more rapidly than the white, as the state experienced explosive growth. In 1830 the black population reached its highest proportion in the state's history, with 24.0 percent of the total population being slaves and 0.7 percent being free blacks. Thereafter the number of blacks continued to increase, but in 1860 Kentucky's 225,483 slaves made up only 19.5 percent of the population, while the 10,684 free blacks constituted 0.9 percent. Several factors contributed to this relative decline. The frontier era had ended in most parts of the state, and the demand for labor had eased. Kentucky's agriculture did not require the numbers of workers used in the cotton, rice, and sugar plantations of the Lower South. This situation led to a considerable slave trade

167

A slave auction on Cheapside in Lexington, probably in the 1850s (from J. Winston Coleman Photographic Collection, Transylvania University Library).

after about 1830, as Kentucky blacks were sold "down the river." Until its repeal in 1849, the Nonimportation Act of 1833 prohibited the importation of slaves into the state for commercial purposes.

Some whites who accepted slavery condemned the slave trade that broke up families without regard to the anguish of those concerned. This trade was pictured as the worst aspect of slavery, and it was often said that the slave traders were despised even in slaveholding communities. That was sometimes true, but some of the major traders were respected members of their society. They were seen to perform a valuable service for owners who needed or chose to sell slaves. Lewis C. Robards, based in Lexington, was the state's chief dealer before 1850. Known as a sharpster in his business, he went broke in 1855, and his property was acquired by Bolton, Dickens and Company, the state's largest slave trading company, which had branches in several southern cities.

Slave Ownership and Distribution

The great majority of white Kentuckians never owned a slave. Some did not because they could not accept the idea that humans were considered as property. There were Kentuckians for whom the Declaration of Independence spoke truly, "that all Men are created equal, that they are endowed by their Creator with certain unalienable Rights, that among

these are Life, Liberty, and the Pursuit of Happiness." More white Kentuckians, however, were not slaveholders because they could not afford to be. The price of slaves varied according to such factors as age, health, gender, location, skills, and economic conditions. During the first third of the nineteenth century, a male slave in the prime working years of eighteen to thirty-five might cost $400-700 in Kentucky; a female in the same age group would cost about $350-450. One slave cost more than many Kentucky farmers earned in cash over two or more years. Prices increased in the late 1840s and early 1850s, putting slaveholding out of reach for most white Kentuckians.

In 1850, when the white population numbered 761,413, only 38,385 (5 percent) were listed as slave owners. That figure is misleading, however, for all of the slaves on a farm or plantation were usually listed as belonging to the head of the household, although other members of the family obviously had close ties to the institution. The truer figure is the number of family units that held slaves. The 1850 census counted 139,920 white families; 28 percent of them owned one or more slaves. Only five of the owners held more than one hundred slaves; 24 percent of the slaveholding families held just one slave. The average slaveholder in the state owned 5.4 slaves; only Missouri had a lower figure. Robert Wickliffe, called the Old Duke, had close to two hundred slaves in the early 1850s and was apparently Kentucky's largest slaveholder.

The distribution of slaves in Kentucky was quite uneven. On the eve of the Civil War Woodford County's population was 52 percent black. Of the state's 109 counties at the time, 21 had a slave population of 30 percent or higher. On the other hand, 23 counties had a slave population of less than 6 percent. The Bluegrass had the heaviest concentration of slaves, but Henderson and Oldham Counties on the Ohio River and Trigg, Christian, Todd, and Warren Counties in south-central Kentucky also had high percentages. Johnson County's black population was only 0.9 percent, and Jackson and Campbell Counties each had only 1 percent. Many white Kentuckians therefore had little or no direct contact with the institution of slavery.

Legal Status

Slaves were legally recognized as chattel property in Virginia, and their status as such continued in Kentucky. In a Warren County court decision in 1838, Judge J. Ewing tried to soften that status without abandoning it. He ruled that slaves were property and had to be treated as such, "but they are human beings, with like passions, sympathies and affections with ourselves." Despite the efforts of antislavery participants, the delegates to the first three constitutional conventions in Kentucky wrote strong proslavery articles into the state's constitutions. Although the term *slavery* did not appear in the U.S. Constitution, that document also recognized slavery as a legal institution. The slave code adopted in 1798 and modified from time to time presented in considerable detail the legal aspects of slavery in the state. The code attempted to regulate the activities and conduct of slaves and their masters, as well as the relationship the slaves had to the general community. Masters often violated the code because they did not want to be restricted in dealing with their own slaves. Some slaves violated it when possible as a part of their resistance to their enforced status. The code was

supposed to provide some protection for the slaves, but those provisions were often ignored, and slaves had little recourse when violations occurred. The testimony of blacks was usually not accepted against whites, and whites were often reluctant to testify against each other. Occasionally, however, a crime was so heinous as to force community action. In December 1811 Lilburne and Isham Lewis, nephews of Thomas Jefferson, killed a clumsy slave named George and dismembered his body. They were burning the pieces when an earthquake toppled the chimney and put out the fire. When the grisly affair was discovered, a grand jury in Livingston County indicted the Lewises for murder. The brothers agreed upon a suicide pact, but when Lilburne shot himself prematurely, Isham allowed himself to be arrested. Then he escaped from jail and disappeared, possibly to die at the battle of New Orleans. In another well-known case, Alpheus and Margaret Lewis brutally beat and burned some of their slaves, including twelve-year-old Martha. Bourbon County authorities seized the Lewises' slaves and sold them at auction, but the law provided that after expenses were deducted, the proceeds of the sale had to be given to the owners.

The slave's economic value was the best protection that that slave had. Only a sadistic or foolish master would punish a slave so severely as to curtail the person's ability to work, for the income of the master would thereby be reduced. If a slave was accused of a crime against the state or its political subdivisions, the master was expected to provide a defense for the accused person. The slave code, however, destroyed some of that protection. If a slave was executed by the state, the court ordered the slave's value paid to the owner.

Punishment posed a problem for owners. Few slaves had property, so fines could not be imposed, and imprisonment denied the master the services of the slave. Corporal punishment was commonly used. Branding and ear cropping were done to identify runaways, and metal rings or weights were sometimes fastened around the slave's neck or leg. Such burdens reduced the slave's mobility and could interfere with assigned tasks. Whipping was by far the most common form of punishment, both by the owner and by the governmental authorities for public crimes. County seats had public whipping posts, as did many small communities. Masters had few restraints upon the punishments they inflicted, and a number of slaves were killed or permanently crippled.

Food, Clothing, and Shelter

Since the typical Kentucky slaveholder in 1850 owned 5.4 slaves, the contacts between master and slave in the state were usually much closer than occurred on large plantations where overseers and gang bosses were used. The provision the small owner made for the slaves depended upon the owner's personal observations of need and the ability to satisfy them. Food rations were based on the three *m*'s of southern diet—meat, meal, and molasses. Pork was the most common meat. Most masters encouraged slaves to raise gardens, to keep chickens, and to fish and hunt such small animals as rabbits and opossums for which a gun was not needed. Special treats such as coffee, oranges, and candy were sometimes given at Christmas or other special occasions.

Clothing was usually made of durable homespun or the long-wearing "Kentucky jeans" material that state factories were producing. Where slaves were numerous, clothing was often issued in annual or semiannual rations. Where slaves were few, distribution was likely to be governed by discerned need. Ribbons, handkerchiefs, and better cloth were sometimes handed out as presents or as rewards for good work.

Slaves on a small farm probably lived in a cabin, with one room and a loft, located not far from the owner's house. As families grew, a lean-to might be added. Stoves were rare; most of the cooking was done at the hearth or outdoors in hot weather. Much of the furniture was homemade and consisted of essentials: a table, chairs and benches, a bed or two with a trundle bed underneath, perhaps a chest of

drawers and a cupboard. Some masters prided themselves upon having frame, brick, or stone slave dwellings, which were often arranged as slave quarters along a short street near the overseer or master so that frequent random checks could be made. The household servants in wealthy families often lived in the "big house" so that their services could be available at any time. Such slaves usually dressed and ate better than did the field hands in the quarters. In the towns, slaves might live in separate dwellings, but they were kept close to the master. Free blacks might congregate in a particular section of town, but slaves and masters in Kentucky's pre–Civil War towns lived in close proximity.

Resistance to Slavery

Historians have given too little attention to the slaves who opposed the system that denied them freedom and human dignity. Many slaves fought back in some way against the institution that enslaved them.

The most common form of resistance was to do as little work as possible while avoiding the whip for working too slowly or too poorly. Some masters countered such slowdowns with contests among workers or gave incentives for work done rapidly and well; others simply resorted to the whip. Occasionally slaves were able to purchase their freedom by means of earned income. Slaves would also sometimes pretend to be ill, and some resorted to self-mutilation, often by cutting tendons in the leg or ankle. Suicide offered an escape from slavery that was occasionally chosen by slaves after an unsuccessful escape attempt or excessive punishment, or by slaves facing an impending sale.

Destruction of the master's property was another form of resistance. It might consist of breaking or losing tools, mistreating horses and other livestock, damaging or destroying crops, or burning barns and other buildings. Fires were common, although arson by a slave carried the death penalty. Stealing food was most common, and many masters assumed that such loss of property was normal; they just tried to keep it under control. Sophie Word, born into Kentucky slavery in 1837, recalled that "we would slip in the house after the master and mistress wuz sleeping and cook to suit ourselves." Stealing property and selling it was considered a much more serious crime.

Resistance against conditions that had become intolerable sometimes resulted in violence against the master or members of the master's family. Aggrieved slaves who had access to the kitchen might try poisoning. Outside workers might use any of the many deadly weapons available on a farm or simply attack with bare hands. In one notorious case, Jim Kizzie, a Daviess County overseer noted for his brutality, was strangled to death by several slaves. Perhaps knowing that Kizzie had brought the result upon himself, a jury found only one slave guilty of murder. As was customary, most of the slaves in the community were marched to the execution site to witness the slave's death.

The haunting fear in a slave society was a slave revolt. The 1831 Nat Turner revolt in Virginia showed how much damage a determined band of slaves could do before being overcome. Many of the restrictions placed upon the slaves' mobility and upon unsupervised meetings were designed to make plotting more difficult. Kentucky experienced acts of violence but no actual insurrection. Enough scares in different parts of the state occurred, however, to keep many whites terrified of what might happen. Rumors spread rapidly across the state around Christmas 1856, and several suspected participants in an insurrection were executed before it became evident that there was no uprising. Abolitionists were usually blamed for stirring up the slaves, and free blacks were often forced to leave an area as a precautionary measure.

Running away was another form of resistance. Sometimes the slave had a temporary goal in mind. A slave might decide that a whipping was acceptable if two or three weeks of hard work during harvest could be missed. Other runaways sought permanent escape from slavery. Even escape to the North was not

sure, for a federal Fugitive Slave Act had been in force since 1793, and a stricter act was a part of the Compromise of 1850. Kentucky offered rewards for people who would apprehend and return fugitives, and there were professional slave catchers. Canada would not return fugitives, and many escapees tried to reach that haven. The number of runaways and the role of the Underground Railroad have been greatly exaggerated. In 1850, when Kentucky had nearly 211,000 slaves, only 96 fugitives were reported. In 1860, with more than 225,000 slaves, the reported fugitives numbered 119. The slaves most likely to escape, or to attempt to do so, were males of prime working age. It has been suggested that fugitive slaves constituted a safety valve for the institution, that those who did escape were the ones who might have been most likely to participate in violence or rebellion had they not left. The Underground Railroad provided little help south of the Ohio River, and even in the North the fugitive ran the risk of being returned to slavery if wrong contacts were made. The safest thing was to approach another black person, but that did not guarantee safety. Some abolitionists, such as Calvin Fairbanks, did help fugitives escape from Kentucky; for that crime he spent from 1852 to 1864 in a state prison before being pardoned. By his count, while in prison he was whipped 1,003 times, for a total of 35,105 lashes.

One of the most heralded escapes was that of Josiah Henson and his family. Henson may have been the model for Uncle Tom in Harriet Beecher Stowe's *Uncle Tom's Cabin.* A slave in Maryland, Henson was ordered by his master in 1825 to conduct the master's other slaves to Kentucky to avoid creditors. Although the group was on free soil in Cincinnati, Henson carried out the promise he had made. In 1828 he received a pass to return to Maryland to see about buying his freedom. He paid $350 and signed a note to pay an additional $100, but upon his return to Kentucky he was told that he owed $650. During the trip he spent some three months in free states and

171

50 DOLLARS REWARD.

Ran away from the subscriber, about the 17th inst. a negro man slave, by the name of

REUBEN,

Twenty-five or thirty years of age, five feet ten and a half or eleven inches high, square and strongly built; very black; his eyes rather inclined to be red or yellow, occasioned from dissipation and night strolling. He has rather a shy, down look, and shews guilt very quick; has had a piece bit out of one of his ears, by fighting; and had on when he went away, a tow linen shirt and pantaloons and an old white fur hat, broad brim—he has other clothes, no doubt, but I do not know what kind they are   He is an artful fellow, calculated to do a great deal of mischief, by roguishness. which he is much addicted to. He has a wife at Mr. Fitzhugh Thornton's, in this county; and, no doubt, will make the principal part of his stay in that neighborhood, being uncommonly fond of his family

I will give fifty dollars, Commonwealth paper, for Reuben, if taken out of the state; ten dollars, Commonwealth paper, if taken in the county, and twenty dollars, Commonwealth paper. if taken out of the county, and delivered to me, or secured in any jail, so that I get him again

FRANCIS TALIAFERRO.

Oldham county, Ky. August 28   615ow

100 DOLLARS REWARD.

Ran away from the farm of A K Alexander, in the county of Franklin, and state of Kentucky, a mulatto man slave, named

GEORGE,

The property of A K. Marshall   George was hired to said Alexander, and some quarrel having taken place with the overseer, he absconded, about the 19th of November, 1823. He is a light mulatto, formerly belonged to the estate of Violett, who, by his will, devised him free; but, said Violett being in debt, George was sold under execution, and purchased by J J. Marshall of the town of Frankfort. George is about 5 feet 9 or 10 inches high; has a slight, genteel person; a brisk, intelligent countenance—but he can be identified beyond dispute, by a scar, which has deprived him of all hair on a large part of his head. He wears his hair long, and attempts to conceal the scar, by combing it smooth over it. He has probably a copy of Violett's will with him, and passes as free; but he is a slave, as above stated. He has been seen in the steam boat Maine, and probably continues in it   The above reward will be paid, upon delivery of said George. in Frankfort, to the subscriber. or by confining him in jail, at Maysville or Louisville, so that he comes to the possession of the subscriber.

J. J. MARSHALL.

august 28   615ow

20 DOLLARS REWARD.

These notices of rewards for the capture of runaway slaves were published in the *Louisville Public Advertiser* in November 1824. The emphasis on "Commonwealth paper" in the advertisement for the return of Reuben reflects Kentucky's banking problems in the 1820s (from The Filson Club Historical Society).

earned $275 preaching. Henson could easily have escaped, but his family was in Kentucky, and he returned to them. When he learned that he might be sold in New Orleans, though, he determined to escape. On a Saturday night in September 1830 another slave rowed the family across the Ohio River. Two children were so young that Henson and his wife carried them in knapsacks. Traveling only at night, they took two weeks to get to Cincinnati, and they walked in hunger much of the way. Henson found a friend in the city who took the family in for a few days before they resumed their difficult trek northward. At Sandusky,

Ohio, Henson found a captain of a trading vessel who carried the family to Buffalo and paid their ferry passage to Canada. Henson founded a community for other fugitives, learned to read and write, penned a well-received autobiography, and became a noted abolitionist speaker.

As antislavery sentiment increased in the North, Kentucky encountered difficulty in getting fugitive slaves returned, despite the harsh 1850 act. In October 1859 a Woodford County grand jury indicted Willis Lago, a free black, for helping a slave named Charlotte escape to Ohio. When the Ohio governor, William Dennison, refused the extradition request, Kentucky sought an order from the U.S. Supreme Court. That body ruled that while Dennison was wrong in his refusal to honor the request, Congress could not compel a state official to perform a duty.

A Black Subculture

Despite their restricted status, Kentucky's slaves were able to build a subculture of their own, one that blended elements of their African heritage with what they had acquired from the dominant white culture. The slave family was a strong institution, although marriage was not required by the Kentucky slave code and family members might be sold without regard to the family unit. Since children born in slavery went with their mother, the woman played a major role in slave families. The church was also an important institution, especially after blacks became able to separate their worship from that of whites. Some churches were then able to provide education for many of their members, and a number of blacks received practical training in business affairs and organizational leadership through the church. A black church also provided a means of voicing opinions and making requests that might have been dangerous for an individual. Thus the black church, with its social and educational functions, offered at least some preparation for freedom.

Breeding and Miscegenation

One of the supposed aspects of slavery that has often received attention in lurid novels of the Old South is the directed breeding of slaves. According to the more extreme tales, this was done both to produce marketable offspring and to breed better individuals. There is little evidence that such a practice occurred in Kentucky. Marriage might make slaves more content with slavery and less likely to run away, and some masters must have viewed an increase in the number of slaves as a growth in their capital investment. But families were large during the antebellum period, white as well as

black, and there is no conclusive evidence that directed breeding occurred.

Miscegenation has also been a favorite theme of novelists, and there is no doubt but that it did occur. A slave woman had few defenses against the demands of white men, and there were also some known instances of intercourse between black men and white women. Miscegenation was not often mentioned in polite society, even when children provided proof of its existence. Miscegenation was probably more common than Kentucky whites admitted and less extensive than abolitionists claimed. Some unhappy incidents took place. In the mid-1850s a respected white man died in Lexington, and an estate sale was held to satisfy his creditors. He had had two daughters born to a quadroon slave. He had given them every care and sent them to Oberlin College in Ohio for an education. They had remained in Ohio, where they were accepted as white without question. When they returned to Kentucky for their father's funeral, they were seized and sold at auction as part of his property. He had neglected to free them.

Overall Treatment of Slaves

Without doubt, slavery was a crime against humanity. It had been discredited and abandoned by most of the nations that nineteenth-century America considered part of the civilized world. Its continuance in the United States was a blot on a society that prided itself upon the practice of democracy. Yet within the institution of slavery in the United States degrees of severity existed, and on that limited basis slavery in Kentucky was milder than it was in the Lower South. That difference was often claimed by defenders of the state's slavery, and it was substantiated by nearly all foreign and domestic travelers who had a chance to compare slavery in different states. The reason commonly given for the difference was that Kentucky masters were more likely to work alongside their slaves than were the plantation owners in the Lower South. It has also been suggested that Ken-

173

tucky masters were more careful to keep slaves from being discontented enough to run away because the state had such a long border with free states. Relative mildness was no excuse for the existence of slavery, but a slave in Kentucky probably received somewhat better treatment than a slave in Mississippi or Alabama.

By careful selection of data, any extreme can be "proved" about Kentucky slavery. Collect only atrocities, and the institution would appear to be devoid of any vestige of humanity. Collect only examples of kindnesses and affection, and the institution would appear to be benevolent and even beneficial to the slave. Few persons who felt strongly about slavery, pro or con, made an attempt to be objective. The treatment of a Kentucky slave depended largely upon the individual master and the individual slave and the relationship that they developed. Yet the dominant fact is that one person held another person in bondage. For that there can be no excuse.

The Defense of Slavery

As the "peculiar institution" came under attack, proslavery advocates offered a defense of slavery. While individuals presented somewhat different ideas, certain points were almost certain to appear. The Bible was cited to show that slavery had existed in biblical days; Old Testament patriarchs had owned hundreds of slaves. Slavery had also existed in all of the great civilizations of the past. The Greeks had shown that slavery could coexist with democracy. Indeed, Greek culture could not have reached its zenith had slaves not been available to do the drudgery. Slavery had saved millions of lives by giving value to captives who would otherwise have been killed. Slavery rescued blacks from Africa and gave them the opportunity to become civilized Christians. Slavery was actually the economic status of the lowest class in society, regardless of what it was called. Slaves, who had to be taken care of when ill, old, and crippled, were actually better off than most of the white factory workers in the North and in

Europe. Besides, slavery had been forced on the American colonies by the British government. Perhaps it would have been better had it never existed in the United States, but wishing did not replace reality. Slaves were here, they were property, and a basic function of government was to protect property. Slaves could not be freed without owners' being paid their full value, and the state could not bear that expense. Slavery was recognized by both the United States and Kentucky as a legal institution. Besides, the argument ran, slaves were from an inferior race, and they simply were not ready for freedom.

The Early Opponents

Antislavery sentiment also existed in Kentucky from early days. Several northern states had abolished slavery before the end of the American Revolution, and some of Kentucky's pioneers agreed that the system should be ended. When efforts to abolish slavery in Virginia failed, the institution was fastened on the District of Kentucky until the constitutional convention of 1792 provided an opportunity to end it. But as Abraham Lincoln said in 1859, "When the Kentuckians came to form the Constitution, they had the embarrassing circumstance of slavery among them—they were not a free people to make the Constitution."

Presbyterian minister David Rice led the opposition to slavery in the 1792 convention. Three months earlier his pamphlet, *Slavery Inconsistent with Justice and Good Policy,* made a comprehensive attack on the institution. Slavery was unfair to black people, Rice asserted, for "as creatures of God we are, with respect to liberty, all equal." It was also harmful to whites, for it reduced moral and political virtue, and it corrupted youths and promoted sloth. If slavery was abolished, Rice predicted that five useful citizens would come to the state for each slaveholder who left it. Taking slave property might seem unjust, but slavery itself was the greatest injustice. Abolition was sure to come; now was the time to end slavery. At the convention, Rice realized that immediate abolition was impossible. He asked for the constitution to reject slavery in principle and to direct the legislature to halt the importation of slaves, provide a scheme of gradual emancipation, and furnish education to prepare the slaves for useful lives in freedom. Rice lost the battle, and the proslavery article 9 was inserted by a vote of 26-16.

The continued opposition from individuals and some church groups proved ineffective. In 1811, when twelve Baptist churches with a combined membership of 300 were antislavery, the state's Baptists numbered 17,511. Most of the largest denominations adopted a policy like that of the Transylvania Presbytery in 1796. Although slavery was an evil, "yet they view the final remedy as alone belonging to the civil power; and also do not think that they have sufficient authority from the word of God to make it a term of church communion." The antislavery advocates made emancipation an issue in the election of delegates to the 1799 convention. The *Kentucky Gazette* even published the gradual emancipation plan of New York as an example. A child born after July 4, 1799, would be free, but a male could be held as a servant until age twenty-eight, a female until age twenty-five. The defenders of slavery stressed the sacredness of property, the prohibitive cost of emancipation, and the slave's unpreparedness for freedom. John Breckinridge suggested that the antislavery people should "satiate their humanity" by buying and freeing slaves. The constitutional slavery provisions passed in 1799 were almost identical to those of 1792.

Baptist preacher David Barrow was unwilling to be neutral on the issue of slavery. Expelled from the North District Baptist Association, he and others founded the Baptist Licking-Locust Association, Friends of Humanity, an antislavery group. Barrow also helped start the Kentucky Abolition Society in 1808 and served as its president for several years. Members pledged to work for a consti-

tutional ban on slavery, education for blacks, better treatment of slaves, and an end to the slave trade. They tried to educate members of the public about the need for their program. In a fifty-page pamphlet published in 1808, Barrow declared that if the blacks were not equal to the whites, it was because they had not had equal opportunities for education. Concerning intermarriage, he asserted that "any woman who is good enough to make a man a concubine, etc. ought to serve him for a wife."

In 1821 the Kentucky Abolition Society decided to publish a newspaper. Before its first issue appeared in May 1822, it had become the monthly *Abolition Intelligencer and Missionary Magazine*. Its twelve issues were edited in Shelbyville by minister John Finley Crowe. It was then one of only two antislavery publications in the nation.

Abolition and Emancipation

A survey of abolition societies in 1827 listed eight in Kentucky, with about two hundred members. Although most of these groups used the word *abolition* in their names, they were emancipationist in their approach. During the early years the two terms were often used interchangeably, but in time divisions between abolitionists and emancipationists became so great that the two groups sometimes seemed to spend more time fighting each other than they did combating proslavery advocates.

Abolition came to mean the demand for the immediate, uncompensated freeing of the slaves. Slavery was a moral evil, and no compromise could be made with it. Human lives had been stolen; a thief should not be compensated for what he had taken. Gradualism was an excuse to prolong the inevitable. Now was the time to act.

Emancipation indicated a more moderate course. Slavery was a moral evil, and it had to be terminated. Still, it was sanctioned by law, and slaveholders had invested much of their capital in slaves. The abrupt end of slavery would disrupt society and the economy in the southern states, so termination should be gradual to allow time for adjustments. Since slavery was legal, compensation should be paid to the owners. Emancipationists had many different plans for achieving these goals.

Colonization

Most white Kentuckians did not believe that a large number of free blacks could or should be absorbed into the general population. Despite their small number, free blacks were so restricted that they were hardly free. The end of slavery could be achieved more easily if no blacks remained after it occurred. Colonization appealed to many persons in both the North and the South, and the American Colonization Society for the Free People of Color was organized in Washington, D.C., during the winter of 1816-17. Henry Clay was a strong supporter of its program.

The Kentucky Colonization Society was established in 1829 as an auxiliary of the national body. By 1832 the state had thirty-one colonization societies. Only Virginia (thirty-four) and Ohio (thirty-three) had more. As Henry Clay emphasized, the society did not attempt to free slaves; it would help those free blacks who were willing to leave the country. Still, many hoped that colonization would encourage more masters to free more slaves. Joseph R. Underwood of Bowling Green was another state politician who gave strong support to the plan.

Opposition was also strong. Abolitionists feared that colonization would weaken their crusade by satisfying some people, some slaveholders concluded that it was a sly plan to end slavery, and most free blacks had no desire to move to Liberia. When Richard Bibb of Logan County freed fifty-one slaves, thirty-two agreed to make the trip to Africa. Others were added, and when the *Ajax* sailed from New Orleans on April 20, 1833, it carried ninety-one former slaves from Kentucky and fifty-one from Tennessee. Illness killed twenty-nine people before the ship reached Key West. The trip exhausted all available funds, and no more

freed slaves were sent from Kentucky until 1840. Establishment of the colony of Kentucky in Liberia, with Clay Ashland as its principal town, revived interest, and more money was raised. When a ship reached Africa in 1846, two colonists looked at the shore and refused to leave the ship. Some became discouraged and returned to the United States, but others adjusted well. As Nelson Sanders wrote his former mistress in 1847, "We enjoy liberty & our lives in a degree which is impossible for the negro to enjoy in any other country."

In 1851 the General Assembly required newly freed blacks to leave the state, and Kentucky's free black population increased by only 673 persons between 1850 and 1860. In 1856 the legislators appropriated five thousand dollars annually to help the resettlement program, but the last sizable group left Kentucky for Liberia in 1857. In the years 1829-59 the Kentucky Colonization Society was able to send only 658 emigrants to Africa; the number of slaves in the state increased from 165,213 in 1830 to 225,483 in 1860. The best efforts of the Colonization Society had almost no effect.

Other Antislavery Approaches

An avowed abolitionist who condemned fainthearted emancipationists, William Lloyd Garrison began publication of the *Liberator* in Boston in 1831. He never had the influence he thought he had, but Garrison became a symbol to many slaveholders of the abolitionist who wrote about a subject on which he knew little or nothing. When he advocated slave rebellion and soon afterward Nat Turner led his bloody insurrection in Virginia, many southerners saw a cause and effect relationship. Most Kentuckians, including the nonslaveholders, saw slavery as a state matter that should be decided without interference from outsiders. The fight to determine the future of slavery in the commonwealth continued.

Since the state constitution that became effective in 1800 did not allow individual amendments, some antislavery agitators sought another convention. Their cause was helped by

Cassius M. Clay's violent encounters with a number of opponents belied his mild views on slave emancipation (from The Filson Club Historical Society).

citizens who wanted other changes made, and in 1837 the legislature proposed holding a convention. The voters rejected the measure by a wide margin, in part because of reaction to the abolitionist attacks on slavery and slaveholders.

The Nonimportation Act of 1833, which made more stringent the law against importing slaves into the state for commercial use, became a focal point for the continuing battle. Some Kentuckians saw the act as a step toward making emancipation easier by limiting the number of slaves; others were convinced that it benefited slaveholders by allowing the price of slaves in the state to increase. The measure was modified, but repeal did not come until 1849.

Cassius Marcellus Clay began his antislavery career in the 1830s after being exposed to antislavery thought while a student at Yale. A wealthy slaveholder who favored emancipation, Clay seldom used moral and religious arguments. Instead, he argued that slavery hampered the state's economic development and victimized working-class whites with unfair competition. His views on legal emancipation were actually quite moderate, but his violent responses to physical attacks brought him to the public's attention. Clay wrote a pamphlet on knife fighting (the secret was to

thrust upward, not strike down), and the Bowie knife was his favorite weapon, as several victims could testify. After his brief editorship of the *True American* in Lexington and participation in the Mexican War, where he was captured, Clay continued to battle slavery on the political front.

Clay was the most spectacular state foe of slavery, but a number of others were also involved. James G. Birney, who moved from slaveholding to colonization to emancipation to abolition, was active but spent most of his antislavery career outside the state. Robert J. Breckinridge favored emancipation and colonization, as did former governor James T. Morehead. In 1833, when the Presbyterian Synod of Kentucky voted to postpone a decision on slavery, Breckinridge stalked out of the hall, declaiming as he went, "God has left you, and I also will now leave you, and have no more communication with you." John C. Young headed a committee that drafted a plan for gradual emancipation and an educational program for blacks, but the synod did not act on it.

Some antislavery advocates were convinced by 1849 that they had a chance to alter the slavery article in the constitution. Meetings in Maysville, Louisville, Bowling Green, and other towns called for gradual emancipation, often accompanied by colonization. Although an emancipation party polled 10,000 votes in 1849, it did not elect a delegate to the constitutional convention. Slavery was discussed at length by the delegates, but Silas Woodson gave the only emancipationist speech. He wanted emancipation to be readily available whenever it was needed. Instead, the convention adopted the 1799 slavery article almost intact.

Antislavery in the 1850s

Some opponents of slavery left the state after their 1849 defeat, but most of them continued the fight. A major weakness was their inability to unite in one group. They often opposed each other, and John G. Fee commented after he and Cassius Clay spoke from the same platform that "there was manifest confusion in the crowd." At least slavery continued to be discussed. It was not allowed to slip into the quiet oblivion that many desired.

One of the critics in the 1850s was William Shreve Bailey, who activated the *Newport News* as an abolitionist paper in 1850. Bailey compounded his perceived sins by becoming a Republican when that party got started. Somehow he kept publishing until he was sent to England in 1860 to raise funds for the cause. When J. Brady, a teacher from New England, tried to establish an antislavery paper in Lexington, he was chased out of town before he got it going.

In the 1850s Cassius Clay concentrated on politics rather than journalism. His exploits had won national attention, and he did considerable speaking in the North. In 1851 Clay announced the birth of the Emancipation Party and declared his candidacy for governor. He knew he could not win, but he expected to get at least 10,000 votes. He received only 3,621. Later Clay worked to form the new Republican Party. With characteristic modesty, he claimed to have influenced Lincoln's antislavery views. In the 1860 Republican convention Clay received two votes for president and was a strong second for the vice presidential nomination.

In an effort to build a political base, Clay turned to the hilly region east and southeast of the Bluegrass, where slaves were few. There he became involved with John G. Fee. Born into a slaveholding family in Bracken County, Fee underwent a spiritual conversion to abolitionism while at Ohio's Lane Seminary. His appalled father ordered him home: "I have spent the last dollar I mean to spend on you in a free state." Dismissed from the New School Presbyterian Synod in 1845, Fee and a few followers started a church in which blacks had equal status with whites. Supported in part by the American Missionary Association, Fee established several other small churches and published antislavery pamphlets to refute the defenses of slavery. He appealed to a "higher law" when reminded that slavery was constitutional. He abhorred violence and refused to carry a weapon or to defend himself. When Fee began to preach in Madison County, Clay encouraged him to move there by giving him ten acres of poor land for a home and school and providing physical protection from those who sought to silence the preacher. John A.R. Rogers was a devout helper among those who came to Berea to join Fee. Rogers and Fee dreamed of a college in which blacks would be welcome along with the mountain whites. Fee attracted unwanted attention from proslavery advocates, but he prayed for members of mobs as they dragged him from his pulpits. A daughter later recalled, "We children never thought anything more about mobs than about thunderstorms. We supposed everybody had mobs." Clay and Fee inevitably split, for their views on the best way to combat slavery were so different. Deprived of Clay's protection, the Bereans were forced to leave their settlement near Christmas 1859.

In 1860 slavery appeared to be as secure in Kentucky as it had ever been. The antislavery advocates had failed to win the support of a majority of the voters, and slavery gave every indication of continuing indefinitely. The crusaders against it had at least kept the issue alive and before the public, but no one could predict how and when the institution might be terminated.

Free at Last

President Lincoln was opposed to slavery, but in his First Inaugural Address he sought to reassure the slave South. "I have no purpose, directly or indirectly, to interfere with the institution of slavery in the States where it exists. I believe I have no lawful right to do so, and I have no inclination to do so." His primary purpose was to preserve the Union, not to abolish slavery. A Kentucky Union soldier wrote on November 5, 1862, "We find ourselves in arms to maintain doctrines, which, if announced 12 months ago, would have driven us all, notwithstanding our loyalty to the Constitution & the Union, into the ranks of the Southern Army." In the summer of 1861 Lincoln quickly reined in General John C. Frémont when he began to free slaves in Missouri. Frémont's actions, Lincoln explained, would "perhaps ruin our rather fair prospects for Kentucky."

The president tried several times to get Kentucky to adopt a scheme of compensated emancipation. If a state would commit itself to a definite date for ending slavery, say January 1, 1882, then he would recommend to Congress that owners receive four hundred dollars for each slave. Lincoln argued that the loyal slave states were prolonging the war, for the Confederacy still hoped that the common bond of slavery would bring them into its ranks. He warned that if the war continued, slavery would not survive: "It will be gone, and you will have nothing valuable in lieu of it."

The members of Congress from the slave states with whom Lincoln met replied that they disagreed about the prolongation of the war. Indeed, the antislavery measures taken by the North strengthened the southern resolve to resist. Slavery was a state issue, not a federal one, and the congressional leaders requested that the president confine himself to his proper constitutional areas. A Montgomery County Union Party convention summed up state opinion in January 1863: "Kentucky does not desire to sell her slaves to the government of the United States at any price." Back in December 1861 the *Louisville Daily Democrat* had stated a belief of many Kentuckians: "The two races . . . cannot exist in the same country, unless the black race is in slavery." If slaves were freed, the editor wrote, they would have to be exterminated.

When Lincoln decided that ending slavery would help win the war, he only declared slaves free in those areas that were in rebellion. His Emancipation Proclamation did not affect Kentucky. Even so, it attracted a storm of protest in the state and from its soldiers in the U.S. Army. The *Lexington Observer and Reporter* of January 7, 1863, declared the proclamation illegal and unconstitutional: "Be assured that a large majority of the people of the United States are for the Union as it was and the Constitution as it is, and are resolved to preserve them against the continued assaults of abolitionists and secessionists."

As Federal troops entered Kentucky in September 1861, they attracted many slaves who slipped away from their masters or who were impressed to do military labor. The erosion of slavery in the state was under way. When Lincoln authorized the use of black troops in December 1862, he excluded Kentucky, but thousands of Kentucky blacks enlisted by going outside the state. A military census showed that the state had 40,285 black males of military age, and that was too important a source of manpower to ignore. Black Kentuckians were enrolled in early 1864 despite bitter protests. Colonel Frank L. Wolford of the "Wild Riders" of the First Kentucky Cavalry (USA) was so enraged that he publicly attacked the president and the administration. At a Lexington banquet in March 1864 he remarked, "What with Abe Lincoln on one side and Jeff Davis on the other, our poor distracted country reminds me of Christ crucified between two thieves." Wolford was dishonorably dismissed from the army he had served well. Near mutiny was reported in a number of Kentucky regiments, but the recruitment went forward. When volunteering slowed, more blacks were impressed into service. The army finally reported that it had enlisted 23,703 black Kentuckians, 13 percent of the 178,895 blacks who served in the Union armies.

Many slave families followed the men into such army facilities as Camp Nelson in Jessamine County, especially after March 1865, when the families of black soldiers were also declared free. The Federal authorities were not prepared to cope with the influx, and some of those in command had no desire to do so. The result was privation and death for many of the women and children who went to the camps. John G. Fee did what he could to alleviate the deplorable situation at Camp Nelson, a number of black churches and benevolent societies were able to help elsewhere, and the army found some commanders who were sympathetic to the plight of the recent slaves.

By March 1865 the U.S. government estimated that 71 percent of the state's slaves had been freed, although many of them remained with their former masters. Some sixty-five thousand people were still enslaved. Stubborn slaveholders persisted in believing that slavery would somehow survive, and slaves in Kentucky continued to be traded through most of 1865, even after the fall of the Confederacy. The Thirteenth Amendment to the U.S. Constitution passed Congress and was submitted to the states for ratification on February 1, 1865. The process was completed and the amendment was declared part of the constitution on December 18, 1865.

The next year, in a senseless gesture of defiance, the Kentucky House of Representatives refused to ratify the amendment.[1] That meant little, for slavery had at last been ended in the state. Unfortunately, emancipation had been achieved only through a bloody and expensive war, and little had been done to prepare the former slaves for freedom.

---

1. The Civil War amendments—the Thirteenth, Fourteenth, and Fifteenth—were ratified in 1865, 1868, and 1870, respectively. The General Assembly, admitting that "this Bicentennial Year is an appropriate time to erase the shadow on Kentucky's history," ratified all three in 1976.

13

The Road to War

Divided Sentiment in Kentucky

When the Civil War began in April 1861, Kentuckians were badly at odds concerning the issues that had brought the nation to open warfare. The commonwealth was truly a border state. Kentuckians were so divided that the state's decision to declare neutrality may have made sense as a temporary measure to gain time. It should have been obvious that the policy could not be permanent.

Ties with the South were strong. Kentucky had been part of the Old Dominion, and many state families still cherished their Virginia associations. Others had come from North Carolina and Tennessee and had connections there. Slavery was an obvious and important tie with the South. Kentucky had benefited from the trade in slaves, livestock, and agricultural products with the Lower South. The state also shared the resentment of other slaveholding states against the abolitionists who attacked slavery, slaveholders, and any state that allowed slavery. The Mississippi River had provided a close bond with the South well before statehood. While the steamboat had increased the river traffic, it had also weakened the tie with the South by increasing upstream trade with Pittsburgh and the North. The first clear statement of states' rights had been in the Kentucky Resolutions of 1798 and 1799.

Yet the ties with the Union were also strong. An appreciable number of Kentuckians had connections with Pennsylvania and other northern states, and Kentuckians were proud of the reputation they had established in fighting for the nation in several wars. They had admired and respected Henry Clay for his devotion to the Union and his success as a compromiser in finding solutions to earlier crises. In recent years the railroad had forged important economic connections with the North and had lessened somewhat the pull of the Mississippi River. Some of the state's citizens did not approve of slavery, and many did not accept the doctrine that led to secession. Was secession the way to make a democratic government work?

The state's society was rent by the Civil War. Families divided, churches split, communities differed over the issues involved. Many participants could not have explained clearly why they chose the side they did. In the Crittenden family, George became a major general in the Confederate Army; brother Thomas held the same rank in the Union Army. Two of Robert J. Breckinridge's sons were in the Union Army, two fought with the Confederacy. Breckinridge was a strong Unionist; his nephew John C. Breckinridge was a Confederate general and cabinet member. Editor George D. Prentice was Unionist; both of his sons were Confederates. Slaveholding Samuel McDowell Starling of Hopkinsville joined the Union Army although he was over fifty years old; he lost one son fighting for the Confederacy, another one fighting for the Union. Such tragedies saddened many Kentucky families.

Sectional Disputes, 1854-1860

The Compromise of 1850 that was supposed to settle the sectional disputes came unraveled four years later. In January 1854 U.S. senator Stephen A. Douglas of Illinois introduced a bill to organize Nebraska as a territory. At least part of his motive was to enhance Chicago's chances of becoming the eastern terminus of a proposed railroad to the West Coast. Other routes were possible, and to get southern support for his bill Douglas agreed to add Kansas and to repeal that portion of the Missouri Compromise that prohibited slavery north of latitude 36°30' in the Louisiana Purchase. Douglas believed that issues should be solved through popular sovereignty: Let the voters in an area decide what they want to do. He grossly under-

estimated the growing antislavery sentiment and the determination of such persons to prevent the further spread of slavery. A struggle began at once to determine the future of slavery in Kansas. With the help of such organizations as the New England Emigrant Aid Society, the North was able to outstrip the South in populating the new territory. The Democratic Party divided over the issue, and the Know-Nothings made sharp gains. Most ominous from the southern perspective was the birth of the Republican Party. Confined to the North, it had no southern wing to compel moderation, and Republicans were adamant that slavery would not be allowed to expand into any new territory, including Kansas.

Kentuckians viewed the controversy with mixed reactions as civil war broke out in "Bleeding Kansas." A rigged election resulted in a proslavery Lecompton Constitution, which Douglas and others would not accept despite the efforts of President Franklin Pierce to get it approved. During this controversy the nation was excited by the news that Representative Preston Brooks of South Carolina had savagely caned Senator Charles Sumner of Massachusetts in the Senate chamber. Brooks resigned from the House, was reelected without opposition, and received scores of canes from southerners to replace the one he had shattered in such a good cause. In 1856 James Buchanan defeated Republican John C. Frémont by an electoral vote of 174-114. The Republicans had made phenomenal progress in just two years; they eagerly anticipated the 1860 election. Buchanan's vice president was John C. Breckinridge of Kentucky.

In 1851 Democrat Breckinridge had won the Whig stronghold that had been Henry Clay's. During his two terms in the House of Representatives (1851-55), he had become an eloquent defender of southern rights. When he refused to run for a third term, one of his Kentucky supporters warned, "You I think are a doomed man—doomed to a political life." In 1856 Breckinridge supported Pierce until his chances faded, then turned to Douglas. The

Kentuckian asked that his name not be added to the nine nominated for the vice presidency, but it was, and he was nominated on the second ballot. "Buck and Breck" won, and at age thirty-six Breckinridge became the nation's youngest vice president.

Buchanan failed to get Kansas admitted as a slave state. It entered the Union as a free state in 1861 after the secession of several slave states. Since a majority of the people in Kansas clearly objected to slavery, Douglas broke openly with the administration. On March 6, 1857, the U.S. Supreme Court handed the South a victory in the *Dred Scott* decision. The court ruled that the slave Dred Scott did not become free by being taken into a free state and free territory. He was not a citizen and could not sue in the federal courts. Furthermore, the prohibition on slaves in the Missouri Compromise had been unconstitutional. The South was vindicated in its contention that slavery could not legally be kept out of a territory. Chances of a compromise decreased. Why, many asked, should the South accept less than the *Dred Scott* decision?

Perceptive Kentuckians closely watched the Lincoln-Douglas debates in 1858 as the two men contested for the position of U.S. senator. At Freeport, Illinois, Lincoln asked Douglas if the people of a territory could legally exclude slavery prior to the formation of a state constitution over the objection of any citizen. Douglas remained true to his doctrine of popular sovereignty: slavery could be excluded by the failure of local authorities to provide protective legislation. Douglas won the election, but few southern Democrats would trust or accept him in the future. Lincoln became one of the leading Republicans.

The slaveholding South was frightened and outraged by John Brown's raid on Harpers Ferry, Virginia (now West Virginia), in October 1859. Virginia found him guilty of several crimes against the state and hanged him. A "Kentucky Gentleman" warned against that action in the *Kentucky Statesman* of November 28, 1859: hanging would make Brown a martyr to abolitionists. He was correct. Ralph Waldo Emerson, for example, wrote that Brown made "the gallows as glorious as the Cross." More southerners, including some Kentuckians, began to wonder if they could remain in the Union with people who held such a view.

The Election of 1860

The Democratic convention met in April 1860 in Charleston, South Carolina. John C. Breckinridge was nominated for the presidency, but he forbade any campaigning as long as James Guthrie's name was before the convention. When Douglas refused to accede to southern demands, many of the slave state delegates walked out of the convention. The convention adjourned to meet later in Baltimore. After another walkout there, in which ten of Kentucky's twenty-four delegates participated, Douglas was nominated by what had essentially become the Northern Democratic Party.

The southern Democratic delegates also met in Baltimore and gave Breckinridge 81 of 105 votes on the first ballot. He accepted the nomination from what was now the Southern Democratic Party. Varina Davis wrote years later that Breckinridge told her, "I trust I have the courage to lead a forlorn hope." He apparently hoped that he, Douglas, and John Bell would all withdraw and the factions would unite in favor of a candidate who could defeat Lincoln. Douglas rejected the scheme, saying that if he quit, many of his supporters would vote Republican.

The Republicans, meeting in Chicago in mid-May, drafted a platform that promised material benefits to various groups but refused to accept slavery in the territories. Lincoln's shrewd managers secured key votes with promises of cabinet positions, and he was nominated on the second ballot. The remnants of the Whig Party and the Know-Nothings, as well as voters who feared the consequences if any of the candidates was elected, joined to create the Constitutional Union Party and to

Vice president of the United States from 1857 to 1861, John C. Breckinridge left his post as U.S. senator in 1861 to become a Confederate general. In 1865 he was appointed Confederate secretary of war. This photograph was taken in Paris in August 1867. Breckinridge did not return to Kentucky until 1869 (from The Filson Club Historical Society).

nominate John Bell of Tennessee for the presidency. This ad hoc party advocated preservation of the Union as its goal.

Douglas violated political mores of that day by waging an exhaustive campaign, including forays into the South, in a vain attempt to reunite his shattered party. He faced squarely the question of secession: even the election of Lincoln would not justify secession by the southern states. Breckinridge made only one campaign address. The clerk of the Kentucky Court of Appeals had died, and his successor was to be elected that summer. The state Democratic convention nominated little-known Clinton McClarty; the Constitutional Unionists selected elderly Leslie Combs, who was also supported by many of the Douglas men. Breckinridge wrote on August 3 that he expected McClarty to win, and "nothing short of a defeat by 6,000 to 8,000 would alarm me for November." Combs won by more than twenty-three thousand votes, and an alarmed Breckinridge decided to defend his position at a great

barbecue held at Henry Clay's estate on September 5.

Although he was not well, Breckinridge spoke for three hours to a crowd estimated at between eight thousand and fifteen thousand. He refused to discuss the charge that he did not own slaves. (He had been a slaveholder, but he apparently was not in 1860. He had sold his home and was living in the Phoenix Hotel in Lexington.) He told the audience that his party accepted the principles announced by the Supreme Court in the *Dred Scott* decision, and he denounced Douglas for stating that the Court should decide the issues and then refusing to accept its decision. Breckinridge denied that he and his party sought to break up the Union: "I presently challenge the bitterest enemy I have had on earth, to point out an act, to disclose an utterance, to reveal a thought of mine hostile to the constitution and union of the States." The Republicans were the disunionists, he charged, because they hoped to take away the constitutional rights of the southern states. As to slavery in the territories, his party's stand had been reaffirmed by the Supreme Court.

In the November election Lincoln got 180 of the 303 electoral votes by carrying every northern state except New Jersey, where he won 4 of 7 electoral votes. Breckinridge secured 72 votes, Bell 39, and Douglas 12. Lincoln had a minority of the popular vote, receiving only 40 percent of the votes cast nationally. Despite his personal popularity, Breckinridge ran second to Bell in Kentucky. Bell received 45.18 percent of the state's vote, Breckinridge had 36.35 percent, Douglas got 17.54 percent, and Lincoln trailed badly with 0.93 percent.

On February 13, 1861, Vice President Breckinridge presided over the joint session of Congress that counted the electoral votes. Then he announced that Abraham Lincoln had been elected president of the United States.

Efforts to Find a Compromise

The sectional crisis became more serious when a South Carolina convention voted for secession on December 20, 1860. That state had already urged others to follow its example, and it was evident that at least some would do so. Once again in a time of crisis, efforts were made to find compromises that would avert the danger. Kentucky was actively involved in the four major efforts, for as a border state its political sentiments were badly mixed.

The House of Representatives established a Committee of Thirty-three, with a member from each state, and charged it to find a solution. Kentucky was represented by Francis Marion Bristow of Elkton. Both radical Republicans and radical secessionists declared that compromise was impossible. The committee recommended repeal of the personal liberty laws in the North, enforcement of the Fugitive Slave Act, and adoption of a constitutional amendment that would prevent Congress from ever interfering with slavery in the states that permitted it. The proposed amendment was accepted by Congress but never ratified by the states.

The Senate set up a Committee of Thirteen, on which John J. Crittenden served. Its members could find no agreement on the vital issue that had eluded the House committee: the future of slavery in the territories. On that point Lincoln refused to consider any compromise. "The tug has to come," he wrote, "& better now than later." He would accept an amendment protecting slavery in the states, and he would approve strict enforcement of the Fugitive Slave Act, but he would not budge from his party's position against the expansion of slavery.

Crittenden presented his own plan to the Senate on December 18. He proposed to reestablish the line of latitude 36°30', with slavery protected south of it; to let future states decide on slavery as they entered the Union; to prevent Congress from ending slavery in the District of Columbia as long as either Virginia or Maryland had slavery; to reimburse the owner if a fugitive slave was not returned; to provide strict enforcement of the Fugitive Slave Act; and to recommend that northern states repeal their personal liberty laws. Southerners would not support the plan unless the Republicans first gave their approval, and that they would not do. On January 3, 1861, Crittenden proposed that his plan be submitted to the people in a referendum. There was no precedent for such a popular vote, and the Republicans rejected the proposal.

The Peace Convention was a conference of delegates from twenty-one states who met in Washington on February 4, 1861, at the invitation of Virginia. Former president John Tyler presided behind the closed doors that many thought might facilitate open discussion. The absence of delegates from thirteen states, five of them from the North, doomed the conference from the start. Kentucky was represented by six delegates. The convention's report on February 27 called for seven constitutional amendments similar to those Crittenden had recommended; the report was rejected. The future of slavery in the territories

John J. Crittenden tried vainly in
1860-61 to find a compromise
to the sectional controversy. His
sons split between the North
and the South (from the
Kentucky Historical Society).

could not be compromised, and so agreement could not be reached.

Governor Magoffin in the Crisis

Beriah Magoffin (1815-85) had been governor for just over a year when Lincoln was elected. He believed that southern rights had been violated in regard to slavery, and he believed in slavery and a state's right to secede. He did not think that Lincoln's election justified such a drastic step, however, for Congress and the Supreme Court would be able to block the president and his party. Magoffin suggested a meeting of representatives of all the slave states to unite upon demands that would then be presented to a conference of all the states. Confronted with such an ultimatum, the North, he predicted, would accede to the southern demands rather than accept the dissolution of the Union. If his conditions were not met, the governor predicted that Kentucky would secede and join the other slave states.

On December 9, 1860, Magoffin sent a circular letter to the governors of the slave states in hopes of halting the move toward secession. He identified six points, outlining measures that he thought had to be accepted if the Union was to be preserved:

1. Amend the Constitution to see that the Fugitive Slave Act was enforced.
2. Provide full compensation to the owner if a fugitive slave was not returned.
3. Pass a law to require that a state render up to legal request any person who had been indicted for helping fugitives escape.
4. Divide the territories at latitude 37° and let that division determine slave or free status.
5. Amend the Constitution to guarantee free use of the Mississippi River to all states.
6. Amend the Constitution to give the minority South a way of protecting itself against oppressive slavery legislation. This protection would probably be accomplished via a sort of sectional veto in the Senate.

In late December Magoffin was visited in Frankfort by representatives from the governors of Alabama and Mississippi, who urged

Kentucky to join the secession movement. The governor on December 27 called a special session of the General Assembly for January 17, 1861. The legislature appointed six delegates to the Peace Conference, but on February 11 it refused to call a convention to determine the state's course of action. Instead, it adjourned until March 20 to see what might emerge from the various peace efforts. In the meantime, a number of the state's political leaders were making their positions known and trying to rally support for their views. Robert J. Breckinridge made a plea for moderation on January 4: Kentucky should not be hasty in leaving the Union to which it had so many ties. Four days later the leaders of the Douglas and Bell state parties met and advised against secession, although they added that the South had been wronged repeatedly. They called for adoption of the Crittenden compromise, and they appealed to moderates in the North to help check the drift toward disunion. But they added that a Union held together by force was not worth having. In effect, the two groups had merged into a Union Party.

Most of the Breckinridge Democrats also hoped for compromise within the Union, but they wanted a convention called to determine Kentucky's policy. Magoffin led the effort to secure it, but the Unionists were determined not to have one. According to the doctrine of states' rights, a convention was necessary to nullify an act of the federal government or to secede from it. Thus, if no convention was called, there was no danger of a stampede for separation. After his term as U.S. vice president ended, John C. Breckinridge had taken the Senate seat to which he had been elected. In the Senate he had become a major spokesman for the South, as senators departed when their states completed the secession process. On April 2 Breckinridge addressed the Kentucky legislature. After explaining his concept of the nation's being a limited confederation of equal states, he asserted that with adequate cause states could leave the Union. He blamed the Republicans for blocking all compromise ef-

forts, but he insisted that Kentucky should continue to work to secure adoption of the Crittenden proposals. Breckinridge called for a border state conference to draft a plan for conciliation to be submitted to the North and the South. If that approach failed, Breckinridge concluded, Kentucky would be "free to pursue whatever course her people may think consonant with her interest and her honor."

Before the conference could be held, the Civil War started when Fort Sumter was fired upon. President Lincoln then requested seventy-five thousand men to suppress the rebellion; Kentucky was asked to supply four regiments of militia for immediate use. Magoffin replied by telegram: "I say, *emphatically*, Kentucky will furnish no troops for the wicked purpose of subduing her sister Southern States." The Central Committee of the Union Party endorsed the governor's stand but insisted that the policy should also apply to requests from the so-called Confederate government. For the present, the Unionists asserted, Kentucky *"ought to hold herself independent of both sides*, and *compel both sides to respect the inviolability of her soil."*

The suggested neutrality was attractive to many Kentuckians who were uncertain of the path their state should take, although a state had no more right to declare neutrality than it did to secede. Crittenden endorsed neutrality in a Lexington speech on April 17, as did the Union Party's Central Committee. Prentice had advocated neutrality in the *Louisville Journal* since January. On April 20 he proclaimed in bold letters: "KENTUCKIANS! YOU CONSTITUTE TODAY THE FORLORN HOPE OF THE UNION." The Union leaders were, however, opposed to the government's use of force to subdue the southern states. In particular, they feared an invasion of Kentucky by the states north of the Ohio River.

Members of the State Rights Party had difficulty opposing neutrality, since it had such popular appeal. Their best hope of getting Kentucky to secede was to use the wave of secessionist excitement that followed the attack

This photograph of a standing Lincoln was taken by Matthew Brady. Because of his height, Lincoln preferred to be seated for portraits (from The Filson Club Historical Society).

on Fort Sumter. Virginia, Arkansas, Tennessee, and North Carolina seceded and joined the Confederate States of America, and Kentucky had close ties with three of these states. But the pro-Confederate Kentuckians were unable to get a convention called, and any deviation from that procedure would lose supporters. John C. Breckinridge said that neutrality was impracticable and untenable, but he hesitated to take drastic action. Some impetuous men wrote to Confederate authorities about raising troops. John Hunt Morgan (1825-64) addressed Jefferson Davis (1808-89): "Twenty thousand men can be raised to defend Southern liberty against Northern conquest. Do you want them?" Some ardent rebels went to other states to enlist in Confederate units; some staunch Unionists went to free states and enlisted in Union regiments.

Magoffin called a special session of the legislature to meet on May 6. He still hoped to get a sovereignty convention, and he believed that even a neutral Kentucky should arm itself. Early in the session the Union Party selected John J. Crittenden, Archibald Dixon, and Judge S. S. Nicholas to confer with State Rights representatives John C. Breckinridge, Richard Hawes, and Beriah Magoffin and to formulate a program for the state to follow. Breckinridge's request for a convention was rejected, and the sextet then agreed upon armed neutrality. The Unionists feared that the governor would not be impartial, and they insisted that a five-man military commission should direct the arming of the state. They agreed upon Simon Bolivar Buckner, the inspector general of the State Guard; each side was to appoint two members. The scheme collapsed when the State Righters named Magoffin to the commission. The Unionists would not accept him.

On May 16 the House resolved "that the State and the citizens thereof shall take no

When he married Mary Todd of Lexington, Lincoln gained another tie to his native state. Mrs. Lincoln enjoyed expensive clothes, and during the Civil War she contracted heavy debts (from the Illinois State Historical Library).

part in the civil war now being waged, except as mediators and friends to the belligerent parties; and that Kentucky should, during the contest, occupy the position of strict neutrality." The resolution passed 69-26, and the House then approved Magoffin's refusal to supply troops to the United States by a 89-4 vote. The Senate did not take action then, but on May 20 Governor Magoffin issued a proclamation of neutrality that sounded as if it had come from a foreign country. He warned both sides against violating the state's neutral status, and he called upon Kentuckians to remain at home, aloof from the struggle. Four days later, just before adjournment, the Senate passed a series of resolutions accepting neutrality by a vote of 13-9.

The 1861 Elections

Two summer elections in 1861 showed that the tide was turning against the State Righters. President Lincoln had called a special session of Congress to convene on July 4, and members of the House were elected on June 20. The Unionists in Kentucky waged an active campaign in an effort to win all ten seats. So many

of the State Righters decided not to participate that the total vote was less than half the number cast in the 1860 presidential election. Henry C. Burnett in the First District (the Jackson Purchase) was the only State Rights candidate to win. At the moment the results were seen as an endorsement of neutrality; later they would be considered as a vote for the Union and a rejection of the Confederacy.

The election for members of the Kentucky legislature was scheduled for August 5. After the June results, most voters assumed that the Unionists would record another victory; their margin of victory was the key issue. Would it be large enough to overturn the vetoes expected from Magoffin? Or would he be able to foil the wishes of the people? A key figure in the campaign was Joseph Holt, a resident of Louisville who had served as commissioner of patents, postmaster general, and secretary of war in the Buchanan administration. Holt had helped secure a peaceful inauguration for Lincoln, and he was determined that Kentucky should take its rightful place among the defenders of the Union. Camp Joe Holt, across the Ohio River in Indiana, was a recruiting center for Kentuckians who were impatient with their state's neutrality. Holt's vigorous campaign was aided by others, and the result was a Unionist majority of 76-24 in the Kentucky House and 27-11 in the Senate, although only half of the Senate seats were involved in the campaign. Once again, many State Righters stayed away from the polls.

After these victories the Unionists held firm control in Kentucky, except for the governorship. When Magoffin demanded that no Federal troops be recruited within the state, Lincoln suggested that the governor did not represent the wishes of the majority of Kentuckians.

A Fragile Neutrality

Kentucky's unique policy of neutrality was more or less respected by both sides for several months. Each feared that an overt violation might drive Kentucky into the other camp. In 1861 Kentucky was relatively a much larger state by population than it is today. In the U.S. House of Representatives, which was then just over half the present size, Kentucky had ten seats; now it has six. In population Kentucky then ranked ninth in the Union; in the value of livestock, fifth; in the value of farms, seventh; in the value of manufactures, fifteenth. In an era when armies still depended heavily upon horses for mobility, Kentucky's horses and mules were of inestimable value. The diversified agriculture of the state produced surpluses of corn, wheat, hemp, and flax. An unproved theory holds that the Confederates lost the Civil War when their supply of bourbon was cut off. If Kentucky joined the Confederacy, the South would have a good defense line along the Ohio River. On the other hand, a southern army poised in Kentucky would threaten to divide the North by driving to the Great Lakes. Kentucky's manpower would be an important asset to either side.

In addition, Kentucky was the most important of the four loyal slave states, and its decision might well determine how the others would go. Lincoln recognized clearly the pivotal importance of the state of his birth. As he wrote a friend, "I think to lose Kentucky is nearly the same as to lose the whole game. Kentucky gone, we cannot hold Missouri, nor, as I think, Maryland. These all against us, and the job on our hands is too large for us. We would as well consent to separation at once, including the surrender of the capital."[1]

Simon Bolivar Buckner (1823-1914) had an important role in the attempt to preserve neutrality. The dormant state militia had been revitalized in March 1860 by a law that he drafted. All white, able-bodied males between the ages of eighteen and forty-five were in the Enrolled Militia. From this group Buckner trained and equipped the Active Militia, better known as the State Guard. By January 1861 Buckner had sixty-one companies available in varying degrees of readiness. The State Guard was perceived as being prosouthern, and Unionists began to organize their own forces, called the Home Guard. Under a compromise reached with some difficulty, control of military affairs was taken from the governor and entrusted to a five-man board. Both forces engaged in a mad scramble for weapons, but the advantage went to the Home Guard when Lincoln sent five thousand "Lincoln guns" into the state for distribution among loyal units. William ("Bull") Nelson, a former naval officer, was in charge of their distribution and other secret Union activities in the state. Standing well over six feet tall and pushing scales upward three hundred pounds, Nelson was one of the most improbable undercover agents of the war. Several near clashes between rival units threatened conflict, but open warfare was avoided.

Buckner made agreements with General George B. McClellan, who commanded Federal troops north of the Ohio River, and Governor Isham Harris of Tennessee to respect Kentucky's neutrality. In July Buckner and

---

1. In 1860 Delaware, the fourth loyal slave state, had 1,798 slaves and 21,627 free blacks in a population of 112,216.

GOVERNOR MAGOFFIN'S NEUTRALITY means holding THE COCK OF THE WALK (*Uncle Sam*) while THE CONFEDERATE CAT (*Jeff Davis*) kills off his Chickens.

Kentucky's neutrality in 1861, as illegal in its way as secession, could be viewed in different ways. This is one interpretation of it (from *Harper's Weekly*, June 29, 1861, the Kentucky Historical Society).

Crittenden went to Washington to get Lincoln to reaffirm his acceptance of the policy. The president denied that he had "any present purpose" to send troops into the state, but he added an ambiguous qualifier: "I mean to say nothing which shall hereafter embarrass me in the performance of what seems to be my duty."

Violations of Kentucky neutrality became more frequent as the summer wore on. A Department of Kentucky had been organized by the U.S. government in May, and active recruiting centered around Camp Joe Holt, across the river from Louisville, and Camp Clay, opposite Newport. On July 1 Nelson was ordered to southeastern Kentucky to recruit three state and five Tennessee regiments. After the Union success in the August elections, he opened Camp Dick Robinson in Garrard County and began open recruiting. Magoffin demanded that the camp be closed and that Nelson leave the state; the camp was a flagrant violation of the state's policy. Lincoln refused the demand. The people of Kentucky wanted Federal assistance, he replied; the governor, who did not appear to want to preserve the Union, did not represent popular opinion. The Confederates had withdrawn recruiting agents from the state, but a steady stream of volunteers went to Camp Boone in northern Tennessee. On August 30 the Confederate Congress voted to recruit within Kentucky, and it made a secret appropriation of one million dollars "to aid the people of Kentucky in repelling any invasion or occupation of their soil by the armed forces of the United States."

By the late summer the prevailing sentiment had become so Unionist that the chief advocates of continued neutrality were secessionists. They realized that if Kentucky made a decision, the state would ally with the Union. The fragile policy of neutrality was in danger of being shattered.

The End of Neutrality

The extreme western part of the state was of great strategic importance because of the Mississippi, Cumberland, and Tennessee Rivers. Confederate general Gideon Pillow, commanding in western Tennessee, was obsessed with a desire to seize control of that area, particularly Columbus on the Mississippi River, but Buckner was able to dissuade Pillow from occupying the town on his own authority. Pillow's superior, General Leonidas Polk, an Episcopal bishop turned soldier, asked Magoffin on September 1 what the Southern Rights Party in Kentucky intended to do: "I think it is of the greatest consequence to the Southern cause in Kentucky and elsewhere that I should be ahead of the enemy in occupying Columbus and Paducah." In late August General John C. Frémont announced his intention of taking Columbus and put Ulysses S. Grant in charge of Union forces in southeastern Missouri. Kentucky's neutrality policy was obviously nearing its end.

191

Pillow and Polk made little effort to consult with Tennessee or with Confederate authorities about Kentucky's neutrality. On August 30 Harris assured Magoffin that Tennessee troops would continue to respect it; three days later those troops invaded Kentucky. On September 2 Polk learned that Federal troops had gone to Belmont, a river loading spot across the Mississippi from Columbus. Fearing that their next move would be to take Columbus, he ordered the eager Pillow to occupy the little river town first. Harris protested the move, the Confederate War Department ordered the troops withdrawn, and President Davis, saying that "the necessity justified the action," countered the order. This advance doomed the efforts of Buckner and other prosouthern Kentuckians to keep the state as a neutral buffer that would protect the Confederacy from attack on that sector.

Two days after Columbus was occupied, Grant moved into Paducah, and soon Louisville and other towns along the Ohio were occupied by Union soldiers. Polk told Magoffin that he would withdraw if the Federals did and if they would promise not to occupy any part of the state again. The *Kentucky Yeoman,* alluding to Nelson's activities, commented, "If Kentucky suffers one of the belligerents to occupy our soil, she cannot expect the other to keep off." Within a few days Confederate general Felix Zollicoffer moved through the Cumberland Gap area and occupied positions in eastern Kentucky to forestall Union advances there.

A Peace Convention was held in Frankfort on September 10 by State Righters, in a last effort to maintain a policy of strict neutrality. Among its delegates were several men who would soon be involved in the formation of a Confederate government of Kentucky. The convention had no success, for the state's Rubicon had been crossed. The troubled neutrality had ended. On September 11 the House by a 71-26 vote instructed the governor to order the Confederates to withdraw from the state.

Then, on a vote of 29-68, it defeated a motion to order both sides to withdraw. The Senate approved the Confederate-only expulsion order, 25-8. Magoffin vetoed it, and the legislature swiftly passed it over his objection. He then issued the order as directed. This pattern would become standard for the governor. He opposed measures he deemed wrong as long as he could, but then he faithfully carried them out. On September 18 the General Assembly again called for the Confederates to be expelled, and General Robert Anderson, the Union hero of Fort Sumter, was given command of the state volunteers he was authorized to enroll. Already in command of the Department of Kentucky, he moved his headquarters to Louisville.

Editor George D. Prentice expressed the sentiments of many fellow Unionists when he wrote, "Well, thank God, we at last have weighed anchor and set out for the haven of safety and honor." He could not know how long that voyage would last.

The Provisional Government of Confederate Kentucky

Some Kentuckians were disappointed and embarrassed by the state's decision to support the Union. On October 29-30 a convention met behind the Confederate lines in Russellville to see what could be done. Most of the delegates were self-appointed, although some military units may have held elections. Henry C. Burnett of Trigg County presided; George W. Johnson (1811-62), a Scott County Confederate activist, was the key figure. Since they could not use the prescribed convention method for secession, the members appealed to the revolutionary power of the people "to alter, reform, or abolish their government, in such manner as they may think proper." Charging that the Frankfort government had been replaced by a military despotism, the convention called for a sovereignty convention to meet in Russellville on November 18. A planning committee included Johnson, John C. Breckinridge, and Humphrey Marshall.

George W. Johnson, the first governor of Confederate Kentucky, was killed at Shiloh in April 1862 (courtesy of the Kentucky Historical Society).

At the second convention, on November 18-20, the delegates severed their connections with the United States and declared Kentucky a free and independent state. They formed a provisional government until such time as a convention could meet to establish a regular one. This government would consist of a governor and a council of ten members, one from each of the ten congressional districts, and such judges and other officials as might be needed. Bowling Green was made the capital, but in a moment of realism the governor and council were empowered "to meet at any other place that they deem appropriate." One of the first acts of the provisional government was to request admission into the Confederate States of America. Despite some qualms over the irregular procedure, the Confederacy admitted Kentucky on December 10, 1861.

George Johnson, the first governor of Confederate Kentucky, was a wealthy fifty-year-old farmer who had become convinced that the "Old Union" was being destroyed by radical groups in the North. He did not believe

that Lincoln's election justified secession, and he hoped for a compromise to the bitter sectional controversy. When he had to accept the secession of eleven states, Johnson reasoned that if Kentucky joined the Confederacy the sides would be so evenly matched as to preclude war. Then the two republics could form a free-trade union and work out amiable solutions to their problems. Johnson had been so prominent in the State Rights Party that he was certain to be arrested, so he fled southward when neutrality ended. After Bowling Green was occupied by Confederate troops, he went there and became a volunteer aide to General Buckner.

Johnson labored with little success to create a viable government. Its jurisdiction extended only as far as Confederate troops advanced, and many Unionists were behind the Confederate lines. When the army evacuated Bowling Green in mid-February 1862 as a part of its withdrawal from the state, Johnson and the council went with it. The capitol of Confederate Kentucky was an army tent.

Age and a crippled arm had appeared to preclude military service for Johnson, but on the evening of the first day's battle at Shiloh in April, he enlisted as a private in Company E of the Fourth Kentucky Infantry. The next day he was mortally wounded, and despite the best efforts of Union doctors, he died aboard a hospital ship on April 8. Near death he attempted to explain the motives that had brought him to Shiloh: "I wanted personal honor and political liberty and constitutional state government, and for these I drew the sword."

The cabinet selected Major Richard Hawes (1797-1877), a Paris attorney and businessman, as Johnson's successor. Active in the State Rights Party, Hawes had become a brigade commissary in Humphrey Marshall's command in eastern Kentucky, and he stayed there rather than become auditor in the provisional government. When Confederate forces invaded Kentucky late in the summer of 1862, Governor Hawes and the cabinet joined them, hoping to establish a government permanently in the state. Hawes was installed in Frankfort on October 4, and in his remarks he predicted that the Confederates would hold the state. But Union guns began to shell the town, the events scheduled for that evening were abandoned, and Hawes and the cabinet departed "in dignified haste." They left the state with the Confederate Army after the battle of Perryville, and they had no opportunity to return to Kentucky during the rest of the war. Confederate Kentucky also had its senators and representatives in the Confederate Congress, but they exerted little influence. When the Confederacy collapsed in the spring of 1865, the provisional Confederate government of Kentucky simply disappeared.

Magoffin Resigns

Governor Magoffin confused his opponents who viewed him as an avid Confederate. When he learned of the formation of the provisional government at Russellville, he denounced it in a letter to the *Louisville Journal*: "Self-constituted, as it was, and without authority from the people, it can not be justified by similar revolutionary acts in other States, by minorities to overthrow the State Governments. . . . My position is and has been and will continue to be, to abide by the will of a majority of the people of the State." This disclaimer did not convince his Unionist critics, and many of his powers and functions were taken away by legislative enactments. Federal brigadier general Jeremiah T. Boyle was his particular foe; the beleaguered governor was convinced that Boyle repeatedly violated the civil rights of suspected Confederate sympathizers. Magoffin sounded plaintive in his July 18, 1862, message calling for a legislative session to begin on August 14: "I am without a soldier or a dollar to protect the lives, property and liberty of the people, or to enforce the laws." His position had become intolerable.

Secret discussions had been under way to resolve the situation, and Magoffin had agreed to resign if his successor, although a Unionist, was "a conservative, just man . . . conciliatory and impartial toward all law-abiding citizens." Lieutenant Governor Linn Boyd had died in 1859, and Speaker of the Senate John F. Fisk, next in line of succession, did not meet the governor's requirements. On August 16, 1862, Fisk resigned as Speaker; James F. Robinson (1800-1882), a moderate conservative farmer-lawyer from Georgetown, was elected Speaker; and Magoffin announced that he would resign at ten o'clock on the morning of August 18. He did so, Robinson became governor, and Fisk was reelected Speaker of the Senate.

14

The
Civil War

Kentuckians at War

Civil War statistics are often inaccurate, and there is no exact count of Kentuckians who participated in the most costly of American wars when measured in number of deaths. The best estimates are that between twenty-five thousand and forty thousand Kentuckians fought for the Confederacy, between ninety thousand and one hundred thousand for the Union. The Confederates were all volunteers, for while the Confederacy started the draft a year before the Union did, the measure could not be applied in Kentucky because of Federal occupation. Many of the Union soldiers were also volunteers, but the draft forced a number into volunteering. The draft secured some men directly, but the provisions for commutation and substitutes raised protests that the conflict was "a rich man's war and a poor man's fight."

Black troops provided great assistance to the Union despite the storm of protest that their use aroused in Kentucky. Editor George Prentice feared a black insurrection in the slave states if the blacks were armed, and many other Unionist Kentuckians opposed the measure. Lincoln heeded the state's views on the issue until the need for manpower became overwhelming. By March 1864 the enlistment of blacks was under way in the state. Governor Thomas E. Bramlette (1817-75), who served from 1863 to 1867, intended to challenge Lincoln on the issue, but Robert J. Breckinridge and three other advisers persuaded Bramlette to accept the law. Black enlistments increased when whites failed to meet the state's quota for men. When black volunteering diminished during the summer of 1864, officials began seizing slaves and declaring them volunteers.

Until 1865 practically all the Kentuckians who fought in the Civil War did so in the western theater, which stretched from the mountains to the Mississippi River. Then, as some of the remaining Confederate units were pushed to the east by victorious Federal units after the fall of Atlanta, many Kentuckians on both sides saw brief service in the Atlantic states. Kentuckians in both armies participated in nearly all the battles and campaigns in the western theater.

The best known of the Confederate units was the Orphan Brigade, the First Kentucky Brigade. Its name may have come from its heavy losses at the battle of Stones River near Murfreesboro, Tennessee, or perhaps from the fact that the unit went for most of the war without seeing Kentucky. John Hunt Morgan's cavalry was another of the famed Confederate units. Colonel Frank L. Wolford's First Kentucky Cavalry, called the Wild Riders, was probably the best-known Union military unit from the state. The Wild Riders clashed often with Morgan's men.

Early Engagements, 1861-1862

On September 10, 1861, General Albert Sidney Johnston, a native of Washington, Kentucky, was given command of Confederate Department No. 2, which stretched from the mountains to the Indian territory. Johnston first established headquarters in Nashville, ordering Buckner to occupy Bowling Green. When Buckner's troops arrived in Bowling Green on September 18, they found that many of the Unionists had fled. One elderly lady who met them clutched her Bible and declared that she was "prepared to die." In October Johnston moved his headquarters to Bowling Green and had the hills in and around the town strongly fortified. He assumed that when a Union army advanced, it would use the Louisville and Nashville Railroad and the Louisville-Nashville turnpike, and Bowling Green would be the site of the critical battle for Kentucky.

With too few soldiers to defend every sector of Johnston's long line, the Confederates held a few strong points across the southern part of the state: Cumberland Gap, Bowling Green, and Columbus. They also held Forts Henry and Donelson on the Tennessee and Cumberland Rivers in northern Tennessee. Henry and Donelson had been constructed south of the state boundary because of Kentucky's neutrality, and both forts were poorly sited.

Neither side was prepared for war. Both needed men, training, and supplies of almost every type. Each commander was sure that his men were greatly outnumbered by his opponent's. When Union commander Robert Anderson's health gave way, he was replaced as head of the Department of the Cumberland by General William T. Sherman in October 1861. Then Don Carlos Buell replaced Sherman in November after the latter had a nervous breakdown. General Henry W. Halleck in St. Louis commanded the western part of the state with Ulysses S. Grant, who soon saw the strategic value of the Cumberland and Tennessee Rivers.

The rival forces began to gain some military experience in a number of small-scale engagements across the commonwealth. The Green River country became a sort of no-man's-land, with a great deal of scouting activity and numerous skirmishes. The most important of the early engagements occurred at Rockcastle Hills, in Laurel County, on October 21, 1861. Confederate general Felix Zollicoffer wanted to move into central Kentucky, but he was checked by a Union force commanded by General Albin Schoepf. General William ("Bull") Nelson forced Confederate troops commanded by Colonel John S. Williams out of the Big Sandy Valley by winning at Ivy Mountain on November 8. When Benjamin Franklin Terry was killed at Rowlett's Station on December 17, 1861, his men decided to call themselves Terry's Texas Rangers, to commemorate their fallen leader and the state from which he and they had come. A clash at Sacramento on December 28 included three men who later became Civil War generals; the most noted was the untrained military genius of the Confederacy, Nathan Bedford Forrest. Other clashes occurred at Hazel Green, West Liberty, Saratoga, Morgantown, Woodbury, and a score of other localities.

When Zollicoffer became convinced that the Federals would attack somewhere west of Cumberland Gap, he shifted most of his troops to Mill Springs, a tiny community on the south bank of the Cumberland River. He crossed to the north side of the river after he heard that General George H. Thomas was advancing in that direction. When George B. Crittenden took command of the Confederate troops, he found them in a dangerous position with a flooded river at their backs. Nevertheless, the Confederates launched an attack on the rainy, foggy morning of January 19, 1862, before Thomas pulled all of his army together. In the confusion of the state's first sizable battle, Zollicoffer rode into Union lines and was killed. After fierce fighting that resulted in 522 Confederate and 262 Union casualties, Crittenden managed to withdraw across the river that night. Thomas shifted westward to cooperate with Buell's anticipated advance on Bowling Green.

Near the end of January 1862, Grant got permission to move against Forts Henry and Donelson. He was aided by Union gunboats, and Fort Henry was so flooded that the small garrison that fought a rearguard action while their comrades escaped to Donelson surrendered to the Union navy on February 6, before the Union army arrived. Johnston had not visited Donelson. Now he sent Generals John B. Floyd, Gideon Pillow, and Simon Buckner there to save it, but he admitted in a letter to Floyd on February 8 that "I cannot give you specific instructions and place under your command the entire force." That decision was an unfortunate delegation of authority: Floyd was a successful politician but an incompetent general. Grant's outnumbered force should have been attacked on its way to Donelson, before it was reinforced. The Confederates instituted no

such action, and on the bitterly cold morning of February 15 hard-fighting Confederates had almost opened an escape route to Nashville when they were ordered to return to their positions. Floyd turned command over to Pillow and escaped on the only available steamboat. Pillow turned command over to Buckner and escaped in a rowboat. Buckner endured the shame of having to accept Grant's demand for unconditional surrender of more than sixteen thousand men. That done, Grant, who had been a year ahead of Buckner at West Point, took Buckner aside and offered him money if he needed any. Forrest, furious at Floyd's stupidity and timidity, escaped with his men before the surrender became final. The sixteen thousand men could well have made the difference at Shiloh in April.

Johnston had realized that he could not hold Bowling Green after the losses at Mill Springs and Fort Henry. Evacuation began on February 11 and was completed three days later. The Confederates destroyed the two Barren River bridges, the railroad depot, and equipment and supplies that could not be removed. Federal artillery briefly shelled the city from the north side of the river, and fires destroyed several businesses around the town square. Union troops occupied Bowling Green for the rest of the war. Almost ignored, Columbus was not abandoned by the Confederates until February 27 and was not occupied by the Federals for another three days.

Johnston could not make a stand in Nashville, for Union gunboats on the Tennessee River could cut his supply line, just as that threat on the Cumberland River had endangered his position at Bowling Green. Many of the supplies massed at Nashville had to be burned, and criticism of Johnston increased. President Jefferson Davis resisted all demands that he remove his friend from command. "If Sidney Johnston is not a general," Davis told a critic, "we have no general." Determined to strike Grant, who was moving southward, Johnston concentrated his army at Corinth, Mississippi, where Generals Braxton Bragg

Part of Bowling Green's main square was burned in mid-February 1862, as the Confederates evacuated the town. This is the only known representation of the courthouse with its cupola (courtesy of the Kentucky Library, Western Kentucky University).

and Pierre G.T. Beauregard brought reinforcements. Johnston planned to strike Grant and his thirty-nine thousand troops before Buell could arrive from Nashville with his army of thirty-six thousand. Johnston had approximately forty-four thousand men.

Planning was poor, and the attack was delayed, but the Confederates achieved tactical surprise on Sunday, April 6, 1862. Johnston declared, "Tonight we will water our horses in the Tennessee River." For a time it appeared that he would succeed in doing so, as the surprised Federals gave ground. But Union artillery cost the Confederates heavy losses, and fire from the gunboats aided the artillery. Some Union units fought well. General Benjamin Prentiss rallied his men in a spot afterward known as the Hornets' Nest, and they beat off eleven Confederate assaults before surrendering about 5:30 P.M. His stand helped give Grant time to rebuild his shattered line. By then Johnston was dead. Shortly after two o'clock a bullet had severed an artery in his right leg. He carried a tourniquet in his pocket, but he was dying before anyone realized that he had been seriously wounded. Beauregard continued to push the attack, but stubborn Union resistance, the exhaustion of the Confederates, and the coming of night brought a halt to the savage fighting.

Buell's troops began to reach Shiloh during the night, and the Union army was reorganized. At dawn the Federals launched an attack and soon recovered the ground lost the previous day. By early afternoon the Confederate army was retreating. The expected battle of Bowling Green had been fought at Shiloh in Mississippi, and the Confederates lost.

The Confederate Invasion, Summer 1862

Until the late summer of 1862 Kentucky was the scene of cavalry raids and skirmishes, as small Confederate detachments tried to cut supply lines and recruit men and horses. In June, Union general George W. Morgan achieved an easy victory by outflanking Cumberland Gap and forcing the Confederates stationed there to withdraw. During this lull in the war, John Hunt Morgan (1825-64) made the first of his famous raids into Kentucky.

Born in Alabama, John Hunt Morgan came to Lexington with his family when he was five. After attending Transylvania University, he saw active duty in the Mexican War, then became a successful businessman and community leader in Lexington. When the state's neutrality ended, Morgan led his elite company of Lexington Rifles to Bowling Green. Even before being mustered into Confederate service, he began the scouting and raiding that became his trademark. A fondness for independent command also became a noted Morgan characteristic. Promoted to colonel in April 1862, Morgan fought at Shiloh. His command was then organized as the Second Kentucky Cavalry. His second in command and brother-in-law, Basil W. Duke, along with an eccentric Englishman, George St. Leger Grenfell, helped supply the discipline and training the men needed. In May Morgan returned to Kentucky with a small detachment and seized trains on the L&N at Woodburn and Cave City. That limited success whetted his desire for a larger raid.

Starting from Knoxville on July 4, 1862, Morgan made a sweep through the central part of Kentucky, going as far north as Cynthiana. His 876-man command included some 370 Kentuckians, some of whom made hasty visits to their families. The unit moved rapidly, and an adept telegrapher, George ("Lightning") Ellsworth, confused Union commanders by sending them misleading orders. The confusion became so great that Lincoln wired General Halleck: "They are having a stampede in Kentucky. Please look to it." In just over three weeks Morgan's men captured seventeen towns, captured and then paroled twelve hundred Union soldiers, dispersed fifteen hundred members of the Home Guard, used or destroyed great quantities of supplies, recruited three hundred men—and lost only ninety from their own ranks. As a result of these actions, thousands of Union troops were stationed far behind the front lines to guard important facilities such as the soaring railroad bridge across the Green River at Munfordville. Back in Tennessee, Morgan's glowing account of his success encouraged others to think of invading Kentucky.

Some Confederates still believed that most Kentuckians only awaited an opportunity to display their true sympathies. Confederate major general Edmund Kirby Smith, commander of the Department of East Tennessee, was itching to invade Kentucky. Like so many

Confederate commanders, he was afflicted with an incurable obsession for independent command. He conferred with Braxton Bragg, his superior, in Chattanooga on July 31. Bragg agreed to an invasion, but he wanted Smith's army to combine with his own and defeat Buell's army in Tennessee before making the attempt at Kentucky. Their plans were vague and subject to different interpretations. Bragg and Smith would operate separately until they met in Kentucky; Bragg would then command the joint forces.

Smith began his move on August 13. Moving through the Cumberland Mountains, the Confederates captured Barbourville on August 18. Humphrey Marshall was bringing three thousand men from western Virginia, and Smith hoped to trap the Union troops guarding Cumberland Gap. Once inside Kentucky, Smith contended that the absence of supplies in that region forced him to advance into the Bluegrass. This left Bragg to fend for himself; there would not be a consolidation of forces in the near future. When Smith learned that Union reinforcements were being rushed to Richmond, he decided to attack before they arrived. Bull Nelson had intended to defend along the Kentucky River, but instead of retiring to that line, General Mahlon Manson advanced south of Richmond to give battle. After several hours of hard fighting on August 30, the Union line collapsed. Nelson, who had rushed to the scene, tried to form another line. Marching his vast bulk back and forth in front of his nervous men, he proclaimed, "If they can't hit me, they can't hit anybody!" Then he was struck twice, although not mortally wounded, and the rout was on. The Union lost over 75 percent of the sixty-five hundred men engaged.

The Confederates captured Lexington on September 2 and Frankfort on September 3. Frankfort was the only capital of a loyal state captured by Confederates during the war. The Union government fled to Louisville, and panic hit such river towns as Newport, Covington, Cincinnati, and Louisville. Smith's army had cut the supply line of Union general George W. Morgan, who held Cumberland Gap, and he had to evacuate his eight-thousand-man force. Expecting General Morgan to use the good roads along the eastern side of the Bluegrass in an attempt to escape, Smith moved his main force of some twelve thousand men to Mount Sterling, in order to reinforce Humphrey Marshall's small army of three thousand men. John Hunt Morgan was sent to scout the Federal movements and to harass the Union soldiers in their flight northward. George Morgan conducted a brilliant retreat through the mountains to Greenupburg on the Ohio River. His exhausted troops ceased to be a factor in the campaign, and Smith had opened the Cumberland Gap route that the Confederates used when they left the state after the battle at Perryville.

Bragg did not leave Chattanooga until August 28. His army had dwindled, in part because he had reinforced Kirby Smith, and he decided to elude Buell and move into Kentucky, where his army would combine with that of Smith. When Bragg reached Glasgow he learned that Buell was moving rapidly through Nashville on his way to Bowling Green. Bragg should have hastened to effect a concentration with Smith, but he had already wasted three days at Sparta, Tennessee, and now he wasted another three at Munfordville, Ken-

tucky, the site of one of the war's most unusual incidents. A Union detachment guarded the vital railroad bridge across the Green River near the town. It beat off some small-scale Confederate attacks, and when thirty-two-year-old colonel John T. Wilder was told to surrender to avoid further bloodshed, he replied tartly, "If you want to avoid further bloodshed, keep out of the range of my guns." Bragg had not wanted to delay at Munfordville, but he decided that the position had to be taken. The Confederates moved to Munfordville and surrounded the defiant Federals, then made a last demand for surrender. Wilder, an iron manufacturer, did not know what to do. Under a flag of truce on the evening of September 16, he paid Simon Buckner a supreme compliment. He asked the Confederate, whom he had never met before, what was militarily correct under such circumstances. Buckner was so caught up in the affair that he conducted the colonel and an aide around the Confederate lines so that they could see that they were hopelessly outnumbered. The next morning Wilder surrendered more than four thousand men. Bragg had spent another three days in that area while Buell's forces flowed northward, to the west of the Confederates.

On September 25 the Federals reached Louisville, where they received heavy reinforcements and supplies. Bragg turned aside

General Don Carlos Buell's army got around the invading army of Confederate general Braxton Bragg and reached Louisville on September 25, 1862. A few days later Buell began the advance that led to the battle of Perryville on October 8 (from Lowell H. Harrison, *The Civil War in Kentucky* [1975; 1988]).

to Bardstown, where he expected to meet Smith but failed to find him. Both Confederate commanders were disappointed in the failure of Kentucky men to enlist under the Stars and Bars. "Their hearts were evidently with us," Smith wrote Bragg, "but their bluegrass and fat-grass [cattle] are against us." Bragg and Smith wanted recruits to help win victories; cautious Confederate sympathizers wanted to see victories before making a commitment. Bragg's comments about cowardly men made him the most unpopular Confederate general with many Kentuckians.

Moving with unexpected speed, Buell left Louisville on October 1. Three columns advanced toward Bardstown while a fourth one moved in the direction of Frankfort. Bragg was not at Bardstown to direct the consolidation of the scattered Confederate units. He met with Kirby Smith and Richard Hawes in Lexington on October 2. Bragg and Smith agreed to install Hawes in Frankfort on October 4; he had been sworn in when he became governor of Confederate Kentucky. One advantage of his installation was psychological: it would help the morale of Confederate sympathizers who had chafed under Union occupation. It would also make possible the enforcement of the conscription law that the Confederate Congress had passed in April 1862. If the Kentuckians would not volunteer, Bragg would draft them. Shortly after noon on a rainy October day, Bragg introduced Hawes to the crowd that packed the hall of the House of Representatives and overflowed into the rest of the capitol. Hawes assured his fellow Kentuckians that his government was there to stay. Later that afternoon, after Union shelling began, the Confederates burned the bridges over the Kentucky River and abandoned Frankfort.

By the evening of October 7 most of Buell's troops were nearing Perryville, where stagnant pools in the Chaplin River held some desperately needed water, a scarce commodity in the drought-stricken state. Some fifty-eight thousand Union soldiers were in the vicinity, and twenty thousand were near Frankfort.

Bragg had ordered a consolidation of his and Smith's armies at Harrodsburg; he expected to fight Buell south of Lawrenceburg. When he learned of the Union advance, Bragg stopped William Hardee at Perryville, then reinforced him with Leonidas Polk's men and another division. The Confederates were to destroy what Bragg believed was a small Union force, then go on to Harrodsburg. Polk and Hardee had about sixteen thousand men, approximately one-third of the Confederate soldiers in the state. Bragg was angry when he arrived at ten o'clock on the morning of October 8 and found that the Union force was not being attacked. He ordered an advance with the main thrust being against the Union left, but Polk was not ready to move until two o'clock. Then in several hours of desperate fighting, the Union First Corps was driven back more than a mile, with some units in shambles. Joseph Wheeler's cavalry held the Union Second Corps in check, and a Confederate brigade engaged the attention of the Third Corps. When Buell finally realized the plight of his First Corps, he sent help. That assistance, darkness, and fatigue halted the Confederate advance. In the state's bloodiest battle of the war, the Union had lost 845 killed, 2,851 wounded, and 515 missing; the Confederate losses were 510 dead, 2,635 wounded, and 251 missing.

When he conferred with his generals that evening, Bragg finally realized the odds his men had faced that day. He decided to withdraw to Harrodsburg and unite there with Kirby Smith. That position was still dangerous, and the Confederates moved to Bryantsville. The vital thing was to save the army, and after consulting with his generals, Bragg ordered a retreat through Cumberland Gap. Joseph Wheeler provided effective rearguard protection, the Union pursuit was lackadaisical, and the Confederates escaped through the difficult terrain. The high tide of the Confederate military effort in the western theater was receding. Many of the Kentuckians who left with Bragg did not see Kentucky again until the war was over. Others never saw Kentucky again at all.

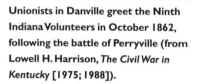

Unionists in Danville greet the Ninth
Indiana Volunteers in October 1862,
following the battle of Perryville (from
Lowell H. Harrison, *The Civil War in
Kentucky* [1975; 1988]).

Humphrey Marshall stayed in the state
until attention was turned toward him. Then
he retreated to his fastness in the western Virginia mountains. (Brigadier General Marshall,
whose bulk rivaled that of Nelson, doted on
independent command. When a friend once
discovered him in a remote mountainous area,
he asked if Marshall was hiding from the
Yankees. "No," Marshall replied, "from Confederate major generals.") Granted permission to raid behind the Union lines, John
Hunt Morgan led his brigade on a long sweep
through Lexington, Bardstown, Elizabethtown, and Hopkinsville to the safety of Tennessee. This gesture of defiance helped sagging
Confederate morale.

General Halleck wrote Buell of the president's displeasure with Bragg's escape. Lincoln,
said Halleck, "does not understand why we
cannot march as the enemy marches, live as he
lives, and fight as he fights, unless we admit the
inferiority of our troops and our generals."
Buell was soon removed from command and
ordered to Indianapolis to await orders that
were never sent.

The Raids Continue

The Confederates did not again invade Kentucky in strength, but raiding continued, although the state was often hundreds of miles
from the main scenes of fighting. The raids
were designed to tie down Union troops and

keep them from the fighting front, to disrupt
the Union supply system, to recruit men and
secure horses and supplies, and to give at least
some Kentuckians a chance to see family and
friends, however briefly.

Morgan continued to follow the pattern
established in his first raid and his swing behind
Buell's army. Despite the hard riding and the
danger involved, there was an air of romance
and adventure about his early forays. The
myths of knighthood were in flower; Sir Walter
Scott might have written the accounts of Morgan's exploits. His 1862 Christmas Raid, starting just days after his December wedding to
twenty-one-year-old Martha ("Mattie") Ready
of Murfreesboro, Tennessee, ended in abominable weather. But in two hectic weeks Morgan's men covered four hundred miles in
central Kentucky, tore up twenty miles of railroad track, destroyed an estimated two million
dollars' worth of supplies, fought four engagements and numerous skirmishes, and captured
and then paroled 1,857 prisoners—at a cost of
two killed, twenty-four wounded, and sixty-
four missing. Some of the wounded and
missing later rejoined the unit.

Then in the summer of 1863 Morgan received permission to enter Kentucky to raid
Louisville, which had never been attacked. His
raid might also distract attention from Bragg's
army as it shifted from Tullahoma to Chattanooga. Morgan did not raid Louisville, and he

ignored an order not to cross the Ohio River; he told Basil Duke that they might ride east and join General Robert E. Lee's army. Morgan's insubordination seemed to trigger a string of misfortunes after the 2,460 men crossed the swollen Cumberland River on July 2, 1863. A rash frontal attack against a Union detachment at Tebbs Bend near Columbia cost seventy-one casualties; nineteen-year-old Tom Morgan, the commander's brother, was killed at Lebanon. Once in Indiana and Ohio, Morgan created so much consternation along the Ohio Valley that one almost forgets that only a few hundred of his men escaped death or capture. When Morgan surrendered in Ohio on July 26, only 363 men remained with him.

After his famous escape from prison in late November, Morgan was restored to command, although doubts about his performance were growing. Anxious to redeem his reputation, Morgan led his fourth raid in June 1864 before he could be stopped. Grenfell had left, and Duke was still in a Union prison; Morgan lost control of his troops. Considerable looting and burning occurred in several Kentucky towns. A Mount Sterling bank was robbed of some seventy-two thousand dollars, and when Morgan's senior colonels pressed for an immediate investigation and punishment of the guilty, the commander replied that there was not time. A brief moment of glory came at Cynthiana on June 11, when the Confederates captured General Edward Hobson and some nine hundred Union soldiers. Morgan ignored warnings that his command should keep moving, and at early dawn the next morning they were surprised and shattered by Union general Stephen Burbridge.

When Morgan still refused to investigate outrages or restore discipline, some of his senior people appealed directly to the Confederate War Department. On August 30, 1864, the Thunderbolt of the Confederacy was relieved of his command. He was to face a court of inquiry on September 10, but in a characteristic reaction, he resumed command when he learned of the approach of a Federal force. John

Hunt Morgan was disobeying a direct order when he was surprised and killed in Greeneville, Tennessee, on September 4. Morgan was a proud man, and he may have preferred to depart that way.

One of Confederate general Nathan Bedford Forrest's raids was into western Kentucky. Forrest held an independent command in western Tennessee and northern Mississippi after telling Bragg that he would never obey another order from him. Forrest had some dismounted Kentuckians for whom he needed horses and supplies, and learning that both were available at Paducah, he led twenty-eight hundred men to that river town in March 1864. Union troops found refuge in a strong fort under the protective fire of Federal gunboats while the Confederates gathered the supplies they urgently needed. The raiders retired so leisurely to Tennessee that newspaper accounts of their foray caught up with them. One story gleefully reported that the Confederates had missed a consignment of especially fine horses destined for the Union cavalry. Incensed by the story, Confederate general Abraham Buford, owner of a fine stock farm near Versailles, took his brigade back to Paducah. On April 14 they drove the Federals back into their fort and found 140 excellent horses concealed in a foundry, where the newspaper had reported they were.

One of the most spectacular raids of the war came in the summer of 1862 and resulted in the first Confederate capture of a Union town north of the Mason-Dixon Line. Adam Johnson, a native of Henderson County, had an exciting career in Texas before returning east in 1861 and becoming a scout for Forrest. In the summer of 1862 he was operating behind Union lines in Kentucky. Disappointed in his efforts to recruit, Johnson decided to go to war with what he had. On June 29 he and two men attacked the Union detachment at Henderson. They killed an officer and wounded ten men before being driven off. On July 5, with a force increased to six men, Johnson assaulted a six-hundred-man Federal camp at Madisonville.

The group drove the enemy out of the camp and inflicted several casualties before having to retire. Leading an army of thirty men, Johnson was disappointed at finding Henderson unoccupied when he returned there on July 17.

When he learned that guns were available at Newburgh on the Indiana shore of the Ohio River, Johnson used two pairs of wagon wheels, a piece of stovepipe, and a length of charred log to mount what appeared to be two cannon aimed toward Newburgh. He and two men rowed across the river while others in his command went to the nearest ferry for passage. The intrepid commander was greatly relieved when eighty armed men surrendered to him. Confronted by 350 Home Guards, Johnson told them that he was there to get guns and other supplies; if they did not interfere, he would soon be gone. Then he directed their attention to the battery across the river. If they interfered, he said, "I'll shell this town to the ground." The Confederates were not bothered as they loaded impressed wagons with weapons and medical supplies and departed after paroling 180 Union soldiers, most of them patients in a hospital. "Stovepipe" Johnson became a Confederate hero.

Most of the Confederate raids were of brief duration, quick slash-and-run affairs conducted before Union forces could be organized to cut off the raiders' escape. Some incursions, however, lasted longer. One such was led by Colonel Roy S. Cluke, commander of the Eighth Kentucky Cavalry in Morgan's brigade. On February 18, 1863, he took his reinforced regiment of some 750 men across the Cumberland River into an area east of Lexington, centering around Mount Sterling. Most of the men were from Bluegrass counties, and as circumstances permitted, Cluke allowed them brief visits to their homes, where they were expected to acquire horses and clothing. Small detachments went out in different directions to confuse the Federal units that were trying to locate and exterminate them. Although his men were plagued by illness, Cluke remained

in the area for more than a month, until ordered to rejoin Morgan. He was reported to have returned with eighteen more men than he had at the start of the expedition, and the Confederacy was relieved of feeding 750 men and horses for that period. This and similar expeditions caused great embarrassment to the Union commanders who were unable to destroy the raiders, but they did not constitute a serious enough problem for the Union leaders to bring troops back from the main campaigns to stop the incursions.

Guerrilla Warfare, 1863-1865

Guerrilla warfare usually consisted of doing damage behind enemy lines while trying to avoid a general engagement. Small parties sought to disrupt communication and supply lines, destroy military property, secure horses, and strike small outposts and isolated units. A distinction should be drawn between regular army units that carried on such activities and groups that operated without official sanction. The distinction was sometimes a very fine one, and the military status of a group was often a topic for disagreement. Unionists often called John Hunt Morgan a guerrilla, but his was a regular unit in the Confederate Army that employed guerrilla tactics. Less definite was Adam ("Stovepipe") Johnson's Tenth Kentucky Cavalry, which operated for more than a year in western Kentucky as a group of partisan rangers. Others, sometimes called war-rebels, had some association with the Confederate military, although the link was often tenuous and was seldom recognized by Union authorities. Then there were outlaws who took advantage of unsettled conditions to operate on their own. They preyed upon anyone, regardless of allegiance to the Union or the Confederacy. During the last two years of the war, and even beyond the war's end, these desperadoes terrorized much of Kentucky. No county was safe from their outrages.

Most notorious of the guerrillas was William Clarke Quantrill, who had gone through an apprenticeship in "Bleeding Kansas" before the war and continued his nefarious career during it. In January 1865 he brought several dozen followers into Kentucky near Canton, then hit such towns as Hartford, Hustonville, and Danville as he worked his way eastward. When Federal troops failed to catch Quantrill and his men, Major General John M. Palmer employed Edwin Terrill, a leader of Union guerrillas in Spencer County, to do the job. Terrill caught Quantrill near Bloomfield on May 10, 1865. Seriously wounded, Quantrill died in a Louisville military prison on June 6 before he could be hanged. The last of his men surrendered on July 26.

"Sue Mundy" had been Captain M. Jerome Clarke in Morgan's command until after Morgan's death. Then Clarke returned to Kentucky in October 1864 and began his own war. The question of his identity and gender intrigued the newspapers and the public, and Sue Mundy received widespread publicity. An informer enabled Federals to capture Clarke and two companions in a tobacco barn in Meade County on March 12, 1865. His plea for military treatment as a prisoner of war was rejected, and he was tried and hanged on March 15.

Among the other men considered guerrillas by the Union authorities were George Jesse, who had remained in the state after Morgan's debacle at Cynthiana, and Henry C. Magruder, who was captured with Sue Mundy and hanged on October 29, 1865.

Union authorities assumed that guerrillas were pro-Confederate. In June 1862 General Jeremiah T. Boyle, the military commander of Kentucky, announced that disloyal persons in any county would pay for damages done to loyal citizens. In August 1864 alleged Confederate sympathizers in and near Morganfield in Union County were assessed thirty-two thousand dollars to cover such losses. In October persons considered disloyal within ten miles of Caneyville had to raise thirty-five thousand dollars. Similar fines were levied in other parts of the state. In January 1864 Gover-

nor Thomas E. Bramlette ordered five rebel sympathizers held hostage for each loyal citizen carried off by guerrillas. That summer General Burbridge ordered four guerrilla prisoners shot for each Union man who was killed. Several legitimate Confederate prisoners of war were apparently executed as a result of this order. In October 1864 Burbridge ordered that "hereafter, no guerrillas will be received as prisoners." Guerrilla warfare was one of the worst aspects of the war in Kentucky. Many civilians suffered from the depredations of guerrillas and from the illegal methods used to combat them.

Civil-Military Relations

Union troops were in Kentucky from September 1861 until after the end of the war, and relations between them and the civilian government were often strained. The Union military commanders had to contend with a major Confederate invasion, numerous raids, and guerrilla warfare that became worse toward the end of the conflict. They knew that a sizable number of Kentuckians sympathized with the southern cause. In late 1864 a Federal War Department agent in the state declared that "a large majority of Kentuckians are today undoubtedly disloyal." In their efforts to maintain control in the state, the Federal military authorities often resorted to measures that were illegal and even unconstitutional. Many Kentuckians, including some of the most loyal, were convinced that they were treated as if their state was in rebellion.

The General Assembly elected in 1861 passed a number of laws restricting Confederate sympathizers. Loyalty oaths were required of teachers, ministers, and jurors, in addition to public officials. Kentuckians who enlisted in the Confederate armies, who encouraged others to enlist, or who invaded the state were subject to severe penalties. A number of ministers were arrested and sent to prisons in the North, as was former governor Charles Slaughter Morehead. Provost marshals were appointed to each county to enforce the Union regulations. On July 1, 1862, General Boyle ordered the provosts "to fit up quarters for the imprisonment of such disloyal females as they may find it necessary to arrest." Later that month he ordered a Newport prison prepared for "rebel females," who would be required to sew for the Federal troops.

Boyle's general order on July 21, 1862, said that "no person hostile in opinion to the government and desiring its overthrow, will be allowed to stand for office in the district of Kentucky." An attempt to do so would indicate treasonable intent and would justify arrest. Federal officials and troops frequently interfered with elections. For example, the August 4, 1862, local elections for county officials resulted in Union Party victories; few opponents were even allowed to run for office. The press was also impeded. Two religious newspapers in Louisville were suppressed by military order in July 1862, and one of the editors was arrested. Such incidents continued during the war, and resentment increased. The Lincoln administration was held responsible, and in the 1864 presidential election the state's voters expressed their displeasure. Democrat George B. McClellan defeated Republican Abraham Lincoln in Kentucky by 64,301 to 27,786 popular votes. McClellan, who had been a ranking Union officer until he was removed from command, won the vote of the state's soldiers, 3,068-1,205. Kentucky, Delaware, and New Jersey were the only states that gave McClellan a majority.

In 1863 General Ambrose E. Burnside declared martial law in the state just before the August 3 election, "for the purpose only of protecting the rights of the loyal citizens and the freedom of election." No disloyal person was to be allowed to vote, and an estimated third of potential voters were kept from the polls. The Unionist candidates won easily. Thomas E. Bramlette, who resigned his commission as a major general to accept the Union Democrats' nomination for governor, defeated regular Democrat Charles A. Wickliffe, 68,422-17,503. As governor, Bramlette secured stringent laws for the suppression of guerrillas, but he strongly

opposed the enlistment of black soldiers, the July 5, 1864, suspension of the writ of habeas corpus in the state, and military interference with elections.

Both Boyle and Burbridge were abrasive and perhaps overzealous in their efforts to maintain military control in the state. Governor Bramlette declared that Burbridge's actions resulted from "the blundering of a weak intellect and an overwhelming vanity." Repeated efforts by Bramlette and the General Assembly to get Burbridge removed as commander of the District of Kentucky finally succeeded in February 1865. The *Louisville Journal* hailed the news that General John M. Palmer of Illinois had replaced him: "Thank God and President Lincoln."

Local military authorities also caused distress and resentment. General E.A. Paine was a notorious example. Stationed at Paducah early in the war, he had been removed when he exceeded his authority, but on July 19, 1864, he was put in charge of the western end of the state. The next seven weeks were described as a "reign of terror." Paine raised a hundred thousand dollars from a special tax to benefit the families of Union soldiers; that money disappeared. Prominent citizens suspected of Confederate sympathies were fined or exiled or both—unless they could purchase exemption from the charges. A 25 percent tax was placed on cotton that had had contact with anyone suspected of being pro-Confederate, and a tax was levied on the mail of Union soldiers. Several persons were executed on Paine's orders without even a pretense of a trial. One victim was a seventeen-year-old schoolboy whose crime was having two brothers in the Confederate Army. The lad met his death with unflinching courage: "I have got enough nerve to face the music; do not tie my hands, do not blindfold me." In early August Paine ordered a useless fort constructed in the Mayfield town square. Hundreds of male civilians, regardless of age and health, were conscripted to the work, but they were excused if they could pay as much as three hundred dollars. Complaints finally led to an investigation, and Paine fled to Illinois. When he was at last tried, a reprimand was his punishment.

The animosity generated by such Federal officials and policies turned most Kentuckians against the national administration. For decades after the war Kentucky consistently voted with the former Confederate states as part of the bloc known as the Solid South.

Economic Aspects of the War

A major economic loss during the war was the capital invested in slaves. The assessed value of slaves in 1860 was $107,494,527; the market value would have been more. The assessed value in 1865 was $7,224,851, as the majority had already become free and the Thirteenth Amendment to the U.S. Constitution was being ratified. Some former owners may have wished then that they had accepted Lincoln's offer of compensated emancipation early in the war.

The decline in the number of farm workers, both black and white, had a devastating effect upon agricultural production. Wholesale farm prices increased sharply during the war. If 1860 prices in Kentucky are considered to be at 100, the index figures for the next five years were 97, 112, 147, 210, and 192. But because of the labor shortage, the state's acres under cultivation declined by some four million by 1865. Hemp production fell by over 80 percent, tobacco by 57 percent, wheat by 63 percent, barley by 15 percent. Prices were good for farmers who had a surplus to sell, but on many farms in the state people made desperate efforts to raise enough to sustain life. Livestock prices also increased as the numbers of animals decreased. Horses in the state declined from 388,000 in 1861 to 299,000 in 1865; mules from 95,000 to 58,000; cattle from 692,000 to 520,000.

Armies cause property losses whether they are friend or foe. State farmers visited by troops found their fences used for firewood. Fruit and roasting ears of corn were eaten by hungry soldiers; chickens and pigs just disap-

peared. Even an overnight halt by a cavalry regiment could cost the unlucky host much grain and fodder. The Shaker communities at South Union and Pleasant Hill were well known for their agricultural production and their hospitality to those who requested it; they were visited frequently by military units from both armies. The losses they suffered undoubtedly contributed to their postwar declines. A Unionist who lost property to a Union outfit had some hope of receiving some compensation at a future date; a Confederate sympathizer had no hope of recovering the value of lost property, no matter who had taken it. Unionist Miles Kelly of Warren County had Federal troops on his property for seventy days; he filed claims of $17,755.80 with the government.

Prices of almost everything went up in the Union during the war. With the general price index at 100 in 1860, the prices of goods in the Union for the next five years were 99, 111, 135, 182, and 179. Since nonagricultural wages rose by only 43.1 percent during the war years, real purchasing power declined for most people. Especially hard hit were those living on fixed incomes and the families of Union soldiers who had to survive on what the soldier could send them. Union privates were paid thirteen dollars a month for most of the war; they received sixteen dollars after May 1, 1864. Pay was often months in arrears. Because of the rapid depreciation of Confederate currency, the pay of a Confederate private became almost worthless. It was also often paid late, and a Kentucky Confederate soldier had little chance of changing his money into U.S. funds and getting it to his family.

During the neutrality period Kentucky enjoyed a booming trade with the South, as the Confederates hastened to acquire war materials as rapidly as possible. The Union had shut off most of the Mississippi River traffic, and the L&N was the main avenue for trade in the Ohio Valley region. The L&N was not in good condition, and its rolling stock of 30 locomotives, 28 passenger cars, and 297 freight cars was inadequate for the increased traffic.

Another problem was that cars went south loaded with goods but most of them had to return empty. Indiana and Illinois tried to restrict goods to the South before the U.S. government became involved. The first Federal order of May 1, 1861, was largely ineffective, but the flow was restricted during the summer. Shipments from Louisville were limited after June 24 to those that had a permit issued by the customs officer, but goods were carried by wagon to stations south of the city and loaded there for forbidden destinations. Goods were also shipped in large quantities to such towns near the Tennessee border as Franklin and Hopkinsville; many of these loads were then carried into Tennessee. The Union later limited the quantities of goods that could be sent to such relay points.

The L&N became increasingly important as the war moved southward. Confederate raiders made the railroad one of their major targets, but experienced repair crews with ample supplies could fix torn-up track quickly. More serious was the destruction of the trestles near Elizabethtown, the tunnels near Gallatin, Tennessee, and the bridge at Munfordville. The Union deployed thousands of troops to keep the traffic running, but during the fiscal year July 1, 1862, to June 30, 1863, the L&N was open along its entire length for only seven months and twelve days. James Guthrie, politician and businessman, was vice president of the L&N during 1857-60 and its president from 1860 to 1868. Albert Fink, a German-born engineer, joined the L&N in 1857 and became superintendent of roads and machinery. Between them they kept the line running. Despite the damage done by Confederate raiders, the railroad made a net profit of more than six million dollars during the war.

For a few months after the war started, the Cumberland, Tennessee, and Green Rivers enjoyed a brisk trade. Then on May 21 and August 2, 1862, the Confederacy made the exportation of cotton, tobacco, sugar, and some minor items illegal when sent through Kentucky and the other border states. After neutrality ended, Union authorities imposed the type of restriction on river traffic that was being imposed on the railroads. Illegal trade continued throughout the war, and the Jackson Purchase region was the center of such activity.

The major economic scandal in Kentucky during the war was the Great Hog Swindle of 1864. The price of pork had increased sharply, so when the Louisville depot commissary said that he could save money by buying hogs directly from the farmers and packing the pork without using the usual contractors, he was told to proceed. He persuaded General Burbridge to issue a proclamation on October 28 prohibiting the shipment of hogs outside the state without a permit and asking farmers to sell to Major Henry C. Symonds. Hog producers were outraged, Burbridge withdrew his order on November 27, and the scheme was abandoned before the end of the year. Symonds claimed that he saved the government at least two hundred thousand dollars; Governor Bramlette said that state farmers had been robbed of more than three hundred thousand dollars.

Kentucky did not have a great deal of manufacturing, and much of the state's industry transformed farm products into whiskey, chewing tobacco and snuff, and flour. The Union Army and the United States had an insatiable demand for almost anything that could be produced, and Confederate raiders never damaged the major manufacturing facilities in Louisville. The Falls City profited more from the war, both in commerce and in manufacturing, than any other town in the state. The townspeople celebrated on Christmas Eve 1863, when a boat arrived from New Orleans with a cargo of sugar and molasses. This boat provided the first direct access they had had to New Orleans in more than two years.

The state government actually improved its debt situation during the war. The $5,698,000 debt in October 1859 was reduced to $5,254,000 in 1865, and the U.S. government still owed Kentucky $1,963,000. The sinking fund was adequate to handle the debt as payments came due. Kentucky spent $3.5 million for direct military purposes during the war. State banks continued making specie payments after major institutions in Boston, New York, and Philadelphia had suspended them. Banking was altered in 1863 by the National Banking Act. Banks could obtain a national charter by investing at least one-third of their stock in national bonds, and they could then issue paper currency worth up to 90 percent of the value of the bonds. A federal tax of 10 percent of the value of state banknotes drove these notes out of circulation, and at last the United States had a standard currency.

Social Aspects of the War Years

Virtually every Kentuckian was affected in some way by the war. Families were broken up, as husbands, sons, brothers, and sweethearts went off to war. Malvina Harlan gave Louisville attorney John Marshall Harlan full support as he agonized over what he should do. "You must do as you would if you had neither wife nor children," she insisted. "I could not stand between you and your duty to the country and be happy."[1] Thousands of Kentucky men never returned from the army in which they served, and other thousands were permanently scarred, physically and mentally. Losses were especially heavy in the group aged eighteen to twenty-five. Too few of these men were left in the generation that had to cope with postwar problems.

Families and communities were divided, often bitterly, by disagreements over the war and its implications for the future. Harriet Means of Ashland found that she had to be careful in inviting guests to her home: "I would not *dare* to give a large party now for fear the ladies would all get into a free fight." Georgetown College refused to grant a Mr. Black a degree in 1862 because he was "a violent secessionist." When Elisha B. Kirtley of the Paradise community joined the Confederate Army in September 1861, he swore that he would not shave until the Confederate States of America was well established. Kirtley died half a century later, still unshaven.

The war intensified previous splits in some churches, and other churches that had held together during earlier crises split during the conflict. Methodist minister George R. Browder in south-central Kentucky was concerned about the loyalty oath and fled to avoid possible arrest before he took it in Russellville in May 1863. He found that attendance was sometimes down at services because people feared that while they were in church their horses would be confiscated. Samuel Ringgold was pastor of the small Christ Episcopal Church in Bowling Green when the Confederates occupied the town in September 1861. He had an immediate problem: Who should be identified in the liturgical prayer for those in authority? Since he could not consult with the bishop in Louisville, he turned to Bishop J.A. Otey in Memphis. After the Provisional Government of Confederate Kentucky was formed, Otey advised Ringgold to pray for the Confederate authorities. More black churches were formed, and churches with both black and white members began vanishing as the slaves became free. Although Kentucky did not consider blacks as citizens until forced to do so by the Fourteenth Amendment to the U.S. Constitution, ratified on July 28, 1868, the presence of thousands of free blacks required many changes in addition to those occurring in the churches.

The progress made in providing public school education by the 1850s was stopped by the war. In 1861 the superintendent of public instruction reported that in one year the number of children in attendance at school had fallen from 165,000 to 90,000. Many of the teachers went into military service or quit teaching to take better-paying jobs. By the end

---

1. Harlan became colonel of the Tenth Kentucky Infantry (USA). He had been recommended for promotion to brigadier general when he resigned in 1863 after the sudden death of his father. Harlan was a noted member of the U.S. Supreme Court from 1877 to 1911.

of 1866 the schools were just getting back to the point at which they had been before the war. Since college students were of prime military age, the colleges that remained open during the war saw severe declines in enrollment. College buildings proved almost irresistible to military commanders, who needed space for hospitals or for housing troops, and the buildings were often used for these purposes. Considerable damage usually resulted from such occupation.

When troops were in a community for an extended period, there was a feverish increase in parties, picnics, dances, plays, band concerts, flirtations, and weddings. Social affairs normally involved only those civilians who favored the garrison troops; civilians who favored the other side boycotted such activities— and longed for the day when their soldiers would return. Confederate sympathizer Agatha Strange later wrote wistfully of the golden days when Bowling Green was Albert Sidney Johnston's headquarters and the capital of Confederate Kentucky: "Our house in those days was visited and made the home of by the intellect and chivalry of the South. . . . These were days of happiness and never can be erased from my memory."

With so many men off at war and labor so scarce and expensive, many Kentucky women did work that they would not have done before the war. Some of them farmed to feed their families, and some found employment in other fields. Women who did not have to turn to employment were often engaged in making bandages, knitting socks and sweaters, and raising funds for the relief of soldiers' families. They were often called upon for nursing duties when the tide of war brought casualties to their neighborhoods. Some mothers tried to continue providing the schooling that their children were being denied.

W.T. Lafferty lived on a prosperous Harrison County farm in 1861 when his twenty-nine-year-old father, John Aker Lafferty, left his twenty-three-year-old pregnant wife and three children to join the Confederate Army. W.T.

Lafferty recalled that "after father's departure, mother, in her usual quiet and thoughtful way, went about putting things in order, and taking up her new responsibilities as planned by father and herself." She had invaluable assistance from slave Will Johnson, who promised his master before he rode off to war, "It matters not what may take place, I will be here when you return, unless I die or am dragged away." When John Lafferty arrived home on June 10, 1865, a bearded, travelworn man in a tattered uniform, his young daughter Sue asked her mother if "that old man" was going to stay all night at their house. Lafferty employed Will Johnson for two years after the war, then gave him livestock and tools when Will bought land for his own farm.

Some events such as county fairs were discontinued for the duration of the war. Both soldiers and civilians needed relief from the wartime pressures, however, and at least in the larger cities plays, musical programs, and other entertainments continued. Proceeds often went to benevolent causes, such as the Ladies' Military Benevolent Association of Lexington. Writers, especially poets, produced a considerable body of patriotic works, but none survived the war with enough distinction to be called literature.

Two Vital Changes

An often-cited cliché asserts that wars never decide anything. The American Civil War, on the contrary, did decide at least two major issues that had far-reaching consequences for the state and nation.

First, the Civil War ended slavery. While it seems incomprehensible that the United States would have entered the twentieth century with slavery still existing in a number of states, the chances for its termination seemed remote in 1860. As long as the fifteen slave states constituted one more than a fourth of the states in the Union, they could block any effort to end slavery by a constitutional amendment. The work of the 1849 constitutional convention in Kentucky and the failure of antislavery

Some Civil War Sites

Some Civil War Sites (courtesy of Neal O. Hammon)

groups in the state to win substantial support indicated that slavery was likely to continue indefinitely in the commonwealth. Only the Civil War and the changes brought about by it ended Kentucky slavery in December 1865, when the Thirteenth Amendment was ratified.

Second, the Civil War placed pragmatic limits on the power of a state to defy federal acts or to secede from the Union. Any system that divides the powers of government between a nation and its states is certain to result in disputes and clashes between them. In arguing over the nature of the Union and the distribution of powers, the advocates of states' rights had some substantial arguments. The question of how far a state could go in defending what it considered to be its rights was still undecided in 1860. Could a state nullify an act of the federal government to which it objected? Could it peacefully secede from the Union? Had there been a definite answer to those questions, the nation would have had a framework within which such troublesome issues as the expansion of slavery in the territories could have been resolved. The Civil War gave an answer: states' rights did not extend as far as its advocates had claimed. At Gettysburg on November 19, 1863, President Lincoln proclaimed "a new birth of freedom" through a national government not of states but "of the people, by the people, for the people."

The Civil War affected many aspects of life in Kentucky and the nation, but it is doubtful that any effect had more far-reaching consequences than the end of slavery and the establishment of limits to states' rights.

The Promise Unfulfilled

The years between the War of 1812 and the Civil War may have been the most promising four and a half decades in the history of Kentucky. Much had been accomplished since 1775, when the pioneers established the first permanent settlements. The fight for survival had been won, and much of the wilderness had been tamed. A nation had been born and a state created, and by 1815 both of them were firmly established. The acquisition of the Louisiana Purchase had solved the vexing Mississippi River problem. Kentucky's population was increasing rapidly, and several towns were offering important cultural amenities. Henry Clay, John J. Crittenden, and John Breckinridge had attracted national political attention. Many Kentuckians were living the good life, whether it was on a Bluegrass plantation, a fertile farm in the Barrens, or a house in one of the growing urban centers. Measurable progress had been

211

made in many areas, and some Kentuckians believed that their state was poised to achieve the promise of the early years of exploration and settlement.

By 1860, however, an astute observer might have been concerned about the state's future. After the 1820s more people had left the state than had entered it, and the rate of population growth had declined sharply. Poor men who had failed to secure land settled into the uneasy life of the landless or left the commonwealth in search of better opportunities elsewhere. Some states newer than Kentucky had pulled ahead in economic development. Manufacturing had trailed far behind agriculture in the state's economy. While belated educational reforms left Kentucky favorably situated when compared with other slave states, it lagged well behind several northern states. Kentuckians had not produced the works of music, art, literature, and drama that would direct national attention to the cultural and creative activities in the state. Many explanations can be advanced to explain why the bright promise of the early years remained unfulfilled. These are the main ones:

The early promise may have been so exaggerated that fulfillment was impossible when Kentuckians encountered the realities of settlement and subsequent development. Attractive as it was, the "Eden of the West" was not utopia.

The chaotic land system plagued Kentucky even before statehood was achieved, and its effects have clouded land titles for more than two centuries. Disappointed seekers of land went elsewhere, immigration was discouraged, endless controversies diverted attention from more profitable enterprises, and numerous quarrels and feuds resulted from disputes over landownership.

The lack of an adequate educational system was a basic weakness. The efforts to improve the common schools near midcentury had come far too late, and the schools were still woefully inadequate.

The absence of adequate leadership on the state level was striking, both in political and economic fields. Henry Clay and John J. Crittenden, the best-known politicians of the era, were more interested in national issues and positions than in state affairs. Clay possessed great leadership abilities, but after his early years in politics he devoted little attention to state issues except as they were part of national goals. Kentucky lacked entrepreneurs to organize the use of the state's natural resources or to build a network of railroads. Leaders were needed who could fire people's imaginations with visions of what was possible and could inspire them to do what was necessary to attain those goals.

Cassius M. Clay was correct when he told nonslaveholding Kentuckians that they and the state were retarded economically by the presence of slavery. Much of the state's capital was tied up in slave property and was thus unavailable for investment in manufacturing and commerce. The presence of slaves and their services may also have sometimes contributed to a slothful attitude on the part of slaveholders.

The state lacked easily used natural resources. The once-promising iron industry had been hampered by its dependence upon scattered deposits of low-grade ore. Coal and timber, the two natural resources most easily exploited, usually benefited absentee owners and companies that had little interest in the long-range development of the state. In many ways, Kentucky of the nineteenth century resembled some of the third world countries of the late twentieth century.

The situation in 1860 was not totally dismal, however. Some Kentuckians had achieved a good life, there were some oases of cultural achievement, and a few citizens had earned national recognition. Kentucky was a lovely state with many admirable people living in it. Still, the state had not achieved what had seemed attainable less than a century earlier. By 1865 the Civil War had shaken the foundations of the state. Could the uncertain future offer an opportunity to recapture the promise that had not been fulfilled?

Part III

Kentucky after 1865

15

1865 and After

The Kentucky World of 1865

One Kentuckian remembered the day vividly: "When we heard of Gen. Lee's surrender pandemonium broke loose and everyone acted as if the world was coming to an end." For people in the state in 1865, one world was in fact ending, and a new, uncertain world built on the wreckage of war was replacing it. But what kind of new world would it be? Would it replicate the old in most fundamental respects, or would it be vastly different? Change, confusion, and chaos often follow war, but this conflict, this civil war, was more destructive and disruptive than any experienced by Americans before or since. More than 600,000 had died (if a similar percentage of the present-day population was killed, some 5 million people would be dead). Among Kentuckians, nearly one in five who left to fight—some 30,000 out of as many as 140,000—never returned. Their graves were scattered across a large, war-ravaged area. Thousands more were wounded, marred for life by bullets or by unforgiving memories of battlefields. Empty sleeves, legless bodies, permanent damage to the mind—all these came home with the veterans of combat, black and white. An entire era had been blighted. What leaders had the state lost among its dead? What art, literature, or statecraft would have resulted from those lives? A generation grew to maturity without those talents, and that personal toll taken by the war could not be replaced. Kentucky's future would be one filled with bitter memories, wartime scars, and long-felt hurts.

The war's effects, however, went beyond the casualties. Perhaps more so than any other state, Kentucky had been sharply divided between the two causes. The conflict had been a brothers' war, as whole families were torn asunder. Friends warred on each other; Kentuckians had looked down their gun barrels at other Kentuckians; churches and communities had split. In time, many of those who wore the Blue or the Gray would grow to respect their former enemies, and the healing would begin. For others, however, the fabric of life, rent by the war, was never mended. The memories remained too strong. "A bitter feeling between neighbors" still prevailed, and this situation made compromise and cooperation difficult and intense violence likely. The dormant seeds of animosity deposited by the Civil War would spring to life later, bringing forth harvests of more bloodshed.

The conflict had left behind its toll of physical destruction as well, for crops had been lost, livestock taken, and property destroyed. There were 89,000 fewer horses, 37,000 fewer mules, and 172,000 fewer cattle in Kentucky in 1865 than at the start of the war. The amount of land under cultivation had declined drastically. Despite wartime inflation, land values in places like Lexington decreased one-fourth between 1862 and 1872. A soldier returned to an eastern Kentucky town and was welcomed by "neglected farms . . . roads and paths overgrown with weeds, and almost no business of any kind being carried on." But that sense of economic setback could be—and would be—easily overcome, for in truth Kentucky had not suffered as greatly as the states farther south. In fact, some locales, such as Louisville, had actually prospered during the war. The commonwealth thus emerged from the conflict hobbled, but strong enough to move ahead, to grow rapidly, even to take a leadership role in a region where other states had much greater handicaps and devastation to overcome.

More damaging than the economic costs was the war's effect on the psyche of the populace. So much of what had once been was no more. The optimism that drove settlers to frontier Kentucky now seemed a rare commodity. Uncertainty caused citizens to wonder

just what this postwar world would hold for them. What was their life going to be like now? They knew already that the War between the States—as southerners preferred to call it—had left an indelible mark on their lives and would likely do so for decades to come. The keys to understanding future developments in Kentucky would be the war, the war, and the war. In politics, for example, the death of Henry Clay's Whig Party in the 1850s had left the arena confused even before the Civil War. Considering the actions taken since then, now what would occur? What would become of the state's educational system, which had made some important progress before the war? It had been hit hard. Could it recover? Would the commonwealth retain its status as one of the nation's leading agricultural states, or would new trade and industrial growth dominate? Kentucky was a land of worry, distrust, and fear, as well as a place of hope, hospitality, and confidence. With so many questions and so few clear answers, the year 1865 seemed an uncertain time indeed.

Yet with all that, one other question seemed in some ways the most important of all at the time. The single most crucial issue, the one topic that filled the pages of the state's newspapers, concerned the place of blacks in the postwar world. For blacks themselves, the debate was simply resolved: Free us from slavery, give us the rights of other American citizens, let us enjoy those freedoms without hindrance, and allow us to go on with our lives as we too seek a better future. Not a single one of these actions, however, would occur without dispute or restriction.

White Kentuckians ruled the state, for only one of every six people in the commonwealth was black in 1870. The former slaves were not close to a majority and could not threaten white dominance except in a very few locales. Yet the issue was never fully a matter of numbers. Slavery had been not only an economic institution but also one of social and racial controls, in which one group ruled another. For many generations it had been emphasized that slaves were not at the same level as the white people around them. Few white Kentuckians—or white Americans, for that matter—could conceive of accepting the idea that blacks were their equals. The world built on that set of racial values was under attack and in danger of being overturned, as political and social equality became the sought-after goal. In large part, white Kentuckians refused to replace the scheme of dominant and subordinate statuses with a system of equality. One newspaper writer would not "submit to a social association perfectly revolutionary to all sensible persons." Such attitudes would breed resistance and cost many lives over many years. For more than a century justice would war against prejudice in a fiercely fought, decidedly uncivil conflict.

The question of civil rights added yet another ingredient to a mix that was already boiling over in the South and in Kentucky in 1865. The attempt to reconstruct a society split by war was difficult enough. With the issue of race and the ferocity of reaction then added, smooth transition into peace became almost impossible. At one extreme, some in the North called for harsh treatment of the South, even for the death by hanging of "traitorous" southern leaders. At the other extreme, some southerners seemed unable to accept the fact that they had lost the war and must accept the consequences. Feelings grew so bitter that various commentators wondered aloud if the war or some guerrilla resistance would begin again. A Kentucky woman wrote that "the war was not over in Kentucky, a state divided against itself." The *Elizabethtown Banner* asked if the country might "be convulsed with the throes of a new revolution, involving the North and South alike, in common ruin." When the former slaveholding states, including Kentucky, refused to accept blacks as free men and women, not to mention as voters or as equal citizens in society, and when force was used to reinforce that stand, northern Republicans responded with stronger actions, some of which raised serious constitutional questions. Those in opposition compared such moves to those

made by the radical Jacobins of the French Revolution and predicted equally bloody consequences. The *Bardstown Leader,* in opposing the national Civil Rights Act of 1866, editorialized that "precious blood has been poured out like water; precious lives have been ruthlessly sacrificed. . . . Now for the sake of three millions of negroes, the white people of this country are asked to submit to the abrogation of the Constitution." Other writers quietly counseled acceptance of the postwar situation and asked their fellow citizens to direct their attention and energies to rebuilding out of the destruction of war, to create a New South, a new Kentucky.

If trying to repair wartime damages, seeking to reintegrate returning soldiers of both armies into society, and working to find a racial arrangement that would satisfy all was not enough to deal with, Kentuckians also had to face what appeared to be serious breakdowns in the legal system. During the war one Christian County diarist had written that young people "seem to think the war will never end & they might as well enjoy them selves as they can." This uncertainty frequently combined with the absence, or loss, of one parent to produce generational conflict. Now in the postwar world those same young adults continued to face an unknown, confused future—as did their elders—and seemed to be searching still for answers and direction. Newspapers printed disapproving stories about bands of roving adolescent boys who drank, stole, fought, and committed acts of violence. Wartime veterans, some of them little more than boys themselves, were struck by the same virus of dissatisfaction and found it hard to adjust to a peacetime situation. Former Union captain John W. Tuttle of Wayne County would later be a successful attorney, but he recalled that when the fighting ended for him, he "contracted a hearty contempt for useful employment of any kind whatsoever so I passed most of my time in gambling, drinking, and rollicking around with . . . 'the boys.'" Add to that mix the new status of the former slaves and the movement of many of them from farm to city, and postwar civilization seemed to be characterized by general unrest and significant uncertainty.

Violence exacerbated the problems and appeared ever-present to Kentuckians of the era. During the conflict the state had been infested with lawless guerrilla bands, made up of outlaws and outcasts from both armies. Many normal protectors were off fighting the war, and little slowed the guerrillas. One Monticello resident recalled:

> Lawless bands were continually prowling about through this region of country stealing, robbing, plundering, burning, and committing all manner of depredations, cruelties, and atrocities upon helpless and unoffending citizens. . . . They howled about the streets like demons, shooting at every man that showed himself on the streets. . . .
>
> It may seem strange that a town . . . should suffer such a gang to run rough shod over it in that manner, but the people knew if they shipped one gang out another larger one would come and destroy the town and perhaps massacre its inhabitants. . . .
>
> Taken all together there is little connected with this period of time that is pleasant to look back upon or desirable to remember.

Such lawlessness did not end with Lee's surrender at Appomattox, and one person who lived in Kentucky during that time recalled later that a virtual reign of terror prevailed in the state from 1865 to 1868. A few returning soldiers were ambushed by those who had supported the opposing side and still had a score to settle. More commonly, criminal bands simply made life dangerous for everyone. One boy remembered that his father slept with two pistols, two rifles, and a machete by his bedside. In Washington County, break-ins were so likely that the bank refused to take deposits; the sheriff himself was robbed of county tax receipts. Across the commonwealth, vigilantes, the Ku Klux Klan, and individual groups killed and lynched blacks with seeming impunity. All that lawlessness caused some of both races—including bright, ambitious people that the state could ill afford to lose—to see little hope

in the "unsettled state of society" and to leave the commonwealth entirely. Those who remained would find it very difficult to eliminate the influence of violence on their lives.

Continuity and Change

Kentucky author James Lane Allen, who could be both an astute critic and an undiscerning onlooker, wrote that out of the postwar period "of upheaval and downfall, of shifting and drifting," his state emerged with "so much the same." Yet Allen in the same book also noted that the war changed things drastically. It was "a great rent and chasm, down into which old things were dashed to death, and out of which new things were born into the better life." Soon afterward, former Confederate Basil W. Duke looked back on the postwar era with its physical and mental destruction, its racial struggles, its violence and unrest, and said of Kentucky and the region that "the life of the post-bellum South no more resembled that of the other than the life of the early settlers . . . was like that they had left on the other side of the ocean." Just as the first Americans had discovered a new world, so too, he argued, Kentuckians after the Civil War found themselves in a new era, in a place vastly different from the one they had known before.

Was life in postwar Kentucky, then, fundamentally a continuation of the earlier lifestyle, or was it profoundly different? Obviously, any generalization about the identity of a physical place bounded by political lines must be tempered by the knowledge that numerous exceptions exist to any broad statement. There were, for example, rural Kentuckys and urban ones, Kentuckys of black and white, rich and poor, young and old. People who lived in the eastern mountains seemed a world away from those in western Kentucky, and people in the countryside had vastly different lives from people in the cities. Divisions of class, race, ethnicity, region, and socioeconomics partitioned the state. To complicate the matter further, little unity existed within each major group. The urban poor, either black or white, might find they had more in common with their rural counterparts than with upper-class society in their own cities. On the other hand, some issues would cause such alliances to break down, and farmers, rich and poor, might join together against urban dwellers. Over the years there would be many Kentuckys, constantly shifting with the various issues that united or divided them.

The state would change as the decades passed, but the degree of change, and its timing, would vary widely across the commonwealth. Each locale had to weigh the costs of every decision, as citizens asked which of the current institutions should be retained and which should be discarded. Each change, no matter how positive it might seem, would affect the way of life that had once been known. The coming of the telephone from 1879 on, for example, allowed merchants to conduct business better, helped bring aid quicker in emergencies, and permitted easier communication among people in a community. Yet the telephone might also cause neighbors to visit less in person; it might add to the impersonal feeling of a growing nation. In the twentieth century, when the dial phone replaced the system in which a local operator made the calls, then the operator's intimate knowledge of the community would be no more. Few questioned the desirability of the telephone or the modifications in it that added to the convenience of the users, but each change made a subtle difference in the way a community worked. The question was one of balance, and in this case the scales easily tipped toward the telephone. But when larger issues arose that had greater consequences, the decisions would not be so simple.

While some places and certain communities embraced new ideas and different outlooks almost immediately, others would remain virtually unchanged for more than a century. In 1865 people all across the state lived on a lingering frontier, isolated and ignored. The nineteenth-century experience of a man who grew up on a farm and by the age of seventeen had never seen a town, not even his county seat,

was not rare. In the first third of the twentieth century, as another Kentuckian recalled, young boys and girls lived within view of the small creek that dominated their lives and went to a small hamlet only a few times a year, "and only then if it didn't rain." By the middle of the twentieth century, despite all the improvements in transportation, a rural high school graduate noted that he had been no farther than the next county. An intense provincialism resulted from such isolated and limiting situations. As one writer remembered, "The conversations of the people were of local subjects. Their intelligence never soared across many water sheds; beyond many streams."

In many such places after the war, the inhabitants could not read—more than one-fourth of Kentuckians over the age of ten were illiterate in 1870—and even in literate homes, books and newspapers might be scarce possessions. Oral traditions were passed down, and with them stories and beliefs of an earlier time. Accounts of ghosts and witches were widespread, and to many people these beings seemed real. In 1869 an Owen County woman was presented to a grand jury on the charge of being a witch. She was not indicted. (Later, in 1898, a woman was supposedly burned as a witch in Fleming County.) Similar fears and superstitions had made a sweeping 1866 rumor believable. Accounts spread that the end of the world was near and that the devil was unchained. A lawyer wrote in his diary that "there was considerable excitement on the streets all day about the coming of the Devil. . . . Some seemed to believe the preposterous stories afloat, some were actually scared." The world of many Kentuckians was one of limited learning, narrow geographic boundaries, and restricted mental horizons. Places of finite options and confined imaginations would long survive.

Yet so too would another, very different world, one peopled by Kentuckians who had broad education and strong vision. They had traveled widely, read well, and learned much. They in their own way had weaknesses and prejudices, and sometimes they could be just as provincial and limited in outlook as their more place-bound fellow citizens. Still, their lives proved very different. Between these two extremes existed almost all variations, and people in practically every group agreed that their own beliefs should be guiding the entire commonwealth.

Despite the differences among Kentuckians, however, certain overall characteristics were evident. First of all, mid-nineteenth-century citizens worshiped an agrarian ideal. Increasingly that would not be so, for an urban ethos would quickly make inroads, and the goals of country gentlemen would be replaced by those of business leaders. But in the nineteenth century the ties to the land remained strong and binding. As Albert E. Cowdrey has noted, a web of traditions linking physical things—the ridges and rivers, the hills and hollows—created a particular "landscape of the mind," a dignity, a strong sense of place. People walked the land they farmed, felt it beneath their feet, knew how it looked, understood its vagaries and variations. They had a camaraderie and partnership with the soil. The bond was often a hard one, but intimate nevertheless. As one Appalachian resident wrote later: "I don't remember even seeing a Van Gogh or Rembrandt . . . but I remember beauty. . . . There was natural beauty enough to fill the eyes and the soul."

A second characteristic of the time was conservatism and a tendency to resist change. Many Kentuckians, particularly the well-to-do, the established, and the landed, believed that there was little need to reexamine the basic arrangement of their lives. They were not reactionary, for they could support improvements, such as in technological matters, for instance. They simply did not see the need to modify the system they knew. That attitude was not restricted to just one class, for many citizens accepted a stable way of life they did not consider terribly bad. Even the poor and landless did not often offer challenges, for such behavior was too dangerous—blacks might lose their lives, poor whites their jobs. Others showed a kind of

resignation. They knew only one way of life, and a hard, unlettered existence left them little time to contemplate options or to put ideas into effect. Still others, of both races, believed that a better life awaited them after death and expected their reward in another world. Such fatalism and passiveness allowed people to accept misfortunes in this life but also created an outlook that resisted change. Indifference and complacency resulted. Amid the uncertainty of postwar Kentucky and beyond, such citizens would provide few challenges to authority.

A third and contradictory characteristic of the era was a rising demand for change and reform of existing ways. Some people spoke out for the idea of progress—whatever that meant to them—because, in their eyes, justice demanded it. Others did so because they and their children had few future prospects under the current system. Thus, throughout the next tumultuous half century—and beyond—various Kentuckians would attempt to alter the status quo. Occasionally such reformers might focus on less vital questions, such as fashion, but more often they dealt with major issues. Questions of politics, race, women's rights, and agrarian change would all demand answers. The struggles to find these answers would be long, hard, controversial, and divisive.

Rural and Small-Town Life

Historian Thomas D. Clark has astutely termed Kentucky a "land of contrast." In 1865, however, there was perhaps less social contrast in the state's population than at any time since the frontier period. The end of slavery had loosened the legal bonds that tied one group to another and at the same time had seriously weakened the financial condition of those who had held slaves. Millions upon millions of dollars had been invested in human property. Early in the Civil War, Kentucky had rejected Lincoln's offer for compensated emancipation. Then, belatedly, compensation for freed slaves—more than $108 million—was sought but was not forthcoming. Families that had been, at least on paper, quite wealthy now became quite poor in fact. A leveling had taken place. In the county housing the state capital, only thirty-six men had incomes of more than one thousand dollars in 1867. On the other hand, blacks began a slow process of gaining wealth and status. For former slaves with little or no money or land, any financial gains would constitute an improvement on the poverty of slavery—and the poverty of the spirit that such bonds had brought as well.

There were still wealthy Kentuckians and still very poor ones. As Allen noted, "a spirit of caste" existed everywhere, and each town of any size had what one woman called "Society . . . with a capital S. . . . You were either in it or out of it." Great racial and gender inequalities continued as well. Yet less wealth existed than before, and the formal divisions made evident by slavery and slaveholding were gone. In a society that was still dominated by rural interests, the lack of money was also less evident, and thus the distinction of class was less clear. Even the Appalachian Highlands, an

area later associated with poverty, did not differ so greatly from the rest of the commonwealth at the time. At least for the moment, the people of post–Civil War Kentucky lived in a relatively less financially defined society and a more classless one.

They also lived in an increasingly homogenous society. Their state was falling in population relative to the United States. Kentucky's growth from 1,321,011 people in 1870 to 2,147,174 in 1900 trailed the nation's expansion. The state population had increased slower than the nation's since 1830 and would continue this trend, with two exceptions, through the late twentieth century. Eighth largest of the states in 1850, Kentucky fell to twelfth by 1900.

Part of that relative decline resulted from an out-migration of residents, many of whom were black. The number of black Kentuckians declined from nearly 17 percent of the population in 1870 to over 13 percent in 1900. Likewise, fewer new faces, particularly of the foreign-born, were arriving in the commonwealth. At a time when great waves of new immigrants flooded America's East and North, Kentucky remained almost untouched, except for a few instances in the coalfields.

Kentucky had a small immigrant presence, for in 1870 only one in twenty citizens was foreign-born. Concentrated along the Ohio River cities—Covington, Newport, and Louisville all had 20 percent or more foreign-born—these immigrants consisted chiefly of Irish and Germans who had arrived before the war. In those places, German would be spoken in churches until the 1910s, and Irish and German newspapers would be printed for decades beyond that. Yet other parts of the commonwealth had no foreign-born residents whatsoever. With few new immigrants and with little in-migration from other states, Kentucky became more and more

Table 15.1
Population of Kentucky, 1870-1990

Year	Population	Kentucky growth rate	U.S. growth rate
1870	1,321,011	14.3	24.0
1880	1,648,690	24.8	30.1
1890	1,858,635	12.7	24.9
1900	2,147,174	15.5	20.7
1910	2,289,905	6.6	21.0
1920	2,416,630	5.5	15.0
1930	2,614,589	8.2	16.2
1940	2,845,627	8.8	7.3
1950	2,944,806	3.5	14.5
1960	3,038,156	3.2	18.5
1970	3,220,711	6.0	13.3
1980	3,660,324	13.6	11.4
1990	3,686,891	0.7	9.8

Sources: P.P. Karan and Cotton Mather, eds., *Atlas of Kentucky* (1977), 17; U.S. Census; *World Almanac and Book of Facts, 1992* (1992); *1996 Kentucky Deskbook of Economic Statistics* (1996)

self-contained. Different ideas and lifestyles brought from outside would prove scarce. By 1910 nearly 90 percent of those living in the state had been born there, the fifth highest percentage nationally.

In the half century after Appomattox, then, the core of life of the average Kentuckian changed only slowly. A resident's lifestyle might vary considerably from class to class, from city to small town and from small town to farm, but at root it remained relatively static. At the center of life stood the family. In the family children learned cultural patterns and ethical norms, character was shaped in ways both open and subtle, and duties and expectations were imparted. Kentucky in 1870 had the highest average number of people per family in the nation—5.67 persons. Each decade that average would fall, so that by 1910 the state's average of 4.6 per family only barely exceeded the national figure of 4.5. Yet larger families remained the norm for the commonwealth during that period.

Families, both black and white, usually lived in a rural setting, for as late as 1910 four of five Kentucky families were in that category. People would typically rise early after sleeping on beds stuffed with goose feathers, straw, or cornhusks. Upon waking, they seldom looked at a clock to find the time, for few timepieces existed in poorer homes. One Caldwell County resident recalled, "I never saw a clock until I was nearly grown." Other families might have a cheap timepiece sold by a traveling peddler, but their lives still remained mostly ruled by nature's hours. If they rose before daylight, they lit kerosene or oil lamps. (Not until the 1940s would most Kentuckians have electricity in their homes.) On cold days many would jump from the warmth of their beds and rush to a place with heat. Many homes, mostly uninsulated, might have only a single fireplace, and spots distant from that central source could feel virtually unheated as the wind whipped through the walls. Family members would undress by the fire at night, jump into their nightclothes, and rush off to

the feather bed and stack of quilts designed to keep them as warm as possible in a cold room, where they could see their breath on a moonlit night. In the morning the mad dash to the fire would be reversed.

A family member charged with bringing in the wood or coal to start the day's fire would have to make certain that embers from the previous day had been preserved, so a new flame could begin. If the embers had died, a trip to a perhaps distant neighbor "to borrow fire" was necessary, since matches remained rare luxuries in many homes until late in the nineteenth century. Warmer weather freed the family from the fire-making chore but brought other problems. Feather beds were hot in summer and might attract fleas. Glass was too expensive for many families, and mesh screens were not typical, so open windows were the usual option for cooling the interior. This option, however, also allowed a variety of flies and other insects to invade the premises. Air conditioning would be used in limited form, such as in theaters, by the 1930s, but not for three or more decades after that would it become commonplace. Until then, handheld and electric fans, open windows, and cooling breezes would be the answers to summer's heat. For a long time in Kentucky, heating and cooling depended as much on nature as on artificial means.

Whether the weather was warm or cold, water used for cooking or washing came from outdoors. Indoor plumbing was not prevalent in nineteenth-century Kentucky, and water often came from a well or nearby creek. Otherwise, rainwater was collected in barrels or cisterns. Sanitary quality varied. Even urban dwellers in Louisville drank unfiltered water straight from the river, and as one resident recalled, "No family was without its case of typhoid." Homes fortunate enough to have a water tank attached to a kitchen stove had hot water readily available, but most people started the morning by washing in cold water instead. Similarly, using a chamber pot indoors or taking a trip to an outside privy—an outhouse—or even to a secluded spot in the woods were the only ways to answer what was euphemistically termed "nature's call."

Many Kentucky families lived almost self-sufficient lives. As in earlier times, people washed themselves and their clothes with a rough homemade lye soap produced from fat waste, wood ashes, and water. They wore clothes made with thread woven at home on a spinning wheel. Yarn was used to knit stockings, socks, and scarves, all colored with dyes fashioned from tree bark or berry juice. Sheep were a vital part of the cloth-making process, for their wool would be sheared, washed in a nearby stream, and then either made into cloth on the premises or shipped to a distant mill, to be returned later. Straw was braided to make men's hats, and leather was formed on stocks to make shoes—although most children went barefoot during the summer months.

Food on the family table came from nearby sources. Hunting and fishing provided some food, while chickens and hogs offered a more constant feature on most farms. With cool weather came "hog-killing" time, and neighbors gathered to help each other. The animals would be shot or axed, their bodies placed in scalding water to remove the hair, and then the carcasses were hung upside down so that the blood could drain out. Finally the meat would be cut up. Some went into sausage— "Unless you have tasted sausage made on the farm," said many, "you have never tasted sausage"—and the rest would be preserved by salting or smoking, to keep out worms. Chickens provided eggs, while cows furnished milk, both for drinking and for making into butter. While some towns had ice companies that made daily deliveries, most places kept food cool only by placing it in a spring or in a specially designed "well house."

Fruit trees and vegetable gardens provided a variety of foods, preserved in many ways. Cellars sheltered potatoes, cabbages, and dried items such as apples, green beans, and peppers. Canning in sterilized jars became common at different times across the state, usually after the turn of the twentieth century. It offered a good way to preserve beets, corn, tomatoes, berries, and similar items. Honey from beehives kept on some farms, as well as molasses made from cane, gave further variety to daily fare. The only food items that many people purchased with regularity were salt, sugar, coffee, and flour. Across Kentucky, people lived in or near self-sufficiency, but this life was one based on long, hard work. When easier options became available, they would be eagerly seized.

The nutritional value of the meals prepared in rural residences fluctuated. Those who

Mathilde Miller makes lye soap at her home in McLean County, ca. 1925 (courtesy of the Kentucky Historical Society).

had access to all the dietary possibilities—the many fruits, the numerous vegetables, the different meats—did quite well. One person recalled a bountiful breakfast of biscuits, sausage, gravy, fried apples, strawberry preserves, butter, and milk. Others remembered equally plentiful dinners (the noon meal) and suppers. Yet some Kentuckians faced meals of little variety, few options, and no luxuries. Their diets more typically consisted of salt pork, corn, coffee, and cornbread. Still others found out that hunger continued to stalk this land of seeming plenty. In the early twentieth century a woman was asked if she had ever been hungry: "Yes, many a time. . . . Some mornings we had just enough meal in the house to make one hoecake. . . . And we had to divide that ten ways."

Whether the meal a family consumed was makeshift or full, it likely had been prepared by women, for a clear division of labor based on gender existed in Kentucky. Young boys might bring in wood for the fire, carry water to the house, and do minor farm chores, such as clearing out chicken houses or feeding pigs. Girls might gather eggs, skim milk, churn butter, roll candles, and generally assist their mother. Grown women faced myriad tasks, ranging from making and mending clothes to washing and ironing them, from cleaning house to caring for the garden. They stored and canned food and prepared meals three times a day. If the family was large and local custom strong, women might well not eat until the men of the household had been served, or they might sit with the children for meals. One man, remembering how his mother balanced all of her work while also raising nine children, concluded simply: "She didn't have much time left." Men, meanwhile, usually worked all day in the fields when weather permitted, plowing, weeding, harvesting. They kept buildings repaired and conducted most of the formal business. In providing food for the table through hunting and fishing, males did have the opportunity to venture away from home more

than women did. Women tended to be more restricted to the household.

For women and men, girls and boys, two institutions provided the opportunity to meet and interact with other Kentuckians of the area. No matter the location or relative isolation of the neighborhood, people would gather at church or at the country store. Churches had a threefold purpose. One obviously was religious, at a time when people's thoughts and words were strongly dominated by religion. Although members of some denominations would deny it, the church also offered a kind of entertainment, for the discourses and music heard there might represent the only group exposure to the arts for isolated Kentuckians. Finally, the churches offered people a place to meet and talk. There new friendships would be made or older ones renewed, and at the country church many young men and women would meet their future spouses. Even when seating was segregated by sex, as it was in places, picnics or walks home afterward provided opportunities for interaction. The church was a social, cultural, and spiritual center.

In a different manner, the country store was just as central a part of people's lives. For an isolated populace, tied to family and home on most days, a trip to the country store seemed almost a journey to grandeur. Each business varied, but most seemed to have a little of everything. On entering the door, the first sense to be assailed would be the nose. The smell of oiled floors (oiled to keep down dust) mixed with the odor of tobacco smoke, combined with the scent of leather and the fragrance of dried herbs, and joined with the aroma of a mix of foods—cheese, coffee, and fruits—to alert visitors to what might lie within. Sounds of delighted children or bargaining customers blended with voices of a local politician seeking votes. The eye could barely take in all that was there. A counter showed off everything from candy to candles. Nearby might be stoves for sale, or harnesses for horses. One Jessamine County resident noted

A Lexington baptism performed by the Rev. Sanford Howard in the 1890s (courtesy of the Kentucky Historical Society).

that the owner of the store near him was postmaster as well as proprietor, and he dispersed "smiles, local news, reminiscences, and everything from hay-rakes to headache pills; from cedar posts to shoes; from ten-quart tin-pails to pencil sharpeners and old-fashioned peppermints." The country store functioned as grocery, clothing store, voting place, credit center, hardware business, post office, and information distribution center. People bartered eggs for canned sardines, mailed and received packages, and traded gossip for more gossip. Front-porch rocking chair debates in summer or pot-bellied stove, spittoon discussions in winter solved, in the participants' view at least, most of the concerns of the neighborhood, or the world.

Country stores would exist well into the twentieth century, for they lived and died based on the isolation and mobility of those around them. But they would not again be so central a part of people's lives as they were in

the late 1800s. With better highways and the coming of the railroad, some stores declined. Others lost trade when mail-order houses brought goods to the doorstep through rural free delivery, particularly after about 1901. Finally, their place at the center of social life and the rural economy went to other institutions.

Improved transportation brought small county seat towns within easier reach of many rural residents. As a result, county court days became as important as the country store to some Kentuckians. On court day, whole families would arrive in town by horse or wagon. Women and girls would go to the small selection of stores and shops, while men and boys mingled with the mob that comprised something that was part folk gathering, part festival, and part marketplace. A minister visited Winchester's court day in 1880 and wrote in his diary: "Pavement as thickly thronged as Broadway, New York. A perfect Babel with the

225

Croley's Hardware and Grocery Store in Barbourville, 1900. The large variety of goods available here typified Kentucky country stores of the time (from Michael C. Mills, *Barbourville, Kentucky* [1977].)

various auctioneers, shouting themselves hoarse, the cattle lowing, horning, hoofing, crowding each other; the drivers yelling . . . ; the various bargainers, buyers, and sellers gesticulating, arguing, protesting; loafers strolling up and down eating peanuts, apples, pawpaws, and enjoying the sights and sounds." Across Kentucky, items as diverse as baskets and bulls, patent medicines and pickles, furniture and farming implements, would be presented to wary buyers. Wealthy merchants talked with tenant farmers, well-to-do estate owners rubbed elbows with laborers, and social distinctions seemed less important than the ability to bargain for a good price. But like the country store, court day saw its glory fade as the nineteenth century died. Although a few examples would live on, the institution had seen its heyday by the time Lexington abolished its court day on Cheapside in 1921.

The Urban Commonwealth

The smaller county seats and other similarly sized towns barely deserved the designation "town," for they frequently remained rough and primitive outposts in the rural landscape well into the twentieth century. Elizabethtown, on the railroad and not far from urbanized Louisville, still was described in the 1880s as a place where hogs roamed the streets, sleeping in the courthouse at night. Only the business section had sidewalks; the rest of the town featured dusty or muddy walkways, depending on the weather. The lack of streetlights meant that people had to carry lanterns if they moved about after dark. When Hopkinsville decided to deal with its own problem of unattended hogs and cows and outlawed the practice of allowing livestock to roam at large, "the community was thrown into an uproar." As late as the 1940s, Hyden in the eastern Kentucky mountains was described as "a slop hole," a "drab and dreary" place filled with roaming bands of cows, hogs, and mules, traveling freely over dirt streets pocked with enormous holes. In 1910 only thirteen cities in the state had more than six thousand people.

Court day in Lexington, 1897
(courtesy of the University of
Kentucky Libraries)

Yet for all their roughness, such places gradually brought to rural Kentuckians new technologies, different ideas, and fresh styles. At varying times, depending on the towns' isolation, they introduced their locales to the wonders of electricity, telephones, indoor plumbing, and much more. A young Muhlenberg County girl arrived in one such urban place in the first decade of the twentieth century and recalled that in the next few weeks she experienced "the first brick paved streets I ever saw, first electric lights, first gas lights, first bathroom and toilet, first board house, first concrete walks, first streetcar, first movies, . . . first pipe organ, first tunnel, first x-ray machine, first love." All was wonderment and romance. As towns grew in size and became part of a real urban setting, however, they faced new concerns, such as "the smoke nuisance" caused by the soot from hundreds of chimneys, the crime and saloons of the city, and the constant struggle to keep streets free of the tons of manure and gallons of urine deposited daily by horses and mules. Small-town Kentucky gradually emerged into urban Kentucky and found both benefits and problems in that transformation.

For a very long time, however, the agrarian ideal lived on, even in parts of the urban commonwealth. In the heart of the Bluegrass, for example, where "the horse is the first citizen," out-of-state observers usually focused on the country estates and thoroughbred farms with their pastoral ethos and noted that Lexington had an English, aristocratic, preindustrial tone. One visitor thought Lexington characteristic of all small Kentucky towns, "slow, easy going and taking but little thought of tomorrow." Native son James Lane Allen

Table 15.2
Kentucky's Largest Cities, 1910 and 1990

1910		1990	
City	Population	City	Population
Louisville	223,928	Louisville	269,063
Covington	53,270	Lexington	225,366
Lexington	35,099	Owensboro	53,549
Newport	30,309	Covington	43,264
Paducah	22,760	Bowling Green	40,641
Owensboro	16,011	Hopkinsville	29,809
Henderson	11,452	Paducah	27,256
Frankfort	10,465	Frankfort	25,968
Hopkinsville	9,419	Henderson	25,945
Bowling Green	9,173	Ashland	23,622

Source: 1910 U.S. Census; Louisville Courier-Journal, Jan. 26, 1991

A homestead in Eddyville (courtesy of the Kentucky Historical Society)

Burkesville, the county seat of Cumberland County (courtesy of the Kentucky Historical Society)

described Lexington and its surroundings as a place where an honored name brought instant respect, where the ideal of the rural gentleman prevailed over the urban business one, and where love of the land dominated the industrial mindset. This "Athens of the South" and other Kentucky cities, such as Paducah, Owensboro, or Ashland, found that an almost rural orientation would long war with the outlook of urban boosterism.

In late nineteenth- and early twentieth-century Kentucky, the urban frame of mind ruled only in two areas—Louisville and the communities near Cincinnati. Covington and Newport, both across the river from Cincinnati, were the second and third largest Kentucky cities in 1900, and the state's only real metropo-lis was Louisville. In 1900, when only one of every five state residents lived in places with populations greater than twenty-five hundred people, nearly half of all urban dwellers in Kentucky lived in Louisville.

Even then, many small- town aspects remained in the urban life of Louisville. Local shops functioned like country stores, poorer areas had outdoor toilets and no sewage disposal, and neighbors helped neighbors. Even the clothes worn by some urban dwellers might resemble those of their rural counterparts. Men dressed in formless brogan work shoes that fit either foot (until the 1880s), unbleached jeans and overalls, and rough shirts. No underwear or shoes would likely be worn in summer. Women typically wore long, shapeless dresses, except for church. Yet clothing patterns did demonstrate the city's differences from rural Kentucky, for a stroll down any well-to-do street would reveal fashionable women wearing tight corsets, wire bustles, high-top shoes, and heavy skirts that brushed the ground. Since a glimpse of a woman's ankles was considered almost scandalous, unseen legs were quietly covered by more utilitarian stockings. These women's male companions might escort them while outfitted in hot, highly starched detachable collars and cuffs, a fancy vest with a watch fob, and a derby or straw hat. Styles would vary, but not until the 1920s would drastic fashion changes take place.

Louisville's size made it different from rural areas, not only in fashion, and magnified the distance between urban and agrarian Kentucky. With two hundred thousand people in 1900, the city at the Falls of the Ohio was the eighteenth largest city in the United States and was five times larger than any other Kentucky place. In some ways, the characteristics of Louisville that visitors observed were simply characteristics of Kentucky writ large. A vot-ing scandal involving a dozen people in a small town might not even be noticed; one in Louisville, involving hundreds, would make front-page news. A dispute between workers and one business in a smaller Kentucky city might never be known, but a labor strike in Louisville would be widely discussed. Brothels or a "fast" woman might exist in almost every small town, but in the Falls City, the houses of prostitution operated so openly that they even published the innocently titled *Souvenir Sporting Guide,* which touted for visitors the attractions of such establishments as those of Madame LeRoy, Lizzie Long, and Mother Mack. A Harrodsburg preacher in 1888 confessed to his diary that three "large, healthy, handsome . . . whores" had accosted him in Louisville, and one "was so kind and cordial, I should have yield[ed] to my low passion. . . . But I escaped."

If labor problems, election fraud, and charges of moral laxity resulted in part simply from the city's size, other differences made Louisville more unique. It was urban; a majority of the state's population would not live in urban areas until 1970. It was prosperous; much of Kentucky was not. Its population included large numbers of blacks and foreign-speaking immigrants; the commonwealth had few such persons in most areas. Louisville could offer those who lived in its environs such things as street vendors, home deliveries of milk and beer, and fresh ice. It also provided easily accessible public schools, fine restaurants, convenient banking, much industry, diverse entertainment, plentiful jobs, and more. Most Kentuckians did not have such options. And if all these benefits came with a price tag that included greater vice, less personal stature, and a dependence on others for livelihood and food, more and more Kentuckians seemed willing to pay that price for urban living as the years passed.

Leisure Time

All across Kentucky, in urban places and rural ones, among both races and sexes and all classes, people continued to find release from

229

their work and woes through a wide variety of entertainment. After the war's end, Kentuckians in the main still followed long-established patterns but eagerly adopted a few new ones.

Little changed in the home, for people looked to themselves for entertainment. They told stories, sang songs, or listened to music played on banjos, fiddles, or perhaps a piano. In other homes, reading individually or aloud to the family proved popular. One woman remembered that, as a result, "the printed word was sacred to us." Kentuckians played board games, such as checkers or Parcheesi, as well as card games. Many families frowned on dancing, but others enjoyed it with passion. They would have "dance parties" in their yards or would form a club that had dances on a regular schedule. Such goings-on disturbed a Livingston reporter, who wrote that "there is a hop every night, the boys and girls seem to have the devil in their heels but nothing in their heads." Yet for all that, the most common form of entertainment was simply conversing with neighbors, relatives, and friends. A young Madison County woman told how she and a visiting friend had spent an enjoyable and simple day, walking in the forest. They had gathered some flowers, stopped and talked, while listening also "to the warble of the birds . . . and the lowing of the cattle in the distance." Plucking a few dogwood blossoms for their hats, they then heard the dinner bell calling them home. Such pleasant and slow-paced pleasures sometimes came at a cost, for certain places seemed to have an endless parade of visitors, who gave tired hosts no rest or time alone. After a period of two months of constant visitors, an exhausted Woodford County woman cried out, "Talk, talk, talk until I was nearly *dead*." Yet for some people in the state, that talk—in reasonable amounts—might be their favorite entertainment.

For others, however, entertainment choices were varied. Food-oriented pursuits, such as hunting and fishing, or work-oriented ones, such as cornhuskings, offered opportunities to meet people and socialize. Picnics, hay

rides, and sleigh rides produced similar results. On a more formal scale, an activity presented as educational—the Chautauqua—did much of the same thing. Most medium- or large-sized Kentucky towns had a parklike Chautauqua grounds, where for a two-week period each summer gatherings would take place. Participants lived in rented cottages and tents amid landscaped walks and lagoons; a dining hall, a library, and an auditorium were also on the grounds. Mornings offered temperance addresses, Bible classes, music lessons, teacher workshops, and talks on civic betterment, while afternoon fare included concerts or education-oriented lectures. In the evening a featured speaker regaled listeners, who then went their own ways in the cool of the twilight, as they strolled and heard more music in the distance. Owensboro's Chautauqua featured a twelve-thousand-seat auditorium, a bowling alley, and train delivery to the grounds. In 1903 popular orator William Jennings Bryan of Nebraska delivered its main address, "The Value of an Ideal," and the next year Louisville editor Henry Watterson presented "Money and Morals." But by the 1910s smaller traveling tent Chautauquas had replaced the more permanent ones. Two decades later a once-formal part of Kentucky life had vanished, a victim of the increased mobility of the people, who traveled to entertainment; of newer challenges, such as radio and motion pictures; and of difficult monetary times. At its peak, however, the Chautauqua provided not only a local out-of-school educational opportunity but also many societal diversions.

Small tent shows, carnivals, country fairs, "Wild West" shows, circuses, and showboats (for those on navigable waterways) also brought audiences a variety of offerings right in their own communities. Performers—who in the absence of access to national models for comparison seemed wonderfully talented—strange animals, hot-air balloons, daring games of chance, fortune-tellers, races, exhibits, prizes—all these things made such shows the high point of the season at many places. Those

230

Boaters enjoy the lagoon at Chautauqua Park in Owensboro (from Lee A. Dew and Aloma Williams Dew, *Owensboro* [1988]).

A carnival in Somerset attracted customers with rides and sideshows (from George Tuggle, *Pulaski Revisited* [1982]).

Kentuckians who could travel to Louisville saw even greater fare, for in 1883 the Southern Exposition provided a regional exhibition. In a building that covered thirteen acres, the exposition's one-hundred-day run brought seven hundred thousand visitors, including the U. S. president. Such popularity made the exposition an annual fixture over the next several years. In 1902 Kentucky began its state fair.

Travel was required for attendance at another popular place—the springs and spas of Kentucky. In relative decline from their antebellum prominence, such places still continued to hold great appeal for middle- and upper-class Kentuckians. Whether at Dawson Springs in Hopkins County in western Kentucky, Rockcastle Springs in Pulaski County to the east, or Crab Orchard Springs in Lincoln County in the central part of the state, the story was similar. Large, spacious hotels in rural settings offered visitors comfortable chairs,

handsome lodging, fine dining, and beautiful ballrooms. Outside, horseback or carriage rides, walks in the woods, swimming in the lake, boating, fishing, tennis, croquet, or visits to the mineral waters all appealed to visitors. Well-dressed Kentuckians danced late into the evening and began their activities again in the morning. But new challenges brought an end to the appeal of the springs, as better transportation took families outside the state and patent medicines made the water's "cures" more readily available. By the early twentieth century most spas had expired.

New forms of entertainment appeared throughout the era, replacing or supplementing the old. Most any town of size, for example, had an opera house, where traveling troupes brought plays and actors who performed both drama and comedy. Minstrel shows featuring white actors in black makeup, vaudeville acts of comedy and singing, and burlesque shows made the rounds as well. By the first decade of the twentieth century, however, that popular fare was challenged by one of the results of a new technological revolution in communication—the motion picture. By 1910 most accessible medium-sized communities had theaters devoted chiefly to showing reasonably priced silent movies. Despite occasional outcries about the "immoral pictures," the new medium had arrived.

Similar changes took place in the field of sports. Some older individual physical exercises continued in the form of swimming, riding, and skating, but the late nineteenth century saw the introduction and acceptance of new sports. By the 1880s bicycling, tennis, and croquet had become popular, and the 1890s saw table tennis and golf begin to make headway, particularly among middle- and upper-class women eager to show their healthfulness. (What has been termed the second golf course in the United States was built in Middlesborough in 1889.) For the first time people became significantly involved in team sports, both as participants and as spectators. The Civil War had spread baseball's popularity, and organized clubs sprang up across Kentucky. The Louisville Grays, a charter member of the National League, had a checkered existence but remained part of the major leagues until 1899. For almost a century, however, smaller clubs formed the heart and soul of the sport. At a time when other team sports were more school-oriented and there were few such institutions across Kentucky, baseball offered communities a variety of amateur, club, and professional teams around which they rallied and cheered. Unlike many other sports, baseball involved all classes.

Football, a college game at the start, was played in Kentucky as early as 1880, when Kentucky University (present-day Transylvania) defeated Centre College 13¾ to 0, under rules very different from today's. Despite attacks on its violence and use of professional players, football gained much support in the

state, and games won front-page headlines by the 1890s.

The newest and least popular of the three major team sports in Kentucky at the start of the twentieth century was basketball. Played chiefly after 1900 and initially by women as much as men, it would grow slowly, only becoming very popular after the 1920s, with the development of high schools and the prominence achieved by coaches at the college level in the state.

For those living in the years after the end of the Civil War, then, Kentucky seemed always changing, with new racial rules, new activities, and new technological developments. The slow death of familiar activities, such as visits to the Chautauquas and the spas, added to the sense of change.

Diaries kept by two young Kentucky women during the post–Civil War period demonstrate just how diverse lives could be in the state. From 1900 to 1914 upper-class Lexingtonian Margaret Preston described days filled with games of cards, tennis, croquet, table tennis, and golf and with seemingly endless visits to friends or visits from her suitors. Days spent reading or listening to phonograph records were followed by nights at concerts, parties, plays, minstrel shows, or club meetings. The presence of maids and a cook freed her to go, by 1910, on "motor-car" rides, football game excursions, and motion picture visits. Only occasionally—such as when her pet bird was eaten by a rat—does the darker side of life appear in her pages.

Twenty-four-year-old Nannie Williams of Graysville, however, told her 1870 diary how she rose at 4:00 A.M. to clean the house before breakfast, then ironed dresses throughout the morning before setting the table for noon dinner. In the afternoon she sewed, then went to the fields to stack a shock of wheat. Married that year to a poor, widowed farmer with four children, she would bear him six more offspring before her twenty-eighth birthday and would raise all ten children. By 1880 the couple's Todd County farm yielded poor crops, and the debt hanging over them caused Nannie to despair that it "is a canker worm that eats the bud out of the flower of happiness. Something will have to be done to pay off or we will suffer." Devoted to her husband and children but frustrated by money problems, she wrote in 1886 that her life was "cares, duties, suffering on one side, Love, faith, and enduring confidence on the other." Her days of hard work broken by churchgoing and a few visits made up a life not unlike that of her mother and grandmother before her.

In the half century after Appomattox, citizens of the commonwealth would live through times of transition and wondrous discovery. But only some were touched, and then only lightly, by the currents of change. Most people still worked and lived in long-established patterns whose roots were more firmly planted in the antebellum world than in the world of the twentieth century. In the main, Kentuckians' lives had not changed a great deal after all in that half century. But change was just over the horizon.

16

Reconstruction, Readjustment, and Race, 1865-1875

Despite much continuity in the postwar lives of Kentuckians, some major changes occurred immediately, chiefly in the areas of race relations and politics. The ending of slavery destroyed many of the old racial rules, and new relationships had to be developed. In the defeated South these new relations would be forged under the aegis of federal Reconstruction. But Kentucky had officially been a loyal, Union state and did not fall under those controls. Many of the same problems and concerns existed in the commonwealth as in the states of the former Confederacy, but solutions resulted from a different set of circumstances. Kentucky's example suggested what might have occurred in a South without Reconstruction; the results proved discouraging. In the end, the federal government did have to intervene, to ensure that blacks received basic rights in this new postwar world, and Kentucky went through a period not of Reconstruction but of Readjustment.

Freedom

Many problems grew out of the piecemeal way slavery ended in Kentucky. The Emancipation Proclamation of 1863 had not affected the commonwealth, since the wartime order applied only to states in rebellion. That fact did not keep some sympathetic Union soldiers and officials from encouraging Kentucky slaves to leave their masters, but equally unsympathetic local and state courts ordered their return. Since enforcement of such court decrees could be sporadic, a kind of de facto freedom existed. Slaveholders in Kentucky had had the opportunity to grasp emancipation with compensation but had totally rejected that course. Had such a route been taken, much of the heartbreak that followed could have been avoided.

In March 1865, shortly before the war's end, the U.S. Congress passed an act proclaiming that all slaves serving as Union soldiers "are made free," and their wives and children were freed as well. Kentucky law did not recognize slave marriages, however, so the whole matter became very complicated. Circuit judges in the state quickly declared the law applying to spouses and offspring unconstitutional, and the case went to appeal before the state's highest court. That process would take eight months, and in the interim Kentucky-born general John M. Palmer of Illinois, as Federal military commander of the commonwealth, consciously disregarded the circuit court ruling and enforced the congressional decree instead. As a result of that and other actions, an estimated 70 percent of the 225,000 former slaves in the state considered their bondage ended. Most white Kentuckians refused to acknowledge the legality of that situation, and the status of blacks in the commonwealth remained unclear. Were they fugitives or free?

Unquestionably, however, some sixty-five thousand Kentucky slaves remained in bondage after the war concluded. Kentucky and Delaware had not ended slavery, and the institution remained legal in those two states longer than anywhere else in the country. Determined to deal with the situation by action if not by law, General Palmer used his powers under the martial law still in force in Kentucky and in May 1865 issued what became known as "Palmer passes." These permits lifted the tight travel restrictions of the old slave codes and permitted virtually free movement. Some ten thousand or more slaves took matters into their own hands—or feet—and simply walked to a boat and crossed the Ohio River to a free state. Others went to Federal army camps, where a forced return to their owners would be less likely. At a July 4 rally, General Palmer was understood to have told a massive crowd of twenty thousand blacks that they were free, and

they took him at his word. Again, most white Kentuckians bitterly opposed the words and the passes as arbitrary and illegal actions. A Louisville court indicted the general for violating the slave code. As one author accurately concluded, "Slavery died hard in Kentucky."

In an attempt to provide some order to the chaos as well as protection to blacks, the state remained under martial law for five months following the surrender of the last Confederate army. On October 12, 1865, however, President Andrew Johnson ordered the end of military rule in the state. This was one of the few federal actions white Kentuckians applauded. Yet some blacks still remained slaves, and others lived in an uncertain legal status, awaiting court decisions to uphold the freedom they understood they had. Now they all lacked the protection of the U.S. Army. Moreover, on December 15, the Kentucky Court of Appeals upheld the earlier lower court decision declaring illegal the federal law regarding the emancipation of black wives and children. These people were still slaves, according to the state decision, and could be returned to their owners. Three days later, however, the entire issue became moot. On December 18, 1865, seven months after the war's end, all Kentucky slaves became free when the Thirteenth Amendment to the U.S. Constitution was declared ratified. The legal question of slavery or freedom was at last answered.

But the question of black rights persisted. Finding answers would take a century or more. Still, for former slaves, the immediate fact was that they were free at last. Liberty came in degrees, in different ways and at different times at various places across the state. In some isolated areas news came slowly, and it might be presented in confusing ways or withheld entirely. As late as 1867 cases were reported of children who were still held in bondage. One woman remembered finally hearing the news: "I got happy and sung, but I didn't know for a long time what to be free was." She learned.

When freedom did come, former slaves generally experienced similar emotions: "When the news came we were free every body was glad," one remembered. A contemporary observer wrote that "the *consciousness* of *freedom* has got hold of them and abides with them." Some white families, long convinced of the loyalty of their slaves to them, were genuinely shocked when they arose not to the smell of breakfast being prepared by slaves but to the silence of an empty house. Their servants had slipped away in the night. One man who lived at the time remembered that in his area only "a very few" slaves did not leave. Such changes added to labor problems and angered white Kentuckians. The situation in some households changed little, however, as former slaves willingly stayed on, working for wages in continued close relationships with white families. But there was a crucial difference: they stayed because they had chosen to do so and could leave when they desired. The working situation may not have been openly modified on the surface, but everyone knew it was different. The former slaves were free.

Freedom brought with it a mobility unknown under slavery, and blacks flocked to towns and cities to get away from former masters, rural violence, and unpleasant memories. Like others, they sought new lives and opportunities in an urban setting. As a result, the black population of Lexington, for instance, increased over 130 percent between 1860 and 1870, at a time when the city's white growth was only a little over 20 percent. Black migrants lived wherever they could—integrated into white areas through housing in back alleys, out-of-the-way streets, and older houses, or self-segregated in newly built shantytowns on the city's edge. The same pattern developed in Louisville and in most towns across the state. But the independence blacks found in cities and towns came at a high cost. They lived in dilapidated housing, endured inadequate food and fuel, and suffered widespread disease. Fever took its toll in Owensboro, and in Paducah destitute people died in the streets. Some white Kentuckians provided aid and support, but anger directed at the newly freed slaves represented a more typical response. Black attempts at self-uplift were viewed almost as an attack on the status quo. When desperate former slaves stole food in order to survive, whites condemned them, and this condemnation became a part of a self-fulfilling prophecy. It seemed as if many whites wanted to prove slavery had been good by seeing the former slaves fail.

Strong black families, however, helped the former slaves survive and succeed in the end. First of all, former slaves who had been separated from spouses and children searched them out and reunited their families. A study of housing in Louisville showed that 70 per-

A black family in Glasgow in the post–Civil War period (from J. Winston Coleman Photographic Collection, Transylvania University Library).

cent of black children lived with both parents by 1880, a figure similar to the white average. Since the law had not recognized the marriages of slaves, those who had been living together before the war sought to solemnize their relationships. An 1866 Kentucky law prohibited interracial marriages, with a five-year jail term as penalty, but it also allowed former slaves to purchase marriage certificates, recognizing antebellum cohabitation as a legal marriage and offspring as legitimate. Many, many Kentucky blacks paid with scarce money to formalize their marriage ties. In spite of all the family divisions and disruptions as a result of slavery, black families within a half decade after war's end were basically similar in structure to white families.

The 1866 marriage law proved to be one of only a few concessions made to the former slaves. A white minister in western Kentucky, on hearing of a black barn dance, remarked in his diary, "This is almost an insult to the moral sense & sentiment of our community." Such attitudes were prevalent. Whites had been reared on stories about the anarchy that would result from the removal of the guiding controls of slavery: blacks would rise up and kill whites, so the stories went, or intermarry with them, or utterly disrupt the labor system. But none of that happened on the scale predicted, and one farmer wrote two years after the end of slavery that "we have tried the system of Free Negro labor . . . and they are doing better than the most sanguine of us had hoped." Yet despite evidence to the contrary, white Kentuckians continued to paint dire pictures of the awful consequences should blacks have anything but a subordinate, slavelike status. As a result, one race had public education; the other did not. One race could sit on juries; the other could not. One race could testify against the other in court; the other could not. And one race could use violence to oppose any action that sought to advance black equality.

Kentucky was a violent state for both races in the 1860s and beyond, but the intensity of the actions directed against former slaves ex-

ceeded anything experienced by whites. Sometimes white antagonism emerged as economic opposition, such as a refusal to sell land to blacks for them to build schools or churches. At other times and places threats would precede violent outbursts, and blacks would be forced to leave whole areas of the state. A band of five hundred whites in Gallatin County, for example, forced hundreds of blacks to flee across the Ohio River. Finally, white hostility could explode directly into physical force. During a two-week period in 1867 some sixteen whites in Kentucky were arrested on separate charges of beating former slaves. The next year brought the account of a black woman who accidentally brushed against the dress of a county judge's wife and was caned so hard by the judge that she acquired a scar. Such events unfortunately were not rare. In a single month in 1868 a black school was destroyed in Monroe County, a school and two churches were burned in Bullitt County, and a teacher of a black school in Mayfield was driven from town by a mob.

Hatred also brought death. Between 1867 and 1871 more than one hundred blacks were lynched in Kentucky, and dozens more were killed by other violent means. Groups of self-styled "Regulators" virtually controlled the central Kentucky counties of Anderson, Mercer, Marion, and Boyle. Groups called Skagg's Men and the Bull Pups, numbering well over a hundred each, lynched people of both races and drove off entire communities of blacks. To counter their actions, another group, Rowzee's Band, organized and killed two of the Regulators. A harried farmer pleaded for aid from the governor: "We cannot lay down at Night in peace we are aroused Shooting and yeling like mad or Deranged men." All across the state such groups or even more formal bands of the Ku Klux Klan terrorized the countryside. A Freedmen's Bureau teacher in Bowling Green received a warning: "KU KLUX KLANS! Blood! Poison! Powder! Torch! Leave in five days or hell's your portion!" A recent study of Klan violence in the period concluded that "outrages in Kentucky equaled those elsewhere in size, frequency, and brutality." In July 1869 a newspaper reported that the Klan had hanged twenty-five people within a central Kentucky area twenty-five miles in diameter and had beaten a hundred more during the previous two years. While some leading citizens and newspapers attacked such extralegal violence and towns like Henderson outlawed the wearing of masks, others in the state media praised "Judge Lynch." Stories written by these people often remarked that "many of the best citizens of the city were members of the clan." It is little wonder that blacks such as former Union soldier Elijah Marrs formed Loyal Leagues for protection. Living at the time in Henry County, a place "overrun with the K.K.K.," Marrs had windows broken in his house, but by sleeping with a pistol under his pillow, a rifle by his side, "and a corn-knife at the door," he remained unharmed. Marrs would go on to be a teacher, minister, civic leader, and political activist, speaking out later against segregation. But an atmosphere of violence like the one in which he lived could only beget more violence.

The bitter, unrelenting opposition to black education, advancement, or rights—indeed, to anything that hinted at the possibility of equality—brought forth a response from the federal government. The extent of the resistance to black self-help efforts and the defiant hostility to efforts at economic independence necessitated outside aid if blacks were to have any reasonable opportunities. The Bureau of Refugees, Freedmen, and Abandoned Lands had been organized to deal with the former Confederacy, and its jurisdiction did not extend to Kentucky. With the state's recent history, however, the head of the organization, General Oliver O. Howard, directed that it supervise the former slaves of Kentucky as well. Opposition was immediate, for the Freedmen's Bureau, aided by a few soldiers, quickly took a limited but active role in trying to secure fair contracts and proper treatment for the state's blacks. Between 1866, when the organization began to operate in the state, and 1869, when its main duties ended, the Freedmen's Bu-

reau proved to be about the best friend former slaves had.

The always underfunded Freedmen's Bureau, which never had more than fifty-seven officials for what was then the 110 counties of the state, provided small amounts of food and clothing to destitute blacks. It operated a hospital in Louisville, and it supervised and, if necessary, voided apprenticeship contracts, which seemed almost an attempt to reestablish slavery. One such typical 1866 contract in Warren County ordered that James Watthall, "a freed boy of color of the age of seven," be bound to a white man "until he arrives at the age of 21 years, to learn the trade, art, or mystery of farming." Most important, however, the Bureau helped establish schools across Kentucky, which were in most instances the only educational facilities available for blacks. By November 1867, 97 schools, employing 117 teachers, had 5,610 pupils; a year and a half later, nearly 250 schools had an attendance of 10,360. Unlike the situation in the former Confederacy, where white northern teachers tended to predominate, 80 percent of the teachers at the Freedmen's Bureau schools in Kentucky were black. Among the seventeen states where the Bureau operated, Kentucky usually ranked third or fourth in attendance and first or second in the percentage of school-age blacks in school. In fact, by 1869 probably a greater part of the black student population attended classes than did the white. Freedmen's Bureau schools provided basic instruction only, but they fulfilled a fundamental need for former slaves.

It is remarkable the Freedmen's Bureau schools did as well as they did, for almost every effort was met by resistance. Schoolhouses were burned, teachers were beaten, and students were threatened and killed. Reports repeated the same story over and over: in 1867 former slaves had been the victims of 20 killings, 18 shootings, 11 rapes, and 270 other cases of mistreatment; in January 1868 "there is certainly a very determined and a very bitter opposition to the education of the negro"; in November

"Armed and Masked bands of men exercise unlimited sway."

The Freedman's Bureau had been established in Kentucky because, as historian Marion B. Lucas notes, the state's citizens had not accepted "responsibility for the human needs of freedmen." The commonwealth's inaction or opposition had brought federal intervention, but the Bureau itself grew to be so hated that even greater violence resulted. The organization became both part of the solution and part of the problem. One study concluded that "Kentucky had the dubious distinction of being in the forefront in its violent opposition to the activities of the Freedmen's Bureau." Whites who were already angry over military rule, federal resistance to state court decrees, and what they perceived as unconstitutional actions concerning slavery struck out against the Bureau as yet another interference in their lives. What white Kentuckians did not see was that through some basic humanitarianism and fairness they could have avoided much of the tragedy that they brought on themselves.

Political Decisions, 1865-1868

If racial adjustments constituted a major part of the shifting ground that made up postwar Kentucky life, political readjustments took place almost in quicksand. The fluid political situation was uncertain, unstable, and unsteady, and for a time Kentuckians tried to make sense of a world that featured three virtually new political parties.

In antebellum times, the Whig Party of Henry Clay had dominated, but with Clay's and his party's death in the 1850s, new challenges had come forth. These were not met before the war came, and the conflict changed all the rules. Now, three groups—former Whigs, former Unionists, and former Confederates—were the prizes the parties sought to gain. Even prewar Democrats were now divided by the causes they had supported, North or South. In the political card game, all earlier bets were off, and new hands were being dealt. All parties wanted to make certain they could win.

In some ways the most clear-cut and stable of what were really all-new parties was what was sometimes called the Union Party. It soon became known as the Republican Party. Representing the victors in the war and the party that controlled national policy, Kentucky Republicans supported Reconstruction in the South and the adoption of the Thirteenth, Fourteenth, and Fifteenth Amendments, giving former slaves rights as citizens and voters. Consisting chiefly of former Unionists, and with former Whigs in its ranks, the party consciously adopted more moderate stances than did the Radical Republicans at the national level. Yet it also sought to have Kentucky perceived nationally as a loyal state deserving of rewards. Republicans in the commonwealth saw themselves as the progressive, "modern" force in the state, the faction that would reshape Kentucky along the lines of the developing North.

Opponents sought to tar Republicans with the brush of radicalism. Calling them Red Republicans, Radicals, Radical Abolitionists, or Jacobins (referring to revolutionary France), those in opposition pictured Kentucky Republicans as bloodthirsty militarists who were seeking, as the *Flemingsburg Democrat* stated, a nation "where liberty is swallowed up by . . . anarchy." Attackers proclaimed that these radicals wanted black suffrage, even racial equality, and would support any actions, constitutional or otherwise, to destroy the rights of white southerners and to promote black privilege.

Leading this attack was what was sometimes termed the Conservative or Southern Rights Party, but more often simply the Democratic Party. Called "the secession Democracy" by its enemies, the party did include many former Confederates and their supporters. But from the beginning it also numbered in its ranks former Unionists who had turned against the national administration over questions involving military, constitutional, and racial matters. Both Democrats and Republicans had former Whigs and former Unionists in their parties, and both parties attempted to attract those former voting blocs. Democrats made their appeals by calling for what amounted to a return to the past, as they opposed, in general, all the constitutional amendments, fought at first any movement toward extending black rights, and indicated that they—and Kentucky—must speak for the South, since only their "free" and "unconquered" state could represent southern interests against the national radicals. While Republicans looked northward for their model, Democrats looked southward. The *Kentucky Gazette,* published in Lexington, presented the Democratic arguments clearly in its July 4, 1866, issue, proclaiming that the question was "whether we will yield up the last vestige of the institutions reared by Washington and Jefferson, and bid adieu to that constitutional liberty . . . or whether we will listen to the syren song of the Jacobins [Republicans], and . . . overturn the Constitution of the country." In response, Kentucky Republicans praised their martyred hero Lincoln and said that his more modern vision must be followed, rather than that of the recent traitors who had sought to destroy the Union.

In all this, however, a third party lurked, seeking votes. Called the Conservative Union or Constitutional Union Democratic Party, it sought to build its base among former Whigs who disagreed with both the "radical" policies of the Republicans and the reactionary ones of the Democrats. It also wooed Unionists who could not stomach alliance with either the increasingly Confederate-dominated Democrats or the black-oriented Republicans. Samuel Haycraft, in a May 1866 letter to a newspaper editor, spoke for those who feared, as he did, voting for an "Abolition" party or a secessionist one. He belonged to "a class of men, old-line Whigs and Democrats" who had supported the Union, but not the end of slavery as it was now occurring. Should either the Democrats or the Republicans adopt extreme stances, then the Constitutional Unionists might develop into a major force.

The three parties engaged in a propaganda war to sell their viewpoints to undecided voters, and the issues were chiefly national ones—Reconstruction in the South, racial concerns, and constitutional matters. Kentucky's political future was being shaped not on state questions but on even broader ones. Citizens had to decide what they wanted their future to be. They made their choice very clear, very quickly.

The initial opportunity to test the strength of the various groups came in the state election held in August 1865. (Some federal elections were held separately, in November.) Some months earlier, the General Assembly had rejected the Thirteenth Amendment freeing the slaves, by a vote of 56-18 in the House and 23-10 in the Senate. What support there was had come from northeastern and southeastern Kentucky. The Thirteenth Amendment remained a key issue; Unionists (Republicans) supported it, and Conservatives (Democrats) opposed it. The state continued under martial law, and the military did influence the vote in some places, but overall the Conservatives carried the day, electing a state treasurer, five of nine congressmen, and a majority of the legislature. Republicans were worried.

Well might they be. The new General Assembly again refused to ratify the Thirteenth Amendment, then angered some Unionists by repealing the Wartime Act of Expatriation, which had deprived Confederates of political and civil rights. As a result, former Confederates suffered no reprisals, and the governor began granting pardons to soldiers under indictment for actions taken during the war. Former Confederates quickly began to retake leadership posts in their communities and state. In fact, the next six governors would either be former Confederate soldiers or men who had been wartime southern sympathizers. The new heroes were not those who had victoriously defended a now less-popular vision, but rather those who had waged war against it. The victors lost the peace.

That fact became even clearer in what would normally have been a minor, off-year race, the race for clerk of the Court of Appeals in 1866. Instead it became a testing ground, with the Democrats running Judge Alvin Duvall of Georgetown. He quickly attacked the "Yankee agents" of the Freedmen's Bureau and that group's "vile usurpation" of state powers. Both the Conservative Union Party and the Union (Republican) Party had candidates in the field, but just five weeks before the election, the two parties united behind former Union general Edward H. Hobson of Greensburg, a man who had captured the Confederate John Hunt Morgan. But Unionist hero status meant less than Hobson's advocacy of the Thirteenth and Fourteenth Amendments, and Democrats labeled him a radical who had supported the "robbery" of one hundred million dollars' worth of slave property through uncompensated emancipation. The passage of the national Civil Rights Act of 1866, giving blacks more rights, became another issue used against Hobson. Bitterness erupted on election day, and some twenty people were killed in disputes across the state. Democrat Duvall won a convincing victory, obtaining 95,979 votes compared with Hobson's 58,035. The pro-Union *Frankfort Commonwealth* summarized accurately the results: Unionists "have been outnumbered or out-generaled, the great engine used against them having been, as usual, the negro."

This election was but one of several preliminary skirmishes before the 1867 battle for major political office, the governorship of the Commonwealth of Kentucky. The victories went consistently to the Democrats. First, the legislature of January 1867 overwhelming defeated, by votes of 62-26 and 24-7, the proposed Fourteenth Amendment to the U.S. Constitution, giving blacks citizenship and certain other protections. Next, in a three-way fight that ended with the Constitutional Union forces combining this time with the Democrats, incumbent U.S. senator Garrett Davis of Bourbon County won reelection for a six-year term. A former Whig and former Know-Nothing, Davis had become a wartime Democrat, and he made the transition to peacetime vic-

tory. Then in May 1867, in a special congressional election, Democrats won all nine seats in races that frequently featured all three parties. A disgusted Republican wrote, "Kentucky is today as effectually in the hands of rebels as if they had every town and city garrisoned by their troops. . . . What is to become of the poor blacks and loyal white men God only knows."

The answer become common knowledge with the gubernatorial race decided in August 1867. Sixty-five-year-old Democratic nominee John L. Helm (1802-67) of Elizabethtown had been a Whig governor of the state in the 1850s; one of his sons had been killed fighting as a Confederate general in the Civil War. While the rest of the ticket included one former Union officer, it also featured a Confederate who had ridden with Morgan and several wartime southern sympathizers. Terming this ticket a "theft of all the offices by the rebels," old Unionists, including current governor Thomas E. Bramlette and Lieutenant Governor Richard T. Jacob, organized a third-party convention, called themselves the Conservative Union Democrats, and nominated William B. Kinkead of Lexington. Both groups chastised Radical Reconstruction policies and opposed granting further rights to blacks. The main difference seemed to be that the Conservative Unionists wanted recognition of their wartime accomplishments and a limit on the growing strength of former Confederates in the Democratic Party. Republicans had been unable to forge another merger with the so-called third party, for their differences on policy were too great, and the Republicans offered instead a slate headed by former Union colonel Sidney M. Barnes of Estill County. His support for the unpopular Fourteenth Amendment overshadowed moderate words suggesting a quick end to military rule in the South, and the results indicated how Kentuckians felt. Democrat Helm won 90,225 votes, Republican Barnes got 33,939, and Conservative Unionist Kinkead polled but 13,167. Two-thirds of the voters had gone Democratic, and Republicans won only

17 seats in the 138-person General Assembly. Happy Democrats rejoiced that they had rid the state of "the Curse of Radicalism." Republican editor William O. Goodloe of Lexington's *Kentucky Statesman* spoke for his side when he angrily cried out, "What [Confederate general] Bragg failed to do in 1862, with his army and banners, the people of Kentucky, five years later, have done; they have given the State over into the hands of those who are and have been the enemies of the Union." Some of his party called on Congress to bring in the military and initiate Reconstruction policies. The *Frankfort Commonwealth* confessed, "The 'Lost Cause' is found again in Kentucky."

Republicans erred in attributing Democratic success totally to the former Confederates in that party. The scope of the Democratic victory showed that many former Unionists simply could not support Republican policies on race and other issues and had joined the opposition instead. In the fight for the former Whigs, both parties had made gains, but that was not enough for the Republicans. To forge a winning coalition, they had needed to bring in even more Whigs. A study of Caldwell County in western Kentucky showed that of those who had opposed the Democratic Party as Whigs in 1848, only 41 percent voted against the Democrats twenty years later. Similarly, a statewide survey of twenty-five prominent prewar Whigs found that thirteen had become postwar Democrats and eleven had become Republicans. In short, the powerful former Whig block had divided fairly equally. Of the twenty counties that had voted Whig consistently before the 1850s, only five—all in the Unionist Kentucky mountains—had voted Republican in 1867. In the struggle for the hearts, minds, and votes of Unionists and Whigs, the Republicans had met defeat.

The year 1867 marked the effective demise of the Conservative Union third-party movement. Ironically, it also marked the death of the man responsible for their immediate defeat. Ill during the campaign, Governor Helm could not leave his home and was sworn in

there. Just five days later, on September 8, 1867, Helm died, and his lieutenant governor, John White Stevenson (1812-86), took over the gubernatorial term. A wealthy, fifty-five-year-old attorney from Covington, Stevenson was the son of a Speaker of the U.S. House from Virginia and had followed his father's path into Democratic politics as a Kentucky congressman and southern sympathizer. Now he inherited a state divided on race, inundated with violence, and mired in debates about federal-state relations. But his immediate task was to win a special election to fill the rest of the unexpired term, a contest that took place in August 1868. Even though the new governor proved to be a less than dynamic speaker, he had no third-party opposition, for a change, and numerous national issues to attack, as usual. The result was a landslide victory over Republican R. Tarvin Baker, on a vote of 115,560-26,605. Winning more than 80 percent of the vote, the Democrats ruled supreme in the state. For almost the next three decades they would continue to do so.

Bourbons and New Departure Democrats

Democrats forged an uneasy alliance, however. They could usually unite at election time and win victories, but many cracks and blemishes developed in their armor.

Part of the problem lay in divisive sectionalism and the divergent interest groups operating in Kentucky. People in different regions of the state—western, central, northern, and eastern—had varied interests and sought to protect and advocate their own positions. Commercial forces struggled with agricultural ones; city competed with city, and leaders with leaders. The old hemp-growing Bluegrass and the new tobacco-growing western Kentucky areas, the railroad towns and those without rails, the old power blocs and the new—all contested for power within the party.

Philosophical differences also arose, and for a time, two major factions split the party that would win almost all the elections for nearly thirty years. On one side stood the so-called Bourbon Democrats. Like the Bourbon royal family of France, they forgot nothing and learned nothing. Led by conservatives like J. Stoddard Johnston of Frankfort's *Kentucky Yeoman* and former Whig George Washington Craddock, the chairman of the Central Committee, they initially controlled the Democratic Party and opposed almost any variations from the old, prewar order. They refused to recognize change brought about by Reconstruction and, according to one writer, "seemed to worship at the shrine of the dead past." Strong advocates of low taxation and limited state and public education, the Bourbons supported an extremely restricted role for government in the lives of Kentuckians.

Opposing them were the New Departure Democrats. So named because they sought to break away from old issues and forge a new Kentucky, the New Departure forces counseled acceptance of the federal amendments so that Reconstruction could be hurried along and ended. They wanted not to refight the war in the press but to put it all behind them and move ahead. Supporting a state and federal role in government and the economy that harkened back to the philosophy of the old Whig Party, they advocated a vision that included support for industrialization, education, and, to a much more limited extent, some black rights. The Bourbons would refer to "the humiliation of this 'new departure' which is a surrender of the whole subject to radical usurpation and revolution." But able New Departure leaders answered that charge easily. On November 8, 1868, major Louisville papers merged and formed the *Courier-Journal*. Led by its young editor Henry Watterson (1840-1921), it soon became the leading newspaper in the South and made Watterson a national spokesman for his party and his region. In the Bluegrass another former Confederate soldier, William Campbell Preston Breckinridge (1837-1904), already was editing the *Lexington Observer and Reporter*. Both men used their papers to spread the New Departure word. Neither man necessarily fa-vored the federal Reconstruction policy, and neither was a racial egalitarian. But both called for acceptance of the amendments, both spoke out against the Klan and violence, and both promoted internal improvements. In October 1866 W.C.P. Breckinridge issued the call for a New South and a new Kentucky: "Extend her railroads; open up her rivers . . . ; dig into her mountain sides and develop her inexhaustible mineral wealth; erect mills and manufactories, and with zeal and energy compete with other parts of the country." More agrarian-oriented Bourbons attacked that vision as only a pale reflection of Republican philosophy, and the factional fight was on.

The Stevenson Administration and Black Rights

New governor John W. Stevenson represented a party that totally controlled the state. The selection of conservative Democratic attorney Thomas Clay McCreery (1816-90) of Daviess County to fill an unexpired U.S. Senate term, the election of Democrats to all nine congressional seats in the 1868 fall elections, and the presidential vote that year all showed the trends. On national issues, Kentucky stood firmly with the southern Democratic viewpoint. As a result, war hero and Republican presidential candidate Ulysses S. Grant received but 39,566 Kentucky votes in the 1868 race, while Democratic hopeful Horatio Seymour of New York carried the state with 75 percent of the vote, a total of 115,889. Kentucky was one of only eight states that supported Seymour (three southern states did not vote in the election). New president Grant brought the hated Radical Republican banner to the White House.

Overall, Governor Stevenson tried to steer a middle-of-the-road course between his party's two factions. He dispatched the state militia to various locales in a largely fruitless effort to stem violence, favored the establishment of a House of Reform for juvenile delinquents, and supported a successful school referendum that provided more tax money for education, all moves the New Departure group

243

supported. Yet at the same time he opposed almost all attempts to expand black rights and did not speak out against moves designed to limit those rights even further, actions the Bourbons advocated. On the question of black testimony, for instance, Stevenson first took the conservative stance. By Kentucky law, blacks could not testify in court against whites. But under the U.S. Civil Rights Act of 1866, when blacks were denied their right to testify, the cases could be taken to federal court, where black testimony would be allowed. Republicans and some of the group that would be called New Departure Democrats advocated that Kentucky pass legislation allowing black testimony, thus returning Kentucky cases to Kentucky courts. The bill failed in 1867, and that year the state's highest court declared the Civil Rights Act unconstitutional in regard to the issue of testimony. Once again the national and state judiciaries stood in conflict, as a federal lower court soon upheld the Civil Rights Act as constitutional. In 1869 the legislature once more refused to modify the state law, and Governor Stevenson supported a move to take the issue to the U.S. Supreme Court. State action thus would be delayed for two more years.

Meanwhile, individuals were taking stands on the issue, often at great political cost. New Departure leader W.C.P. Breckinridge, for instance, ran for commonwealth's attorney in 1868 and at a gathering was accused of supporting black testimony. He responded: "Fellow-citizens, the charge my opponents urge against me is true. I am aware that this avowal will most likely defeat me in this canvass, for you are not ready to view this question calmly and dispassionately. Your prejudices blind your judgement. . . . In the after days, when the passions of this hour shall have cooled, when reason shall assert her sway . . . in that hour you will approve though now you condemn me." Facing certain defeat after that open acknowledgment of his views, he withdrew from the race. Not until 1871 did Governor Stevenson support black testimony, but his last legislature

defeated it once more. With local judges now being indicted in federal court for denying black testimony, however, the General Assembly in 1872 finally passed a bill giving blacks the same legal rights held by whites in the state's courts. Ironically, only a few months later the U.S. Supreme Court gave some support to Kentucky's appeal, but the matter had been decided by then.

In the meantime, an even greater fight was going on. The proposed Fifteenth Amendment to the U.S. Constitution gave black men the right to vote, but the state legislature in January 1869 had rejected the proposed measure by votes of 27-6 and 80-5. Yet as each month passed, more and more states ratified the amendment, and it was only a matter of time before the proposition would become the law of the land. The *Covington Journal* protested the "infamy" of the idea, the *Paris True Kentuckian* called the proposal "a villainous innovation," and Bourbon leader Craddock termed it unconstitutional. Angry Democrats said that theirs must be "a white man's party," free of any black voters. When the amendment was declared ratified on March 30, 1870, it enfranchised thousands of blacks, most of whom were expected to vote Republican—if they could. Some towns and cities imposed lengthy residence requirements for voting or changed their boundaries to omit areas of significant black population and thus remove potential voters. Those subterfuges eventually failed. More commonly blacks voted, amid some violence but without major problems. A few scratched the Democratic ticket, but most voted for the party of Lincoln. They and their descendants would continue to do so for the next seven decades. Many previously Democratic areas with sizable black populations suddenly saw a two-party system develop overnight, as blacks began to vote Republican. In the 1870 election in Danville, for example, the winning Republican count of 276 consisted of 59 votes from whites and 217 votes from blacks. The losing Democrats had 203 votes; only 5 of these came from black voters.

Governor Stevenson would not have to face these new voters directly in the future, for he had been selected by a joint vote of both houses of the legislature to replace incumbent McCreery as U.S. senator from Kentucky. Since senators continued to be elected by the legislature and not by popular vote, and since the General Assembly remained heavily Democratic for decades, the senatorship would stay solidly in that party's hands. In February 1871 Stevenson resigned as governor to take up his new position the next month, leaving behind an administration constantly troubled by turmoil and conflict. Since Stevenson had vacated the lieutenant governor's post to become governor when Helm died, the president of the Senate, Preston H. Leslie (1819-1907), now became governor—the third person to fill the office in the four-year term.

The Leslie Years, 1871-1875

Facing an August 1871 election for a full four-year term, Governor Leslie tried not to alienate either faction of his party and thus to ensure his reelection. He had always followed such a path. Born in present-day Clinton County, Leslie had overcome poverty and a limited education to enter the legal profession. A successful Whig

legislator, Leslie had turned to the Democrats after Clay's death and had gone through the war years as a slaveholder opposed to secession but sympathetic to the southern cause. Now in 1871, he ran on a states' rights platform that opposed the "revolutionary" spirit of the "unconstitutional" Fourteenth and Fifteenth Amendments and just about everything connected with the Republican administration of U.S. Grant.

With blacks voting in a governor's race for the first time, Republicans voiced more optimism, particularly once their gubernatorial choice was made. John Marshall Harlan (1833-1911) represented the "new" Republican of the commonwealth, although he came from an old Kentucky family. Son of a Whig congressman, he had been a prewar Whig state adjutant general at age eighteen. When war came, the well-educated and capable Harlan had joined the Union Army, then resigned later to accept election as attorney general of Kentucky. A slaveholder who opposed the Thirteenth Amendment and the Freedmen's Bureau, he had first joined the postwar third-party forces but with their demise went to the Republicans. Harlan was one of those leaders who matured in politics. When his earlier, conservative racial

John Marshall Harlan, Kentucky Republican leader and later U.S. Supreme Court justice (courtesy of the Library of Congress)

stands were pointed out, he replied simply: "Let it be said that I am right rather than consistent." He soon was recognized as one of the most able Kentuckians and would be named to the U.S. Supreme Court in 1877. In his thirty-three years on the bench there, Harlan became known as the Great Dissenter, famous for his defense of black rights—a stance perhaps influenced by the fact that he had grown up with a mulatto man who was often referred to as his half-uncle or half-brother. Harlan would later be named one of the Supreme Court's dozen greatest justices.

By the 1871 governor's race, the Republican Party, like its Democratic counterpart, had finally stabilized and had taken on the characteristics it would retain for the next several decades. The Republican Party was a party of contrasts, made up chiefly of economically disadvantaged blacks and eastern Kentucky whites, but led by wealthy and probusiness urbanites such as James Speed and Benjamin H. Bristow, both of Louisville. The combination also included what were termed Post Office Republicans, who joined the party primarily to benefit from the patronage of what were usually Republican administrations in Washington. Some two thousand federal jobs came to the state. But fights over the spoils of office would divide the party, as would disagreements over the role of blacks. In the end, votes of blacks were accepted and sought, and some further rights were advocated, but Republican candidates statewide remained as white as those the Democrats proposed. Even then, for some in the commonwealth Republicanism was akin to heresy. One politician noted much later that in one Democratic stronghold, "If Christ came to Earth, even the strong Baptists up there wouldn't vote for him if he were on the Republican ticket."

In the 1871 election Harlan appealed to the New Departure Democrats on mostly state issues, as he called for support for education and railroads, an end to lawlessness, and acceptance of the federal amendments. Tall, muscu-

lar, and a strong speaker, the red-haired Harlan dominated his bearded friend, the less oratorical and less imposing Leslie, in joint debate, but in the end it did not matter. The Democrat began to take more moderate stands, stressed federal instead of state issues, and found that most Kentucky voters simply could not bring themselves to endorse the Republican record nationally. By a vote of 126,455-89,299, Leslie won the race. Even with a strong candidate and the support of black voters, the Republican Party could not break free of the shackles of the war and Readjustment. The Republicans' immediate electoral future seemed clear—continued defeat.

A Lexington newspaper had editorialized earlier that "the Kentucky Democracy is a party that hangs very loosely together. The least difference, the smallest dissatisfaction creates a split." Governor Leslie quickly discovered the truth of that conclusion, as a major conflict split not only his party but also the state.

At issue was the Cincinnati Southern Railroad bill, which would support building a line through the central part of Kentucky and tying that area to the South via Chattanooga. Sectionalism quickly arose as supporters of the powerful Louisville and Nashville Railroad opposed this challenge to their near monopoly of the state's rail system, especially a challenge led by "Yankee" commercial rival Cincinnati. The question was one of power, money, and dominance, and the bitter battle lines divided parties and factions. Some usually prorailroad New Departure leaders, such as Louisvillian Henry Watterson, opposed the bill, while more conservative central Kentucky Bourbon Democrats favored it. But in 1870 and 1871 votes, the legislature had rejected the bill, despite pleas from one-time presidential candidate and lionized Confederate hero John C. Breckinridge of Lexington. Now in the 1872 General Assembly, Leslie opposed the measure, but it passed the Kentucky House and gained a tie vote in the Senate. Lieutenant Governor John G. Carlisle of Covington cast his deciding ballot in the bill's favor, and it became law. Sectionalism and the L&N had been defeated. That would not always be the case.

Despite passage of this bill that he did not support, Leslie usually collaborated well with the legislature during his term of office. Some much-needed legislation was enacted. Black testimony was allowed, funding for asylums and correctional institutions was increased, more stringent laws against violence were enacted, a geological survey to determine the state's resources was established, a pharmacy board was created, and, in a particularly important action, a public system of black schools was begun. An advocate of temperance who did not serve liquor at state functions, the "Coldwater Governor" also signed a law providing for local option elections to decide whether intoxicating drink would be sold.

Politically, Leslie's administration held few surprises. Former Confederate congressman Willis B. Machen of Lyon County was selected to fill an unexpired term in the U.S. Senate, and on-again, off-again Senator McCreery won a full term in 1872. Democrats continued to control the congressional and legislative delegations. The only confusion appeared in the 1872 presidential election, when reform-minded Republicans at the national level rejected what they saw as Grant's scandal-ridden administration, nominated Horace Greeley of New York as their candidate, and called themselves the Liberal Republican Party. Nationally, the Democratic Party recognized that it could not win the election and endorsed Greeley as well. Henry Watterson led a reluctant Kentucky into the Liberal Republican fold, but to no avail. Greeley carried the commonwealth by a vote of 100,212-88,816, but of the thirty-seven states, he carried only five others.

At the conclusion of the Leslie years in 1875, then, the patterns for the next decades seemed established. The Freedmen's Bureau was gone, and Reconstruction was fading as an issue. The third-party movement had died, for the moment. Party factionalism appeared to be receding, and the divisive Cincinnati Southern issue had been resolved. All the voting blocs were now securely attached to one party or another. In short, many of the concerns troubling Kentucky in the Readjustment years now seemed solved.

Much had been decided, but the role of blacks had not. In some areas gains had been made. Whites in Kentucky now begrudgingly accepted blacks as citizens and as voters and would not deprive them of their voting rights (unlike the situation farther south). Blacks could now testify in court. By 1876 they were sitting on some federal juries, and by 1882 on state ones (although that would change). Black lawyers Nathaniel R. Harper of Louisville and George A. Griffith of Owensboro had been accepted to the bar in 1871, and a new cadre of leaders had come to the forefront, including Dr. Henry Fitzbutler, Kentucky's first black physician and editor of Louisville's *Ohio Falls Express*. Blacks could attend an integrated institution at Berea College, where the 237 students in 1875 included 143 blacks. Blacks also lived physically among whites in cities across the state; Louisville in 1870 had black families residing on three of every four blocks on average. Blacks began to run for and win minor political offices. In Hopkinsville, for example, a black man sat on the city council from 1895 to 1907, and others of his race served as deputy sheriff, county coroner, and county physician. In Mount Sterling between 1901 and 1918, at least one black man won election to the city council. In certain locales, blacks and whites sat together at religious services and worked beside each other in coal mines. The integration of blacks into some facets of Kentucky life had occurred.

Yet as the years wore on after 1875, segregation increased in other areas. There were no sudden changes, and just about every community had its own rules and exceptions. But in some places vagrancy laws were used to enforce a status for blacks not dissimilar to slavery. More formally, the state penitentiary in 1882 segregated the races at its church services; two

Nathaniel R. Harper, admitted to the bar in 1871, practiced law in Louisville (from A. P. Lipscomb, ed., *The Commercial History of the Southern States ... Kentucky* [1903])

years later the Kentucky Institution for the Education of the Blind set up a separate "Colored Department." Public schools started out segregated and remained so. Residential integration grew less prevalent, and increased segregation in all areas seemed the future for Kentucky blacks. That situation and the continued presence of violence stimulated an out-migration of black residents, particularly to Kansas in the late 1870s. The promised land lay elsewhere.

With all that, black and white children continued to play and eat together all across the state. Strong bonds remained between some adults in both races as well. But only an optimistic leader such as W.C.P. Breckinridge could look beyond a present without great hope for blacks to a time when "barriers will be removed, prejudices will die, class distinctions be obliterated. Not at once; not in our day; not without fierce contest; not without heroism and sacrifice; but yet slowly, surely [that] day grows stronger."

17

Decades of Discord, 1875-1900

Politically and socially, the first fifteen years of the last quarter of the nineteenth century were relatively static, save for a scandal here and there. But the last decade of the era proved to be one of the most turbulent in the state's history. Throughout the period from 1875 to 1900, Kentucky unfortunately developed a reputation as one of the most violent places in the United States. Feuds grew almost commonplace, and an Appalachian stereotype entered the American consciousness.

Despite the decades of discord, the state's political order displayed the characteristics that would form the core of the system for many decades into the twentieth century. It was a world of patronage and personal politics, localism and sectionalism, lobbies and little kingdoms, voting blocs and bosses.

The Political System

In a general sense, party affiliation defined how people voted more than anything else. On occasion it ruled individual lives, for some families simply did not associate much with other families of a different political faith. Yet at the local level, when it came to specifics, politics was first and foremost personal. The *Henderson Journal* remarked, "No people in the world are more given to confidence in the value of family strains than our people." While this was an exaggeration, the comment did indicate the importance of family to voting. Past leaders tended to perpetuate their families in office; families often voted as a bloc, and winning candidates combined as many of those families as possible. Kinship ties remained a key to political success.

Rewards were expected for political support. Voters did not cast their ballots necessarily because of a particular candidate's qualifications or fitness for office over the opposition. Many understood the system to be one in which those who favored the victor should receive benefits for their aid. At the local level, few challenged a winning candidate's right to name family members to office, and nepotism ran rampant. Fewer still questioned a victor's right to place supporters in appointive offices, even though this practice meant frequent turnover and little opportunity to develop a professional staff. Each community had its leaders around whom voters gathered; each had strong kinship connections that had to be recognized; each had particular local interests to protect.

Added to that localism was a system of county government that made those units semiautonomous, or as Robert Ireland has called them, almost "little kingdoms" unto themselves. Each officer had important powers at a time when relative isolation made the county about the only place where citizens had any contact with government. The county judge, for example, could dispense liquor licenses at his discretion, the sheriff gathered taxes, the justices of the peace—there were two thousand in the state in 1889—served as local jurists hearing cases concerning petty crime, the county clerk recorded legal documents, and the county assessor evaluated property for tax purposes. Local government—not state—built most roads, enforced most laws, collected most taxes, and dispersed all poor relief. It did not always do so fairly or effectively, but it did so locally. By the time of the creation of Kentucky's last county (McCreary) in 1912, Kentucky counties were, on average, the smallest in area in the United States. Citizens therefore had a very intimate connection with the officials they elected in the state's 120 counties, and elections became even more personal and important. As a minister wrote in 1886: "Politics is the all absorbing question."

Outside the more rural and isolated areas, similar forces operated on a somewhat different stage. In Louisville, for instance, "Papa John" Whallen and to a lesser degree his brother James built a powerful machine by the 1880s, one based in the Catholic and Irish population centers of the Falls City. By providing jobs, particularly in the police force and city government, assisting those in need with rent or meals, and giving baskets of food and clothes on special occasions, the Whallens built a supportive network, one whose votes they could control. Their Buckingham Burlesque Theater offered scantily clad showgirls and a popular saloon, but behind those areas, in the green room of "the Buck," political careers could be made or broken by the "Buckingham Bosses." Almost every smaller town and city had its own version, perhaps with a different base but with the same goals—to control votes and win elections.

Various forces could disrupt that local power, particularly powerful lobbies. The most powerful of those in the late nineteenth century was the Louisville and Nashville Railroad, which paid 40 percent of all rail assessments in the state in 1900. Its longtime chief executive officer, the capable and cold Milton Hannibal Smith, openly stated that "all legislative bodies are a menace. In action they are a calamity." He thus determined to reduce the perceived risk to his lines by controlling such bodies as much as possible. Numerous legislators were on the payroll of the L&N as its attorneys in counties through which its lines passed. Others received free travel passes for themselves and their families. Still more benefited from L&N's "suggestions" to its numerous workers on how they should vote in elections. Almost all partook of the railroad's lavish entertainment, being "freely furnished with whiskey, &c." It is little wonder that one observer noted in 1900: "A man could not be elected justice of the peace or school trustee without the sanction of the Louisville and Nashville politicians."

Other lobbies would come and go. An active lobby for the lotteries, for example, existed through the 1880s, and various agricultural forces asked for legislative support. In the early twentieth century the coal interests and the thoroughbred groups each developed strong forces in the legislature as well.

The lobbies, the localism, and the expectation of rewards for votes—all created an atmosphere that tacitly accepted or condoned corruption in the voting booth. In 1879 a minister visited a Simpson County canvass and told his diary: "Oh the rabble . . . men aspiring to high offices treating to whiskey & buying up votes." Vote buying, said one observer, "is as common as buying groceries." Even after Louisville pioneered the use of the Australian, or secret, ballot in 1888, problems continued to grow. One 1909 estimate indicated that up to one-fourth of all votes in the average Kentucky county could be purchased. Two years later a gubernatorial candidate suggested that seventy thousand ballots were bought each year.

The practice went on far into the twentieth century. One county judge recalled that in his mountain county, up to half of the votes would have to be paid for, usually for a dollar or some whiskey. His counterpart in another area recalled voting before friendly election officials when he was but fifteen. Later, he reported, he would pay black transient miners to vote for his party, then would take them en masse to another precinct and have them vote a second time. After that he would have them change their clothes and vote a third time elsewhere. A white voter in another eastern locale remembered selling his vote for four dollars, but, he said, "I was thoroughly rebuked by my father . . . for not holding out for the going rate of seven dollars and a half pint of Heaven Hill bourbon." Fraudulent activity did not end with the buying of votes, for the practice (continued until 1936) of counting the ballots at 10:00 A.M. the next weekday after the election gave time for returns to be "fixed." As one county judge noted, it was standard practice to call party headquarters to see if the election was tight "and ask them how many they need." In close races, each party held back local totals as long as possible in order to counter suspicious late results favorable to the other party. Democracy in Kentucky often had several helping hands on election day.

General Violence

Elections took place in a state plagued by violence, and reports make it appear that almost every voting area featured fights and gunplay on the day the votes were cast. The commonwealth seemed immersed in a culture of violence. Once unleashed, the violence that had become so prevalent in the immediate postwar period would not go away. Formally constituted lawless groups, such as the Ku Klux Klan, did not long survive the time when black rights were under debate, but the Klan's name would be often attached to more informally organized, self-styled "Regulators" who operated for the rest of the nineteenth century and tried to place their own interpretation of the law on those around them. In a few instances, Regulators may have given some order to isolated counties with ineffective law enforcement, but that result was atypical. Such groups usually contributed to the lawlessness. While they sought to justify their actions by suggesting that they were merely implementing justice, in fact they decided guilt and inflicted punishment arbitrarily and willfully. They allowed no trial by one's peers, heard no evidence, and offered no appeal. Each time they acted, justice in Kentucky became a little more lifeless.

Threats and beatings became commonplace where Regulators ruled, and lynchings sometimes occurred. Between 1875 and 1900, at least 166 lynchings took place, and two-thirds of the victims were black. Mobs murdered with impunity. In October 1899, for example, a Maysville mob took accused killer Richard Coleman from the sheriff, who did not resist. As hundreds watched and then fed the flames, Coleman was set on fire and died a slow death. Later the mob dragged the body through the streets, and people cut off the fingers and toes as souvenirs. No one wore masks; everyone knew who was involved. But no charges were filed, and the lesson for Kentuckians was that the law was not supreme.

Many other examples supported that conclusion. The production of whiskey at home stills had been commonplace and legal for many years, but in 1862 a new federal tax on whiskey production changed that. Failure to pay the tax made "moonshining" illegal, and revenue agents began to try to seize illegal stills and place violators of the law in custody. In 1881, for example, 153 arrests were made. But many communities tacitly accepted the moonshiner, and a wall of silence often met the attempts of the revenuers at law enforcement. One county newspaper in 1881 openly proclaimed that "shooting matches and moonshine whiskey are as common as corn bread." Once more, community mores seemed more powerful than established law.

That supposition became even clearer in the way certain communities reacted to individual acts of retributive violence. If a gentleman's honor and reputation were challenged, deadly responses seemed acceptable. In April 1883, for example, Congressman Philip B. Thompson Jr. of Harrodsburg killed a man he claimed had "debauched" his wife. A jury easily acquitted him. A few years later, *Louisville Times* journalist Charles E. Kincaid reported that married congressman William P. Taulbee of Magoffin County had been found "in a compromising way" with a young woman in the U.S. Patent Office. The story ended Taulbee's career, and when he encountered Kincaid in Washington, D.C., in 1890, the two argued, and threats were made. Two hours later they met again, and a shot rang out in the halls of the U.S. Capitol. The unarmed Taulbee had been wounded, and he died some days afterward. Kincaid confessed but was found not guilty in a District of Columbia court on the grounds that he had reacted to threats as a gentleman would. In a similar instance, an irate husband discovered his wife in Louisville with the son of former governor John Young Brown in the 1890s. He killed both of them but was acquitted under the "unwritten law" that in essence permitted personal revenge in such cases. Many elements of Kentucky society

seemed, then, to approve of individual retribution, Regulator violence, and illegal moonshining. The law took second place.

What made the challenges to the system even more accepted was the poor condition of the legal process itself. In some places the entire judiciary was tainted. A Kentucky attorney general found one county's grand jury "made up of the criminals, their close kin, and steadfast friends and admirers." Other locales saw one party or faction or family firmly in control of the whole system, and those in opposition could find little justice. Grand juries that would not indict, or courts that would not convict, resulted. Even if a conviction did occur, governors often rewarded political allies by pardoning their friends in the penitentiary. Convicts seemingly incarcerated for life might be free in a matter of months.

Being an enforcer of the law also became dangerous. Even the justices of the state's highest court were vulnerable. In March 1879 John Milton Elliott, a former U.S. congressman and now a judge, was approached on the streets of Frankfort by Thomas Buford of Henry County. Upset over a judicial decision of Elliott's, Buford shot him at point-blank range with a double-barreled shotgun. Declared not guilty by reason of insanity, Buford later escaped from an asylum, fled to Indiana, and remained free from Kentucky law for two years before he returned voluntarily to the asylum, where he died in 1885. Group support of the law was shown to be dangerous as well. Three men in Ashland had been arrested for some brutal murders, and a mob lynched one of the men. The state militia was called out in 1882 to protect the remaining two, and officials were in the process of moving them by water to a safer place when a mob fired on them from a boat and from the shore. After a furious hail of bullets, the "battle of Ashland" ended with several wounded soldiers and at least four dead civilians.

Some commentators recognized the effect that all of the lawlessness was having on the state. A central Kentucky editor in 1878 called for "a revolution in the moral sense of the community, so that the man-slayer instead of being exalted as a sort of hero, and actually worshipped for the very qualities which ought to make all men shun him, will be esteemed for his real worth, and blood guiltiness be regarded as it is—as the worst and blackest of crimes against nature." Four years later, after the Ashland tragedy, another editor in the commonwealth found that little had changed: "Murders are more frequent, punishment is lighter, pardons more numerous, and abuses are more flagrant. . . . The most alarming feature of all is the indifference of the public. . . . Shocking tragedies at their very doors do not startle them to a realization of the evils that are cursing Kentucky . . . and presenting us to the eyes of the world as a reckless, God-defying, reeking band of law-breakers and murderers."

In truth, the violent situation these writers decried did not differ markedly from the situation in the South generally at the time. The partisan *New York Times* recognized that fact, even as it unfairly declared that the Elliott assassination "could scarcely have taken place in any region calling itself civilized except Kentucky, or some other southern state." The commonwealth partook of a regional subculture heavily oriented to violent behavior. So it was violent but not unique. In the three decades after 1875, however, another form of violence developed, one centered in Kentucky and one that identified the state with a particular, almost unique, kind of killing. Feuding would create a stereotype that would curse Kentucky for a century or more.

Feud Violence

It is important to recall that one definition of a feud is "a lasting state of hostilities between families or clans marked by violent attacks for revenge." In short, feud violence must take place over time, must involve family, and must have the motive of revenge. Often, actions labeled as feuds did not meet these criteria, and the term was carelessly applied to violence that differed little from that taking place elsewhere.

Even narrowly defined, however, feud violence did exist aplenty in Kentucky, and place after place saw lives snuffed out and families destroyed.

Most of the feud violence took place in Appalachia after the Civil War, but one of the earliest identifiable feuds did not. The Hill-Evans feud of Garrard County traced its roots back to an 1820 controversy but erupted in full force in the 1850s, was renewed during the Civil War, then concluded in 1877, when, according to one report, only one male participant remained alive.

Confused and biased reporting of all the feuds makes a clear picture of what happened elusive. The so-called Underwood-Stamper or Underwood-Holbrook feud in Carter County, for example, may have been more a struggle between outlaws and Regulators than a feud. But the fighting erupted out of an "old grudge" and an earlier "Kinney-Carter war," and in 1877 some ambushes rekindled the old feud flames. Defending themselves in "Fort Underwood," that family faced, at various times, the Stampers, a law-and-order citizens' group, and a state militia force. Various arrests ended with few convictions. As many as thirty deaths may have occurred. A brief period of calm had ended by 1880, when reports once more filtered out of the hills, telling of a band of two hundred Regulators who enforced their clan's version of justice. By that time, though, events in a neighboring county were seizing the headlines.

The Rowan County War of the 1880s, or the Martin-Tolliver-Logan feud, resulted in at least twenty murders and sixteen woundings during a three-year period, in a county whose population never exceeded eleven hundred. Beginning with some political disagreements in the 1870s, the feud erupted in an 1884 election dispute that left one man dead and two more, including John Martin, injured. A former Underwood ally, Martin met "Big Floyd" Tolliver in a saloon months afterward, accused him of the earlier shooting, and killed him. Eight days later the Tolliver faction seized Martin from the authorities with a forged order and fired seven shots into his body. Each side took turns with retaliatory killings, but the Tollivers gained virtual control of the city of Morehead and of the court system. Finally Daniel Boone Logan, an attorney whose two cousins had been killed after they had surrendered to the Tollivers, requested aid from the governor. When the chief executive rejected his request, Logan purchased rifles and ammunition, armed a group of 120-200 men, and surrounded the Tollivers and the town. In a western-style shoot-out in June 1887, the Tollivers were forced to flee a burning building. They were caught in a crossfire, and their leader and three others were killed. Pardons were issued to the Logan faction. In quieter times, a legislative investigating committee called officials in the county inept, inefficient, corrupt, and "depraved." The committee's recommendation that Rowan County be abolished was not accepted.

Deeper in the mountains, three more feuds also attracted much attention in the 1880s. The Howard-Turner feud in Harlan County had its origins in the pre–Civil War period, and isolated murders had occurred during the 1870s. By June 1889, however, hostilities had become so open that a pitched battle took place, and the Turners withstood a long siege in the courthouse. By the end of the month it was estimated that fifty people had died over the decades of the feud. Similarly, the French-Eversole feud in Perry County saw the two opposing bands meet in a two-day battle in the streets of Hazard in 1880. By the 1890s the violence had declined, but the legacy left was bullet holes and empty buildings, forty to fifty deaths, and nearly fifty orphans.

Ironically, what would become the best known of the feuds was not the bloodiest, the longest-lasting, or even the most spectacular of the family "wars." Instead, the Hatfield-McCoy feud received much attention from the media, involved two state governments in its dispute, and became synonymous with feuding. In many ways, the "war" was not unusual: Randolph ("Old Ran'l") McCoy led the Pike

County, Kentucky, clan; William A. ("Devil Anse") Hatfield directed the West Virginia group, who resided across the Tug Fork. Disputes concerning the Civil War, failed justice, a hog, economics, and a romance were all prelude to what resulted on election day in 1882. A fight between a Hatfield and three McCoys left the Hatfield mortally wounded. Angry members of his family, distrustful of Kentucky justice, seized the three McCoys, tied them to bushes, and, in an almost ritualistic manner, riddled their bodies with some fifty bullets. One fifteen year old's head was virtually blown away by a shotgun blast. Scattered violence took place over the next five years. Then on New Year's Day in 1888, Old Ran'l McCoy's home was surrounded and burned, and a son and daughter were killed. An illegal raid by a Kentucky deputy sheriff ended in some Hatfield deaths and arrests and a court case that involved the governors of both states and eventually the U.S. Supreme Court. A lawful execution by hanging took place in 1890, and some semblance of peace followed. Overall, from twelve to twenty deaths had resulted from a feud that the *New York Times* said "caught the attention of the whole nation."

As that feud was fading, the Baker-White feud in Clay County heated up in the 1890s. Rising out of an 1840s case when a clearly insane Dr. Abner Baker had murdered a man, and then stimulated later by some business rivalries, the feud culminated in a pitched battle at the Manchester courthouse. One person's estimate of fifty dead was likely too high, but the death toll was still large.

The final major Appalachian feud was one of the longest-lasting. Breathitt County had been plagued by violence since the "little hell" that was the Civil War there, and the Amis-Strong-Little feud marked the formalization of the killing. In 1874 one faction fortified the courthouse, and the militia was called in. Four years later a member of the Little family was arrested for murdering his pregnant wife. As he was being taken to trial, ambushers killed the county judge. The circuit judge disappeared.

Stock images, such as this one showing members of the Hatfield clan posed around "Devil Anse" Hatfield (*seated, at center*), helped shape the conception of the feuding mountaineers (courtesy of the West Virginia Department of Archives and History).

A mob again seized the courthouse, several were wounded, and virtual anarchy reigned. Once more the militia marched in and enforced an uneasy peace in a county where some said a hundred had already died. By the 1890s a new generation of leaders had come to the fore in Breathitt County, and out of the Amis-Strong-Little feud grew its successor, the Hargis-Marcum-Cockrell-Callahan feud. Democratic county judge and businessman James Hargis, aided by Sheriff Ed Callahan, led one group; Republican attorney James B. Marcum and town marshall Tom Cockrell led another. Each group had ties to the earlier feud. In separate fights Hargis's brother and half-brother were killed; in July 1902 Cockrell's brother Jim was murdered as Hargis and Callahan watched. By November of that year some thirty deaths had resulted, and Marcum would not venture out in public without a young child in his arms, for he knew his enemies would not risk killing a baby. But in May 1903 an unescorted Marcum was shot in the back, then in the head. Two convictions followed, but neither Hargis nor Callahan was found guilty. Their punishments came in other ways. In 1908 Hargis was killed by his drunken son; four years later Callahan answered a telephone call by a store window and was assassinated. In essence the feuds in "Bloody Breathitt" and other Appalachian counties had ended. But people went on paying the costs, and like a ghost haunting the state's hills and hollows, the bloody specter of the feuds would long bedevil the people of Kentucky.

Kentucky Images and Appalachian Stereotypes

While each feud differed in details and causes, several characteristics did stand out. In the first place, many of the leading citizens of a county were involved. Entrepreneurial business types often headed one or both factions, although, conversely, virtual outlaws sometimes served as feud leaders. In either case, what one observer called almost "a large, paid army" operated under the guidance of a person who functioned mainly as a medieval feudal lord caring for his men. The fighters might center around a family but could include others who were little more than "hired guns."

A second characteristic, sometimes submerged at the time by writers who told of the "code of honor" of the mountains, was that the actions taken were generally cruel and cowardly. Honor seldom appeared when ambushes and assassinations proved the favorite method of murder. Pitched battles, usually centered around the symbol of justice, the courthouse, did occur, but usually only because one side found itself trapped and outnumbered. Young boys tied to bushes and executed, unarmed women beaten or shot as they fled a burning house, men shot in the back—these kinds of violence left deep mental scars with the living and produced deeper desires for further revenge.

Finally, while causes of feuds differed, a few key elements appeared in what people of the region called "the troubles." Anger escalated into violence because of such factors as Civil War memories, the presence of whiskey at elections, political partisanship, economic rivalries, the prevalence of concealed weapons, and an intense localism fed by a restrictive isolationism. A kind of urban-rural conflict, where external forces intervened to pressure more local and traditional ones, may have been a factor as well. But in the end, the main source of feuds was the ineffectiveness of the law and the consequent lawlessness. When no responses or legal redress could be obtained from a legal system "rotten to the core," other answers would be sought. A form of family-oriented vigilantism developed, one in which interwoven ties, fed by a limiting environment, produced a bloody personal code. Each resulting act only worsened the situation, and revenge, not justice, soon guided most actions. A widow in the Baker-White feud explained how her "chief aim" in life became the avenging of her husband's death: "Each day I shall show my boys the handkerchief stained with his blood, and tell them who murdered him." The circle of violence grew wider with each generation.

The result of feud violence for Kentucky and Appalachia would be broad and far-reaching. The immediate effect of most feuds proved to be an out-migration of some citizens, a business depression in the affected counties, and suspended growth. Those effects usually did not last, though, for the great coal boom that struck the region gave some feud-desolated places a rebirth of sorts.

More crucial long-range results grew out of the publicity generated by the feuds and the stereotypes that developed. Once almost forgotten by Kentucky and the nation, Appalachia now was suddenly "discovered," and two somewhat contradictory images grew out of the

resulting deluge of print stories and silent movies. One stereotype presented the mountain people as "our contemporary ancestors," a people from frontier times, cut off from the world by isolation. As a result, they spoke—so sayeth the commentators—"the English of Shakespeare's time," maintained the earlier ways of life, and preserved old customs. In this benign and pastoral view, hospitable mountain people lived self-sufficient and happy lives as they sat in front of their little log cabins, sang ballads, and played their dulcimers. In this image they perpetuated the past and represented a hope for the future.

A second, much starker and darker stereotype presented Appalachian people as ignorant and immoral, backward and blood-thirsty, poor and primitive. It featured not the homespun pioneer but a gaunt, bearded feudist with moonshine jug in one hand, rifle in the other, and murder in his eye. That image grew over time into a picture of a people who chiefly "fuss, feud, and fornicate." By 1934 historian Arnold Toynbee concluded that "the Appalachian 'Mountain People' at this day are no better than barbarians."

That stereotype expanded to include all of Kentucky, and the commonwealth as a whole began to be labeled as a violent, lawless place that should be avoided. Between 1878 and 1883, for instance, the *New York Times* called Kentuckians "unreclaimed savages" and "effective assassins," proclaimed the state a "delightful" place to live, "especially if one enjoys anarchy and mobocracy," and concluded that "there is no state in which lawlessness and bloodshed prevail to such an outrageous extent as in Kentucky." The *Chicago Tribune* in 1885 said the commonwealth's civilization had been tested "and found to be barbarism," while an article in *Leslie's Popular Monthly* in 1902 described the author's trip to bloody feudist country "where the sun set crimson and the moon rose red." The stories went on and on, so that the stereotype of violent Kentucky became firmly embedded in the national consciousness.

Both images—the forgotten pioneer and the violent hillbilly—had a basis in fact. Some elements of the romantic view did exist. Kentucky was also a very violent state, comparatively, until at least the 1940s. But neither stereotype represented Appalachian Kentucky fully or fairly. Many writers, for example, based their accounts on a quick trip to the area, and their stories often ignored the region's complexities. As one 1901 article noted, correctly, "very great differences exist among the people." While there was poverty, there was also wealth. While there were log cabins, there were also houses that would have been fashionable in upper-class urban settings. While there was a traditional society, there was a coexisting modern one. That "other" Appalachia seldom appeared. What writers have called an "urban provincialism" often colored the attitudes behind the stories, and a cultural colonialism shaped the results. Once established, however, the stereotypes would prove to be extremely hard to demolish. There may have been some truth to the lament in the *Hazard Herald* that "one little crime in the mountain section will receive more front page comment than a dozen murders . . . in the cities." A congressman complained that authors "make a universality out of an incident." Whatever the correctness of that view, there was still little doubt that in the late nineteenth century Kentucky garnered a stereotype of violence, and Appalachia several stereotypes. All of this hurt the state's and the region's image and subsequent development for decades to come.

The McCreary Administration and Health Care, 1875-1879

Violence stood out as one of the key issues in the gubernatorial campaign of 1875, as Democrats pledged to contain the violence while Republicans criticized them for failing to do so. But that was but one of many issues, as the party of Lincoln again put forth its strongest candidate and best speaker, the young attorney and former Unionist John Marshall Harlan. Opposing him was an even more youthful

barrister, former Confederate colonel James B. McCreary (1838-1918) of Madison County. McCreary—like his predecessors and successors—played on his ties to the South, as did many candidates for local offices. One nineteenth-century observer noted that "worthy and capable ex-Confederate soldiers (especially if maimed)" would "invariably" be elected, and Alben W. Barkley exaggerated only a little when he wrote that "for years after the Civil War, a candidate for political office in our part of Kentucky who had not had at least one limb shot off while fighting for the Confederacy might as well have whistled down a rain barrel." While Harlan hammered state issues, McCreary focused on national ones and Reconstruction and successfully reiterated his Confederate ties. He won by a vote of 130,026-94,236. Governor McCreary came to office as the youngest governor ever elected to that time, and he quickly found new issues awaiting him, matters that created conflict and controversy for the next quarter century.

Labor demanded a larger voice in the state, and the outcry came both from the farm and from the city. The more numerous agrarians saw much of the attention devoted to railroad and business issues, they saw the value of farm products decline in the state by 27 percent during the 1870s, and they saw their people—"the very bone and sinew of our country," one Kentuckian called them—their world, their ideal, under attack. They struck out against that change.

The first formal organization to expound the agrarians' view was the Patrons of Husbandry, more commonly called the Grange. While conservative in many of its demands, the Grange also called for actions that were more radical for the time. The Grangers sponsored the formation of farmers' cooperatives in the form of stores and warehouses and supported a revision in the nation's financial structure, which they argued favored business. Such appeals found favor in Kentucky, and in 1875 the commonwealth had some fifteen hundred Granges with more than fifty thousand members, one of the largest state totals in the South. The organization had planted the seeds of agricultural discontent that would grow over the decades. Sometimes that dissatisfaction spilled over into politics, as farmers supported first the so-called Greenback Party, which advocated the printing of more money, thus creating an inflated currency. By the 1880s the Agricultural Wheel and the Farmers' Alliance took up the cause as well, calling for a money policy of inflation and a political policy of agrarian pride. Tightly organized and sometimes almost evangelical in their fervor, the various agrarian groups represented a threat to the existing political order in Kentucky. Just when the old Democratic Bourbon–New Departure divisions seemed to be healing, the party now had to face angry farmers, who might bolt the Democrats or even form their own party if their wishes were not met. The problem for McCreary and his successors was how far to go to meet those demands without alienating the other forces in the often-fragile Democratic coalition.

At the same time, labor unrest in the cities developed, particularly in connection with a prolonged "long-wave" depression that lasted much of the rest of the century. When the L&N and other railroads slashed wages in 1877, workers struck in protest in Louisville. In July of that year some two thousand laborers shouted down the mayor during a talk and inflicted some minor damage to several buildings. The militia was called out, but no further conflicts of any significance developed. The formal organization of unions increased, however, and by 1880 the Knights of Labor had thirty-six assemblies in Louisville. During the next two decades, that city alone experienced at least 140 strikes, chiefly over wages. In 1887, for example, working women struck the Louisville Woolen Mills, but lack of funds or laws sympathetic to labor doomed their effort. Similarly, a depression in 1893 left an estimated ten thousand unemployed in Louisville and many more suffering from wage cuts. A two-month strike to better that situation failed. Labor won

few victories over management in the nineteenth century, but workers increasingly coalesced as an important voting bloc. They too represented a fresh force that the dominant Democratic Party had to face.

Despite the new threats, Democrats continued to win state elections. In the 1876 presidential race, Kentucky editor Henry Watterson emerged as perhaps the leading national advocate for Democratic nominee Samuel J. Tilden of New York. For the first time in two decades, it appeared that state Democrats might be on the victor's side in a presidential canvass. Republicans considered as a possible presidential choice a native Kentuckian. Benjamin H. Bristow (1832-96) of Elkton had had a distinguished career as a Union soldier and had been the nation's first solicitor general, as well as secretary of the Treasury. But Rutherford B. Hayes won the nomination and, in a controversial way, the election. Democrats carried Kentucky by a vote of 160,445-98,415, won all ten congressional seats (through some resourceful gerrymandering of the districts), and believed they had elected Tilden as president. When questions arose over the count, Kentucky party members passed resolutions asserting that "an appeal to arms is the last desperate remedy of a free people in danger of being enslaved." An angry Watterson called for ten thousand Kentuckians to march to Washington to show their displeasure at events. Wiser heads prevailed, violence was avoided, and a compromise put Hayes in the White House. But Kentucky Democrats, feeling cheated of victory, put the election of 1876 in their campaign arsenal to be used against Republicans.

In state politics, the Democrats still ruled in the legislative halls. Since the Grange had a dominant voice, though, many of the laws passed during McCreary's tenure had an agrarian orientation. Various acts established a Bureau of Agriculture, reduced the property tax—the main source of state revenue—by some 11 percent, lowered the maximum interest rate to 6 percent, instituted a conservation measure for fish, and made the Agricultural and Mechanical College (later the University of Kentucky) an independent school. Almost ignored in all that activity was a bill creating a State Board of Health, one of the first in the nation.

Such an action was desperately needed, for Kentuckians did not live in a healthy state. Major epidemics of cholera, smallpox, yellow fever, and typhoid had left thousands dead. Drinking unsterilized milk or contaminated water (which might come directly from a sewage-polluted source) or eating food prepared in the absence of health regulations added to the incidence of disease. One study of a meat slaughterhouse found "conditions barbaric in the extreme. . . . The meat is dressed by unwashed hands, covered with flies . . . , [and] hung upon hooks that are never cleaned." Lack of sanitation in the home, where whole families drank from the same water dipper, spread diseases quickly; the absence of shoes on summer feet resulted in bodies riddled with hookworm; poor ventilation in homes added to the high rate of tuberculosis. As late as the 1910s perhaps one-third of all Kentuckians had hookworm, and one-fourth of those in some areas had trachoma, a disease that could cause blindness. The river town of Paducah in 1900 had the nation's second highest rate of typhoid fever and the third highest level of malaria.

Medicines available to treat these diseases ranged from adequate to ridiculous. With little or no regulation of drugs, patent medicine firms covered newspapers with their advertisements, offering "cures" for virtually everything. For one dollar a bottle, for example, Dr. Radway's Sasaparillian Resolvent would cure tuberculosis, syphilis, ulcers, sore eyes, skin diseases, ringworm, "female complaints," and "nocturnal losses." Most such offerings proved to be either heavily alcoholic or a laxative. Other Kentuckians innocently sought relief through morphine, cocaine, and opium, which were sold legally in many drugstores in the nineteenth century. Unexpected addictions brought other newspaper advertise-

ments for more "cures" of "the habit." The cure was often worse than the problem.

The new State Board of Health, under the longtime direction of Bowling Green's Dr. Joseph N. McCormack (1847-1922), sought to improve that situation, although its annual budget never exceeded five thousand dollars until 1901. The board began by addressing the question of medical preparation. An 1878 study found that one thousand of the commonwealth's five thousand doctors had never attended a medical school. Another report a few years later termed Kentucky "the worst quack ridden State in the union" and called physicians little more than "ignorant vampires." Even attendance at a medical "college" might be meaningless, for, without regulation, some institutions served more as diploma factories than places of instruction.

A second concern was the quality of the food Kentuckians ate. By 1898 a state Pure Food Law—later revised and strengthened—brought inspection of processed and prepared items. Through the efforts of people like Robert McDowell Allen, who became a national leader in the field, major change soon occurred. One sampling of certain foods, for instance, found that 80 percent were adulterated in some way. Punishment of violators quickly reversed the situation, and by the first decade of the twentieth century good medical education, stronger food and drug laws, and a better-educated citizenry began to make positive differences in the health of Kentuckians.

The Blackburn Governorship and the Prison Issue

Plagued by statewide violence and by political infighting within his own party, Governor McCreary had served amid a climate of financial retrenchment and limited initiatives. To face those concerns as his successor in 1879 would be either the young Republican nominee, former Union soldier Walter Evans of Louisville; the Democratic choice, Dr. Luke Pryor Blackburn of Woodford County; or the National (Greenback) Party candidate,

259

C.W. Cook. Cook, representing the agrarian and labor interests, eventually polled more than 8 percent of the vote, supported chiefly by those usually in the Democratic ranks, but Blackburn still won easily over Evans by a count of 125,799-81,882.

New governor Luke Blackburn (1816-87) came to office amid controversy and remained mired in strife throughout his term. During the campaign one issue had been physician Blackburn's earlier unsuccessful attempt to aid the Confederacy by infecting northern cities with yellow fever. Balancing that perfidy, however, was his postwar humanitarian efforts to fight the same disease across the South. His work during an 1878 yellow fever epidemic in Kentucky won him the appellation the Hero of Hickman and brought the former Whig legislator the gubernatorial nomination and the election victory.

Most of Blackburn's subsequent work as governor focused on a single issue—prison reform. At the time Kentucky's prison population lived—and died—in miserable conditions. Seeking to operate the system as a business, the state government leased the penitentiary at Frankfort and its inmates to the highest bidder. Maximizing profits, each lessee kept expenses low, worked convicts hard at various tasks, such as chair making, and sold the products. With literally a captive labor force, lessees ignored the human element, and what one paper called a system of "absolute slavery" existed. As a result, the penitentiary became a place of slime-covered walls, open sewage, "graveyard coughs," and general unhealthiness. An 1875 study had found that 20 percent of the inmates had pneumonia; the year Blackburn took office another report revealed that three of every four prisoners had scurvy, owing to poor diet. More than 7 percent of the nearly one thousand prisoners had died during the year. Others had lived on in a hellish existence, cramped two to a poorly heated cell less than seven feet long and four feet wide. Their untrained guards owed their jobs to political patronage, and these officials changed as frequently as the administration.

Prison lessees sought favor with the legislators whose votes would select them by providing the solons with cheap washing, free meals, and other benefits. Legislators, in turn, averted their investigative eyes from the frequent whipping of prisoners, the cockroaches in the food, the rats in the hallways, the thumbscrews, the sickness, and the death.

With no parole system in existence, the only way a prisoner could be released before the full sentence was served was to die or to be pardoned by the governor. The pardoning power had previously been much criticized, for the friends of political allies, or those whose families contributed to campaigns, seemed to receive a disproportionate share of the pardons. Luke Blackburn examined the "degrading" situation in the state prison, concluded that something had to be done immediately or more deaths would follow, and began an unprecedented pardoning policy. The net effect was to relieve overcrowding and to provide a second chance for prisoners previously without hope. In practice, however, his decision earned him widespread criticism as "Lenient Luke." Before his term ended, the governor had pardoned more than a thousand people, including nearly four hundred Regulators from eastern Kentucky. Such actions, amid increasing state violence, angered many.

Attempts at reform took place in the legislature as well, for the 1880 session authorized but did not fund a new prison (eventually located at Eddyville), set up a warden system in which responsibility for prisoners rested with the commonwealth and not the lessee, and provided for a crude system of parole. But one supposed reform only added to the woes of the prisoners. In an attempt to end overcrowding immediately, the General Assembly allowed contractors to lease convict labor and to employ the inmates on public works outside of prison walls. Abuses arose at once, for contractors had no one supervising their handling of the prisoners. At one camp, half of the fifty leased convicts perished; at another, inmates officially reported as escapees had, in fact, died of malnourishment, overwork, and beatings. Attempts to regulate the contractors failed, chiefly because there was no longer any place to put the prisoners should they be returned to the penitentiary. Laboring at mines, railroads, and reservoirs, inmates continued to live in virtual death camps until the 1890s, when the new state constitution prohibited convict leasing.

So in the end, Blackburn's efforts at prison reform only partly succeeded: the governor's free use of pardons still had not helped the overcrowding a great deal, the new penitentiary would itself be full almost immediately, and the convict leasing system represented a step backward. Over the coming decades, more prison investigations would find more problems, and the same story would be repeated.

By the conclusion of his four-year term, the politically inexperienced and somewhat naive Blackburn had almost no allies. He was shouted down and booed by his own party as he sought to defend his record. Democrats, after all, had once more carried the state in the 1880 presidential race, this time for Winfield

Scott Hancock, and had reelected U.S. senator James B. Beck. Besides reforming prisons, Blackburn and the legislature had raised property taxes, cut state salaries by one-fifth, improved river navigation, and reorganized the court system. The press ignored most of these achievements, however, and instead wrote about the pardon record of the man whom one paper called "the old imbecile." In truth, Blackburn's overall accomplishments varied little from those of most other governors of his era. His tenure saw some reform, some financial actions, and some problems with violence. If his reform agenda had been limited, at least he—unlike some others—had tried to do much more.

Knott, Buckner, and "Honest Dick" Tate, 1883-1891

Some Democrats worried that the unpopularity of the Blackburn administration would hurt their party's chances of retaining the governorship, but that concern proved needless. Republican nominee Thomas Z. Morrow, a

The Kentucky State Penitentiary in Frankfort (courtesy of the Kentucky Historical Society)

former Union officer and attorney from Somerset, faced a difficult race, for his Democratic opponent was the popular six-term congressman J. Proctor Knott (1830-1911) of Lebanon. Knott owed much of his political fame to a very witty speech made in 1871, in which he sarcastically commented on a federal project near Duluth, Minnesota. In an era that praised oratory, and at a time when average people could become major leaders on the strength of their speaking abilities, Knott's "Duluth speech" garnered him national acclaim. It also helped propel him in 1883 to the governorship, which he easily won by a vote of 133,615-89,181.

Between the end of the Civil War and the turn of the twentieth century, virtually all Kentucky governors made recommendations to their legislatures that proved to be far more reform-oriented than their administrations turned out to be. The influence of powerful lobbies, party factionalism, and the limitations of a local-oriented mindset all combined with the presence of mostly conservative legislators, so that the General Assembly did little. Stronger chief executives could have challenged that situation more, but in the end their limited vision and restricted philosophy of government held them back.

Proctor Knott was no exception. A learned, intelligent, and well-liked individual, he still could do little regarding the violence in Rowan County and other areas of eastern Kentucky. He also continued to pardon large numbers of prisoners, and he usually advocated local actions over state ones. His administration did create the Kentucky State Normal School for Colored Persons in Frankfort (now Kentucky State University) and enacted a major overhaul of the educational system, but Knott's major achievement lay in the area of revenue reform. A new law not only fixed new taxes and raised the property tax, but it also established more uniform assessments, providing, for example, that railroads and other corporations be taxed at the regular property rate. The action concerning corporations alone added ninety million dollars' worth of property to the taxable property lists. As a result, state government revenues increased to $3.6 million by 1890, representing 50 percent growth over the 1880 figure. All this had occurred despite one other fiscal action during the Knott years. The governor opposed but the legislature enacted a bill backed by the L&N that granted newly constructed rail lines—about one-fourth of those operating—a five-year period free of taxes. Powerful forces still operated in the General Assembly.

For the Democratic Party of Proctor Knott, perhaps the greatest achievement took place outside Kentucky. In the 1884 presidential election, the issues varied only in detail from before: Democrats attacked the "horrors" of Republican Reconstruction and the character of Republican nominee James G. Blaine of Maine (a man who had once taught in Kentucky), while calling for a low tariff on foreign goods so workers would have access to cheaper merchandise. Republicans, in turn, countered with the observation that the character of the Democratic nominee, Grover Cleveland of New York, hardly seemed pure, given the fact that he had acknowledged paternity of an illegitimate child. They also defended a high protective tariff, arguing that it allowed American manufactures to grow. Such issues mattered little, it appeared, for the commonwealth followed its usual pattern and went Democratic—as it had for twenty years—by 152,961 to 118,122 votes. This time, however, Republican divisions and mistakes at the national level proved fatal, and Cleveland won. Kentucky Democrats looked forward to long-delayed political rewards from a president from their own party.

The Knott administration was nearing its end. Would the Democratic Party be able to hold the reins of office in the commonwealth in the gubernatorial contest of 1887? Republicans put forth a strong candidate for governor, forty-year-old attorney William O. Bradley of Garrard County. A strong orator, "Billy O'B." openly called for black support. His opponent, the stereotypical goateed southern gentleman Simon Bolivar Buckner (1823-1914) of Hart County, brought both strengths and weaknesses to the race. A former Confederate general who had grown wealthy from business ventures after the war and had been a pallbearer at Grant's funeral, Buckner had never held political office. His advocates seemed willing to forget political records and praised instead the family record of the sixty-four-year-old general, his thirty-year-old wife, and their newborn son. Ignoring the fact that Buckner's wife's name was Delia, they cried out, "Hurrah for Bolivar, Betty, and the baby!" Despite a sizable Union Labor Party vote in northern Kentucky and a strong race by Republican Bradley, the Democratic appeals were enough. The "Confederate Dynasty" continued—barely. In the closest contest since the war, Buckner won with 51 percent of the vote. He polled 143,466 votes against Bradley's 126,754, and more than 12,000 more ballots went to third-party candidates. The vote showed that the long-successful Democratic coalition had developed serious problems.

Those problems grew worse under Buckner. Dominated by rising agrarian interests in the form of the Farmers' Alliance, his legislatures successfully pushed for a property tax reduction that left the commonwealth so short of cash that the governor had to make a personal loan of more than fifty thousand dollars to the state treasury in order to keep Kentucky solvent. Other laws passed by the General Assembly so angered Buckner that he vetoed more than a hundred bills, issuing more vetoes than his ten predecessors combined. At the same time, the actions of the L&N lobby brought forth a legislative investigation that concluded that the railroad company had used money, passes, and influence in "an extraordinarily powerful effort to dominate the legislature." Additionally, the Hatfield-McCoy feud dragged Buckner into a convoluted legal controversy with the governor of West Virginia, one that had to be settled by the U.S. Supreme Court. Even that issue, however, paled in comparison to a sensational political scandal that suddenly erupted.

Beginning in 1867 and continuing every two years thereafter, Kentucky voters had elected James W. ("Honest Dick") Tate of Frankfort as state treasurer. Praised for his integrity and affability, Tate was so trusted that other state officials did not even bother to carry out their duties and double-check his accounts. On March 14, 1888, Tate packed some bags for a trip to Louisville and Cincinnati. He was never seen in Kentucky again. A few days later, worried officials began to scrutinize his books. They found a chaotic, confused system that was no system at all. Bills had been laid aside and forgotten; others had been paid but not so recorded; more seriously, some had been marked paid when they had not been. State funds had also apparently been offered by Tate as personal loans to various friends and officials, including at least one governor. The treasurer had used the commonwealth's money to speculate in land and coal mining ventures of his own. Finally, a clerk recalled that Honest Dick had filled two large sacks with gold and silver coins and had taken a large roll of bills with him on his final trip.

Eventually, investigators found that Tate had embezzled more than $247,000 from the state. He had doctored bills, deleted accounts, and forgotten transactions in a fairly crude way, but the loose controls had allowed him to continue his fraud for fifteen years. Worried about the possibility of a routine check, he finally fled. The Kentucky House of Representatives quickly impeached Tate, and the Senate removed him from office. Criminal charges were filed against him in civil court. Belatedly, the legislature created the office of state inspector and examiner.

Behind the scenes, chaos reigned. Worried officials tried to distance themselves from Tate or to minimize the damages in a scandal that reached the highest levels. Long-unpaid IOUs to Tate were suddenly redeemed. The current state auditor, like his predecessors, had been clearly derelict in his duty, but he got off with only the censure of the public. More uncertain was the fate of a series of wealthy, influential, and trusting people who had signed as bondsmen for Tate, as required by law. Supposedly any fiscal shortage by him would have to be met by them. But given the magnitude of his defalcation, several people's fortunes would be lost if the state collected. In the end, the state's highest court, in a decision not openly reported because of political consequences, decided that the bondsmen would not be held liable.

Back in 1876 the city treasurer of Covington, a son of former Confederate governor of Kentucky Richard Hawes, had embezzled fifty-seven thousand dollars, only to be among those pardoned during Governor Blackburn's term. The Tate affair thus seemed a continuation of a trend. Distrust of all public officials increased dramatically, and angry critics charged that a cover-up had occurred.

What happened to Honest Dick Tate and the state's money after he left Kentucky? The wife and daughter he left behind, as well as a family friend, said later that for a brief time they received secret letters indicating he had gone to Canada, the Orient, California, and finally Brazil. No further word came from Tate after that. Whether he returned to the United States under an assumed identity or lived and died in a foreign country is unknown, one of the mysteries of Kentucky history. His actions would have an enduring effect on the state, however, particularly in regard to the new constitution soon to be drafted.

A New Constitution

The constitution of 1850 clearly required at least revision, for it still sanctioned slavery and did not adequately deal with new issues such as corporations and railroads. Calls for a new convention had been made for two decades, but finally an 1889 vote made that possibility a reality. One hundred delegates, representing each district in the Kentucky House of Representatives, were selected. They convened in Frankfort on September 8, 1890, met for 226 days,

and signed the result of their deliberations on April 11, 1891. The process was long, controversial, and not always fruitful.

Not unexpectedly, the delegates were a varied lot. There were sixty attorneys, twenty farmers, thirteen doctors, and seven business leaders. Almost one-fifth of them had been elected as representatives of the Farmers' Alliance and spoke out chiefly on those issues of importance to agrarians—limited government, control of corporations, railroad regulation, and the like. The delegates at the convention included a former governor, the current governor, a future governor, and the uncle and brother of two other governors. About a dozen middle-level political figures formed the core of those involved in most deliberations, however. In short, the group of delegates was competent but not exceptional.

Unfortunately, the delegates often operated like oarsmen in a boat with no one steering. With no particular person to lead and with a piecemeal rather than a considered approach to constitution making, the convention seemed to flounder. Delegates spent long hours offering resolutions or debating procedural or minor matters. What one delegate termed lengthy, "aerial flights of oratory" emanated on virtually every subject. Delegates ignored William M. Beckner's advice that they should fashion a flexible document, to "give posterity a chance." Unable to agree on broad statements, they instead degenerated almost to making laws in the form of a constitution through very specific sections, which, as it turned out, were often quickly outdated. Fresh from the Tate scandal, the delegates did not trust government or its leaders very much. They therefore limited officials' time in office and fashioned a restrictive document that reflected their suspicion of power and those who wielded it.

The document they drafted in 1890 and 1891 would change drastically over the years, as a result of various constitutional amendments. Its chief provisions at the time included the following:

1. The basic Bill of Rights from the 1792 constitution was retained, except for the slavery provision.

2. The General Assembly would consist of a House of Representatives of one hundred members elected to two-year terms, and a Senate of thirty-eight members serving four-year terms.

3. The executive branch would consist of the governor and other constitutional officers, all elected for four-year terms, with restrictions on selection. On the chief executive's absence from the state, the lieutenant governor automatically assumed the power of the office (this provision was later amended).

4. The judicial branch would consist of a Court of Appeals, made up of five to seven members elected for eight-year terms, and a system of circuit, quarterly, county, justice of the peace, and police courts. The General Assembly was forbidden to create any courts other than those in the constitution (later amended).

5. Under more general provisions,

    a. The Railroad Commission was given constitutional sanction to help its regulatory powers.

    b. Lotteries were abolished (later amended).

    c. Salaries of state officials were restricted to five thousand dollars per year (later amended).

    d. State elections would be held in November instead of August, would be by secret ballot rather than voice voting, and would be limited to males over the age of twenty-one (later amended).

    e. "An efficient system" of schools had to be maintained and must be racially segregated (later amended).

    f. The creation of new counties was made more difficult.

Almost as soon as it was written, the new constitution attracted critics, including Watterson, who opposed its limitations and restrictions as well as its bundle of statutes disguised as a constitution. Others disliked some of the reform elements, such as the strengthened Railroad Commission, and the L&N campaigned against adoption. But the framers had reflected the will of a state fearful of power, distrustful of politicians, and careful of prerogatives, and the constitution was adopted by a statewide vote of 212,914-74,523. Then, in a strange move, the delegates reassembled for almost a month, made several changes, some of them significant, and signed a new, "final" draft. Not voted on in that form by the people, the document was tested in the courts but was eventually approved. At long last the constitution of 1891 was complete. The problems it would create, however, had only begun.

Populism in the Chaotic 1890s

The postwar Democratic Party consisted of many elements—former Whigs, former prewar Democrats, former Confederates, former Unionists, rural interests, urban interests, wealthy Bluegrass farmers, poorer western Kentucky agrarians, leaders of a Bourbon bent, politicians of New Departure views, and much more. Bonded in a weak philosophical way by a devotion to low tariffs, a limited role for government, and an opposition to Republicans, Democrats had never had a fully united party. One element seemed always in conflict with another, whether it was Bourbon versus New Departure earlier, or agrarians against the established leadership in the 1880s. Over the years, different factions had broken off, either in passive rebellion or in small third-party movements. Now those divisions threatened to grow into full-scale revolt.

Farmers grew even more worried about their place in American life and in Kentucky politics. Many argued that corporations, especially railroads, discriminated against them; others noted the long-term debt many agrarians owed to bankers or other lenders; still more complained, as did an 1891 writer in Rock Bridge, about the "defeated feeling in the minds of the people of this part of the state that they have not rec'd. the recognition they were entitled to, in the division of state offices." Simply put, as historian Edward L. Ayers notes, "Rural people sought to claim a share of the New South's promise, to make a place for themselves and their children in the emerging order."

Various groups had sought to do that, ranging from the Grangers to the Greenbackers, from the Agricultural Wheel to the Farmers' Alliance. The Alliance had been organized in Kentucky in 1886, with S. Brewer Erwin of Hickman as president. Within five years, the Alliance—under the formal name of the Farmers and Labor Union—claimed more than 125,000 members in some twenty-four hundred subunions in eighty-eight counties. Its endorsement was eagerly sought, and its influence on the political scene was important. But all of that power had come about within the structure of the existing two-party system. By 1891 it was not at all clear whether the situation would continue, and in an open letter to Democrats, one agrarian summarized the atmosphere, in a "Word of Warning." He told of the "unrest" in the minds of many who usually voted Democratic, for "this element, chiefly farmers, are honestly impatient as to existing grievances."

The agrarians grew more concerned once the Democratic nominee for governor in 1891 was chosen. John Young Brown (1835-1904) of Henderson did represent western Kentucky and helped calm sectional fears, but he also represented the old leadership more than had his defeated party rivals. Disgruntled agrarians who had attended a national farm protest meeting in Cincinnati crossed the river to Covington, founded the People's—or Populist—Party in Kentucky, and offered a slate of officers for the 1891 governor's race. Led by candidate Erwin, the Populists did not stress some of the issues that would be important when the national party organized in 1892, such as a graduated income tax, the direct election of U.S. senators, and greater regulation—even to the point of government ownership—

of transportation. Although far from revolutionary in their demands, the Populists were perceived by the "old guard" of both parties to be quite radical, chiefly because of their stand on the money issue.

During economic hard times, those in debt sought relief. More than sixty years before, conflicts on that issue had erupted in the Old Court–New Court struggle. Now the same kinds of concerns brought forth new responses but similar divisive reactions. Self-described "slaves of the money powers and corporations," the debt-ridden agriculturalists called for the free and unlimited coinage of silver at a set ratio to gold. Perhaps few understood this action in principle, but many knew that it would create an inflated currency. Higher prices for farm products would mean that farmers could use cheaper dollars to pay off old debts. The Republicans and one part of the Democratic Party vehemently opposed the proposal and called for "sound money." A large—and growing—faction of the Democrats cried out instead for "free silver." The fight was on.

Populists began to draw votes from both parties, but the Farmers' Alliance refused to endorse the third party. That decision gave the victory to Democrat Brown, who received 144,168 votes. Republican Andrew T. Wood of Mount Sterling had 116,087, Populist Erwin polled 25,631, and a Prohibition candidate won 3,292. But the Democrats had not won a majority of ballots cast (only 49.9 percent); the Populists had garnered nearly 9 percent of the vote, and the potential for future problems was clear. The slow erosion of Democratic votes over the years had continued, and the party's western bastion had drastically lessened its support. Of the forty-four counties where Populists had gained more than 10 percent of the vote, most were in the agriculturally distressed western farm belt. Populists had elected at least thirteen members to the General Assembly, and the presence of numerous Alliance-backed Democrats gave agrarians a majority in the legislature. Free silver and agricultural reform issues would have to be addressed by Democrats, or their party could face the rarest of events—future defeat.

Governor Brown presided over a schizophrenic and chaotic administration. Operating under the new constitution for the first time, the legislature had to reexamine old laws and, as a result, stayed in session almost continuously from December 1891 until July 1893, an action that pleased few and earned the body the name the Long Parliament. Brown so feuded with his cabinet and his lieutenant governor that the administration split into two factions, and the political situation in Frankfort grew increasingly bitter. Meanwhile, legislative actions varied between the reactionary and the reform-minded. The General Assembly passed a much-needed law that at last gave property rights to married women, but at the same time it enacted a separate coach law (opposed mostly by Republicans and some Populists), which racially segregated passengers in railroad cars. It passed a limited but basic coal mine safety act but terminated as too expensive the important geological survey. Brown himself vetoed a revenue bill that would have increased railroad taxes but then turned against the railroads by preventing the merger of the L&N with the second-largest carrier in the state, the Chesapeake and Ohio. No one seemed to be in charge or to know where the state was going.

Similar problems plagued the Democratic Party at the national level. The 1892 presidential election brought Grover Cleveland back to the White House, a move endorsed by Kentucky voters, who gave Cleveland a 40,000-vote majority over incumbent Republican president Benjamin Harrison. Populists had garnered a smaller but still respectable 23,500 votes (7 percent). President Cleveland and his Kentucky-born vice president, Adlai E. Stevenson of Illinois (1835-1914), recognized the role of the Kentucky Democrats by appointing John G. Carlisle (1835-1910) as secretary of the Treasury.

Then the most prominent national political figure from Kentucky, Carlisle had studied law under former governor Stevenson.

From his northern Kentucky base of Covington, he had won election as lieutenant governor, U.S. congressman for seven terms, and U.S. senator. He had also been Speaker of the U.S. House. Looking cold and austere dressed in his traditional black suit, Carlisle was usually described as intellectual, analytic, and brilliant, and many expected him to use the cabinet position as a springboard to the presidency. But a national depression and the money issue made the Cleveland administration and Carlisle very unpopular, even in Democratic Kentucky, and doomed his political hopes. A sound money man, Carlisle spoke in Covington in 1896, and when free silver supporters pelted him with rotten eggs, he made that occasion his last public speech. Carlisle left the state to live elsewhere, his career having fallen victim to the issues that were dividing the commonwealth.

Political, Tollgate, and Other Wars

In the 1895 race for governor, the money issue and other questions threatened to end the dominance of the Democratic Party in Kentucky. With an unpopular Democratic president and governor, with a depression still ongoing, with the third-party Populists present to siphon votes from the majority party, and with the free silver issue splitting the Democrats further, Republicans could taste victory at last. They put forth their strongest candidate, William O. Bradley.

In a bitter convention fight, Democrats repudiated incumbent governor Brown's choice, selected P. Wat Hardin of Harrodsburg, and endorsed a party platform in support of the gold standard and sound money. Hardin's plank fell apart quickly, for the Democratic candidate repudiated the platform and came out for free silver, to try to hold agrarians in the party. Meanwhile, Governor Brown refused to campaign for Hardin, and conservative Democrats abandoned Hardin for the Republicans. Populists put forth a fairly prominent former Democrat, Thomas S. Pettit of Owensboro, and he gained the support of one of the largest black newspapers in the region, Louisville's *New South*. Overall, however, blacks generally remained loyal to the Republicans.

Bradley further divided the already-splintered Democratic ranks by courting the estimated 20,000-30,000 votes of the American Protective Association, a secret fraternal group opposed to Catholics and immigrants. The group had been credited with the defeat of a Catholic who was running for Congress in Louisville in 1894, and it now favored the Republicans over the party associated with Catholic ethnic groups. Forty years earlier, similar elements and feelings had erupted in the "Bloody Monday" riots, but the election of 1895 passed with no unusual violence. What once seemed almost impossible in Kentucky had happened. The Republicans won. Bradley gained 172,436 votes to Hardin's 163,524. Although in decline as a formal party, the Populists had garnered 16,911 ballots with Pettit, and the Populist candidacy made the difference in a race decided by fewer than 9,000 votes.

The election of 1895 marked the beginning of more than three decades of strong two-party competition in Kentucky at the state and national levels. Legislatures and local politics remained solidly Democratic, but Republicans would win four of the next nine governor's races. In the presidential election of 1896, the state went for the party of Lincoln for the first time since the Civil War, as William McKinley defeated the silverite and Populist-oriented William Jennings Bryan by a margin of fewer than 300 votes. To Kentucky agrarians, Bryan was a hero who spoke for them "on behalf of the masses against the classes." To more conservative elements in the state, he represented a "dangerous," radical spirit. With many of the old key leaders—including Watterson, Breckinridge, Carlisle, and Buckner—in opposition to Bryan, some Democrats left their party for the Republicans, while others gave their votes to the National—or Gold—Democrats. Another splinter third party, the Gold Democrats had as their presidential nominee Kentucky native John M. Palmer of

Illinois, and their vice presidential choice was former Kentucky governor Buckner. They won only 5,108 votes in the 1896 election in Kentucky, but had those ballots gone to regular Democrat Bryan, he would have won the state. Some of the wayward voters would return to Democratic ranks, but others would not.

Similar issues resulted in the rejection of the once-popular U.S. senator J.C.S. ("Jo") Blackburn (1838-1918) of Woodford County and the selection—after fifteen months and 112 bitter ballots in the General Assembly—of the state's first Republican senator, William J. Deboe of Crittenden County. A realignment of parties was taking place, and as a result the Republicans, once the more reform-minded of the two major parties, grew more conservative. On the other hand, Democrats would increasingly be viewed over the next few decades as the reform party of the commonwealth, except in racial matters. Yet in the end, both parties retained reform and reactionary wings, eschewed extremes, and remained moderate.

Despite the string of Republican victories in political races, new governor Bradley did not taste great success otherwise. Much of his time was spent dealing with violence, both legal and illegal. The so-called Tollgate Wars resulted from a system whereby private companies met the need for local roads by building them, then charging tolls to pay off their investment, and eventually earning a profit for their stockholders. By 1890 more than three-fourths of all hard-surfaced roads in the state were under the toll system. But people less able to pay opposed the roads, charging that their rates were exorbitant, especially in such depressed times. The call went up for "free roads." State and local government hesitated to get involved, and faced with inaction, angry agitators began to take matters into their own hands. Tollhouses were burned, gates destroyed, and gatekeepers threatened and beaten. One Mercer County man received a warning which read, in part: "We ask you Not to collect no more tole. You must Not collect one cent[.] if you do we are Going to Destroy your House with fire and Denamite. . . . We want a Free Road and are agoing to have it, if we have to Kill and Burn up everything. Collect No more tole[.] We mean what we say." By 1897 eleven gates had been destroyed in Mercer County, and a keeper had been seriously wounded. "A state of siege" existed. Other counties, mostly in central Kentucky, saw masked Regulators destroy virtually every tollgate in the area.

A kind of class warfare seemed to be occurring, and business leaders spoke of anarchy and communism. An angry Governor Bradley called for retribution toward "lawbreakers" and "outlaws," but a Democratic legislature that may have been quietly sympathetic to the agrarian goal of free roads refused to act against the tollgate attackers, saying the matter was a local one. Such decisions probably encouraged conservative Democratic Party members to look to the Republicans. By the turn of the century the wars had ended, for tollgate companies either had sold their stock to local groups, who then opened the roads without charge, or had simply been driven out by the violence. The lesson some people seemed to have learned was that violence worked. It would be a deadly lesson for Kentucky's future.

Kentuckians' desire to channel their violent energies found an outlet in 1898 with the start of the Spanish-American War. Eventually, four Kentucky regiments and two troops of cavalry served in the conflict but saw little action. Their suffering came not on the battlefield but at army camps in the United States, where official ineptitude, crowded conditions, inadequate clothing, poor sanitation, impure water, and spoiled food all took their toll. With sick soldiers awaiting transportation back to Kentucky, the state government found that it had no funds to pay for the hospital trains needed to return them. Governor Bradley ended up borrowing the money from a bank, trusting the General Assembly to reimburse the loan. Eighty-four Kentuckians did not make that trip back, and their deaths reminded

others that the conflict may have been "a splendid little war" with easy victories, but it had a cost even at that.

Goebel!

Governor Bradley had another problem in 1898, and it concerned a person who was becoming the most controversial man in Kentucky. William Goebel (1856-1900) seemed a strange leader of the Democrats, for that party had been guided by the Confederate Dynasty; Goebel's father had fought for the Union. In a state that praised its British ties, Goebel had been born to German immigrant parents and had spoken the German language early in life. In a commonwealth whose politicians stressed their long lineage in the Bluegrass, Goebel had been born outside the state. And in a place where hearty greetings, strong oratory, and warm camaraderie characterized most politicians, Goebel displayed none of those traits.

Aloof and cold in public, uneasy when mixing with crowds, and just barely an effective speaker, Goebel overcame his faults by reading widely to become well informed and by winning his victories behind the scenes through a strong organization. Politics was his life, and he had few male friends and even fewer female ones. As a result, his waking moments were devoted to his search for political power. Brilliant and bold, ambitious and audacious, he seldom compromised and won allies by his will, his inner force, and his program. Heading a new group of young Democrats unhappy with the old leadership, Goebel called for aid to the laboring class and greater controls on corporations and their lobbies, particularly the L&N. He was pictured as the friend of the "common man." Such appeals found a ready audience, but Goebel's forceful and antagonistic manner of making them resulted in an equally strong-willed opposition. No one of his era aroused such passions, and one of his enemies—a former Confederate from his own party—had met Goebel on a street in their hometown of Covington in 1895. Each man drew a pistol

Ambitious and uncompromising,
Pennsylvania-born William Goebel was the
most controversial figure of his era
in Kentucky politics (courtesy of the
Kentucky Library, Western Kentucky
University).

and fired one shot. His opponent fell dead; Goebel went free; the widow went to the insane asylum. To those who battled against "Boss Bill" Goebel, the Kenton King, the shooting was but another indicator of the man's ruthless nature. To them he was a murderer.

Now he sought the governorship of Kentucky, to be decided in 1899. As a state Senate leader, he pushed through the so-called Goebel Election Law in the 1898 session. The act established a Board of Election Commissioners, with members basically selected by Goebel, that would choose all local precinct officials and would judge disputed gubernatorial races. Furious opposition arose from both parties, as warnings of one-man rule and one-party tyranny came forth. But enough Democrats remained loyal to override Governor Bradley's veto. The act became law.

In the 1899 governor's race Goebel did in fact win his party's nomination but in a manner that so angered his opponents at the turbulent Music Hall Convention in Louisville

that some bolted and organized a third party, the Honest Election League. These Democrats soon took a name from their popular nominee, former Democratic governor John Y. Brown, and as Brown Democrats went on to garner 12,140 votes. A dying Populist Party took 2,936 more. But in the end the election came down to a contest between Goebel and Republican William S. Taylor (1853-1928) of Butler County. The state attorney general, Taylor was not the strongest of candidates, but the growing opposition to Goebel plus the financial largess of the L&N gave him a chance for victory. Goebel, meanwhile, continued to attack: "I ask no question and I fear no foe." On election day the count was too close to call. Each side claimed victory and charged the other with fraud. Finally the Board of Election Commissioners, thought to be in Goebel's control, surprised almost everyone by declaring that Taylor had won with 193,714 votes to Goebel's 191,331. Once more the third parties had taken away the votes that could have won the election for the Democrats. In December Taylor was inaugurated as the second governor from the Republican Party, and the matter seemed resolved.

The conflict was only beginning, however. The Democratic majority in the General Assembly voted to investigate the election to determine whether fraud and illegal military force had been used. A change of only a few votes could make Goebel governor. An investigating committee was formed, and in what was likely a prearranged drawing, ten of the eleven names picked were Democrats. Republicans expected the committee to recommend removal of enough ballots so Goebel would have a majority, and then the legislature would approve that finding. Such an action would be similar to measures taken a few years before regarding a Republican governor in Tennessee. Desperate Republicans tried to put pressure on the General Assembly and brought in a "Mountain Army" of supporters, a move suggesting that force might be used. Both sides issued threats and counterthreats, and another volatile element was added to an already combustible political mix.

In that atmosphere, Goebel and two of his supporters walked toward the state capitol on January 30, 1900. Within days Goebel might become governor. His long-term desire would at last be realized.

Then a shot rang out.

18

Progressivism, Prohibition, and Politics, 1900-1920

Assassination of a Governor

Goebel had been shot. Mortally wounded from a rifle bullet that had passed through his body, he was taken for treatment to a room in a nearby hotel. Governor Taylor declared that a "state of insurrection" existed, called out the militia, and ordered the legislature to reconvene in a safer location, in this case the Republican stronghold of London, Kentucky. Democratic legislators refused to recognize the legality of that action, but they found armed soldiers barring them from meeting in the capitol or in several other public places in Frankfort. Gathering secretly in the hotel, with no Republicans present, they accepted the contest committee's report regarding the disputed election, threw out enough votes to reverse the results, and on January 31, 1900, declared Goebel governor. He was sworn in, and in his only official act he ordered the militia to leave and the legislature to reassemble. Soon the new Democratic government called out a friendly militia force to face the Gatling guns staring across the capitol lawn. Republicans in turn cried out about the "steal" of the election and refused to recognize the constitutionality of any of the Democratic actions. Two governments, each with its own force of more than a thousand armed men, faced each other, and the level of tension rose higher and higher. A stray shot could spark bloody violence and perhaps even another civil war, only this time along party lines.

At 6:44 P.M. on February 3, 1900, William Goebel died of his wounds. The only governor in American history to die in office as a result of assassination, he had been chief ex-

On January 30, 1900, William Goebel was assassinated outside the Kentucky state capitol. He was sworn in as governor the next day but died on February 3 (from the *Cincinnati Enquirer*, Jan. 31, 1900).

ecutive of the commonwealth for three days. The forty-four-year-old northern Kentuckian had survived the assassin's bullet for only a little over a hundred hours. His last words, at least as reported by the Democratic press, ensured that he would live on as a martyr: "Tell my friends to be brave, fearless, and loyal to the great common people."

With the death of the controversial Goebel, more rational discussions began to take place, and the danger of warfare lessened. Goebel's lieutenant governor, J.C.W. Beckham (1869-1940) of Nelson County, now took the reins of leadership for the Democrats, and both sides waited for the courts to decide who legally was governor and who was not. Meanwhile, state government ground to a halt, since no one knew who was in charge. Banks refused to honor checks from either side. Finally, in May, with John Marshall Harlan dissenting, the U.S. Supreme Court ruled that it could not examine the issue since no federal questions were involved. Thus the actions of the Democratic majority in the legislature would stand. The Republicans were out, and the Democrats in.

Governor William S. Taylor, under indictment from a partisan jury as an accessory to the crime, fled the state. Numerous others were arrested, and eventually three men were convicted of the assassination: Republican secretary of state Caleb Powers of Knox County, the man said to be the mastermind of the plan; Henry Youtsey, a clerk from northern Ken-

tucky, said to be the aide to the assassin; and James B. Howard, a man involved in the Clay County feud and the supposed assassin. But the whole legal process was flawed. Juries were packed with Democrats, most trial judges had been partisan supporters of Goebel (one had been a Democratic lieutenant governor), and several witnesses perjured themselves in giving testimony. Two of the three convicted men appealed and won the right to a new trial from an equally partisan high court that had a Republican majority. As a result, Howard went through three trials, and Powers through four, during a seven-year period. The long, drawn-out process only added to the bitterness and the bad publicity for the state. As one national observer noted: "How deeply the bitterness of the Goebel killing has entered into the life of Kentucky no outsider can fully realize. The animosities engendered by it have brought about literally scores of fatal quarrels. Business partnerships have been dissolved; churches have been disrupted; lifelong friendships have been withered; families have been split; there is no locality so remote, no circle so clearly knit, as to escape the evil influence."

In 1908, eight years after the assassination, after the last Powers trial had ended in a hung jury, the governor pardoned Howard and Powers, and later he pardoned others still under indictment. In 1916 Youtsey was paroled, and he was pardoned in 1919. After Powers went free, he quickly ran for a seat in the U.S. House of Representatives and won. As he liked to say, he then served as many years in Congress as he had in jail. The other two men lived quieter lives, although they were frequently asked, "Did you kill Goebel?" Because of the contradictory evidence and partisanship surrounding the case, the answer to the question of who killed William Goebel still remains mired in mystery and intrigue.

The effects of the assassination on Kentucky are a bit clearer. First, the event strengthened Kentucky's reputation as a violent place. Second, party lines solidified, as each group looked at the other with greater and greater distrust. Republicans would cry out that Democrats had stolen the governor's office from them; Democratic orators would figuratively wave the bloody shirt of Goebel before voters and label their opposition as murderers. A third effect is less clear-cut. Some have argued, then and now, that the death of Goebel snuffed out the reform spirit in the state. That really was not the case, for reforms did occur and progressive legislation was enacted, and it is far from certain whether Goebel's record would have been much different from that of some of his predecessors. What the assassination did show, however, was that personality and reform were joined. Bold moves and successful challenges to the establishment could take place, but the tactics had to be carefully chosen. Political bosses who lacked charisma and popularity had to move slowly. The Goebel affair was to the wise politician not a roadblock to action but rather a caution. In that sense it did have an effect on reform in Kentucky.

In the midst of the Goebel trials, with partisanship at fever pitch, a former legislator and judge delighted a 1902 banquet audience with a poem that would be endlessly reprinted over the years. The concluding lines of the last verse of James H. Mulligan's "In Kentucky" summarized the state of politics in the commonwealth not only then but in the future as well:

> The song birds are the sweetest
> In Kentucky;
> The thoroughbreds are fleetest

> In Kentucky;
> Mountains tower proudest,
> Thunder peals the loudest,
> The landscape is the grandest—
> and politics—the damnedest
> In Kentucky.

Bosses and Beckham

John Crepps Wickliffe Beckham (1869-1940) was called the Boy Governor. Coming to office as a result of Goebel's death, J.C.W. Beckham at age thirty was barely old enough to meet the constitutional requirements of the office. In truth, he probably owed his place on the Goebel ticket to the fact that he was what Goebel was not—from an old Bluegrass family. Beckham's grandfather Charles A. Wickliffe had been governor of Kentucky, and his uncle Robert C. Wickliffe, the chief executive of Louisiana. An attorney, Beckham had been Speaker of the Kentucky House, and from that position he became the party's nominee for lieutenant governor. Looking as young as his years, he also projected a sense of handsome, aristocratic dignity and reserve. Many were uncertain whether he would even survive a special election in the fall of 1900 to fill the remainder of Goebel's term. As it turned out, Beckham showed very quickly his political acumen and became one of the state's major political leaders over the next three decades.

But was the governor of Kentucky really the ruler of the state? For five or more decades after 1900, a series of political bosses wielded much of the real power, usually behind the scenes. Almost every town and county had someone who could "get out the vote," and electoral success often depended on how many of those key people could be brought into a candidate's camp. Some individuals had influence beyond their small area, and they became the major players. Foremost of those was William Purcell Dennis ("Percy") Haly (1874-1937), who had started out selling newspapers on the streets of Frankfort. He became a confidant of Goebel's and stayed in the dying man's room day and night. While Goebel had wanted both the spotlight and the power, Haly needed

J.C.W. Beckham assumed the governorship upon the death of Goebel. Known as the Boy Governor, Beckham was only thirty at the time he took office (courtesy of the Kentucky Historical Society).

only the latter. With Boss Bill's death, Haly quickly transferred his allegiance and talents to Beckham. The two men became politically inseparable and won numerous victories as a result. Although intelligent and an exceptional planner, Haly was not a good speaker or public figure, and he achieved his aims away from center stage. His only important office was an appointed one as adjutant general, but "the General" preferred to command votes, not troops. An insomniac who lived in a hotel and never married, Haly devoted his many waking hours to the political game he so enjoyed and mastered.

Numerous other political bosses vied for power all across Kentucky. In the western part of the state, Thomas S. Rhea and then Emerson ("Doc") Beauchamp controlled Logan County and other areas, while the Broadbent family of Trigg County proved important later. Louisville's Whallen brothers were succeeded by Michael J. ("Mickey") Brennan, then by "Miss Lennie" McLaughlin and the Fourth Street Machine. Maurice L. Galvin controlled votes in northern Kentucky, as William F. ("Billy")

Klair did in Lexington. Bardstown, the home of Beckham, was also home to a bitter enemy of his, "Boss Ben" Johnson, and Johnson's son-in-law J. Dan Talbott. The eastern part of the commonwealth saw Albert W. ("Allie") Young, called the Morehead Manipulator, become a powerful political force, while Marie Turner of Breathitt County filled that place later.

The lives of the various bosses exhibited few common characteristics. All but Galvin were Democrats, for that was the party in power in most local areas. A large number were Catholic: Haly, the Whallens, Brennan, Klair, Johnson, and Talbott all recognized that they could not win statewide office because of their religion. To gain power they had to operate in a less open manner.

Otherwise, differences distinguished the various bosses. Some, such as Ben Johnson, were born to wealth, while others, such as Haly, Brennan, and Klair, came from poorer German or Irish immigrant bases. Some used their positions to garner additional funds either for themselves or for their political organizations. Yet in the end, power, not money, motivated

275

most. Klair's contacts brought a large share of the state's insurance business to his firm, while Brennan in Louisville attracted funds from political activity. One would-be candidate was told by Brennan that if he paid two thousand dollars, Brennan would ensure that the city precincts would all vote for him. He paid, and they did. Some of the bosses sought or held no political office, while others pursued their own political goals: Rhea ran for governor, Beauchamp was lieutenant governor, Johnson a congressman, Young a state senator. Most gained their fame, however, not from the positions they held as much as the power they controlled.

They gained that power by fulfilling a need. In an era of little governmental involvement in relief efforts, the bosses provided aid to destitute families, whether in the form of a pair of shoes, a load of coal in winter, a turkey at Christmas, a loan, or a job. Brennan, for instance, used the funds given him by political candidates and daily took cash from his Louisville bank account and ordered it distributed to the needy. In return for such actions, bosses asked for people's allegiance—and their votes. They could then offer those votes to politicians, in exchange for rewards—usually in the form of contracts or the promise of jobs. Distributing patronage, they gave allies positions in fire and police departments, and later in highway departments, or in prisons or hospitals. If this political circle did not benefit democracy, it did benefit those who were part of the game.

Of course, if the occasion demanded, some bosses were not averse to taking action that made certain their pledges of political victory could be honored. A widely circulated story, for instance, told how Percy Haly manipulated the vote of a Franklin County precinct so that his ally Beckham won by a vote of 219-0. On examination of the suspicious returns—so the accounts said—it was discovered that such voters as A. Apple, B. Beans, C. Corn, P. Pear, P. Plum, R. Raspberry, as well as B. Broom, F. Fence, H. Hog, L. Log, R. Road, and

R. Rock, had all cast ballots—in alphabetical order! Less ingenious or daring bosses simply used the names of voters who resided in the local cemetery on election day.

Yet for all the corruption and power politics, the bosses provided aid and support when others did not. They often were reform-minded, for their constituencies generally were the poor and forgotten, but they would be attacked for the perceived evils they brought to politics. Their influence was mixed, and for half a century or longer their role was all-important. They were the kingmakers.

In the fall of 1900 Governor Beckham faced an election that would decide whether his term would continue. Called to fill the remainder of Goebel's term, the contest—for a change—did not include any significant third-party threat, for Populists had generally returned to the Democratic Party, while many disgruntled Brown Democrats voted Republican. Thus a close vote was expected, as in the two previous governor's races. Beckham and Haly made two shrewd moves that may have been decisive. Openly, a special session of the legislature was called, and it repealed the unpopular Goebel Election Law. That action removed what had become one of the main Republican campaign issues. Behind the scenes, a representative of Beckham's met secretly with a recent and powerful enemy, Milton Hannibal Smith of the L&N, and Smith agreed that if the attacks on railroads ceased, he would support the Democrats. As he noted later, "The procedure suggested was followed." All of this effort was needed, as it turned out, for Beckham still barely beat the Republican candidate, John W. Yerkes, a law professor from Danville, by a count of 233,052-229,363. Losing by fewer than 3,700 votes, Republicans charged fraud, particularly in the boss-dominated Louisville precincts, but they did not have the legislative majority that had enabled the Democrats to give a victory to Goebel in 1900. Beckham was elected.

Could he be reelected in 1903? The constitution specified that the governor "shall be ineligible for the succeeding four years after the expiration of the term for which he shall have been elected." A high court friendly to Beckham ruled that since Goebel, not Beckham, had been elected to the original term, Beckham could run again, and he did. In the period since Beckham's first race, the governor and the General had together built an effective political machine—this became the issue for Republicans—and had attracted some wayward Democrats back into the fold. One who had not returned cried out against his former party's appeal: "It is pitiful," he said, "to have William Goebel's wounds torn open at every election and his bones dragged from the grave to secure votes." The result of such tactics, however, was a Democratic victory in 1903, and for the first time in sixteen years that party won a majority of the votes cast. The incumbent's 229,014 votes outdistanced wealthy Louisville businessman Morris B. Belknap's 202,764. As a result, Beckham ended up serving all but two months of two full terms. He had time to do much.

Beckham's administration left a decidedly mixed record of achievements. Basically the governor hesitated to take strong stands if opposition arose, and he sought to heal many of the wounds left by the Goebel affair. His legislatures passed a child labor law, acts concerning conservation, and a statute regulating insurance companies. Using funds received from the federal government for a long-delayed Civil War claim, Beckham ended the state's debt and began construction of a new capitol. Two new colleges—Eastern Kentucky State Normal School and Western Kentucky State Normal School—were established, chiefly to train teachers. A Racing Commission was set up to regulate horse racing, and the state fair was begun.

Yet these more progressive actions were offset by others of a less noble bent. The governor's declaration that Kentucky was "exceedingly generous toward her schools" did not help education. Under Beckham, Berea College, the last integrated college in the South, was ordered to become segregated, and a limited franchise

for women was ended as well. The administration's numerous pardons and its close ties to the Hargis faction in the feuds in "Bloody Breathitt" brought much criticism. Fraud in the 1905 municipal election in Louisville had been so pervasive and open that the state's highest court declared that the election had not been "free and equal" and invalidated the whole process. All the Democratic victors were thrown out of office. In addition, in another ruling the court voided the creation of Beckham County by the General Assembly, since the county did not meet the guidelines in the new constitution. The time-honored process of naming counties for governors might finally cease, it seemed.

In some ways, Beckham's chief accomplishment lay in the political arena, for Democrats resurged and won most major elections. In the 1900 presidential race in Kentucky, a huge turnout—86 percent of the voters—gave William Jennings Bryan a majority over incumbent president William McKinley; four years later Democrats once more carried the state, for Alton B. Parker over Theodore Roosevelt. Again the efforts of Kentucky Democrats proved of no avail, for the Republicans won nationally in both contests. In 1900 Democrat J.C.S. Blackburn took one U.S. Senate seat, and two years later former governor James B. McCreary defeated incumbent William J. Deboe for the other. Near the end of Beckham's term, nine of the eleven members of the U.S. House from Kentucky were Democrats. It appeared that the party had made a comeback. But factionalism, that old devil of the Democrats, had been growing as well, and in his quest to build a base of power, Beckham had alienated major leaders, including Henry Watterson. One other issue in his term widened those divisions.

Prohibition and Progressivism

Progressivism meant different things to different people in the first two decades of the twentieth century. In a sense, some of the reforms so long advocated by farm groups had been taken up by middle- and upper-class Kentuckians of urban and commercial backgrounds and in their hands now became respectable ideas, considered worth pursuing. Viewed as more moderate and less disruptive than the agrarians, such reformers found more support and had more success, as they tried to modernize their world while remaining true to many of the traditions of their past. They worried about the current situation, one filled with social unrest and much injustice, but remained optimistic about their generation's ability to change all that. With faith in a future of progress, they were convinced that they could eliminate many of the evils around them.

Historian Willard Gatewood has written that southern progressivism "was a diffuse, amorphous movement, embracing a complex of reforms designed to promote corporation regulation, political democracy, public health and welfare, efficiency, and morality." So it was in Kentucky. Not all interested groups or individuals supported all aspects of the political and social reform movement that gave the period 1900-1920 the label of the Progressive Era. Coalitions shifted, at times crossing party lines, at other times strengthening them. In the end, individual Kentuckians had to decide the extent of their own personal commitments to change.

Putting the ideas and theories of progressivism into practice required that citizens accept a "new interventionism," a different concept of government's role. In reality, this new view meant that trusts would be controlled by regulation of corporations, utilities, railroads, and the like. It meant that corrupt politics and bossism would be offset by laws forcing the direct election of U.S. senators (instead of their being elected by the state legislature), the selection of party candidates through direct primary votes (instead of via political connections in "smoke-filled rooms"), and even, perhaps, the votes of women. Reformers would call out for acts against corrupt practices, more restrictions on lobbyists, and an extended civil service. They advocated social justice through child

labor laws, factory safety inspections, and systems of workers' compensation. Food and drug controls for consumer protection, tax reform through a regulated income tax, attempts to fight poverty and give the dispossessed a better life, greater protection of natural areas and natural resources—all these issues were part of some people's progressivism as well.

It was in the area of social control, however, that Kentuckians had their greatest differences regarding progressivism. In large urban areas of the United States, some argued that true reform required a restriction on immigration; in the South, the same contention produced so-called voting reforms that resulted in white supremacy and a segregated voting system. Those conservative elements of progressivism had less appeal in Kentucky, for with comparatively few immigrants and blacks in the state, white, native-born residents did not see such groups as threats to the same extent as their counterparts did elsewhere. Instead, progressivism in Kentucky turned its full fury in the area of social control to one other part of progressivism—the prohibition of alcoholic drink.

Prohibition found many allies in the home of bourbon. At the same time that whiskey production in the state was growing from 5,870,000 gallons in 1871 to 30,386,000 in 1882, a strong movement was forming to control "Demon Rum" in the commonwealth. In 1874 the legislature passed a general local option bill, which allowed towns, cities, and other legal entities to enact Prohibition if a majority of citizens so voted. Two years later Kentuckian Green Clay Smith ran for U.S. president on the platform of the National Prohibition Reform Party, although he gained only 828 votes in his home state. John Hickman led a powerful temperance group, the Independent Order of Good Templars. Carry Nation (1846-1911), born in Garrard County, soon attracted greater national attention with her hatchet-wielding forays against saloons; in Kentucky, however, such religious-based groups as the Women's Christian Temperance Union

(WCTU) and, after 1904, the Anti-Saloon League probably changed more attitudes. Two people led the fight, both operating from Lexington, both strong orators and national figures. George Washington Bain (1840-1927) took the early leadership role, as presiding officer of the twenty-four-thousand-member Order of Good Templars and as editor of the *Temperance Advocate* newspaper. Through the active involvement of WCTU president Frances Estill Beauchamp (1857-1923), more than three hundred chapters of her organization were established across Kentucky. Temperance advocates asked citizens to look around themselves, for virtually every town experienced fights and deaths resulting from drunkenness. The Prohibition forces argued that drinking destroyed families, corrupted elections, and provided power to a "Beer Trust" or a "Whiskey Party." To their minds, drinking ripped apart the social fabric of society.

Those opposed to Prohibition praised the individual's right to choose whether or not to imbibe alcohol, pointed out how much money and how many jobs the liquor industry brought to Kentucky, argued that drinking could not be legislated out of existence (as shown by moonshining and bootlegging in "dry" areas), and noted that with the water and milk quality so poor, alcoholic beverages often provided safer alternatives. In a culture where saloons provided not only free meals with drinks but also an almost sacrosanct male meeting place, the Prohibitionists' attacks brought forth spirited defenses in return.

The anti-Prohibition forces, however, found themselves losing fight after fight. In the 1906 legislature a bill passed that permitted an entire county to vote to decide whether to allow liquor sales (and be "wet") or to restrict them (and be a "dry" county). Tardily, Governor Beckham came out in support of Prohibition, and the party split widened. As a result of the county unit law, by 1907, 95 of the state's 119 counties were dry. The fight now turned to statewide Prohibition, and that issue would be very divisive. It also proved to be a very emo-

tional issue, as a political candidate's poster made clear: "Are you willing to redden your hands with human blood by voting to protect the Whiskey and Beer Trust . . . ? If it strikes down your own boy, and sends him to a drunkard's grave and a drunkard's hell, how will you answer to the bar of God . . . ?" Prohibition and, indeed, progressivism in all its facets would provide major defining issues in Kentucky life for many years.

The Black Patch War and the Night Riders

One element of the Progressive Crusade was its attempts to restrict trusts, to bring back Jeffersonian values, to heal rifts between classes rather than to divide them further. With farmers across Kentucky facing a tobacco trust that controlled them, their actions could be viewed as part of progressivism, but in reality the roots of their rebellion lay in the nineteenth-century revolts of Populists, the Farmers' Alliance, the Grange, and other such groups. In those long-distressed areas of western Kentucky, the situation had grown worse and worse. Finally the farmers could take no more, and a massive popular uprising took place, which would spread to other parts of rural Kentucky. It was war.

Tobacco had become the salvation crop for more and more Kentucky farmers, who were attracted by its high prices and strong production from small plots. Whether the new light-colored burley or the dark tobacco of western Kentucky, the crop replaced others on farms, and less diversified production resulted. In good times this system worked well to yield greater rewards; but if prices fell, then all the farmer's fortunes were tied to "the filthy weed." By the turn of the century the agricultural situation was, in fact, becoming almost hopeless. The American Tobacco Company, together with two overseas groups, dominated the market, and the three agreed not to compete against each other when purchasing tobacco. A virtual monopoly resulted and left farmers no choice in selling their crop. They had to take

279

what was offered, which was not much. Prices continued to fall, to levels below the cost of production. Agrarians had long been concerned about their declining economic fortunes in Kentucky, and now they grew desperate. Something drastic had to happen, they believed, or they would not survive.

Their answer proved to be a massive grassroots effort that united tobacco growers in an economic struggle against the tobacco trust. In September 1904 a large number of farmers met at Guthrie and soon formed the Planters' Protective Association (PPA), a two-state cooperative. Agrarians would pool their tobacco and hold it off the market until they were given the price they desired from the tobacco companies. In central Kentucky the Burley Tobacco Society organized in order to decrease production and increase demand. But success depended on cooperation, and if significant numbers of farmers defected, then the pool would not be effective. Some farmers, particularly those strapped for funds, did agree to continue to sell to the trust, and these so-called Hillbillies soon became the focus of violence, particularly in the dark patch tobacco areas of western Kentucky.

Known as the Night Riders, or the Silent Brigade, lawless vigilante bands of men donned masks, took oaths of secrecy, obeyed the orders of leader Dr. David Amoss of Caldwell County, paid dues, and rode across the region to "persuade" farmers who remained outside the pool. Warnings would be issued, perhaps tied to a bundle of sticks thrown on a porch. Then the tobacco plant beds would be destroyed or the crops burned in the fields. If this action did not produce results, people were beaten—sometimes with thorn bushes—and others were even killed. As one person noted, "To join the Night Riders was both fire and life insurance."

The violence spread, and soon Night Rider armies of hundreds of men took over entire towns and burned trust tobacco stored in warehouses. In Todd County and in Princeton, Hopkinsville, Russellville, Eddyville, and else-

where, flames, bullets, and burned-out buildings represented the Night Rider legacy from 1905 to 1909. Unsupportive county officials either cowed to threats or were beaten. Huge divisions marked western Kentucky, as rural elements fought with urban ones, as Night Riders warred on Hillbillies. Homes became armed fortresses across the Black Patch. With some thirty thousand members in the PPA, more in the burley group, and an estimated ten thousand in the paramilitary Night Riders, the tobacco farmers formed a formidable group. Political leaders either openly or tacitly supported the PPA and usually the Night Riders as well. Those who were fighting saw the conflict as a people's war against a monopoly that strangled them, and all means were justified. Others saw property being destroyed and individuals being hurt, and they cried out against the use of illegitimate violence to achieve legitimate goals. When other area elements used the opportunity to harass, beat, or kill black families in the region, the whole movement began to take an ugly racist turn and whirled more out of control.

By the 1907 gubernatorial election, the Night Riders had become a major campaign issue. Governor Beckham, proclaiming that "our people are contented and prospering," had done virtually nothing about the situation. His party's nominee, state auditor Samuel W. Hager, had to bear that fact and the other burdens of his predecessor. Once an ally of Haly and Beckham, Hager disagreed with them during the race, and they offered him only limited support thereafter. Republicans knew they had a good opportunity to reclaim the office of governor. Their nominee, Augustus E. Willson (1846-1931), appeared to have the needed attributes. A sixty-year-old, Harvard-educated attorney from Louisville, Willson had been in a firm with the state's two major national Republican leaders, Benjamin Bristow and John Marshall Harlan. On the negative side, he had once served as a lawyer for the American Tobacco Company, and he had never before won a major elective office. He criticized Beckham's

A masked Night Rider, 1909 (from Christopher R. Waldrep, *Night Riders* [1993])

"bossism," pledged to end the violence of the Night Riders, and presented himself as the best choice of Prohibition forces. He won with 51 percent of the vote; 214,481 votes were cast for Willson, and 196,428 for Hager.

As governor, Willson soon activated several state military units and sent them to more than twenty tobacco counties in central and western Kentucky. He also dispatched detectives to uncover more details and even suggested publicly that he would pardon anyone who killed a Night Rider. The irony of a tacit endorsement of vigilantism—against the Silent Brigade—coming from a law and order governor was not lost on his critics.

Yet in the end, other actions had more to do with ending the Black Patch War. Finally some court convictions resulted, while in 1909 A.O. Stanley guided a bill through the U.S. Congress that removed an oppressive national tax on tobacco. Two years later the U.S. Supreme Court ruled that the American Tobacco Company had violated antitrust acts. The "cut out" of a whole year's crop—said by one historian to be the only successful agricultural strike in the nation's history—together with the pooling of crops had helped the situa-

tion as well. Higher prices for farmers resulted. But internal problems and the inability of agrarians to stay united during prosperity doomed the PPA and the Burley Tobacco Society. Both dissolved. What remained was a Pyrrhic victory, one of temporary gains for agrarians but long-term losses for Kentucky. The violence had again seriously damaged the state's image, and the tobacco issue still had not been settled.

Governor Willson was criticized by both sides during the "wars," for doing too much or too little. In some ways that was the story of his administration, which had a decent record of achievement. That achievement, however, came from a General Assembly under Democratic control. The major accomplishment proved to be passage of an educational reform act, which established high schools in every county and gave the newly renamed State University needed funds. Limited progressive acts emerged, with a stronger child labor law, a new juvenile court system, a better pure Food and Drug Act, and an eight-hour day for laborers on public works. The state legislature also ratified the Sixteenth Amendment to the U.S. Constitution, which authorized the federal income tax. But attempts to enact broader laws concerning Prohibition failed, and that issue continued to make or break political fortunes.

In 1908 the General Assembly by joint ballot would again select a U.S. senator, and hopeful Republicans put forth their colorful former governor William O. Bradley to meet the newly retired Democratic former governor, J.C.W. Beckham. When the votes were counted, seven mostly "wet" Democratic legislators had failed to support their party's "dry" nominee and had voted for others. No one had a majority. Over the next seven weeks, vote after vote was taken, with similar results. Political figures called on Beckham to step down so that another, less controversial party member could unite the Democrats and give them victory. He refused. Finally, on the twenty-ninth ballot, four "wet" Democrats switched to Bradley, and he was elected. Termed traitors, none of the four won reelection; Bradley later hired one as his private secretary.

That same year of 1908 saw national Republicans win the presidency once more, as William Howard Taft overcame Henry Watterson's colorful characterization of him as "a mess of pottage and a man of straw." With 83 percent of Kentucky's eligible voters casting ballots, the commonwealth had given its electoral votes to old hero William Jennings Bryan, 244,092-235,711. The efforts of the Bryan voters were of no avail. It was a Republican, outgoing president Theodore Roosevelt, who laid the cornerstone of the new Abraham Lincoln Memorial near Hodgenville in 1909; it was a Republican who held the governor's office when the new state capitol was christened in 1910. It seemed that a Republican tide had swept Kentucky. As it turned out, however, there was much ebb and flow still in party currents.

The Politics of Progressivism

For a long time many Kentuckians had been concerned about the situation both in the state and in the nation. In the commonwealth, the scandals, like the Tate affair, the party factionalism and third-party movements, the endless

violence, the farm revolts, the corruption, and the inequities had all brought some citizens to call for a reform of the political system. Both parties contained elements of that reforming force, but since the invasion of Alliance and Populist elements into the Democratic Party, the Democrats had become increasingly supportive of change. Some party members, however, had either temporarily or permanently left the party, finding the reformist elements too radical. Now, though, the progressivism movement that was seizing the Democratic Party was led by different forces, ones more acceptable to the middle- and upper-class leadership elected by lower-class votes. Reform had become respectable, and both old and new leaders embraced it eagerly and readily.

Representing the old guard was one of the most accomplished political survivors of Kentucky history, former governor James B. McCreary. Since serving as chief executive of the state from 1875 to 1879, the former Confederate colonel had been in many political camps. When governor he had balanced between Bourbon and New Departure factions; as congressman during the monetary debates, he had first supported the sound money faction, then, as the votes changed, the free silver group. Initially opposed to Goebel, he had finally endorsed his campaign. He then became a Beckham supporter and won a U.S. Senate seat in 1902, but lost it later in a primary to onetime ally Beckham. Now, seeking to leap out of political oblivion and gain the governorship in 1911, he had once more tied his aging star to young Beckham and General Haly. Given all that waffling, it was no surprise that McCreary was nicknamed Bothsides. According to a popular story of the time, McCreary had once been observing black sheep in a field, and someone remarked on their color: "Well, they do appear to be black on this side at least," he responded. Such extreme cautiousness carried over to his political attitudes; he was asked once how he stood on the divisive question of Prohibition. McCreary replied, "If the people of Kentucky are for prohibition, I'm for it. If the people of

Kentucky are against prohibition, I'm against prohibition. Does that answer your question, my friend?" The seventy-three-year-old candidate would seldom lead voters, but he very carefully would gauge their wishes, then almost never oppose the views of the majority. With voters supporting reform, McCreary—ironically—would follow them into progressivism. As a result, the vain man with the dyed hair, the politician so slippery on issues that he was called Oily Jeems, became associated with major reform.

Two western Kentuckians represented the younger wave of progressive Democrats— A.O. Stanley and Ollie Murray James. Both men were superb orators; both could descend into demagoguery on occasion; both exhibited little sympathy for black rights; both supported the Night Rider movement; both advocated numerous reform measures. Although not always united, the two men soon formed a new faction in the Democratic Party, one opposed to Beckham.

A.O. Stanley (1867-1958), the son of a minister who fought for the Confederacy, grew up in central Kentucky, but after becoming an attorney he moved to Henderson. There in 1902 he won election, at age thirty-five, to the U.S. House and soon gained huge voter acclaim for his role in repealing a tobacco tax. A fierce opponent of trusts, he became nationally known for his actions in a congressional investigation of the U.S. Steel Corporation. But it was the man rather than his programs that people most remembered. Eloquent, flamboyant, and intelligent, Stanley would stand before an audience, loosen his tie, and start his talk. Then as his passion increased, he would throw off his vest and coat and leave his audience shouting for more oratory. The subject of many of his harangues was his bitter enemy J.C.W. Beckham. Both men drank, but the former governor led the "dry" forces, a move that infuriated Stanley, who was opposed to Prohibition. Beckham, Stanley shouted, "would sell out the world to go to the Senate. This house is full of squirming cowardly prohibitionists just

like him. . . . I have not been a canting two faced hypocrite." Sparing few words, Stanley called his bête noire "a fungus growth on the grave of Goebel" and painted word pictures of him "with one dimpled hand placed trustingly in the cadaverous clutch of Percy Haly." In addition to their differences on Prohibition, Stanley and Beckham also took different attitudes toward corporations and trusts. Beckham had allied with the L&N, serving as its attorney, while Stanley had inflicted political damage on tobacco, steel, and railroad companies. Corporations representing all three interests would oppose Stanley, with Milton Smith of the L&N calling him "a demagogue" and Beckham "a very good man." In truth, Beckham stood closer to the progressive camp than Stanley indicated, but the personal gulf between the two was too great to bridge. Even their campaign styles exemplified their differences, for Beckham relied on Haly's behind-the-scenes organizational talents, while Stanley trusted in his oratorical gifts. In the end, the only answer was a factionalism that further split the party.

Joining the Stanley faction was another relative newcomer, Ollie Murray James (1871-1918). In his Crittenden County home, James lived across the street from one-time Republican senator William J. Deboe. Elected to the U.S. House the same year as Stanley, James moved to the U.S. Senate in 1913 and supported measures to create an income tax and to elect senators by popular vote. A thorough progressive, he—like Stanley—gained national acclaim for his eloquent and forceful speaking style. Standing six-feet, six inches tall and weighing well over three hundred pounds, he was, as one admirer recalled, "an enormous man with an enormous voice." James supported horse racing and disapproved of Prohibition—which placed him in opposition to Beckham on both counts—and he thus joined Stanley. But in some ways he went beyond his ally, for James compromised more and left fewer feelings of ill will behind as a result. He gained numerous national allies and in 1912 gave an important keynote speech at the presidential convention. Four years later, speaking as permanent chairman of the Democratic National Convention, he brought forth a large roar and a large demonstration when his booming voice praised the president as a peacemaker who was keeping the United States out of World War I, thus demonstrating "that principle is mightier than force, that diplomacy hath its victories no less renowned than war." Delegates discussed the possibility of James as a presidential candidate in 1920, and he appeared to be a good possibility. Then in 1918, at the age of forty-seven, he suddenly died of Bright's disease. It would be more than a quarter century before another Kentucky politician would again be seriously mentioned as a presidential candidate.

While James was making his impact in the nation's capital, James B. McCreary was doing the same in Frankfort. His election as governor in 1911 had not been easy. At the Democratic convention Beckham and other supporters of McCreary had passed a platform supporting Prohibition, which alienated Watterson, James, Stanley, and other "wets." Moreover, earlier in the race candidate Ben Johnson had dropped out, citing opposition to his Catholicism. The moral and religious questions, however, were offset by Republicans' own problems, for their candidate, Judge Edward C. O'Rear of Montgomery County, had supported the law segregating Kentucky education and thus risked losing the usually Republican black vote. He had also favored several reform measures that made moderates uneasy, while ignoring his predecessor's record. Governor Willson's friends gave him little support. McCreary won with 226,771 votes to O'Rear's 195,436. Northern Kentucky Socialist Party candidate Walter Lanfersiek gained most the remainder of the ballots, with 8,718 votes.

McCreary's win resulted, in part, from the fact that he had a much better funded campaign than did his opponent. The reason for that was John C. Calhoun Mayo (1864-1914). Born in Pike County, he later settled later in Paintsville and abandoned school-

teaching for the business world. He traveled across eastern Kentucky, stopping at homes and farms, chatting with the owners, then offering them scarce hard currency in the form of gold coins in exchange for the option to mine the minerals on their land. Using such "broad form deeds," he collected hundreds of thousands of acres of options, formed companies, and sold options to other major producers of coal. That sparked the development of the Eastern Coalfield. All this made Mayo incredibly wealthy, and he used that power in politics. With timberman Rufus Vansant of Ashland and horseman Johnson N. Camden Jr. of Woodford County, Mayo formed what was called the Millionaires' Club. Club members supported Beckham and Haly and, through them, McCreary. In return, the new governor saw to it that some of Mayo's suspect titles to mineral lands were validated. But Mayo's role as political financier was cut short in 1914, when at the age of forty-nine he died of Bright's disease. At his death, he was reputed to be the wealthiest man in Kentucky. Within the decade, then, each faction had seen one of its major figures die from the same disease—Beckham had lost Mayo, Stanley had lost James.

Despite McCreary's actions regarding the Mayo land titles, his administration had a very good record and justified the accolades he was given as a progressive governor. Some women were given the vote regarding school matters, a Department of Public Roads was created and funded, and a mandatory statewide primary system for selecting candidates was established. The legislature created numerous new regulatory groups, the Kentucky Illiteracy Commission, and a stronger child labor law, while funding construction of the new Governor's Mansion, strengthening the local option law, and lengthening the school term. It also rewarded McCreary by creating a county in his honor, which turned out to be the last of the state's 120 counties.

For Democrats, however, perhaps the greatest achievement came outside Kentucky.

The 1912 presidential race saw the usually victorious national Republican Party divided between incumbent president Taft and former president Roosevelt, whose followers eventually formed the Progressive, or Bull Moose, Party. Kentucky Republicans similarly divided, and Democrats had an excellent opportunity for victory. Two native Kentuckians, Oscar W. Underwood of Alabama and Champ Clark of Missouri, pursued the prize, with Clark being the choice of the delegates from the Bluegrass State. But in the end, a man whom an angry Henry Watterson called "cold, nervy, and unscrupulous," Woodrow Wilson of New Jersey, became the candidate, and on his shoulders the Democrats rode to victory. Republicans in Kentucky split their votes, with Taft getting 115,512 votes and Roosevelt 101,766. Roosevelt was bolstered by a particularly strong showing in Louisville. Socialist Eugene Debs received 11,607 votes, mostly in northern Kentucky. But a united Democratic Party won 219,584 votes, garnering the electoral votes of Kentucky, and Democrat Wilson won the nationwide election.

The race of 1912 proved important to the future of Kentucky political parties. With Woodrow Wilson firmly committed to progressive legislation as president, and with most Kentucky Democrats firmly supporting the chief executive, the party began to take much stronger stands on reform issues than before. At the same time, the more reform-minded elements of the commonwealth's Republican Party—those who had broken ranks and supported Roosevelt's Bull Moose Party—soon found themselves in a second-class status. Increasingly, conservatives would dominate Republican councils. For a time in the 1920s, there would be little difference between the two parties, until the next Democratic president once again made the Democrats the party of change.

A change of gubernatorial administration would take place in 1915, and the race that year turned out to be perhaps the most entertaining in the state's history. Beckham had

finally become U.S. senator in early 1915, and with him removed as a political possibility, A.O. Stanley won the nomination for the Democrats, to face his close friend, Republican Edwin P. Morrow (1877-1935) of Somerset. The son of a defeated Republican candidate for governor and the nephew of former governor Bradley, attorney Morrow was one of the few men in Kentucky who could match Stanley's speaking on the stump. The two men seemed to savor the situation and traveled together to towns and hamlets across the state, verbally ripping each other apart in daytime speeches, then often sharing the same hotel room and, some said, the same bottle at night. In a rollicking campaign marked by little substantial difference between the two platforms, the election came down to oratory and style. Morrow would blame Democrats for corrupt government and call for a Republican administration, since, he said, "You cannot clean house with a dirty broom." Stanley, in turn, would criticize past Republican governors as corrupt: "Why a snake in a spasm isn't that crooked." With former Republican gubernatorial candidate O'Rear speaking with Democrat Beckham across Kentucky in favor of "dry" candidates, the liquor issue remained a potential threat to Stanley. Progressives from the Republican camp opposed Morrow and made their support a matter of concern for him. But personalities proved more of a decisive factor. The most widely repeated story told of Stanley's too free imbibing of his favorite beverage. Under the effects of a hot sun, he vomited in full view of the audience, while Morrow was speaking. When it came his turn to talk, a pale and weakened Stanley walked to the podium, then in a strong voice said, "That just goes to show you what I have been saying all over Kentucky. Ed Morrow plain makes me sick to my stomach."

Election day brought no resolution to the contest. The election was too close to call, and each side hesitated to report returns until it saw how many votes were needed to win. A week after the election, knowing that Democrats controlled the legislature and that contesting the results would end in failure, Morrow finally conceded. The official count later showed Stanley had won by 471 votes, 219,991-219,520, in the closest governor's race in state history.

Governor Stanley did not acknowledge that the election had been less than an overwhelming mandate for his views, and he proceeded to fashion an excellent record of accomplishments. With his term of office, the Progressive Era reached its apex in Kentucky. The General Assembly passed a Corrupt Practices Act, a bill forbidding railroads to offer free passes to public figures, and a state antitrust law. In a special session, the solons created a State Tax Commission, set up the first budget, and modernized the revenue system, shifting the burden from property taxes to other forms of taxation. Given more funds, the legislature then appropriated needed fiscal support for education and government. Ironically, the "wet" Stanley recognized the trends and agreed to let the people vote on a state constitutional amendment that would put in place statewide Prohibition. In 1919 the voters adopted Prohibition by a ten-thousand-vote majority, and the home of bourbon became officially dry before the nation did. When national Prohibition went into effect in 1920, under the Eighteenth Amendment to the U.S. Constitution, one divisive state issue seemed settled at last. But other controversial issues had to be addressed as well.

Child Labor, Women's Rights, and Race Relations

Young children often worked long hours, from daylight to dusk, six days a week, on farms and in factories all across Kentucky. Families counted on the labor or meager salaries of children to help alleviate economic want. Youth ended early in such situations, and small bodies wore out quickly.

Reformers who sought to limit child labor argued that the state had a right to protect its future generations when they were powerless to protect themselves. Opponents stressed that

children's work was an individual choice and said that the commonwealth had no right to interfere in what was essentially a family matter. As early as 1894 a law had forbidden children to beg or to peddle goods on the streets or to engage in jobs of unusual danger. But that measure left most young laborers untouched. In 1902 the first real child labor law for the state made it unlawful for industries to employ a child under the age of fourteen, except with a parent or guardian's signed consent. Farm work was exempt. A labor inspector soon after that found a Maysville factory in which forty children, aged eight to thirteen, worked from 5:45 A.M. until 6:15 P.M., with a thirty-minute break for lunch. All the children had permits; they all were legal under the new law; they all worked twelve hours, and each child earned twenty-three cents a day.

In 1906 the law was amended to limit child labor to a maximum of ten hours per day and sixty hours, with the age raised to sixteen. Eight years later, under Governor McCreary, the limits were lowered to a forty-eight-hour week and an eight-hour day. No child under the age of fourteen could work during school hours. With that law, Kentucky's child labor statutes were considered to be among the best in the nation. But inconsistent enforcement allowed many places to continue hiring young boys and girls in violation of the law. Kentucky cared better for its children as a result of Progressive Era reform, but it still neglected them all too often.

A much more controversial question focused on the role of women in Kentucky, and that fight had been building for decades. All agreed that there was a double standard for men and women, and the two groups did not share equal rights. In the nineteenth century most Kentuckians also agreed that that situation was how it should be. They defended the status quo with two somewhat contradictory arguments. The starker one simply said that women were not men's equals and should be subordinate to them as their "helpmates." A state senator in 1880 quoted the Bible's saying that wives should submit themselves to their husbands as the head of the family. Then he concluded: "Give me a wife that can love, honor, and look up to me as her lord and shield, or give me separation and death."

The second defense turned that argument around and said that women were subordinate to men in the public sphere but were superior to them in the home arena. Writers waxed poetic about nature's intended place for women. In the words of a governor, women are "but ministering angels in the quiet loveliness of our homes." Under "a cult of woman-worship," women occupied a higher moral plane than men, and to involve them in public life would "overburden" them and destroy their innate superiority. As late as 1914 Senator James—who would eventually vote for woman suffrage—said: "I believe woman should remain in her sphere. Her power is greater where it is, than it would be in the mire and maelstrom of politics." Those who agreed with such perspectives would view any action to change the existing order as revolutionary, as an attack on the home and family and the whole social fabric.

Soon after the Civil War, fledgling and isolated groups began to question the status quo regarding women, probably beginning with an 1867 organization in Hardin County. National leaders such as Carrie Chapman Catt and Susan B. Anthony toured the state after that, and in 1881 the Kentucky Woman Suffrage Association was founded, the first such group in the South. Seven years later it transformed itself into the broader-based Kentucky Equal Rights Association (KERA).

Other women-oriented organizations formed in the same period, and most eventually gave the women's rights movement support in one way or another. The Daughters of the American Revolution, cofounded by Kentuckian Mary Desha in 1890, turned away from equal rights more as time passed, but groups such as the Women's Christian Temperance Union and the Kentucky Federation of Women's Clubs—the latter was founded in 1894—

did not. Increasingly, members of such groups saw the vote as a way to achieve Prohibition, educational reform, and other goals.

Changes taking place in society also caused some people to question the "home sphere" argument. A labor inspector wrote in 1903 that "women in the business world are no longer regarded as intruders," and by 1910 some 11 percent of Kentucky factory workers were female—although they received discriminatory wages. A study conducted in 1905 showed that the average daily wage was 87.5¢ for women and $1.63 for men. Still, change was in the air.

The first target was the state's discriminatory laws. Before 1894 Kentucky allowed divorce for adultery only if the wife was the offender. If a wife earned wages, they went to her husband. If she wanted to make a will, she had to get her husband's consent. If she wanted to enter into a contract or own property while her husband lived, she could not. Finally, in 1894, laws gave married women property rights and the right to prepare a will. Six years later married women were allowed to keep their wages; a decade after that the state legislature raised the age of consent at which women could marry to sixteen years, up from twelve years.

More and more, the highly symbolic issue of suffrage held the key to opening the doors to full equality. Over time, greater numbers of middle-class and upper-class women began advocating their right to the vote, as a simple matter of justice. Because of their involvement in temperance reform, some women wanted the ballot in order to "clean up" politics; others simply saw it as a way to leave behind a second-class citizenship status. Because of the level of leadership, the crusade became a call for respectable, not radical, reform.

Women such as Josephine K. Henry of Woodford County and Eliza Calvert Obenchain of Bowling Green were important, but the acknowledged leader of the nineteenth-century fight was Laura Clay (1849-1941) of Madison County and Lexington. Ironically, her father, Cassius Marcellus Clay, had been a leading antislavery reformer, but he bitterly opposed women's rights. The inequalities involved in the divorce of Cassius Clay and his wife, Mary Jane Warfield Clay, prompted action on the part of their daughters Laura, Mary, Annie, and Sallie. All four women became strong advocates for the cause of women's rights. For twenty-four years Laura Clay served as president of the KERA, and by the 1890s she was recognized as the leading southerner in the National American Woman Suffrage Association (NAWSA). Progress came slowly in Kentucky, however, and just as hopes for success grew high in the early twentieth century, Clay left the KERA. Disagreeing with the organization's strategy to seek a federal constitutional amendment and supporting states' rights arguments instead, Clay joined a splinter southern group, which used more racially charged arguments. Sadly, others would have to take up the suffrage banner she had borne for so long.

A younger woman, Madeline McDowell ("Madge") Breckinridge (1872-1920), hardly hesitated and energetically pushed forward to victory. A great-granddaughter of Henry Clay, she had lived part of her life at Clay's Ashland in Lexington and then furthered her already strong aristocratic credentials by marriage to Desha Breckinridge, editor of the *Lexington Herald*. Madge Breckinridge's sister-in-law, Dr. Sophonisba P. Breckinridge, had probably been the first woman lawyer in Kentucky and served as a national leader in the field of social work as

a professor at the University of Chicago. With that support, a reserved but confident Madge Breckinridge began her personal crusade. She did so despite great suffering, however, for she had lost part of a limb to tuberculosis of the bone when still young and wore a wooden leg the rest of her life. When thirty-two, she suffered a stroke and later experienced other unhappiness in her private life as well. But she became president of the KERA in 1912, and vice president of the national group a year later. The most influential woman in the state, she used new tactics, such as suffrage marches, as well as her speaking ability and humor, to gain more support. In a strong voice coming from a slim and often weak body, she told audiences to look at male-led Kentucky, with its poor schools, violence, and corrupt politics, and asked if the question should be not whether women were fit for suffrage but whether men were. She criticized one governor for his response to her questions, noting that "Kentucky women are not idiots—even though they are closely related to Kentucky men."

Slowly, gradually, her appeals made headway. In 1902 the legislators had taken a step backward and had repealed, supposedly because of racial arguments, a law that allowed women in second-class cities to vote on school matters. In 1912 the General Assembly returned that right to literate women, in more areas across the state than before. Various attempts to secure a state amendment to allow

Laura Clay (center, with umbrella) leads a delegation of the Kentucky Equal Rights Association to the Democratic National Convention in 1916 (courtesy of the University of Kentucky Libraries).

Women's rights leader Madeline McDowell ("Madge") Breckinridge in Lexington, 1913 (courtesy of the Kentucky Historical Society)

women to vote failed, but with President Wilson's support for a national constitutional amendment, enough legislators fell in line. On January 6, 1920, Kentucky ratified the Nineteenth Amendment and became one of only four southern states to do so. The commonwealth, and Clay and Breckinridge, had long been leaders in the women's rights fight in the region and set the example to the end.

In November 1920 Kentucky women voted and for the first time had equality in suffrage matters. Within weeks after that election, Madge Breckinridge died at the age of forty-eight. Her tragedy was that she voted but once; her triumph was that she and others had voted, at last.

World War I

While women were fighting for political equality, people of both sexes had been fighting their own battles, both domestic and foreign, in a real war. In 1914 World War I broke out in Europe, and Americans easily adopted a policy of neutrality. Kentuckians experienced

some prosperity as overseas demand brought an agricultural boom—farm prices went up 110 percent between 1915 and 1917 in one town, for instance—but overall they seemed more interested in local political conflicts than in struggles between France and Germany. Bellicose editors Watterson of the *Courier-Journal* and Breckinridge of the *Lexington Herald* cried out for early entry into the war, but immigrant-oriented newspapers in Louisville criticized those appeals. Generally, citizens around the state evinced no real war spirit. Yet when Congress finally declared war in April 1917, most Kentuckians joined the national effort with little hesitancy and much fervor—in fact, almost too much fervor.

On the home front, anything German became a target, and any action that questioned official policy was viewed as traitorous. Hearing Watterson's editorial advice, "To Hell with the Hohenzollerns and the Hapsburgs," the legislature forbade the teaching of German in schools, an act Governor Stanley vetoed. The German Insurance Bank of Louisville changed its name

289

to Liberty Insurance Bank, some of the churches that still had Sunday services in German now ceased that practice, and sauerkraut became "liberty cabbage." Criticism of the government earned jail terms for some Kentuckians, and those who did not buy bonds to help finance the fight were criticized as "enemies of their country."

Meanwhile, Councils of Defense in each community supervised the war effort at the local level. People sacrificed, with "Fireless" Mondays, "Meatless" Tuesdays, or "Wheatless" Wednesdays, and they enacted stronger laws regarding morality. Not only did Prohibition emerge from the war, but red-light districts across the commonwealth were shut down to protect supposedly innocent soldiers from such professional enticement.

In fact, Kentucky in places took on the appearance of an armed camp. Troops patrolled bridges and public buildings. Fort Thomas in northern Kentucky and Camp Stanley in Lexington functioned as staging areas for soldiers sent elsewhere, while Camp Knox opened in 1918 as a training facility for artillery. But the major post became Camp Zachary Taylor in Louisville. Overall, about 125,000 soldiers received training there; some went on to fight—and die—overseas.

Unlike the situation in earlier conflicts, state identity was not retained in units, so soldiers found themselves scattered in all sorts of organizations. Eventually, 84,172 Kentuckians (13,584 of them black) served in the conflict, and 2,418 gave their last full measure of devotion. Thousands more came home with debilitating wounds or with lungs damaged by poison gas. Finally, on the eleventh hour of the eleventh day of the eleventh month in 1918, it all ended. A Kentucky soldier wrote: "I cried because I was so glad it was all over. . . . We heard the last big roar die away and the world seemed quiet."

The suffering and deaths had not ended, however. In that same fall and winter, Spanish influenza struck Kentucky and the nation. At Camp Taylor eleven thousand soldiers were stricken, and an estimated fifteen hundred did not recover. Across the state, the "Spanish Lady" took its victims, and before the flu was over in early 1919, more than fourteen thousand people died. Schools, churches, and places of amusements closed; political rallies ceased; industries stopped; even funeral services halted. With the epidemic raging at war's end, few celebrations took place. The "war to end all wars" came to a quiet conclusion, and soldiers began to trickle back to their homes.

What had been the result of the war for Kentuckians? First of all, it initially stimulated, then eventually dampened the reform spirit. Women had worked in public campaigns during the conflict, and a few more took jobs as a result of the absence of men. That situation, plus the argument that democracy should extend to both sexes, helped the suffrage movement succeed. For those who viewed Prohibition as a reform, the war sped that movement forward as well. Yet Kentuckians, and Americans, had entered the conflict with the spirit, as one state paper explained, that "we wage not our own, but humanity's war." The Progressive Era had widened the idea of community to extend beyond the locality to the nation, or even the world. As historian Larry Hood notes, "The war was to be the final crusade, the full flowering of progressivism." Yet it was not to be. Those who returned from the battlefields spoke little of glory; the hardships, the deaths, and then the epidemic at home did not seem rewards for noble actions. Doubts arose about America's mission, and the peace treaty seemed to leave many goals unrealized. As a result, Kentuckians turned inward, back to their locales. In the end, the war wounded the humanist spirit of the people. Their recovery would be slow and uncertain.

Other results were more definite. Some prosperity had occurred, but it would turn out to be fleeting; more lasting was the damage done to schools, which suffered from a scarcity of teachers, and to health care. Blacks became a part of the war effort and participated in broad ways, but they found few new freedoms as a result. One decorated black soldier was warned not to return to his Hickman hometown in the uniform he had honored, because the police chief did not like blacks in uniform. This soldier's experience was not uncommon. Improved race relations would not be an outcome of this war. But almost all soldiers, black or white, did return home changed men. They had been to parts of the United States they had never before seen and had experienced foreign lands for the first time. New contacts, new people, new ideas, all resulted. Some came back eager to change the land they had left behind. But most appeared more resigned to try to forget the horrors of trench warfare and to retreat into a world of quiet and peace. They had seen too much. Like them, most Kentuckians retreated from reform and retrenched in a reactionary world.

19

Bourbon Barons, Tobacco Tycoons, and King Coal: The Economy, 1865-1995

Agriculture

Before the Civil War, agriculture had been the economic lifeblood not only of Kentucky but also, in large part, of the nation. At a time when farm products formed a major part of economic wealth, Kentucky was a wealthy state. It ranked high or led nationally in the production of hemp, tobacco, corn, wheat, and livestock. Yet in the decades after the Brothers' War, Kentucky slowly lost its leadership position, in part because of decisions made within the commonwealth, in part because of events taking place in the United States. Overall, the country was becoming an industrial nation, and agricultural wealth declined in importance. Kentucky did not match the nation's pace of industrialization. But even in agriculture, problems arose. The opening of the great corn and wheat belt in the Midwest, for instance, introduced that region as a major producer that would soon eclipse Kentucky. Overall, five trends characterize the state's agrarian history between 1865 and 1995: changing crop patterns and, for a time, less diversity; a greater role for livestock; increased involvement of the federal government; a decreasing agricultural workforce and the decline of the family farm; and the professionalization of agriculture as a science and a business.

Changing Crop Patterns

Hemp had been the major cash crop for many antebellum central Kentucky farmers, with its use in ships' riggings and as bale rope and bagging for southern cotton. Kentucky's economic isolation from the South during the Civil War, however, had forced cotton planters to look elsewhere for alternatives. That trend continued after the conflict's end, and jute bagging and iron bands for baling cotton gradually replaced hemp. At the same time, ships began using wire rigging, and another part of the hemp market declined. In 1860 the United States produced almost seventy-five thousand tons of hemp; a decade later the nation grew less than thirteen thousand tons. Kentucky's crop had declined from nearly forty thousand tons to less than eight thousand. Farmers needed alternate crops.

Some hemp growers did turn to other crops. A few held on. By 1890 the commonwealth grew 94 percent of all the hemp produced in the United States, but only a thousand farmers still worked those fields. Their crops yielded a thousand pounds per acre, brought an average price of $96.82 per ton, and gave them earnings of $800 each—for a total value of nearly one million dollars. When World War I halted foreign imports, the crop experienced a brief revival, but by 1940 only four Kentucky farms still grew the fiber. The next year, however, another war brought further shortages as a result of the Japanese capture of the Philippine jute fields. Encouraged by governmental supports, Kentucky farmers went back to hemp, and thousands of acres once more blossomed over the Bluegrass. Entrepreneurs constructed hemp factories as well. The spurt proved brief, though. Buildings were sold as war surplus, and hemp effectively died as a Kentucky cash crop—or so it seemed.

The use of hemp in the form of marijuana cigarettes had become known by the 1920s. A national tax was instituted in 1937, and World War II hemp production had strict controls imposed on it. For several decades after that, the crop seemed forgotten. Yet James F. Hopkins, the author of *A History of the Hemp Industry in Kentucky,* may have been more prophetic than he knew when he wrote in 1951 that "once more perhaps the distinctive odor of growing hemp will hang heavily in the summer air, and the fields of emerald green may once again add beauty to the Kentucky landscape." By the 1980s hemp was adding not only beauty but also green dollar bills to an underground economy. By then moonshine production had nearly ceased, but the spirit behind it lived on through illegal hemp/marijuana production. "Wars" between federal and state officials and some Kentuckians broke out once more. In 1988 officials estimated that they destroyed half a billion dollars' worth of hemp plants in Kentucky, but that half of the crop was harvested and sold. If so, then hemp may have again become the commonwealth's chief cash crop, for tobacco brought in only $471 million that same year. In 1992 more than nine hundred thousand plants were exterminated, and more than five hundred people were arrested in Kentucky. The commonwealth's officials found that the crop dating back to statehood resisted strongly the attempts to eradicate it from the state's economy.

The decline of the hemp industry after the Civil War and the growth of other production centers for certain crops had helped make tobacco the undisputed ruler of Kentucky agriculture. Bringing in a sizable return on a small plot, tobacco added dollars to farmers' income, but it also had longer-term effects on the state that would be debated for decades. In 1869, for example, the *Columbus (Ky.) Dispatch* warned readers of the health hazards of tobacco and asked smokers to restrict their puffing to private smoking rooms. Nearly a century later, in 1965, the U.S. surgeon general reported tobacco's hazardous effects on health.

For all of the nineteenth century and much of the twentieth, however, few people seriously challenged tobacco's place in American life. Through chewing tobacco, pipes, and cigars and then, after the 1880s, through the popularity of factory-produced cigarettes, tobacco consumption rose. By the Roaring Twenties, daring women increasingly smoked. As a brief inspection of almost any motion picture of the 1930s and 1940s indicates, smoking

Tobacco and hemp grow side by side in a Woodford County field, 1931 (courtesy of the
Kentucky Historical Society).

had by that time become accepted in the middle class.

Kentucky farmers sought to fill the demand for tobacco. The work was not easy, and tobacco long proved resistant to labor-saving mechanization devices. But the major change affecting Kentucky tobacco cultivation came soon after the Civil War, apparently by accident. State farmers grew a dark-fired tobacco, "cured" by hickory smoke in tightly enclosed barns. In the 1860s, however, some seeds were planted—first on either a Brown County, Ohio, or a Bracken County, Kentucky, farm— and they unexpectedly matured into a lighter-colored leaf. White burley tobacco was born. From that beginning, the crop spread rapidly across the central Kentucky area, where hemp's decline had left a void. The new variety also began to replace the dark-fired version, since it could be harvested earlier and could be more safely air-cured in barns, where panels could be opened or closed to control moisture. White burley seemed a godsend to farmers increasingly strapped for cash. Gradually, more and more Kentucky farms turned away from a variety of crops and focused on the golden tobacco leaf. In Scott County, for instance, burley tobacco production jumped from 43,000 pounds in 1880 to 3.5 million pounds nine years later. Tobacco fever in Washington County brought

an increase from 90,000 pounds in 1888 to nearly 2 million pounds by 1900; the county was producing almost 10 million pounds by 1920. Cumberland County's tobacco crop increased fivefold between 1890 and 1940. The story was the same across Kentucky, as good prices made the switch attractive. In more difficult times, however, the increasing dependence on one crop and one price gave agrarians fewer options. For better or worse, Kentucky farmers had made their choice and had to accept the results.

The raising of tobacco continued almost without change, decade after decade. In a difficult, labor-intensive process, farmers plowed the land, sowed a protected seed bed, transplanted the shoots to a larger field, and began the endless weeding of the crop. They periodically "topped" the blooms to stimulate leaf growth, they removed worms, and they watched the weather for floods, hailstorms, and high winds. In late summer the whole family helped cut the crop, bring it to a barn for curing, and then strip the stalks. If the weather held and if prices were high, bills could then be paid and income saved. All too often the reverse occurred, and suffering resulted. Yet even then Kentucky could not bring itself to let go of a plant that held the state hostage and also paid the ransom.

Tobacco production statewide increased steadily from over 105 million pounds in 1870 to 180 million pounds three decades later. From 1865 through 1928 Kentucky led the nation in tobacco production. Yet that position came at a very real cost to farmers. The large amount of tobacco brought prices down, from a high of 13.7¢ per pound to 6.6¢ per pound during a twenty-year period ending in 1894. That decrease in price of over 50 percent offset the advantages of the increased poundage grown and brought angry farmers into the Grange, the Farmers' Alliance, and the Populist movement. When the American Tobacco Company formed a virtual buying monopoly and prices went down even more, the anger spilled over into violence, in the Black Patch and in the burley region. Resolution of these problems proved difficult, but the market seemed to be on its way up by the time World War I began.

Increased demand during the war years brought a 1916 Kentucky crop of 462 million pounds, worth nearly $59 million. Prices continued to rise; farmers grew more and more tobacco, and the days were good for the industry. Then peace brought resumed production overseas, and markets suddenly declined. Hope had made the 1919 crop the largest the state ever grew; reality, in the form of overproduction, brought 1920 prices to 13.4¢ per pound, down from 34¢ per pound the previous year. Lower averages the next year shut down the market. Once more, planters lashed

out at the invisible enemy of poor prices and formed another cooperative marketing organization. Joint action resulted in higher prices for a time. As in the Black Patch War earlier, however, impatient farmers could not remain united, and the cooperative had failed by 1926. Once again agrarians had to turn to auctioneers, whose final cries left them still searching for answers to their financial problems.

Relative stability finally came to the tobacco fields as a result of the governmental controls and supports initiated during the New Deal years of the 1930s. Through the efforts of the University of Kentucky Experiment Station, more disease-resistant tobacco plants were also introduced. Crops and prices steadied to a degree, and by 1990 tobacco remained Kentucky's number one cash agricultural commodity, representing 37 percent of all crop values, and tobacco was grown on two-thirds of the state's farms. The 366 million pounds produced in 1990, which brought an average of $1.68 per pound, made Kentucky the second-largest producer of tobacco (behind North Carolina) and the leading burley grower. In 1993 tobacco brought $836 million to the state's economy. By that time, however, smoking, which had once been a frequently copied and almost glorified social activity, was under criticism and increasing restriction. Tobacco remained an important and controversial part of Kentucky's agricultural present.

Even in the best of economic times, tobacco had not reigned unchallenged. Various

Transplanting tobacco plants from a seed bed to the field remained a labor-intensive job. The workers at the back are "setting" the plants in the row (courtesy of the Kentucky Historical Society).

crops sprang up to dispute that dominance, but none offered a sustained value that would bring farmers to abandon tobacco. By 1870, however, before burley's great growth, Kentucky remained diversified, ranking not only first nationally in hemp production but also fifth in rye, sixth in corn, and eighth in wheat. In 1890 the state stood third nationally in apple production. All of those crops, however, faded relatively before tobacco, other states' dominance, and farmers' preferences. Wheat production, for example, doubled between 1870 and 1900, but a decline followed. Only near the twentieth century's end did wheat production in the state climb back to nineteenth-century levels. Oats never did. A crop that in the 1880s had been grown on twice as many acres as had tobacco, oats had become chiefly a cover crop a hundred years later, yielding only five hundred bushels for sale in 1990.

Most of the agricultural variety in twentieth-century Kentucky came from three crops—hay, corn, and soybeans. Between 1889 and 1907 the acreage devoted to hay increased 40 percent, and annual production approached a million tons by 1909. Eight decades later, in 1989, over 5.5 million tons were harvested. Similarly, in 1900 nearly half of the state's six million acres of cropland was planted in corn, and this figure would rise and peak in the wartime year of 1917. Production increased from 63 million bushels in 1896 to well over twice that figure in 1989.

The greatest change in the state's agricultural mix of crops came in the growing of soybeans. The crop was virtually ignored for much of the century; only five thousand acres were harvested in 1928. By 1990, however, over 1.1 million acres produced nearly 37 million bushels of soybeans, valued at over $215 million. That made Kentucky the nation's fourteenth-leading producer of the crop. Capable of two crops in one growing season and used in various forms, soybeans appeared the most likely candidate of choice if farmers ever decided to abandon tobacco.

Livestock

Crops represent only one of the farmer's sources of income. By 1990, in fact, Kentucky cattle sales brought in as much money to state agriculture as did tobacco, and cash receipts from livestock overall, at $1.67 billion, considerably exceeded the money generated from crop sales, $1.26 billion. Yet reaching this level of livestock production—chiefly of cattle, sheep and lambs, hogs, and poultry—had taken a long time and had required drastic changes in the production processes.

Hogs and pigs were early mainstays of Kentucky agriculture, used both for home food purposes and for sale to nearby markets in Louisville and Cincinnati. Like other livestock, swine for many years roamed free on open ranges, to be collected at the time of sale. Soon after the Civil War's end, the state had more than 2.1 million hogs, but a steady decline followed, and the numbers reached their lowest level in 1931. After that time the number of hogs remained fairly steady. The state had nearly a million head in 1990. Sheep experienced even more drastic declines. In 1867 Kentucky had 1.1 million sheep, constituting an important part of self-sufficient farms, where families used the wool to produce homespun materials. As store-bought clothes filled that need more and more and as other markets opened, sheep production almost ceased. The state total reached a low of twenty-one thousand in 1980. Similarly, poultry had long furnished meat as well as eggs, not only for home use but also for barter at country stores and for cash sales. Needs and markets changed, however, and from a high of more than 14 million chickens in 1944, the numbers dropped to 6 million in 1961 and 2.1 million in 1990, the lowest figure on record. By then Kentucky ranked fourteenth nationally in numbers of hogs, thirtieth in sheep and lambs, and thirty-first in poultry. It was a far cry from 1870, when Kentucky had stood fourth nationally in numbers of swine and tenth in sheep.

The cattle industry in Kentucky did not suffer such drastic changes. Damaged by the Civil War, cattle production in the state required almost two decades to attain its pre-war level. Then western markets, railroad refrigerator cars that brought western beef to eastern processing centers, and new diseases in Kentucky herds all slowed relative growth. As historian James E. Wallace has noted, cattle remained at the 1 million level for nearly four decades after 1886. Better animal feed, improved breeding methods, and increased popularity of Hereford and Angus herds were offset by agricultural depression and the drought of 1930. Major increases began after 1940, and production rose to 3.75 million head in 1975. But declines followed, and the 2.4 million cattle and calves in Kentucky in 1990 represented the lowest number in more than twenty-five years. Almost 200,000 of the total were dairy cows, producing more than 2.3 billion pounds of milk annually on more than seven thousand farms. In short, even though Kentucky farmers had turned away from hogs, sheep, and chickens and more toward cattle, and even though the commonwealth still had more cattle than any state east of the Mississippi River, the cattle industry had experienced inconsistent growth. From the mid-1970s to 1987, one-third of all cattle farms ceased production. For that reason, the role of livestock in Kentucky's future remained uncertain.

Then there were the horses. Almost from the time of statehood Kentucky had been known as a place for quality thoroughbreds and, later, standardbreds. Yet the Civil War had hit the commonwealth particularly hard in regard to horseflesh, quality or otherwise. The census of 1870 showed that the 350,000 horses then in Kentucky represented a decrease in numbers of more than 60,000 animals from a decade earlier, before the war. Mules, which had survived military raids better, made the state a major market for that four-legged beast, and Kentucky ranked third nationally in the number of mules in 1870. By 1900 the state

still held an important place, with 190,000 mules within its borders. But with increased mechanization in the twentieth century, the need for horses and mules, either to work on farms or as methods of transportation, declined with each passing year. From 450,000 at the turn of the century, the number of Kentucky horses fell to 155,000 six decades later.

Throughout that time, however, thoroughbred farms in Kentucky continued to produce major racing champions. In 1926, 44 percent of the thoroughbred foals registered with the Jockey Club were from Kentucky. But changes soon affected the numbers. Competition from other states, a more unfavorable national tax structure, and other factors lessened the state's dominance of the industry. By 1992, however, Kentucky still produced almost one-fifth of all the foals registered in North America. Between 1982 and 1991 the state produced more than one-third of all major racing stakes winners. Overseas buyers drove up sale prices drastically in the 1980s, when one horse sold for $13.1 million, but by the 1990s those heady days had passed. In fact, in 1989 horse sales and stud fees totaled $524 million, causing the horse industry to fall to second in Kentucky's livestock receipts, behind cattle sales. While the state's image nationally remained tied in part to the thoroughbred, some worried citizens grew concerned about the ability of the industry to persevere and grow.

"The Feds," the Family Farm, and Agribusiness

Those who formulated New Deal farm policy in the 1930s recognized that overproduction had long plagued tobacco farmers. Through the Tobacco Control Act of 1934, tobacco growers could vote for mandatory quotas, in exchange for a minimum price (parity) guaranteed by federal funding. State farmers agreed to that scheme, and in 1936, for example, they reduced their harvest by 28 percent while increasing overall income by several million dollars. The limits on acreage (and later poundage), plus the huge increase in demand during the war years—consumption went up 75 percent between 1939 and 1945—brought a boom to tobacco. Ironically, in the period after 1965 the federal government would subsidize production while criticizing and limiting tobacco products in the marketplace.

If federal policy aided certain parts of the agricultural community, virtually all sectors felt the effects of broader changes in the agrarian world. Generally, farm homes lagged behind the rest of the commonwealth in receiving the advantages of "modern" America—good roads, electricity, indoor plumbing, and the like. As late as 1940, for instance, four of every five rural dwellings in Kentucky had no electricity, no telephones, no refrigeration, and no access to hard-surfaced roads. Ninety-six percent had no running water. As technology and transportation bypassed much of rural Kentucky, particularly the Appalachian area, the ideal of agrarian life seemed unalterably tarnished. Kentucky could not keep its population down on the farm.

In 1880 more than two-thirds of the state's labor force worked on farms (versus a U.S. average of fewer than one in five workers). In 1940 slightly more than one-third of that force still worked in agriculture. By 1990 less than 4 percent of the state's labor force did. As a result, the number of farms in Kentucky declined from a peak of 270,000 in 1920 to 93,000 seventy years later.

Yet despite all that, Kentucky remained a significant agricultural state, if for no other reason than the fact that the mindset of rural areas remained agrarian. After all, compared with the rest of the nation, numerous Kentuckians still farmed. In 1990 the state stood fourth nationally in the number of farms, chiefly because of the small size of average holdings. From the end of the Civil War until the start of World War II, state farm size declined, from an average of 158 acres in 1870 to a low of 80 acres in 1940. But as people left the farms after that, larger farms became more commonplace, and the average farm size increased to over 100

acres in 1955 and over 150 acres in 1990. Still, the average farm in Kentucky was less than one-third the size of the typical American farm.

During 1865-1990 Kentucky agriculture had three advantages. First of all, it had survived the Civil War better than agriculture in the South, and in 1870 Kentucky had more acres in agriculture than any southern state save one. As late as 1900 the value of Kentucky's farm products surpassed that of all southern states except Texas. Kentucky also depended less on tenant labor, comparatively, than did other southern states. At a time when about one-half of most farms south of the Mason-Dixon Line were operated by tenants, only between one-fourth and one-third of Kentucky ones were. Moreover, very few black Kentuckians were tenants—only 8 percent of all tenants in the state in 1900 were black—and the chances for racially unfair treatment remained lower. Finally, Kentucky farms remained relatively mortgage-free. In contrast to the images of the debt-ridden agrarian, an 1890 report indicated that 96 percent of the state's farmers were free of debt on their property (72 percent of the nation's farmers were mortgage-free). Twenty years later, at the close of the era of the tobacco wars, 85 percent of Kentucky farmers were without mortgages.

Yet despite all that, the real statistics of importance show the relative poverty of Kentucky farmers, even when they formed the mainstay of the state's economy. Rural Kentuckians did not live on valuable plots—the 1920 average value of state farms was not much beyond one-third of the national mean, and the commonwealth ranked forty-first of forty-eight states in that regard. While the state ranked high compared with the South in the value of farm production in 1900, the South was poor. Overall, Kentucky stood only fifteenth nationally that same year. By 1994, the state ranked twenty-second in the United States in farm marketing receipts.

During years of great change, Kentucky had seen drastic agrarian modifications as well. In fact, the farmers of 1890 little resembled their counterparts a century later. The earlier era featured small, family-operated farms, with mules or horses pulling plows through unfertilized fields, acreages little improved by conservation efforts. While a variety of livestock helped make such places more self-sufficient, already a dependence on one crop was the seed for future problems. Farmers lived a life governed by daylight and the weather.

A century later, much had transpired to change all that. Terms that had once seemed foreign to Kentucky farmers, such as *crop rotation* and *soil conservation,* were accepted without question. The beginning of the state fair in 1902 had helped showcase new agricultural successes; by the 1920s county extension agents operating under the aegis of the University of Kentucky College of Agriculture began to have an effect, as they told farmers about new methods and different options. Hybrid plant strains, chemical herbicides and pesticides, education about the values of fertilizer—all had an influence. No longer did tobacco farmers have to work as hard to control the problems of caterpillars or worms. Other crops benefited as well. By the 1980s some farmers did not plow their fields, using chemicals instead in the "no-till" method.

Production per acre drastically increased. Tobacco poundage went up from 550 pounds per acre in 1874 to 1,100 pounds per acre in 1945, and two decades later the figure had doubled. The average bushels of corn produced expanded from 27 bushels per acre in 1904 to 116 bushels per acre eighty-five years later. Wheat's yield of 4 bushels per acre in 1885 escalated to 54 bushels a century afterward. As a result, the shrinking amount of land devoted to farming produced more and more, with less effort. For those who had struggled in the hot summer sun for meager returns, those changes seemed almost miraculous.

In a sense, farming became more professional and less personal. Other labor had replaced that of children on larger farms; tractors had taken the place of mules; mechanization had displaced hand planting; machines, not

people, milked cows or fed livestock. No longer could successful large farmers plant the same seeds in the same field, year after year, with little knowledge of outside events and forces. Kentucky farmers had to have global vision, for the markets for tobacco, live animals (including horses), and feed grains extended beyond national boundaries. In 1992 the state sold nearly $880 million in agricultural products abroad, representing some 27 percent of state production. Instead of using a stubby pencil to write notes in a worn notebook, farmers now could use a computer tied in to a widespread communications network. They focused on interest rates, investments, and income potential and lived in air-conditioned homes that usually featured all the conveniences of the city. The gap between farm and city had narrowed considerably.

As the end of the twentieth century neared, Kentucky agriculture had a twofold division. On the one hand, about half of those who operated farms did so because farming was their primary occupation. They made their living from "agribusiness" and followed the latest agricultural bulletins, experimented with new hybrids and herbicides, and seemed far removed from the often provincial agrarians of the century's first decades, those who had trusted the weather and had waited. They might still grow many of the same crops as before, for 95 percent of all crop values came from tobacco (37 percent), hay (24), corn (21), and soybeans (13). They might still be affected by broad trends, prospering in the 1970s, suffering in the depression of the 1980s. Yet chance played a much smaller role in their lives than in those of their ancestors.

The other half of those listed as farmers were very different. About 60 percent of the commonwealth's farms had sales of less than ten thousand dollars, and most of the laborers in those fields worked as part-time farmers. For them the agrarian way of life still had importance, but farming was a secondary consideration, providing a supplementary income. The family farm of yesteryear had increasingly disappeared from Kentucky, and the ideal of a nation of small, self-sufficient farms whose yeomen formed the backbone of the country seemed as far away as a distant star. By the 1990s only nine Kentucky counties depended on farming as the keystone of their economies. Yet those who continued to work a small plot, perhaps in the evening or on weekends, showed that the smell of the earth, the view of crops blowing in a breeze, the feel of the land itself, remained an important part of the Kentucky psyche even yet.

Commerce

Even though Kentucky would long honor the agrarian ideal, with each passing decade after the Civil War residents would increasingly praise the goal of a more commercialized and industrialized commonwealth. Slowly, more and more people in Kentucky accepted the idea that future progress was tied to industrial growth. Few questioned exactly how that growth should occur, or at what price, for the United States was developing industrially, and state government and business leaders feared being bypassed. City leaders fought to attract new industry to their locales, and urban boosterism pushed the businessman as the new ideal.

Yet Kentucky had great difficulty attaining the commercial success its leaders desired, as two examples indicate. The state's timber, for instance, provided a vast resource, worth millions of dollars. Small subsistence farmers needed cash to pay taxes and bills, and often their only real source of money was the timber around them. They would cut the trees, take

them down aptly named "snake roads" to log dumps, where a "splash dam" had backed up enough water to float the logs. Tied together in great booms, which might typically be sixteen feet wide and fifty to a hundred feet long, the logs would be released into the waters of the Kentucky, the Licking, the Big Sandy, or a few western Kentucky rivers when a high "tide" caused by rains finally occurred. Over the next several days, loggers would guide their rafts through treacherous waters, in a process that cost some loggers their lives. Finally they would reach a mill, at Beattyville, Irvine, Frankfort, Catlettsburg, Ashland, Clay City, or other places, and sell the logs. In 1890 a sizable raft would yield between $150 and $300; at that time those sums represented one or two years' worth of wages for a laborer. If the loggers could resist the temptation to spend their new cash on the worldly temptations near the mills, they could return home and pay off bills. If not, they at least could come back with new memories of an exciting time.

That system presented many problems, however. Those in poverty needed money and cared little about renewable resources. As a result, whole forests were stripped and never replanted. As early as 1868, the *Bowling Green Democrat* warned that small forests in the area had already been exhausted and others would follow "unless a different system is adopted." In 1887 the governor called on the legislature to reforest denuded land and preserve the remaining timber. No one acted. The head of the Bureau of Agriculture, Labor, and Statistics worried in 1905 that state forestlands were

This post card shows logs moving on the Kentucky River (from Wade Hall, *Greetings from Kentucky* [1994]).

being devastated "without regard for the future." Barren County, he reported, remained "nude of even firewood." His successor in 1909 predicted that the "suicidal" cutting of timber resources would strip the state of all good trees within eighteen years. Not only lack of income but also soil erosion and flooding would result.

The timber boom continued for a time. From 1870 to 1920 flush years brought large sales. In the peak year of 1909, over a billion board feet of lumber was sold. As predicted, however, the timber began to run out, and in 1927 production had fallen to less than 30 percent of the previous high. The glory days had passed, and timber rafts became rare sights in the rivers by the 1920s. The huge Mowbray-Robinson Company in Perry, Knott, and Breathitt Counties depleted fifteen thousand acres of timber, and the area industry that had employed five thousand workers had vanished by 1922. The deforested area and a million dollars were donated to the state university, the sawmills were torn down, and the railroad lines were abandoned. But perhaps the greatest tragedy for Kentucky's economy, other than the exhaustion of the land and the partial devastation of timber as a resource, was the fact that those raw materials would not form the basis for some other home industry, such as furniture building. In a story that would be told and retold in the commonwealth's economic history, many of the benefits of Kentucky's sizable timber industry would go outside the state. When by the 1990s the commonwealth made its way back to become the nation's fourth-largest producer of hardwood lumbers—furnishing 11 percent of American production—still three-fourths of that lumber would be shipped, unprocessed, to other states.

A second example of the problems facing Kentucky's commercial sector affected the area around Cumberland Gap. For years, Kentucky had been an important producer of iron, through furnaces scattered across the state. The Ashland Furnace, started by John Means, for instance, produced over thirty-five tons daily in 1869. But depletion of ore and

timber resources, the middling quality of the local product, and the easier availability of iron to out-of-state buyers through better transportation all hurt the industry. The Boone Furnace in Carter County ceased production in 1871, the Estill Furnace in Estill County stopped blasting in 1874, and the Raccoon Furnace in Greenup County did not operate after 1884. The story was repeated across the commonwealth, as the industry declined from the number three position nationally that it had held in 1830. The dream died hard, though, and in 1886 Alexander A. Arthur looked out at the half dozen houses in a valley near the Gap and saw visions of greatness. As president of the British-owned American Association Limited, he bought huge tracts of untouched coal and iron reserves and started construction of a railroad tunnel under the Gap, to this new place called Middlesborough.

By 1889 the area was being transformed into what was expected to be a major steel manufacturing center in the United States, much on the order of Birmingham, Alabama. In a violent and raucous boomtown atmosphere, Englishmen in silk hats, monocles, morning coats, and spats mixed with upper-class easterners and mountaineers in the Marvelous City. Steel mills were established, coal mines dug, railroads completed, and businesses built. On a wide main street designed for future growth, ten blocks of stores sprang up; town lots sold at unheard-of prices of more than four hundred dollars per square foot. Impressive stone and brick Victorian homes were constructed on spacious lawns. In this "New Eldorado," a massive hotel served by an electric railroad became the center of social life, while the state's first golf course attracted attention. It was a heady time for investors.

In 1890, though, a fire destroyed the core of the city. That same year a bank failure in England cost foreign investors heavily and left Arthur without the capital necessary to go forward. In the United States, a national business depression struck. Then it was discovered that the iron deposits so central to growth were of a mediocre quality. The boom ended with a thud, and land values fell nearly to nothing. The four banks all failed, and half the population left. Those who remained included people who were once wealthy but now were penniless or even insane as a result of their losses.

Middlesborough's experience in many ways represented the pattern of future development in the state. The capital for growth had come from outside the commonwealth, and that circumstance would characterize Kentucky's economy after 1880. Saying that the state became part of a colonial economy, with control located outside of the commonwealth, may be an overstatement, but the analogy is not too inaccurate. Even though Kentucky-owned businesses continued and prospered, as time wore on the finances directing the state's growth, as well as the stockholders and boards of directors of the major business institutions operating in the commonwealth, increasingly came from outside the state. The wealth went elsewhere, and Kentuckians lost more control of their economic destiny.

What was attempted at Middlesborough took place on a smaller scale at other locales in eastern Kentucky, as new coal communities changed the face of the land. Some towns rose and fell with the fortunes of the minerals; others expanded and grew on their own. Similarly, towns all across the commonwealth might spring up and prosper for a time, because of their location along a new railroad line or because of a sudden oil or timber boom in the area. Many of those places, some of which were sizable communities, fell back into quiet obscurity as the boom ended.

More commonly, urban areas in Kentucky grew or declined in commercial activity at a slower pace. Most smaller cities might have an industry or two, but they generally gave the impression recorded by an 1881 traveler: "There are no manufactories in these towns; they make one think of villages in rural England." Most of the growth took place in the larger urban areas. Towns expanding in the late nineteenth century and the early twentieth

generally were located in the eastern or western regions of the state. In the east, Ashland's strength in timber, petroleum refining, and iron rolling mills brought a doubling of population to twenty-nine thousand during 1920-30. In the west, Owensboro, the site of a major wagon company, tobacco factories, and, after 1900, a light bulb manufacturing plant, almost quadrupled in population between 1880 and 1920, reaching nearly twenty-three thousand. At the same time Paducah, then slightly larger than Owensboro, almost tripled in size. Cities in the central and northern parts of the commonwealth grew as well, but at a slower pace. Once at the forefront of commercial activity in what was the New West of the early nineteenth century, Lexington had languished since then, and an 1886 visitor accurately described it as "a pretty village," living on "frequent memories of fugitive greatness," a place whose dreams of glory had passed. By 1900 it had fallen to fourth in population among the state's cities, behind the growing Covington and the static Newport, which both benefited from the expansion of adjacent Cincinnati. Lexington's economic fortunes would change within half a century, but some communities could never adjust from being a supplier to a surrounding agrarian world to being an industrial place. The residents of some towns may not have wanted such a change.

In truth, Kentucky had only one truly industrial and commercial city. After all, in 1890 only six cities in the commonwealth had more than ten thousand inhabitants, and commerce in those places concerned relatively small establishments. For most of the nineteenth and much of the twentieth century the only sizable manufacturing center in the state was Louisville.

The Falls City and Urbanization
Virtually untouched by the Civil War, Louisville, in fact, benefited from it economically. The Falls City emerged at war's end as a center of trade for the still-devastated South. Traveling salesmen, called drummers, spread the gospel

of trade to small stores and homes across the region, all the time preaching the virtues of Louisville's goods. Those economic missionaries capitalized on Kentucky's southernness and usually introduced themselves by a military title, obviously won in the Rebel cause. They told stories, entertained the locals—and made sales. In 1874, a year in which the Falls City sold 287,000 bales of southern cotton, one paper in Arkansas said that people there knew "no market but Louisville."

Louisville-based J.P. Morton and Company had become "publishers to the Lost Cause," and the *Louisville Courier-Journal* had for a time the largest circulation of any southern newspaper. Capitalizing on these connections, the drummers rode the L&N Railroad, took orders, and sent them back to the Falls City to be filled. There J. Bacon and Son's mail-order department or the W.B. Belknap Hardware and Manufacturing Company, or dry goods stores such as Bamberger and Bloom, the largest in the region, or the New York Store (later Stewart's Dry Goods) did the rest. Louisville had the largest plow factory in the world, B.F. Avery's, and near the end of the nineteenth century the city was the nation's chief producer of cast-iron pipe, the largest banking capital in the South, the chief leaf tobacco market in the world, the second-largest tobacco manufacturing center in the United States, and the home of the largest textile industry west of the Appalachians. The city at one time featured the largest leather market in the United States and served as one of the major paint and varnish centers, as well as a significant liquor headquarters, with thirty-five distilleries on the eve of World War I. It continued to be an important pork-processing center, though economic rivals Cincinnati and St. Louis made inroads there, as in other areas. Still, Louisville's prosperity brought its exuberant spokesman, editor Henry Watterson, to cry out that "a union of pork, tobacco, and whiskey will make us all wealthy, healthy, and frisky."

Notwithstanding the question of the Louisvillian's frolicsome and robust nature, the people and the city certainly prospered. Within the thirty-year period 1870-1900, population doubled to more than two hundred thousand, making Louisville the nation's eighteenth largest city. Visitors to the urban metropolis saw a place that had the look and feel of a big and vibrant city. One observer in 1888 wrote that the "friendly" city "has the unmistakable air of confidence and buoyant prosperity." Louisville featured theaters, such as Macauley's; a growing system of parks, designed in part by Frederick Law Olmsted; racing at Churchill Downs; and 175 miles of street railways by the first decade of the twentieth century. The second largest city in the South offered telephones, electric lights, daily ice delivery, and much more, plus a strong literary tradition. In places such as St. James Court and nearby Central Park, a new elite and old families mixed. Later, summer homes grew up away from the core of the city, and then permanent residences connected by street railways broke up the earlier unity to a degree, but the orientation remained toward downtown. Each generation, however, faced the problems of slums, violence, and racism. For better or worse, Louisville was the place where Kentucky first confronted the industrialization of the new United States.

Louisville's growth continued at a less spectacular but still steady rate through the first decades of the twentieth century, and the city ranked twenty-second nationally in the value of manufactured products in 1920. At the end of the twenties, manufactories in or near Louisville provided over half of the value added by state industries. But by the late 1930s one author included the city in a group of five he studied in their "old age." Calling it "a museum piece," untouched by waves of immigrants or by new economic patterns, he concluded that the Falls City was approaching "an ossified dotage." At almost the same time as he wrote, the huge Ohio River flood of 1937 devastated the town. Yet those two events may have helped transform Louisville's psyche, as leaders and the populace worked to rebuild from both a natural and a public relations disaster. Stimulated by

World War II, and a new leadership that included Wilson W. Wyatt, Louisville began a rebirth, both culturally and economically. The 1950s became a Louisville decade in Kentucky: General Electric built Appliance Park, the largest such complex in the nation, and the state constructed the Fair and Exposition Center, the largest indoor facility at that time. The city's peaceful racial integration of schools won national praise, while activity in the arts brought further recognition.

Yet Louisville's dynamic spirit of the 1950s did not continue at the same level. That situation was not surprising, for Kentucky cities generally have experienced periods in which businesses, or leaders, or a combination of other forces have for a time made them vigorous and progressive places, attracting energetic men and women. Lexington had experienced such vitality during the state's first decade of statehood but had relinquished its position later. In the 1970s and afterward it would again be revitalized. Northern Kentucky cities had been strong in the late nineteenth century, then had slowed in growth. Paducah, Owensboro, Hopkinsville, and other western Kentucky cities had shown similar trends at different times. Louisville in the 1960s and beyond continued to develop, but at a different and more mixed pace. Older, individually and locally owned firms such as B.F. Avery, Ballard, and W.F. Axton consolidated with larger, national ones, and at the same time a city whose fortunes had been tied to the assembly line began to lose jobs. Race-oriented violence in 1968 and 1975 hurt Louisville's image; labor strikes slowed production; and the growth of suburbs, each constituting its own little municipality, fragmented efforts toward unity and affected downtown trade. Yet the city remained the financial and economic core of Kentucky, and in 1994, of the state's ten largest public companies, measured by revenue, six were in Louisville.

Fragile Finances

One of the mainstays of Louisville's—and Kentucky's—economy has been the liquor industry. Aided by wartime imbibing and more accessible postwar transportation, whiskey production nearly tripled in the state between 1871 and 1880, and by 1882 thirsty Americans had doubled the 1880 figure again, to more than thirty million gallons. Within the commonwealth, drinking proliferated; by 1886 there was one saloon for every fifty-five adult males in Owensboro, for example. Five years later Kentucky's 172 distilleries had the largest daily mashing capacity in the nation and produced 34 percent of the distilled spirits manufactured in the United States. Little uniformity in production existed, however, until federal acts in 1897 and 1936 defined standards to be followed.

At the same time, the industry faced huge challenges. A national business depression in 1893 drastically curtailed production, while the growing temperance movement added to liquor's problems. National Prohibition in the 1920s and beyond seriously injured the state's manufacturing standing, particularly in relation to southern states not so tied to the spirits industry. Louisville alone lost an estimated eight thousand positions when its distilleries closed, and the state lost 5 percent of its jobs. Towns dependent on nearby distilleries almost vanished: Tyrone in Anderson County declined from a place with one of the largest plants in the world and nearly a thousand inhabitants to an unincorporated village. The empty buildings were left to vandals and the weather.

Ironically, out of another depression came the impetus to repeal Prohibition and provide more employment. In the 1930s the Kentucky distilleries once more filled the air with the aroma of sour mash. Symbolic of the new growth was the 1937 opening of Seagram's Distillery in Jefferson County, billed as the world's largest at the time. By 1943 the state furnished 68 percent of U.S. liquor production. Despite changing American patterns of consumption over the years and a greater dependence on foreign markets for sales, the industry continued strong. At the beginning of the 1990s, Kentucky produced an estimated 70 percent of the nation's distilled spirits and nearly 90 percent of its bourbon. Companies such as Brown-Forman spread the state's name worldwide.

The shifting fortunes of the liquor industry symbolized a trend that affected many mainstays of the state's economy. Three bedrock industries—liquor, tobacco, and thoroughbreds—all at one time or another have been restricted. Prohibition stopped legal liquor production, the federal controls on tobacco increased from the 1960s on, and the racing industry almost ended in the 1920s and continued to face challenges into the 1990s. In addition, a once-strong lumber industry went into decline before later rebounding; certain major factories, such as those that made carriages, disappeared; and the commonwealth's coal industry experienced a periodic rise and fall. The combination of such trends resulted in an uncertain economic future for the state by the late twentieth century. Traditional sources of growth might continue to provide economic possibilities, but change seemed a more likely and promising option. To Kentucky's credit, the state economy did move into other areas, but often slowly and tardily.

The Late Twentieth-Century Economy

By the latter decades of the twentieth century, some observers argued that Kentucky had always been in a second-class status on economic matters and lagged behind both the nation and the region. Yet the picture they painted did not exactly reflect the reality of the not-so-distant past. Even though post–Civil War Kentucky never stood at the forefront of the nation's industrial states, neither did it always trail. In 1870, for instance, the commonwealth's manufacturing worth placed it first in the South and sixteenth in the United States; thirty years later it stood in almost the same position. Generally, then, Kentucky entered the twentieth century in a role as a regional leader.

Between 1900 and 1930, however, the state fell further and further behind. During the first decade of the new century, which saw violence in the Black Patch, feuds, and gubernatorial assassination, only two southern states grew slower than Kentucky. Other southern states continued to grow at a faster rate than Kentucky during the World War I years; during that time the commonwealth suffered an absolute drop in manufacturing. The decline of the lumber and liquor industries by the 1920s only added to the industrial decline, and one study showed that by 1930 the southern manufacturing base had expanded three times more rapidly than had Kentucky's. Only Ohio River cities had experienced much prosperity, and between 1920 and 1930 interior counties had actually suffered a decrease in the number of wage earners. The national depression of the 1930s kept Kentucky from falling further behind. However, the increased prosperity growing out of World War II did not benefit the commonwealth as much as it did most of the South. By the mid–twentieth century Kentucky's economic future had dimmed considerably compared with the bright promise of 1900.

Slowly, the state's economy diversified and began to reflect overall national patterns to a greater degree. Kentucky made a largely successful shift from agricultural employment to other sectors. By the 1960s General Electric in Louisville, International Business Machines in Lexington, and Armco Steel in Ashland represented the most visible aspects of the change. In 1980 the state's largest employers were in the fields of electronics, machinery, textiles, food, metal industries, and chemicals, and by the end of the decade Kentucky had about the same percentages of people employed in most work categories as did the rest of the United States. Only in the financial and service areas did the state lag.

Out of these changes came a state economy that led the nation in few new fields, but one still very different from that of earlier years. Kentucky continued to play a significant role in the liquor and tobacco industries, but it also had become an important automotive center. Kentucky's own attempts at building horseless carriages, such as the Ames, the Dixie Flyer, the Lexington, and the Bowman, had failed. But a Ford plant started assembling Model T's in Louisville in 1913, and Ford later expanded, making heavy and light trucks and utility vehicles in the state. By 1987 Ford plants in Kentucky had produced more than 8.5 million vehicles. In 1980 a General Motors plant in Bowling Green became the only factory building Corvette sports cars, and Toyota Motor Company opened its Georgetown factory in the late 1980s and started turning out Camrys, which won national awards for quality. Such activity made Kentucky the fourth-leading producer of motor vehicles nationally in 1993.

Similarly, the commonwealth advanced as a health care center, particularly with the growth of a new company that started as a simple nursing home, born out of the entrepreneurship of David A. Jones and Wendell Cherry. The enterprise that became the multifaceted Humana Corporation would be listed in 1989 among the most valuable companies in the United States and would have 1991 revenues of almost six billion dollars.

In the food products line, young businessman John Y. Brown Jr. capitalized on Colonel Harland D. Sanders's product, purchased Kentucky Fried Chicken in 1960, and made the company's name an international byword. Other chains, such as Jerrico (later Long John Silver's), were also born in the Kentucky economy. The overseas connections of such companies only symbolized Kentucky's growing export trade, and the state ranked in the middle of the states in that regard by the 1990s. In 1994, for example, Kentucky sold items worth some $5.3 billion outside the United States. Ex-

port products chiefly comprised transportation equipment, machinery, food, coal, and livestock, sold to Canada, Japan, France, Mexico, and Germany.

Yet those positive economic indicators could not obscure a trend that had perhaps increased in importance as the century progressed: much of the state's wealth still went to companies with headquarters outside its borders. In the banking industry, for example, several sizable and independent state banks in the 1980s and 1990s became part of larger national financial institutions that had their corporate centers in Ohio, Pennsylvania, North Carolina, or elsewhere. Privately held newspapers, with the *Louisville Courier-Journal* being only the best-known example, followed the same trend, as did other businesses. In a 1995 ranking of the one thousand most valuable companies in the United States, only seven were in Kentucky, and none of these were ranked in the top quarter. Kentucky remained primarily

Table 19.1
Gross State Production, 1990

Industry	Amount (millions of dollars)	% of total
Manufacturing	$16,860	25.0
Services	9,594	14.2
Finance and real estate	8,970	13.3
Retail trade	6,482	9.6
Transportation and communication	6,153	9.1
State and local government	5,164	7.7
Wholesale trade	3,493	5.2
Mining	2,714	4.0
Construction	2,586	3.8
Federal government	2,152	3.2
Farms	1,976	2.9
Federal military	1,049	1.6
Forestry and fisheries	298	0.4
Total	$67,491	100.0

Note: The Deskbook gives the total amount as $67,492.

Source: 1994 Kentucky Deskbook of Economic Statistics (1994)

what one scholar has called a peripheral region, where products are processed locally but where dollars flow out of communities rather than into them. Extractive rather than constructive actions more often result. That situation makes even more praiseworthy those Kentucky-based people and companies—such as William T. Young, the Bingham family, Ashland Oil, Humana, and Brown-Forman—who have returned some of their funds to better the quality of life of Kentucky.

King Coal and the Mineral World

As young mountaineer John C.C. Mayo rode across the eastern Kentucky mountains in the late nineteenth century, he represented, in one sense at least, the future of Kentucky's coal industry. At the time, most coal was produced in small community mines, for local use. As one observer noted on her trip to Appalachia, "We saw coal-mines all along the road, just sticking out of the mountains." Some thirteen hundred of those shaky affairs dotted the region. Only slowly had Kentucky sold coal for shipment outside its borders: in 1870 the state produced just 150,000 tons of coal, but a decade later it had passed the million-ton mark. As late as 1900 some 60 percent of the coal dug in the commonwealth was still used in Kentucky. Early mines generally remained in local hands, and talented immigrants who had had experience with mines overseas were usually involved. The largest operation in Kentucky in 1900, for example, had as its superintendent a man born and educated in Germany, who brought his mining engineering degree to the United States after the Civil War and settled in Kentucky by 1886. The center of coal produced for sale was western Kentucky. In 1884, for instance, 57 percent of all coal mined in the commonwealth came from the Western Coalfield, and this area would continue to lead until 1912. Mayo sought to change all that. From the end of the Civil War on, people knew about the vast coal reserves in eastern Kentucky, but poor transportation, feud violence, and other factors had slowed development of

those resources. Others had already taken advantage of the so-called broad form deed, which gave the purchaser rights to the minerals on the land in exchange for a set fee, but Mayo used this instrument extensively to acquire mining rights to thousands of acres—usually at a dollar per acre. Appalachian essayist Harry M. Caudill concluded that "no man has had so profound an impact on the economic life of Kentucky."

Mayo symbolized the revolution taking place in eastern Kentucky, one that changed the face of an agrarian region. As railroads inched their way into formerly isolated areas, a transformation occurred, sometimes virtually overnight. In Letcher County, a valley containing a lone cabin became in a few days the booming coal town of Jenkins. That coal camp town featured more than a thousand buildings, including a school, a library, a hospital, an electric plant, and churches. Tennis courts, playgrounds, motion-picture theaters, and several shops added to its appeal. Nearby in Harlan County, the town of Lynch brought forth similar promise: it had ten miles of paved streets for some sixty-five hundred people by 1920. By 1924 nearly two-thirds of the state's miners lived in company housing. The urban world thus came to parts of rural Kentucky with little time for adjustments or evaluation.

To people eking out a subsistence on a farm without electricity, far distant from stores and communities, the new life offered by the coal boom held great appeal. Those who came to the coal camps in the first generation mostly did so eagerly, for they gambled that mining could give them a better life, new opportunities, and a more promising future. As one recalled: "I didn't have any choice. I had a family. They had to eat. There wasn't anything else to do. . . . You couldn't make a living on the farm." And so they came from within the state, as well as from across the region and overseas. Immigrants and blacks moved to the mining areas and added an ethnic mix to a population that had previously been almost totally Anglo-Saxon. Still, as the boom times

Miners' houses and a coal tipple near Hazard, 1928 (courtesy of the Kentucky Historical Society)

passed, only remnants of those new groups would remain. In the good times, though, everyone enjoyed the higher wages, the entertainment options, the goods to be purchased, the schools, the medical care, the higher hopes. For the new miners and their families, a long-established way of life had ended, for they now lived in different homes, surrounded by different people speaking strange languages. They were working different jobs and adjusting to different family structures.

Prosperity often came at a high price, however. The vaunted Appalachian independence, self-reliance, and self-sufficiency now had to be submerged to officials who ran company towns like little kingdoms. In the worst cases,

the companies controlled everything, with no debate. Miners were expected to vote as the company desired; they paid high prices at monopolist company-owned stores; they were treated by doctors paid by the company; they lived where they were told to live, in areas segregated by race or ethnic origin; they often suffered in silence if abuses arose. In short, their lives became socially, physically, and psychologically controlled by a corporate fiefdom.

Some coal areas, on the other hand, continued to be managed well. These places were still dominated by the companies, but at least more benevolence was involved. Many families experienced prosperity for the first time; many children of miners now had the benefit of education and went on to success in other occupations. Still, when hard times hit the coalfields and when profits declined, even the best of the company towns suffered. The physical infrastructure could not be kept up, and unpainted houses gathered the ever-present coal dust hanging in the air and turned gray. Sanitation declined, as creeks filled with litter and garbage remained uncollected. At those moments, the gulf separating the operators living on the hill from the miners in the valley suddenly seemed much broader. Over time, the miners and their families would not suffer in silence. Protests and strikes would be an ever-present part of the reign of King Coal.

Those who entered the mines to dig coal risked much every day. Changes would take place over the years, as the oil lamp on the hat became a carbide one, as the tracks of the car that took workers into the mines turned from wood to steel, as the power that moved those cars evolved from mule to motor, as the tools for digging the mineral converted from hand tools to cutting machines. But certain things varied little. The Office of State Inspector of Mines was created in 1884, but it more

---

Table 19.2
Kentucky Mine Deaths, 1890-1980

Period	Deaths
1890-99	95
1900-9	274
1910-19	754
1920-29	1,614
1930-39	1,203
1940-49	1,328
1950-59	689
1960-69	451
1970-79	379
1979-80	242

Source: Claude E. Pickard, "The Western Kentucky Coal Fields" (Ph.D. diss., University of Nebraska, 1969), 97; Kentucky Department of Mines and Minerals, *Mines and Minerals Report* (1991)

often chronicled the problems rather than solving them. In the half century after that date, seventy-three dust and gas explosions occurred in the state's mines, collapsing roofs remained a danger, and ventilation problems persisted. One miner remembered that he and others in the coal mining communities "not only knew the pain of broken bones, but also the pain of broken hearts." As more and more mines opened, and as larger numbers of workers ventured underground, deaths rose (see table 19.2). A 1903 report found most mines in a "deplorably bad condition," and it meant little to the forty-two people who died in Kentucky mines in 1912 that the number of deaths compared with the number employed in Kentucky was lower than the U.S. average. There is little irony in historical markers in Harlan County, which show that far more people have died in the mines there than in military actions. Going into the mines was sometimes like going to war.

But go the miners did, both with courage and fatalism, and their work resulted in the production of massive amounts of coal from both the western and eastern Kentucky fields. A million tons was produced in 1879, and that figure increased to more than 5 million two decades later. Between 1900 and 1907 production doubled, then nearly doubled again by 1914, and almost tripled between 1914 and 1929. By 1920 Pike County alone produced almost as much coal as the whole state had in 1900. High demand through World War I was followed by a slump in the early 1920s, and again during part of the 1930s. Then the industry experienced adequate demand in the 1940s, a bad market in the 1950s, and a large jump in prices per ton following the 1973 oil embargo. Kentucky coal prices, adjusted for inflation, increased 100 percent between 1973 and 1978—above the national average—and new fortunes were made before the 1978 peak year. The dominant pattern of coal production in Kentucky, however, continues to be one of boom and bust.

Three other trends have characterized the coal industry since 1950: the mechaniza-

Two miners work in an underground coal mine, 1920s (courtesy of the Kentucky Historical Society).

tion of the mines and overall loss of jobs, the increase in strip mining, and the changing pattern of consumption. Between 1885 and 1929, for example, the coal workforce increased from forty-five hundred to more than fifty thousand, then peaked in 1940 at sixty-three thousand. Mechanization began to replace men in the mines, and that fact, coupled with the depressed 1950s market, drastically reduced the numbers of miners to twenty-seven thousand by 1972, on the eve of the oil embargo. After a temporary rise as production increased, employment from 1978 and 1987 declined another 37 percent. Between 1990 and 1993 more than a thousand mines closed, leaving 752 in operation. Jobs grew scarcer.

During the three decades after 1940, more and more Kentucky coal was mined above ground. Although some surface mining occurred as early as 1919, by 1940 only 2 percent of the state's "black gold" was mined by that method. By 1960 a third of the state's coal came from the so-called strip mining method, and in 1974 over half did. Stronger standards governing reclamation of the land were adopted after 1966, and the number of surface mines slowly declined in relation to underground mines. By 1993, 60 percent of all Kentucky coal once again came from deep mines. Although a safer method, strip mining had taken its own toll on Kentucky, and various writers compared the state's coalfields to battlegrounds. Once-scenic lands, unreclaimed from the ravages of the strippers, soon featured deep gashes on the hills and soil erosion in the valleys. Water and land pollution resulted. While bringing jobs, salaries, and some economic wealth to Kentucky, King Coal also brought scars to the countryside.

By the 1990s virtually all the increase in local consumption of coal came from the use of utilities, for trains had switched to diesel oil and few homes still used coal for heat. As a result, coal's future seemed as dark as the mineral itself. But the industry continued to be significant. The state had gone from being ranked ninth in coal production in 1910 to third by 1929, and by 1978 it stood first in production of bituminous coal. Over 17 percent of U.S. coal came from Kentucky in the 1980s. Although coal is a nonrenewable resource, large reserves still remained for the 1990s and be-

yond. With all its benefits and all its debits, King Coal still ruled, although it rested on a shaky throne.

Other extractive industries in Kentucky took a secondary place to coal. In 1865 the legislature granted charters to some 140 oil or oil and mining companies, and the first of many postwar oil booms was on. In county after county at various times during the following century, a boom would bring "wildcatters" to a town, and some profits would be followed by a return to normalcy. Overall state production fluctuated greatly, with 63,000 barrels in 1900 being followed by 1.2 million six years later and 9.2 million in 1919. The peak was reached in 1959, at 27.3 million barrels, but another decline followed. At no time did the commonwealth become a major oil producer, although one petroleum company, Ashland Oil, did attain significant status.

Beginning as a refining operation in 1924, what became Ashland Oil grew under the leadership of Paul G. Blazer (1890-1966) and others to become one of the fifty largest American industrial companies by revenue in 1994. Emphasizing refining and marketing rather than production, and developing major inland waterway networks, the company acquired other properties, diversified, and developed to become the largest Kentucky-based corporation, with thirty-one thousand employees by 1994. The involvement of Ashland Oil in education, through corporate support, stressed the contrast often shown between Kentucky companies and those with headquarters elsewhere. The colonial-style economy affected the state in many ways.

Fluorspar from Kentucky made up over half of the U.S. production of that mineral in the 1920s, and on the eve of World War II the state still ranked first in the production of fluorspar. A half century later, however, foreign imports and a declining market had ended production of the mineral in the commonwealth. By then Ken-

Table 19.3
Kentucky Coal Production, 1870-1990

Year	Amount mined (thousands of tons)
1870	150
1879	1,000
1892	3,025
1900	5,329
1907	10,753
1914	20,383
1920	38,892
1929	60,705
1947	88,695
1954	58,600
1974	136,800
1987	165,192
1990	173,322

Note: When figures from different sources disagree for certain years, what seems to be the most official source is cited.

Sources: Willard Rouse Jillson, "A History of the Coal Industry in Kentucky," *Register of the Kentucky Historical Society* 20 (1922): 21-45; Commonwealth of Kentucky, *Report of the Inspector of Mines,* later the *Report of the Department of Mines and Minerals;* data from the U.S. Energy Information Administration

tucky did rank second in the production of ball clay (used in ceramics) and fourth in lime. Still, by 1991, 87 percent of the value of all mineral products in Kentucky came from coal. Crushed stone, natural gas, and all the rest never threatened to topple the throne of King Coal.

Rivers, Rails, and Roads

Transportation was a key element of Kentucky's commercial and agricultural development. At the end of the Civil War, the state's rail system was damaged in some places and consisted of relatively few miles of track anyway. A boom would soon bring town after town seeking out iron rails for itself, but rail expansion would take time. With the exception of a few roads of worth, the commonwealth's system for horses and carriages was either poor or virtually nonexistent. As had been the case for nearly half a century, then, the state's most extensive transportation network in 1865 remained its rivers.

With well over a thousand miles of commercially navigable waterways, Kentucky offered numerous possibilities for river travel. People on the rivers knew the horror of accidents like one in 1868, when the *America* and the *United States* collided and sank, with significant loss of life, near Warsaw. They also knew pride: in 1870, for example, the two captains in the famous steamboat race between the *Natchez* and the *Robert E. Lee* were both Kentuckians. Most important, however, was the economic benefit of river travel. Kentuckians could transport their goods to market easier and quicker, whether they were shipping lumber on the Big Sandy, crops from the Upper Cumberland to Nashville, or various items on the Ohio. People located on or near a river had reasonably easy access to other places along the rivers, for visiting, travel, or amusement. Rivers also provided traveling entertainment at times, in the form of showboats, with their plays, music, comedy, and occasional bawdiness. Although scattered remnants would long remain, the showboats reached their peak around the turn

of the century. Several generations of Kentuckians from Ashland to Paducah, however, had thrilled to the cry "Showboat's coming!"

River travel declined as other modes of transportation improved. By the 1870s and afterward, congressional and state appropriations resulted in more locks and dams on key rivers, improving access while "canalizing" the waters. But river forces were fighting a rearguard action in a technological battle they had already lost. By the 1930s most secondary rivers had lost their showboats and their riverboats. Barges on the Ohio and a few other waterways continued to provide an important service for the rest of the century, but the era of the rivers as the vital arteries in Kentucky's transportation network had long ended.

The new transportation god that Kentuckians worshiped came cloaked in steam and smoke. As it made its way into town, some saw it as a devil, while most proclaimed it as a savior to their communities. The advantages the railroads brought were many and obvious. A Glasgow paper in 1869 noted that the train would allow people to travel a hundred miles in four hours, rather than in days, as before. Markets would thus be brought closer, so fewer goods would spoil, and prices of goods available in the town would decline, since transportation costs would be less. People could visit friends and relatives easier; they could go to large towns, such as Louisville, and be back the same day; they could see a whole new world of possibilities opening before them, as they would have a mobility never before thought possible. Such advantages, and the perceived disadvantages of not being on the rail lines, encouraged towns across Kentucky to donate land or rights of way or to vote for taxes to pay off bonds whose funds would go to attract railroad companies. The Glasgow paper, in pleading for voters to approve such a tax in 1869, noted, "We heard a sensible gentleman living in the country remark a few days ago that the difference between the present price of eggs and butter in the market and the price when we get the Railroad would more than pay the tax which it is proposed to vote on."

Counties that refused to provide adequate support for many human services eagerly went into debt for the railroads. In many cases, the decision proved a wise one, for some places not on the railroads withered away. But often the railroad companies had already made their choices, and the money that towns offered only made the financial deal better for the lines. Unfortunately, some places lost entirely, as residents voted for bonds and handed the funds to a new company, only to see it go into bankruptcy while they still had to pay off the bonds. In others, railroad mania controlled citizens' better judgment, and they made financial commitments beyond their capacity. By 1878 local governments began to experience debt problems, and nine counties and one city defaulted at least once on payments. Green County went without a sheriff from 1876 to 1920 because no one would accept the office, the duties of which included collecting tax payments to pay off a failed railroad bond.

___

Table 19.4
Railroad Mileage in Kentucky, 1870-1994

Year	Mileage
1870	1,017
1880	1,530
1886	2,098
1890	3,000
1900	3,060
1929	4,062
1984	3,356
1994	2,929

Source: Kentucky Railroad Commission, *Eleventh Report of the Railroad Commission* (1891), 6; J.J. Hornback, "Economic Development in Kentucky since 1860" (Ph.D. diss., University of Michigan, 1932), 145; Kentucky Department of Economic Development, *Kentucky's Locational Advantages for the Auto Parts Industry* (1984); *Worldmark Encyclopedia of the States* (1996)

Other disadvantages rode into Kentucky life with the railroads. As the first major businesses in the state, the rail companies raised issues that required new answers. Kentucky railroad mileage almost tripled between 1870 and 1890, and the L&N, headquartered in the state but with tracks all over the region, became the chief corporate citizen of the commonwealth. As various parts of the rail system came under attack, particularly from farm groups, the railroads reacted by using their power to influence politics generally and political decisions affecting transportation specifically.

In 1884 Milton Hannibal Smith became chief executive officer of the L&N, an office he would hold for more than thirty years. By the time he took over, people such as German immigrant Albert Fink, who had engineered what was at the time the world's largest truss bridge, over the Ohio River at Louisville, had made the line strong. But a weak Railroad Commission had been created by the legislature in 1880, and Smith feared the future. Attempts at influencing politics caused more resentment toward lines that already charged high or inconsistent rates in some areas. The issues coalesced in the Goebel race, and following the governor's assassination, the Railroad Commission in 1900 was given the power to fix rates. Court cases weakened the commission's actions for some fifteen years, however, and during that time Kentucky exercised less state control over the railroads than any other southern state. By 1930 the commonwealth's attorney general argued that Kentucky's economic growth had been limited by discriminatory rates by railroads, which "have taken the advantage of us." It cost more, for instance, to ship items from Louisville to Bowling Green, a distance of 114 miles, than to ship the same materials to St. Louis, some 280 miles away. Steel could be sent 158 miles from Ashland to Danville at the same cost required to ship it 450 miles north. The attorney general argued that agricultural and industrial rates were much lower north of the Ohio River and that Kentuckians had higher costs as a result. Others noted that in 1909 the major railroads in the state, the L&N and the Chesapeake and Ohio (C&O), had twenty-two directors, and of those only two were from Kentucky. Outside control once again became an issue.

Railroad excesses, however, often blinded critics to the benefits the railroad had brought to the state. As a Lewisburg observer recalled, "We had trains, of course, which was the life's blood of all the small towns in Kentucky." Although early train riding was not always comfortable, since cinders and soot could blow back through open windows and closed ones left cars hot and stuffy, train travel improved over the years. Diesel began to replace coal as a fuel in 1939, and other improvements followed. At least through the 1940s, rail travel provided the core of the state's transportation system. But that core steadily eroded, as symbolized by the end of passenger service in the state. Most of that service was curtailed in the 1960s, but nearly all of it was gone by 1971. Mergers brought new names to Kentucky lines, and by the 1980s, nearly 90 percent of the state's railroads came under the control of three lines—the Chessie System (which represented the C&O), the Seaboard System (which included the L&N), and Illinois Central. In 1986 the first two merged and formed CSX, a holding company with headquarters in Virginia. The Norfolk Southern's lines also passed through Kentucky. Railroads in the state by the 1990s chiefly handled freight and coal, and the golden age of railroading had become only a misty memory.

At the same time that railroads became important across Kentucky, the state's cities began to replace mule-driven street railways and trolley cars with electric ones. By 1890 places such as Louisville and Lexington offered electric streetcars, and by the first decade of the twentieth century smaller communities, such as Somerset, offered commuters that luxury. Larger cars with service to outlying areas

soon followed, and interurbans featured hourly runs at relatively high speeds. Such activity encouraged the growth of suburbs and of commuting, but a new form of transportation ended these services. The last interurban ran to Henderson in 1928, and the last to Louisville in 1935. The last streetcar made its way to the shops in Lexington in 1938, and the last in Louisville a decade later. A newer form of transportation had made them unprofitable and unused. The automobile age had arrived.

Many factors slowed the arrival and acceptance of automobiles in Kentucky. The expense of the early vehicles meant that fewer citizens in a poor state could afford them, but more important was the condition of roads in the commonwealth. Other than the toll roads, which had been outlawed or purchased after the Tollgate Wars in the 1890s, Kentucky had few serviceable roads as the twentieth century opened. One traveler in the eastern mountains found "not a single well-made wagon road." Future president Franklin D. Roosevelt echoed those remarks in 1908, when he wrote his wife about the "horrible" roads leading to Harlan. He went over "a so-called wagon road— positively the worst road I have ever seen or imagined and one which was not very easy to traverse on horseback." Across Kentucky, dusty roads in summer became quagmires of mud in the rain and frozen ponds in winter. In bad weather many people simply did not even try to travel. Nor did the system of maintenance in most locales help. Kentucky still used a legal system of forced labor, with origins back in England, whereby most males of a certain age had either to work on roads or to pay a fee to avoid doing so. Poor results usually followed.

In 1914 almost one of every six Kentucky counties was not served by a railroad. People in those areas received few of the benefits of modern transportation. Only poor roads were available for buggies, runabouts, carriages, and wagons, so many Kentuckians remained isolated. As late as 1928 Burkesville, the seat of Cumberland County, was connected to the "outside" world only by water; a year later a report remarked on the "pathetic" roads in other counties.

As a result, automobiles became commonplace at far different times in different places in the commonwealth. Central Kentucky towns saw the first cars in 1900, and towns like Somerset, London, and Bowling Green had their first automobiles before 1910. In 1928, however, it took one man five days to drive his new Model T from Irvine to Booneville—a distance of some forty miles—because of poor roads, and many mountain counties had few cars before 1930.

In most parts of rural Kentucky, though, the automobile age came earlier. The number of cars rose from nearly 20,000 in 1915 to more than 127,000 six years later. Kentuckians had 272,000 passenger vehicles in 1928 and more than 1 million three decades later. Bus lines provided public transit for even more people. The new transportation not only provided more freedom and greater recreational opportunities, but it also promoted consolidated schools, the growth of suburbs, job mobility, and new factory locations. Vacation patterns changed for families, as did courtship rituals. No longer would male-female contacts be chiefly limited to parlors or porches in a home, for the automobile gave mobility to the young as well—with the attendant worries by parents about such liberation.

Such advantages brought increased demands on state government to take a role in promoting better highways. Candidates sought to outdo each other in support of highways, so much that Governor A.O. Stanley noted in 1915: "To say that you are in favor of good roads is like saying you are in favor of good health or good morals." In 1912 a fledgling Highway Commission was organized, and two years later a system was planned to connect county seats. In 1916 and 1921 federal acts provided support; using gasoline taxes and licensing fees, the commission began to spend large amounts of money. Later a vehicle usage and weight distance tax further supported the road fund. The last stagecoach line in the state had ended in 1911, when a coach made its final run from Monticello to Burnside. That cessation symbolized the start of the new age, one which by 1930 brought forty-four hundred miles of state-maintained roads. That year Kentucky devoted 47.6 percent of its state funds to highways. The old macadamized, wood block, or brick streets in cities began to be replaced by asphalt, and real rural roads began to be constructed for the first time. Haphazard planning, however, often resulted in incomplete connections, and the commonwealth for a time earned the nickname the Detour State. By World War II many parts of rural Kentucky still remained unserved by good roads.

Kentucky's answer to the question of poor roads in some areas was to build highways financed by state bonds, to be retired by toll receipts. In 1956 the first of those, the Kentucky Turnpike from Louisville to Elizabethtown, opened; nineteen years later all tolls were removed from that road, far ahead of schedule. The pattern, like the earlier pattern in bridge-building, was repeated across the state. The toll roads, combined with the chiefly federally funded interstate highway system authorized in 1956 and with the state's continued devotion to road construction, meant that by the late twentieth century Kentucky had a strong road network, one that aided commercial and agricultural interests while promoting more regional ties. In the mid-1980s the commonwealth's 25,000 miles of state-maintained roads included 739 miles of interstate highways and 631 miles of toll roads.

By that time the greatest twentieth-century innovation in transportation had finally become commonly used as a method of movement. Air travel had required Kentuckians to make greater leaps in acceptance than any other. No longer would they be earthbound, as people had been for eons, for they could now fly through the air at great speeds. For those who remembered horses and car-

A biplane flies over Louisville's Bowman Field, ca. 1929 (courtesy of the Kentucky Historical Society).

riages, such things seemed almost impossible. But change did occur, albeit slowly. Louisville's first airport, Bowman Field, was initially used in 1919. A terminal was constructed there a decade later, and finally concrete runways were built nearly ten years after that. The construction of a new airport in Louisville, Standiford Field, and a major one in northern Kentucky, serving that area as well as Cincinnati, indicated the growing acceptance of passenger travel by air. Later United Parcel Service made Louisville's airport a hub. The sounds of planes overhead—once an occasion of wonder—had become commonplace.

Kentucky had changed a great deal since 1865 in regard to agriculture and commerce, but perhaps no change had been greater than the innovations in transportation. A people largely limited in a day to a trip that would take them no farther than their county seat could by the late twentieth century be continents away in the same time. Such mobility made the late twentieth century seem, by comparison with the past, almost another world. In many ways it was.

20

Culture and Communications, 1865-1995

By the start of the twentieth century, writers usually considered Kentucky as part of the South and often described its cultural mores in negative ways, echoing the manner in which southern culture was frequently portrayed. The commonwealth's violence before and after the turn of the century only added to an emerging image of a culturally benighted Kentucky. At least into the first third of the 1900s, and perhaps beyond, such national views of the state persisted. Yet the state had made contributions in art, architecture, dance, motion pictures, music, photography, sculpture, and theater; and Kentuckians had real strengths in literature and journalism, both on a regional and national scale. Only slowly, however, did the commonwealth begin to shake off its "barefoot and backward" cultural image.

The Press

By the end of the Civil War and the start of Kentucky's Readjustment, the newspaper was the choice reading material of most Kentuckians. In 1872 some ninety state papers had a circulation of nearly two hundred thousand. Many of those readers chiefly perused a local weekly. These county newspapers seldom told of matters beyond the nation's borders and usually focused on events very close to home. Syndicated stories on religion, health, morals, and style appeared after 1865, and standard patent medicine advertisements helped pay the bills for a time, but usually the editors filled their pages with local fare. The weather, farming, fashion, morbidity, lawlessness, race, religion, and, of course, politics dominated the columns. Since names make news, such sheets, according to Thomas D. Clark, seemingly tried "to print the name of every . . . man and woman in the county at least once a year." Readers apparently sought such fare, for by 1930 the seventy-odd weeklies of 1872 had grown to two hundred. But modified markets, new media, and higher costs brought changes to presses that had often been run by a small staff, out of a few rooms, with little profit. From the 1960s on, local papers increasingly became part of newspaper chains. Often the local voice could still be heard, but "safe" editorial stands and less idiosyncratic views usually resulted. At the same time, however, various specialty presses continued to find a readership, albeit usually a small one. Through all those newspaper columns, an individual style of journalism still emerged on occasion, a fragile memory of an earlier era when Kentuckians chiefly read a local paper, edited by a person most of them knew personally.

Many Kentuckians long received their news through the pages of a community weekly, but more and more turned to larger-city dailies as the decades passed. Some people subscribed to both. In certain parts of the commonwealth, the newspaper of choice might be one published nearby, though outside Kentucky's borders. Some in western Kentucky read papers from St. Louis or Memphis; in south-central Kentucky, from Nashville; in the southeastern part of the state, from Knoxville; and in northern Kentucky, from Cincinnati. More readers, however, perused either a Kentucky paper from a nearby large city or the paper that for nearly a century was the state's single major newspaper.

On November 8, 1868, a significant event took place in Kentucky journalism, for on that day subscribers to the *Louisville Courier* and the *Louisville Journal* found that those papers had merged. A new newspaper, the *Louisville Courier-Journal,* had been formed. With the inclusion of the *Louisville Democrat* soon afterward, the merger was complete. The paper's twenty-eight-year-old editor, Henry Watterson, would make the *Courier-Journal* the

leading southern journal for a time, with the largest circulation in the region for some twenty years. He also would make the *Courier-Journal* the state's major paper, as he became a spokesman for Kentucky, the South, and the Democratic Party.

Henry Watterson (1840-1921) was the leading Kentucky journalist for a half century after 1868. Son of a Tennessee congressman, Watterson briefly served in the Confederate Army, but even before the end of the Civil War, he entered the newspaper business. As editor of the *Courier-Journal,* he would prove to be moderate on many issues, conservative on some, progressive on others. His real strength, however, would be not his philosophy but his ability to write, to turn a memorable phrase, to make a dull subject lively, to entertain. When discussing a possible Democratic president in 1892, for example, he said that renomination would lead the party "through a slaughterhouse into an open grave." Refusing to support another party candidate four years later, Watterson cried out, "No compromise with dishonor." When some criticized his opposition to candidates from his own Democratic Party, he responded, "Things have come to a hell of a pass / When a man can't whip his own jackass." On another issue, woman suffrage, the editor took a very conservative stand, calling the women's rights leaders "blatant zealots" and "immoral" "he-women." In another editorial he termed them "Crazy Janes and Sillie Sallies" and said that if women got the vote, "the wench and the harlot will muster at the polls."

No matter what his editorial stances, Watterson took them with flair, gusto, and showmanship. Blind in one eye, nearsighted in the other, and missing part of one thumb, the editor wrote his column by hand with a pen, a practice that constantly created problems for typesetters who could not read his prose. Once his expression "forty miles of conflagration" became "forty mules of California." The prototype of the southern colonel, Marse Henry—as he became known once his hair and mustache

Henry Watterson, editor of the *Louisville Courier-Journal,* was the leading journalist in the South for half a century (courtesy of The Filson Club Historical Society).

turned white—also caused concern at times in the financial department. Generally he left business matters to his capable publisher, Walter Haldeman, but on occasion Watterson would take petty funds from the cash drawer for some paper-related expenses. The accountants asked him to leave a record of what he took; Watterson's note the next time read simply, "Took it all." It was this man who likely had more influence nationally than any late nineteenth-century southern editor and who won a Pulitzer Prize in 1917.

As it turned out, the 1917 prize marked the beginning of the end for Watterson as editor. His wartime editorials angered some; his stances against Prohibition, woman suffrage, and the League of Nations contradicted those of a new owner. In 1919 he retired as editor, and in a sense the personal journalistic style began to leave the Kentucky scene as well. On Watterson's death in 1921 the *New York Times* wrote about "that Wattersonian style, pungent, vivid, superlatively personal, those adhesive epithets, that storm of arrows, . . . the swift sar-

casm, the free frolic of irresistible humor—it was as if the page was not written but spoke and acted before you."

The new owner of the *Courier-Journal* was Robert Worth Bingham (1871-1937). For the next sixty-plus years, the Bingham family would leave a mark on the paper as indelible as Watterson's. Over time, various papers challenging the *Courier-Journal*'s supremacy died out, ranging from the Republican *Louisville Commercial* to the merged *Louisville Herald-Post.* With the latter's demise in 1936, the *Courier-Journal* and its companion, the afternoon *Times* (begun in 1884), had the major newspaper field of the Falls City to themselves. Politically active in one faction of the Democratic Party, Robert Worth Bingham used the papers as a forum for his views; his ties to President Franklin D. Roosevelt brought him the ambassadorship to Great Britain in 1933, and his involvement with the papers lessened. Bingham's death in 1937 ushered to the forefront his son George Barry Bingham (1906-88), who soon made the papers nationally known as leaders in reform causes. The morning *Courier-Journal* and the afternoon *Times* took stands generally more liberal than those of most Kentuckians, on issues of race, education, ethics, conservation, and other matters. In 1946 writer John Gunther called the *Courier-Journal* "one of the best newspapers in the country . . . a splendid liberal force," while *Time* magazine in 1952 listed it among the nation's four best newspapers. It continued to garner high rankings in later surveys. Publishers such as Mark F. Ethridge and Barry Bingham Jr. and talented columnists such as Allan Trout, Joe Creason, John Ed Pearce, and C. Ray Hall joined good reporters on both the state and national levels to give both papers a deservedly strong reputation that won them six Pulitzer Prizes. Internal conflicts in the Bingham family, however, ended in the sale of the papers to the Gannett chain in 1986. The afternoon *Times* soon ceased production, in a cost-cutting measure, and observers watched to see the full effect of the change from a Kentucky-owned, family-dominated paper to one connected more to national ownership.

By that time the *Courier-Journal*'s primary position in Kentucky was under challenge from the *Lexington Herald-Leader*. That paper traced its origins to different sources. In 1895 two Democratic papers, the *Lexington Daily Press,* started in 1870, and the *Morning Transcript,* founded in 1876, had merged to form one paper, which soon became the *Morning Herald*. With its editor Desha Breckinridge, it was perhaps the most reform-minded paper in the state in the first two decades of the twentieth century, taking strong Progressive Era stands on woman suffrage and racial matters. The subject of many of the Breckinridge editorials on politics was the afternoon *Kentucky Leader,* founded in Lexington in 1888 to thunder the Republican cause. Following the death of Breckinridge in 1935, the two papers merged in 1937 under the ownership of John G. Stoll, while keeping their separate political outlooks and separate names. The newspapers took more conserva-

tive stances, however, and refused, for example, to print stories about local civil rights activities in the late 1950s and early 1960s. In 1973 the papers were purchased by the Knight (now Knight-Ridder) national newspaper chain; a decade later the two papers merged into the single edition *Herald-Leader*. In that form, the Lexington paper won a Pulitzer Prize and had the state's second-largest circulation. It was dominant in central and eastern Kentucky, while the *Courier-Journal* had wide circulation in south-central and western Kentucky, with some enclaves elsewhere, left over from the days when it was the unchallenged statewide newspaper. The old personal-style, often-vitriolic journalism in which Breckinridge crossed verbal swords with Watterson or Bingham had softened into calmer, more politically oriented differences in later decades, only to be replaced by competition directed by national chains, in papers whose political orientation and overall philosophy sometimes seemed difficult to pinpoint.

While the *Courier-Journal* and the *Herald-Leader* increasingly dominated Kentucky journalism, many strong editors had long made their own contributions, sometimes from smaller towns. W.P. Walton of the *Stanford Interior Journal,* Harry A. Sommers of the *Elizabethtown News,* the Dyches of the *London Sentinel-Echo,* the Joplins of the Somerset papers, and Al Smith of the *Russellville News Democrat,* for example, had all contributed to the vitality of journalism in the commonwealth.

Others made their mark in somewhat larger-circulation markets. In Paducah, three newspapers—the *Sun,* the *Daily News,* and the *Democrat*—went through a series of mergers that produced the *Paducah Sun-Democrat* in 1929. Various members of the Paxton family have led the paper since then. Similar actions took place in Owensboro, where Urey Woodson edited the *Messenger,* founded in 1877, while in 1909 former gubernatorial candidate Samuel W. Hager purchased the rival *Inquirer,* set up in 1884. In the late 1920s the two merged as the *Messenger and Inquirer,* and the paper was long operated by members of the Hager family. In northern Kentucky, newspapers were identified more with Cincinnati parents than as independent sheets. In 1890 the *Kentucky Post* was founded as one of the Scripps's "penny papers" and began to build a solid subscription base. In Frankfort, the Republican *Commonwealth,* edited by elderly Albert G. Hodges, shut down its presses in 1872 rather than support a party candidate the editor opposed; the Democratic *Yeoman* of S.I.M. Major, with editorials from the pens of Henry T. Stanton and J. Stoddard Johnston, never had such serious pangs of conscience and put out various editions—weekly, triweekly, or daily—depending in part on whether the General Assembly was in session. But the *Yeoman* did not see the start of the twentieth century either, and by 1912 a series of mergers brought forth the *State Journal,* which became a politically influential paper in a very political city. Across Kentucky, newspapers started, prospered, folded, merged, and finally emerged as healthy papers.

Other presses sought to reach a more specialized audience. In Louisville, for example, the *Anzeiger* published news in a German-language edition until its demise on the eve of World War II. The *Kentucky Irish American* met the reading needs not only of the sons and daughters of Eire but also of the labor union forces initially and, later, of Catholics generally. With witty writers such as John Michael ("Mike") Barry, the *Irish American* continued until November 1968. Also in the Falls City, the black press found some support for the *Louisville News* (established in 1912) and the *Louisville Leader* (1917-50). Not until the founding of the *Louisville Defender* in 1933, however, did black Kentuckians have a strong and lasting editorial voice in the state. Under the guidance of Frank L. Stanley Sr. and his successors, the *Defender* spoke out for integration and racial equality. Away from the state, Kentucky-born Alice A. Dunnigan became a major black journalist at the national level, while Arthur Krock of Glas-gow won four Pulitzers early, and Helen Thomas later served as White House bureau chief for United Press International.

Literature: The Rise to Prominence

In a book published in London, England, in 1870, an author who had visited Kentucky some years earlier remembered the state's citizens as urbane, polite, agreeable, and "remarkable for intellectual activity, but not for literary accomplishments." His analysis of the literary landscape at that time was correct. Low educational levels, a provincialism born out of rural isolation, an orientation by the talented to other fields—all slowed the development of literature in the state. Yet that situation would change by the beginning of the twentieth century, and for most of the subsequent decades Kentucky played a significant role on the national literary scene. It is difficult to determine what caused greatness in Kentucky writers, what common factors existed in their lives, what brought them to achieve. A survey of the careers of Kentucky authors shows a wide variety of backgrounds: some grew up poor, others did not; many had unhappy childhoods, many did not; they came from all regions of the state. Perhaps the most common feature was that they felt comfortable creating in the loneliness that writing entails. But whatever the source of the fine writing, the Kentucky cultural patterns that both shaped authors and gave them subject matter for their books in the end helped produce strong literary achievements in the commonwealth.

By the late nineteenth century, writing that centered on a particular region, exploiting that landscape and place, had gained much favor among American reading audiences. The so-called local color school brought to the forefront two Kentucky authors, James Lane Allen and John Fox Jr., who would be among the most respected and best known of their generations. In a sense, their rise to prominence marked the emergence of Kentucky as a place of significant literary achievement.

In 1892 Lexington's James Lane Allen (1849-1925) wrote that "Kentucky has little or no literature," but already he had begun to change that status. Tall and handsome yet distant, with aristocratic manners, few friends, and a vain personality—he once became angry when an acquaintance yelled for him to come on into a room, rather than opening the door for him—Allen first taught school, then turned totally to writing in the 1880s. In a series of articles and books, he portrayed the romance, gentility, and honor of earlier times. An excellent collection of short stories, *Flute and Violin* (1891), brought him some acclaim, and *A Kentucky Cardinal* (1894) and its sequel, *Aftermath* (1895), added to his reputation. But it was *The Choir Invisible* (1897) that made Allen nationally and internationally known. Set in frontier Kentucky, the novel deals with a man's love for a married woman. Duty and honor eventually conquer passion, and he leaves behind "a love that was forbidden." Appearing at a time when the United States seemed to many to be setting aside ethics and morality, the well-crafted work became immensely popular.

Angered by slights, real and imagined, and unhappy with the treatment he received at times in his home state, Allen left Kentucky in the 1890s and came back only occasionally. Virtually all of his novels, however, continued to be set in the Bluegrass, for Allen could not leave behind that world of his imagination. Interestingly, at the peak of his popularity, he turned to other themes, as he sought to make a transition by combining romance with realism. His *Reign of Law* (1900) dealt with the controversy between religion and evolution, earned him considerable ministerial opposition, and again made the best-sellers' list. Three years later *The Mettle of the Pasture* won both popular and critical acclaim, as it dealt forthrightly with double moral standards for the sexes. Another Allen book would not emerge for six years, and like its many successors, *Bride of the Mistletoe* did not achieve much recognition. The reading taste of America had changed, and Allen's prose had as well. The man once called the nation's greatest novelist was almost forgotten by the literary world when he died in 1925.

Novelist James Lane Allen of Lexington achieved international acclaim for his 1897 novel *The Choir Invisible* (courtesy of the Kentucky Historical Society).

Allen's Kentucky successor in the American mind was a former student of his, John Fox Jr. (1863-1919) of Paris, Kentucky. In many ways, Fox represented the antithesis of Allen. Small and sinewy, he enjoyed the company of people, liked sports, and attracted friends. Whereas Allen wrote of the central Bluegrass, Fox chose Appalachia and became the first Kentucky writer of note to deal with the evolving character of that region. While Allen had been educated in Kentucky but left the state to write, Fox went to Harvard and took a job at a New York newspaper but returned to the region to achieve his fame. Short stories, such as "On Hell-fer-Sartain Creek" and "A Mountain Europa" (1892), were followed by novels set in Appalachia. Fox's first major best-seller combined the eastern Kentucky region and the Bluegrass, as it told the story of a mountain orphan who comes to Lexington, becomes accepted in an aristocratic household, finds his new family and his new love torn apart by the Civil War, but returns from battle to see "the sundered threads, unraveled by the war . . . knitted together fast." *The Little Shepherd of Kingdom Come* (1903) would sell more than a million copies and would later be made into several motion pictures.

After some less successful works, Fox then wrote his best book, *The Trail of the Lonesome Pine* (1908). *Little Shepherd* had presented a somewhat sentimental and outdated picture of the Civil War, but Fox's new novel broke fresh literary ground. It portrayed the struggle taking place in the mountains, as the forces of change and modernization warred with the culture of tradition and stability. Through the love story of a young mountain woman and an "outsider" man, Fox presented a generally balanced and sympathetic picture of a region struggling to find a new identity. When Fox died of pneumonia in 1919, that struggle was still continuing.

Other authors of the era also used the Appalachian region as the setting for their prose, though none of them would be able to write as well or as understandingly as had Fox.

Charles Neville Buck (1879-1930) of Midway and Louisville, for instance, spent two decades, starting in 1910, writing numerous popular novels featuring standard plot formulas, stereotypical feud characters, and exaggerated mountain drama. In the same period Lucy Furman (1870-1958), in books such as *The Quare Women* (1923), wrote of events she experienced at Hindman Settlement School.

In another part of Kentucky, however, a very different kind of writing had been taking place, and it too proved popular to a national readership. Louisville and its environs at the turn of the century and after had attracted a large literary colony, which included patrons such as the Belknaps and the Speeds, journalists such as Henry Watterson, poets such as Cale Young Rice and Madison J. Cawein, geographers such as Ellen Churchill Semple, and novelists such as Charles Neville Buck. But the women of the Authors Club formed the core, and three of those writers dominated—Annie Fellows Johnston, Alice Hegan Rice, and George (Georgia) Madden Martin.

Annie Fellows Johnston (1863-1931) had written little before the death of her husband in 1892 left her with three stepchildren. While visiting Pewee Valley in Oldham County, she became enchanted with the lifestyle, which she perceived as very much like life in antebellum times. Using that setting, she wrote *The Little Colonel* (1895), the first of a dozen works in a popular series that usually sold a hundred thousand copies per book. A witty woman with "a kind of spiritual aristocracy" about her, Johnston wrote stories stressing Victorian, nineteenth-century values. In *The Little Colonel* a bright and innocent child, through her sweetness, brings together a family split by wartime memories and postwar actions. Such themes proved long popular, and a line of clothes and a series of motion pictures bore the Little Colonel name. Such sentimental writing was not great literature, but it was very popular.

Similar themes came from the pen of Alice Hegan Rice (1870-1942). Her inspiration for writing resulted from philanthropic work in a Louisville slum area, where she met an optimistic and cheerful woman. Using that model, Alice Hegan wrote *Mrs. Wiggs of the Cabbage Patch* (1901), a widely successful, sentimental book that eventually sold more than 650,000 copies in a hundred printings. It combined a developing national interest in the urban poor with a solution that focused on individual achievement in the face of adversity. The book ends with Mrs. Wiggs saying, "Looks like ever'thing in the world come right, if we jes wait long enough!" Hegan married Cale Young Rice the next year, and other best-sellers with not dissimilar themes followed: *Lovey Mary* (1903), *Sandy* (1905), and *Mr. Opp* (1909) among them. An intelligent, caring woman, Rice in her books seldom took her interests to a higher level, and the books remained popular more for their charming optimism than their literary worth. Rice died in 1942, and her poet husband, "a lost soul" without her love, committed suicide the next year. In a sense the Rices' deaths symbolized the death of innocence expressed in the works of writers like Annie Johnston and Alice Rice.

Two other women authors in the same Louisville milieu achieved some national recognition, though they focused their writing in different ways. George (Georgia) Madden Martin (1866-1946) wrote the very popular Emmy Lou stories, which told of a young girl, but later books—*Selina* (1914) and *Children in the Mist* (1920)—looked more at women in the changing century. As the chair of the Association of Southern Women for the Prevention of Lynching, Martin worked actively in reform efforts as well. Eleanor Mercein Kelly (1880-1968) came to the commonwealth in 1901 as a result of marriage and began to write first about Kentucky and then about the world. Her career would span enough years to link the Authors Club generation to a new group of Louisville-based authors.

Outside the Falls City, some scattered authors also published works of interest. In northern Kentucky John Uri Lloyd (1849-1936) gained national fame as a plant scientist

and chemist and regional recognition as the author of the local color novel *Stringtown on the Pike* (1900) and more than a half dozen other books, including the early science fiction novel *Etidorhpa* (1896). In Bowling Green women's rights leader Eliza Calvert Obenchain (1856-1935), who wrote as Eliza Calvert Hall, gained recognition for her short stories, the best of which appeared in her popular book *Aunt Jane of Kentucky* (1907). Farther to the west, Paducah produced Irvin S. Cobb (1876-1944), who moved successfully from newspaper reporter and editor to author of the popular Judge Priest stories, which were collected in book form and made into a motion picture. Cobb was also a humorist and raconteur, as well as a scriptwriter and actor. Friendly and sociable, Cobb continually stressed his state ties, calling himself the Duke of Paducah. Nationally known, he became a Kentucky version of his friend Will Rogers. In short, all across Kentucky, authors were writing prose that was being read by millions of Americans.

The Maturing of the Literary Craft

Of the ten books on the *Publisher's Weekly* best-sellers' list in 1903, five were written by Kentuckians. Two decades later, however, many of the authors who gave the state its literary strengths in the first years of the century had either died or had passed the peaks of their popularity. It seemed that the commonwealth might revert to the barren literary days of the nineteenth century. Within a few short years, though, a new generation of Kentucky-born or Kentucky-based authors would come to the forefront and would in many ways eclipse their popular predecessors.

The first of these new writers was Elizabeth Madox Roberts (1881-1941) of Springfield. Having read widely in her youth and listened to "phantom books" in the oral stories of her father, Roberts taught school for a time, but the poor health that plagued her all her life interrupted that activity. The reserved, tall, slender woman became almost a rustic recluse, except that she went to the University of Chi-

Springfield novelist Elizabeth Madox Roberts drew on the history of Kentucky for her novels, including *The Great Meadow* (1930) (courtesy of the Kentucky Historical Society).

cago in 1917 and left there confident and in-spired to write. Her first novel appeared when she was forty-five years old; her last came a doz-en years later. In that time Roberts became one of the nation's most-praised writers. The initial review of her work in the *New York Times* concluded that "there has not been a finer first novel published in this country for many years." Critics compared her with Ernest Hem-ingway, Theodore Dreiser, and Sinclair Lewis, often suggesting that she eclipsed them all. One critic said that Roberts was America's greatest writer.

Her first novel, *The Time of Man* (1926), touched on most of the themes displayed in her important works. In flowing and slow-paced prose, Roberts tells the story of the voiceless rural people and portrays their strength and vitality and "the glory in the commonplace" of their lives. Her characters display a strong will, a "power of the spirit," that allows them to fight the larger external forces always threaten-ing their emotional lives. In *My Heart and My Flesh* (1927), everything is taken from a woman of prominence, but she overcomes what one writer called her "descent into the living veins of her soul." Roberts's next book, *The Great Meadow* (1930), remains perhaps the best his-torical novel set on the Kentucky frontier; in

it the heroine once more demonstrates the power to achieve from within. All three books have women as the chief characters, and Ellen Chesser, Theodosia Bell, and Diony Hall are strong examples "of hopes ever defeated and ever renewed."

Other books, some of short stories and poetry, came from Roberts's pen, but contin-ued ill health brought the writer's life to an end in 1941, at the age of fifty-nine. Unfortunately for her literary reputation, she became less and less read and studied as time passed, only to be recognized again much later. In her time she personified Kentucky literature. As one critic wrote, the state stood like "an immense territo-rial ghost" in her life: "Its past, still animated in her imagination, accompanied the present."

Roberts had led the way, but in the 1920s through the 1930s, as William S. Ward notes in his *Literary History of Kentucky*, a notable group of writers burst forth on the Kentucky land-scape, including Robert Penn Warren, Allen Tate, Caroline Gordon, Jesse Stuart, James Still, and Harriette Arnow. Part of what has been called the Southern Literary Renascence, these writers brought to Kentucky its own dis-tinguished literary rebirth as well. In contrast to Allen, the Authors Club of Louisville, and others before them, the members of the new

Robert Penn Warren of Guthrie is the only writer to have won Pulitzer Prizes for both fiction and poetry (courtesy of the Center for Robert Penn Warren Studies, Western Kentucky University).

generations, like Roberts, grew up in small-town and rural places and mainly wrote of agrarian themes. Their world of reference was the western Kentucky of Warren and Gordon or the Appalachia of Stuart, Still, and Arnow. More diversity, different outlooks, and fresh approaches resulted.

The most honored of this group of authors was Robert Penn Warren (1905-89) of Guthrie. Before his life ended, he became the only writer to win Pulitzer Prizes in both fiction and poetry, and in 1986 he was named the nation's first poet laureate. With Murray-born Cleanth Brooks, he coauthored the immensely influential *Understanding Poetry* (1938), which ushered in the New Criticism, with its emphasis on a close analysis of literary works.

Most of all, Warren wrote. Growing up in Todd County, the tall, thin boy saw around him a subculture of violence, exemplified in the Black Patch War of the region. His schooling at Vanderbilt University exposed him to the intellectual questioning of the Fugitives group there and resulted later in a contribution to their agrarian paean, *I'll Take My Stand* (1930). Spending much of the rest of his career as a college professor, "Red" Warren wrote short stories, poetry, and prose and excelled in all three areas. His novels often used Kentucky settings and generally dealt with what James Justis has identified as the themes of "the Ambiguity of Truth, . . . the power of the past, the painful path to self-knowledge." Warren's first novel, *Night Rider* (1939), was followed by a second

work, then his Pulitzer Prize–winning *All the King's Men* (1946), set in Louisiana with a Huey Long figure at the center. Four years later Warren returned to a Kentucky setting, retelling the story of Jereboam Beauchamp's tragic life in *World Enough and Time* (1950). One of his strongest works, written in a kind of narrative poetry, came next. It is a book that eludes easy clarification. In *Brother to Dragons* (1953) Warren revisited in his imagination the effects on Thomas Jefferson of his nephews' murder of a slave in antebellum Kentucky. (The historical story would be well told in 1976 by Boynton Merrill Jr. in his *Jefferson's Nephews*.) In Warren's novels *Band of Angels* (1955) and *The Cave* (1959), based on the Floyd Collins rescue, he used his home state once more as the basis for his stories.

In a sense, these works marked Warren's turn back to poetry, and he won his second Pulitzer for *Promises: Poems, 1954-1956* (1957). A plethora of books (on such matters as civil rights), essays (including a well-known analysis of Coleridge's "Rime of the Ancient Mariner"), and poems (winning Warren a third Pulitzer Prize) continued to flow from Warren's mind as he became arguably the most respected man of letters in the United States. Near the end of his life he once more returned to the Kentucky he had physically departed but that seldom left his writing consciousness, in his books *Jefferson Davis Gets His Citizenship Back* (1980) and *Portrait of a Father* (1988). Throughout his life of writing fiction, Warren had portrayed the conflict of evil and idealism within, and the agony of souls in search of self-salvation, of places where "In the turpitude of time / Hope dances on the razor edge." In 1989 the most renowned and honored author that Kentucky ever produced died. Yet unlike the situation in many of his books, at his death no ambiguity existed regarding his life and his contribution to literature: they had been monumental.

Three other Kentucky-born authors had careers in which Warren played an important role. Cleanth Brooks (1906-94) left Kentucky when young. He was at Vanderbilt at the same time as Warren, and later he coauthored three important textbooks with the man from Guthrie: *An Approach to Literature* (1936), *Understanding Poetry* (1938), and *Understanding Fiction* (1943). Together the two Kentuckians also founded the all too short-lived *Southern Review*, one of the strongest literary quarterlies ever prepared in the United States. Brooks would go on to write other important works as one of the nation's foremost critics.

Allen Tate (1899-1979), like Brooks, was born in Kentucky (near Winchester). He also went to Vanderbilt, where, like Warren, Brooks, and so many others, he fell under the influence of John Crowe Ransom and also was a classmate of Warren's. Like Warren, he wrote an essay in *I'll Take My Stand* and became a college professor. Unlike "Red," however, Tate seldom used Kentucky settings in his writings. Interestingly, however, his poem "The Swimmers," which was identified as taking place in the commonwealth, may have been his best poetic work. The man who later held the chair of poetry at the Library of Congress had a distinguished career as critic, teacher, and writer.

Caroline Gordon (1895-1981) had connections to Robert Penn Warren in two ways. She too had been born in rural Todd County, almost a decade before Warren, and their families had known each other. It was through Warren that she met Allen Tate, and in 1924 Gordon and Tate were married. In places such as New York, various cities of Europe, and

Clarksville, Tennessee, the two hosted many of America's leading literary figures and became known for their own work. (They divorced in 1946, remarried that same year, and divorced again in 1959.) Joy Bale Boone wrote that they "collaborated, supported, and destroyed each other." Gordon stressed the role of agrarianism, of family, of place, of historical ruin in the South, as she wrote of the world of her youth, with books often set on the Kentucky-Tennessee border. Works such as *Penhally* (1931), *Aleck Maury, Sportsman* (1934), *None Shall Look Back* (1937), and *The Garden of Adonis* (1937) gained much critical praise, but Gordon's detachment from her characters left a popular readership unsatisfied. In later years she, like Elizabeth Madox Roberts, would be less honored than in her lifetime, but the fact that a 1987 book on fifty post-1900 southern writers included Gordon showed her importance in the literature of Kentucky, the South, and the United States.

All these authors—Warren, Brooks, Tate, and Gordon—had been born between 1895 and 1906, had come from an agrarian, western Kentucky background, and had written about a Kentucky and a South searching its history and its present for moral and personal answers. In eastern Kentucky another group of writers emerged from very different backgrounds, and their writing touched themes important to Appalachia.

First to burst on the scene—and burst he did—was Jesse Hilton Stuart (1906-84) of Greenup County. Son of a virtually illiterate father, Stuart grew to be a person who almost could not stop writing. In fact, his literary reputation would likely have been even stronger had he accepted editors' advice to tighten more of his work or even not to publish some of it. As it was, the physical act of writing gave him pleasure, and he wrote with uncontrolled zest and zeal. After education at present-day Lincoln Memorial University in Harrogate, Tennessee, Stuart went to Vanderbilt, where another of the Fugitives who had influenced Warren and the others became one of his mentors. Donald

Davidson's advice—"Stick to your hills, Jesse, and write about the people you know"—proved valuable, and from his W-Hollow home, schoolteacher, principal, and author Jesse Stuart began to tell the myriad stories of his hill people.

In 1934 a large collection of poems, *Man with a Bull-Tongue Plow,* gave Stuart instant recognition. Two years later what probably is his best collection of short stories, *Head o' W-Hollow,* appeared, to be followed by an autobiographical account and then his first novel, *Trees of Heaven* (1940). Next, *Taps for Private Tussie* (1943) sold more than a million copies, as it presented a satiric and broadly boisterous look at a mountain family. Some criticized it for perpetuating stereotypes; others praised it. The comic *Foretaste of Glory* (1946) and Stuart's excellent and poignant account of his years of teaching, *The Thread That Runs So True* (1949), added to his readership. A tall and powerfully built man, he survived a massive heart attack in 1954—he would die from the effects of another three decades later—and he continued to write, lecture, and visit foreign lands. He always returned to W-Hollow, and his vigorous and raw energy and his powerful words made him the most popular Kentucky author in his native state. For all Stuart's weaknesses, Kentuckians still liked the man who wrote

> I take with me Kentucky embedded in my
>   brain and heart,
> In my flesh and bone and blood
> Since I am of Kentucky
> And Kentucky is part of me.

Although he grew up in Alabama, James A. Still (b. 1906) lived an early life somewhat similar to Jesse Stuart's. Like Stuart, he was born in 1906, went to Lincoln Memorial University and then to Vanderbilt, became associated with a Kentucky school (as librarian at Hindman Settlement School in Knott County), and lived in a log cabin, near Wolfpen. But there most similarities ended, except that both men wrote of the eastern mountains they knew. As one critic noted, "James Still is

realistic where Stuart is melodramatic, poetic when Stuart is often sentimental." He was also unlike Stuart in that his output was limited. For a long time, three slim volumes published within four years represented his book-length work: *Hounds on the Mountain* (1937), a collection of poems; his best-known book, *River of Earth* (1940), a novel whose simple, clear, and strong prose tells the story of a family in transition in the coalfields; and *On Troublesome Creek* (1941), a compilation of his short stories. Still wrote more short stories and poetry after that initial output, but he seemed almost forgotten until two collections of short stories appeared, *Pattern of a Man* (1976) and *The Run for the Elbertas* (1980). Well received by critics, as most of his work was, they sparked a kind of Still revival.

Stuart may have had more popular success and less critical praise than he deserved; Still, the reverse. But another of their generation tasted success from both the public and the critics and may have been the strongest novelist of the three. Born two years later than Stuart and Still, the diminutive Harriette L. Simpson (1908-86) grew up in Wayne County, attended Berea College, taught school briefly, went back to graduate from the University of Louisville, then taught again, published her first book in 1936, and married a newspaperman and subsequently wrote as Harriette Simpson Arnow. In 1944 the couple moved to Michigan, and she lived there the remainder of her life. Like so many who left the commonwealth, though, Arnow built on her experiences, memory, and observations and used Kentucky characters or settings in most of her writing. In *Mountain Path* (1936) she portrayed Appalachian life of earlier times, while *Hunter's Horn* (1949) told a symbolic story of a fox hunter's obsession during a depression generation's decaying life. A *Saturday Review* poll placed *Hunter's Horn* first among the novels of that year, outdistancing George Orwell's *1984,* for instance. But Arnow's masterpiece, and one of the most powerful novels written by a Kentuckian, was *The Dollmaker* (1954), which won the National

Book Award. In the book, Gertie Nevels's family moves from Kentucky to Detroit, and the life she once knew is taken away by the industrial North. In a grim and tragic portrayal, this strong woman fights a failing battle with a dehumanizing and impersonal foe. The small and slight Arnow was more than just a tough, realistic novelist, however, and in two social histories based on solid research, she portrayed the life of the frontier along the Cumberland River. *Seedtime on the Cumberland* (1960) and *Flowering of the Cumberland* (1963) join with a memoir of her early life, *Old Burnside* (1977), to give a more nostalgic view of a land in change. Arnow told the story of her people honestly and well.

Coming later to the state scene but touching on some of the same Appalachian themes was Arkansas-born Janice Holt Giles (1905-79), who moved to Kentucky in 1939. After marriage, she settled first in Louisville and then in south-central Kentucky, and she told of the urban-rural conflict in a strong book, *The Enduring Hills* (1950). A year later, *Miss Willie* touched on similar topics, as an outsider to rural Kentucky finds that values of importance exist in her new world as well. Soon afterward, Giles turned to writing historical novels from her Adair County home and became well known for books set on the Kentucky frontier—*The Kentuckians* (1953), *Hannah Fowler* (1956), and *The Land beyond the Mountains* (1958). She also wrote of other times: *The Believers* (1957), for instance, deals with the Shaker experience in the state. Her husband, Henry Giles, wrote several strong volumes as well.

Another historical novelist of the same generation was A.B. ("Bud") Guthrie Jr. (1901-91). Like Janice Holt Giles, Guthrie was born outside the state, but he spent the years 1926-53 in Lexington as a reporter. While there, he wrote the first two parts of his trilogy of the westward movement, *The Big Sky* (1947) and *The Way West* (1949), the latter of which won a Pulitzer Prize in 1950.

Numerous other writers of that generation left their mark on the state as well. Their work ranged widely, from the protest novels of Leane Zugsmith (*The Reckoning*) and Edith Summers Kelly (*Weeds*) to the supposed humor of Cordia Greer-Petrie (the Angeline series) and the historical fiction of Isabel McMeekin and Dorothy Park Clark (who collaborated in writing as Clark McMeekin), Ben Lucien Burman, Felix Holt (whose book *The Gabriel Horn* [1951] sold more than a million copies), Alfred Leland Cobb, and Gene Markey. But one of the most interesting of the group was Elizabeth Hardwick (b. 1916), born and educated in Lexington. Although her novels received mixed reviews (except for the much-praised *Sleepless Nights* [1979]) and her short stories varied in quality, Hardwick found her niche and made her impact as an essayist and critic, helping found the *New York Review of Books*. Immensely influential in New York and national literary circles, she said of her home state: "This was, is, truly home to me, not just a birthplace." Kentucky remained fertile literary ground.

A very different kind of writing came from an unexpected source in Kentucky. Three days after the attack on Pearl Harbor, on December 10, 1941, a strong, short, and stocky man, Thomas Merton (1915-68), entered the Abbey of Our Lady of Gethsemani near Bardstown and began the process of prayer and austerity that would eventually make him a Trappist monk. This choice followed his birth in France, years of wandering, and a varied educational background. In those monastic halls of silence, however, Merton wrote prolifically on matters theological, philosophical, and historical. During the next twenty-seven years he produced some fifty volumes of poetry and prose. His 1948 autobiography, *The Seven Storey Mountain,* sold a million copies and brought international acclaim to him and royalties to the monastery. Later books such as *The Sign of Jonas* (1953) and *No Man Is an Island* (1955) made him one of the nation's best-known and most read religious and philosophical writers. By the 1960s Merton's growing concern with social justice brought him to travel more, explore Far Eastern and Indian religions, and write more militantly about nuclear war, race relations, and religious rap-prochement. On one overseas trip in1968—on the anniversary of the day he entered Gethse-mani—Merton died from electrocution, having apparently touched a fan with faulty wiring while bathing.

New Generations of Writers

Over the years certain places had attracted writers connected with Kentucky like a magnet: nineteenth-century Lexington, with Allen and Fox; turn-of-the-century Louisville, with its Authors Club of Johnston, Rice, Martin, and others; post–World War I Vander-bilt University, where Warren, Tate, Brooks, Stuart, and Still went; and, in the late 1950s, the University of Kentucky, in Lexington.

Between 1956 and 1962 a half dozen writers who would go on to win acclaim re-ceived degrees from the university: Walter Tevis, Wendell Berry, Ed McClanahan, James Baker Hall, Gurney Norman, and Bobbie Ann Mason. The university at that time was not a literary mecca. It was, however, a place where at that moment in history those talented people were touched by professors and events in a way that sparked and developed their interest in writing. Like other authors from Kentucky, many would leave the commonwealth; unlike earlier writers, however, they would come back. By 1990 the five still living—that is, all but Tevis—resided in Kentucky. Yet none of these writers had ever left it in their prose.

Wendell E. Berry (b. 1934) in some ways most evoked the Kentucky spirit in es-says, poetry, and fiction that stressed agrarian concerns and the place of people and personal responsibility in this era and on this earth. His novels include *Nathan Coulter* (1960) and *The Memory of Old Jack* (1974), the latter of which remains one of the best fictional works in a Kentucky setting. Berry's strongest presenta-tion of his themes, however, came in a series of essays, including *A Continuous Harmony* (1972) and *The Unsettling of America* (1977). In these works he criticized the impersonal cor-porate and governmental influence on tradi-

tional farming, which, together with societal changes, made it more a business than a way of life. With that shift, he feared, would come a death of important parts of an agrarian lifestyle that brought strengths to a rapidly changing world. Berry tells his readers that bigger is not better; that home, neighbors, and community come first; that quality work, of whatever kind, is reward enough; that individuals must not worship technology nor forget ecology; and that without history, learning, and a sense of place, "We are adrift in the present, in the wreckage of yesterday, in the nightmare of to-morrow." Teaching either full-time or part-time at the University of Kentucky, living a simple life on a farm in rural Henry County, Berry remains the conscience of Kentucky and of the United States.

Walter Tevis (1928-84) came to Ken-tucky to live when he was ten years old, went to college in the state, and used experiences gath-ered while working in a poolroom near the university campus as the basis for his first suc-cessful book, *The Hustler* (1959), and its later sequel, *The Color of Money* (1984). Both were made into motion pictures, as was his science fiction novel, *The Man Who Fell to Earth* (1963). Bothered by personal problems that almost ended his career, Tevis left his professorship at Ohio University and again took up writing full-time, but he died of lung cancer at the age of fifty-six.

James Baker Hall (b. 1935) of Lex-ington, Edward P. McClanahan (b. 1932) of Bracken and Mason Counties, and Gurney Norman (b. 1937) of Hazard had been friends at college. All received prestigious fellowships at Stanford University, and all taught in institu-tions of higher education outside Kentucky before returning to the commonwealth. As Hall noted, they needed "to escape provincial-ism," then to return to capitalize on the same trend: "Kentucky breeds an intense identifica-tion of oneself as a Kentuckian, which focuses you in on things local. That . . . is useful to fic-tion writers and poets [whose] . . . stories come most successfully from embodied lives, not ideas." Hall, through his combined interest in poetry, photography, and prose; Norman, through works such as the immensely popular *Divine Right's Trip* (1971), which sold two million copies, and his Appalachian-based *Kinfolks* (1977); and McClanahan, through his earthy and marvelously funny *The Natural Man* (1983), all demonstrate the creativity that resulted from physical and spiritual journeys to and from the state.

"People think my first name and my middle name are Mayfield Native. Everything I've ever read in the paper started out 'Mayfield native Bobbie Ann Mason.'" Mason (b. 1940) did indeed grow up in western Kentucky and wrote of that area in most of her work. Literally not "one of the boys" in the group of budding writers at the university, she left Kentucky to write first for movie magazines, then earned a Ph.D. in literature and began composing fiction. On her twentieth submission to the *New Yorker,* she was accepted, and as a late bloomer at age forty, she had arrived. *Shiloh and Other Stories* (1982); *In Country* (1985), which became a motion picture; *Spence + Lila* (1988); *Love Life* (1989); and *Feather Crowns* (1993), which won the Southern Book Award, all stamped her as a major American writer. The modest Dr. Mason and her husband returned to Kentucky in 1990, to live in a rural setting where she could continue to craft works that deal with societal change and its effect on everyday lives.

A whole host of writers with Kentucky ties remain on the contemporary scene, some with reputations already made, others making them still. Some authors write from university settings, such as Guy Davenport, others independently, such as Sallie Bingham. Certain novelists, such as popular mystery writer Sue Grafton, do not show a conscious state influence in their work, while others, such as James Sherburne and Taylor McCafferty, do. Some writers, such as Joe Ashby Porter in *The Kentucky Stories* (1983), use the short story form, while others, such as Betty Layman Receveur in *Oh, Kentucky!* (1990), take the historical narrative approach. Certain literary figures successfully create in the fields of poetry, fiction, and nonfiction, such as Wade Hall and Jim Wayne Miller, while others remain true to only one genre. Some authors, such as black novelist Gayl Jones, speak for an underrepresented group in Kentucky fiction, while others write from a long-common background. Rising literary stars, such as Barbara Kingsolver (b. 1955), in books such as *The Bean Trees* (1988) and *Animal Dreams* (1990), plus novelists such as Fenton Johnson and so many others all show the diversity that represents Kentucky literature at the end of the twentieth century.

Bobbie Ann Mason grew up in western Kentucky, and her work reflects that heritage (photo by Marion Ettlinger, courtesy of Bobbie Ann Mason).

Historical Writing

Two very different historians dominated the writing of Kentucky's history, Richard H. Collins and Thomas D. Clark. Collins (1824-88) was more a compiler and reviser than a historian, but his two-volume work, *A History of Kentucky* (1874), became the research bible for several later generations. Taking his father's earlier history, editor and attorney Collins got numerous people to contribute material, wrote part himself, and produced a book filled with facts, lists, and information. Over the next half century numerous authors added to the story produced by Collins, or put the story in more narrative form. Many state histories basically started with Collins's *History,* including works by Nathaniel S. Shaler (1884), Zachariah F. Smith (1885), W.H. Perrin, J.H. Battle, and G.C. Kniffin (1887), Elizabeth S. Kinkead (1896), Robert M. McElroy (1909), E. Polk Johnson (1912), William E. Connelley and E. Merton Coulter (1922), and Temple Bodley and Samuel M. Wilson (1928). Most of those authors were not trained historians. Such a trend would continue later in the persons of authors such as Willard Rouse Jillson and Lexington's J. Winston ("Squire") Coleman Jr., whose prolific writings covered a wide range of topics. Similarly, in a later era, attorney Harry M. Caudill of Letcher County would become what might be best termed a historical essayist. Although his history would be criticized by some, Caudill drafted powerful, advocacy-style prose that brought national attention to his native Appalachia. In books such as *Night Comes to the Cumberlands* (1963), *My Land Is Dying* (1971), and *The Mountain, the Miner, and the Lord* (1980), he wrote eloquently about the coal land and what he saw as the strengths and weaknesses of the people who inhabited it.

The era of writing from the pens of professionally trained historians can best be dated to September 14, 1928, when Mississippi's Thomas Dionysius Clark (b. 1903) came to graduate school in the commonwealth. With a Ph.D. from Duke University in hand by 1932, Clark would teach at the University of Ken-

tucky from 1931 until 1968, serving as chair of the history department for many of those years. During that time excellent historians, particularly in the field of southern studies, made the University of Kentucky one of the best history schools in the nation, with W. Clement Eaton, Holman Hamilton, and Albert D. ("Ab") Kirwan among the faculty.

Clark himself wrote books in numerous fields—southern history, western history, the frontier—and served as president of most of the professional organizations in each area. First and foremost, however, he wrote of Kentucky. Not only did he research his topics in libraries, but he also traveled the back roads of the state, knew the people, and understood their diversity. Perhaps his best-named book was *Kentucky: Land of Contrast* (1968). Throughout his career, Clark wrote of that place of contrast, and his *History of Kentucky* (1937) was the standard for six decades. He also worked to ensure that future historians would have better access to materials from which they could write their own revisions. He helped build up the University of Kentucky's Special Collections, pushed for the funding of the state archives, and, when he was over ninety years old, encouraged the formation of the Kentucky Historical Society's History Center. In 1990 Clark was named the state's historian laureate for life.

By that time the landscape for writing state history had changed, and dozens of professional historians at historical societies, where Hambleton Tapp operated, or at regional universities were presenting various facets of the state's past through increasingly well-written and well-researched works. Representing the most prolific of these was Lowell H. Harrison of Western Kentucky University, who wrote biographical studies of Kentucky governors, John Breckinridge, and George Rogers Clark, as well as books on Kentucky's road to statehood, the antislavery movement, and the Civil War. At the same time, authors representing groups who had previously written little of the state's history began to present new interpretations

Historian Thomas D. Clark at the University of Kentucky, 1968 (courtesy of the University of Kentucky Library).

of the commonwealth's past. Kentucky-born black historian George C. Wright told of racial violence and of black life, then joined with Marion B. Lucas of Western Kentucky University to produce the pathbreaking two-volume *History of Blacks in Kentucky* (1992). Similarly, women historians began to issue fresh examinations of the female experience in Kentucky history. All in all, the writing about Kentucky's past had become more diverse and more professional, but much still remained undone. Clio, the muse of history, continued to cry out for more toilers in the field.

Historians, both amateur and professional, found more publications available to them as the years passed. In 1903 the *Register of the Kentucky Historical Society* began, and then in 1926 *The Filson Club History Quarterly* also started providing an outlet for scholarly articles and reviews. A growing public library movement, supplemented by bookmobiles, made books more easily available across Kentucky. In the 1940s the University of Kentucky Press began, offering Kentucky authors a state publisher to produce their books. A number of universities and colleges, plus two historical groups, formed a consortium in 1969, and as the renamed University Press of Kentucky the new institution achieved even greater regional

respect as a publishing house. Through the efforts of directors Bruce F. Denbo and then Kenneth H. Cherry, the University Press of Kentucky showed the strengths of a cooperative approach. Perhaps the highlight of the press's efforts came in 1992, with the publication of *The Kentucky Encyclopedia,* edited by John E. Kleber. Garnering rave reviews and huge sales, it became a model for other states.

Poets, Artists, Architects, and More

Many of Kentucky's best poets had strengths in other areas as well, as the careers of Roberts, Warren, Stuart, Still, Merton, and Berry attest. When the lives of those who primarily owed their success to their output of poems are examined, a very mixed picture results. In contrast to the field of fiction, poetry in Kentucky did not become one of the state's cultural strengths. Of the late nineteenth- and early twentieth-century poets, some owed their fame chiefly to a single work, such as Henry T. Stanton's "The Moneyless Man" or James H. Mulligan's endlessly quoted "In Kentucky" (1902). Others voiced the otherwise silent thoughts forged in forgotten aspects of Kentucky life. Black poet Effie Waller Smith (1879-1960) of Pike County wrote three volumes of verse by the time she was thirty, but she virtually

333

disappeared from the state literary scene until being "rediscovered" near the end of the twentieth century. Louisville's Joseph S. Cotter (1861-1949) is generally regarded as the state's first significant black poet. While serving as a teacher and administrator in the Falls City's black schools, he achieved some national recognition for his many volumes of lyric poetry; his son and namesake was a poet of much promise as well but died at the age of twenty-three in 1919. When *A Brief Anthology of Kentucky Poetry* appeared in 1936, neither Smith nor the Cotters were included among the ninety-three poets listed. Segregation separated races even in the arts. The anthology also discriminated based on religion, for it did not include Israel J. Schwartz (1885-1971), a man called the author of the first important Yiddish literature produced in America. The Lithuanian-born Schwartz came to Lexington in 1918 and wrote his book-length narrative epic poem, *Kentucky*, over the next four years. Published first in a journal, then in 1925 as a book, it told of an immigrant's experiences in this new world and his attempts to reconcile the past with the future.

More traditional sources of poetry included Robert Burns Wilson of Frankfort, James T. Cotton Noe of Washington County and Lexington, and Edwin C. Litsey of Lebanon, all of whom attracted some regional attention. Wilson, also a fine visual artist, came to the state in the 1870s and chiefly wrote melancholy verse, but his poem "Remember the *Maine*" was put to music and became the anthem of the Spanish-American War. Of Professor Noe's many volumes of poetry, his best known was *Tip Sams of Kentucky* (1926), and the verses that that book contained brought him the honor of being the state's first official poet laureate. Litsey worked as a banker by day but found time at night to produce solid short stories, novels, and poetry. He too would be named poet laureate, and his daughter Sarah Litsey also wrote successfully.

Of all the poets who lived in the half century after the Civil War, however, one—a

strange one—dominated and achieved an international reputation. Born into a Louisville family in which the mother was a spiritualist and the herbalist-farmer father spoke only in German, Madison J. Cawein (1865-1914) combined the influences of his parents in producing verses that both celebrated nature and filled it with dryads, demigods, nymphs, and fairies. He had to work in a poolroom and betting parlor to make a living and often did not return home until late at night. He rose early, before his job started, and wrote then. Beginning with his *Blooms of the Berry* (1887), the too-prolific Cawein averaged more than a volume of verse a year. Later, Joyce Kilmer called Cawein "the greatest nature poet of his time," and modest success brought an end to the Kentuckian's poolroom days. Later financial reverses, however, again brought him near poverty. In his poems, the shy and lonely Cawein could write:

> This is the truth, as I see it, my dear,
> Out in the wind and the rain:
> They who have nothing have little to
>   fear,—
> Nothing to lose or to gain.

But he felt he had lost much, and he died of apoplexy at the age of forty-nine. The voice of "the Kentucky Keats" was stilled early.

Following Cawein, Elizabeth Madox Roberts and then a host of other writers began to produce excellent poetry that far departed from Cawein's traditionalism. Later, through the pages of the literary magazine *Approaches* (later called *Kentucky Poetry Review*), under the editorship of Joy Bale Boone and then Wade Hall and others, contemporary poets found a good outlet for their production.

In the field of visual art, Kentucky produced even fewer nationally recognized figures than it did in poetry. Before the Civil War, several artists had made a living chiefly by concentrating on portraits and by traveling to various states. With the increasing popularity of photography, some of the demand for portraiture declined, and Kentucky artists of the late nineteenth century became better known for their landscapes. Some of the more respected prewar artists saw careers end in the postwar period. The painter of horses, Edward Troye, moved to Alabama and died there in 1874. Samuel Woodson Price had become a Civil War general and returned to studios first in Lexington, then Louisville. His career in portraiture ended in 1881 with blindness brought on by a war wound; he lived on in darkness for thirty-seven more years and dictated two historical works.

German-born Carl C. Brenner (1838-88) came to prominence through his landscapes, particularly those featuring beech trees in the Louisville area. His father denied him attendance at an art academy in Munich, and Brenner had worked first as a house and sign painter in Louisville after the family came to the United States in the 1850s. His career ended prematurely with his death before the age of fifty. Charles Harvey Joiner (1852-1932) followed much the same path, working as a journeyman house and sign painter before opening a studio in Louisville in 1880. He too featured beech woods in his landscape views; in 1907 he left the state and painted several outstanding western scenes. During that same era poet Robert Burns Wilson settled in Kentucky, started painting in Frankfort after 1875, and produced portraits and landscapes in oil, watercolors, crayon, and charcoal. Works such as *Little Bo Peep: Mary Hendricks Swigert Moore* (now at the Kentucky Historical Society) show the multiplicity of Wilson's talents. Louisville-born and -based Patty Prather Thum (1853-1926) studied under William Merritt Chase and Thomas Eakins, served as art critic of a Louisville newspaper, and painted landscapes and portraits that were widely exhibited. Dixie Selden (1868-1935) of Covington also studied under Chase, used the same subjects as Thum, and displayed her more impressionist-style works across the United States.

The most popular among the Kentucky landscape painters of the late nineteenth and early twentieth century was Paul Sawyier (1865-1917). Unfortunately for the Ohio-born

Sawyier, much of his popularity came after his death, and his life was filled with constant struggles to make enough money to live. Studying under Chase and painting his watercolors of river and city scenes around the Frankfort area, he appealed to a sense of nostalgia even in his own time, as he used his colorful, eclectic combination of tonalism and impressionism to portray Kentucky places. The withdrawn Sawyier resided for a time on a houseboat, but he finally left the state where he had lived for forty-three years and went to New York, seeking a better climate for his art. He found little respite there, but by the time of his death he had left a large body of works, such as *Scenes on Elkhorn Creek* and *Old Capitol Hotel,* which later gave him a strong reputation within the state.

All of these artists were minor masters, however, with only limited national reputations. Only one Kentucky artist of the first half century after the Civil War could be said to have achieved national prominence. That was Frank Duveneck (1848-1919) of Covington. Leaving Kentucky to study at the Royal Academy in Munich in 1870, he spent much of the next twenty years in Europe. His 1875 showing at the Boston Art Club Exhibit brought him instant acclaim, as he bridged American and European realism through introduction of the Munich style. His broad brush stokes, his warm and dark tonality, and his powerful but delicate realism all showed the strengths displayed in *Whistling Boy* and *The Turkish Page,* as well as in cathedrals in his hometown. In 1888 his young American-born artist wife died, and a grief-stricken Duveneck returned to Covington to live and to the Cincinnati Art Academy to teach. There he became influential and popular as a warm and personable mentor, including among his students Kentucky artists Selden, Sawyier, John Bernard Alberts, and William Welsh.

Still, whatever sparked the creative genius of Kentucky authors touched state visual artists only seldom, and no lasting tradition influenced later artists. The vitality shown in

Paul Sawyier's painting *View of Wapping Street* depicts a Frankfort scene (courtesy of the Kentucky Historical Society).

the New Deal–commissioned public building murals did not endure. Only in the field of folk art did the state achieve much success, as exemplified in the simple but powerful figures of artists like Edgar Tolson and in traditional textiles and pottery.

In other fields of artistic endeavor, individual Kentuckians achieved some national recognition, but widespread achievement remained elusive. In Louisville, cartoonists Paul Plascke and, later, Hugh Haynie enlivened journalism, while Fontaine Fox's "Toonerville Trolley" series at its peak appeared in more than 250 newspapers. Interest in photography in the state sparked the establishment of the Kentucky-Tennessee Photographers Association near the turn of the century, and this was one of the first such organizations in the South. Around the same time William G. Stuber left Louisville to direct the Eastman Kodak Company's sensitive-material laboratory; in 1924 he became president of the company. Later Ralph Eugene Meatyard (with his gothic symbolism), Robert May, F. Van Deren Coke, and others

in the Lexington Camera Club made their mark in the field. In 1969 Moneta J. Sleet Jr. of Owensboro became the first black American to win a Pulitzer Prize for feature photography. The sculpture of Enid Yandell of Louisville, as exemplified in the Daniel Boone statue in Cherokee Park, represented all too rare success for a Kentuckian in the field of sculpting.

James Lane Allen wrote in the 1880s that Kentucky's postwar architecture featured no "native characteristics" and had become like that of much of the rest of the United States. In a sense he was correct, for the new technology, with circular saws, machine-made nails, and easy transportation, helped standardize construction. Architectural journals spread national trends to regional locations, where they were soon adopted. The state's premier postwar architects, Henry Whitestone and Charles Julian Clarke, helped professionalize the field, and in 1890, the year the state's first skyscraper was built, the University of Kentucky also graduated its first engineering student. In 1900, 118 architects, 2 of them women, worked in the state. By then Kentucky had seen the influence of High Victorian Gothic Revival styles after 1860; Italianate; and the heavy solid stone construction of the Romanesque Revival, introduced to the commonwealth by Mason Maury in 1886 and best exemplified in the Fayette County Courthouse. From the 1890s to World War II the Colonial Revival style proved very popular, particularly in the architecture of horse farms. Post–World War II business and public buildings had a more functional, styleless form, one characterized by its critics as shapeless, dull, and utilitarian. For these observers, the distinctive postmodernist style of the Humana Building, constructed in Louisville in 1985, proved a welcome, if controversial, relief.

For individual families, the large, rambling two-story frame houses, with extensive porches, continued to be common in rural areas, while simple box houses dominated in coal camps. Increasingly, though, town and city dwellings took on a different face. The parlor of the early post–Civil War era had been the public buffer shielding the private places in the house; the front porch had been a place of meeting and relaxation; for some, servants and their quarters had been a part of the mix. By the 1920s much of that had changed. The cottage, then the bungalow (or California) style, featuring small, affordable one-story homes with low roofs, had become very popular. Another national form, the prairie style, did not become commonplace, and indeed, the Frank Lloyd Wright–designed Ziegler House in Frankfort represents perhaps the only example of that style in the South.

With the growth of the automobile suburb, particularly after World War II, the ranch style invaded Kentucky and found little resistance. Throughout, various revivals—Tudor, Italianate, Renaissance—appeared and found support as well. A late 1980s comparison of one Kentucky town with twenty others across the nation showed that it had more ranch-style homes (42.7 percent) than the norm, fewer two-story dwellings, fewer garages, about the

same percentage of porches, and much more brick construction (43.4 percent versus an average of 25.2). In short, the fairly typical Kentucky town was characterized by a brick ranch-style home with a porch. But perhaps the major and most welcome post–World War II trend in Kentucky architecture was the restoration of old homes. Into the 1960s such actions proved sporadic, and many historic structures were lost to parking lots. Ironically, however, the slow growth of some Kentucky towns and cities left many older structures still intact when historic preservation began to become more commonplace. As a result, many parts of the commonwealth have been able to combine past and present through architecture.

The Sounds of Music

In the areas of poetry, drawing and painting, photography, sculpture, and architecture, Kentuckians had made only marginal marks on the national scene. But people of the commonwealth would make a significant impact in their music. A rich tradition of song had long existed in the state, particularly in the folk ballads. Those songs remained mostly unheard and uncollected until the twentieth century. Books such as *A Syllabus of Kentucky Folksongs* (1911) and *Kentucky Folk Songs* (1920) changed that, as did those who collected and sang the old tunes. Such a revival occurred in a more formal way with Louisville-born John Jacob Niles (1892-1980), who gathered songs across Appalachia, then performed with his dulcimer all over the United States, operating from a Clark County base. Even more Appalachian in background was Jean R. Ritchie (b. 1922), who grew up in a "singing family" of fourteen children, became a Phi Beta Kappa graduate of the University of Kentucky, and then began recording traditional ballads in their original form in 1952.

Change was coming to the mountains and to all of Kentucky, even as the old tunes were being preserved and recorded. What one author has called "the music of the damned—not the elect" was becoming popular by the

1920s, and the availability of radio gave "hillbilly" music a way to reach almost everyone. What by the 1950s would be called country music gave the voiceless an outlet; it gave people a way to express their hopes, fears, frustrations, and life stories; it gave comfort in time of need or just simple enjoyment at the end of a hard day. Kentucky became a major producer of the people and songs that made country music popular.

At first the music came through recordings, and Philipine ("Fiddlin' Doc") Roberts of Madison County became the most widely recorded fiddler, a tradition continued by "Blind Ed" Haly and then Clifford Gross. But the real boon came when Chicago's WLS radio station began its "National Barn Dance" program in the 1920s. There Garrard County's Bradley Kincaid became a star, and his songbooks sold hundreds of thousands of copies. In 1939 John Lair and others brought the idea to the Bluegrass State and started the "Renfro Valley Barn Dance," which rivaled Nashville's "Grand Ole Opry" for a time. Louisville's WHAS radio broadcast live music into the 1930s as well. From those bases individual bands like the Prairie Ramblers and the Coon Creek Girls with Lily May Ledford began to be widely heard.

So too did a series of individual stars. Clyde J. ("Red") Foley (1910-69) grew up near Berea and by 1930 joined the WLS team. His "Peace in the Valley" would become the first million-seller gospel song, while "Chattanoogie Shoe Shine Boy" was the first country recording to go to the top of the popular music charts. Louis M. ("Grandpa") Jones (b. 1913), born to sharecroppers in Henderson County, toured with Bradley Kincaid and became a regular on the "Grand Ole Opry." Four months after Jones's birth, the performer who became known as Pee Wee King was born in Wisconsin. He later moved to Louisville. While there he composed many of his most popular works, including "Tennessee Waltz," country music's most recorded and most sold song. All three

men would be inducted into the Country Music Hall of Fame. A second wave of performers followed, with Loretta Webb Lynn (b. 1935) of Butcher Hollow in Johnson County being perhaps the best known. Singing of a life that saw her born a "coal miner's daughter," she married at age thirteen and was a mother of four by age eighteen and a grandmother by twenty-nine. In 1972 she was selected as the first female Country Music Association entertainer of the year, and eight years later she was named entertainer of the decade in her field. Others in that second generation included Mary Frances Pennick (b. 1931) of Dry Ridge, who sang as Skeeter Davis; Tom T. Hall (b. 1936) of Olive Hill; and Diana ("Naomi") Judd (b. 1946) of Ashland, who joined with her daughter to perform as the Judds. Newer lights on the music stage include Billy Ray Cyrus and John Michael Montgomery.

Most of the Kentucky-born country music performers found success away from Kentucky, but a study of country music in the state saw that as only one characteristic. Most performers also took a strong sense of place and heritage with them and sang about their experiences, and virtually all used a popular style that made their music readily accessible. The state sent out more than just talented performers; Bluegrass music became, as one writer said, "Kentucky's most famous export." The acknowledged Father of Bluegrass was William S. ("Bill") Monroe (1911-96) of Rosine in Ohio County. Influenced both by Kentucky and Carolina ballads, he perfected the mandolin style and high-pitched rendition that brought success in "Blue Moon of Kentucky" and other tunes. His Blue Grass Boys band was the prototype for the performance of that type of music, and Monroe's twenty-five-million record sales attest to the popularity of the man who also joined the Country Music Hall of Fame. Out of that same tradition came such performers as the Osborne Brothers, J.D. Crowe, Ricky Skaggs, and Merle Travis (also in the Hall of Fame). Don and Phil Everly, as the Everly

Charlie and Bill Monroe of
Rosine, 1936. Bill Monroe is known
as the Father of Bluegrass
(courtesy of the Country Music
Foundation Library).

Brothers, found success in the crossover "rocka-billy" style. By 1980 Kentucky had contributed more "stars" to country music than any other state except Texas.

Coming from a different background but born out of the same human needs were blues and jazz. The so-called Father of the Blues, Alabama-born W.C. Handy, lived in Henderson in the 1890s and wrote later that "there I learned to appreciate the music of my people. . . . The blues were born because from that day on, I started thinking about putting my own experiences down." In Louisville, whose Walnut Street became a scaled-down version of Memphis's Beale Street, similar influences operated on guitarist Sylvester Weaver, trumpeter Jonah Jones, singer Sara Martin, vibraphonist Lionel Hampton, singer Helen Humes (who in 1938 replaced Billie Holiday in the Count Basie band), and a score of other important blues performers. Jazz guitarist Jimmy

Raney proved to be an extraordinary innovator in his field. Yet as in country, many of the best blues and jazz musicians left the state and performed elsewhere.

While all these important new forms were influencing American music, more traditional music continued popular. William S. Hays (1837-1907), a Louisville native who wrote for the *Courier-Journal,* achieved fame as one of the nineteenth century's most popular songwriters. Following in the tradition of Stephen Collins Foster, he wrote gentle, sentimental lyrics, and his more than three hundred songs sold more than twenty million copies. Classical music remained popular through all eras, but not until 1937, when Robert S. Whitney became conductor of what would become the Louisville Orchestra, was there a strong, sustained classical presence in Kentucky. During Whitney's tenure, the orchestra commissioned new music, and the city gained some

339

fame as a musical center. At various times, smaller symphony orchestras also found success in Lexington, Owensboro, Paducah, and elsewhere. Although Louisville's Roland Hays became the first black American to have a successful career as a concert singer, his career represented a rarity for Kentuckians, black or white, in that area.

A meeting place of northern and southern influences, Kentucky produced various kinds of music and musicians. Not all would be appreciated in their times, but the words of one Kentuckian rang true. He said that he would rather listen to Bluegrass than Beethoven, but that did not mean he was uncultured; it only meant that he had different tastes in music than other critics. Some in the state liked one style, some another. There were many musical Kentuckys, and in most of them citizens of the commonwealth made major contributions to the national scene.

Theater, Radio, and Film

Kentucky has attracted and presented plays, in many ways, better than it has produced stage actors and actresses and playwrights. Mary Anderson (1859-1940) of Louisville became internationally known as an actress in the nineteenth century, but she was an exception. Better known were the theaters at which Anderson debuted. Louisville's Macauley's Theatre had opened in 1873 and was one of the first great theaters west of the Appalachian Mountains; it would later present the initial American production of Ibsen's *A Doll's House*. The final play at Macauley's came in 1925, the year the original building was demolished; years afterward, the name would go to another Louisville theater. In some ways more successful was Actors Theatre of Louisville, begun in 1963. Under the direction of Jon Jory and through the annual Humana Festival of New American Plays, it became perhaps the nation's best regional theater. Premieres of works such as Beth Henley's *Crimes of the Heart* and John Pielmeier's *Agnes of God* earned it deserved praise. In 1996 a *Time* magazine article con-

cluded, "From now on, maybe Broadway should be called 'Off-Louisville.'" When combined with such institutions as the Louisville Ballet, one of the oldest such companies in the South, and strong local patronage of the arts, Actors Theatre gave the Falls City and Kentucky a strong cultural presence.

Individuals such as playwright Cleve Kinkead (*Common Play*) and drama critic John Mason Brown, both from Louisville, made an early impression, but not until after 1950 did Kentucky playwrights make a significant impact on the national stage. Louisville's John Patrick (Goggan) (b. 1906) won a Pulitzer Prize for drama in 1953 for *Teahouse of the August Moon* and wrote several successful screen adaptations as well. Thirty years later, another Louisvillian, Marsha Norman (b. 1947), won the same prize for her *'night Mother,* first presented at Actors Theatre. Her other plays, such as *Getting Out* (1977) and *D. Boone* (1992), won acclaim as well. Frankfort's George C. Wolfe (b. 1954) attended an all-black school but found more diversity in New York later when he created the award-winning musical *Jelly's Last Jam* and produced and directed other successful works.

While theater continued to be popular through the years, in the late nineteenth century it had been dominant. Other forms of entertainment came with the twentieth century, radio among them. Louisville's WHAS, owned by the Bingham family, served as the state's major voice over the airwaves after its 1922 opening. In its first two decades WHAS produced much innovative and original programming, but financial demands finally made the station like others across the commonwealth, not dissimilar to those across the country. Other than musical personalities, few national radio figures came forth. Perhaps the best-known was Harlan County's Cawood Ledford (b. 1926), who gained national acclaim for his sports broadcasts.

In the area of motion pictures, Kentucky made a much stronger impact, both as a subject and as an influence on individuals. No more important person appeared than the man called the Father of Film—David Wark Griffith (1875-1948) of Oldham County. Coming from southern roots that included a slaveholding Confederate father, Griffith moved from acting in bit parts to become arguably the most influential director in film history. He changed moviemaking forever. First at the Biograph Company, where he worked with Mary Pickford and Lillian Gish, and then through his own efforts, he made the craft look at itself in new ways. Experiments in camera movement, film length, editing, fade-outs, close-ups, color, and lighting, among other innovations, made him a model for international filmmakers. Yet the brilliant Griffith was a paradox: a man whose most famous and successful film, *The Birth of a Nation* (1915), brought about racial tension and aided in the formation of a new Klan movement, yet who in *Broken Blossoms* (1919) gave a very sensitive and touching treatment of race; a person who made strong and powerful antiwar motion pictures but also a strong film supporting World War I; a Kentuckian who stressed artistic freedom and the evils of bigotry in his masterpiece, the film spectacular *Intolerance* (1916), yet contributed in other films to prejudice. Director of the

first important feature-length film, called "the greatest creative genius that cinema has ever known," D.W. Griffith would have been given even larger later praise had he not reflected his southern, Kentucky racial roots so well. By the 1920s his era had ended, and his last years were spent in alcoholism and poverty, mostly back in the region of his birth. His director's mantle was worn, more imperfectly, by a student of his, Charles A. ("Tod") Browning of Louisville, who directed *Dracula* (1931) with Bela Lugosi, as well as the cult classic *Freaks* (1932). The emphasis on the horror genre would be taken up later by director John Carpenter of Bowling Green.

Numerous actors and actresses with Kentucky ties performed in films over the years, in all kinds of roles, and a listing of some names suggests the variety of talent: Una Merkel of Covington, Irene Dunne of Louisville, Tom Ewell of Owensboro, George Reeves of Ashland and Versailles, Victor Mature of Louisville, William Conrad of Louisville, Oscar-winner Patricia Neal of Packard, Warren Oates of Depoy, Rosemary Clooney of Maysville, Florence Henderson of Owensboro, and Ned Beatty of St. Matthews. More recently, Lily Tomlin of Paducah; Lee Majors of Middlesborough;

D.W. Griffith of Oldham County became an influential film director (courtesy of the Kentucky Historical Society).

Harry Dean Stanton and Jim Varney, both of Lexington; Tom Cruise of Louisville; and Johnny Depp of Owensboro continue the state's long involvement in film.

Yet in many ways, the most important aspect of all was the portrayal of the state in film, through a large number of motion pictures, particularly in the early years of the industry. Four themes resulted from the depiction of Kentucky on celluloid: Land of Plantations, as shown in a series of *Uncle Tom's Cabin* films; Land of Horse Racing, as exemplified in *Kentucky* (1938); Land of Feuds and Moonshine, as presented in dozens of silent movies, several done by D.W. Griffith; and Land of the Pioneer, as portrayed in *The Great Meadow* (1931). To those in the public whose views of the commonwealth were formed chiefly from

the screen, Kentucky came across in stereotypical fashion as either a place of mansions and racehorses or as a home for feuding mountaineers. In fact, in the formative years of the industry, the Appalachian theme dominated, in the same way that Westerns would later. Almost nothing that showed twentieth-century Kentucky, except an occasional Derby, would appear in the films featuring Kentucky, and in the public image the state remained mired in times past, suspended from modern America.

Nevertheless, Kentucky had cultural strengths not usually emphasized. The Kentucky stereotypes seldom included cultural Kentucky, which was a rich resource in many areas of the state. Benighted Kentucky would be the common image, not enlightened Kentucky. The commonwealth's cultural strength, interestingly, would be in areas involving words, in literature, music, and, to a lesser degree, film. The oral traditions, whether in the "phantom books" stories told to Elizabeth Madox Roberts, or the songs sung to Jean Ritchie, or the tales of southern heroism learned by D.W. Griffith, all heavily influenced talented Kentuckians to achieve in their respective areas. Often those people had to leave the state to put all the traditions into perspective, but the most successful built on that heritage and often used it in their work. Some returned with a different outlook and found they actually could go home again, with success. In short, while weak in some areas, Kentucky overall had a long history of solid cultural achievements. These have not been fully appreciated, but at the same time they have proved vitally important in shaping the lives not just of citizens of the commonwealth but also of the nation and, sometimes, of the world.

Catherine Christianson and Gladden Schrock in **D. Boone** by Marsha Norman at Actors Theatre of Louisville (photo by Richard Trigg, courtesy of Actors Theatre of Louisville).

21

The Transitional Twenties

The 1920s were years of transition in Kentucky, not because the state and its people suddenly moved from one era to another, but because citizens of the commonwealth confronted change. In that decade modernism moved into Kentucky, but fundamentalism followed with its own counterattacks. The forces of reform and reaction each won victories, but in the end the state rejected extremes and took a course of conservative moderation. The twenties alerted Kentuckians to what might lie ahead, for modern America could not be totally rejected; the years prepared them for the greater changes coming from the New Deal of the 1930s.

Mindsets, Morals, and Manners

To many Kentuckians, the world after the Great War seemed to be falling apart before their eyes. The rise of Lenin and communism (or Bolshevism, as it was also called) sparked drastic fears of revolt and revolution. In the commonwealth the "Red scare" brought Desha Breckinridge of the *Lexington Herald* to declare that Russian agents in the United States were a greater threat to the nation than the recently defeated German armies had been. Nationally, bombings by anarchists, numerous race riots, the Boston police strike, and then, later, the scandals of the Warren Harding presidency all made chaos seem the norm. Coming after a searing war and the debilitating influenza epidemic, such events suggested little future hope, at least to some. Henry Watterson, now retired from the *Courier-Journal,* was troubled further by Prohibition and woman suffrage—both now in effect. He told a friend in 1920 that "the

343

world is on the way to another collapse. . . . Another Dark Age interlude and another civilization with its strange gods." He predicted that by the year 2013, with the Bolsheviks having dominated Europe, Asia, and Africa, Prohibition "having degenerated America," and the aftereffects of woman suffrage having allowed females to dominate males, "the flag will drop," and all would be lost.

Others saw the situation differently. While they did not approve of the violence or the manner in which change was coming, they did see a need to move on from one era to another. As one Kentucky youth wrote later, after the Great War "henceforth forever the door was closed to innocence." The thoughtful author Elizabeth Madox Roberts concluded in a later letter to a friend, "It was about that time the great change came to all places." Some of that change, such as electricity, was welcomed. Other aspects of change were debated, and elements of the population opposed certain alterations. When the twentieth century finally knocked on the doors of many Kentuckians, they hesitated to answer.

In 1910 Kentuckians had lived generally as had those of a half century earlier. Out of a population of 2,289,905 in 1910, 88 percent had been born in Kentucky; only 40,000 residents were foreign-born. Kentuckians had only begun to be touched by new currents of change sweeping the nation. By 1920, however, those waves were proving harder to resist, if resistance was even sought. For the rest of the century, change would come quicker and quicker, giving each generation less time to adapt. Kentuckians, like other Americans, had to try to keep the best of their past and reconcile tradition with change, while not slipping into a blind resistance to anything new or an equally sightless acceptance of all that was fashionable. Hard decisions lay ahead.

For much of Kentucky, the new era of the twenties affected the citizenry only little. Rural and some small-town populations remained similar in certain ways to their earlier counterparts; even some people in larger urban areas changed little. Yet everyone saw or heard about the new ideas, the fresh outlooks, and the different lifestyles that were becoming the pattern for the United States. Many did not like what they saw.

All the old rules of conduct seemed to be modified, particularly for women. Now the national model appeared to be the youthful "flapper," with her short skirts, boyish figure, rouge-covered face, and bobbed hair. She smoked a cigarette (the first advertisements focusing on women appeared in 1919), drank illegal whiskey and bathtub gin, and danced strange new dances to the sensuous tones of the saxophone. All these trends at least touched Kentucky. A girl at Bethel Woman's College in Hopkinsville was expelled for bobbing her hair. Another woman recalled that when her schoolteacher mother began wearing pants in the early 1920s, that action aroused much negative comment: "And, oh, it was bad when she started riding her horse astride instead of side-saddle!" The dance crazes that featured the bunny hop, turkey trot, fox trot, tango, and Charleston could earn admiration for agile participants, as one girl noted in her diary: "Mills sure can knock off the Black Bottom." But they also brought censure from numerous places. A member of a central Kentucky Purity League had earlier denounced the "sin-crazed age" with its dances "and all the other twists and squirms," and speakers in numerous church pulpits continued to echo those sentiments. As late as 1930 a Baptist congregation in Paducah split when members were suspended for dancing, card playing, and attending motion pictures. Three years later a Kentucky Birth Control League was organized in Louisville, with Jean Brandeis Tachau as its president.

Many blamed the automobile and the movie theater for what they saw as the problems of the state. Kentucky had 127,500 motor vehicles in 1921, and if the popular press was to be believed, every one of those conveyances was the scene of "petting parties." Almost as bad were the very popular motion picture shows,

The "modern" woman and the "sinful" automobile both worried some Kentuckians in the 1920s (courtesy of AAA Kentucky).

sparked by the innovations of D.W. Griffith and the beginning of the star system. Regular theater with its "scanty attire" had long been criticized, but the widespread availability of film and the 1920s subject matter added to the fault-finding. A judge declared that "the majority of delinquent boys are movie fiends," while a state senator tried (and failed) to set up a censorship board to control viewing. The films went on, and by 1925 moviegoers of the newly emancipated age were viewing, without restriction, such fare as *The Painted Flapper, Eve's Secret* ("Love in a Modern Eden and He Learned about Women from Her"), and *I Want My Man.*

The new mass-media culture propelled sports into the national spotlight as well. In Kentucky, the Derby became a national event, so that Irvin S. Cobb could proclaim, "Until you go to Kentucky and with your own eyes behold the Derby, you ain't never been nowheres and you ain't never seen nothin'!" Across the United States, boxing, tennis, golf, football, and, most of all, baseball were also avidly followed, and fans cheered their favorite heroes and teams. Kentuckians supported John D. ("Jughandle Johnny") Morrison of Owensboro, a pitcher who won more than a hundred games, with his best year in 1923; Liberty's Carl Mays, a pitcher whose submarine delivery won him more than twenty games a year five times in the 1915-29 period; outfielder Bobby Veach of McLean County, who played with Ty Cobb and from 1912 to 1925 had more than two thousand hits; Maysville's Don Hurst, who averaged over .300 from 1929 to 1932 and led

the 1932 league in runs batted in; and outfielder Earle B. Combs of Owsley County, who batted over .300 nine times and led the league in numerous categories while in the Yankees' "Murderers' Row" lineup that included Babe Ruth. For his feats, Combs, called the Gray Fox, would become the state's first Hall of Famer in baseball. The widespread interest in sports also affected colleges and high schools, where organized sports became a more important part of activities, although not always with unanimous approval. The University of Kentucky held the first night football game in the state in 1930, and the rise in interest in basketball came soon after that. Big-time sports had invaded the commonwealth. As the years passed the focus on sports would bring positive and negative results, but in the 1920s few questioned the trend.

Mass communications also meant that what might formerly have remained isolated incidents now became international spectacles. One Kentucky case illustrated that phenomenon vividly. On January 30, 1925, an obscure thirty-seven-year-old explorer named Floyd Collins became stuck and partially buried in Sand Cave, not far from Mammoth Cave. Efforts to rescue him gained national attention, and a young *Courier-Journal* reporter, William B. ("Sheets") Miller, would win a Pulitzer Prize for crawling into the narrow shaft and talking to Collins. But the whole matter resembled a carnival, as cutthroat on-site radio reporters vied with sensational print journalists while a young Charles Lindbergh flew film from Kentucky to waiting urban centers. Bal-

345

lads were composed in what students of the matter have called "one of the first truly *national* media events." In a rescue dig complicated by arguments over strategy and command responsibility, workers finally reached Collins some two weeks after he had been trapped; he had been dead three days. Later the body was removed and placed in a glass-covered coffin for tourists to view in another cavern. Robbers stole the corpse a few years afterward, but Collins's remains, minus a leg, were recovered, to go on display again. Only much later did the body find the solitude of a grave. Collins in his lone explorations had joined what in the 1920s was a "floodtime for heroes."

The Counterattack: Evolution and the Klan

By the early 1920s some Kentucky places of worship, chiefly in urban areas, had accepted a liberal theology that sought to reconcile science and Darwinian theory with religious teachings. In other churches, however, observers found very different outlooks. Two studies of mountain religion both stressed the supernatural and superstitious aspects of worship there, for instance, and across the state a strong conservative strain dominated, producing defenders of traditional theology. Out of this milieu a militant evangelicalism emerged. Protestant fundamentalists saw evolution as the key reason that American society had strayed so far from the righteous path, and they sought to correct the situation.

As early as 1900 the evolution issue had provoked controversy, for author James Lane Allen had defended his religious questioning in *Reign of Law* before attacks from a theology school president. By 1921 Baptist minister John W. Porter of Lexington led a fight to purge evolution from schools. His book *Evolution: A Menace* (1921) implored that Christ "shall not be crucified on the cross of a false philosophy, called evolution," while his church's Board of Missions resolved to enact laws to stop the teaching of such a "false and degrading theory." Former presidential candidate William

Jennings Bryan pledged his aid when he spoke in the state that year, and he returned the next January to address a joint legislative session. A day after Bryan's talk, bills were introduced in each house of the General Assembly to prohibit the teaching of "Darwinism, Atheism, Agnosticism, or the Theory of Evolution." Kentucky had become the first state where fundamentalists had enough power to propose antievolution bills. The fight was on.

Later, in some other southern states, key leaders stood aside when the issue arose, doing little. In Kentucky the governor stayed out of the fight, but others in opposition did not. Their involvement, their willingness to take a chance, made a difference. Three men played the most important roles. Two religious leaders, Dr. E.L. Powell of Louisville's First Christian Church and Dr. E.Y. Mullins, president of the Southern Baptist Theological Seminary in Louisville, spoke before the General Assembly in opposition to the antievolution bill and showed the diversity of religious thought on the issue. Dr. Frank L. McVey, president of the University of Kentucky, said forthrightly in a public letter that evolution was taught at his school, for failure to do so would make the university a laughingstock in the scientific community. He did add, however, that "there is no conflict between the theory of evolution and the Christian view." Backed by leading state newspapers, all three men called for tolerance and for the separation of church and state.

In March 1922 the antievolution bill in the Kentucky House came up for a vote. A tie resulted, and each side rushed to find a representative willing to break the 41-41 deadlock. Breathitt County legislator Bryce Cundiff finally cast the deciding ballot that defeated the bill. The next year Kentucky Wesleyan College suspended a faculty member for his support of evolution; in 1925 Paducah-born and University of Kentucky–educated John T. Scopes became the center of attention as the defendant in the famous "Monkey Trial" in Dayton, Tennessee. In 1926 and again in 1928, antievolution bills introduced in the Kentucky General

Assembly went nowhere. With that the effort ended, at least for many decades. A religiously conservative state, Kentucky had been the first major battleground in the antievolution fight, but in the end it had beaten back the forces of anti-intellectualism, time after time. Ironically, about the same time, another Kentuckian, Dr. Thomas Hunt Morgan (1866-1945), was leading a Columbia University research team in fruit fly experiments that strengthened the genetic theory behind evolution. A great-grandson of Francis Scott Key and a nephew of Confederate general John Hunt Morgan, Thomas Morgan had grown up in Lexington and had received a master's degree from the present-day University of Kentucky, before leaving the state for further schooling and research elsewhere. His efforts culminated in a Nobel Prize in 1933. Home of evolutionists and antievolutionists, Kentucky continued to be a place of contrasting views.

At the same time the antievolution forces were declining from their peak strength, another group began rising to oppose the forces of change in America. The so-called second Ku Klux Klan, in the words of historian David Chalmers, "was reborn in the war-time, weaned during the immediate post-war unrest." Partially stimulated by Griffith's 1915 film *The Birth of a Nation,* the group represented a protest against modernism and gave voice to the belief that only white Protestant Anglo-Saxons should guide the nation's fortunes. While it included blacks on its list of enemies, as the earlier KKK did, the revived Klan focused even more on immigrants, Catholics, and Jews.

Given the composition of Kentucky's population, the state did not appear to be particularly fertile ground for the rapidly growing movement. In 1926 the commonwealth's religious census enumerated 126,000 Catholics and 15,000 Jews, and the two groups together comprised only about 8 percent of the adult population. Moreover, while prejudice against both groups had been periodically evident throughout Kentucky's history, so too had acceptance. For a decade beginning in 1871, Paducah's mayor had been Jewish, and when Somerset was incorporated as a city in 1888, its first mayor was of that faith as well. But other than in Louisville, the number of Jews in the state was minuscule. The same held true for the foreign-born, for immigrants made up less than 2 percent of the commonwealth's population.

Thomas Hunt Morgan won a Nobel Prize in 1933 for his research in genetics (courtesy of the J. Winston Coleman Photographic Collection, Transylvania University Library).

Blacks constituted a somewhat more sizable bloc—9.5 percent of the population in 1920—but in recent decades they had experienced declining rights and increasing segregation rather than successful challenges to the emerging racial status quo. The 1892 act segregating railroad cars had been the beginning of a series of formal actions that made the black and white worlds even more separate. Such changes did not take place all at once, but gradually. Both races had used Henderson's city park for years, but in 1903 blacks were restricted to one area only. In Lexington in 1916 and Louisville in 1924, parks for blacks only replaced the formerly integrated system of sharing pools, tennis courts, and baseball fields. In the Kentucky Derby, blacks had ridden fifteen of the first twenty-eight winners, but after 1911 the race became an all-white affair. Memories grew dim of three-time winner Isaac Murphy, who took his mount to victory in 44 percent of all his rides. By the mid-1920s, then, Kentucky had segregated racing, transportation, parks, hotels, theaters, library systems, orphans' homes, restaurants, funeral parlors, and more. Louisville's police force, fire fighters, and jail employees had become segregated by 1890. In other areas, such as juries, blacks were excluded altogether. Segregation had planted deep roots in Kentucky soil, and blacks reasonably wondered whether their rights would wither away further in the future.

In some places increased segregation was not enough. Night Riders had earlier forced blacks out of parts of western Kentucky, and in 1919 the actions shifted eastward. In October an armed mob of some 150 whites in Corbin, angered by rumors of an attack by blacks on a white man, seized itinerant railroad workers in the dark of night, placed them in a barricaded area ("like cattle," one recalled), then forced them to board a train and leave town. Between two and three hundred black residents left; only a few elderly people remained. Less spectacularly but just as effectively, through various means, other towns did the same over time and proudly boasted of their whiteness.

The victories won by blacks proved even more significant, given the climate in which they occurred. Weak attempts by whites to take away the vote all failed, for instance, although violence and gerrymandered districts sometimes gave the desired effect. In 1914 Louisville and other Kentucky cities passed segregation ordinances that forbade both blacks and whites from buying homes in areas where the other race predominated. A Kentuckian by birth, the wealthy William English Walling had, more than perhaps anyone, been responsible for founding the National Association for the Advancement of Colored People (NAACP) in 1910. Now a branch opened in Louisville, and C.H. Buchanan, a white man, and William Warley, a black man, brought a test case of the segregation ordinance. Eventually heard by the U.S. Supreme Court as *Buchanan v. Warley* (1917), the case resulted in the Court's rejection of the Louisville ordinance, in a rare national victory in that era for black rights. Warley's action cost him his job at the post office. Victories took their toll.

Such successes were few for blacks, but despite that and despite the relatively small numbers of immigrants, Jews, and Catholics in Kentucky, the newly formed KKK spoke out about the supposed threat to the United States from such groups. But the Klan never found Kentucky a very comfortable home. Indiana to the north was a center of Ku Klux activity, and the Klavens were strong to the south, but the Klan philosophy never took hold in the Bluegrass State as strongly as in those areas. The KKK did have strength and influence: a contemporary estimate placed membership at fifty thousand to two hundred thousand, very likely an overestimate. More recently a historian suggested that thirty thousand Kentuckians joined the Klan's ranks. The Klan did gain support, as rallies drawing crowds of five thousand or more took place in communities as diverse as Paintsville in the east and Owensboro in the west. The message came through clearly in a document issued by the Warren County Klan: "We believe in the Protestant Christian Religion;

348

White Supremacy; Separation of Church and State." It portrayed Jews and Catholics—"these representatives of the Pope"—as controlling Bowling Green's government and called for "pure blooded 100% American" rule.

As in the antievolution fight, however, Kentucky leaders spoke out against the Klan, often at some political risk. In Lexington, Owensboro, Louisville, Pulaski County, Hopkins County, Laurel County, and elsewhere, judges, mayors, and city council members either publicly attacked the KKK or refused to allow its members to meet on public property. A similar stance by Paducah mayor Wynn Tulley showed the dangers inherent in such a position: he alone on the Democratic ticket did not win reelection in 1923. Still, when the minister who had authored *The Kall of the Klan in Kentucky* (1924) spoke, he found little official sympathy. Owensboro arrested him on conspiracy charges (later dropped), and similar harassing activities dogged him as he spoke across the state, blaming the ills of the United States on blacks and aliens. By the last half of the 1920s, inept and corrupt national leadership, violent actions, and an unresponsive citizenry in Kentucky had brought the Invisible Empire to its knees. It would have lingering influence for a time in some places, but the Klan's effect on the state, though significant, had been brief.

As the world around them continued to change, some Kentuckians still worried about the ways all that was occurring. Longing for an aristocratic control as in days of old, W.G. Clugston wrote in 1925 in H.L. Mencken's *American Mercury* magazine about "the collapse of Kentucky." Arguing that "the manners, the customs and the ideals of the people are so completely altered that there is little left of the old stripes and patterns," he concluded that "every circle of society is changed." In reality, however, while certain old traditions had been modified or even lost, some had adjusted to the new era and had emerged even stronger. Others remained virtually untouched. Despite all the fears and concerns, Kentucky had not fallen

apart when confronting modernism. In fact, some of the constant nature of the state showed very clearly—unfortunately—in the politics of the twenties.

Bosses, the Bipartisan Combine, and the Governors

In May 1919 A.O. Stanley had resigned the governorship to take a seat in the U.S. Senate, thus making Lieutenant Governor James D. Black (1849-1938) of Knox County the chief executive of the commonwealth. Governor Black immediately set about to win election to a full four-year term, but he had to face the popular, barely defeated 1915 candidate Edwin P. Morrow (1877-1935). Black ran a weak, careful campaign, defending Stanley's "wet" views and overall record and President Wilson's handling of a coal strike; he lost handily, receiving 214,114 votes to Morrow's 254,290. In December 1919 Morrow became the fourth Republican inaugurated as governor since 1895; in that same time, five Democrats had served in the office. The two-party system seemed strong in Kentucky.

Yet as Morrow and other governors elected during the next decade would discover, "party" was a fluid concept in the 1920s, and the real power centers remained not the voting booths but the headquarters of the political bosses, who had their greatest influence in those years. Moreover, new players were joining the political game, and they would bring to the table more money and different agendas, further complicating elections. The two most visible of the fresh faces were James B. Brown and Robert Worth Bingham, both Louisville millionaires.

Bingham had grown up and been mostly educated in North Carolina, and he had come to Kentucky following a marriage that would later end tragically in a train accident. He had served as county attorney, as an appointed short-term mayor of Louisville, and as an appointed judge, afterward operating for a time as a political independent, supporting one party or the other. The defining moment in his life came following the death of his newly married second wife in 1917. One of the wealthiest women in the United States, she left Bingham five million dollars, to the surprise of her family. The circumstances of her death brought rumors from Bingham's enemies, and while nothing criminal had occurred, the stories would haunt the Binghams for decades. Bingham used part of his inherited wealth to purchase the *Louisville Courier-Journal;* he allied with former governor Beckham and the political boss Percy Haly (who went on the newspaper's payroll) and formed a faction in the Democratic Party. Aristocratic in bearing, with a stable of polo ponies and dozens of purebred hunting dogs, Bingham loved things British, used his wealth to aid friends and good causes and to oppose enemies, and represented a curious combination of reformer and conservative.

Bingham's one-time ally and later opponent, Jim Brown (1872-1940), had fewer paradoxes. Kentucky-born, he had worked his way up through the banking ranks, with the help of boss John Whallen, and had made millions. "Colorful, careless, and reckless," Brown would take friends to casinos at French Lick, Indiana, and pay their gambling losses. He once spent fifty-nine thousand dollars in one outing. Working into the night, sleeping, vampirelike, in the day, he too purchased newspapers—the *Louisville Herald* and the *Louisville Post*—and combined them to give him a voice to oppose Bingham. Brown led the largest financial institution south of the Ohio River, and the two very rich men soon became factional political enemies.

Meanwhile, all around them, the behind-the-scenes power brokers—Ben Johnson, J. Dan Talbott, Billy Klair, Allie Young, Mickey Brennan, Maurice Galvin, and Thomas Rhea, among others—still dominated, still made deals. That so-called invisible government offered the real key to electoral success.

Operating in such an atmosphere, Morrow had to tread carefully, but he did have some success. Unlike previous Republican governors, he had control of the House, and he persuaded a Democratic senator to defect, creating a party balance in the upper house. A tie in the Senate could be broken by vote of the Republican lieutenant governor. Still, Morrow faced a legislature torn by factionalism, regionalism, and bickering. By his second legislative session, he also had a Democratic-controlled General Assembly—with the first woman legislator, Mary E. Flanery, in it—and had to deal with a hostile political party. Still, Morrow had a fairly productive term, despite his veto of much-

Robert Worth Bingham (*left*) stands beside President Calvin Coolidge in 1925, eight years before Franklin D. Roosevelt appointed Bingham as ambassador to Great Britain (courtesy of the *Louisville Courier-Journal*).

A Lexington mob surges forward just before shots were fired in the Will Lockett riot, 1920 (courtesy of the J. Winston Coleman Photographic Collection, Transylvania University Library).

needed additional appropriations for the University of Kentucky and his silence during the antievolution fight. His administration ratified the woman suffrage amendment and created a bipartisan Board of Charities and Corrections and two new teacher-training colleges for whites at Morehead and Murray. A one-cent per gallon gasoline tax (the fifth in the nation) helped finance road projects, while a racetrack levy supported an increase in teachers' salaries. Convict labor was prohibited in highway construction, a Child Welfare Commission was established, and the tobacco cooperative movement was aided. Indicating the search for nostalgia in an era of change, a monument to Jefferson Davis in Fairview was authorized, and Federal Hill in Bardstown, known as My Old Kentucky Home, was purchased by the state.

Some of Morrow's finest moments as governor, however, concerned blacks in Kentucky and took place outside the halls of the capitol. In February 1920 a black man named Will Lockett was arrested for the murder of a white woman, and rumors of an attempted lynching were heard. Morrow provided a National Guard force to protect the prisoner, and

Lockett stood trial in Lexington. A large crowd faced the soldiers as the court heard testimony. According to one account, a cameraman called on the some four thousand citizens to "shake your fists and yell" for his pictures. But as they did so, others took up the action, and the mob surged forward, intent on taking Lockett. The Guard opened fire, killing six people and wounding perhaps fifty more. Army veterans from Camp Taylor soon joined the Guard, and martial law was established. Meanwhile, Lockett was convicted, in a trial characterized chiefly by its brevity, and was later executed. The national press, however, praised the "Second Battle of Lexington" for showing that "Lynchers Don't Like Lead." Law had triumphed over the mob. An antilynching law was passed by the legislature, and during the next four years, four county officials in four different places were removed from office when they allowed mobs to take prisoners from their jails. Those prisoners had been killed, however, and the people responsible for their deaths had gone free. The state still had a long way to go to rid itself of lawlessness. The Lockett affair had sent a strong signal to the South, but even in Kentucky not everyone got the message.

351

Kentuckians did listen to the siren song of politics, as usual. The key issue in the early 1920s seemed to be whether Morrow's win had been a personal rather than a party triumph, or whether the Republican Party had become a consistent challenger to the Democrats. Election results gave a mixed response. In 1920 and 1922 Republicans won only three of eleven congressional seats but did capture Louisville's, showing that the party had become, in Walter Baker's later words, a "coalition of rich and poor, black and white, town and mountain." In the presidential race of 1920 Kentucky's electoral votes went to Democratic choice James M. Cox, who barely edged out fellow Ohioan and eventual winner Republican Warren G. Harding by 4,000 votes, 456,497-452,480. In the first election in which all Kentucky women could vote, the state had resisted the Republican presidential tide that swept over the other border states.

Kentucky also led the nation in voter turnout, when 71.2 percent of its citizens voted, including a large number of women. The votes of women may have been significant in the one other important race in 1920, that for U.S. senator. Incumbent J.C.W. Beckham had not achieved an impressive record. He also had not voted on the suffrage issue and in a private letter had called the extension of the franchise to women "a serious mistake." Sensing Beckham's vulnerability, Republicans put forth a virtually untested wealthy corporation lawyer who worked in Cincinnati but lived in Covington. His workplace plus the fact that his mentor, boss Maurice Galvin, was brother to the Cincinnati mayor made critics argue that Richard P. Ernst (1858-1934) sought to be Ohio's third senator. Attacking the League of Nations as "unjust and un-American," the Republican sought to capitalize on postwar discontent, Beckham's weakness on suffrage, and Democratic factionalism. Aided by some questionable late returns from the mountains, Ernst won the race by 5,000 votes, 454,226-449,244.

The real test of Republican strength would come in the attempt to win the governor's race two times in a row with two different candidates. As it turned out, such a double victory would not occur in the twentieth century. Democrats appeared confident that 1923 would be their year, and each of the factions put forth a strong candidate. The acknowledged front-runner, J. Campbell Cantrill of Scott County, had long served in Congress, where he had opposed suffrage and Prohibition, and had been a leader in the central Kentucky tobacco cooperative fight. The old Stanley wing and most of the veteran politicians supported Cantrill.

The challenger also came from Congress but represented western Kentucky and the small farmers of the protest movements there. Paducah's Alben W. Barkley (1877-1956) would become well known, but during the 1923 Democratic primary race he was a forty-five-year-old relative newcomer to the state scene. When Barkley, in an unusual move for Kentucky, actually took stances on controversial issues, he shaped the race. Chastising the labor and railroad lobbies, attacking the racing interests by promising to end pari-mutuel betting, and calling for a production tax on coal, Barkley brought the Bingham, Beckham, and Haly triumvirate to his side. But most of the other bosses stood behind the conservative Cantrill, and Barkley's definition of the issues united the eastern half of the state against him.

Born in a log cabin, Barkley would become the dominant state politician in the twentieth century. He was already showing the strengths that would win him election after election. A reporter in 1923 saw him as "the most vigorous personal campaigner and speech-maker ever seen in Kentucky." Barkley, called the Iron Man, gave ten to fourteen speeches a day. As a later writer noted, Barkley could turn a speech "delivered from the bed of a hay wagon into something resembling the Sermon on the Mount." But that was not enough in 1923, and Barkley lost the primary by nine thousand votes, the only defeat of his career. In a regional outcome, he won almost all the counties west of a line running from Louisville to Middlesborough, while Cantrill carried almost all the counties east of there.

When Cantrill died of a ruptured appendix soon after the primary, however, a new nominee had to be selected by the Democratic state committee, under Jim Brown's control. It chose Congressman William J. Fields (1874-1954). Known as Honest Bill from Olive Hill, the onetime traveling salesman had a good voting record and few enemies. His Republican opposition, Attorney General Charles I. Dawson of Bell County, had once been a Democrat, and Dawson's attempts to tar Fields with the appellation "Dodging Bill from Olive Hill, who answers no questions and never will" were matched by Fields, who labeled Dawson "Changing Charley." The race ended with an easy Democratic win: Fields garnered 356,035 votes to Dawson's 306,277.

Fields came to office without a great deal of respect, for he owed his selection to Cantrill's death and his election to a weak opposition. He did not help his situation by his actions. On the day of his inaugural, Fields, a simple man, prohibited any dancing in the executive mansion; later his frugality caused him to keep dairy cows on the lawn of the governor's house. Both acts brought condescending sneers from urban critics. A wider group condemned Fields's nepotism. As the term wore on, Fields reacted to the *Courier-Journal*'s attacks by responding in petty public letters that discredited their author. Finally, even though Fields was an honest man pursuing worthy goals, he could never disengage himself completely from the bosses who backed him.

From the very beginning of Fields's term, it seemed that the factions and parties were using the time to rehearse for the 1927 gubernatorial show. With Beckham early seen as a candidate, Bingham's paper and the allies of the onetime Boy Governor began to paint a picture of a corrupt force that transcended party and

had to be stopped. They called their opposition the bipartisan combine. In truth, various groups were working to protect their own turf, whether that involved racing, coal, or other interests. But such activity rarely took place as a formal, concerted conspiracy; rather, those with the common enemy of Beckham, Bingham, and Haly generally coalesced in an informal way. Thus, both Democratic factions actually had elements of reform and reaction within, and both sought the same end—power.

All that is not to say that the Jockey Club was not a formidable foe, for it was. The state's Racing Commission, formed in 1906, quickly outlawed the then-prevalent betting practice of bookmaking and replaced it with pari-mutuel wagering. In 1918 prominent men—including, initially, Bingham—had formed the state Jockey Club as a further aid to a thoroughbred industry under siege. By the 1920s only three states still had legal betting at racetracks. But as the attacks on racing increased, so too did the Jockey Club's response to them. Like the L&N lobby before, the monopolist Jockey Club grew more powerful. At one time the club reputedly had thirty legislators on its payroll.

Standing in opposition were forces that emerged from both the earlier crusades for Prohibition and the new moral concerns of the 1920s. Urban reformers joined religious fundamentalists and some Klansmen in support of a strong anti–pari-mutuel gambling movement. The supporters of this movement wished to end betting at tracks and to cleanse the body politic of what was seen as a corrupting influence. Lotteries had been abolished in the 1890s; perhaps now gambling at racetracks could follow.

All of the forces operating in the decade seemed to come together in 1924. In the legislature a bill to outlaw pari-mutuel betting passed the House easily but lost by a 14-24 split party count in the Senate. By a 10-vote margin the state retained racing. That controversial issue was matched by an attempt to change the composition of the Board of Charities and

Corrections from a bipartisan makeup to a partisan one, and to give the governor, not the board, the power to select those heading the various institutions.

The state supported a series of eleemosynary places—the Eastern, Western, and Central State Asylums for the Insane, two Houses of Reform, a Home for Incurables, the Institution for the Education and Training of Feeble-Minded Children, the Kentucky Children's Home Society, the Kentucky Home Society for Colored Children, the Kentucky Institution for the Education of Deaf-Mutes, and the Kentucky Confederate Home. Segregated, always underfunded, usually overcrowded, these institutions faced continual problems. In 1901, for example, the Eastern Kentucky Asylum for the Insane noted that it had annually received $200 per patient up to 1880 but only $150 since 1895. Thirteen percent of the patients at the Central Kentucky Asylum died in one twelve-month period. In that same year of 1901, seventy-five of the pupils at the state school for the deaf in Danville had to sleep on mattresses placed in hallways. A 1901 report stated that at Frankfort, where the mentally retarded were housed, males came on the grounds to "enter into contacts unholy" with unsuspecting females there. The auditor's office also complained about the "costly and dangerous" practice of paying seventy-five dollars annually to individuals to take care of "pauper idiots" in their homes. By the mid-1920s most of those matters had improved only marginally.

Symbolic of attempts to reform, modernize, and professionalize the state's institutions was what was happening in the prisons. Since Governor Blackburn's time, some changes had occurred, but problems remained. One study reported in 1921 that 41 percent of the inmates at the Frankfort prison had syphilis, that sanitation continued to be poor, and that overcrowding in the "Black Hole of Kentucky" persisted. The whipping post had been abolished only in 1913. In 1920 Joseph P. Byers, a respected national authority, had been chosen

as commissioner of public institutions to bring needed change. He hired expert non-Kentuckians for some key professional jobs, fired one warden, and generally tried to remove the prisons from the game of political patronage. Byers's activity angered political figures who used the prison spoils system to reward supporters and who assessed contributions from those employees. They almost gleefully used against Byers a 1923 riot at Eddyville, which left three officers dead. More than twenty-five thousand rounds had been fired before military men found one prisoner dead and two others the victims of a suicide pact. In the 1924 legislature a bill sought to remove Byers, and despite opposition from all the state's major newspapers, it barely failed to pass, by a 44-46 count. Not pleased at the prospects for his future, Byers resigned the next year. Significant change in the prison system came slowly.

When Governor Fields proposed a seventy-five-million-dollar bond issue to build highways, provide additional money to education and the prisons, and eliminate the state debt, with funding coming from a road and gasoline tax, he expected support. Instead he got opposition, particularly from one faction of his own party. Seeing boss Billy Klair as a man active in road bonding, fearing "a lifetime burden of taxation," and distrusting the placement of so much money in Fields's hands, Bingham and the *Courier-Journal* faction strongly opposed the idea. The ensuing debate grew bitter. The governor called the editor a "carpet-bagger from North Carolina," while the *Lexington Herald* asked, "Can't we be pros for a little while instead of perpetual antis?" People in the mountains, with their poor roads, particularly spoke out for the bond issue, which in truth would have provided the state a needed influx of funding. The General Assembly passed the decision to the voters, setting up a referendum in the fall elections.

Those 1924 elections would prove to be important ones for Kentucky. The Senate race found incumbent A.O. Stanley opposed by the "dry" forces (who had a long memory) and the "dry" governor of his own party, by the Ku Klux Klan, and by a handsome, wealthy, and well-educated former New Englander who had never held elective office. Republican Frederic M. Sackett Jr. had married into the prominent Speed family of Louisville and had gained the support of the *Courier-Journal* and Stanley's old enemies, Beckham and Haly. No Kentucky senator had won reelection in some forty years, a writer declared. Would that situation change now? The presidential race did not help Stanley a great deal either. Democrat John W. Davis stirred little enthusiasm, although his opponent, Calvin Coolidge, hardly proved a campaign dynamo either. Still, the presence of Progressive Party candidate Robert M. La Follette suggested that both parties would lose votes to him.

The results of the 1924 elections shocked some Kentuckians. For the second time ever, a Republican carried the state in the presidential race: Coolidge received 398,966 votes, and Davis got 374,855. La Follette gathered 38,465 votes, mostly among laborers in the cities and coal counties. With apathy prevalent, voter turnout fell greatly from the 1920 level. The results in the Senate race were similar to the presidential contest: Democrat Stanley lost to Sackett, 381,623-406,141. As the loser had said of Sackett, "His ten millions are a power." In March 1925 Kentucky would have two Republican senators. The bond issue, garnering 275,863 votes for, 374,328 against, went down to defeat. Kentucky would have to "pay as you go," though it might not go very far as a result. Only in the congressional races, in which new House member Frederick M. Vinson won, did the faction-ridden Democrats hold fast. A Republican tide, aided by Democratic divisions, had swept the state.

If anything, the 1920s showed that political currents could change rapidly. The 1925 city elections in Louisville proved so corrupt that the winning Republicans were later swept from office by a court decision. Then on January 11, 1926, Republican congressman John W. Langley of Pikeville formally resigned his seat

after the U.S. Supreme Court upheld his conviction for violating the Prohibition laws. Paroled that same year, he published a book entitled *They Tried to Crucify Me* (1929). The evidence, however, suggested that "Pork Barrel John" had accepted a bribe in order to assist in the withdrawal and eventual illegal sale of more than a million gallons of bourbon whiskey. If his district's voters could not reelect John Langley, they could select his politically astute wife, Katherine G. Langley. In 1927 she became the state's first (and the nation's eighth) female member of Congress. She would serve for four years. The electorate seemed to be all too forgiving of political corruption.

To the man challenging Republican incumbent senator Ernst in 1926, such developments proved fortuitous. Congressman Alben Barkley saw that "Coolidge prosperity" had not touched Kentucky as much as elsewhere and that his opponent had little popular appeal. Ernst's opposition to a bonus for veterans, his age (twenty years older than Barkley), and his lack of support for fellow party member Langley during his legal troubles all hurt. But the key factor was Democratic unity. Members of one faction wanted Barkley to win so they could be victorious; supporters of the other faction wanted him to win so they could get him out of the state, out of the way in Washington. That combination brought victory to Barkley and the Democrats by a 20,000-vote margin, 286,997-266,657. But the party's "love feast" of 1926 was soon over.

Beckham and Betting

Now, finally, the curtain raised on the 1927 governor's race. As expected, Beckham's hat flew into the ring, and his faction backed that action wholeheartedly. In fact, A.O. Stanley, defeated by Sackett in 1924 and angry at Governor Fields for his role in the loss, even announced that he would support his old and bitter enemy Beckham. But powerful Democrats, including those allied with the racing and mining interests, as well as the governor, backed the Canadian-born former Speaker of

the Kentucky House, Robert T. Crowe of Oldham County. Nevertheless, the better-known
Beckham, winning heavily in western Kentucky, took the primary by nearly twenty-four
thousand votes.

On the Republican side stood Flem D.
Sampson (1875-1967) of Knox County. A college roommate, then a law partner, of Goebel
conspiracy figure Caleb Powers, Sampson had
been chief justice of the state's highest court
and had the full backing of mountain Republicans. He offered free textbooks, opposed the
tonnage tax on coal, indicated that the pari-
mutuel issue should be a legislative matter, and
generally tried to avoid controversy: "I'm just
plain old Flem. When I'm elected Governor of
Kentucky, come into my office and sit down
and say 'Howdy Flem!'" Beckham Democrats,
in turn, said the Republican should be called
"Flim-Flam Flem" instead, and their candidate
made the differences between himself and
Sampson clear as he again called for an end to
racetrack betting. Ironically, the pari-mutuel
bill had its origins in Beckham's own gubernatorial administration, and his opposition
pointed out the reversals on the issue by both
Beckham and Bingham. But the onetime Boy
Governor countered with attacks on the Jockey
Club lobby, suggesting that it was pouring large
sums of money into Sampson's campaign coffers. Many of Beckham's fellow Democrats,
including Governor Fields, Billy Klair, and Jim
Brown, deserted their party's candidate as the
issue became clear. Would it be Beckham or
betting?

When the results came in, every Democrat was elected except one—J.C.W. Beckham.
Sampson won easily, 399,698-367,567, as
Democrats had split their tickets. But making
certain that the rest of the Democratic field
won may have taken much hard work manipu-
lating the returns, since the margins in those
races were microscopic. Lieutenant Governor
James Breathitt Jr. won by 159 votes out of
more than 700,000 cast, for example. There
may not have been any formal agreements
that anti-Beckham Democrats would vote for a

Republican as governor in exchange for taking
the rest of the offices, and there likewise may
not have been a formal bipartisan combine.
Nonetheless, the racing and coal interests and,
indeed, the Republicans seemed pleased with
the outcome. Beckham was beaten.

The new governor quickly discovered
that any coalition that had existed during
the race slowly vanished amid the reality of
partisan politics. Initially, though, the situation looked strong for the Republicans. The
national Democratic nomination of Al Smith
of New York, with his "wet" views, ties to the
Tammany Hall "machine," eastern accent, and,
most of all, Catholic religion, made the 1928
presidential campaign a very difficult one for
the state party. Sampson asked voters to select
Herbert Hoover "if you want to preserve the
churches." Senator Barkley, who seconded
Smith's nomination, recalled later that the religious issue split Democrats "worse than an Oak
Ridge atom." Rural, "dry" Protestant Democrats simply could not bring themselves to vote
for the New York Catholic, and Republican
Herbert Hoover's 177,000-vote win in Kentucky gave his party the state's biggest majority
to that time, as well as Kentucky's electoral
votes. Democrats, who won only 41 percent of
the ballots, also suffered a major setback in the
congressional races, as nine of the eleven congressmen rode Hoover's coattails into office.
The state Democratic Party was in tatters.

The next battleground also seemed to
produce a Republican victory. Sampson had selected the Democrat "Boss Ben" Johnson to
head the Highway Commission, the price for
Johnson's support. There Johnson and his commissioners ruled over a small fiefdom. With few
restrictions, the Highway Department spent
nearly 45 percent of the state's total budget,
employed some ten thousand people, and directly influenced fifty thousand more through
contracts or family ties. Legislators wanting
highways for their districts easily swapped votes
for roads; people seeking jobs commonly offered to pay a portion of their salaries if a
position could be attained; the party in power

generally built thoroughfares to their supporters first. When elections grew near, more weed cutters and road workers went on the payroll, and their votes went to those who hired them. Legislative control, party financing, patronage—all this meant that the Highway Department had become "the most politically significant function of the state government." The governor could not leave a post that powerful in the hands of someone he could not control, and in December 1929 he dismissed Johnson. Although Sampson seemed to have won, the power of the bosses showed that such victories were illusions.

The 1930 General Assembly quickly rendered Governor Sampson politically powerless. First, two contested seats went to Democrats, and with a sizable majority, the party passed "ripper" bills, which ripped the power of appointment from the chief executive and placed it under Democratic control. The Highway Commission was reorganized, and to the surprise of few, Johnson soon regained his post of power.

The key fight, however, centered on one of the state's most scenic areas, Cumberland Falls. In 1927 a hydroelectric company had purchased the site, and Samuel Insull's powerful influence came into play as he sought to use the falls to generate electrical power. Sampson, citing the jobs to be gained, favored the Insull plan. Meanwhile, conservationists, led by journalist Tom Wallace and with the support of over 90 percent of the state's newspapers, favored acceptance of the offer of Louisville-born millionaire T. Coleman du Pont of Delaware. He indicated that he would buy the Falls and present it to Kentucky as a park. In a mostly party vote, both houses accepted the du Pont plan. Sampson immediately vetoed the bill, saying that it would hurt industrial development, but his veto was easily overridden. The Cumberland, at the Falls, remained undammed.

That autumn, in the 1930 elections, a relatively unknown Democrat, Kentucky Court of Appeals judge M.M. Logan of Bowling Green, defeated conservative Republican congressman John M. Robsion for the Senate seat vacated when Sackett accepted appointment as ambassador to Germany. Democrats also won nine of the eleven congressional seats, and the delegation in Washington was strongly Democratic once more. Politically, the Republicans' once-bright prospects had dimmed so much as to be almost invisible. The party's dark period had begun, and it would largely last for many decades.

Kentucky's 1930 population of 2,614,589—ranking the state sixteenth in the nation—represented only a 59 percent increase over the 1880 figure, while the United States had seen a 144 percent rise during the fifty-year period. The decade of the twenties had not been one of Kentucky's best eras. Bootlegged whiskey, from Golden Pond and elsewhere, to-

Governor Flem D. Sampson (*left*) visits Cumberland Falls, 1929. Sampson had supported a plan to dam the Cumberland River to generate electrical power (courtesy of the University of Louisville Photographic Archives).

gether with gunfights between revenue agents and moonshiners, had added to the state's violent image. On the agrarian landscape, however, little had changed, in some ways. Despite advances, only 2.8 percent of farms had tractors (one-fifth of the American average); only 4.3 percent were lighted by electricity (one-third the national mean); and only one-fourth had telephones (versus one-third of U.S. farm homes). A man returned to the Marshall County home he had left forty years earlier and first saw the changes—timber cleared, the old homestead abandoned, the trees grown large, the creek deeper. But then he went to a relative's home, ate, and talked to the people, and he concluded that "everything there seemed more like old times than anything I saw during the day." Like the physical changes that man saw, changes taking place in American society in the twenties had chipped away at Kentucky character and lifestyles, but beneath the surface much remained as before. Attempts to reverse the modernization process, in the form of Klan activity or in the antievolution bills, had failed. Efforts to rekindle the moral crusades against gambling, as in earlier times, had not succeeded. Yet it was not so much that Kentuckians had embraced the changes around them or that they even wanted most of these changes. Rather, they simply accepted the times and went on with the basics as before. In the upcoming years all that would change.

22

Old Problems and a New Deal

Economically, the 1930s would prove to be one of the most difficult decades in Kentucky's history. The 1920s, however, had well prepared the state's residents for hardship.

Economic Want

Farmers suffered the most. Techniques that depleted and eroded the soils combined with a depressed market for agricultural products in the 1920s to produce agrarian distress. The tobacco economy collapsed soon after the end of World War I, while corn acreage decreased nearly one-fifth between 1920 and 1930. In the five-year period ending in 1928, Kentucky ranked forty-seventh among forty-eight states in farm income; its 1930 per capita farm earnings average of $148 stood well behind the Southeast's $183 mean, which itself trailed the national norm. The state's farmers were in trouble.

Then came 1930 and an unprecedented drought. In some places it did not rain at all for a month and a half; in most, precipitation averaged less than half the normal summer levels. Ice factories stopped production, water rationing began, farm animals suffered, and the Bluegrass turned "so brown that there did not seem to be a vestige of life remaining." In Franklin County the agricultural agent reported that only 15 percent of the corn crop had survived. By August the value of state crop losses exceeded one hundred million dollars. Debt-ridden farmers could hear the voice of disaster growing louder.

Sadly, that cry echoed all across Kentucky, and not just in rural areas. The stock market crash of October 1929 marked the beginning of a national economic depression that would leave few untouched. To a state already hurt by the effect of Prohibition, a declining coal economy, and a decade-long agricultural depression, the new blow struck hard. Nor was the commonwealth prepared to deal with the staggering numbers of people in need. At the time, the prevailing system of "poor relief" dictated that the county court magistrates heard each request, each month, and then decided whether to grant relief through an order to pay or to reject the claim. One study indicated that counties could average as little as nine cents per capita in aid, and "money is given with no regard to the available resources of the applicant or the community. No attention is paid to the mental or social fitness of the recipients." Limited funds, favoritism, politics, and other factors, the report concluded, made local relief efforts an utter failure. If no other options were available, the needy would go to what was called an almshouse or poorhouse or pauper farm to live. Small and underfunded, such institutions could not adequately meet needs either.

It became increasingly clear that something different would have to be done, for the scope of the problem exceeded anything seen before. The Red Cross director for Kentucky reported in 1930 that "the picture of distress . . . in the eastern part of our state is almost unbelievable. . . . There is a growing army of itinerants traveling on foot." That same year a Danville newspaper proclaimed that the area was suffering "from the greatest depression as well as the greatest drought that this country has ever known." Whereas 5 percent of the city's population lived on local charity in 1927, by 1932 some 25 percent did. In Louisville in 1932, 23.5 percent of white workers and 37.2 percent of black workers were unemployed. The story was repeated across Kentucky. In 1930 a medical worker in the mountains predicted starvation if nothing was done; the next year she described "a state of acute famine." One of her Bluegrass relatives told an out-of-state friend that the commonwealth was facing "a damn bad situation." In 1932 an Inez attorney noted the lack of jobs and the hard times and concluded that "the people feel that there is something radically wrong." From Pikeville to Paducah, people wandered from place to place, walking, riding, "moving on," seeking work, a job, some hope. Few found what they sought.

As the depression took its toll on Kentucky, *Life* photographer Margaret Bourke-White captured this arresting scene in Louisville during the 1937 flood (courtesy of *Life Magazine*, Time, Inc.).

In some ways, state banks symbolized the despair. Over the decades a few banks had failed every year. In 1928, for instance, three near Hazard closed their doors in one week owing to the state of mining. In the Great Depression, however, few failures now became many. In 1930 some 5 percent of the state's more than four hundred banks ceased doing business; the next year another 8 percent closed; in 1932 nearly 12 percent more followed. Deposits that had peaked at $385 million in June 1929 had fallen to under $230 million six years later and would not again reach the 1929 figure until 1943. The greatest bank failure was that of the state's—and the South's—largest financial institution, the BancoKentucky Company. Poorly managed by Jim Brown, with his insider loans, unsecured notes, and misappropriated funds, the bank closed its doors on November 16, 1930. That action caused widespread panic and the closing of other banks, including two black banks that had funds deposited at BancoKentucky. Brown, his financial empire, and his newspapers all went bankrupt. The city, the state, and the people of the commonwealth only slowly would take financial risks in the future, for the BancoKentucky example long haunted them. Unable to face even tomorrow, two bank presidents in Paducah committed suicide.

Kentuckians had trusted banks and had placed their savings there. Some lost a lifetime of work. Gradually, many of the banks reopened, but usually they returned only part of the funds to those who had entrusted their money to the banks' care. In 1936, for instance, the sixteen banks that completed liquidation proceedings paid anywhere from 5 percent to 100 percent on earlier deposits, with a per-bank average of around 60 percent. For depositors who received the average return, 40 percent of their funds had vanished almost overnight, and all of their money had been unavailable, owing to legal proceedings, while the depression raged around them. They did not want that ever to happen again.

The depression held Kentucky firmly for many years. When federal aid became more available in 1933, almost whole counties went on relief. In Morgan County, over 85 percent of families accepted federal support; in Magoffin County, the December 1933 figure was 68 percent; in other places the needs were similar. Farm values dropped nearly 30 percent in the five years after 1930, and by 1940 they still remained below the 1930 average. As late as 1938 over one-third of Kentucky's counties appeared to be nearing default on their debts, while an additional one-fourth were overdue on payments. On top of all that, in the cold of January 1937 a flood submerged large parts of the state. On the Ohio River, two-thirds of Louisville's businesses were under water, and thousands of people had to be evacuated. Up and down the river, particularly in Paducah, the same results occurred. Dead animals filled the streets and rivers; homeless people sought shelter throughout the area; the economy once more was devastated. Two years later, in 1939, the Frozen Creek flash floods in eastern Kentucky killed dozens of people there. Nature was not helping Kentucky recover.

Yet the commonwealth weathered the drought and the floods and survived the depression better than many places. The end of Prohibition and the continuation of smoking aided the state economy in those sectors, the general absence of industry meant relatively little damage there, the overall lack of wealth left people only a little way to fall, and the rural nature of the commonwealth allowed families to live off the land. In fact, people returned to Kentucky, and the decade of the 1930s saw the state's population increase faster than the national average for the first time since before the Civil War. From distant places, those who had migrated in search of jobs that were now gone came home to crowd in with their families in hollows, hills, and other places throughout the state. By 1940 the state's 2,845,627 people lived less in urban areas than a decade before (29.8 percent of the population was urban in

1940). When trouble came, Kentuckians had returned to their rural roots.

Depression Era Politics

The portly, balding, and cigar-smoking Ruby Laffoon (1869-1941) of Madisonville looked like the stereotypical politician. Born in a log cabin, he had become an attorney, entered politics, lost more races than he won, then served as circuit court judge. It did not seem a strong background for a gubernatorial candidate, but supported by the bosses and his politically powerful cousin Polk Laffoon, he became the Democratic nominee in 1931, the choice of the only Democratic gubernatorial convention after 1903. His youthful opponent, Louisville's Republican mayor, William B. ("Billy") Harrison, gained the support of the *Courier-Journal,* attacked the supposed bipartisan combine, and benefited from opposition to the Catholic bosses backing Laffoon. But all Laffoon had to do was to mention Sampson's failed governorship, Hoover's problem-laden presidency, and the depression, and victory was his. He won by a huge margin, 446,301-374,239.

Laffoon spent most of his administration trying to deal with a depressed economy and searching for funds. State expenditures in 1931 had been $46 million; in Laffoon's first full year they were $34.5 million. The commonwealth went deeper into debt by issuing more and more promises to pay, in the form of interest-bearing warrants. Warrants as a percentage of total state receipts increased from 24.2 percent in 1931 to 40.2 percent in 1932; by the end of the governor's term, warrants exceeded twenty million dollars. Faced with that fiscal disaster, having already made huge cuts in the budget (especially in education), and having to pledge more funds to match new federal relief programs, "the Terrible Turk from Madisonville" asked the legislature to enact a sales tax. Political disunity in the Democratic Party resulted, both from that action and as bosses who sought political spoils now found that few crumbs could be offered. Merchants opposed the tax proposal, as did money-poor citizens, and in

March 1932 a mob of some one hundred stormed the Governor's Mansion, damaging some items inside. The tax failed to pass. The next year Laffoon had angry demonstrators fed in a warehouse after he called a special session to try to get the tax passed once more. Again the General Assembly refused.

Convinced that the opposition sought his political ruin, Governor Laffoon lashed out at the *Courier-Journal* as "Public Enemy No. 1" and suggested that the attacks by businessmen were led by a "bunch of New York Jews." During Laffoon's term, the Board of Charities was made partisan, the Highway Commission was reorganized with the chief executive's supporters, and various powers were "ripped" from the lieutenant governor and auditor, who opposed Laffoon. Next, the governor allied with the Republicans in exchange for patronage and got a needed reorganization bill passed. He also more than doubled the whiskey levy and finally got his sales tax through in 1934, but inexplicably, he also reduced the real estate tax to one-sixth its previous level. Overall, though, the state finally had achieved some needed fiscal stability. That had come at a great cost, however, both politically and personally. A sad figure by term's end, Laffoon lived in the mansion under guard to keep another mob away, went into a sanatorium to be treated for exhaustion, and then had to have surgery for appendicitis. In 1935 Laffoon left an office that had overwhelmed him.

Laffoon had been crippled in a childhood accident, and ironically, another politician with a physical disability, Franklin D. Roosevelt, had entered the national political stage during Laffoon's term. Unlike the Kentuckian, who faltered before the heat of the spotlight, FDR gloried in it. He projected confidence and gave listeners the sense that things could be better. As the nominee for president on the Democratic ticket in 1932, he had the election in hand before he began, for all the reasons that had given Laffoon his victory a year earlier. One Kentucky political boss said of FDR that "I believe he could go home and go to sleep and wake up elected. . . . Everybody broke and out of work." On election day, Roosevelt won by the largest margin ever recorded in Kentucky, as he defeated Hoover by 580,574 votes to 394,176. At the same time, something happened that had not occurred in the twentieth century—a sitting U.S. senator from Kentucky, in this case Alben Barkley, won reelection. Even better for the majority party, an attempt at reapportionment had been voided by the courts, so the nine candidates with the greatest statewide vote totals would be selected to go to Congress. Districts that were normally Republican were swamped by the vote over the commonwealth, and Democrats won all nine seats. It was a massive sweep. With only a few exceptions, Democrats would dominate state elections in Kentucky for the next six decades.

At the time that Roosevelt came into office, many people, like the editor of one Kentucky newspaper, were "gravely apprehensive," for unrest was everywhere. Certain commentators feared that the entire system might be in jeopardy. But the president's immediate and active response, causing people to hope once more, helped change attitudes. The same editor in March 1933 wrote that "the spirit here really . . . is very much better." The state also had some hope of change because FDR included numerous Kentuckians in his administration. In 1937 Barkley would become majority leader of the U.S. Senate, while Frederick M. Vinson later became important in several capacities. The president appointed Stanley Reed of Maysville to the Supreme Court, where he joined two other Kentucky-born justices, and made Bingham ambassador to Great Britain. Several other citizens of the state served in key positions.

With these appointments, plus the actions taken in the New Deal, Roosevelt became virtually unbeatable in the state. In 1936 he won 58.4 percent of the state vote; four years later, in his controversial third-term bid, he took 57.4 percent; in 1944, in the midst of war, Roosevelt garnered 54.5 percent. In all those elections the state outcome never stood

in doubt, and he carried two-thirds of all Kentucky counties. At the same time, the New Deal programs that aided labor unions and blacks brought about a change in the makeup of the Democratic Party in the commonwealth. Before Roosevelt, virtually all blacks registered and voted Republican, the party of Lincoln. But the scant support given during the Hoover term combined with the aid provided by the New Deal to bring about at least a gradual shift. It would take nearly twenty years for that change to become a constant, but by 1936 the Louisville black voting wards were giving a majority to Roosevelt. Similarly, the New Deal's prounion actions brought the Eastern Coalfield to turn from the Republicans as well. Whereas the Democrats carried only eight of thirty-two eastern counties in 1924, by 1936 they carried a majority of them. A new, broader, and more powerful Democratic coalition was being forged.

The New Deal

Much of the Democratic success resulted directly from the effects of the New Deal. A generation who had known mostly economic distress in Kentucky now saw the possibility of better days. As Robert Penn Warren noted, many had thought that "things lay beyond any individual effort to change them," but now the crisis demanded action "because you had to have action or die."

Federal action addressed problem after problem, in an often bewildering array of programs, most of which became known by their acronyms. A need existed to provide security for the young? The result was Aid to Dependent Children (AID), through which in 1939 some forty-five thousand Kentucky families received an average of $8.73 per month. The National Youth Administration (NYA) gave part-time work or aid to young people of high school and college age, allowing them to remain in school. What about security for the elderly? The Social Security Act of 1935 provided that for the first time. And what about financial security? A series of acts helped Kentuckians refinance mortgages or, in the case of the Federal Housing Administration (FHA), get new low-interest loans. Bank deposits were guaranteed to a certain level under the Federal Deposit Insurance Corporation (FDIC).

The greatest efforts went to help those without jobs. Immediate needs were met on a short-term basis by direct payments under the Federal Emergency Relief Administration (FERA). Longer-range solutions focused on providing relief funds in return for labor on public projects. Professionals found an outlet, as out-of-work teachers provided instruction to illiterate citizens, artists painted murals through the Federal Art Project, and various people worked in the Federal Writers Project, which, among other activities, produced archival guides and several histories. Other Kentuckians worked in sewing rooms and the like, but the largest group labored in the Public Works Administration (PWA), which built sewers, post offices, and river facilities, and particularly in the Works Progress (later Projects) Administration, or WPA.

A Henderson woman with diabetes was "right down in despair" until her husband started working on a WPA project: "First off he bought us some groceries, things that would last. . . . Then he had a chance to get that little heatin' stove for two dollars and . . . some coal. . . . They got us some mattresses from the relief to take the place of our straw and husk ticks." For a family in Newport, "those were mighty hard years. . . . Our savings were gone.

We had a hard time getting enough to eat." Then the husband began working on a WPA project, but poor health forced him to stop; the wife received WPA relief employment at a sewing center, and that "started to get [us] on our feet." For those two families and for the nearly sixty thousand people employed by WPA by Christmas 1935, such work saved them. The WPA built or improved numerous buildings and greatly helped in the modernization of the state's infrastructure. Workers constructed schools, gymnasiums, recreation centers, parks, privies, roads, bridges, culverts, and more, and many of these projects served to break down isolation.

The land itself received attention as well. The Agricultural Adjustment Act had to be reexamined after the first version was declared unconstitutional, but in the end the Agricultural Adjustment Administration (AAA) controlled production in an attempt to raise prices. Some livestock was killed in order to do that, and restrictions were placed on tobacco production. Despite indifferent success among small farmers, especially in eastern Kentucky, the project succeeded in bringing more money, overall, to state farms. The commonwealth's forests benefited from the Civilian Conservation Corps (CCC). Eighty thousand young Kentucky CCC workers reforested the land, helped control soil erosion, built lodges, cabins, and trails in parks, and thereby helped awaken the people of Kentucky to environmental matters. The damming of rivers through the

The WPA created jobs for many Kentuckians. Here WPA workers build a sewer in Paducah (courtesy of the University of Kentucky Libraries).

Tennessee Valley Authority (TVA) together with the Rural Electrification Administration (REA) provided cheap and widespread electricity throughout the region, but especially in rural areas. TVA's construction of Kentucky Dam, completed in 1945, in a sense signaled the end of the New Deal. That massive dam, the federal narcotics hospital at Lexington, and the U.S. Bullion Depository at Fort Knox, however, only symbolized all that had occurred.

The most significant change of the New Deal had been mental rather than physical. The roads and buildings all made a difference, but acceptance of the involvement of the federal government in the lives of Kentuckians was a greater change. Need overrode a philosophy centered in localism and individualism. Now programs that provided security to farmers, laborers, the elderly, and the young were accepted. The individual was not solely responsible for his or her well-being; society had a role to play as well. Governmental involvement had given more stability to the economy and more protection to consumers. Not everyone accepted that, and some bitterly criticized Roosevelt's actions. Certain programs had not worked; some had benefited certain groups more than others. People recognized that important compromises had been made and some important things had been given up. Most, though, readily accepted what had taken place, for their lives and, most important, their future hopes had improved as a result of the New Deal.

Labor and the Coal Wars

Labor unions had existed in Kentucky since before the Civil War, but most had had only limited success because of hostile courts, unsympathetic government and governors, and plentiful strikebreakers. Only in 1935, with the passage of the federal Wagner Act and the creation of a National Labor Relations Board, did that situation change drastically. The new law provided that employees had the right to join unions and to bargain collectively, and it also gave governmental protection to those rights.

Several fundamental issues were thus settled, but in some ways the law came a few years too late to spare the state from an episode that further damaged Kentucky's image.

In the years soon after the Civil War, various unions of skilled or semiskilled workers had been organized, mostly in Louisville and northern Kentucky. In 1877 some two thousand laborers marched in Louisville, bringing out a large militia force in answer; in 1893 a large strike against the L&N failed. The Knights of Labor had local assemblies in Kentucky by the late 1860s but had virtually disappeared by 1900, when the national convention of the American Federation of Labor (AFL) met in the Falls City. Soon afterward, the Kentucky State Federation of Labor, with James McGill as president, was established. By 1902 about 12 percent of Kentucky factories were unionized. Sporadic strikes, a few victories, and many defeats followed, with the Newport Rolling Mills Strike of 1921-22 being one of the most bitter. Following a 1919 steel strike that left a half dozen people wounded in an exchange of shots, troops, machine guns, and tanks fired into strikers in early 1922, trying to keep company workers from crossing picket lines. Injuries and arrests followed.

Of the 223 Kentucky strikes listed in one account for the 1880-1900 period, however, 81 occurred in the state's coalfields. It was there that the most violent opposition arose. In 1873 a "miners' union" was established in Boyd and Carter Counties, and from that beginning the impulse spread. The issues of concern were not just job security and higher wages but also safety and fair practices. From 1876 to 1878 strikes in Rockcastle County sought to raise miners' wages from four to five cents per bushel of coal (a bushel of coal contains about eighty pounds). Other similar work stoppages took place elsewhere. In 1890 the United Mine Workers of America (UMW) formed. Kentucky workers joined nationwide strikes in 1894 (involving thirty-seven local unions, with more than thirty-five hundred men), 1919 (involving twenty thousand Kentucky miners), 1922, and 1924. The depressed coal industry of the 1920s offered little hope for success, however, and UMW membership in the state fell from nineteen thousand in 1912 to fewer than one thousand by 1931. As one miner succinctly explained, "If you kicked too much, or complained too much about [working conditions] . . . you would soon be hunting for a job." Since coal companies often operated their own towns, strikers could be evicted from their homes as well.

Yet as the depression spread throughout the eastern Kentucky coalfields, conditions grew so bad that workers believed they had no choice but to challenge the mine owners. In one Kentucky county, operators remained more intransigent than elsewhere, and abuses seemed more flagrant. Out of those conditions arose the image of "Bloody Harlan" and the Harlan County Coal Wars of the 1930s.

Harlan County had experienced a huge population increase in the years before 1930, and with that expansion came massive societal disorganization for the sixty-five thousand people. The once-proud coal towns had fallen on hard times in the 1920s as coal prices dropped, and what profits there were often went to stockholders, not toward making repairs. Tensions rose, violence increased, and class animosity intensified. Then came the additional problems of the national depression. By 1932 one-third of Harlan County's mines had closed, and four thousand miners had lost their jobs. Relief from the New Deal was in the future, so hungry, desperate, jobless people roamed the region, looking for work or just food. Company evictions left many homeless and hungry, and even more just angry. In May 1931 what became known as the battle of Evarts took place: over a thousand shots were exchanged between miners and the coal company's paid deputies, sometimes called "gun thugs." In an ambush of company cars, one miner was killed, and three died on the operators' side. With the UMW virtually absent, the Communist-oriented National Miners' Union (NMU) came in to fill the void and to offer

help, through soup kitchens. Although few Harlan County miners supported the NMU, its presence caused the conservative owners to fear the worst. The owner of the Creech Coal Company proclaimed, "They'll bring a union in here over my dead body." Each side armed itself, but the operators controlled the county and its legal machinery. No one could be neutral, and a folk song asked, "Which side are you on?" People had to choose.

All attention seemed to focus on Harlan County. A group of national writers, which included Theodore Dreiser and John Dos Passos, visited the area, and one of their number called the situation "the most outstanding example of industrial despotism and official depravity in the history of coal mining." Soon an NMU organizer was killed by a deputy, some writers were beaten, and out-of-state student groups who came to investigate conditions were refused admission to the county. The NMU soon left, but other union organizers remained, and several were beaten. In September 1935 a car bomb killed the county attorney, and more murders followed. Yet by the time the conflict ended, only six miners had died, with thirteen wounded, while five company men were killed and five other people were injured. The publicity in some ways exceeded the reality, for union conflicts in other places in the United States took a larger toll. But the very ferocity of the fight, the uncompromising nature of the operators, and the length of the struggle made Bloody Harlan nationally known.

In 1935 a state investigating committee reported that "coal mine operators in collusion with certain public officials" had created "a virtual reign of terror." Two years later, national government hearings by the La Follette Committee focused more attention on the situation and reached similar conclusions. Finally, with the provisions of the Wagner Act in operation, the Harlan County Coal Operators' Association reluctantly capitulated and signed a contract with the union. UMW membership in Harlan County rose to fifteen thousand by 1940, and while the violence had ended only for a time, the legitimacy of unions seemed settled at last. Miners began to speak of their lives as divided into two parts—"Before the Union" and "After the Union"—for it made that much difference in their lives.

What turned out to be most damaging to the miners in the long run, however, was mechanization of the coalfields. Workers almost worshiped national UMW president John L. Lewis as he stood up to even the president in calling strikes. But following a crucial work stoppage, a 1950 wage agreement was signed by Lewis, which practically freed companies to reduce their labor costs by mechanization (see table 22.1).

Between 1950 and 1965 mechanization caused the number of employees in Kentucky's underground mines to fall by 70 percent. The average amount of coal mined per person per day had gone from 4.75 tons to 14 tons. Many young, displaced miners could find no other jobs in the area. Harlan County lost twenty thousand people during the 1950s, and across the coalfields massive migrations took place.

From the 1940s into the 1980s, unions, both in the coalfields and in other areas of Kentucky, played an important role, not just in economic matters but in political ones as well. Union endorsements meant votes, and labor lobbies had a major influence on legislatures. Despite a strong start, however—Kentucky ranked thirteenth nationally in union member-

ship in 1939—the state soon settled into the middle ranks. It did have more strikes and more lost time than the American norm in the three decades after 1952 and had a relatively higher percentage of labor union members than did the rest of the South. Overall, however, Kentucky had only an average amount of union activity. By the early 1980s less than 20 percent of the manufacturing plants in the state were unionized. Reflecting national trends, the numbers continued to drop after that. With less cohesion, influence, and control, unions became far less important in political races, and by the last part of the twentieth century the golden age of unions appeared to be over.

Happy

The 1930s saw many transformations take place in Kentucky, as unions became powerful after years of weakness, as the New Deal brought an entirely new outlook on federal-state relations, and as the older political leadership began to pass from the scene, to be replaced by a fresh cadre. One of the newcomers, Albert Benjamin ("Happy") Chandler (1898-1991), burst onto the Kentucky scene almost overnight. State senator, lieutenant governor, and governor, all by the age of thirty-seven, he would go on to become one of the dominant Kentucky political figures of his era, serving later as U.S. senator, again as governor, as baseball commissioner, and as a faction leader in the Democratic Party. A following that was more personal than political became the core from which he operated for more than thirty years. During that time Chandler would throw off the bosses who had orchestrated his rise and would be dominated by no one. He was Happy. That said it all.

Born near Henderson, Chandler saw his mother leave him when he was four. He worked hard, but he could also

Table 22.1
Coal Production and Employment, 1950-1965

Year	Underground coal production (tons) (Ky.)	Employees (Ky.)	Employees (Harlan Co.)
1950	54,725,201	66,636	13,619
1960	32,041,574	26,744	3,968
1965	37,740,473	20,144	2,433

Source: Jerry Napier, "Mechanization and the Central Kentucky Coal Fields" (unpublished manuscript)

call on a strong speaking (and singing) voice, some athletic skills, and a will to achieve. Very early he came to believe he was destined to be president, and he moved steadily, and for a time successfully, toward that goal. Politically allied to the Beckham-Haly-Bingham faction, Chandler became a pariah in the Laffoon administration, and what powers he had as lieutenant governor were stripped from him. But a key constitutional strength remained: at the time, a Kentucky governor who was outside the state lost all powers to govern. The Laffoon forces planned to call a convention, which they could control, and thus they would select the person that they wanted to be the party nominee. But when Laffoon went to Washington to address some relief matters, acting governor Chandler called a special session of the legislature for the purpose of enacting a primary election law. A furious Laffoon hurried back and cancelled the call, but the courts ruled Laffoon's action illegal. When the session met, Laffoon forces, expecting elderly J.C.W. Beckham to be the nominee of the opposition, enacted a possible two-stage primary, which would wear down the old politician.

For personal reasons, however, Beckham did not run. The youthful Happy Chandler, backed by Bingham money, did. Political boss and Laffoon choice Thomas Rhea soon found himself facing an extremely tough campaigner. Wearing white suits, singing songs like "Sonny Boy," hugging voters, and kissing babies, Chandler dominated a gathering with his flamboyant personality. His speeches were short for the time, and he conducted assemblies like revival meetings, making asides to people in the crowd whom he would call by name. Beneath the exuberance and brassy enthusiasm, though, also lay a hard, determined soul, and Happy did not spare his opponents. Rhea he labeled "Sales Tax Tom," and he called on his audience to redeem the state from "Ruby, Rhea, and Ruin." A veteran reporter watched all this and concluded that Chandler was the best campaigner he had seen during the last thirty years: "By methods he probably doesn't understand

himself he has become one of them," that is, one of the crowd itself. It was a show, a personal tour, and the charismatic Chandler was the star.

Known as the Sage of Russellville, or the Gray Fox, Thomas Rhea was a shrewd politician who knew that he had few strengths on the political stump. His forte had been behind-the-scenes organization, and he now had to depend on that for victory. The first primary ended with Rhea ahead and Chandler second by nineteen thousand votes, but Rhea did not get enough support to avoid a runoff. In a large turnout, Chandler won this time, 260,573-234,124. The two-primary strategy had cost the Laffoon-Rhea forces the election. Embittered, Laffoon and Rhea, together with most of the highway commissioners and others in the administration, refused to support the nominee and went with the Republican candidate, King Swope of Lexington. No real policy differences separated Swope and Chandler, though, and the legacy of Hoover versus the New Deal doomed the Republicans. In the largest vote cast in the state up to that time, Chandler won by a 556,262-461,104 count.

Hardly hesitating, the new governor began to put his stamp on the state government. He received resignations from or fired thousands of employees, replacing them with loyal Chandlerites, but to his credit, he also brought to Frankfort numerous college professors, whose innovative ideas helped streamline the bureaucracy. A needed Government Reorganization Act in 1936 not coincidentally gave the governor more power, but it also made the government run more efficiently. A law calling for a single primary replaced the two-primary law that had won Chandler the governorship. Philosophically a follower of Virginia's Harry F. Byrd (a godfather to a Chandler child), Happy not only used Byrd's ideas about reorganization but also followed his fiscal conservatism. Bitterly opposed to a sales tax, Chandler got the General Assembly to abolish that Laffoon legacy and replaced the revenues with liquor and cigarette taxes. With Prohibition ended, the alcoholic beverage industry brought new money into the state's coffers. Combined with federal dollars, the new taxes gave Chandler the opportunity to reduce the state's debt significantly. The fiscal windfall also allowed construction of a new penitentiary at La Grange, since the 1937 flood had forced evacuation of the outdated prison in Frankfort. Finally, the influence of Louisville's Charles W. Anderson Jr. (1907-60), the first black person elected to a southern legislature in the twentieth century, combined with the availability of state money to allow passage of a law giving a total of five thousand dollars annually to fund attendance by black students at out-of-state graduate schools, since segregation denied them such opportunities in Kentucky. Overall, the flush fiscal times allowed Chandler's "pay-as-you-go" philosophy to work. In later years, under different circumstances, such a view would create problems.

In one way, Chandler had been lucky in financial matters. He also benefited and received some credit from the federal government's new programs aiding the elderly and others. The new Boy Governor further gained from political circumstances. As it turned out, Percy Haly and Robert Worth Bingham both died in 1937, and Beckham's demise followed three years later. With the leadership in that long-standing faction virtually gone, Chandler moved into the void and led the remnants of the group. All this was heady stuff for the new governor, and he now looked to take his success to the national stage, as U.S. senator. In the 1936 primary, incumbent senator M.M. Logan had defeated Beckham and rising political newcomer John Y. Brown Sr. (in the first of Brown's seven unsuccessful attempts for that office) and had, like Barkley, won reelection over a Republican opponent. Logan's seat would not be open, it seemed, until 1942. That was too long for Happy to wait. Chandler thus decided to challenge Alben Barkley in the 1938 U.S. Senate race. It would be a battle of giants.

Chandler went into the race supremely confident. He had never lost, had a generally popular administration, and had built a strong political organization. Like others before him,

he did not hesitate to involve state government in the election, as employees were solicited for funds while new workers were hired in exchange for their and their families' votes. The "Old Bear," J. Dan Talbott, served as the governor's patronage czar and used his powers effectively. Most of all, though, Chandler's strength was Happy Chandler the campaigner. He expected to overwhelm "Old Alben."

What Chandler did not expect was that Barkley could match him on the campaign trail and could draw support from the federal government to counter the state effort. Like his mentor Byrd, Happy did not philosophically support much of the New Deal, and its leader, Franklin D. Roosevelt, knew that. Roosevelt also called Chandler a "dangerous" person, of the populist, Huey Long type he disliked. Besides all that, FDR had handpicked Barkley for the post as Senate majority leader, and defeat would amount to a repudiation of the president. Roosevelt said some favorable things about Chandler as he made a series of whistle-stop talks across the state, but his clear choice was Barkley. As Edward F. Prichard Jr. remarked, the president's words about the governor seemed to say, "You're a good boy, but you won't do." Behind the scenes, the federal relief agencies, particularly the WPA, worked for Barkley's election in such a brazen way that Congress would soon make such action illegal. Each machine—federal and state—geared up for the vote.

Barkley might well have won without all that extra help, though, for he had always been a popular, if long-winded, campaigner in his own right. Although sixty years old (versus Chandler's forty years), the tireless Iron Man probably made more speeches each day than his opponent. It was hard to vote against Barkley, for he had become nationally known for his strong keynote addresses at the 1932 and 1936 Democratic conventions and had acquired many allies by speaking as a party loyalist in other races. Backed by the *Courier-Journal* and by the labor unions—both of which had supported Chandler when he ran for governor in

President Franklin D. Roosevelt, Governor A.B. ("Happy") Chandler, and Senator Alben W. Barkley in northern Kentucky during the 1938 Senate race (courtesy of the *Louisville Courier-Journal*)

1935—Barkley had a great many allies. He also could capitalize on opportunity. When Chandler fell ill from drinking some water, and when it was weakly suggested that the liquid had been poisoned to slow Chandler's bid, a laughing Barkley announced that he would put "an ice water guard" on his staff. When he spoke and started to drink from a glass, Barkley would purposely hesitate, shudder, and put the glass away, to much laughter. Chandler had a dynamic personality and some state allies, but Barkley had more support, including the president's endorsement. The incumbent won easily, 294,391-223,149. While a good ally of his friends, Chandler was also a good hater, and he never forgave Barkley and Roosevelt. He spoke bitterly of them the rest of his life. After all, they had defeated destiny.

World War II

Ironically, fortune smiled once more on Happy Chandler. In 1939, when Senator Logan died, Chandler resigned as governor and was appointed to the vacant Senate seat by the new governor, Keen Johnson. Then Chandler won the seat in a special election. He joined his enemy Barkley in the Senate just as the nation began to face a challenge even greater than the depression. Across the face of the globe, militant governments threatened weaker nations, drawing the world closer to war. Kentuckians had seen the Italians take Ethiopia, the Germans seize Austria and Czechoslovakia, and the Japanese conquer part of China. During that

time the state's congressmen had voted with the majority on legislation concerning neutrality acts and defense spending, except for the reactionary isolationist mountain Republican John M. Robsion, who, it seemed, opposed anything and everything. But with the Japanese attack on Pearl Harbor on December 7, 1941, all the discussion regarding peace or war ended.

The start of World War II meant that lifestyles and the usual ways of doing things changed, often drastically. As in most wars, governmental intervention in the economy, and thus in everyday lives, increased, but the federal actions of the New Deal had set the stage, so such intervention did not seem so unusual. Still, governmental rationing of sugar, coffee, butter, and meat, together with gasoline (around three gallons a week for most people), tires, fuel oil, and shoes all meant sacrifice on the home front of at least a limited scope. But "victory gardens" on small plots furnished up to one-third of the vegetables consumed nationally in 1943, and the overall good crops of the wartime years helped overcome shortages. Unlike people in many parts of the world, most Americans did not go hungry.

The war required raw materials, and scrap drives brought in junk iron and aluminum for the effort. Factories switched from making consumer goods to producing battlefield equipment. The maker of Louisville Slugger baseball bats, for example, converted to the building of rifle stocks. When the huge Ken-Rad Company of Owensboro refused to

Women worked in factories in increasing numbers during World War II, as exemplified in the Reynolds Medal Company in Louisville in 1943 (courtesy of the Photographic Archives, University of Louisville).

sign a contract with a union in 1944, the government intervened and took over the plant. An agreement quickly followed. New factories also sprang up to fill new needs. Louisville, for instance, became the nation's largest producer of synthetic rubber, since most overseas rubber areas were in enemy hands. Still, despite a booming economy, Kentucky did not offer as much as did places elsewhere, and everyone was searching for workers. A mass exodus to better-paying jobs in the North and East resulted, with some 13 percent of the population leaving the state between 1940 and 1950. Occasional labor shortages in Kentucky showed that, in contrast to the depression decade, now anyone who wanted to work could do so. For many, the wartime economy provided long-sought financial security.

Those labor shortages brought, for the first time, large numbers of women into the workforce. Not only did they toil in factories, but they also entered what had once been solely male domains. In Lexington, women drove taxicabs and stood guard at the gates of the new Blue Grass Ordnance Depot, for example. In job after job, women showed that they could do the same work as men. Once the war ended and soldiers returned, however, many women had to give up their jobs to the veterans and go back to more traditional "women's work." But a start had been made.

Away from factories, women helped the war effort in other ways. To conserve cloth, short sleeves were touted, and bathing suits became smaller. The scarcity of nylon hose induced more women to wear trousers, a break with tradition that brought forth much discussion in some circles. In whatever form of dress, women staffed USO canteens for soldiers, prepared surgical dressings, led neighborhood collection efforts, aided hospitals and the Red Cross, and conducted war bond drives. With a huge rise in income all across the economic spectrum, but with no new cars or durable consumer goods on which to spend that money, savings soared. By buying bonds, civilians financed the war effort; cashing them in after the conflict ended would produce a postwar consumer buying spree.

Signs of the war stood all around Kentuckians. Military bases at Fort Knox and the newly formed Camp Campbell and Camp Breckinridge expanded greatly, while the U.S. Army Corps of Engineers built ordnance works in Henderson, plus Darnall General Hospital in Boyle County and Nichols General Hospital in Louisville to care for troops. The gold vault at Fort Knox became the temporary home of the Declaration of Independence and the U.S. Constitution. The Army Air Force took over Bowman Field, and it served as the site of the nation's first glider pilot combat training.

Aircraft, soldiers, the wounded—all made the conflict visible to the people of the commonwealth.

Yet for all the changes, daily life remained remarkably stable. Although several colleges suspended sports, the Derby went on. Listening to radio programs or going to a motion picture became even more popular pastimes. Milk was still delivered daily to homes, and mail still came twice a day, as before. Even segregation continued, but it seemed ironic that in a war against fascism and for democracy, German POWs could eat in some Kentucky restaurants while their black guards could not. That struggle for equality would be fought after the current war was won.

For those serving in the military, fighting in forgotten places across the oceans, the relative calm, the prosperity, the peace of wartime America seemed a lifetime away. Whether in the Pacific theater, with its heat and rain and malaria, or in the European arena, with its cold and mud and frozen feet, stretches of utter boredom would be mixed with periods of utter terror and death.

Kentuckians' involvement began early, for it was a military chaplain from Murray who at Pearl Harbor cried out, in the middle of the attack, "Praise the Lord and pass the ammunition!" The unfortunate commander of the naval forces at the base was another Kentuckian, Admiral Husband E. Kimmel of Henderson. A seaman from Louisville who had been on the sinking U.S.S. *Arizona* later recalled his reaction: "The whole harbor was on fire. . . . I went into a state of shock." For those who had recently been in a tank company in the Kentucky National Guard but had been sent to the Philippines just days before, the hell lasted much longer than at Pearl. Of the sixty-six men who left Harrodsburg, twenty-nine died before war's end. After the group surrendered in the Philippines, they had to endure the Bataan Death March, where their captors bayoneted men, buried others alive, beheaded some, and left other prisoners dying from dysentery or malnutrition. Only years later did the survivors return from prison camps to tell their stories or to bury them in their memories.

A Lexingtonian recalled hearing the news of Pearl Harbor: "You knew the military was going to be part of your life. You just knew it." A college student in the same city would write later of his leaving: "From the train I gave a final salute to the years of youth that had died at Pearl Harbor. I never saw myself again." Before it all ended, 306,715 Kentuckians entered the armed forces, and they fought in virtually every theater. At the leadership level, Admiral Willis A. ("Ching") Lee of Owen County led battleships in the Pacific, while General Simon B. Buckner Jr. of Hart County commanded army forces at Okinawa, where he was killed. Throughout all the ranks, though, men fought and died. They were symbolized in the person of Franklin R. Sousley of Fleming County, one of the Marines in the famous picture of the raising of the American flag on Iwo Jima. Sousley was killed soon afterward, and he became one of the nearly eight thousand Kentuckians who never came back. Too many Gold Star Mothers wept across Kentucky.

War's end in 1945 returned to the commonwealth many people with changed attitudes; they joined others who had stayed and evolved as well. The lives of women and blacks would not be the same again, for brief glimpses of possibilities would not be forgotten in later years. Nor would Kentucky remain the same, for the mass migration had taken away many of the young, seldom to return. The greatest change, though, came among those who had left to fight. Some brought back wounds, others scarred memories. A Warren County captain had gone to a liberated German concentration camp, but it was too late for the hundreds of dead he saw, "stacked like cordwood" ready to be burned before the Americans arrived: "The tragedy . . . hangs like a shadow over the place even now." He could not forget that, or the faces of combat and the dead young men. For others, however, the travel to distant places and the contact with people from other parts of the United States proved a maturing experience, which left them more sophisticated and broadminded. Still other soldiers simply came home, at least on the surface unchanged from the experience, as they took up the life they had left when they went to fight with others against a common enemy. In the end, the United States had faced massive military might, had beaten it, and had done so in a way that left the homeland unscathed and even prosperous. Americans now wanted to reap the benefits of their action in a postwar world.

Wartime Politics

When Happy Chandler resigned in October 1939 to become U.S. senator, his lieutenant governor took the reins of office, less than a month before the general election for a full term. Keen Johnson (1896-1970), though, had already been campaigning for the post and had beaten John Y. Brown Sr. in the primary. The new governor was very unlike his predecessor, for Johnson was usually quiet and reserved. Moreover, he had represented the Laffoon-Rhea side in the 1935 election and thus had not been a Chandler ally initially. He had made peace with Chandler, however, and Happy backed Johnson as he faced the once-defeated Republican gubernatorial choice, King Swope. The Democratic candidate won easily, 460,834-354,704. The journalist from Richmond became governor soon after war began raging in Europe; before he left office, the conflict had encompassed the United States and the world.

Johnson presided over what he himself called a cautious, frugal, and conservative administration, but one with solid accomplishments. Despite lowered road receipts due to rationing, the state debt was paid in full, and a surplus accumulated. Various groups, particularly in education, argued that more funds should have been spent. Funding for the Teachers' Retirement Act, an enabling law that allowed TVA to proceed, and a thorough legislative redistricting—the first in nearly fifty years—all passed. A constitutional amendment to allow the use of voting machines instead of paper ballots met with the voters' approval in 1941 as well. Other than the war and all the restrictions it brought, though, the key event in the Johnson administration was the rebirth of internecine factionalism in the Democratic Party.

When Chandler ran for a full Senate term in 1942, a now-bitter enemy faced him in the primary and accused the incumbent of using his office to receive favors—especially the construction of a swimming pool—during wartime restrictions. Namesake of a former governor but not related, John Y. Brown Sr. was the son of a tenant farmer and came from western Kentucky roots not unlike Chandler's. Brown believed that Happy had promised to support him for senator earlier and had reneged, and he now became almost a perennial candidate. Brown lost, and Chandler took the race handily, in both the primary and the general election. Two years later, Senate majority leader Alben Barkley won reelection easily as well, although his break with the president on a veto that year angered FDR and may have cost the Kentuckian the vice presidency, which went to Harry Truman. The real party bitterness, however, came from within Johnson's administration, as an ambitious attorney general brought up various problems, real or imagined, while a muckraking *Courier-Journal* reporter unearthed more. When the Democratic primary for governor started in 1943, the usually gentle Johnson grew so angry at his own party's attacks on him that he called one candidate a Casanova and another a phony farmer and a "carpet bagger from North Carolina." In the end, Johnson's choice, J. Lyter Donaldson of Carrollton, won and faced a formidable Republican, for a change.

Simeon Willis (1879-1965) appealed to voters as a political outsider, for he had not held office for a decade by 1943, having left a seat on the state's high court and returned to a law practice in Ashland. The tall, dignified-looking Ohio-born son of a Union veteran, Republican Willis echoed the corruption and bossism themes of the losing Democrats in the primary and presented himself as the reformer, above partisan bickering. He also advocated repeal of the income tax, a stance his opponent would not take. Donaldson ran what observers termed "a very leisurely and indifferent campaign," one based on national issues of wartime unity. In a close race decided by fewer than 9,000 votes, Willis won, 279,144-270,525, and for the first time in a dozen years a Republican sat in the gubernatorial office. As it turned out, an even longer time would pass before that phenomenon occurred again. Willis's victory had been more personal than political.

Facing a Democratically controlled legislature and a wartime situation, Willis had many problems, both party-oriented and otherwise, but his scandal-free administration greatly increased aid to education and old-age assistance, funded a series of state tubercular sanatoriums, and provided new support for black rights. Wartime inflation, the relative prosperity owing to the economy, and additional federal dollars brought a budget increase from thirty-one million dollars in 1943-44 to more than fifty-two million by the end of Willis's administration. Leaders in neither party gave much support to a repeal of the income tax, and a huge budget surplus resulted. Who would spend it in the next administration, Democrats or Republicans?

In November 1945 Senator Chandler resigned his seat to become baseball commissioner. The race to fill the remainder of the term came down to Democrat John Y. Brown (again) versus a Republican newcomer, John Sherman Cooper (1901-91). Born in Somerset and partly educated in Ivy League schools, Cooper had won election as county judge and, at first glance, seemed destined to go little higher. Not a good public speaker, habitually late, often forgetful, he seemed to do only

one thing right on the campaign trail—win. Cooper, a liberal, could secure the vote of the conservative Republicans; he could appeal to factional Democrats, especially Chandler, who often supported him; and he could typically count on the endorsement of the now usually Democratic *Courier-Journal* with its urbane young editor, Barry Bingham Sr. Cooper's very weaknesses appeared to endear him to voters, and in 1946 he defeated Brown, 327,652-285,829. That victory seemed to bode well for Republicans in the governor's race the next year. But Chandler's absence lessened factionalism, and the generally united Democrats faced a Republican Party now infected with the virus of factionalism. As had occurred with Johnson four years earlier, Willis's own party candidate criticized his governorship; that stance won the primary in 1947 but doomed the Republican in the general election. Once more Democrats won.

By then a series of studies had emerged, focusing on what actions Kentucky should take in the new postwar world. They noted that the state had been through an agricultural depression in the 1920s, a massive drought in 1930, a nationwide general depression in the 1930s, a damaging flood in 1937, and a searing world war in 1941-45. A whole generation had faced problem after problem. During that time parts of the face of Kentucky had changed through New Deal construction projects and through wartime building. In some ways even more important parts of the commonwealth's psyche had changed, as the longstanding localism and states' rights views had been severely tested by the effects of the Roosevelt revolution. Less clear, particularly given recent Republican success, was the change taking place in the electorate. Democrats had formed a new and stronger coalition that included labor, urbanites, and, increasingly, blacks. The effects of the depression under a Republican president plus a New Deal under a Democratic one severely damaged Kentucky Republicans, who had successfully competed for a quarter century. Only sporadically and slowly would the new Democratic dominance in state elections be threatened.

Yet for all the modifications taking place in Kentucky life, many of the old problems still remained, ranging from party divisiveness to a struggling economy, from sizable out-migra-tions to segregation and educational neglect. Kentucky had gone through a trying period, but in some ways the problems still to be faced would prove even more demanding and more difficult to solve.

23

Education and Equality, 1865-1995

When soldiers, black and white, returned from World War II, they found a chaotic educational system that stood near the bottom nationally in most categories. It featured bad facilities, underfunded districts, poorly paid teachers, racial segregation, and political meddling. It also included dedicated people and students who loved learning. Neither characterization represented recent, wartime developments, for behind each stood a long history.

Commentators on Kentucky had long recognized the importance of education to the commonwealth's development. A geologist-historian in 1884 concluded that "the educational problem is by far the most serious of all the difficulties before this state." More than six decades later a study said, "There is an amazingly high degree of correlation between what a state invests in education and the standard of living of its people." Some thirty years after that a former governor declared that "you can't have a progressive state without an adequate educational system." Unfortunately, analysis and action did not always coincide.

Shaping the System, 1865-1908

In the first forty years after the Civil War, people who became teachers generally did so out of desperation or dedication. Young men seeking to rise up the economic ladder often started their professional careers as teachers, but they usually moved on; young unmarried women in many locales had few other choices if they wanted an independent existence. In some of those same places, however, local custom dictated that if women married, they would leave schoolteaching behind. That outlook continued into the early part of the twentieth century. A few teachers, men and women, stayed in education because they had no further options; others remained in the ranks because they enjoyed the work and could see that they made a difference in people's lives.

Dedication was often required, for teachers had to go through a great deal just to secure and keep their jobs. With no seniority or tenure system in existence until the mid–twentieth century, teachers as a rule found themselves underpaid, underprepared, and underappreciated. Yet some sought the job. The hiring process centered on the school district. Wherever up to one hundred school-age children lived, a district was formed; by 1907 Kentucky had some eighty-five hundred districts. Each served as a distinct and separate unit, with its own governing system, headed during most of the late nineteenth and early twentieth centuries by three elected trustees. This system meant that by 1907 nearly twenty-five thousand Kentuckians—almost one in ninety of the state's entire population—served as a school trustee. While such a scheme certainly ensured local control, three serious problems also arose. One was apathy. In some places no one sought the position of trustee, and those who did responded to the schools with the indifference they brought with them to office. That lack of interest contributed to the second problem, since a trustee's job requirements remained lax. By 1907 an estimated five thousand trustees—one-fifth of the total—could not read or write. Illiterates led some school systems. The third problem reversed the first; that is, sometimes there was too much trustee involvement.

Trustees had almost total local power, for they set taxes, hired teachers, and fixed salaries. As a result, local trustee elections often brought out more voters and inspired hotter debates than presidential contests. A dispute in one such 1933 race at Prather Creek in Floyd County ended in thirty gunshots and three wounded people, plus five dead ones. In many districts, teachers applying for positions had to pay trustees to be hired and had to pledge to support the trustees in political races. When the state instituted examinations for applicants for teaching positions, in order to restrict entrance of the uneducated into the system and to classify those in it, what were termed "unscrupulous" trustees skirted that process. They installed their favorites by selling exam questions to applicants or to "question peddlers," who did the selling for them. The local examination system continued until 1920. Even after an elective county superintendent's position was established in 1884, the trustee system continued, in one form or another, for another half century. But the trustees' local interjection of politics into education would live on, and in some places at least, the county superintendents later became virtual political bosses. They might supervise the biggest payroll in the county in small places, and through bus drivers, cooks, janitors, and teachers they could command a significant voting group. The ability to decide who received contracts to provide the necessities for the schools gave superintendents even more power. As a result, learning sometimes was not the chief goal of a county's educational system.

Once a teacher was hired, he or she—and in 1907, 58 percent of Kentucky educators were women—was assigned to a school. In most cases it was a one-room school, for even in 1920, half of all Kentucky children and three-fourths of all rural students went to one-teacher schools. As late as the 1940s, 65 percent of the commonwealth's nearly six thousand schools remained under the control of just one teacher.

In the late nineteenth and early twentieth centuries, the school day started at 8:00 or 8:30 A.M., featured a recess in the morning and another in the afternoon, included an hour for the consumption of a lunch brought from home, and ended at 4:00 P.M. Months of attendance varied, often depending on whether the school was in a rural area, where schools operated around farm needs, or in an urban setting.

Legally the minimum term ran five months (increased to six in 1904 and to seven a decade later). By the 1910s pupils usually began in July and finished in January, or went to school from September to March.

New teachers faced an assortment of students, for the one-room school included various grades and many ages. One Logan County teacher began work as soon as she finished high school and found that nine of her forty-nine students were older than she. Overall, the number of pupils per teacher varied a great deal, not only from one place to another but also during the year. Average attendance in 1882 stood at 33 percent of the eligible school-age population; according to the state superintendent of public instruction, this poor figure was due in large part to indifferent parents. Finally, in 1896 the state passed a weak compulsory education law, the first one in the South. Still, daily attendance in 1900 stood at only 36 percent. Even then, calls for farm labor in growing or harvesting seasons—the so-called tobacco vacations—further decimated the school ranks in rural areas.

In fact, significant differences existed between rural and urban education. One study found that the average rural school term lasted only two-thirds as long as the city terms and that students in rural schools tested about two and a half years behind those in urban districts as a result. Schools in large cities also offered greater options earlier. In 1891, for example, kindergarten became part of the public system in Lexington, apparently the first city in the South to make this opportunity available to young children.

While many of the differences between rural and urban schools resulted from local attitudes, more significant was money. Studies showed that the taxable wealth per teacher was twenty times higher in Louisville than in the poorest Appalachian county in 1921, and property assessments in the state's wealthiest areas stood over thirty times higher than those in the poorest areas in 1945. Thus, poverty-ridden places found it practically impossible to

secure anywhere near the funds available to the richer places. In 1901 the state's fifteen largest cities raised $600,000 from local taxation, while all the rest of the state together produced only $250,000. Not all of the disparity resulted from inequalities in wealth, however, for rural districts had a well-deserved reputation of not supporting education through local taxes. An 1895 educator acknowledged that "local taxation by districts, subject to the will of the people, is a failure." Aside from the differences in wealth among districts, the greatest problem in Kentucky educational funding was (and would long remain) the apathy, indifference, or even opposition to local taxation to support adequate schools.

In 1882 one superintendent lamented that "the people generally are opposed to voting a tax to pay the teachers better." It showed. Salaries in the 1880s ranged from $9.33 to $28.00 per month, and by 1900 the average across the state stood at $215.00 per year, about the wage of a general laborer. Author Elizabeth Madox Roberts taught in Washington County in 1907 for a total salary of $198.03. It was little wonder that one-sixth of the state's teachers left the profession each year.

Students entering the one-room schoolhouse to face their new teacher knew little about such issues. They did know, though, that the building itself did not promote learning. The worst type was described by Kentucky governor Preston Leslie in 1874:

A little square, squatty, unhewed log building, blazing in the sun, standing upon the dusty highway or some bleak and barren spot . . . without yard, fence, or other surroundings suggestive of comfort to abate its bare, cold, hard, and hateful look, is the fit representative of the district schoolhouse of the Commonwealth. . . . The benches—slabs with legs in them so long as to lift the little fellows' feet from the floor. . . . The desks—slabs at angles, cut, hacked, scratched. . . . Full of foul air and feculent odors. These are the places in which a cruel parsimony condemns childhood to pass its bright young days. . . . The school-house . . . seems to have been built simply for a pen for prisoners, at the smallest possible outlay. . . . It stands [as] an offense to justice, kindness, taste. . . . It invites no one to its interior, and sends a shudder through the frame of the pupil, daily, who approaches it.

A Rockcastle County educator echoed that analysis in 1881, calling the log schools in his district "places of punishment rather than learning." The cruelest cut came in the superintendent of public instruction's 1905 report, which declared that "hundreds of farmers in Kentucky have more comfortable barns in which to shelter their stock than they have school-houses in which to train the minds and mould the characters of their children."

The log buildings declined rapidly, though, and of the 8,115 schools in 1917, only 123 were log; 87 percent were still one-room, though. Generally, those white frame buildings sat on stone pillars, with the wind whipping beneath the floors, and in the worst cases they featured a leaky roof, broken windows, and a dusty floor. More often they were tight little buildings with an insufficient pot-bellied stove but little else. Water would be hauled from a well or stream—sometimes far distant—and would be made available in a common drinking bucket, with a community dipper. Fortunate students had frame outdoor toilets; others went into the woods, or as one remembered, "the boys went up the creek . . . while the girls went down the creek."

Inside, teaching tools remained limited or nonexistent. An eighteen-year-old Jessamine County teacher in the early twentieth century received her year's supply from the superintendent: a box of chalk, some erasers, a coal bucket, a mop, and floor oil. A chalkboard or perhaps a globe might offer the only aid to students, who typically used either the McGuffey books (whose author once taught in Kentucky) or publications from the Louisville firm of Morton and Griswold, featuring the Goodrich reader. One survey of nearly six hundred school libraries in Kentucky found that they each contained only forty-three books on average. Teachers had little support available.

Yet teachers persevered, endured, and, in some cases, succeeded. Despite all the problems—the poor physical facilities, the political overtones, the underpaid teachers, the unequal funding, the local apathy—learning still took place. In the mostly one-room schools, students often helped other students, and the good teachers did well and left a lasting impression on many of their pupils. Overall, the situation was in dire need of change if the state's educational promise was to be fulfilled; nevertheless, some individuals overcame all the obstacles and educated generations of students.

Separate and Unequal

The effect of the Civil War on Kentucky's schools had been nearly disastrous. During the conflict, one state superintendent wrote that

This one-room school in Mason County, with its central stove and shared desks, was typical of many Kentucky classrooms of the late nineteenth and early twentieth centuries (from Jean Calvert and John Klee, *The Towns of Mason County* [1986]).

the lack of funds, the fighting, and the general disruption had "thrown backward" the system: "Entire counties have been utterly prevented from keeping up a single school." In 1862 only 159,000 students attended classes, compared with 286,000 two years earlier, in a more peaceful time.

Recovering from that situation was hard enough in the postwar world, but Kentucky also had new challenges to face. Thousands upon thousands of freed slaves now desperately sought education for their children, and emancipation alone would bring large numbers of new students into the system. But inclusion of blacks in the public schools was not supported by most whites, for some wanted the former slaves educated only as workers, through a limited, second-class approach. In 1866 the state did pass a law that dealt with education for blacks, but significantly it mandated an entirely separate system. For almost a century, then, Kentucky would fund a costly dual system, with two sets of schools, two sets of administrators, two sets of teachers and supplies. The state's few resources were stretched thin.

The problem with the 1866 law was that only taxes collected from blacks could be used in the schools for black children; funds from whites would support white education only. Then two years later the General Assembly further limited the "Colored School Fund" by ordering that any money from taxes collected from black residents would go to paupers first, before being spent on education. Given the fact that most blacks came out of slavery without money or property, their property taxes yielded a very small total, only $2,232 as late as 1871. After funds from that source went to the poor, no money was left for education. Black public schools remained virtually nonexistent. The Freedmen's Bureau sought to fill the void, and by 1869, 267 of its schools provided education to thirteen thousand blacks. Yet like most Freedmen's Bureau activities, the schools attracted strong—and violent—opposition. School after school was burned, and teacher

after teacher was whipped or driven away. Yet for some three years soon after the close of the war, those schools and teachers gave black Kentuckians their chief opportunity for learning.

In an 1869 election white voters agreed to raise school finances through a fourfold increase in taxes, and overall funds jumped in one year from $283,000 to $968,000. Most black schools, however, continued to languish under the separate system, because of the small amount of taxable property owned by blacks. Finally, in 1874 the federal government dangled the lure of $60,000 before the state if Kentucky would establish a uniform system of black schools. Superintendent of Public Instruction H.A.M. Henderson, a former Confederate general who opposed "mixing" whites with "ignorant Africans," could not resist the bait. The change took place, but the inequality of the segregated system still showed in 1880, when annual expenditures per student totaled 48¢ for black students versus $1.45 for whites.

That disparity brought blacks, led by John H. Jackson, the first president of the Colored Teachers State Association, to call for a law combining the two school funds, so that equal monies could be appropriated to the two separate systems. When the proposal failed to receive legislative support, the scene shifted to the federal courts. In April 1882, in the case of *Kentucky v. Jesse Ellis,* the existing state funding plan was ruled unconstitutional. Members of the General Assembly responded with a plan to establish a combined funding system with the same per capita rate for black and white schools, to raise the tax rate, and to abolish the poll tax, paid only by blacks. Put before the voters in an August 1882 referendum, the plan was adopted by nearly a 17,000-vote margin. The plan applied only to state funding, though; local systems still discriminated. In August 1883 Judge John W. Barr, in the case of *Claybrook v. Owensboro,* ruled such discrimination "void," since it violated the Fourteenth Amendment to the U.S. Constitution. The two systems could remain separate, but in regard to calendar, curriculum, and funding, they must—on the surface at least—be equal. The state's superintendent of public instruction, like his predecessor a former Confederate officer (although he was a chaplain), agreed that "all the pupil-children of the commonwealth should enjoy equal privilege for preparing for intelligent citizenship."

The dual system of segregated schools could not do that, though, for the separation in itself suggested inequality. Moreover, in practice, school buildings for black pupils generally did not match those for whites, and blacks often received as their textbooks the worn-out leftovers from white classrooms. Nonetheless, despite all the handicaps, black schools still remained a highly prized part of community life. The state's 714 black public high school students and 93 graduates in 1900 led the segregated South, for example, and in 1907 a higher percentage of black youths attended school daily than did whites. Since the teachers in the black schools had often found their choice of occupation limited by segregation, some of the best and the brightest went into education, a highly honored profession among blacks. With fewer blacks than whites using teaching as a springboard to other jobs, more stability and a better educated teaching corps characterized many schools. In 1921, for instance, only 23 percent of white teachers had had a year or more of college, but 46 percent of black educators did. Pay discrimination did exist—Fulton County in 1904 paid white teachers $43.50 per month and blacks teachers $25.71—but the overall picture was more mixed. Because of their higher educational levels and classifications, black teachers in nineteen Kentucky counties earned a higher average salary than their white counterparts in 1904. In fifty-eight counties, though, the reverse held true. By 1916 the average salary for a white teacher stood at $322.76, for a black teacher at $310.05. While discrimination could in some cases be overcome, it remained an ever-present reminder to blacks of the badge of inferiority assigned them by white society.

One Kentucky school practiced a different philosophy, one that honored racial equality. Berea College had been founded by abolitionist John G. Fee and almost from its earliest times had offered equal access to education. Black students outnumbered whites every year but one between 1866 and 1894, and individuals from both races held leadership positions in various campus organizations. For twenty years interracial dating was permitted. Such a policy of equality never found widespread acceptance among the state's whites, though, and the *Lexington Observer and Reporter* in 1870 called Berea "a miscegenation school," one "of the meanest Yankee type." But some five years later the president of Berea College told of the goals sought by the school: "The great work of Berea looks to a vast and fundamental change in the views, tastes, feelings, and customs of society. White and colored people must be perfectly equal before the law." For nearly four decades the school held firm to that commitment, although it emphasized education for Appalachian students more heavily near the end of that period.

As increasing segregation took place in Kentucky life in the late nineteenth and early twentieth centuries, however, Berea's policy of racial integration found more and more critics. Finally, in January 1904 legislator Carl Day of Frozen Creek in Breathitt County called for an end to the "contamination" of white students at the college and introduced a bill "to prohibit white and colored persons from attending the same school." Since privately funded Berea College was the only integrated college in the South, Day's target was clear and his aim good. Supported by the superintendent of public instruction and not opposed by Governor J.C.W. Beckham, the Day Law became reality. Berea's president, though more racially conservative than his predecessors, led an appeal through the courts. In 1906, however, the commonwealth's highest judicial body ruled the key parts of the law constitutional. Meanwhile, black graduates of Berea, led by minister James Bond (1863-1929), began a

At Berea College in the 1890s, black and white students worked side by side in this integrated "homecooking" class (from Elisabeth S. Peck and Emily Ann Smith, *Berea's First 125 Years, 1855-1980* [1982]).

fund-raising drive to establish a separate school should a final appeal fail. In 1912 Lincoln Institute opened its doors in Shelby County as a high school and teacher training school, but the orphan never realized its founders' hopes of becoming a new black Berea. The school gained status in the black community when its first black principal, Whitney M. Young Sr., took over in 1935, but by then other institutions had seized much of the leadership role in black education.

In November 1908 the U.S. Supreme Court ruled in the case of *Berea College v. Kentucky.* Justice John Marshall Harlan, a Kentuckian, dissenting from the majority opinion, asked, "Have we become so inoculated with prejudice of race that [Kentucky] . . . can make distinctions between such citizens in the matter of . . . meeting for innocent purposes simply because of their respective races?" His fellow justices in essence answered yes, as they turned down Berea's appeal. The Day Law remained in force, and biracial education in Kentucky and the South legally ended for nearly a half century.

Whirlwinds and Doldrums, 1908-1954

Like sinners who knew the errors of their past ways and were ready to repent, Kentucky leaders by the early 1900s saw an educational revival sweeping the South and decided that they too wanted to join the crusade. Such an attitude had been so foreign previously that a superintendent of public instruction in the

1860s had complained about a legislature "almost uniformly unfriendly, indifferent, and evasive" to educational support. Historians in the 1880s proclaimed the typical legislator of their era "lamentably indifferent" to school improvements. The evil of the local trustee system, the parsimonious allocations, the expensive segregated system, and so much more cried out in support of such assertions. Yet even during those years Kentucky had stood reasonably well compared with other southern states. Now state after state began devoting more attention—and funds—to education. Virginia in 1905 and 1906 took major steps in that direction and in the succeeding decade saw school revenue triple and per capita expenditures double. Kentucky had to act or fall behind.

The 1906 General Assembly first looked at the vexing issue of teacher training. It was then handled by summer county institutes lasting only a few days or by the normal (teacher training) departments of some private schools and the present-day University of Kentucky, which proved too far distant for many to attend. In response, the legislature created two regional normal schools, which became Eastern Kentucky University, at Richmond, and Western Kentucky University, at Bowling Green. (In 1922 two additional normal schools were authorized for Murray and Morehead.)

Major reforms earned the 1908 General Assembly the title Education Legislature. With the strong support of the Kentucky Federation of Women's Clubs and of Superintendent of Public Instruction John G. Crabbe of Ashland, a bill was passed that required public high schools to be established in each county and a minimum school tax to be enacted. It also abolished the small school districts and their trustees and made the county the fundamental unit. Subdistrict trustees remained, and members of the county boards of education were elected from those smaller areas, but a broader system still emerged. Higher education received more funding as well.

Unwilling to rest on their educational laurels, advocates of Kentucky's schools followed with what were called Whirlwind Campaigns. During a two-month period in late 1908, nearly three hundred talks were given to audiences totaling more than sixty thousand people; even more read the discourses in newspapers and pamphlets. The summer of 1909 saw more than a hundred speakers go forth on a second campaign in an effort to keep the reform spirit alive. Local funding increased fivefold in a year, and the 1910 census showed that over 57 percent of the school-age population attended school, nearly the national average and far above the 48 percent figure of 1900. Between 1911 and 1919 the number of high schools in the state increased from 157 to 400. The educational winds seemed to be blowing strong.

Illiteracy among adults still loomed as a significant problem, however. In 1900 the state's illiteracy rate had been 16.5 percent, which, though second best in the South, trailed the national figure of 10.7 percent. One in six Kentuckians over the age of ten could not read or write. A decade later more than two hundred thousand Kentuckians (12.1 percent of the adult population) remained illiterate. Seeking to correct that situation, the energetic and controversial Cora Wilson Stewart (1875-1958) in 1911 organized classes to be held at night—thus their name, moonlight schools—and demonstrated that such methods could work in her native Rowan County and elsewhere. Three years later she received a legislative appropriation of five thousand dollars and set up the Kentucky Illiteracy Commission, which in

its brief six-year existence did much good. Textbooks were published, literacy was made a condition of parole for prisoners, and numerous new readers were trained. But Stewart's publicity efforts overstated her importance and the results. By 1920 the state's literacy rate was 8.4 percent; the decline since 1910 represented about the same drop as in the decade before the commission was formed. Continued effort was what was needed, though, and the death of the commission in 1920 hurt the state's efforts to combat illiteracy for generations.

Attacks on the state's educational problems came on several fronts. In addition to the focus on public school reform and the fights against illiteracy, some private citizens turned their attention to rural education in the isolated parts of the Kentucky mountains. Born out of the urban settlement schools of London, England; New York; and the Hull House of Chicago, the rural settlement school movement had several varied elements. While all the schools sought to change the population around them, most did so through an approach centering on industrial arts and vocational training, although a few, such as a school at Caney Creek, stressed a classical education. Many teachers came from New England or had been educated in the new women's colleges there, but others had their roots in Kentucky. All the teachers, however, approached their work as missionaries intent on doing good. While their fund-raising efforts required that they portray the area as a place of great needs, thus perpetuating stereotypes of the region, at the same time they did provide an education to children who had no other options.

In 1902 Katherine Pettit (1868-1936) of Lexington and May Stone (1867-1946) of Louisville founded Hindman Settlement School on Troublesome Creek in Knott County and thus started what has been called the first rural social settlement school in the nation. Eleven years later Pettit and Ethel de Long of New Jersey founded Pine Mountain Settlement School in Harlan County and started a similar program. In 1915 Alice Geddes Lloyd (1876-

1962) of Boston came to Knott County and set up her community center. With June Buchanan (1887-1988) of New York, Lloyd established Caney Junior College (later Alice Lloyd College) in 1923, at Pippa Passes. The school required its students to conduct "no unauthorized meetings with the opposite sex" and to pledge to remain in Appalachia once their education was completed. The three schools joined with numerous others to give mountain youth a needed educational option into the 1940s, but most of the settlement schools would have to find alternative ways of operating once better transportation and public schools arrived.

The Education Legislature of 1908, the Whirlwind Campaigns, the Kentucky Illiteracy Commission, the settlement schools—all seemed to demonstrate that a true educational awakening was taking place in the Bluegrass State. The reform, however, was not as deep or as long-lasting as it appeared, and Kentuckians had not even kept up with the educational change taking place all around them. In 1900 Kentucky had stood fourth in the South in educational spending per student, and in the twenty years after that the state had increased expenditures per pupil by 238 percent. But the nation's and the South's figures had gone up even more in that period, and by 1920 the state ranked only eleventh in the South. Its per pupil spending, which had been only half the national average in 1900, had fallen to just one-third the norm by 1920. Kentuckians thought that they had accomplished a great deal in those decades, and they had, but it was not enough. The promise had not been realized, and not for many, many more decades would the will be present once again. Generations of Kentuckians were doomed to an educational system that soon stood near the bottom in most national categories.

The years between 1908-9, when the Whirlwind Campaigns occurred, and the 1950s were not barren of action. In 1918 the legislature established a Division of Vocational Education. Two years later a law made the county

school board popularly elected and gave the board the power to select a county superintendent and all employees. Twelve years later, however, the county superintendent would again become an elected official. The 1920 act also gave the state Department of Education responsibility for the teacher certification process, ending the problem-ridden teachers' examinations at the local level, and required a high school diploma for elementary teachers after 1936. By 1935 a bachelor's degree was required for high school teaching. The 1930s saw several major changes take place: in 1930 a stronger State Textbook Commission was formed; in 1934 a major new school code was funded, following the recommendations of a committee appointed by Governor Ruby Laffoon a year earlier; and in 1938 the first Teachers' Retirement Act was passed, with full financing to come much later. By 1952 the school term had been lengthened to nine months.

Nevertheless, a series of studies, from the 1920s through the 1940s, showed that many of the actions taken had only a limited effect on a bad situation. Kentucky stood fortieth in the nation in expenditures per pupil in 1912, forty-fourth in 1920, and forty-first in 1930. The year before Pearl Harbor, the commonwealth spent forty-eight dollars per student per year, while the U.S. average was ninety-four dollars. The state's capital outlay for schools increased 214 percent between 1934 and 1952, but the South's shot up 667 percent during the same period.

The same trends existed concerning attendance and the length of the school term. By 1943 Kentucky students spent sixteen fewer days in the classroom than the average American student, a statistic that ranked the state last nationally. For students ages ten to fourteen, the commonwealth in 1900 had ranked first in attendance in the South, both for white and black students; by 1940 it ranked last and next to last in the two categories. By 1940 some 95 percent of the children in the United States received an elementary school education, but only 63 percent of Kentucky children did. It was little wonder that by 1945, at the end of World War II, the commonwealth ranked absolutely last in the nation in the percentage of the population over twenty-five who had a high school diploma. Given the dismal educational picture overall and the fact that only seven states in 1940 paid their teachers less than the $1,507 average salary that instructors in Kentucky received, one observer noted that Kentucky's greatest export was not bourbon or thoroughbreds but schoolteachers.

In 1954, however, one action gave some promise that the future might be better. The inequality between wealthy and poor districts had long plagued the system. In an attempt to change that situation, voters in 1941 approved a constitutional amendment that allowed 10 percent of school funds to be appropriated on some basis other than pupil population. A 1949 amendment increased this figure to 25 percent of funds. These actions gave poorer districts much-needed money. After the passage of another constitutional amendment four years later, the 1954 General Assembly went one step further and established the Minimum Foundation Program, in an effort to provide greater balance in public school funding. There was thus some hope that the years ahead in Kentucky education would be brighter. Greater opportunities were also heralded that same year by changes in the system of school segregation.

Before *Brown*

Change had been in the air for more than a decade before the critical year of 1954. The first major suggestion that the state's system might be modified came from outside education, when in 1938 the U.S. Supreme Court in *Hale v. Kentucky* overturned a Paducah man's conviction because of "a systematic and arbitrary exclusion of Negroes from the jury list." For well over thirty years, no blacks had sat on a state jury deciding an interracial case. That practice, said the court, clearly violated the Fourteenth Amendment and must stop.

In education, some progress had occurred as well. In 1942 the city of Louisville equalized the salaries of black and white teachers, and that same year the two racially separate teachers' unions merged. A public study by one of the postwar planning groups, the Committee for Kentucky, obliquely suggested that the "waste and inefficiency" resulting from segregation should end. Problems still remained, however, as a 1940s survey of state educational facilities showed. It found that black school buildings had half the value of white ones; the doctrine of "separate but equal" seldom addressed the second part as well as the first. More than that, the spiritual deprivation arising from segregation continued to be worse than any building inequities.

A new black leadership led by a Louisville cadre that included Charles W. Anderson Jr., the Reverend Charles E. Tucker, and *Louisville Defender* editor Frank Stanley Sr. began to probe for ways to desegregate the whole system. In 1941, black student Charles L. Eubanks applied for admission to the segregated engineering school at the University of Kentucky, on the grounds that no other such educational opportunity existed in the commonwealth. The school refused his application, and a legal challenge followed. After dragging on for years, the case was dismissed on technical grounds in 1945. That same year troops returning from World War II found that the two races, whose members had died together on foreign battlefields, could not be educated together in Kentucky's schools.

In 1948 the first legislative session during the administration of Governor Earle C. Clements (1896-1985) made a dent in the formerly ironclad Day Law when it provided that black medical personnel could take postgraduate courses in white public hospitals. At the same time Lyman Johnson (b. 1906), a navy veteran and black history teacher from Louisville, applied to take courses at the graduate school of the University of Kentucky. Once more the petition was denied, and attorneys began to prepare their cases. Hurried attempts were made to set up a makeshift program at the black college in Frankfort. That activity fooled no one, though, and in March 1949 Judge H. Church Ford of the U.S. District Court ruled that Johnson was being denied equal access to education and must be admitted to the university. After a bitter meeting of the university's trustees, the school did not appeal. In the summer session of 1949 more than a dozen black students joined Johnson on the campus. For the first time in forty-five years, both races took classes together at a Kentucky school.

Such developments worried some citizens. A St. Matthews woman asked the governor to strengthen the Day Law to prevent further black attendance at state schools. "I would hate to think that my sons would attend a school with a negro; eat in the same room; play on the same team and learn to accept them socially." Another Kentuckian asked a University of Kentucky dean, "Who gave you the right to compel our children to sin Against God, by compelling them to intermix with Negro's?" According to the courts, the U.S. Constitution gave that right; according to other people of the commonwealth, simple justice did. In 1950 the General Assembly further amended the Day Law to allow colleges to desegregate if they offered classes not available to blacks at segregated colleges. That year Berea College and several Catholic schools did just that. In fact, before 1954 nearly six hundred blacks had enrolled at formerly white campuses. Secondary and elementary education, however, still remained segregated.

Ironically, it appeared that the rapidly crumbling wall of constitutional segregation would be finally torn down at the national level by a Kentuckian. In 1946 President Harry Truman had named his friend and soulmate Frederick M. Vinson (1890-1953) of Louisa as Chief Justice of the United States. The new appointee's already distinguished and varied career included stints as congressman, federal judge, wartime director of economic stabilization, and secretary of the Treasury. Known for his good memory, mathematical ability,

checker-playing prowess, political astuteness, and bushy eyebrows, Vinson was described in 1946 as a tall man with a mountain twang in his voice, a leader with "a sense of American continuity in time." Truman hoped that Vinson's calm, sociable, and patient attitude could unite a divided Court that included fellow Kentuckian Stanley Reed and, for a time, former Kentuckian Wiley Rutledge. The Chief Justice's attempts to compromise and forge a united Court often failed, however, and dissenting opinions continued to be commonplace. Still, his actions would set the stage for a predecessor who would be able to accomplish those goals.

Basically pragmatic, with a tendency to support the state over the individual, Vinson soon found his Court confronting segregation and racial prejudice piece by piece. In *Sweatt v. Painter* (1950) Vinson spoke for a unanimous Court in ordering a black student admitted to the previously all-white University of Texas Law School. The Court also struck down aspects of segregation in *McLaurin v. Oklahoma State Regents* (1950) and *Henderson v. United States* (1950) and in so doing came very near to declaring that separate education could never be equal. By 1953 another key case drew near a decision, and it seemed only a matter of time before the Court would rule that the nation's system of segregated schools was unconstitutional and illegal. Whether Vinson could get a unanimous decision or even induce Reed's support was uncertain, however.

On September 8, 1953, Chief Justice Vinson died of a massive heart attack. The segregation case the Court had been hearing would be decided by a group now headed by Chief Justice Earl Warren. In a unanimous decision in 1954, the Court ruled segregation illegal, in *Brown v. Board of Education of Topeka, Kansas*. By declaring that "in the field of public education the doctrine of 'separate but equal' has no place," for such a policy is "inherently unequal," the U.S. Supreme Court accelerated a slowly developing civil rights movement.

What would be Kentucky's reaction to the decision? It quickly became clear that across the South massive resistance to integration was the common response. Such an attitude by state leaders would not be unpopular, for the commonwealth's racial mores differed chiefly only in degrees from those of the rest of the South. Yet at the same time, Kentucky had been moving independently to dismantle the system of segregation bit by bit during the past few years. Acceptance of the decision or resistance to it both seemed possible.

Implementing Integration

Strong leadership came to the forefront and made Kentucky an early model of peaceful integration for the South and for the nation. That leadership came at three levels. The commonwealth's chief newspaper at the time, the *Courier-Journal*, came out in favor of acceptance of the *Brown* decision and supported the actions of others who did so. In the political arena, both U.S. senators spoke in favor of the decision, while Governor Lawrence W. Wetherby (1908-94) resisted southern efforts to oppose *Brown*. On March 1, 1955, the governor stated clearly that "Kentucky will meet the issue fairly and squarely for all." In the gu-

bernatorial elections of 1955 and 1959, no candidate for either party took a prosegregation stance.

The victor in the 1955 race was Happy Chandler. His mail bag quickly filled with dire warnings of doom should integration occur. A Hopkinsville woman concluded, for example, that if such a step took place, "we might as well open the doors of Hell." From Lexington a woman warned that the races might next be swimming together in pools. The governor's background provided clues that he could support either southern extremists or the Court. As a U.S. senator he had voted against antilynching and poll tax repeal bills. In 1948 he had headed the racially conservative Dixiecrat movement in the state, had entertained its candidate J. Strom Thurmond in his home, and had given little evidence that his racial views varied drastically from those of others of his generation. Yet at almost the same time, he had faced the question of integrating baseball in his position as commissioner of that sport. While Chandler would overstate his role later, it remains correct to say that had he opposed the move, integration of baseball would have been much more difficult. Instead, he supported the action.

Fred Vinson of Louisa was the first Kentuckian to be appointed Chief Justice of the United States. President Harry Truman sent Vinson to the Supreme Court in 1946 (courtesy of the Kentucky Historical Society).

The man who integrated baseball in the twentieth century was Jackie Robinson, who had had a less than ideal experience during his military service at Kentucky's Camp Breckinridge and who had been roundly booed when he appeared in a minor league game in 1946 in Louisville. Yet when Robinson entered the major leagues in 1947, his chief supporter and friend on his team, the Brooklyn Dodgers, was Louisville's Harold ("Pee Wee") Reese, later elected to baseball's Hall of Fame. In a sense, Robinson's varied experiences with Kentuckians represented the divisions existing within the society.

In 1956 Governor Chandler indicated publicly that the Court's decision was the law of the land and he would enforce the law. Privately in letters he said he did not know whether he as an individual favored integration, but "I do not think it is Christian, and I know it is not lawful, to deny any of our fellow citizens equality of opportunity and protection under our laws." Already blacks were attending public institutions of higher education in Kentucky, and in 1955 the commonwealth's highest court finally ruled the Day Law unconstitutional. That summer a young black woman entered Lafayette High School in Lexington, and soon afterward several students integrated the Wayne County system during the regular school term.

On August 31, 1956, nine black children enrolled in the Union County school at Sturgis. When classes began four days later, a crowd of several hundred people opposed the attempt to integrate the school. While the situation seems to have been resolved locally, press reports spurred Governor Chandler to bring in police and troops, and that action intensified the dispute. On the night of September 6, a prosegregation white citizens' council held a meeting attended by a thousand people. Nevertheless, calm followed. Meanwhile, at the nearby town of Clay, similar events and reactions brought National Guard forces there as well. The state's attorney general issued an in-

terpretation of the *Brown* decision that allowed the local school board to reject integration for the moment but to draw up a plan for it to take place in the future. The some one thousand state troops and soldiers were withdrawn, a court case ordered full desegregation the next year, and in 1957 blacks and whites sat in the same classes at Sturgis High School. A boycott by some students ended quickly when they were given unexcused absences. In 1965 the once all-black high school closed, and integration was complete. Symbolically, however, the incidents at Sturgis and Clay showed Kentuckians that the state government would support the integration process, by force if necessary. No further incidents of that scope occurred, and school segregation began to end peacefully.

Leadership also came from school officials themselves. In Louisville, superintendent Dr. Omer Carmichael (1893-1960) instituted a plan that rapidly integrated the city's major system and gave Louisville a national reputation as a model for the South. Under the plan, the entire system was redistricted without regard to race, and pupils were assigned to the nearest school. Voluntary transfers were allowed, however, which meant that in practice the plan was far less sweeping than it seemed on the surface. Future problems would result from that situation, but by the fall of 1956 fifty-five of the city's seventy-five schools, containing 73 percent of the students, had integrated without major opposition. A reporter for the *New York Times* watched classes open and announced: "Segregation died quietly here today."

In one sense, integration and the state's reaction to it showed how far Kentuckians had come in a little more than eight decades. During the immediate post–Civil War years, white people of the commonwealth had matched those elsewhere in resistance to black rights. Lynchings and segregation had continued well into the twentieth century. In the 1950s white citizens were still far from racial egalitarians, and they would not be deaf to racial appeals in later years. Nor was integration in the state quite so widespread as journalists pictured it. Yet the press, the politicians, and the school officials had set the standard and the examples at a crucial time. When confronted by racial questions in the 1950s, Kentucky reacted in a way that made it a leader in integration. It was a strange but welcome position for the state.

Civil Rights in the Sixties and Beyond

Kentuckians still had a long way to go on racial matters, however, and the state's leadership position would rise and fall over the next few decades. Education had been only the first fight on the integration front, and attention soon turned toward achieving equal rights in other areas.

In politics, Kentucky blacks had continued to vote, so the struggles taking place elsewhere in the South regarding voting rights were largely absent in the state. Gains did take place in other areas, however. In 1961 the first black woman, Amelia Tucker, was elected to the legislature; six years later Georgia Davis (later Georgia Davis Powers) became the first black woman elected as state senator; in 1968 the city of Glasgow, where white voters outnumbered blacks by ten to one, made educator Luska J. Twyman Kentucky's first black mayor elected to a full term. Still, despite the individual gains,

by 1970 blacks comprised less than 1 percent of elected officials in the commonwealth.

Away from the political world, change was taking place in ways both small and large. When the Mississippi Valley Historical Association held its national meeting in Lexington in 1953, one hotel in the city opened its doors to black guests for the first time. The next year the city directory there dropped the *c* (for *colored*) designation after people's names. In 1955 the state Court of Appeals banned segregated public recreational facilities. The most significant victories, though, were won in the 1960s. At the beginning of that decade, stores, restaurants, theaters, pools, and other public places remained segregated in many areas of Kentucky. In Hopkinsville, for example, the 30 percent of its population that was not white found housing, public toilets, theaters, restaurants, motels, and county fair competitions still segregated. Two of the twelve councilmen and four of the thirty-five policemen were black, however, and the library, sporting events, and religious services had been integrated. Faced with such situations across Kentucky, blacks, and their white allies, began in 1960 an eventually successful series of "sit-ins," "stand-ins," and boycotts of lunch counters and stores, particularly in Lexington, Frankfort, and Louisville.

Protesters in Louisville stage a sit-in to challenge segregation, 1961 (courtesy of the *Louisville Courier-Journal*).

That same year the Kentucky Commission on Human Rights was formed and began to issue reports on civil rights. It found in 1961 that state parks and bus terminals were open to all races, but that twenty-six of eighty-seven drive-in theaters surveyed were not. The next year it noted that six cities still had "whites only" pools but that thirty-five of forty Little League baseball programs had been integrated. In fact, sports became a key area for gains by blacks, and in 1967 University of Kentucky football player Nat Northington became the first black athlete to play in the Southeastern Conference. Increasingly, whites who had decried integration would find themselves cheering the sporting accomplishments of a black high school or college player on their favorite team.

Resistance to integration continued, though, and it became clear that further action would be needed to bring about full change. At the national level, Kentuckian Whitney M. Young Jr. (1921-71) led the National Urban League through the decade and became a major spokesman for racial moderation: "We must learn to live together as brothers or we will all surely die together as fools." At the state level, Governor Bert T. Combs (1911-91), in the last year of his term of office, issued a Fair Services Executive Order and a Code of Fair Practices,

which affected those dealing in state contracts. The major achievements, however, came under new governor Edward T. ("Ned") Breathitt Jr. (b. 1924). Attempts to pass a statewide public accommodations bill in 1964 brought the Reverend Martin Luther King Jr., the Reverend Ralph Abernathy, and Jackie Robinson to a March rally attended by thousands at the state capitol. Neither the original Norbert Blume draft nor a compromise bill could secure enough votes to get out of committee before the session ended, however. Months later a national civil rights bill became law; the two Kentucky senators and Representative Carl D. Perkins voted for it, and four other Kentucky congressmen opposed the bill. That national action, accomplished under a Democratic president, helped the situation in Kentucky when a stronger antidiscrimination bill came before the General Assembly in 1966.

Backed by Governor Breathitt and legislative leaders, the resulting Kentucky Civil Rights Act passed easily and was signed into law at the base of the statue of Abraham Lincoln in the capitol rotunda. The first such act in the South, the law opened public accommodations to all races and prohibited discrimination in employment in firms with eight or more workers. That same year Bardstown took the lead in enacting a local open housing ordi-

Whitney M. Young Jr. of Shelby County, president of the National Urban League, confers with Lyndon Johnson (courtesy of the University of Kentucky Libraries).

nance. In 1968 the commonwealth became the first state in the South to pass a comprehensive Fair Housing Act.

At that time Kentucky seemed to have avoided the racial tragedies that had ended in beatings and death elsewhere for those supporting civil rights. But the successes blinded too many to the still unsolved problems, issues smoldering beneath the surface tranquillity. Following the murder of Dr. Martin Luther King Jr. in 1968, a May rally in the black Parkland section of Louisville erupted in some minor disorders, the police moved in, and then, as one observer noted, "all hell broke loose." Before the rioting ended, many black businesses were destroyed, two black teenagers were killed, dozens of people, black and white, were injured, and nearly five hundred individuals were arrested. More than two thousand National Guard members joined city and county police in restoring order. Across Kentucky that summer several black churches and businesses were bombed, and a September exchange of shots between blacks and a white supremacy group meeting near Berea left two whites dead. The state had prided itself on its moderate stance on race, but the summer of 1968 left a scar, reminding Kentuckians that the fight for racial equality could not stop.

In the field of education, the promise of the 1950s seemed to be continuing. The number of schools with students of both races rose from 41 in 1955 to 685 a decade later, while the percentage of blacks in desegregated classrooms increased from 46 in 1962 to 68 in 1964. But by 1968—the year of the riot—the city once held up as a national model now saw headlines that read, "Schools Move Back Toward Segregation." Ten Louisville schools remained either all-black or all-white; in twenty-five others, over 95 percent of the students were of one race. The situation worsened between 1968 and 1974, as the growth of suburbs drew whites from the city, and the federal judiciary became involved. A district court's decision favorable to the existing system was overturned at a higher level, which ordered the city and

county school systems to merge "not only to eliminate the effects of the past but also to bar future discrimination." Court-ordered busing for racial balance brought forth a violent reaction by whites, especially in the southwestern parts of Jefferson County. School buses were damaged, stores looted, and other property destroyed in September 1975 riots, which resulted in fifty injuries and nearly two hundred arrests. State and local police, together with eight hundred members of the National Guard, brought an uneasy peace.

Louisville's—and the state's—once-strong record on race appeared to be only a distant memory. Yet the integration taking place across the commonwealth was resulting in drastic change. In 1974 some 29 percent of Kentucky blacks went to schools that were over 90 percent black; six years later none did. Two national studies, based on 1986 and 1991 figures, proclaimed that Kentucky schools were the most integrated in the nation.

Kentucky Education Reform Act

The educational history of the commonwealth in the four decades after the 1954 *Brown* decision was marked by historic peaks and valleys. Higher requirements for teachers, for instance, caused the percentage of teachers with college degrees to grow from 51 percent in 1950 to 94 percent fifteen years later. In the 1960s, the end of segregated systems and funds from the new sales tax provided state schools with an influx of money. State aid to education more than quadrupled in the decade after 1964, more than the national average in that expansive time. The commonwealth's expenditures on higher education rose nearly 400 percent from 1960 to 1968. In that same decade Kentucky Educational Television began its successful operation under the guidance of Leonard Press. In expenditures per pupil in average attendance, the state's figure was 65 percent of the national figure in 1963 and 79 percent in 1969.

Constant, consistent support did not characterize later years, though, and educational valleys proved more prevalent. Various chief executives of the commonwealth might periodically infuse more budgeted funds, and the physical facilities might grow adequately, but more often whatever occurred simply kept Kentucky at its previous level. It really had no place to fall. Despite being number one in the nation in the percentage of salary increases for teachers in the 1960s, the state still ranked forty-second in teachers' pay in 1968, forty-sixth in 1976, and fortieth in 1978. In 1970 Kentucky's population stood last in median years of schooling (9.9 years versus the U.S. average of 12.1) and tied for forty-eighth in the years of high school completed. A decade later it ranked last in the nation in the percentage of high school graduates (53.1 percent as opposed to the national figure of 66.3). By 1976 Kentucky was forty-sixth in overall per pupil expenditures. The state cowered at or near the bottom in almost all educational categories. Given the increasing need for a better-educated workforce and population, state leaders feared for the future.

Governor Martha Layne Collins (b. 1936), a former schoolteacher herself, got some significant reforms passed in the 1985 and 1986 sessions. But an action was under way that would soon transform the entire system. In a court case led by former governor Bert Combs, some sixty-six underfunded school districts sued the state, and in 1988 circuit judge Ray Corns supported their position regarding the lack of equity in distribution of funds. Appealed to the state's highest court, the case of *Rose v. Council for Better Schools* (1989) brought an even more far-reaching decision by the Kentucky Supreme Court, led by Chief Justice Robert Stephens. The court ruled that "Kentucky's *entire system* of common schools is unconstitutional" and ordered the General Assembly, in essence, to start over and "re-create" an efficient and fair system. Beginning with a clean slate, the legislature crafted an entirely new approach, financed by an increase in the sales tax. House Speaker Don Blandford, Sen-

ate president pro tempore John ("Eck") Rose, and budget leaders Joe Clarke and Mike Moloney joined in an uneasy and not altogether smooth partnership with Governor Wallace G. Wilkinson (b. 1941) to enact what became known as the Kentucky Education Reform Act of 1990 (KERA).

KERA combined elements of strong local control with strong central powers. An antinepotism section and passages that restricted more blatant forms of local patronage could be enforced by the state Department of Education, which could (and did) take over some local systems that did not operate as required under the new guidelines. A statewide testing system was established to determine progress and accountability, with financial rewards accruing to districts that met established goals. Yet in other areas, more control flowed away from Frankfort to schools. Local councils of teachers, parents, and administrators had greater powers to determine curriculum and other such matters than before. The reforms stressed hands-on activities, individual progress, and an ungraded primary system with teams of teachers. Finally, KERA raised school district revenues by an average of 30 percent in four years, greatly increased teachers' salaries in the poorer school districts, and funded computer technology for each classroom and for the state. Even at that, the state's earlier funding problems in the 1980s meant that the new monies only brought the state per pupil spending to national spending ratio back to what it had been in 1979. Much remained to be done. KERA represented an almost unprecedented modification of an entire school system, however, and other states began looking to Kentucky as a model.

Not everyone agreed with the changes, and alterations soon followed. The key point, however, may not have been the form or the details of KERA, but rather its spirit. The act placed education in Kentucky at center stage and declared that the state considered learning crucial to the future. By 1995 Kentucky school spending per pupil had risen to thirty-second in the nation, and teachers' salaries ranked twenty-ninth overall. The state stood seventh in providing computer access to students. But the question remained for the future: Would Kentucky continue to support that growth and the spirit behind it, or would it, as in the early 1900s, let the opportunity slip away?

Higher Education

Emerging from the Civil War, the state's system of higher education stood in disarray if not in shambles. What had once been the best of the prewar schools, Transylvania University, had barely survived, and other struggling institutions had seen enrollments drop drastically. Numerous institutions had the name *college* attached to them but offered no more than a secondary level of education. Most such schools had a teacher or two, taught students of one sex, and struggled annually for existence. Private colleges generally started that way, or as a normal (teacher training) school, often connected to a particular religious group. They then usually transformed into colleges offering a two-year program, in the process changing locations at least once. Kentucky Wesleyan College, for example, opened in 1866 as a Methodist school at Millersburg, moved to Winchester in 1890, then to Owensboro sixty years later. What became Spalding University started as Nazareth College, for women, in 1920, changed its name in 1963, merged with Nazareth College in Nelson County in 1971, and became coeducational two years later. Alice Lloyd, Campbellsville, Cumberland, Lindsey Wilson, and Pikeville Colleges were all junior colleges by the 1920s and began offering baccalaureate degrees between 1957 and 1986.

On the other hand, some institutions that had existed before the Civil War functioned fairly steadily as four-year colleges soon after the conflict ended. Georgetown College, which had closed for a few months at the beginning of the Civil War and had only 35 students in 1863, by 1870 numbered 145 in its preparatory and college departments. When the separate female seminary merged with the men's college in 1892, enrollment jumped to 397, and growth continued after that. Berea College, which had opened briefly as a secondary school before the Civil War, welcomed its first college-level students in 1869, but as late as 1890, of its total enrollment of 355, only 28 students were taking college courses. Under President William G. Frost, that number rose to 215 by 1920. Berea's emphasis on student work and tuition-free education gave it a special status as the decades passed. In Danville, Centre College became the strongest of the state's private colleges in the late nineteenth and early twentieth centuries. Although it had only seven graduates during the war year of 1863, the school grew to include a law department, then merged in 1901 with another Presbyterian institution, Central University in Richmond. Soon after the Centre College football team won what was called the greatest upset in that sport's first half century in a 1921 game with Harvard, the Danville school grew to enroll 315 students; by 1926 it became coeducational, although women students did not move onto the campus until the 1957-81 presidency of Dr. Thomas A. Spragens, who also doubled the student body and greatly expanded the physical facilities and endowment. The school had developed a strong academic tradition as well.

Not all colleges succeeded, however, and the 1868 closing of Shelby College in Shelbyville marked an equally common trend. The names of Logan Female College in Russellville (founded in 1846, closed in 1931), Gethsemani College near Bardstown (1851-1912), and Eminence College in Eminence (1857-95) stand as testimony that some tried and failed. Even then, they failed in only one sense, for the schools had educated generations of students.

Most of the nineteenth-century discussion of higher education in the commonwealth, however, focused on the state's role in what was occurring in Lexington. After the

Table 23.1
Selected Private Four-Year Colleges and Seminaries, 1995

College	Location	Founded
Alice Lloyd College	Pippa Passes	1923
Asbury College	Wilmore	1890
Bellarmine College	Louisville	1950
Berea College	Berea	1869
Brescia College	Owensboro	1950 (1925)[a]
Campbellsville College	Campbellsville	1924
Centre College	Danville	1819
Cumberland College	Williamsburg	1889 (1913)[b]
Georgetown College	Georgetown	1829
Kentucky Christian College	Grayson	1919
Kentucky Wesleyan College	Owensboro	1866
Lindsey Wilson College	Columbia	1903 (1923)[c]
Midway College	Midway	1847
Pikeville College	Pikeville	1889 (1918)[d]
Spalding University	Louisville	1920
Thomas More College	Fort Mitchell	1921
Transylvania University	Lexington	1780
Union College	Barbourville	1879

Seminary	Location	Founded
Asbury Theological Seminary	Wilmore	1923
Clear Creek Baptist Bible College	Clear Creek	1926
Episcopal Theological Seminary	Lexington	1834 (1951)[e]
Hopkinsville College of the Bible	Hopkinsville	1883
Lexington Theological Seminary	Lexington	1865
Louisville Presbyterian Seminary	Louisville	1901
Southern Baptist Theological Seminary	Louisville	1859

[a] Brescia, so named in 1950, was preceded by Mount St. Joseph College, established in 1925.

[b] Founded in 1889, Williamsburg Institute was renamed Cumberland College in 1913.

[c] Founded in 1903, the Lindsey Wilson Training School expanded its curriculum and became Lindsey Wilson College in 1923.

[d] Established as an elementary and secondary school in 1889, Pikeville College began offering college courses in 1918.

[e] Episcopal Theological Seminary was reestablished in 1951, following many years of closure.

Source: John E. Kleber, editor in chief, *The Kentucky Encyclopedia* (1992)

main building of Kentucky University in Harrodsburg (formerly Bacon College) burned in 1864, the energetic John B. Bowman engineered a move that he hoped would result in a great "university for the people." In 1865 the legislature agreed that Transylvania University would merge with and take the name of Kentucky University. At the same time, the commonwealth established the Agricultural and Mechanical (A&M) College, to be financed through the proceeds of the sale of some public land, under the national Morrill Land Grant Act. A&M would be an independent college but, together with a law department and a college of the Bible, would be part of the new Kentucky University. Funded by public and private funds and operated by both church and state, the hybrid school had problems from the start. Financial concerns growing out of the Panic of 1873 and debate over denominational control added to the difficulties. Finally, in 1878 the A&M College had only sixty students on its campus on Henry Clay's old estate of Ashland, and the General Assembly separated it totally from Kentucky University. That private school retook the name Transylvania College some three decades later, and its law school closed, reopened, then closed for good in 1912. After struggles and successes common to most private colleges in Kentucky, Transylvania University emerged as a small and strong liberal arts college with a good academic reputation.

Meanwhile, across town, the A&M College, under its benevolent dictator-president James K. Patterson, was trying to find success in its role as the commonwealth's chief public institution of higher learning. Leaving its old Ashland campus, the school started life anew on some city parkland. Additional acres were added for a developing agricultural experiment station, started in 1885. The state established a property tax to give the institution a financial base, required the college to offer free tuition to two students from each county, and created a teacher training department (which admitted the first women students on campus in 1880). In 1908 the school's name was changed to State

University, and a college of law was authorized; eight years later it became the University of Kentucky.

In higher education, however, as at other levels, a dual system existed. With the exception of Berea College until 1904, blacks found their options restricted to segregated colleges. In medical education, for instance, Louisville National Medical College, under the leadership of Dr. Henry Fitzbutler, opened in the fall of 1888. The next year it conferred the first M.D. degree to a black person in the state's history and in 1891 graduated the first woman doctor educated in the state, of any race. But the first institution of comprehensive higher learning for blacks, and for many decades the strongest, was the Kentucky Normal and Theological Institute, established in Louisville in 1879. Five years later the name was changed to State Colored Baptist University, and under the presidency of former slave and Civil War veteran William J. Simmons (1849-90), it grew to include law and medical schools. After President Simmons left to found Eckstein Norton Institute at Cane Springs in Bullitt County, Charles H. Parrish Sr. succeeded him. The institution's name was eventually changed to Simmons University, and it gave blacks their best college instruction in the state. By 1930, however, problems with debt caused the University of Louisville to purchase Simmons's property. The school was renamed Louisville Municipal College and opened in 1931 as a physically separated and segregated branch of the then-private University of Louisville. Twenty years later, as the walls of integration were falling, the institution's students, and one of its faculty members, merged into the University of Louisville system. Louisville Municipal College was no more.

Within a decade after emancipation, blacks in Kentucky had called out for a state-supported school for their race, since they could not, by law, attend A&M College (later the University of Kentucky). Accordingly, in 1886 the General Assembly established in Frankfort what was then called the State Normal School for Colored Persons, later known as Kentucky State University. Underfunded, used for political patronage by whites to reward black supporters, and devoted to a philosophy of industrial education as advocated by Booker T. Washington, the institution grew slowly, functioning chiefly as a teacher training school with only elementary and secondary level classes. A 1917 national study criticized its factional leadership, "unsatisfactory" discipline, lax accounting methods, and unhappy students. Finally, under the thirty-three-year presidency of Rufus B. Atwood (1897-1983), the school became a strong four-year college, moving away from the emphasis on industrial education. Enrollment increased from 200 in 1929 to 590 eight years later, and a strong faculty was recruited. Like many conservative black college presidents whose appropriations depended on white votes in the state legislature, Atwood had to walk a fine line. He had to be the spokesman for blacks in Kentucky, yet he could not alienate white allies or his funding would be cut and black education would suffer, and he could even be out of a job. He had to push for integration as a leader of his race, but achieving that goal would diminish his school's role in the black community. It was a dilemma he and others could never fully solve.

The state supported one other black college during the early twentieth century, for in 1918 David H. Anderson's industrial school in Paducah received legislative funding. As West Kentucky Industrial College, it fought to rival Kentucky State but never did. With Atwood's urging, the General Assembly ceased state funding for the Paducah school in 1938 and merged its collegiate functions with the Frankfort college. By that time Kentucky blacks had two basic choices—Kentucky State or Louisville Municipal College.

By contrast, white students were seeing a proliferation of state-supported schools in the twentieth century. Teacher training schools established at Richmond and Bowling Green in 1906 and at Morehead and Murray in 1922

began to grow, and their exact roles in the overall system would be long debated. Over time they evolved into multifaceted universities. At what sometimes would be proclaimed the state's flagship university, the University of Kentucky, appropriations—and perhaps will—kept it from attaining status for a long time as anything other than just another school for Kentuckians. Its president noted in 1904 that the commonwealth gave the school some $36,000 to operate, while Wisconsin supported its university with $471,000, and other places did even more. By World War I the school had only fifty-four out-of-state students. New president Frank L. McVey served from 1917 to 1940 and built a stronger academic base, so the goal of developing a strong, major university had come nearer. The growth of the school's athletic programs created controversy but also aided its visibility in the 1940s and 1950s. In 1956 the state's second medical school was authorized for the University of Kentucky's campus, and in 1962 the legislature approved a community college system of two-year colleges, to be administered by the university. Often set up in locations chosen as political rewards, the community colleges proliferated to fourteen by 1995 and educated a quarter of the state's college students.

Other actions, though, increasingly confused the picture of how the state-funded system of higher education should operate and began to spread the available resources even thinner. The Council on Higher Education helped planning somewhat, but its lack of strong central authority restricted its power. The four regional colleges developed strong political constituencies and grew rapidly (see table 23.2), particularly when soldiers returned home after World War II and in the general growth associated with the "baby boomers" of the 1960s. Then in 1968 the state created what became Northern Kentucky University, merged a community college into the newly built campus at Highland Heights, and later agreed to support an Ohio law school that affiliated with the university. At about the same time, in 1970, the previously private and municipally funded University of Louisville, with its medical and law schools, entered the state system as well. Located in large metropolitan areas, both of the new state schools expanded their student populations and physical plants very quickly; state appropriations to the University of Kentucky fell from 54 percent of the total in 1970 to 41 percent in 1979. The long-existing rivalry for state educational money grew even stronger.

Yet for all the changes, many elements of the universities varied only in degree. At the leadership level, boards and governing bodies, or even governors, often forced furious fights with college presidents. Politics brought about the removal of several Kentucky State University presidents early in the century, while the actions of the state's chief executives in the 1940s caused Morehead State University to lose its accreditation briefly. In the midst of the student unrest in the late 1960s, Governor Louie B. Nunn (b. 1924) complained about the "filth and smut" coming from the University of Kentucky, while his ally on the university's board, former governor Happy Chan-

dler, wrote of the Communist infiltrations of the school. Such hostile attitudes hastened the resignation of the university president. In 1970 the burning of a building on campus during another protest brought Nunn to call out the National Guard and impose a curfew. Overall, however, student protests in the state remained generally peaceful. Another governor, in the 1980s, asked all members of the Murray State University Board of Regents to resign, so he could control a controversy involving the school's president. Later in that decade a different state chief executive took actions that hastened the departure of another University of Kentucky president.

More changes took place in student life. Immediately after the Civil War, colleges and universities operated under strict rules. At Kentucky University (Transylvania), for example, students were required to attend chapel daily and on Sunday, and they had to abstain from drinking, smoking, profanity, card playing, or criticizing the university. These rules were apparently broken with abandon. Moreover, scholars were forbidden from attending "exhibitions of immoral tendency; no racefield, theatre, circus, billiard-saloon, bar room,

Table 23.2
Enrollment at State-Supported Colleges and Universities, 1930-1990

Institution	1930	1950	1970	1990
Eastern Kentucky Univ.	1,179	1,861	8,872	15,371
Kentucky State Univ.	138	716	1,279	2,512
Morehead State Univ.	846	824	5,315	8,622
Murray State Univ.	902	1,665	6,320	8,097
Northern Kentucky Univ.	—	—	1,328	11,260
Univ. of Kentucky	3,245	8,476	16,251	23,081
Univ. of Louisville	—	—	7,193	23,610
Western Kentucky Univ.	2,739	1,833	9,760	15,240
Community College System	—	—	5,835	40,758

Note: Dashes indicate entities not in existence or not part of the state system at the time.

Source: Kentucky Legislative Research Commission, *Report,* no. 14, n.s., 66; *Kentucky College and University Enrollments, 1970* (1970); *Kentucky College and University Enrollments, Fall 1990* (1991), 6-7

or tippling house," although they went any-way. By 1922 the student paper criticized first-year students for not wearing their man-datory caps and, when they did wear them, for not tipping them to professors. Four decades later, the turbulent 1960s brought an end to most such rules, including semiformal dress for candlelight suppers each evening.

Schools across the commonwealth went through similar transitions. In the late nine-teenth century, the A&M College (University of Kentucky) operated much like a military school, with some two hundred published rules and a 5:30 A.M. wake up, daily room inspec-tion, compulsory chapel, afternoon military drill, and a scheduled seven hours of required study each day before the sound of taps at 10:00 P.M. As late as the 1960s, women stu-dents had to be in their dormitories by a specified time or face sanctions. At nearby Georgetown College in the 1890s, students had to attend chapel every school day, had to be in their rooms by 7:00 P.M., and had to refrain from attending "any exhibitions of an immoral tendency" or frequenting "any barroom or tip-pling house." In 1968 a decision to allow stu-dent dancing—which had been banned until then—brought much criticism from George-town's Baptist governing board. Alice Lloyd Junior College had always prohibited con-tact—in conversation or in classrooms—between the sexes and required uniforms for women and coats and ties for men, but in the 1960s those rules were relaxed as well.

Throughout the decades, however, much remained the same in students' lives. Across the years, they complained about tu-ition and difficult professors, rebelled against certain rules, and wrote letters home asking parents for more money. Student pranks seemed ever present: in the nineteenth century a University of Kentucky president once found a horse in a second-floor chapel room, and in the next century April Fool editions of campus newspapers proliferated. College authorities continued to deal with student transgressions, whether panty raids of one era, or nude streak-ing of another, or demonstrations in several. Some students attended college during periods of activism regarding social issues, while others did so in times of apathy. No matter what the time frame, students at campuses across the state most of all learned, thought, dated, and graduated.

For all the problems education in Kentucky faced at all levels, success stories numbered thousands upon thousands. Billy Duvall grew up poor and had to drop out of school to help earn money for his family. Vir-tually illiterate for most of his life, and facing

An early dormitory room at the University of Kentucky (courtesy of the University of Kentucky Libraries)

racial prejudice as well, he only much later learned to read and write. But his son went to college and then graduate school. In the same era, William N. Lipscomb Jr. (b. 1919) received his elementary, secondary, and undergraduate college education in the state; in 1976 he won the Nobel Prize in chemistry. The illiterate man who raised a college graduate and the Nobel laureate both demonstrated that

Kentucky education, with all its weaknesses and variety, still had many successes in virtually every classroom, every year.

24

A Half Century of Kentucky Politics

In 1947 Republican governor Simeon Willis turned the reins of office over to his Democratic successor. That event would mark the beginning of twenty uninterrupted years of governorship by Democrats, coupled with similar control of the state legislature. In the presidential and U.S. senatorial contests, however, the Republicans won the important races in the state more often than did their opposition. By the time Republicans took the governorship again in 1967, when Louie B. Nunn began his term, it seemed that a new majority party might be forming in Kentucky. That was not to be, though, and after Nunn left office in 1971, Democrats again ruled supreme at the state level for the next two decades and beyond, while dividing national presidential and senatorial races with Republicans. Only in the last decade of the century did the state's longtime minority party begin to make serious inroads into the electoral process, and that change came amid several other significant shifts in party politics.

Democratic Ascendancy

Taking the oath of office as governor in 1947 was a man who would quickly become the state's most powerful politician over the next decade and a half and who would form and lead one of the state Democratic Party's two factions. Earle C. Clements (1896-1985) had made his way up through the ranks from his Union County base, serving as sheriff, county clerk, county judge, state Senate majority leader, and two-term congressman. Allied to the Thomas Rhea faction and to Alben Barkley, Clements almost naturally became a Chandler foe. He soon led those opposed to Happy. Such a split, though, might have occurred no matter what, for Clements sought power in his own right and usually found it.

Governor Clements would be most often described as a consummate politician, in the positive sense of that term. Not a particularly good campaigner, not a man the press trusted, not a person who could hide a strong temper, he won few of his victories in open forums. To him politics was a game, a serious one, and the former football player and coach played it outside the glare of public lights. Intelligent, detail-oriented, methodical, secretive, sometimes cold and tough, "Cautious Clements" could also be personable one-on-one, and he skillfully formed behind-the-scenes alliances to achieve his goals. Once he decided on a course of action, his word and his commitment were good. More than anything, he simply had the best organizational skills of anyone of his generation in Kentucky politics.

Clements's 1947 victory also symbolized the ascendancy of western Kentucky in the Democratic Party. Barkley was already powerful, and four of the first seven post–World War II Democratic governors would emerge from the western part of the state. Moreover, with Chandler strong in the central Bluegrass but an anathema in Louisville, Clements quickly formed a powerful alliance with the "Fourth Street" political leaders in the Falls City. The well-organized Clements faction sought to counter the personality-oriented Chandler faction in the fight for dominance in the state.

As governor, Clements did not deal with the General Assembly with a soft hand. The unfriendly *Kentucky Times-Star* of Covington referred to "the Clements steamroller" in the 1948 session, while the not overly supportive *Courier-Journal* called the 1950 gathering "the most ruthlessly operated in anybody's memory." With a three-to-one Democratic margin in both houses, the governor saw his major programs all passed in the first session, and overall, he got a great deal accomplished. Without much fanfare, the legislature lowered racial barriers by twice amending the Day Law;

it increased the gas tax to help fund rural roads, raised the distilled spirits tax, and instituted the first tax on pari-mutuel betting, then used those new funds to raise teachers' salaries and lower the inheritance tax. Clements also created a state police force to supersede the sometimes inefficient and partisan highway patrol, and he funded what became the Legislative Research Commission. He stressed economic development and the state parks as well.

Clements also took a keen interest in the 1948 presidential and senatorial races, for Republican John Sherman Cooper held a Senate seat, and Republicans fully expected to capitalize on problems of housing, prices, strikes, and more to win the presidency from Harry Truman. The nomination of Alben Barkley as Truman's vice presidential choice made the Democratic task in Kentucky easier, for the Iron Man remained immensely popular. Truman's civil rights policy, however, had been unanimously opposed by Kentucky delegates to the party's convention, and some southern politicos had expressed their own disapproval by forming the States' Rights Party, or Dixiecrats, led by J. Strom Thurmond of South Carolina. In the end, though, Kentucky Democrats remained loyal to their favorite son. The Truman-Barkley ticket won a massive victory in the state, with 466,756 votes to Thomas Dewey's 341,210; the Dixiecrats, who carried four southern states, took only 1.3 percent of the ballots in the commonwealth. President Truman's razor-close national victory ensured a continued Democratic presence, and Kentucky influence, in Washington. In January 1949 Chief Justice Fred Vinson of Kentucky swore in Truman as president, while Associate Justice Stanley Reed of Kentucky administered the oath of office to the veep, Barkley.

Nineteen forty-eight also marked the beginning of a series of complex actions regarding Kentucky's two Senate seats. Between January 1949 and January 1955 eight men served as senator. For one seat, incumbent Republican Cooper was challenged in 1948 by "Mr. Tobacco," the longtime Democratic congressman

Virgil M. Chapman of Bourbon County. Not sympathetic to civil rights or labor unions and rumored to have a drinking problem, Chapman would not normally have seemed a serious challenger. In fact, Cooper did receive 100,000 more votes than his party's presidential candidate that year. Barkley's presence on the ticket, though, brought out a huge Democratic majority, and Chapman rode those coattails to defeat Cooper by almost 125,000 votes. Ironically, Senator Chapman would die in an automobile accident in March 1951, and Cooper would win the election to fill the rest of the term.

The other Senate seat had been Barkley's, but when he left it for the vice presidency, Clements appointed an ally to serve for a year and a half, then ran for the full term himself in 1950. Easily defeating the very conservative Republican and earlier gubernatorial candidate Charles I. Dawson, Clements resigned as governor and took his seat in the U.S. Senate. Within a very short time the newcomer gained the attention of Senator Lyndon B. Johnson, became his close confidant, and was selected assistant floor leader. To add to the Democratic success, after the end of Alben Barkley's vice presidential term in 1953, seventy-six-year-old Barkley challenged Senator Cooper in 1954 for that seat. Indirectly, Barkley had cost Cooper the 1948 race by his presence on the national ticket; now he directly caused his defeat by more than 70,000 votes. In January 1955 Kentucky had two major Democratic leaders in the Senate.

Clements's resignation as governor, effective in November 1950, meant that his lieutenant governor was now chief executive, a year before the general election. New governor Lawrence W. Wetherby (1908-94) had been a fairly minor juvenile court trial commissioner before his selection, but Clements had wanted a Louisville–Jefferson County person, and Wetherby had been chosen. Although he would stress that he came from Middletown rather than nearby Louisville, Wetherby was only the second person from the state's most populous county to serve as governor in the twentieth century.

A gregarious person and an avid sportsman (one photograph shows him driving a sulky pulled by an ostrich), Wetherby had to overcome a popular press presentation of him as a less than serious chief executive. In truth, he had a good administration, with a good record. He did have the disadvantage of serving as governor during the unpopular Korean War (1950-53), in which 1,025 Kentuckians lost their lives, and of governing after the Republicans regained the presidency in 1953. Like others of his era, he also had to operate under the considerable political shadow of his mentor, Clements. Wetherby, however, achieved on his own. Facing a 1951 election for a full term, he called a special session in March of that year and used a fiscal surplus to provide more funds to teachers (who represented a substantial voting bloc). In the election itself, Wetherby faced an old guard Republican judge, Eugene Siler of Williamsburg. Stressing his fundamentalist, anti-Catholic, and antiliquor views, Siler made inroads in rural areas but virtually forfeited the growing urban vote. Wetherby won, 346,345-288,014.

The governor worked well with his General Assembly. In education, a Minimum Foundation Program began, the school term was lengthened, and teacher tenure was strengthened. Wetherby also spoke out forthrightly for the U.S. Supreme Court's decision in *Brown v. Board of Education*. A Highway Authority, with the power to issue bonds to raise revenue for construction, began the first of what would be a series of toll turnpikes (usually connected to a governor's home region). The Wetherby legislatures also created a Department of Mental Health and a Youth Authority, issued initial but weak strip mining regulations, increased the so-called sin taxes, and passed a state constitutional amendment that gave eighteen-year-olds the vote (approved by the state's voters in 1955). As the Wetherby administration ended in 1955, then, the Clements faction could point to two constructive gubernatorial terms. No Democratic faction in the century, though, had elected three straight candidates. Everyone knew that the factional opposition in the 1955 governor's race would be formidable indeed.

Happy Days Again?

Happy was back. Denied a second term as baseball commissioner by unhappy major league owners, A.B. Chandler had returned to his Versailles law practice in the summer of 1951. He had been too late to influence the governor's race that year but had used the four years since to rebuild his political base and to renew old contacts. Now he sought a second gubernatorial term in 1955.

The selection of a candidate to oppose Chandler in the Democratic primary presented a problem for the Clements-Wetherby forces. Kingmakers such as William H. May of Brighton Engineering recognized that their most politically astute and available candidate was Lieutenant Governor Emerson ("Doc") Beauchamp, but his unimposing appearance, gravelly voice, and connections to boss-dominated Logan County all were deemed liabilities. To the surprise of almost everyone, Earle Clements virtually handpicked a long-shot candidate, Bert T. Combs. An eastern Kentuckian who spoke with a mountain twang, Combs sat as judge on the state's highest court, but that experience was virtually the extent of his political background. Untested and relatively unknown, he did have a reputation for integrity and intelligence. But would that be enough against the veteran campaigner Chandler?

Since Combs really had no record for Happy to attack, Chandler focused his attention instead on the factional leaders and went for their political jugular. Referring to "Clementine and Wetherbine," he cried out that "Old Earle" called up "that little Hitler" Wetherby and told him exactly what to do. Not only that, roared Chandler, but Wetherby had frivolously spent the state's funds to air-condition the

capitol: "We could raise the windows; there are shade trees around." The governor, said Happy, had also wasted the people's money by buying a new twenty-thousand-dollar rug. An invoice showing that the cost was twenty-seven hundred dollars did not slow the salvos. Then Happy turned to the new toll road from Louisville to Elizabethtown: "It doesn't start anywhere, it doesn't go anywhere," it should never have been built. Likewise, he said, the new state fairgrounds and Freedom Hall, both in his favorite target of Louisville, should not have been constructed either. As soon as Clements, Wetherby, or Combs started to defend against one attack, Chandler would shift to another, all presented in his entertaining style. A British observer called him "a rare natural spokesman. . . . His sentences were short and they balanced like a chant." His loudspeakers blared out: "Be like your pappy and vote for Happy."

Combs helped Chandler, for in his low-key campaign-opening address, he honestly admitted that a sales tax might be needed to solve the state's fiscal concerns. With Chandler's antitax reputation, such a stance represented a form of political hara-kiri in Kentucky. Not only that, but the candidate read his dry speech poorly. The saying immediately went up: "Combs opened and closed on the same night." Doc Beauchamp, who had been rejected in part because of his poor speaking ability, reportedly told Clements, "And you said *I* couldn't give a speech!" The results surprised few: Chandler won the primary by some 18,000 votes. In the general election, Republicans put forth still another lackluster candidate, Edwin R. Denney, a reserved U.S. attorney from Rockcastle County. Chandler dominated the race. His meetings seemed like evangelical gatherings, while his opponent's, said a *New York Times* reporter, took on "some of the chilling qualities of a wake." A 129,000-vote margin—the biggest in a governor's race to that time—and 58 percent support showed Chandler's continuing appeal.

Chandler's presence in the Governor's Mansion would play a key role in three elections scheduled for 1956—the presidential contest, the regular U.S. Senate race, and a special election to fill the other Senate seat. The special election had been called as a result of what had happened on April 30, 1956. That day Senator Barkley gave an address to students at Washington and Lee University in Virginia, and in the midst of the talk he collapsed and died of a heart attack. A politician could have asked for no better final remarks than the last words he spoke to the audience: "I would rather be a servant in the house of the Lord than to sit in the seats of the mighty."

Barkley's death not only meant that the most powerful political player from Kentucky in the century was gone, but it also meant that the state would elect two senators the same year, which also happened to be a presidential election year. For president, Republicans renominated popular incumbent Dwight D. Eisenhower, who had almost carried Kentucky four years earlier. On the Democratic side, Chandler set his eyes on the prize and went to the national convention as a "favorite son" choice. His acrid enemy, Mike Barry of the *Kentucky Irish American,* wrote, "Any time Chandler is referred to in Chicago as 'Kentucky's favorite son,' it should be made unmistakably clear that the sentence is incomplete." As it turned out, Happy got virtually no votes outside Kentucky, Adlai Stevenson was renominated to run again, and an unhappy governor returned to Kentucky and gave the national Democratic ticket little support. Eisenhower eventually won Kentucky's electoral votes by a margin of nearly 100,000 popular votes.

In the senatorial races, Clements was up for reelection, and the lateness of Barkley's death had left the selection of the other Democratic nominee in the hands of the state Central Committee, still dominated by people loyal to Clements. They chose Wetherby as the second nominee. The party knew that the hard task would be electing Wetherby, but they expected Clements to win. After all, in one term he had already been named in a *New York Times* story as one of the four top Democratic leaders. When Lyndon Johnson suffered a heart attack, Clements became the acting Senate majority leader. Unfortunately for the state party, this task kept him away from the campaign trail quite a bit in 1956. What time he did have he often devoted to Wetherby's campaign, in an effort to help him achieve victory.

An additional obstacle for Clements and Wetherby was their party's own governor. Of Chandler, a reporter wrote Clements: "The fellow on the first floor, I am convinced, means nothing but ill for both you and Lawrence [Wetherby]. He may publicly say he is for you, but he's not going to urge anyone else to be in your camp." The administration used none of its resources to work for a ticket that the governor did not like at all. In essence, Chandler supported the Republican nominees.

For that reason and others, Republicans felt they had an excellent opportunity not only to carry the state for "Ike" but also to elect one senator. Eisenhower had lured away from his diplomatic post in India the party's veteran campaigner John Sherman Cooper, to run against Wetherby. Former senator Cooper was well known, and he did not have to contend with the Barkley factor any longer. Still, it surprised seasoned observers every time Cooper won, for he seemed to do so much wrong. Journalist John Ed Pearce wrote: "Watching him in action, it is easy to sense but hard to explain why John Cooper is a formidable campaigner. He is not a dramatic speaker. His delivery is halting, low. He violates all the rules. . . . Yet to all of this there is agonizing sincerity—in the sad, soft smile and the slow, soft speech—that entraps audiences and infuriates his opponents." Despite being divorced, despite an earlier nervous breakdown (which no one mentioned during his races), despite his halting manner, he had appeal. Later, a Paducah attorney noted that "so many Kentuckians . . . feel Cooper is a good Democrat [who] just gets registered wrong." Backed by an infusion of funds from the Taft family of Ohio, John Sherman Cooper had an excellent chance for victory.

Not so his Republican running mate. Thruston Ballard Morton (1907-82) came from the wealthy "River Road Crowd" in Louisville, and his grandfather had been lieutenant governor under Edwin P. Morrow. A fresh postwar face, the handsome and hardworking Morton had been elected to Congress, then had served as an assistant secretary of state in Washington, but in 1956 he had had little statewide experience. Moreover, his campaign style was not typical for Kentucky. His shy and quiet manner coupled with his Louisville, millionaire background made him appear almost aloof at times. But he could also be very pleasing on television and did well in smaller crowds, where he felt more at ease. Morton, as one reporter recalled later, also had another side: "He's a very earthy guy. He's a gut fighter. He's a nice guy, gut fighter." That side he kept hidden, but he would need it to defeat Clements.

Actually, the two Republicans were not so different as their south-central Kentucky and Louisville backgrounds suggested. Both had graduated from Yale, both moved easily in eastern and upper-class circles, both had good relationships most of the time with Barry Bingham Sr. and the *Courier-Journal,* both had a World War II military background, and both seemed to dislike formal campaigning. Yet both could fight hard (and not always on the high road), and both could be effective vote getters in their own special ways.

And get the votes they did. With eighteen-year-olds voting for the first time in a general election in 1956, Eisenhower won big, and his victory helped the Republican Senate races in Kentucky. Chandler's opposition to Clements and Wetherby, and Clements's absence from the state, contributed to the outcome. Cooper defeated Wetherby by 65,000 votes, and Clements was in a surprisingly close contest as well. As a key Republican insider recalled later, "We began to call eastern Kentucky . . . and tell them to slow down their

count . . . and hold back 'til we got the votes in from western Kentucky, so that we'd know what we needed instead of them knowing what they needed." By whatever methods, Republicans (and Chandlerites) got enough votes so that Clements lost by some 7,000 votes out of more than 1 million cast. "Landslide Morton" joined Cooper as a U.S. senator. As it turned out, not for sixteen years would Democrats elect another senator.

The defeat shocked Clements, who had not lost an election in his thirty years of public office, and it hurt his considerable ego greatly. Given his ties to later president Johnson, he very likely would have become Senate majority leader in the future, as had his mentor Barkley, and Kentucky would have had a major influence in the nation's capital. Instead, Clements—a man of pride—never ran for political office again, and he focused his immediate efforts on defeating the Chandler faction that was partially responsible for his loss. Not only Republican victory but Democratic bitterness were the legacies of 1956.

Politics dominated Chandler's legislative sessions, and the accomplishments of his second term as governor were much more limited than those of his first term. Opposition by the "rebels," a group of Democratic legislators friendly to the Clements faction, meant that Chandler had to ally openly with the Republicans, giving them patronage in exchange for General Assembly votes. The result, said one newspaper, "was less of a legislative session and more of a political convention." Trying to balance campaign promises on taxes with the state's financial needs (as pointed out by Combs), the Chandler coalition first lowered racetrack taxes and later raised them, broadened the income tax base and then reduced it, and finally expanded the truck, corporate, and liquor levies. The State Health Department's headquarters was moved from Chandler's bête noire of Louisville to the capital city, and a bill passed that authorized the Highway Department to use its own workforce rather than award contracts, a move the opposition saw as an attempt to build a stronger political machine for the administration.

Several other actions strengthened that perception. Chandler abolished the merit system coverage of the Children's Bureau that protected employees from political interference. According to a National Civil Service League publication, he then replaced the employees with those of less training—and more loyalty to the administration. In the Division of Probation and Parole, which had once been heavily influenced by politics, a new law required competitive exams and strong qualifications. But as the director of that division noted in February 1956, "We have now had seven new officers employed in the last 60 days. At no time have I talked with any of these officers before they were employed and have known nothing concerning their qualifications prior to their employment." He soon resigned. A year later, scandals in the Highway Department brought the resignation of its commissioner. And when a vacancy occurred in the position of clerk of the Court of Appeals, the court appointed one person and Chandler another. The governor ordered the Finance Commission not to pay the court's choice; the judges and attorney general told the state treasurer to issue the checks. Finally both sides agreed to a constitutional test of the situation, and eventually the interpretation of the Court of Appeals was upheld.

Still, despite all the controversy, the political positioning by both factions, and the building of political armies for the next governor's race, Chandler had, above all, taken the high ground on the explosive question of racial integration. Possibly with gritted teeth, a journalist for his old enemy, the *Courier-Journal*, wrote in May 1958: "No governor south of the Mason and Dixon line has been so forthright and as consistent as he in upholding . . . the concept of law and order." Bingham even penned a personal letter, saying that Happy "acted with commendable dignity and determination." Demagogue and democrat, political alley fighter and statesman, Chandler at the

end of his second term still defied easy definition, except that he was Happy, sui generis. That was all that need be said.

The Sixties

In the 1959 gubernatorial primary, the Chandler faction gave its full support to Lieutenant Governor Harry Lee Waterfield. The western Kentuckian was a strong candidate in his own right, but having the administration behind him gave even more advantages, as a series of letters showed.

The campaign's organizational chairman wrote the Department of Revenue: "I am told that . . . [two men] of your Department are not helping our cause. . . . Please check into this." The same man wrote the Department of Public Safety: "We have several complaints that the State Police are recommending wrecker service in Pulaski, Laurel, Knox, and Nelson Counties to garages that are our opponents. . . . Please look into this matter and straighten it out." The Department of Highways received a letter from Waterfield: "It is desired that you set up the following [seventeen] temporary maintenance jobs in the counties indicated below." The organizational chairman wrote a Bardstown man: "I hear the rumor that the Henry and Oldham County Highway Garages have stopped paying their 2% [of salaries into campaign coffers]." The Department of Economic Security heard from the same individual: "Our good political friends at the Shelbyville Coca-Cola plant are anxious to put a coke machine in your Economic Security Building across the river. How about it?" A field report from Owsley County indicated that "one State Highway employee has at this time succeeded in getting 33 Republicans to re-register as Democrats with the promise of building a large concrete-pipe culvert." The writer of a field report for the Department of Industrial Relations said: "I attach special significance to Mr. Nickell's request [for a road] as he has expressed a willingness . . . to cooperate in naming Republican election officers who are in sympathy to our cause." From Johnson County, a field report commented: "Laurel Creek Road. Mullins wants this down the south or Paintsville side of the creek. . . . Mullins says the north side is Republican while the south side is much more Democratic. He says don't consider contracting down the north side until after the election."

The anti-Chandler forces faced two significant problems. An obvious one was the support the current state administration could give Waterfield. Even more serious, however, was the fact that those who opposed Chandler were not united. Former Louisville reform mayor Wilson W. Wyatt (1905-96) had managed Adlai Stevenson's presidential bid in 1952 and brought to the race a good record, a good mind, and a good initial base of support. The question remained, however, whether Wyatt could extend that support statewide and overcome perceptions such as that of a local attorney who "considered him an egghead and not his kind of folk or people, and that he would probably not do anything helpful for his section." The other anti-Chandler faction candidate was Bert Combs, back for a second run. Divided, the faction could not defeat Waterfield and the Chandler group, as the polls showed. The old professional Earle Clements brokered a January 1959 meeting at the Standiford Airport Motel in Louisville, showed Wyatt that he trailed the field, and, in an all-night session, worked out an arrangement whereby the two camps could merge, with Wyatt running for lieutenant governor and gaining promises of support for later races.

The race was now Combs versus Waterfield, the Clements faction versus the Chandler one, the former judge against the former journalist, eastern Kentucky opposite western Kentucky. Both men had lost earlier primaries, and both had learned from those experiences. But again the best target was the sitting administration, and Combs turned the political tables on Chandler, whose actions now came under fire. One example was the so-called crippled goose incident. Happy had

been accused of shooting at some geese a few minutes before the allotted legal time began and had been fined. His refusal to pay first brought forth duck and geese calls at Waterfield rallies, and then later the Combs forces paraded ducks with signs around their necks that read: "Happy Killed My Pappy." Similarly, it had been rumored that Chandler forces had placed the 2 percent assessments from state employees in a Cuban bank, where the funds could not be traced. But when Castro seized the Cuban government, those funds had been taken as well, so the story went. Combs pictured Chandler looking out over the water, crying out, "Castro! Castro! Send back my 2 percent!"

Chandler countered, calling Combs a "Bertie of Paradise," and a "Clements parrot," while Waterfield pointed to his opponent's legal effort on behalf of coal operators. The election had been decided at the Standiford Airport Motel, though, and even earlier, when Combs learned from his 1955 defeat. He garnered 292,462 votes to Waterfield's 259,461, with the difference coming in Wyatt's home county. In the general election against another weak Republican candidate, Combs defeated John M. Robsion Jr. by 180,000 votes, 516,549-336,456. Combs was in, and Clements was back.

Fortune smiled on the new governor, and he backed that up with some shrewd political moves. Military veterans had been pushing for a bonus, and Chandler forces, confident that the proposal would lose, had agreed to allow a popular vote on a sales tax to fund such a bonus. But the measure had been approved by some 38,000 votes, and Combs's legislature had to shape the details. It was generally agreed that a tax of one-half of 1 percent could fund the bonus, and most expected a 1 percent tax. But the Combs camp knew the state needed money, particularly for education, and boldly advocated—and got—a 3 percent tax. As a journalist said later: "It was a fraud, but it was the greatest fraud of this century." By 1963 some four hundred thousand veterans and their

Former governors Keen Johnson, Earle C. Clements, and Lawrence W. Wetherby (*left to right*) stand behind Lieutenant Governor Wilson W. Wyatt (*left, seated*) and Governor Bert T. Combs (courtesy of Edward T. Breathitt Jr.).

beneficiaries had received more than $126 million as a bonus, but the real winners were those who benefited from the many millions more that went into the state budget, year after year. Unlike many chief executives who faced tight budgets, Combs had money to spend.

The result was one of the most progressive gubernatorial administrations of the century. For the first time, an extensive state merit system was established by law (which also meant that Combs's allies would not be ousted by a future unfriendly administration), and by executive decree public accommodations were desegregated. A Human Rights Commission was created, statewide use of voting machines was required, and assessing political campaign funds from state employees was established as a felony. The state's first billion-dollar budget increased school funds 50 percent, formed a community college system, and fully funded— ironically—the Albert B. Chandler Medical Center at the University of Kentucky. A one-hundred-million-dollar bond issue provided even more money for a system of toll highways and for state park construction. One study showed that by 1962 Kentucky had increased its appropriations faster than any state over the

last five years, with per capita expenditures doubling in that period. Even the courts helped, for a 1962 ruling decreed that the state's (amended) constitutional limitation on salaries could be interpreted to mean limited salaries as adjusted for inflation. The so-called rubber dollar ruling helped government attract more professionals.

The one major negative of Combs's administration was chiefly a media creation. This was ironic, since Combs as a rule had excellent publicity both at the state and national levels. (One state journalist, for instance, wrote certain Combs speeches, then praised them editorially the next day.) But Earle Clements had wanted to be named as head of the powerful Highway Commission, and Combs had done so. Then a news story broke that suggested that the state was getting ready to purchase some trucks at a very favorable rate from a dummy firm controlled by Combs's former finance chairman. Some argued that "the truck deal" problem would have been caught and corrected through the review process; others said that it was a political payoff and that Clements had been trying to carry it out for others; some indicated it was a Clements deal, pure and simple. Combs cancelled the proposed lease and contradicted his highway commissioner's testimony, and Clements took these actions as a personal and public rebuke. "Very bitter," Clements resigned his post. When asked at a news conference if he would have fired Clements had he not resigned, Combs answered, "No comment." To Clements, that response was an insult and a betrayal of trust. Thereafter he took every opportunity to oppose his former ally and his supporters. Yet it was the beginning of the end of the Clements domination of that Democratic faction.

All this activity proved crucial in the 1962 U.S. Senate race, which pitted incumbent Republican Thruston Morton against Lieutenant Governor Wyatt. Democratic prospects, at one level, did not seem good, for in 1960 Republican senator Cooper had easily defeated former governor Keen Johnson in his bid for reelection to the Senate. That same year Republican Richard Nixon had carried Kentucky by a sizable margin—80,000 votes—as well. The results of the 1960 presidential race, however, had been skewed by the Catholicism of Democrat John F. Kennedy. The *Western Recorder,* the voice of Baptists in Kentucky, came out against the Democrat, and considerable anti-Catholic political literature was spread over the state, often from in front of Protestant pulpits on Sunday mornings. Republicans did not speak out openly against the anti-Catholic attacks, and religion permeated all parts of the race. Catholic Al Smith had gotten 41 percent of the state's votes in 1928; Catholic Kennedy received 46.4 percent thirty-two years later. The increase was not enough. But Democrats could argue that religion was not an issue in the 1962 Senate race and that they had a popular administration behind Wyatt.

They also had a split party, for old former foes Chandler and Clements now combined to oppose the Combs-Wyatt alliance. Morton did not depend on Democratic factionalism alone, however, and his campaign became what one observer called one "of misrepresentation, smear, and confusion." Wyatt's

early advocacy of Americans for Democratic Action was presented as support for socialism; his call for what later became Medicare was legitimately used against him among members of the health care profession; his opposition to a loyalty oath was seized upon to brand him "soft on communism." Wyatt had a campaign brochure printed, for distribution on election day in black wards in Louisville, which showed a black hand grasping a white one in unity. Republican strategists got a copy early, reproduced it by the thousands, spread it among whites in western Kentucky, where the integration question was particularly volatile, and gained votes as a result. What even the incumbent's son termed a "nasty" race ended in a Morton victory by almost 50,000 votes, but the senator had lost friends, including the Binghams, in winning as he did. Disturbed by that, Morton, the former chairman of the Republican National Committee and the first Republican to win two full consecutive terms as senator, would not seek reelection six years hence. Wyatt never sought public office again either. In effect the 1962 race ended the careers of two key party leaders.

National and even international issues continued to be more and more dominant in state political races in the 1960s. Civil rights, the cold war and communism, and the Vietnam War all entered into state campaigns. So too did another issue that affected only parts of the United States, but certainly had an impact in Kentucky. That was the so-called War on Poverty. In 1963 Harry M. Caudill's *Night Comes to the Cumberlands* appeared. Not particularly strong in its history, it was forceful and passionate in its call for action and attacks on the pillaging and pollution of a place and its people. The story told by its pages and by other studies was not a pleasant one.

The mountain region was not poor, but as one author noted, its people were. By 1960 the coal mines had been in a period of general stagnation for nearly four decades; mechanization had produced unemployed miners who received little aid from the operators. For some the only salvation had been out-migration to places like Chicago's Uptown or Dayton's East End, where the former Kentuckians became "O-tucks" (Ohio-Kentuckians). Between 1940 and 1950 nearly a quarter million people left the state's Appalachian counties; the next decade saw a net migration of 340,000 people, 32 percent of the area's population. It was an exodus akin to the great overseas migration from Europe in the nineteenth century.

Worse for Kentucky, those who departed Appalachia were the young and those, on average, who were better educated. They left behind a region of great promise and much natural beauty, but one plagued by pollution, illiteracy, poor medical care, bad roads, few colleges, substandard housing, and absentee ownership. (As late as 1980, 42 percent of the surface land in the region was corporate-owned.) Whereas in 1950 some 63 percent of U.S. homes had hot water, a bath, and an indoor toilet, only 2 percent of the houses in Wolfe County, Kentucky, did. It was little wonder that Leslie County experienced a net loss of 60 percent of its population from 1950 to 1960, or that Harlan and Letcher Counties lost nearly half their populations between 1940 and 1970. By 1960 two of every five households in Appalachian Kentucky had incomes below the poverty line; U.S. congressman Carl D. Perkins testified that one-third of the workers in his congressional district were unemployed in 1961. Poverty was a Kentucky problem and a national one.

President Kennedy had seen Appalachian poverty during his election campaign and had later initiated actions to deal with the issue. Following his death, those actions reached maturity under President Lyndon B. Johnson, who visited the region in April 1964. The approach taken was both pragmatic and idealistic and had both successes and failures. The Volunteers in Service to America (VISTA), the Appalachian Volunteers (AVs), Head Start, the Appalachian Regional Commission (ARC)—all were attempted solutions. While the ARC focused on infrastructure, other groups sought

to educate or empower local citizens. Some of those efforts had the desired effect, but others fragmented and failed. Certain ventures challenged long-established local elites, who struck back. Two civil rights activists, Anne and Carl Braden, again became the focus of legal action, while Alan and Margaret McSurely came to Kentucky from Washington, D.C., angered Pike County officials, and were arrested for criminal syndicalism. The "radical" books confiscated ranged from works by Karl Marx to the writings of Barry Goldwater. The couple eventually went free, after much negative publicity for the region.

Poverty was not eradicated, but the war against it weakened its hold on eastern Kentucky. Out-migration slowed drastically in the 1960s, and the region's per capita income as a percentage of the national average rose from 45 percent in 1965 to 66 percent in 1979. The infant mortality rate by 1990 was one-fourth what it had been three decades earlier. By the early 1980s, however, ten of the nation's twenty-five lowest-income counties were still in Kentucky; in that decade the state's overall poverty rate increased from 17.6 percent to 19 percent of the population. By 1990 some twenty of the state's counties—one in six—had over 35 percent of their people living below the federal poverty line, and all but one of those counties was in Appalachian Kentucky. The number of children living in poverty in the commonwealth increased from 21 percent in 1979 to 25 percent by the mid-1990s. In Owsley County two of every three children fell in that category. Even more troubling, the problem was no longer simply a rural one, for some 60 percent of the overall numbers of children in poverty came from urban areas. In the 1960s, amid much debate, some anger, and considerable political infighting, a start had been made to combat poverty, and some successes had resulted. The War on Poverty had been but a skirmish; the main battle had not been won.

Political fights loomed on the horizon as well, and they soon erupted in another contentious Democratic Party primary in 1963. Happy Chandler sought an unprecedented third term and began his familiar attacks on the sales tax and on expenditures by the opposition. Targeting the floral clock that Combs had built near the capitol, for example, he would say that in Frankfort, the time must be "two petunias past the Jimson weed." Opposing the old campaigner was a surprise choice. As Clements had done with him, Combs unexpectedly selected Edward T. ("Ned") Breathitt Jr. (b. 1924) of Hopkinsville, and Combs's administration put all its support behind the thirty-eight-year-old former legislator. Nephew of a Democratic lieutenant governor, grandson of a Republican attorney general, related to the nineteenth-century governor who shared his surname, Breathitt came across on the increasingly important television screen as a fresh and enthusiastic young man. Chandler never quite adapted to the new campaign methods, and his attacks fell flat. When young, he had represented the new approach to campaigning; now his opponent did, and the circle was complete. Chandler went down to defeat by more than 60,000 votes, losing all but one congressional district. Shocked by his first personal defeat in a quarter century, he would later charge that "it was stolen." The large margin of victory and a lack of evidence, however, give that argument little force. It was

hard for Happy to see that political time—as measured on the floral clock or elsewhere—had passed him by. He would win no other races. The Chandler era had ended.

For a change, victory was not automatically assured for the Democrats, however. To his credit, Chandler had not really incited racial tensions in his primary bid. The general election would not follow the same pattern. That factor, combined with recent Republican victories and the now-familiar support by Happy for the Republicans, gave the GOP optimism. The Republican candidate was the capable Louie B. Nunn (b. 1924) of Glasgow, and he, with the aid of his brother Lee, would seek out the opposition's weakest link and then hammer at that over and over. Called "ruthless" by one political scientist, Nunn capitalized on Combs's executive order concerning open housing in an attempt to get votes, particularly in western Kentucky. Appearing on television with the flag, a Bible, and Kentucky statutes around him, Nunn pointed to the civil rights order and said, "My first act will be to abolish this." The unfriendly *New Republic* accused him of conducting "the first outright segregationist campaign in Kentucky," but Nunn knew that he had no chance of victory through the standard Republican arguments of the past twenty years. He wanted to win, and he came very close to doing so, losing to Breathitt by 13,000 votes, 436,496-449,551. The *New York Times* commented sadly on the "marked reversal for the forces of racial moderation in this border state whose whites had heretofore supported moderate to liberal candidates."

Yet the liberal candidate had won, and Ned Breathitt proceeded to forge a good record, despite having to overcome budgetary disadvantages never faced by Combs. Hindered in his first session by the death of long-time legislative leader Richard P.

Table 24.1
Personal Income per Capita, 1930-1990

Year	Kentucky	U.S.	Kentucky as % of U.S.	State rank
1930	$ 321	$ 611	52.5	40
1940	315	585	53.8	43
1950	988	1,497	66.0	46
1960	1,623	2,258	71.8	44
1970	3,138	4,047	77.5	43
1980	8,051	9,940	80.9	43
1990	14,747	18,666	79.0	44

Source: 1996 Kentucky Deskbook of Economic Statistics (1996)

Moloney, the new governor had only mixed success. In what is usually the weaker, lame-duck second session, however, he dominated. Sometime Chandler ally Lieutenant Governor Waterfield was stripped of his powers, former governor Wetherby—now in the state Senate—was selected president pro tempore, and the control was so complete that the budget was introduced on January 4, 1966, and passed in virtually the same form ten days later, garnering margins of 99-0 and 31-5. Overall, the Breathitt administration could point to a major state-wide Civil Rights Act, a strong strip mining law, a new Corrupt Practices Act, more funds for rural roads and education, and initial funding for Kentucky Educational Television. Its chief defeat came when a proposed new constitution, based on national models, was submitted to the voters. Opposed by county leaders, it lost by a huge margin, 510,099-140,210.

At the same time, the expanding Vietnam War sparked increasing demonstrations and unrest. The first Kentuckian died in Vietnam in 1962. Eventually about 125,000 Kentuckians served in Southeast Asia; more than 1,000 died, and others returned with

wounds physical and mental. Back home, anger between those who opposed the conflict and the larger group of those who supported the government's prosecution of it divided generations, communities, and whole families and left its own scars on those involved. Young Kentuckians went off to fight—"I felt the typical invincibility of a teenager," one recalled—and had to bear what another termed "the haunting cross of combat." The hardest burden came later, in June 1969, when elements of an activated National Guard unit were attacked at a forgotten place called Fire Support Base Tomahawk. In one night five men were killed from Bardstown, and that small town suffered perhaps the greatest lost per capita of any community in the country.

Easily victorious in his 1966 bid for reelection over John Y. Brown Sr., Senator Cooper had been among the first political leaders to question the war, and his sponsorship of the Cooper-Church Amendment to cut off funds to Indochina reflected his desire to forge a peace. By 1967 two other World War II veterans, Republican senator Morton and Congressman Tim Lee Carter of south-central Kentucky, both broke with the admin-

Governor Edward T. Breathitt Jr. signs the 1966 Civil Rights Act before the statue of Abraham Lincoln in the state capitol rotunda (courtesy of the Kentucky Department for Libraries and Archives).

University of Kentucky students protest the Vietnam War (courtesy of the University of Kentucky Libraries).

istration and became critics of American policy. Strong feelings remained prevalent in the state, however, and Vietnam and the civil rights movement would be important issues as the commonwealth moved toward still another governor's race, in 1967.

Republican Resurgence and Retreat

With factionalism fading, Chandler's and Waterfield's separate 1967 attempts to defeat the Combs-Breathitt candidate in the Democratic primary failed badly, and the party's nomination went to a well-qualified and well-prepared former journalist, legislator, and public official, Henry Ward of Paducah. Hopeful Republicans experienced one of their hardest-fought and bitterest primaries, with possible gubernatorial victory as the great lure. Marlow W. Cook (b. 1926) had been elected Jefferson County judge in 1961 and reelected four years later. Together with fellow Louisville Republicans, including Mayor William O. Cowger, Cook had put together a strong urban base. Opposing him was the defeated candidate of four years earlier, Louie Nunn. Facing an attractive and strong

candidate, Nunn attacked the "liberal, former New Yorker" from the urban area, then struck out at what he saw as Cook's weakest point, his Catholic religion. Some Nunn allies also criticized what they termed Cook's "Jewish backers." Such anti-Semitic overtones brought Senator Cooper and Representative Carter to speak out against such tactics and to support Cook, while Louisvillian Morton—aided by Nunn in his earlier Senate race—remained silent. Rural votes and religious influences helped Nunn beat Cook in the primary by a small margin.

Using racially oriented tactics four years earlier, Nunn had barely lost to Breathitt, an attractive candidate backed by a strong administration. Now, in 1967, Ward proved much weaker on the campaign trail and generated little enthusiasm. As usual, Chandler supported the Republicans. Nunn in turn capitalized on the race issue and the uneasy mood of the nation, since riots, demonstrations, and general unrest appeared in the news seemingly daily. That anger was expressed by a *Hazard Herald* writer who was "tired of beatniks, hippies, and civil righters," and by a conservative Ken-

413

tucky Republican congressman speaking for Nunn, who blamed the societal "degeneration" on bearded protesters and the promises of LBJ's "Great Society." The result was the first Republican victory in a Kentucky governor's race in twenty-four years: Nunn won by a count of 454,123-425,674. Even then, the victory represented something of a personal triumph for Nunn, for half of the other elected offices, including lieutenant governor (Wendell H. Ford), went to Democrats, and that party continued to control both legislative chambers. Still, Republicans held the governorship, both U.S. Senate seats, and three of the seven House posts.

The next year Kentuckians would give Richard Nixon their presidential electoral votes, as they did every time he ran. Faced with the choice for U.S. senator of Catholic Marlow Cook on the Republican side or a Democratic woman, Katherine Peden, Kentucky voters collapsed the religious barrier first. Cook took Morton's vacated Senate seat in 1968. Predictions became commonplace that Kentucky—like many southern states—was turning Republican.

In that heady atmosphere, Governor Nunn came to Frankfort, bringing with him a group of young and fresh "whiz kids," reminiscent of Chandler's first term. Working with the Democratic legislature, Nunn presided over an administration characterized by much accomplishment and much controversy. Even though party cohesion is not usually strong in the Kentucky General Assembly, the specter of a Republican governor, a Democratic lieutenant governor, and a Democratic legislature haunted the sessions, and Nunn successfully vetoed 25 percent of the bills passed in 1968 and 14 percent two years later. The General Assembly also enacted the first statewide open housing law south of the Ohio River, a bill drafted by black legislators Georgia Davis (Powers), Mae Street Kidd, and Hughes McGill. Governor Nunn, who had campaigned on a platform of restricting such actions, let the bill become law without his signature.

But the key issue concerned money. Faced with a budget deficit, Nunn squarely proposed and the legislature passed an increase in the sales tax to five cents per dollar. That tax hike allowed large amounts of money to go into education and permitted the University of Louisville and Northern Kentucky University to be brought into the state system.

At the same time, events outside the capital occupied much of the governor's attention. He sent troops to Louisville during the May 1968 race riots that left two dead, and to the University of Kentucky in May 1970, following the destruction by arson of a building on campus in what was likely an antiwar-related action. Saying that the campus was in "clear and present danger," Nunn ordered armed soldiers to enforce a curfew that also affected the week of final examinations.

In between these two events, Nunn showed that he still kept a sense of humor. When hosting the Republican Governors Conference in 1969, for instance, he gave his guests a thoroughbred. Shortly thereafter, the Poor People's Coalition presented a surprised and not particularly sympathetic governor with a mule named Hope. Nunn noted that he would look at the animal's face and think of the sadness among the poor, and then look at its back and be reminded of the burden on the backs of the taxpayers helping the poor. Then he concluded: "And then as the mule walks away from me and I look at the rear quarters of this mule, I shall always be mindful of the conduct and the behavior of some of those who made this presentation." The gift of Hope was not accepted, and the mule was returned to Knox County to work in a sorghum mill.

Hope of another kind had come to Frankfort with the Republican victory in 1967. Yet despite the accomplishments and despite the prediction of a wave of Republican wins in the future, the Nunn administration from 1967 to 1971 marked the gubernatorial high-water mark for the party for the next quarter century. Why did the Republican resurgence die, while in other southern states it persisted?

First of all, as riots ended, as the racial question faded, and as integration became basically accepted, race declined as a divisive issue in elections. Since the state did not have a sizable black population, the later concern of white voters did not reach the same level as elsewhere. Second, the sales tax increase hurt the Republicans a great deal, even though it was passed with Democratic votes. When the state retail sales tax had been approved in 1959, the people had voted on it, and if the amount did turn out to be larger than expected, many had been paid hundreds of dollars in a veterans' bonus and could not really repudiate their votes. But no such mitigating factors affected Nunn, and like most candidates he had spoken out against more taxes. Then came the increase to five cents per dollar, called Nunn's nickel. Finally, the Republican Party itself was injured by the Watergate episode that ended in Nixon's resignation in 1974, and also by a string of gubernatorial candidates that presented little challenge to a Democratic opposition. Not until generational replacement shifted allegiances much later would Republicans win sizable numbers of victories. Until then, a Democratic tide swept the state once more.

The 1971 Democratic primary for governor ended the political career of one leader and started the rise of another. Lieutenant Governor Wendell H. Ford (b. 1924) of Daviess County had been Bert Combs's executive assistant, but now he hoped to win the nomination from his old boss. Combs sought to leave his federal judgeship for the governor's office, but Ford ran a better-organized campaign, which focused on the 1960 sales tax, Combs's age, and the former governor's desire to leave the better-paying federal post. In a relatively quiet race, Ford confounded the experts and defeated overconfident Combs voters by more than 40,000 votes. "This is the end of the road for me politically," said Combs. He was right, although he would continue to be active in public affairs, including educational reform. Republicans put forth young attorney Tom Emberton, who had grown up in south-central

Kentucky, and he ran a solid race. But the former Nunn aide had to try to defend the sales tax increase and never could generate voter excitement for his cause. The seventy-three-year-old Happy Chandler, running as an independent, third-party candidate, added to the mix, but in the end he only received 39,493 votes. Emberton garnered 412,653 votes, and Ford won with 470,720.

Democratic factionalism was dead for just about the only time in the century. Combs, Clements, Chandler—all had gone from center stage, and a basically united party resulted. The first beneficiary of that situation was Wendell Ford. The son of a state senator, he had been in the insurance business and then had risen up the political ladder. During Ford's gubernatorial administration, the sales tax was removed from food products, state government was extensively reorganized, the commonwealth's first severance tax on coal was authorized, and considerable funding was given to education, environmental protection, and the infrastructure. Moreover, when John Sherman Cooper announced that he would not seek reelection as U.S. senator in 1972, Ford's campaign manager, forty-six-year-old Walter D. ("Dee") Huddleston, defeated Nunn for that seat by nearly 34,000 votes. (Cooper, who had been ambassador to India and Nepal and had served on the Warren Commission investigating President Kennedy's assassination, later was appointed ambassador to East Germany.) Two years later, in 1974, Ford ran against incumbent U.S. senator Cook and defeated him easily. Kentucky had two Democratic senators for the first time since 1956. Ford would go on to win reelection after reelection to the Senate, at one time serving as majority whip. Freed of factional attacks, the quieter Ford rivaled Barkley in his ability to win.

What factionalism existed in the Kentucky Democratic Party resulted from the rivalry of the supporters of Ford and of his lieutenant governor, Julian M. Carroll (b. 1931) of Paducah. Yet that contention was muted, for the Carroll forces supported Ford for senator, since his election and resignation as governor would make their man the state's chief executive. On December 28, 1974, Carroll became governor. Eleven months later, after a lackluster race, he won election to a full term, carrying every congressional district and defeating coal company owner Republican Robert E. Gable by the record margin of 470,159-277,998.

The first governor from the Jackson Purchase, Carroll entered his full term with a mandate, an ample treasury, and perhaps as much experience as any of his twentieth-century predecessors. An attorney and excellent stump speaker, he had served ten years in the legislature (four as Speaker of the House), three in the lieutenant governor's office, then one as governor. He brought an extensive knowledge of the details of government to the job and so controlled his first legislative session that an observer said, "A cockroach couldn't crawl across the Senate floor without an OK from the governor stamped on his back." During Carroll's term he was able to pump considerable money into the secondary and elementary schools, expand the state park system, provide aid to the poor to help pay fuel bills, and abolish the bail bonding system. Moreover, the governor implemented a constitutional amendment quietly approved by the voters in 1975, which drastically reorganized the state's legal system and made it a model for the nation. Under this amendment the position of county judge became totally administrative; the state's highest court was renamed the Supreme Court; a new Court of Appeals was created to hear cases from the circuit courts; and a district court system formed the core of the revamped judicial plan (and would hear nearly six hundred thousand cases in 1988-89).

Yet Carroll experienced little good fortune outside state government. Floods, severe winters, the Scotia mining disaster that cost 26 lives in Letcher County in 1976, and the Beverly Hills Supper Club fire in Campbell County that left 165 dead in 1977 brought much grief and eventually some regulatory reforms. Carroll's problems compounded when

he briefly left the commonwealth in 1978. Acting governor Thelma Stovall—the state's first woman lieutenant governor—used her powers to call a special session of the legislature, as her onetime ally Chandler had done before his first election. A candidate for governor in 1979, Stovall likely hoped to help her chances, and the General Assembly obliged by passing House Bill 44, a measure that limited annual property tax increases. Nor did Carroll help himself by certain actions. Sensitive to criticism, he reacted to attacks—some from his politically ambitious auditor—with an attitude that induced enemies to call him Emperor Julian. Charges that his administration had favored its friends through leases and preferential personal service contracts gained credence when Carroll's choice as party chairman resigned in the wake of a FBI investigation and eventually was sentenced to two years in prison. A scandal involving the state's insurance policies netted two further convictions—one of a cabinet secretary—but those were overturned on appeal. While Carroll left office in 1979 under a cloud, the sound and fury exceeded the eventual results. Still, it was a warning of what was to come later.

New Politics or No Politics?

The 1979 election proved to be something of a watershed, dividing the past form of political campaigning and candidates from what would be the immediate future form. At first the Democratic primary seemed to be rather traditional, with Terry McBrayer, backed by the Carroll administration, fighting off challenges from western Kentucky congressman Carroll Hubbard Jr., auditor George Atkins, and the Bingham-backed millionaire and former Louisville mayor Dr. Harvey Sloane. The initial front-runner, Lieutenant Governor Stovall, faltered badly owing to health problems.

Then forty-five-year-old John Y. Brown Jr. (b. 1933) unexpectedly entered the race, and everything changed. Son of a politician father who had run often and won little, Brown had married a former Miss America,

Phyllis George, ten days before his announcement. Now he interrupted his honeymoon for his first political race ever. Wealthy through his involvement in Kentucky Fried Chicken, Brown—like so many before him—promised to run government like a business. The difference this time was that his self-funded campaign sold that image well in carefully crafted television events and advertisements, and the handsome candidate and his attractive wife appeared, as Governor Carroll noted later, "as sort of a fresh breath of air in a stale campaign." Brown surprised everyone by winning the primary with 165,158 votes, receiving 25,000 more than Sloane, his nearest competitor. He had received less than 30 percent of the total vote, but in a crowded field that proportion was enough by far. Brown's victory upset the Republican plans, for they believed the other candidates all had major liabilities on which their hard-hitting candidate, former governor Nunn, could capitalize. About the only thing Nunn could attack now was his opponent's flashy lifestyle, and that approach went nowhere. Continuing what was called his show-biz campaign, Brown won by more than 176,000 votes, 558,088-381,278. The former salesman had successfully sold himself to Kentuckians.

Brown's race and his subsequent term as governor showed four trends that would continue for some time. First of all, television became the all-important medium, as film editing increasingly replaced local organizations as a key. Political scientist Jasper Shannon wrote that "policy and philosophy yielded to personality and images," and voters became spectators watching from their living rooms, rather than organizers and participants. This situation brought about a second trend, the emergence of the self-funded, wealthy candidate. If any twentieth-century Kentucky governor had been a millionaire before Brown, he had only been marginally so at best. At least three of the four governors elected between 1979 and 1991 would be in that category, however. With no real limits on campaign spending, they would

have a great advantage in the battle for television time.

The new governor had called his style the New Politics; veteran party leaders worried that it might be no politics. All patronage came from the Brown camp, not from Democratic Party headquarters, and the chief executive virtually forgot local party organizations. Instead, the future would be based not on party or factional allegiance but on shifting personal alliances, a third trend. Finally, Brown—who rode a motorcycle to his office on occasion—displayed a very casual attitude toward governing. His hands-off attitude took him on vacation during one of his two legislative sessions, and his lieutenant governor, Martha Layne Collins, served as chief executive for the more than five hundred days Brown was out of state during his four-year term. That fourth trend allowed the General Assembly to become very independent, perhaps for the first time.

Well-liked by the press, Brown received the *Courier-Journal*'s praise at the end of his gubernatorial term for his "unparalleled" record. The newspaper cited his reduction of state government personnel, strong increases in the compensation to remaining employees, the use of competitive bidding, and passage of a weight-distance tax on trucks. But on examination, Brown's overall cupboard of accomplishments was actually fairly bare. Seeking a constitutional amendment that would allow him a second term, Brown saw that proposal fail by a large margin. The state jobless rate went from 5.6 percent the year he became governor to 11.7 by the time he left, the highest figure in more than a decade. In 1983—the last year of the Brown administration—the state's per capita income was lower in relation to the nation's than it had been five years before. Despite claims about cuts in spending, overall expenditures increased 33 percent during Brown's term, although very little of those funds went into the financially strapped educational system. Bad publicity resulted when the governor admitted withdrawing $1.3 million in cash from a Florida bank, mostly to cover gambling debts, and when his office tried to hide the seriousness of his condition after a 1983 heart bypass operation resulted in the loss of his pulse for a time and the partial collapse of a lung. Recovering from that experience, Brown could look back on a scandal-free administration, at least within the government, and could take pride in some of the internal reforms that had occurred. Yet his term ended with a sense of much left undone.

As usual, a host of candidates sought to become governor in 1983, to try their hand at the office. Back for a second race in the Democratic primary was Dr. Sloane, as was the Brown administration's eventual choice, Dr. Grady Stumbo from eastern Kentucky. Yet the winner, in the closest primary in recent times, was Lieutenant Governor Martha Layne Collins (b. 1936). By 4,532 votes out of more than 640,000 cast, she won. Collins received 223,692 votes, Sloane polled 219,160, and Stumbo got 199,795. The Republican candidate was James P. ("Jim") Bunning of northern Kentucky. Formerly a superb major league baseball pitcher, Bunning found that in this contest at least he came to the political plate

with several strikes against him—his Catholic religion and attendance at schools in Cincinnati, his sometimes less than personable manner on the campaign trail, and his inability to find issues that would cause normally Democratic voters to support him. With front-runner Collins speaking carefully, the race was called "one of the dullest . . . in years." The results, however, were pathbreaking, for Collins's 107,000-vote win (561,674-454,650) meant that the state would have a woman governor for the first time.

The forty-six-year-old Collins had grown up in Shelby County, graduated from the University of Kentucky, and then taught school. Active in precinct-level politics in her new home of Woodford County, she gained Ford's support and in 1975 won election to the office of clerk of the Court of Appeals. In 1979 she squeaked out a surprising 4,500-vote win in the Democratic primary and went on to become lieutenant governor during Brown's administration. His frequent absences and willingness to let her represent him at statewide functions immensely aided her bid to become governor. One study noted that typically some 10 percent of the primary voters in Kentucky

Martha Layne Collins was elected governor of Kentucky in 1983 (courtesy of the Kentucky Historical Society).

have actually seen a candidate in the year before the election; some 36 percent saw Collins, and she apparently made a good impression. Yet her victory puzzled some observers, for Kentucky—in their view a conservative state—had elected one of the first half dozen women governors in the nation. Perhaps they forgot that the state had been a leader in the women's rights struggle early in the century. More than that, the commonwealth's vaunted individualism may have caused voters—some of whom were perhaps hesitant to support women candidates in theory—to judge Collins on her merits, based on their personal contacts with her. For whatever reason, as she noted on election night, "We made history, Kentucky."

Collins's first full year as state leader in 1984 was not a memorable one, however. The General Assembly rejected her proposals and program, and her husband's financial activities were already starting to attract the attention that would eventually land him in prison. That same year the state lost its most influential member in Congress, when the quiet and unassuming but politically astute Carl D. Perkins died. Congressman for more than a quarter century, fourth in seniority in the House, he had long aided the poor and supported education, and he would be missed. Democrats also lost another important player when the results of the 1984 Senate race came in. Senator Huddleston had forged a good record, had won reelection rather easily in 1978, and had been expected to win again over Republican judge executive A.M. ("Mitch") McConnell of Louisville. A former legislative assistant and speechwriter for Senator Cook (who supported Huddleston in the canvass), McConnell used what became known as the effective "hound dog" commercials and simply ran a better race than the incumbent. The surprising results gave Republicans and McConnell a 5,800-vote win, 645,530-639,721. Then, two days before Christmas of that year, a key party adviser died.

In the 1940s Edward F. Prichard Jr. (1915-84) had been viewed by many as the most politically talented and intellectually

gifted Kentuckian of his generation. Law clerk to U.S. Supreme Court justice Felix Frankfurter and legal counsel to the president before the age of thirty, Prichard numbered among his friends Katherine Graham of the *Washington Post* and historian Arthur Schlesinger Jr. But if he had received seemingly endless gifts of talent from the gods, they had also given him a fatal flaw, what he called later "a moral blind spot." In 1948 he helped "fix" a meaningless election and in a politically charged atmosphere was convicted. His appeal could not be heard by the U.S. Supreme Court, for too many justices had to disqualify themselves since they knew him. In 1950 President Truman pardoned him, five months into his federal prison term, but "Prich" lived in his own private prison of humiliation for years more.

Slowly he made his way back, behind the scenes, to be a key adviser to the Clements-Combs camp, and "the Philosopher" helped fashion their wins and programs. Opponent Chandler once sought to make Prichard an issue and labeled him a "jailbird." Prich replied: "It is true that I have served time in the federal reformatory. I have associated with murderers, robbers, rapists, and forgers, criminals of all kinds, and let me say, my friends, that every one of them was the moral superior of A.B. 'Happy' Chandler." Finally, near the end of his life, a blind Prichard helped initiate the educational reform movement that would bear legislative fruit after his death. Like a figure from a Greek tragedy, Prichard had been shown the highest laurels, only a fingertip away, but then had been driven to the lowest depths. At last he had rebuilt his shattered life, and he died a highly honored Kentuckian. But now he too was gone.

Despite the 1984 setbacks for Collins and for her party, by the time she left office in 1987, she would receive wide praise for what had taken place on her watch. Hardworking, Collins grew in office, was considered for the vice presidency in 1984, chaired the Democratic National Convention that year, and then had two successful legislative sessions. A 1985 special called session resulted in an additional three hundred million dollars for education, to reduce class size, increase teachers' salaries, and construct more classrooms. The former schoolteacher had made educational reform fashionable. She also had success in economic development, with the capstone coming in December 1985, when Toyota announced the construction of a billion-dollar automotive plant near Georgetown. A sizable incentive package tied to the Toyota plant brought Collins some criticism, but the growth of allied industries connected to the plant, as well as its later expansion, muted that censure quickly. Finally, Collins had a good working relationship with the legislature by the time she left office, something that would not be said of a Kentucky governor over the ensuring decade.

The Democratic primary still effectively decided who the next governor would be, and the 1987 primary seemed a repeat of eight years earlier. John Y. Brown Jr. was back, as was 1983 candidate Grady Stumbo, former governor Julian Carroll, plus administration-backed Lieutenant Governor Steve Beshear. This time, however, the fresh face with the seemingly unlimited bankroll was another political newcomer who rose outside the party structure, forty-five-year-old Wallace G. Wilkinson (b. 1941). After growing up in Casey County, Wilkinson had made several fortunes, through bookstores, real estate, and other ventures, and now he advocated a state lottery as a way to distance himself from the other candidates. That tactic worked, as his 35 percent of the total gave him nearly 58,000 votes more than his nearest competitor, Brown. Wilkinson's success spilled over to the general election, particularly since a strong Republican candidate unexpectedly withdrew from the race. Wilkinson carried 115 counties and won over Republican state legislator John Harper of Shepherdsville by a record vote of 504,674-273,141.

Unlike fellow millionaire Brown, who almost avoided legislative involvement, Wilkinson took a hands-on and sometimes confrontational approach, which did not make

for a very happy relationship between the executive and legislative branches. With Wilkinson's election seen as a mandate for a lottery, the General Assembly passed an amendment that, when approved by the voters, allowed a state lottery after a hiatus of nearly a century. In that same election citizens endorsed another important constitutional amendment, which over-turned a 1956 court ruling and required landowners' approval before surface (strip) mining could occur, thus negating much of the old broad form deed. When the state Supreme Court ruled Kentucky's entire educational system unconstitutional, action had to be taken on that issue by the governor and legislature in the 1990 session. After many disputes, Wilkinson reluctantly agreed to modify his funding package and to support instead an increase in the sales tax to six cents per dollar, in order to finance educational reform. He and the legislative leadership also used a healthy number of promises of roads and projects in exchange for votes to pass the Kentucky Education Reform Act (KERA). A compromise, for which no individual nor any branch of government could claim sole credit, the educational reform package was the key action taken during the Wilkinson years. With a good record on prisons and the environment, with a weaker one regarding appointments, state leases, and bond sales, the governor had focused attention on rural areas and illiteracy. But his style almost overcame his actions, and many found it hard to forget the first as they evaluated the second.

BOPTROT and Beyond

In 1951 a losing candidate for governor had attacked the political immorality and corruption in the state capital, "our Ninevah on the Kentucky River." That was nothing new, for criticism had long existed regarding the influence of lobbies, the way votes were secured, and, on occasion, the general quality of the elected officials themselves. Journalists in the 1950s and later noted that the liquor lobby kept a twenty-four-hour open house, with free drinks, for any member, "a temptation that proved fatal to many a lawmaker away from home and the cold eye of the Baptist Church." One member was known for drinking out of a milk carton on the chamber floor; it was less well known that the carton contained a mixture of half milk, half vodka. And antics could be very open. When a bill passed as a result of some political dealings, or even a monetary payoff, it was labeled a turkey bill, and members would yell out, "Gobble, Gobble, Gobble," as the vote was taken. In 1972 a live turkey was released on the House floor, with the name of a bill on a sign around its neck. Capers such as that brought a versifier to conclude:

> Our ancestors settled the country
> when it was wild and dense,
> then politicians took over
> and it's been unsettled since.

In the three decades after the end of World War I, the pattern for the Kentucky legislature had been rather settled, however. The typical legislator was a white, middle-aged male who attended a Baptist church, practiced law, voted Democratic, and during the successful sessions usually followed the governor's wishes on key votes and in the selection of leadership. While turnover in the state Senate generally matched national trends, House members changed at a much more rapid rate, owing in part to the practice of rotating the nomination among the counties constituting a district.

At a time when a rate exceeding 50 percent was deemed "excessive turnover," in the decades of the 1940s and 1950s nearly 62 percent of the legislators in the House changed in each ten-year period. Slowly, though, those rates decreased. A strong committee system developed, members were better informed, and professionalism grew. The General Assembly attracted more members oriented to their legislative careers and, not coincidentally, less likely to accept gubernatorial guidance. The general characteristics did not change, except that the typical legislator had an average of three years of experience in 1970 but nearly nine years in 1990 (see table 24.1). The state continued to be very near the bottom nationally in the percentage of women legislators and did not rank high in minority representation either. One change in the composition of the General Assembly had taken place, however. In 1960 Catholic members made up less than 13 percent of the total; in 1970 the figure still stood at only 16 percent; but by 1990 Catholic members represented 29 percent of state legislators. Over one-third of the Senate was Catholic in 1990. One longtime barrier to elective office in the state had been broken down, but others remained.

While the state legislature was undergoing change, most of it positive, one other element of Kentucky politics—corruption at the local level—seemed to resist modification. In the two years after 1976, for instance,

Table 24.2
Characteristics of the Kentucky Legislature, 1970-1990

Year	Democrats	Republicans	Average age	Average years experience	Men	Women	Minorities
1970	95	43	47	3.0	133	5	4
1980	104	34	46	5.7	130	8	4
1990	100	37	50	8.8	130	7	3

sheriffs or deputies in five eastern Kentucky counties were convicted of extorting funds from bootleggers. The 1980s began with the Fayette County sheriff resigning after pleading guilty to mail fraud, and the county judge executive of another locale had the same experience the following year. In 1992 the Muhlenberg County judge executive pleaded guilty to spending county funds for personal use, and the next year the county attorney in Lexington and the sheriff in Jefferson County both went to jail. Political corruption at the local level may not have been any worse than in earlier times, but law enforcement agencies now vigorously prosecuted such fraud, and the media publicized it. The local level, though, was only part of the story.

Members of the General Assembly came out of that local political environment, and in Frankfort, they continued some long-traditional practices, despite a changing situation. Moreover, by 1979 and afterward, the legislature had become increasingly independent and was in a state of transition as a result. Whereas deals before had been made in the governor's office with one person in charge, now deals had to be made with many. The once-considerable power of the chief executive to influence legislative outcomes decreased, and the vote of each legislator took on more importance. When the decline of party allegiance was added to the mix, suddenly lobbyists found themselves playing by a whole new set of rules. The result was a long and major political scandal that drew national attention to Kentucky and hurt the image of the evolving independent legislature.

Federal investigators named their operation BOPTROT, for the Business Organizations and Professions Committee (BOP) and for the trotting track involvement (TROT). By the end of their probe in 1995, twenty people and one organization—the Jockey Guild—had been convicted or had pled guilty to a variety of crimes. Sixteen of the twenty individuals were legislators or former legislators, from both parties, and they included the Speaker of the

House. Another was Governor Wilkinson's nephew and appointments secretary; yet another was a former state auditor and gubernatorial primary candidate. A few were guilty only of lying to the FBI; most were involved in bribery, extortion, mail fraud, racketeering, or a combination thereof, and crimes were usually captured on camera or videotape. Generally, those convicted had been given a small bribe by a racing lobbyist or a more sizable amount by the vice president of a health care concern to vote for bills of importance to them, particularly in the 1990 session. While Kentuckians traditionally have displayed a high degree of tolerance for political corruption, what seemed to disturb them most about BOPTROT was the smallness of most of the bribes (a few hundred dollars). As one historian noted: "It's embarrassing that our legislators were bought off so cheap—almost for a mess of pottage."

But even that was not all. In 1993 the husband of former governor Collins was convicted of extortion and tax fraud involving forced investments in his businesses and kickbacks from firms doing business with the state. A state legislator was convicted in the same year of extorting money from a woman in order to help her win leniency for her husband on a federal charge. In 1994 former nine-term congressman Carroll Hubbard pleaded guilty to felony charges of using campaign funds and congressional workers for his personal benefit, while former congressman Chris Perkins also pleaded guilty to bank fraud and misuse of campaign funds. For a time, citizens wondered whether anyone would be left untouched by what the *Economist* called "one of the worst political scandals in Kentucky's history." BOPTROT cast a long shadow over the state's subsequent actions.

Kentuckians went to the polls to elect a governor in 1991 knowing almost nothing of all that. Instead, they could see new trends. The shift of dominance from western Kentucky to the central part of the state was clear in the primary, for six of the seven candidates in the two parties came from Lexington or an adjacent county. The three previous governors—Brown, Collins, and Wilkinson—all fit that pattern as well. That area had boomed in the 1970s and beyond and had attracted the young and the ambitious. Soon a fourth straight governor from the area would be elected.

For Democrats, the field of serious candidates narrowed as Martha Wilkinson, the governor's wife, dropped out because of a lack of support, while a long-shot candidate running on a platform of legalizing marijuana saw his chances go up in smoke. The eventual victor was Lieutenant Governor Brereton C. Jones (b. 1939), who had grown up in West Virginia, had served as Republican minority leader in the legislature there, and had then moved to Kentucky, changed his registration to Democratic, and operated a thoroughbred farm in the Bluegrass. In the Republican primary, congressman Larry Hopkins barely overcame a late challenge from Lexington attorney Larry Forgy. But in the general election, Hopkins's negative advertisements, mistakes about his record, and his involvement in the U.S. House scandal involving "bounced" checks all hurt him, for Jones carried all but thirteen counties and won by almost a quarter million votes, 540,468-294,452, representing the largest gubernatorial margin in the state's history.

Widely perceived as a reformer, a supporter of "good government," Jones came to office with much support from opinion makers and legislators, as well as a voter mandate. All that brought high expectations. Early on, however, the state's two largest newspapers became critical of the governor and remained so. Moreover, a good working relationship between the executive and legislative branches never really developed, and some harsh language worsened divisions. Yet beyond the rhetoric, the Jones administration and the General Assembly actually fashioned a good record. It did not come easily, for one regular session ended without a budget, and one of the many special sessions accomplished almost nothing. Still, the legislature passed one of the strongest ethics laws

in the nation. Heavy restrictions were placed on lobbyists, and campaign finance reforms limited the advantages that wealthy candidates once had. A runoff primary was enacted, whereby a second primary would be held—as when Chandler had won the governorship in 1935—if no candidate received 40 percent of the vote. (Had that rule been in effect earlier, all three governors before Jones would have had to run in a second primary race.)

The voters also approved a constitutional amendment, which did not apply to the sitting governor. It permitted future chief executives to serve a second consecutive term, ended the remission of the governor's powers when leaving the state, and caused the governor and lieutenant governor to run as a slate instead of separately. Other actions taken during Jones's term included a mandatory seatbelt law, the establishment of a new health care system, additional funds for a revitalized park system, a four-year phase-out of the inheritance tax, and provision for the largest budget reserve trust fund (or surplus) in the state's history—coming from the core taxes that bring monies into the state, including sales, income, corporate, coal severance, and property taxes. The governor also appointed the first woman, Sara Combs, to sit on the state Supreme Court.

During the Jones administration, Democrats also carried the state for successful presidential candidate Bill Clinton, who won 665,104 votes in Kentucky, compared with Republican George Bush's 617,178 and independent candidate Ross Perot's 203,944. But in the ten elections for president stretching from 1956 to 1992, Democrats had won Kentucky's vote only when southerners—Lyndon Johnson, Jimmy Carter, and Bill Clinton—were the party candidate. In all the other races, Republicans won, usually by a sizable margin. In a state in which Democratic voter registration remained constant, at almost 68 percent of the electorate between 1975 and 1987, a lot of "closet Republicans" hid behind Democratic labels. By 1994 they appeared to be emerging from the closet in larger numbers, for Republicans won four of six congressional seats, controlling that delegation for only the second time. One of those winning Republican candidates filled the seat of the powerful Democrat William H. Natcher, who died that year, after casting a record 18,401 consecutive votes in Congress.

Such trends caused Democratic concern as the 1995 governor's race began, and early prognosticators predicted a pathbreaking victory by Republican Larry Forgy as he faced Lieutenant Governor Paul E. Patton (b. 1937) of Pike County. Yet when the results came in on election day, Democrats found themselves in the unfamiliar position of having won as one-time underdogs in the race, by a margin of more than 21,000 votes, 500,787-479,227. What had happened? Simply stated, Forgy lost, and Patton won. Forgy lost, in part, owing to three factors. First of all, he became identified with the Christian right, and that had a dual effect, causing some in his own party to desert him, particularly in Louisville, and making him less of an option to moderate Democrats, especially in Lexington. Second, his attacks on KERA seemed another move away from the center to the right, and some Republican supporters of educational reform looked elsewhere. A bipartisan pro-KERA response also followed. In both cases, Forgy's actions seemed, on the surface at least, unnecessary, for votes from both the Christian right and the anti-KERA forces were likely his already. Finally, he was also unlucky, for the budgetary actions of the Republican majority in the U.S. Congress on issues affecting the elderly were used against him, taking some of the focus away from the unpopularity of the Clinton administration in Kentucky.

Forgy did not only lose, however. Patton also won the election. One voter spoke of "sleeping Democrats. With the campaign so close . . . it prompted us to get active." For the first time in a long while, the once-traditional Democratic voting blocs—labor, education, blacks—came out in force and made a differ-

ence in Louisville in particular. Running well in his native region and recapturing much of western Kentucky for the Democrats, Patton won in the closest race in thirty-two years and became the first eastern Kentuckian chosen governor since 1959. He also became the fifth of the past seven governors who had used the office of lieutenant governor as a stepping-stone to the Governor's Mansion. All those people had been Democrats. In the fifty-year period since the end of World War II, Republicans had won only one gubernatorial election in Kentucky.

Even with all the close races in the 1990s, both parties worried about voter turnout. By 1976 Kentucky had fallen to forty-first in the nation in that category, and in the hotly contested 1991 Democratic primary, only 39 percent of eligible voters went to the polls. Three years later in the congressional races, less than 28 percent of those who could cast ballots in the commonwealth did so—the next to lowest turnout in the nation. In the state in which the 1900 turnout of 83 percent almost led the nation and where the 1920 figure did lead, in the commonwealth where politics is "the damnedest," in a place where a newspaper editor once complained about the "manic preoccupation" of the people with the subject, voters now seemed apathetic and bored. They stayed away from the polls in droves. The nearly 44 percent turnout in the close 1995 race marked a swing upward, but still more than half of the state's registered voters did not participate. Whether some candidates or some cause could re-ignite their interest remained to be seen.

Everyone agreed that the politics of the twenty-first century would differ in some ways from the campaigns of decades and centuries before, but would important traditions live on? Would the colorful stories of the Stanley-Morrow race ever be matched? Would the oratory of individuals like Henry Clay, John C. Breckinridge, Billy O'B. Bradley, Alben Barkley, or Happy Chandler ever again be an important part of political success? Would a well-crafted media image be more important than local organizational ability? Would the results of political polls be more crucial than a candidate's ability? Would Kentucky see—or did it want to see—a rebirth of past campaigns? Answers awaited a new century.

25

New Challenges, Old Traditions

In the half century after World War II, Kentuckians experienced the greatest changes in their recorded history. The atomic age arrived. Men walked on the moon. Women's rights expanded. Segregation ended. Television, air conditioning, and automobile ownership became commonplace. Almost instant communications resulted from the presence in virtually every home of radios, telephones, and televisions, as well as fax machines and computers in many. The world grew smaller, and opportunities to visit foreign areas grew wider through easily available airplane travel. Trips that took months a century before now took a day; information that would formerly have taken days or weeks to assemble and transmit now issued in minutes or hours. The state moved from an agricultural and coal economy to a more diversified base, and for the first time statistics showed that the state was more urban than rural.

Yet at the same moment, many elements of Kentucky life continued. Some individuals fought hard to resist change, seeking to carry forth worthy parts of the past into the new millennium. The commonwealth struggled to find and keep its identity in a rapidly changing world.

Images

Some of the conceptions Americans held of Kentucky disappeared over the years, such as the gambling and vice associated with Newport, just across the Ohio River from Cincinnati. Other perceptions proved much harder to eradicate and, in fact, sometimes grew more enduring. Paducah-born author Irvin S. Cobb wrote that "ghosts walk Churchill Downs on

Derby Day. . . . The whole place . . . is crowded with memories." Through the efforts of promoter Matt Winn and others, the Kentucky Derby, held on the first Saturday in May, became the nation's greatest horse race, and the commonwealth's identification with the thoroughbred grew stronger. Nor was that image a false one. In presenting a special subscription offer in 1965, Mike Barry of the *Kentucky Irish American* added a proviso: "This offer may be withdrawn at any time. Any time we have that Real Good Day at the track." The day after the Derby the same Mike Barry would be given time at Sunday mass to explain to the congregation exactly what had taken place on Derby day. Such interest, together with the presence of other major tracks, such as Latonia (later Turfway) and Keeneland, made Kentucky the home for horses.

Allied to this view of Kentucky was the image of the Colonel. In the nineteenth century cartoonists had made Henry Watterson almost the personification of the South; Kentuckian D.W. Griffith had perpetuated that stereotype in film, as did other filmmakers; Annie Fellows Johnston's book *The Little Colonel* and similar publications included the same representation; and governors furthered the myth by issuing thousands of Kentucky Colonelcies. Then came Harland D. Sanders (1890-1980). Not particularly successful in the first decades of his life, the Indiana-born Sanders made a modest start at a Corbin restaurant, began to franchise Kentucky Fried Chicken in 1953, and by the end of the decade had more than two hundred fast-food outlets. The image of Colonel Sanders spread across the country. Although Sanders sold his interest in the domestic part of the company's operations for two million dollars in the early 1960s, he became an even greater part of the corporation's advertising strategy. Continued publicity made him an internationally known figure—and a part of the nation's mythology of Kentucky.

Add to all that the identification of the state with bourbon, and the archetypical Kentucky Colonel was complete. He sat on the veranda of his white-columned mansion, drinking a mint julep or bourbon and water, watching his thoroughbreds run in the fields of bluegrass, with a Stephen Collins Foster melody playing softly in the background. The fact that almost no Kentuckians lived that life did not make the image any less real as a representation of the state and its people.

A very different alternative image existed as well. In this scenario the Kentuckian sat propped up against a log cabin instead of on the porch of a mansion, drank moonshine rather than bourbon, and enjoyed the sport of feuding over racing. The long-suffering hillbilly lived on. One author counted more than three hundred silent films that focused on moonshining and feuding between 1910 and 1916 alone. A stereotyped media presentation of Appalachia continued after that; some representations were specific to Kentucky, and some were more general, but all contributed to the image of a region and its people. In 1934 comic-strip characters Li'l Abner and Snuffy Smith appeared, and Li'l Abner eventually appeared on stage and in a motion picture. Television programs such as *The Real McCoys, The Beverly Hillbillies, Green Acres,* and *The Dukes of Hazzard,* while often showing the lead characters in positive ways, all fed the image. In 1992 the Pulitzer Prize–winning play *The Kentucky Cycle* presented a sordid picture of the region.

Attention resulting from Lyndon Johnson's War on Poverty produced books, articles, and television stories, rarely focusing on the positive aspects of the places or people under study. Some citizens in the Appalachian region, not surprisingly, grew defensive; others saw themselves almost as a minority group, assailed by prejudices from without. And the image of eastern Kentucky was often expanded to describe the entire state. A citizen could answer the inquiry "Where are you from?" with the response "Kentucky" and be greeted with "Oh, a hillbilly." That image ignored much reality, but it lived on nationally for generation after generation.

This image from a penny postcard represents one of the stereotypical views of Kentucky: the white-suited colonel, preparing to drink a mint julep (courtesy of the Kentucky Historical Society).

Not as persistent, or perhaps not as prevalent, were three other images, which can be classified as beauty, boxing, and basketball. When George Gallup polled Americans in 1956, Kentucky was cited as one of the "most beautiful" states. That strength became the basis of a strong state park system focused on lakes, scenic areas, and historic sites. According to one accounting, by 1993 tourism had become the commonwealth's second-largest private employment sector; it was the third-largest revenue-producing industry, generating some $6.8 billion annually. Yet paradoxically, all places of beauty were not always treated well. In 1972 author Wendell Berry flew over the mountain region and cried out about the strip mining: "This industrial vandalism can be compared only with the desert badlands of the west. The damage has no human scale. . . . It is a domestic Vietnam." The environmentalist concluded of his native state: "We have despised our greatest gift, the inheritance of a fruitful land." By 1994 more than one-third of the public lakes in Kentucky had pollution problems, eight of the state's counties experienced ozone pollution, and almost half of the commonwealth's private wells—20 percent of the population relied on such sources—tested positively for bacterial contamination. Yet overall, protection of the environment was growing stronger in the last decades of the twentieth century, and the state seemed to be better heeding Berry's call. More time would be needed, however, to determine whether Kentuckians would fully protect a strength of the state—its natural beauty and historic resources—for generations yet unborn.

The motion picture *2010* was set in that future, in outer space. In the film, the main character, an American, gives his Russian counterpart some bourbon from Kentucky. She asks him what else they have in this place, Kentucky, and he answers that they play good basketball there. The image of Kentucky as a basketball-playing state remains in the minds of many Americans. In the 1989 *Encyclopedia of Southern Culture,* under the entry "Basketball," the writer concluded that "if there is one

team and one region of the South that is most noted for its basketball it is Kentucky." He traced that situation to a man from Kansas, Adolph F. Rupp (1901-77).

Coming to the University of Kentucky in 1930, Rupp coached there for forty-two years, winning a record 875 games and four national championships. Despite a gambling scandal involving players that caused the cancellation of the 1952-53 schedule, Rupp's Wildcat teams dominated the college game in the decade after 1945, with an undefeated stretch ending in 1954 and a record 129-game home winning streak that concluded the next year. A driven, forceful, colorful man, "the Baron" in his trademark brown suit reluctantly retired in 1972, to be succeeded by Joe B. Hall of Harrison County, who coached the UK team to a fifth national championship. By that time, as one reporter noted, one of the few things uniting the state was a love for Wildcat basketball. A 1991 poll revealed that outside Louisville, 68 percent of the people who followed sports were University of Kentucky fans, 8 percent were University of Louisville fans, and smaller percentages followed other schools or none at all. With no major professional teams in the state, college basketball had become the only game

around, the sport of choice, part of the state's culture. Rupp and other coaches had brought a rich tradition of success to a state often ranked at or near the bottom in other national categories. A love affair was born, and every loss was like a death in the family. In 1996, under Coach Rick Pitino, the Wildcats won yet another national championship.

Basketball in Kentucky went beyond the activity at one university, however. Along with Rupp in the national Basketball Hall of Fame are three of his players, Cliff Hagan, Frank Ramsey Jr., and Dan Issel, but also six other Kentuckians: former Western Kentucky University coach Edgar A. Diddle of Adair County, whose 759 victories ranked fourth on the major-college list; Paducah native Clarence ("Big House") Gaines, who won more than 800 games at North Carolina's Winston-Salem State; University of Louisville coach Denny Crum, who brought two national championships to his school; Kentucky high school player and later professional star Dave Cowens; University of Louisville center Wes Unseld; and Murray State University player "Jumping Joe" Fulks, who led the professional league in scoring in one year. Kentucky, Louisville, and Western combined to make the commonwealth the first state to win one hundred tournament games, while at the small-college level, Kentucky Wesleyan won six titles and Kentucky State University three. Indicative of the commonwealth's priorities, one minister recalled a Louisville wedding at which he officiated in the 1980s. It was time to begin, but the groom and his friends were watching a tightly played contest involving their favorite team. After some discussion with her intended, the bride came to the preacher and said, "Why don't we just delay the wedding until after the game?" Forty minutes late, the marriage took place. It is not recorded whether it endured, but devotion to the college game certainly does.

High school games have also sparked intense interest. Howard ("Howie") Crittenden of Pilot Oak in Graves County was the last of ten children, and he lived in a house without electricity or indoor plumbing. On December 25, 1947, at the age of fourteen, he received the first Christmas gift he had ever gotten, and the first item he ever owned that was new. It was a basketball. Five years later, as a member of the 1952 Cuba Cubs, Crittenden was a starter on the state championship team. He later became a school principal. Such stories of success through sports fed the dreams of many Kentuckians, although from 1932 to 1974 girls' basketball was not played, apparently because it was deemed "too strenuous." The absence of divisions in high school basketball meant that every school had the chance to win the state tournament, the Sweet Sixteen, no matter what the enrollment. While urban institutions generally dominated these tournaments, victories by rural teams such as the undefeated Brewers of Marshall County in 1948, or teams from Edmonson County in 1976 and Breckinridge County in 1965 and 1995, became part of the lore that kept interest strong. Still, attendance at most high school games decreased as the century neared its end; different interests and the presence of top games on television took precedence. High school basketball may never again achieve the popular support it enjoyed between 1920 and 1970.

Numerous other sports have attracted Kentuckians over the years. Danny Sullivan and Darrell Waltrip drove to victories in auto racing, Gay Brewer Jr. and Bobby Nichols both won major professional golf tournaments in the 1960s, Mary T. Meagher brought home three gold medals for swimming from the 1984 Olympics, and even the Birchfields of Stamping Ground in Scott County, father and son, captured the U.S. Croquet Association national doubles championship in 1982. Older sports, such as hunting and fishing, continued to be popular, and conservation measures increased the available wildlife. The state's deer population, for instance, grew from a meager 2,000 in the 1940s to more than 380,000 in the 1990s. Bloodier contests, including organized dog fights with pit bulls and cockfights with roosters, still occasionally occurred. And much newer sports for the state, such as soccer, experienced steady increases in popularity from the 1980s on.

Yet despite all the interest in basketball and the growth of other sports, the most recognizable person from the commonwealth in the last half of the twentieth century was likely the man who grew up in Louisville as Cassius M. Clay Jr. (b. 1942). He later changed his name to Muhammad Ali. Descended from slave great-grandparents of Logan County, Ali rose to become world heavyweight boxing champion in 1964, but he later had his title stripped because he refused induction into military service for religious reasons. His conviction was overturned years later, and he won the title a second time (1974-78), lost it briefly, then regained the championship from 1978 to 1979. Colorful—"Float like a butterfly, sting like a bee"—and controversial, Ali joined earlier boxer Marvin Hart and later ones Jimmy Ellis and Greg Page in wearing that crown, but none wore it with the flair or excitement that he did. To many he was, as he proclaimed himself, "The Greatest."

Thus when the word *Kentucky* is spoken, the images in the American and world mind are many and varied: bourbon and bas-

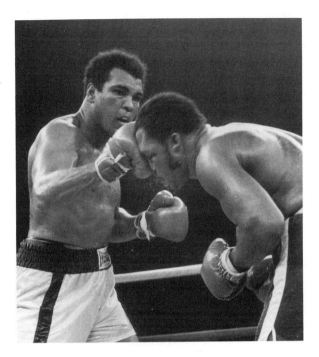

Muhammad Ali lands a right to the head of Joe Frazier during their famous 1975 fight in Manila (courtesy of AP/Wide World Photos).

ketball, natural beauty and strip mines, Muhammad Ali and Colonel Sanders, the goateed colonel and the white mansion, the bearded mountaineer and the log cabin, the Derby and more. Such images perhaps ignore more than they include and in some ways hinder a full understanding of the state as it is. Yet these stereotypes shape the view of the commonwealth held by many people, and they are the things some see as distinctively Kentuckian. Influenced and shaped by such stereotypes, Kentucky cannot avoid them. The question for the future is how the state will deal with those images and whether it can build on the positive parts of its past, for its future.

Trends I

A college professor writing in 1995 noted that "'Kentucky' does evoke, if one subtracts the glamor of the Derby and UK basketball, the image of a rural, backwoods state to too many people. Yet, the state is largely urban. . . . It is a state with a sophisticated transportation system, distinguished public parks, important uni-

versities, and industries with worldwide ties and markets." While parts of that analysis could be debated, the underlying theme is sound: changes over recent decades have transformed many aspects of people's lives and, indeed, the face of the commonwealth. Long-established images—some reflecting reality, some not—often overshadow significant trends that are, in many ways, more important to understanding this place called Kentucky.

The decades after World War II brought forth change with increasing speed. The 1950s saw an affluent society, a consumer economy, affordable homes, flashy large cars, suburbia; it also featured drive-in theaters, the growth of television, Communist "witch hunts," discount stores, game shows, "cruising," crew cuts, Elvis and rock and roll, Marilyn Monroe, *Playboy,* Civil Defense shelters and worries of World War III, polio vaccines, Sputnik, and the U-2 incident. By the end of the 1960s, 94 percent of the state's households had a television set, and during that decade Kentuckians watched protests concerning civil rights and Vietnam and learned about the Cuban missile crisis, the

431

Beatles, JFK and Camelot, urban renewal, interstates, the Pill, bra burning, and the murders of John and Robert Kennedy, Martin Luther King Jr., and Malcolm X. Later decades included Watergate, shopping malls, streaking, the Moral Majority, AIDS, space shuttles, computers, and the fall of the Berlin Wall, among other things. Some national and world phenomena affected the state less than they did many other places; the number of AIDS-related deaths in Kentucky in 1988, for example, numbered only slightly more than forty, ranking the state forty-second in the nation—although that ranking brought little comfort to the family and friends of these individuals. Other, single events had a special interest for Kentuckians; U-2 spy plane pilot Francis Gary Powers was from the state. Most changes occurring during the second half of the twentieth century, however, influenced the people of Kentucky and their lives a great deal.

One of the major changes taking place during those decades concerned women. Achieving the right to vote in 1920 had only represented one step toward equality, and in the years before World War II, only halting progress had occurred. The depression of the 1930s actually reversed several trends, and women lost some of the ground they had earlier won. Wartime demands of the 1940s opened new doors of opportunity, but in many cases the return of soldiers closed some of those again. By 1950 men and women were marrying younger than they had since the government began keeping such statistics. As historian John Diggins notes, "If there was a women's movement in the fifties, it led directly to the wedding chapel."

Change had been taking place over time, however, that made the 1950s only the dark before the dawn. The freedoms unleashed by the war were remembered, new appliances made tasks in the home easier to perform and allowed time for other pursuits, the declining number of children per family meant fewer years spent in child-rearing and more time available to work once that phase of life

had ended, and the need for an additional income in families still below the poverty level remained high. All these factors brought increasing numbers of women into the public working world in Kentucky. In 1940, just before America's involvement in World War II, 17.6 percent of the women in the commonwealth were in the workforce; by 1960, some 27 percent were—one-fourth of them married. On the eve of the women's movement of the 1960s, the state's female workforce had increased in median age from thirty-two in 1940 to forty, and women were employed chiefly in clerical, technical, and service jobs. Women comprised 96 percent of the private household workers in Kentucky, 80 percent of the food servers, 79 percent of the laundry operators, 75 percent of the cooks, and 67 percent of the clerical force. The earlier prohibitions against married teachers had fallen, and most professional women were educators. Otherwise, women workers generally remained in low-paying jobs. Considerable changes took place during the next two decades, however. The percentage of working-age women in the labor force climbed from 27 percent in 1960 to 50 percent in 1980 and then to 54 percent in 1995 (still ranking Kentucky low among the states). In the two decades after 1960, women began to make inroads into selected professions as well.

An existing law providing that property gained by joint effort during a marriage belonged to the husband was transformed, while major modifications took place in societal mores. Later, poet and children's book author George Ella Lyon recalled that when she entered Centre College in 1967, women could not wear slacks on Danville's Main Street. Across Kentucky, schoolgirls were not permitted to don pants unless the temperature dropped to low levels. That soon ended. But as historian Margaret Ripley Wolfe notes, the greatest change during the 1960s may have been the new availability of birth-control devices: "This may have done more for southern women . . . than all the laws ever written and enacted."

What did all these transformations mean for women in public life? Dating from the late nineteenth century, when women first served as county superintendents of public instruction, women in Kentucky began to make slow advances into holding public office. Frankfort elected women to its city council in 1923, soon after the passage of the Nineteenth Amendment to the U.S. Constitution; Louisville selected its first woman alderman six years later. At the state level, the first woman member of the House, Mary E. Flanery of Catlettsburg, took her seat in 1922; the first woman senator, Carolyn Conn Moore of Franklin, came to office twenty-eight years later. Emma Guy Cromwell was the first woman to hold a constitutional office in the executive branch when she won election as secretary of state in 1923; Thelma Stovall took the oath as the commonwealth's first female lieutenant governor in 1975; Martha Layne Collins became governor eight years later. In the judiciary, the first woman to preside over a court was Kathleen Mulligan of Lexington, who served as a municipal judge in 1928. A greater problem, though, was simply getting women on juries. The first woman to sit on a case in Johnson County did so only in 1926; the first time people of both sexes served together on a jury in Garrard County came two decades after that. When voters in 1993 elected Janet Stumbo to the Kentucky Supreme Court, to succeed the first woman to serve there, Sara Combs, the election marked the culmination of a long struggle in the legal realm.

Yet despite the advances, step by step, year by year, and despite some actions—such as the election of Governor Collins—far in advance of the nation, Kentucky continued to lag behind in achieving equality for its female citizens. Seventy-five years after women gained the vote, only about sixty women overall had been elected to the General Assembly, and the state ranked next to last nationally in the percentage of women legislators (8 percent, as opposed to the U.S. average of 21 percent). No women were on the November 1995 ballot for statewide office, and of sixty-six hundred elected officials at that time, only a few more than one thousand were women. Yet Kentucky was a state that had led in the southern women's rights movement and had ratified the Nineteenth Amendment; it was one of a minority of states in the South to support the unsuccessful Equal Rights Amendment of the 1970s; it elected one of the first women governors in the nation. Kentucky remains a place of paradox. The commonwealth's women do a disproportionate amount of the housework and provide for the care of both young and old, but they have more personal independence than ever; they increasingly suffer from the feminization of poverty, but they have greater economic possibilities than before; they win public office as individuals, but not as a group; they eschew most aspects of what critics call a radical feminism but strongly advocate equality under the law. They support those who choose to work in the home, but stress the importance of having the freedom to make a choice.

Relationships between the sexes cannot be fully understood either, for behavior within the home often remains hidden, except for an occasional glimpse. A minister in eastern Kentucky, for instance, told in his recent memoirs

Table 25.1
Women and Careers, 1960 and 1980

Occupation	Women as % of total, 1960		Women as % of total, 1980	
	Ky.	U.S.	Ky.	U.S.
Lawyer, judge	2	3	9	14
Physician	5	7	13	13
Engineer	1	1	4	5
Banking manager	13	13	28	34

Source: Catherine O'Shea, "Success and the Southern Belle," *Southern Magazine* 2 (Aug. 1988): 42

about the first wedding he performed, decades earlier. The young bride brought all her earthly possessions with her, in two pillowcases. The groom seemed to be of a patriarchal spirit, and at the conclusion of the quiet service, his wife meekly walked behind him, lugging her belongings. But once the young husband thought he was out of sight of the minister, he took her burden and put his arm around her. The two walked down the road to their new home, beside each other, as partners. While women in Kentucky may not all yet be walking in full step as complete partners, their road to equality is much smoother than before.

For Kentucky women, and men as well, another postwar trend concerned violence in the commonwealth. In 1882 the *Nation* reported that Kentucky, with 1.6 million people, recently had more homicides than eight other states combined, with an aggregate population of more than 10 million. At the turn of the century a Chicago paper compiled statistics from the previous decades and found that Kentucky's average of 398 reported murders per year ranked it sixth among the states. In the middle of the depression, in 1933, Kentucky's homicide rate of 14.5 per 100,000 people placed it eighth highest in the country. Two years later 530 murders took place in the state. The commonwealth was a violent place. Slowly and gradually, however, Kentucky's place on murder row was taken by other states, and the commonwealth became comparatively safer. By 1976 its murder rate stood fourteenth in the nation; thirteen years after that, it ranked twenty-first.

Among the state's urban areas in 1993, Covington, Newport, and Paducah had the highest crime rates, Owensboro and Elizabethtown the lowest. The state's two largest cities fell in the middle in the commonwealth but low nationally. In the Louisville metropolitan area, for instance, the number of murders fell from 122 in 1974 to 58 in 1993. Overall, Kentucky ranked thirtieth in the United States in violent crime and only forty-sixth in property crime in 1993. Thus, while a well-founded

earlier image of violent Kentucky still existed in some stereotypes, and while better communication resulted in citizens' having greater knowledge about violence statewide, in truth, a larger population experienced many fewer murders than Kentuckians of a half century earlier. Kentucky, compared with the nation at least, was a safe place to live.

It was also a place of much greater mobility than ever before. While the end of most passenger train service—in Glasgow in 1955, Owensboro in 1958, and Lexington in 1971, for example—hurt transportation in the state, the widespread road building program helped assuage the loss. Toll roads, most of which had

Table 25.2
Homicide in Kentucky

Year	Homicide rate (per 100,000 residents)
1933	14.5
1940	14.1
1950	8.9
1960	6.0
1970	10.3
1983	7.4
1989	7.9
1993	7.0

Year	Number of Homicides
1929	455
1930	487
1935	530
1940	400
1950	262
1963	200
1970	331
1976	344
1989	293

Sources: Bulletin of the State Board of Health of Kentucky; Kentucky Vital Statistics Reports; FBI Uniform Crime Reports

become free of tolls by the 1990s, added to the existing interstates and a strong rural roads system to give Kentucky a well-connected network. People could commute greater distances for jobs, and they had easier access to shopping, cultural events, and entertainment than before. In the 1970s, attorney Tom Waller of Morganfield and Paducah recalled what all that meant in his lifetime, beginning in the 1920s:

> To go from my home to Frankfort, then, I could either go by mud roads or dust roads or the railroad. To go by rail meant that I'd leave Morganfield at 9:00 o'clock in the morning, go to Henderson . . . , then at 2 get a train to Louisville, then at Louisville . . . next morning take a slow train [to Frankfort]. . . . By the time you got home you'd lost at least three days.
>
> As soon as automobiles became prevalent we began making that trip by automobile. In the winter the roads made it generally impossible to get there. In the summer the dust was unbelievable. I'd leave Morganfield at noon and spend the night in the vicinity of Leitchfield or Elizabethtown. . . . The next day . . . [I'd] get into Frankfort by 10 o'clock. . . . We had lots of blowouts, lots of bearing failures. The roads were bad. You couldn't drink the water hardly anywhere because of the danger of dysentery. And you dare not drink milk at all because it'd give you all kinds of maladies. You slept where you could get to. You sometimes encountered bed-bugs. That was just the risk you had to take. You . . . had a public bathroom at the hotel [and] in a small town you had no bathing facilities at all. An outdoor privy. Flies were very prevalent. We had no pesticides. Mosquitos were bad.
>
> Then came an era when we got roads from county seat to county seat. They were all-weather roads. . . . We used tax money. We employed health people. We cleaned up the hotels. Today I can leave my home at 5 o'clock in the morning and be in Frankfort . . . for a session of the court. I don't have to have a bath. There's no dust, no flies, no mosquitos. You can drink water. You can drink milk whenever you want to. . . . I can be home for dinner. While that seems to have changed us, it hasn't changed us a particle. We are just able to do things we couldn't do before. Just as now we are unable to do things we will be able to do later on.

Whether or not the people changed, their options certainly did as a result of transportation trends.

Better roads transformed communities and counties, in both positive and negative ways. Isolation had caused some locales to develop a variety of individual businesses, and roads would dry up the need for those services. Health care, professional requirements, and economic wants now could be satisfied by driving to a larger town, in less time than it took an ancestor to get to the county seat. In the late nineteenth century, for example, Owsley County had six physicians, nine attorneys, two jewelers, and two shoemaking shops; by the late twentieth century it usually had one doctor, two barristers, and no real specialty stores. Other places saw what was called the Wal-Mart invasion, as larger, all-purpose stores built on the edge of town took away downtown trade and hurt small businesses in the area.

By the 1990s, then, urban and semiurban places in Kentucky had developed into at least three general categories: crossroad towns, county seats, and cities. The crossroad towns had perhaps developed from a country store where roads met or had grown because of specific local circumstances—a situation near a railroad or river stop, proximity to timber or coal, or a central location offering services to scattered farmers. By the late twentieth century these places might be characterized by a flashing traffic light, a church, a small post office, a branch of a bank, a grocery, a service station, and an eclectic collection of homes. Houses ranged from one or two large columned ones, either new or old, to older frame ones and newer brick domiciles, seldom connected by sidewalks or lit by a public system of streetlights.

Of Kentucky's 120 counties, 78 in 1990 had a county seat whose population did not exceed five thousand people. In those county seat towns—over half of which lost population from 1980 to 1990—downtown activity usually revolved around a courthouse, where attorneys' offices mixed with scattered stores, sometimes featuring antique shops. Other professionals—a few doctors, employees at the federal and state government offices—operated in a variety of places. But in many of those locales the downtown still lived, and surrounding it were eating places, banks, churches, auto dealerships, a post office, and a library. An area slightly more removed from the center integrated businesses with aged houses, a few old and impressive, a few old and decaying. Then in the next circle of activity might be the former edge of town, with small groceries, some eating establishments, agricultural stores, and a scattering of economic enterprises. Finally, the new business section—too small to be called suburbia—featured small stores, convenience-type groceries, fast-food places, and, in larger towns, a shopping center and larger chain stores. Newer homes surrounded all that.

Finally, the larger towns, usually themselves county seats, grew by near the end of the twentieth century to become regional centers or almost extended suburbs of sizable cities. These places of ten thousand to fifty thousand people presented more contrasts. Many of their downtowns became stagnant, as new and extensive suburban shopping areas developed in ways that made them little distinguishable from other such places across the United States. Near the courthouse area, several noble mansions remained as reminders of a preautomobile age when people walked or rode a trolley to the town's core. But poorer homes usually characterized the courthouse fringe. In the suburbs, new schools, parks, and playgrounds dominated. Many residents found that making trips to the shopping fringes or to malls in nearby cities seemed more convenient than waiting through downtown traffic lights and locating suitable parking. Towns more removed from the larger metropolitan areas became regional centers themselves and built their own malls, motion-picture theaters, and the like, in turn creating satellite communities.

Despite the urbanization of the state by 1970, however, statistics showed that Kentucky

slowly became more rural again after that. The old ideal of agrarian living, now coupled with the availability of city pleasures, remains strong in Kentucky. Increasing mobility through better roads and growth of a communications infrastructure has liberated rural dwellers and made their goals attainable once more. Many Kentuckians still prefer to see before them a rural landscape rather than an urban one. The city still has not won the hidden heart of the state.

Trends II

Better transportation and increased mobility, lower crime rates, the opening of opportunities to women—most Kentuckians welcomed such trends. The results of other developments in the state, however, left a more mixed legacy.

Kentucky continued to face problems in health matters, for example. The state's citizens used traditional products of the commonwealth in sizable amounts: a 1987 study showed that despite the presence of seventy-seven "dry" counties, Kentucky led the nation in the consumption of bourbon—one case per year per seven people. Statistics from 1993 indicated that the state also ranked second nationally in the percentage of the adult population who smoked—29 percent. As a result, critics noted, the commonwealth stood second in the United States in deaths from coronary heart disease, sixth in chronic respiratory disease, and first for men and sixth for women in deaths from lung cancer. By the bicentennial of its statehood, Kentucky had the third highest overall rate of death in the nation, and citizens' average life expectancy of seventy-three years ranked the state forty-first on the mortality scale.

Many medical advances had occurred in Kentucky and in the nation during the twentieth century, however. Women like Linda Neville, who helped reduce trachoma, and Mary Breckinridge, whose frontier nursing service provided nurse-midwives and health care to the mountains, aided greatly in the medical field. Individuals of both sexes worked so that deaths from tuberculosis in the state dropped from 1,748 in 1943 to 77 three decades later and to almost none after that. Polio virtually vanished, as did several other once-dreaded diseases. The adjusted death rate declined by 37 percent between 1930 and 1960, and people lived longer. In 1900 only 77,000 Kentuckians (4 percent of the total population) were over the age of sixty-five; by 1990, 465,000 (13 percent) were. By that time citizens of the commonwealth enjoyed the best health care ever. Still, the problem of the distribution of physicians remained acute, as Fayette County had among the highest numbers of doctors for the population in the United States, while some rural counties had among the lowest. Problems of poverty added to the concerns, and some 14 percent of the state's people had no health insurance in 1992. For a few, the option of being an apostle of clairvoyant Edgar Cayce of Hopkinsville, who gave trance-induced health readings and had a national following long after his death in 1945, seemed the only alternative.

Another statistic, troubling to some Kentuckians, concerned the aging of the people. Statistics showed that the commonwealth's 13.7 percent population increase during 1970-80 was higher than the national average, for only the second time since 1810-20. But during 1980-90 the state population remained virtually static at less than 3.7 million people, ranking the state twenty-third in size nationally. The lack of real growth resulted from two key factors, the familiar one of out-migration—171,000 people—and the newer one of a very low birthrate. In fact, by the late 1980s Kentucky's birthrate was the sixth lowest in the nation. Fewer children lived in the state in 1990 than had in 1900. Average household size—which had once been very high—declined from 4.1 in 1940 to 3.1 in 1970 and to 2.6 in 1990, while the median age of the state's residents jumped from twenty-one years in 1900 to twenty-nine years in 1980 and to thirty-three by 1990. Kentucky grew older.

By the 1990s several other demographic trends had become clear. First of all, Kentucky remained very homogeneous. The state's population—52 percent of whom were women—stood fourth nationally in the percentage of natives who lived in their home state. Moreover, it was also among the "whitest" of states, with a black population of 7 percent and with almost no Hispanics, Asians, or Native Americans (about 1 percent total). In 42 of the commonwealth's 120 counties, blacks comprised less than 1 percent of the population, and 10 counties each contained fewer than 10 blacks. Of the 263,000 black people who lived in Kentucky in 1990, half lived in Lexington and Louisville. One author surveyed such statistics and concluded that the state had little population diversity and one of the highest percentages of English-speaking people in the United States.

Men and women of all races attended church. In 1990 Kentucky ranked high—thirteenth among the states—in the percentage of people who identified themselves as Christians. Some 60 percent of the population was part of a specific religious group, and one study of the 1990 census concluded that the commonwealth had 7,255 churches, one for every 508 residents. That analysis found that the largest number of adherents were Baptists (963,000, 42 percent of the total), followed by Roman Catholics (365,000), Methodists (227,000), independent Christian churches and Churches of Christ (91,000), black Baptists (90,000), and Disciples of Christ (67,000). The Church of Jesus Christ of Latter-Day Saints (Mormons) numbered 16,000, while state residents of the Jewish faith, including the mayor of Louisville, numbered 11,000 (about .3 percent of the population).

As a group, Kentuckians did not rank high in wealth. Fairly consistently, the commonwealth stood somewhere in the forties among the states in per capita income (forty-third in 1995). At the same time, 14 percent of the state's residents received federal aid in the

437

form of food stamps. In Appalachia, 28 percent of the elderly were classified as living in poverty; in the entire state, 27 percent of children fell in that category. Yet after years of high unemployment rates, the state's overall figures for the mid-1990s fell below the national average.

Those who worked and those who did not were all part of a poorly educated population, compared with the United States generally. Kentucky ranked at or near the bottom in the proportion of the population that had graduated from high school and college. In 1994, 35 percent of Kentuckians had not completed secondary school (versus the U.S. average of 25 percent); only 13.6 percent of the population had finished a college undergraduate degree (compared with a national figure of 20.3). One study placed the commonwealth fortieth in literacy. Yet at the same time, the merged Lexington–Fayette County city population stood sixth highest in the United States in the percentage of college graduates. Despite success stories such as that, those who wished to upgrade the state's educational level had much to overcome in the race for a well-educated citizenry.

In 1992 the Kentucky General Assembly created a Long-Term Policy Center and charged it with drawing conclusions about the decades ahead. Three years later the members of that group pointed out several dozen trends affecting the state's future. They noted the homogeneity of the people and their rural character and predicted only moderate population growth. The center pointed to the commonwealth's sharply declining birthrate and concluded that "the aging of our population is perhaps the most striking population trend affecting Kentucky." Regarding the economy, they stressed the danger signs for coal and tobacco, emphasized the tourist potential of historic attractions, recounted the dramatic gains made by the state in manufacturing, and accented the importance of small business to future growth. The center recited concerns over income inequality, child poverty, health care,

and environmental integrity and called for action on each issue. It noted the state's prominence and progress in educational reform but made it clear that at present, "By virtually every measure, Kentuckians are undereducated and ill prepared to meet the challenges the future will bring." Finally, the Long-Term Policy Center affirmed that the most successful and prosperous communities in the state featured high levels of civic involvement. People, they concluded, could make a difference.

Most of the matters on which the planning group focused dealt with statistics, numbers, and measurable trends. But there was another part of Kentucky life that was harder to define and articulate, but one equally crucial to the future. This aspect might be called the soul of Kentucky.

Change and Nostalgia

Over the years, observers, both foreign and domestic, praised what they saw as special qualities of Kentucky. The British observer and member of Parliament James Bryce wrote in 1898 that among the southern states, Kentucky was one of the two that he found had the most individuality, with its dignity, polish, and strong leaders. He found it "a sort of nation within the great nation." Less than a decade later, in 1906, the *London Daily Mail* published the observations of "an English litterateur of much repute" who had lived in the United States more than eleven years. He called Kentuckians "undoubtedly the finest people in the states," pointing to their manners, hospitality, courage, and confidence. "With all their freeness and easiness," he noted, "they are still self-poised and self-contained." The writer ended with perhaps his greatest praise: "I will even go so far as to say that even their lawyers look less dishonest than [other] lawyers."

The perceptive novelist Elizabeth Madox Roberts looked at her native state and concluded, in much the same tone, that "Kentucky has form and design and outline both in time and space, in history and geography. Perhaps the strongly marked natural bounds which make it a country within itself are the real causes which gave it history and a pride in something which might be called personality." Another chronicler of the state, in the 1942 book *"Weep No More My Lady,"* approvingly repeated the quote given him by "a gentleman of the old school": "Kentucky is not so much a political unit as a soul; an achievement in character." Various commentators over time did not completely agree on the aspects of the Kentucky character that made the place special to them, but they—and others—understood that the people shared a common memory and a common heritage that gave the state some degree of distinctiveness. But too much should not be made of all that either, for other American places had a special quality as well. The question was not whether the state was distinctive—for all places have at least some degree of that—but how it was special, and what such uniqueness meant to the people in their own era and to the future.

Perhaps the only real constant in Kentucky's history had been change. Robert Penn Warren, born in 1905, noted, "My father's was a different world." A *Courier-Journal* reporter in 1940 looked at a part of the state and concluded, "The pattern of life as our grandfathers knew it is broken and we don't know what to put in its place." Two decades later an editorial in the *Cumberland Tri-City News* reminisced, "Often now, we talk of the time when prices were low, days were not so rush, rush, and there was time to spend with friends, without a feeling of pressure with many things to do and no time to do it in. We all recognize that those days are gone forever." He then quoted the president of the 1890 constitutional convention— "Times change and we change"—and summarized, "We know that the good old days were wonderful ones but few, if any of us want to travel a backward path."

Life had changed in the lifetimes of Warren and his father, as well as the journalists. In an earlier era, events revolved around home and church, and perhaps school and the country store. But generations saw the decline of the family farm and the abandonment of once-prosperous villages. Time brought with it longer lives, fewer diseases, better sanitation, improved educational levels for the general populace, increased mobility, convenient labor-saving devices, and more. At the same time, new technology made former luxuries almost necessities; mechanization permitted people to do more but at the same time produced less need for community-oriented, cooperative efforts.

The fate of the front porch symbolized all that change. As Kenneth Jackson noted in his *Crabgrass Frontier,* American homes in the nineteenth century and much of the twentieth were places "to get out of." They were hot in the summer, and screening was not introduced until the 1880s. Insects swarmed through open windows, or else closed ones left no ventilation. People moved to front porches, where they greeted promenading friends, did chores such as "breaking beans," and even courted. The ideal house had a front porch shaded from the afternoon sun. By the late twentieth century, however, home buyers paid better prices for homes whose barbecue-site backyards were in the shade of the early evening. Porches often disappeared completely. People traveled by automobile instead of by foot and did not wait for others to come to them. Larger homes and smaller families gave individual members of the household more privacy and separateness; air conditioning and entertainment via television left families closed away behind shut doors. Barry Bingham Sr. looked at such trends and asked, "Does that same child ever look out of the real window . . . any more? Does he open it to hear the sounds of ordinary people living around him?"

John Egerton, who grew up and was educated in Kentucky, looked at the evolving landscape of his home area and of the nation and penned a book he called *The Americanization of Dixie: The Southernization of America.* He and other observers noted a national sameness: similar newspapers to read, food to eat, stores to visit, television programs to watch, and clothes to wear. All that helped give a sense of national unity, but it warred with regional distinctiveness. A person could get on an airplane in one part of the country, arrive in another region at an airport like all others, go down streets lined with fast-food places just like those left behind, and then stay in a hotel or motel whose name and rooms matched exactly those in many other locales. Venturing into the suburbs, the same visitor might see homes whose architectural styles looked like those he or she had left. At a shopping mall, few of the store names would be unfamiliar. Many places in many Kentucky towns and cities looked like hundreds of others across the country.

Some Kentuckians welcomed such change with open arms; others accepted it and adapted to it; some resisted bitterly. As a reporter said of one Kentucky town in 1991: "Mayfield will take its changes in little doses, sometimes even going ahead to the past." At the other end of the state, an observer noted that same year, "I think there was a feeling for a long time that Maysville didn't want to change. It was happy the way it was. It didn't want to be bothered by the outside world. That's changed." Historian Arthur Dudden looked at the process of change over time and affirmed: "It is indicated from their history again and again that important segments of the American people, though driven like tumbleweed before the buffeting winds of change and upheaval, attempted to do nothing more than remain where they stood, to keep old ways familiar, even to flee the present and the future into a nostalgically golden yesteryear secluded somewhere far off among remembrances of things past." He defined that sense of nostalgia as a preference for things "as they are believed to have been."

Throughout the decades, citizens of Kentucky had sometimes retreated into nostalgia. Now, in an even more rapidly changing world, Kentuckians had to be careful to honor their past but not to be chained to history. They had to be positive that they went into the future with a sense of perspective and not as prisoners of presentism; they had to preserve worthy traditions and strengths but avoid uncritical nostalgia and insular complacency; they had to face change armed with a sense of their history and what was important to them, while realizing that change was important and part of history too. It was a difficult balancing act. Such hopes were perhaps best expressed when Bingham told what Louisville sought, which in a sense was what Kentucky sought as well: "What we want is a modern city that still remembers the past, as old bricks remember the sun of many summers and the soft rains of a hundred autumns. That is what gives them character and beauty." Kentucky sought to build its future from those same solid foundations.

Continuity

The Americanization of Kentucky was real, but it also had a false front. Behind that, another Kentucky still lurked, one with traditions and a culture that proclaimed that a distinctiveness lived on. Living lives tied loosely to the past, recreating parts of a world left behind, helped twentieth-century Kentuckians deal with the great changes occurring all around them.

Amid the modifications taking place, certain aspects of earlier times continued to endure, including those focusing on the human character. Historian David Kennedy explained that there are

> timeless contrasts in the life of persons and societies about which historical study speaks eloquently: sorrow and happiness; success and defeat; effort and reward; effort and failure; love and hatred; birth, guilt, shame, pride, compassion, cruelty, justice, injustice, death. These in one form or another are the great fixed elements in the lives of all people, everywhere and at all times. History provides us with a means of vicariously sharing in their travails and triumphs . . . even as our own experiences themselves become a part of the story. In this way we are all . . . bonded to our fellow mortals, living, dead, and yet to be born.

For Kentuckians that common heritage was part of a collective memory that many citizens sought to preserve.

What that meant to individuals was personified by Addie King Ledford and Curtis Burnam Ledford. Born on Coon Branch in Harlan County in 1876, Burnam Ledford spent his early years milking cows and bringing in wood for the open fireplace where his mother cooked. Their log home had in it a Bible, a dictionary, and regular issues of the *New York Tribune.* In 1889, however, feud violence drove the family to Garrard County, where Ledford lived the rest of his life. He briefly returned to Harlan County to marry Addie King, who had been born there in 1885. They had thirteen children—three of whom died young—before she ceased childbearing at age forty-three. As their chronicler, John Egerton, notes, "Like the vast majority of Americans past and present, they had been relatively anonymous people, just ordinary folks; they had not 'made history,' in the customary usage of the term. But they had seen history and lived it."

Burnam Ledford had spoken to his great-grandmother, who remembered when George Washington was president; he recalled church services at which Republican Unionists sat on one side, Confederate Democrats on the other, and blacks in the balcony; he heard Goebel speak, voted in his first election against him, and recounted learning of Goebel's murder; he remembered the assassinations of all presidents killed except Lincoln. Addie Ledford grew up amid the Howard-Turner feud, voted for the first time in 1920—"I wasn't very proud of it. I got used to it though, and I've never failed to vote since then"—and saw by 1978 her thirty-two grandchildren and thirty-nine great-grandchildren growing to maturity. When those younger family members visited, they found that all people have stories that make history more than a lifeless abstraction. By February 1983 Burnam was one hundred six years old, and Addie was ninety-eight. "In their reconstruction of it, history was a con-

crete and personal thing, a continuous story in which they and their forebears and their descendants were directly involved. In their eyes, it bound the past to the present, the distant to the near-at-hand; it made unknown people important, ordinary places extraordinary, common things significant. History gave meaning and continuity to their lives." And to the lives of those around them.

Family reunions that reinforce generational ties and memories, searches of the genealogical landscape that bind groups together, preservation of historical places that keep alive the meaning of the activities of those who went before, construction of aspects of a folk culture that carries forward past traditions—all these indicate that the hand of tradition still lies heavily on the commonwealth. Singer Rosemary Clooney told of her favorite memory of her home state: "The memory keeps coming back, and I review it every summer. On the drive from Augusta to Maysville, there's a kind of meadow that drops down to the river. On summer nights, that meadow has fireflies that almost light up the earth. I've driven my grandchildren there to show them this, and they're filled with as much wonder as I was when I was a child. It's the most beautiful thing I've ever seen." Her transference of experiences to a new generation meant that through the children those memories would live on. In that sense, the future of the state as a place of some special distinctiveness lies less in the physical aspects of Kentucky—the fast-food outlets, the sameness of places—than in the people themselves. A Shepherdsville man recounted, "My favorite thing about the town is the people. . . . We've got people that if you need something, there are people here you can turn to."

University of Kentucky president Otis A. Singletary Jr., who came to the commonwealth later in life as the school's chief officer, noted in 1979, "I have always divided the world into two camps, places I can live and places I can't. I can live in Kentucky because it has ghosts. Your past is not all that remote to you. You are not alienated from it. . . . Your folk characters . . . keep our folklore, our customs, our history alive. That's why Kentucky is so charming and different. I think that while that may change, it will change slowly."

Those ghosts of the past have appeal to many Kentuckians and, as Singletary noted, give the state strengths. Yet at the same time, slavish adherence to that history can be as bad as too little, and the results can haunt Kentucky. Various commentators have complained over the years about the resistance of the state's citizens to positive change; on the other hand, others have criticized those who bring about change by destroying distinctiveness and the things that make the state special to some who live in it. The task of future generations will be to be future-oriented *and* history-minded, to honor their ancestors *and* to prepare their world for their grandchildren to look globally and locally. It can be done. Whether it will be done right is the question.

One of the state's several history-minded governors was Bert Combs. In his last speech as chief executive, he said, "These have been years of great change in the world and in our state. . . . Yet . . . it is the spirit that survives, and the spirit of Kentucky is strong. We may change . . . but the spirit of Kentucky endures."

That spirit was present in December 1991, when Combs was buried in a cemetery overlooking his Clay County birthplace. After the graveside service concluded, with those present joining hands to sing "Amazing Grace," the procession of the famous and the friends went back to a church, where a large assortment of food was waiting for those who had made their way over long distances. John Ed Pearce was one of those affected by the neighborliness, by the warmth, by the caring people: "How long it had been since I had felt that wave of loving care lap around me." Those people holding hands, singing that favorite song, told him what community meant. He knew why Combs had returned there, to his home, once more.

Such a sense of community and of place could be in rural Kentucky or urban Kentucky, or it could be absent in either place. It could be taken too far and result in parochial, restricted visions, or it could give needed stability in a sea of change.

Frontiers

Change came with increasing speed as the decades passed, and adjustments had to take place faster, if they were made at all. But much of what seemed unique to an era often was not. Virtually every generation complained about the young, saying things were "not like that" when they were that age. People of almost every era criticized new fashions in clothes, or new dances, or strange, different musical tastes. The scandals might involve dresses showing ankles in the early 1900s, or a flapper's outfit of the 1920s, or a miniskirt of the 1960s. They might focus on shocking actions, such as women wearing slacks, or both sexes wearing shorts in public. To a later generation, each debate might seem tame and the outcry surprising. But to those at the time it seemed to signify dangerous trends. Yet in fact, those who decried the indecent pictures or the state of morality, or the high taxes, or the violence, or the corrupt officials, existed in every period from frontier times to the present. That in itself was part of the continuity of the state.

Through the eras, the commonality of the human experience at least matched the great changes taking place, as attorney Tom Waller argued: "Folks are folks. . . . People are born, reach maturity, old age, and die. . . . Human emotions never change. They were the same 200 years ago as they are now, and will be 200 years from now. . . . [But] we are always heading toward a better day for more people. And it's all right. It's all right." In 1971 state attorney general John B. Breckinridge made the same point about the problems faced by each era: "They may change from generation to generation. But basically they're the same problems arising out of ignorance and prejudice and bias and selfishness and avariciousness. And every generation . . . will have in it that vanguard that will contain within it the seed of progress."

Yet too much should not be made of that universality, for differences did—and do—exist from generation to generation, and distinct new influences in each era to some degree created new reactions. Still, worlds that seemed far apart—frontier Kentucky and the twentieth-century commonwealth—were not so far distant from each other as generations thought. After all, Burnam Ledford of the 1980s had spoken to a person living in the 1790s.

People of the frontier settlements admired nature but also abused it, as did their modern-day descendants. They lived in solitary homes sometimes without close ties to neighbors, but they did occasionally become involved in group activities such as church meetings, weddings, and the like, not unlike those of the twentieth century. They sought economic well-being, a better life for their children, and security, as did those who came after. Even in the variety, similarities lived on. The frontier had its heroes, usually men who could shoot and kill, or women who could nurse a wound or raise a strong family. By the late twentieth century the new hero might be a sports figure or a humanitarian. The frontier was made up primarily of people with little

formal education, as opposed to those of later times, yet the settlers might have read the rhythms of the land better, as a balancing educational factor. While modern-day citizens point to the wonders of technology, is their awe any greater than that of those who first saw airplanes fly or, earlier, those who looked before them and experienced the wonders of a new land, beckoning to them?

Boone and others looked over a physical frontier and sought to meet its challenges. In the present day, some frontiers are more distant in miles, such as those in space, but others are the same frontiers challenging the human mind, from settlement times on. Strengths grow out of Kentuckians' history and their decades of living on the land. But problems persist, as they have for centuries. Much remains undone. Each generation has had to meet the challenges of new frontiers.

That the spirit present in each era lives on becomes clear when thousands of Kentuckians gather to watch a sporting event. The strains of the national anthem are followed by the antebellum verses of the state song, "My Old Kentucky Home," and more people sing the state song than the national one. The emotions felt and expressed show that this place of once-artificial boundaries, this place called Kentucky, still is important to them and still means something to those who call it home.

Appendix A

Some Facts and Figures

When the boundaries of Kentucky were finally fixed, the state lay approximately within 36°30′ and 39°6′ North latitude and 82° and 89°33′ West longitude. The state contains 40,395 square miles, of which 745 are water surface and 39,650 are land. The area in square miles translates into 25,376,000 land acres and 476,800 acres of water. The commonwealth ranks thirty-seventh in size among the fifty states. The greatest distance east-west is about 458 miles; Kentucky measures 171 miles at its widest north-south point. Seven other states touch Kentucky's boundaries. Big Black Mountain in Harlan County, at 4,145 feet, is the state's highest point; the lowest elevation is 257 feet at a site in Fulton County on the Mississippi River. The average elevation is about 750 feet.

Prehistoric Kentuckians probably told each other, "If you don't like the weather, wait until the sun moves a hand's width. It will change." The state's weather can and does change quickly. The mean annual temperature for the state is 55° Fahrenheit; the averages for the state's regions vary between 40° and 60°. Temperatures are judged to be extreme in Kentucky if they exceed 100° or fall below −10°. The normal mean precipitation varies from about 50 inches in the southern part of the state to about 38 inches in the mountains; the state average is close to 46 inches. In most years little precipitation falls in the form of snow, although heavy snows do occur. The growing season ranges from 190 to 210 days.

Kentucky's motto is "United We Stand, Divided We Fall." The official state bird is the cardinal, the flower is the goldenrod, the tree is now the tulip poplar (it was formerly the Kentucky coffeetree), and the song is "My Old Kentucky Home" by Stephen Collins Foster.

Appendix B

Kentucky's Governors

Isaac Shelby (1750-1826), 1792-96 and 1812-16; of Lincoln County; native of Maryland; active in American Revolution and frontier campaigns against the Indians; counties in nine states named in his honor. Democratic Republican.

James Garrard (1749-1822), 1796-1800, 1800-1804; of Bourbon County; born in Virginia; Revolutionary War soldier; first to live in Governor's Mansion (today the residence of the lieutenant governor); only Kentucky governor to serve two full successive terms. Democratic Republican.

Christopher Greenup (1750?-1818), 1804-8; of Mercer and Fayette Counties; born in Virginia; soldier; one of the first two Kentucky representatives in Congress after Kentucky entered the Union; elected governor in 1804 without opposition. Democratic Republican.

Charles Scott (1739-1813), 1808-12; of Woodford County; born in Virginia; soldier; officer in Braddock expedition (1755); represented Woodford County in Virginia Assembly. Democratic Republican.

George Madison (1763-1816), 1816; of Franklin County; born in Virginia; Revolutionary War soldier; Indian fighter; hero of War of 1812; captured at River Raisin; elected governor in 1816 but died the same year. Democratic Republican.

Gabriel Slaughter (1767-1830), 1816-20; of Mercer County; born in Virginia; farmer; regimental commander at the battle of New Orleans; twice lieutenant governor; became governor upon Madison's death. Democratic Republican.

John Adair (1757-1840), 1820-24; of Mercer County; born in South Carolina; Revolutionary War soldier; fought in Indian wars; aide to Governor Isaac Shelby in 1813 battle of the Thames; elected to U.S. House of Representatives for one term, 1831-33. Democratic Republican.

Joseph Desha (1768-1842), 1824-28; of Mason County; born in Pennsylvania; soldier in Indian campaigns; commander in battle of the Thames (1813); state legislator; served in U.S. House of Representatives, 1807-19. Democratic Republican.

Thomas Metcalfe (1780-1855), 1828-32; of Nicholas County; born in Virginia; stonemason; nicknamed Old Stonehammer; soldier in the War of 1812; served ten years as U.S. congressman and senator; died during cholera epidemic of 1855. National Republican.

John Breathitt (1786-1834), 1832-34; of Logan County; born in Virginia; lawyer; served in Kentucky legislature and as lieutenant governor; died in office. Jackson Democrat.

James Turner Morehead (1797-1854), 1834-36; of Logan County; as lieutenant governor succeeded to the governorship upon death of Breathitt; U.S. senator, 1841-47; political ally of Henry Clay. Whig.

James Clark (1779-1839), 1836-39; of Clark County; born in Virginia; served in Kentucky legislature; as state circuit court judge, rendered decision that started Old and New Court fight; died in office. Whig.

Charles Anderson Wickliffe (1788-1869), 1839-40; of Nelson County; lawyer; six-term U.S. representative; became governor upon death of Clark; postmaster general for President John Tyler, 1841-45; grandfather of Governor J.C.W. Beckham. Whig.

Robert Perkins Letcher (1788-1861), 1840-44; of Mercer (later Garrard) County; born in Virginia; lawyer; served in state legislature and U.S. Congress; American minister to Mexico, 1850-52. Whig.

William Owsley (1782-1862), 1844-48; of Lincoln County; born in Virginia; lawyer; served in state legislature; long service as justice of Kentucky Court of Appeals. Whig.

John Jordan Crittenden (1786-1863), 1848-50; of Woodford County; lawyer; saw service in War of 1812 as aide to Isaac Shelby and was present at the battle of the Thames; resigned governorship to become U.S. attorney general; served a total of twenty years in U.S. Senate. Whig.

John Larue Helm (1802-67), 1850-51 and 1867; of Hardin County; as lieutenant governor succeeded to the governorship after Crittenden resigned in 1850; elected in his own right in 1867; state legislator; openly sympathetic to Confederate cause. Whig, then Democrat.

Lazarus Whitehead Powell (1812-67), 1851-55; of Henderson County; lawyer; state legislator; U.S. senator; favored Kentucky neutrality during Civil War. Democrat.

Charles Slaughter Morehead (1802-68), 1855-59; of Nelson County; lawyer; two-term Whig member of Congress; elected governor on American (Know-Nothing) Party ticket.

Beriah Magoffin (1815-85), 1859-62; of Mercer County; lawyer; after being permitted to name his successor as governor, resigned because of his Confederate sympathies. Democrat.

James Fisher Robinson (1800-1882), 1862-63; of Scott County; lawyer; Whig state senator. Staunch Union Democrat.

Thomas Elliott Bramlette (1817-75), 1863-67; of Cumberland (now Clinton) County; lawyer and circuit judge; commissioned in Union Army. Union Democrat.

John White Stevenson (1812-86), 1867-71; of Kenton County; born in Virginia; as lieutenant governor succeeded to the governorship upon death of John L. Helm; U.S. senator, 1871-77. Democrat.

Preston Hopkins Leslie (1819-1907), 1871-75; of Clinton County; lawyer and state legislator; accepted appointment in 1887 as governor of Montana Territory; died in Montana. Democrat.

James Bennett McCreary (1838-1918), 1875-79 and 1911-15; of Madison County; lawyer; soldier with Generals John Hunt Morgan and John C. Breckinridge in Confederate service; served eighteen years in U.S. House and Senate; first to occupy new Governor's Mansion (1914). Democrat.

Luke Pryor Blackburn (1816-87), 1879-83; of Woodford County; only physician to serve as Kentucky governor; volunteer in cholera and yellow fever epidemics in Kentucky and throughout the South; prison reformer. Democrat.

James Proctor Knott (1830-1911); 1883-87; of Marion County; lawyer, congressman, and noted orator; attorney general of Missouri before returning to Kentucky in 1862; one of the framers of the present Kentucky constitution. Democrat.

Simon Bolivar Buckner (1823-1914), 1887-91; of Hart County; West Point instructor; served in Mexican War and later with Confederacy; editor of *Louisville Courier.* Democrat.

John Young Brown (1835-1904), 1891-95; of Hardin County; lawyer and congressman; his "three-year legislature" adjusted laws to the new constitution. Democrat.

William O'Connell Bradley (1847-1914), 1895-99; of Garrard County; lawyer; U.S. senator, 1909-14; uncle of Governor Edwin P. Morrow. First Republican governor.

William Sylvester Taylor (1853-1928), 1899-1900; of Butler County; lawyer; Kentucky attorney general; lost the governorship to William Goebel in a contest decided by the legislature. Republican.

William Goebel (1856-1900), 1900; of Kenton County; born in Pennsylvania; lawyer; state senator; declared governor after being shot by assassin on the grounds of the Old Capitol; only governor in U.S. history to die in office as result of assassination. Democrat.

John Crepps Wickliffe Beckham (1869-1940), 1900-1903, 1903-7; of Nelson County; lawyer and state legislator; Speaker of Kentucky House; elected lieutenant governor on Goebel ticket and succeeded to governorship upon Goebel's death; U.S. senator, 1915-21; grandson of Governor Charles Anderson Wickliffe. Democrat.

Augustus Everett Willson (1846-1931), 1907-11; of Jefferson County; born in Mason County; law partner of John Marshall Harlan; lost bids for U.S. House or Senate five times. Republican.

Augustus Owsley Stanley (1867-1958), 1915-19; of Henderson County; born in Shelby County; lawyer; served six terms in U.S. House; elected to U.S. Senate in 1918; resigned as governor in 1919; later chaired International Joint Commission to mediate disputes arising along the U.S.-Canadian border. Democrat.

James Dixon Black (1849-1938), 1919; of Knox County; lawyer; state legislator; first assistant attorney general of Kentucky; as lieutenant governor succeeded to governorship upon Stanley's resignation; defeated for election in his own right. Democrat.

Edwin Porch Morrow (1877-1935), 1919-23; of Pulaski County; lawyer; served in Spanish-American War; U.S. district attorney; nephew of Governor William O. Bradley. Republican.

William Jason Fields (1874-1954), 1923-27; of Carter County; resigned after almost thirteen years in U.S. Congress to become governor; called Honest Bill from Olive Hill. Democrat.

Flem D. Sampson (1875-1967), 1927-31; of Knox County; born in Laurel County; lawyer; circuit judge; chief justice of Kentucky Court of Appeals. Republican.

Ruby Laffoon (1869-1941), 1931-35; of Hopkins County; lawyer; chaired first Insurance Rating Board in Kentucky; Hopkins County judge. Democrat.

Albert Benjamin Chandler (1898-1991), 1935-39 and 1955-59; of Woodford County; born in Henderson County; lawyer; state senator; lieutenant governor; U.S. senator; commissioner of baseball; nicknamed Happy. Democrat.

Keen Johnson (1896-1970), 1939-43; of Madison County; born in Lyon County; publisher of *Richmond Daily Register;* as lieutenant governor succeeded to governorship upon resignation of Chandler, who went to U.S. Senate; elected in his own right that same year. Democrat.

Simeon Willis (1879-1965), 1943-47; of Boyd County; born in Ohio; lawyer; appointed to state Court of Appeals; member of Republican National Committee. Republican.

Earle Chester Clements (1896-1985), 1947-50; of Union County; served in U.S. Army during World War I; sheriff; county clerk; county judge; state senator; U.S. representative; resigned governorship to assume seat in U.S. Senate. Democrat.

Lawrence Winchester Wetherby (1908-94), 1950-51, 1951-55; of Jefferson County; lawyer; judge of Jefferson County Juvenile Court; lieutenant governor on Clements ticket; became governor upon Clements's resignation; elected in his own right in 1951. Democrat.

Bert T. Combs (1911-91), 1959-63; of Floyd County; born in Clay County; served in

World War II; lawyer; judge on Kentucky Court of Appeals, 1951-55; judge of U.S. Court of Appeals, Sixth Circuit, 1967-70. Democrat.

Edward Thompson Breathitt Jr. (b. 1924), 1963-67; of Christian County; lawyer; served in state legislature, 1952-58; later a railroad executive; called Ned. Democrat.

Louie Broady Nunn (b. 1924), 1967-71; of Barren County; lawyer; elected county judge of Barren County; city attorney of Glasgow. Republican.

Wendell Hampton Ford (b. 1924), 1971-74; of Daviess County; state senator; lieutenant governor; resigned governorship to assume seat in U.S. Senate. Democrat.

Julian Morton Carroll (b. 1931), 1974-75, 1975-79; of McCracken County; member of Kentucky House of Representatives, 1962-71; Speaker of Kentucky House; as lieutenant governor succeeded to governorship upon resignation of Ford; elected to the office in his own right in 1975. Democrat.

John Young Brown Jr. (b. 1933), 1979-83; of Fayette County; attorney; successful business executive with Kentucky Fried Chicken; involved in the ownership of professional sports teams. Democrat.

Martha Layne (Hall) Collins (b. 1936), 1983-87; of Shelby and Woodford Counties; public school teacher and home economist; elected clerk of Kentucky Court of Appeals in 1975 and lieutenant governor four years later; only woman to be elected governor of Kentucky; president of St. Catherine College, 1990-96; became director of International Business and Management Center, University of Kentucky, 1996. Democrat.

Wallace Glenn Wilkinson (b. 1941), 1987-91; of Casey and Fayette Counties; prominent business leader and real estate developer;

instrumental in revitalization of downtown Lexington; author of *You Can't Do That, Governor!* Democrat.

Brereton C. Jones (b. 1939), 1991-95; born in Ohio; served in West Virginia legislature as Republican; horse farm owner in Woodford County, Kentucky; Democratic lieutenant governor; as governor called record number of special sessions. Democrat.

Paul E. Patton (b. 1937), 1995-; born in Lawrence County; active in many aspects of the coal business; judge executive of Pike County; chair of Kentucky Democratic Party, 1981-82; secretary of Cabinet for Economic Development; lieutenant governor. Democrat.

Governors of Confederate Kentucky

George W. Johnson (1811-62), 1861-62; of Scott County; wealthy planter and slave-holder; Democratic state legislator; key member of two 1861 Russellville conventions that formed the Confederate state of Kentucky; elected governor by second convention; killed at Shiloh.

Richard Hawes (1797-1877), 1862-65; born in Virginia; lawyer and business leader in Clark County; moved to Bourbon County; Whig member of state legislature and U.S. Congress; became Democrat; refused post of auditor in the Confederate government of Kentucky; commissioned brigade commissary as major in Confederate Army; upon Johnson's death, appointed to succeed to the governorship; postwar lawyer and judge.

Appendix C

Kentucky's Counties

County	Date Established	County Seat
Adair	1801	Columbia
Allen	1815	Scottsville
Anderson	1827	Lawrenceburg
Ballard	1842	Wickliffe
Barren	1798	Glasgow
Bath	1811	Owingsville
Bell	1867	Pineville
Boone	1798	Burlington
Bourbon	1785	Paris
Boyd	1860	Catlettsburg
Boyle	1842	Danville
Bracken	1796	Brooksville
Breathitt	1839	Jackson
Breckinridge	1799	Hardinsburg
Bullitt	1796	Shepherdsville
Butler	1810	Morgantown
Caldwell	1809	Princeton
Calloway	1822	Murray
Campbell	1794	Alexandria
Carlisle	1886	Bardwell
Carroll	1838	Carrollton
Carter	1838	Grayson
Casey	1806	Liberty
Christian	1796	Hopkinsville
Clark	1792	Winchester
Clay	1806	Manchester
Clinton	1836	Albany
Crittenden	1842	Marion
Cumberland	1798	Burkesville
Daviess	1815	Owensboro
Edmonson	1825	Brownsville
Elliott	1869	Sandy Hook
Estill	1808	Irvine
Fayette	1780	Lexington
Fleming	1798	Flemingsburg
Floyd	1799	Prestonsburg
Franklin	1794	Frankfort
Fulton	1845	Hickman
Gallatin	1798	Warsaw
Garrard	1796	Lancaster

County	Date Established	County Seat	County	Date Established	County Seat
Grant	1820	Williamstown	Mercer	1785	Harrodsburg
Graves	1823	Mayfield	Metcalfe	1860	Edmonton
Grayson	1810	Leitchfield	Monroe	1820	Tompkinsville
Green	1792	Greensburg	Montgomery	1796	Mount Sterling
Greenup	1803	Greenup	Morgan	1822	West Liberty
Hancock	1829	Hawesville	Muhlenberg	1798	Greenville
Hardin	1792	Elizabethtown	Nelson	1784	Bardstown
Harlan	1819	Harlan	Nicholas	1799	Carlisle
Harrison	1793	Cynthiana	Ohio	1798	Hartford
Hart	1819	Munfordville	Oldham	1823	La Grange
Henderson	1798	Henderson	Owen	1819	Owenton
Henry	1798	New Castle	Owsley	1843	Booneville
Hickman	1821	Clinton	Pendleton	1798	Falmouth
Hopkins	1806	Madisonville	Perry	1820	Hazard
Jackson	1858	McKee	Pike	1821	Pikeville
Jefferson	1780	Louisville	Powell	1852	Stanton
Jessamine	1798	Nicholasville	Pulaski	1798	Somerset
Johnson	1843	Paintsville	Robertson	1867	Mount Olivet
Kenton	1840	Independence	Rockcastle	1810	Mount Vernon
Knott	1884	Hindman	Rowan	1856	Morehead
Knox	1799	Barbourville	Russell	1825	Jamestown
Larue	1843	Hodgenville	Scott	1792	Georgetown
Laurel	1825	London	Shelby	1792	Shelbyville
Lawrence	1821	Louisa	Simpson	1819	Franklin
Lee	1870	Beattyville	Spencer	1824	Taylorsville
Leslie	1878	Hyden	Taylor	1848	Campbellsville
Letcher	1842	Whitesburg	Todd	1819	Elkton
Lewis	1806	Vanceburg	Trigg	1820	Cadiz
Lincoln	1780	Stanford	Trimble	1837	Bedford
Livingston	1798	Smithland	Union	1811	Morganfield
Logan	1792	Russellville	Warren	1796	Bowling Green
Lyon	1854	Eddyville	Washington	1792	Springfield
Madison	1785	Richmond	Wayne	1800	Monticello
Magoffin	1860	Salyersville	Webster	1860	Dixon
Marion	1834	Lebanon	Whitley	1818	Williamsburg
Marshall	1842	Benton	Wolfe	1860	Campton
Martin	1870	Inez	Woodford	1788	Versailles
Mason	1788	Maysville			
McCracken	1824	Paducah			
McCreary	1912	Whitley City			
McLean	1854	Calhoun			
Meade	1823	Brandenburg			
Menifee	1869	Frenchburg			

Note: Each date given is the year in which the county was established by statute. Some counties were formed in the year following their legal approval.

Sources: Kentucky County Data Book, Kentucky Historical Society Research Contribution, no. 8 (n.d.).

Selected Bibliography

Abbreviations

Antiques	*The Magazine Antiques*
CWH	*Civil War History*
FCHQ	*The Filson Club History Quarterly*
JAH	*Journal of American History*

JNH	*Journal of Negro History*
JSH	*Journal of Southern History*
MVHR	*Mississippi Valley Historical Review*
Register	*Register of the Kentucky Historical Society*

The sources for Kentucky history are voluminous, and only a small number of them are listed here. J. Winston Coleman Jr., *A Bibliography of Kentucky History* (1949), is quite complete for books and pamphlets published before 1948 but does not include articles. Some of the works published between 1949 and 1981, including nonbook materials, are discussed in James C. Klotter, "Clio in the Commonwealth: The Status of Kentucky History," *Register* 80 (1982): 65-88. A few more recent works are listed in the bibliography of James C. Klotter, ed., *Our Kentucky* (1992). John E. Kleber, editor in chief, *The Kentucky Encyclopedia* (1992), is indispensable for any work in Kentucky history, both for its information and its guide to additional sources. Martin F. Schmidt, *Kentucky Illustrated: The First Hundred Years* (1992), depicts many aspects of state history before the advent of good photography.

While the Kentucky *Senate Journal* (1792-) and *House Journal* (1792-) do not report debates and discussions in the respective bodies, they contain material such as messages of the governors, and they trace the fate of bills. The *Acts of the General Assembly* (1792-) indicates which bills survived the legislative process and the scrutiny of the governors. Most major organs of the Kentucky state government have issued reports and documents from time to time, and most of these have been published. Among the most important are the *Reports* of the superintendent of public instruction, the *Reports* of the Court of Appeals, and the *Reports* of the Bureau of Agriculture, Horticulture, and Statistics. Such reports became more frequent after the Civil War, with the formation of new divisions of the state government. Also important is Adelaide R. Hasse, comp., *Index of Economic Material in Documents of the States of the United States: Kentucky, 1792-1904* (1910). Vital for the prestatehood years are William W. Hening, comp., *The Statutes at Large: Being a Collection of All the Laws of Virginia, 1619-1792,* 13 vols. (1809-23); James R. Robertson, *Petitions of the Early Inhabitants of Kentucky* (1914); and *The Calendar of Virginia State Papers and Other Manuscripts,* 11 vols. (1875-93).

The *Register of the Kentucky Historical Society* (1903-) and *The Filson Club History Quarterly* (1926-) contain articles on most aspects of the state's history. Each has an annual index, and the summer 1989 issue of the *Register* has a general guide to its articles through 1988. A comprehensive index to the *FCHQ* is being prepared. The *Mississippi Valley Historical Review* (1914-64) and its continuation as the *Journal of American History* (1964-), as well as the *Journal of Southern History* (1935-), have published numerous articles on Kentucky history. Many other journals and magazines have carried occasional pieces.

The standard history of the state since 1937 has been Thomas D. Clark, *A History of Kentucky* (1937), revised in 1950 and 1960. Steven A. Channing, *Kentucky: A Bicentennial History* (1977), was limited by the format of the series in which it was published. Of the pre–Civil War histories, John Filson, *The Discovery, Settlement, and Present State of Kentucke* (1784), is more of a travel account than a history, but it also contains the "autobiography" of Daniel Boone, which Filson wrote. Humphrey Marshall's partisan *History of Kentucky* (1812), revised and enlarged to two volumes in 1824, is still useful, but Mann Butler, *A History of the Commonwealth of Kentucky* (1834), is a better account. Lewis Collins, *Historical Sketches of Kentucky* (1847), was revised and expanded by Collins's son, Richard H. Collins, into *History of Kentucky*, 2 vols. (1874). The Collinses' works contain a great deal of information but little analysis. That assessment is also true of Mrs. William Breckinridge and Harry V. McChesney, eds., *Kentucky in Retrospect: Noteworthy Personalities and Events, 1792-1967* (1967, updated from 1942). Three one-volume histories appeared in the 1880s: Nathaniel S. Shaler, *Kentucky: A Pioneer Commonwealth* (1884); W.H. Perrin, J.H. Battle, and G.C. Kniffin, *Kentucky: A History of the State* (1887); and Zachariah F. Smith, *The History of Kentucky* (1885). All three were published in later editions. Shaler's account is the most readable; Perrin, Battle, and Kniffin's contains the most information.

Several multivolume works were published during the first half of the twentieth century. Each devoted half or more of its contents to uncritical genealogical and biographical sketches of Kentuckians, most of them men. The best of these histories are E. Polk Johnson, *A History of Kentucky and Kentuckians*, 3 vols. (1912); William E. Connelley and E. Merton Coulter, *History of Kentucky*, edited by Charles Kerr, 5 vols. (1922); Temple Bodley and Samuel M. Wilson, *History of Kentucky*, 4 vols. (1928); and Frederick A. Wallis and Hambleton Tapp, *A Sesqui-Centennial History of Kentucky*, 4 vols. (1945). Additional biographical references can be found in *Biographical Encyclopedia of Kentucky* (1878); *Biographical Cyclopedia of the Commonwealth of Kentucky* (1896), reprinted in 1980; H. Levin, *Lawyers and Lawmakers of Kentucky* (1897), reprinted in 1982; and J. Winston Coleman Jr., *Kentucky's Bicentennial Family Register* (1977). Also useful are such specialized sources as Lowell H. Harrison, ed., *Kentucky's Governors, 1792-1985* (1985); *Biographical Directory of the United States Congress, 1774-1989* (1989); Francis B. Heitman, comp., *Historical Register and Directory of the United States Army*, 2 vols. (1903); and David Porter, *Bio-*

graphical Dictionary of American Sports: Basketball and Other Indoor Sports (1989).

Much of the study of Kentucky has focused on manuscripts and on state and local records. Many of the government records are found in the original or in microform at the Kentucky Historical Society and the Kentucky Department for Libraries and Archives, both in Frankfort. The state universities, as well as the Kentucky Historical Society and The Filson Club, all hold special collections of manuscripts, books, photographs, oral interviews, and microform copies of research materials. The largest university collections are at the University of Kentucky, the University of Louisville, Western Kentucky University, and Eastern Kentucky University, but smaller collections may offer excellent coverage of certain subject areas. Berea College, for example, has an outstanding collection of slavery and antislavery materials. Many important collections, however, are located out of state in such depositories as the Library of Congress, the National Archives, the University of Chicago, Duke University, and the University of North Carolina. The Draper Collection at the State Historical Society of Wisconsin contains a wealth of information on Kentucky and Kentuckians, most of it for the period before 1850. The major guides to state collections are *A Place Where Historical Research May Be Pursued: An Introduction to Primary Research Sources in the University of Louisville Archives, William F. Ekstrom Library* (1981); Jeanne Slater Trimble, comp., *Guide to Selected Manuscripts Housed in the Division of Special Collections and Archives, Margaret I. King Library, University of Kentucky* (1987); Mary Margaret Bell, comp., *Manuscripts of the Kentucky Historical Society* (1991); and James J. Holmberg, James T. Kirkwood, and Mary Jean Kinsman, comps., *Guide to Selected Manuscript and Photograph Collections of The Filson Club Historical Society* (1996). Cary C. Wilkins, comp., *The Guide to Kentucky Oral History Collections* (1991), is most valuable for the twentieth century.

Since 1978 the Kentucky Guide Project, under the auspices of the Department for Libraries and Archives, has undertaken a comprehensive survey of the state's 285 repositories. A general overview, *Guide to Kentucky Archival and Manuscript Collections,* was published in 1988. By 1997 only the first two detailed volumes had appeared: Barbara Teague, ed., *Albany–Burkesville* (1988); and Jane A. Minder, ed., *Cadiz–Eminence* (1992). By 1996 the Library of Congress had published twenty-nine volumes of its *National Union Catalog of Manuscript Collections* (1959-), listing some 72,300 collections in 1,406 repositories. Many valuable collections have not been reported to NUCMC, however, and the future of the program is in doubt.

Doctoral dissertations on aspects of Kentucky history reflect a great deal of research and often contain information not found elsewhere. Warren F. Kuehl has compiled three volumes of *Dissertations in History: An Index to Dissertations in History Departments of the United States and Canada.* The volumes cover the period 1873-June 1980: *1873-1960* (1965), *1961-June 1970* (1972), and *1970-June 1980* (1985). Research libraries often have copies of at least some of the Kentucky studies, and individual photocopies of most of them can be purchased from University Microfilm International, Ann Arbor, Michigan. Many of these dissertations were later published, wholly or in part, in book and article form. There is no comprehensive listing of M.A. theses. Many of the state's counties and towns have histories that are helpful for various phases of Kentucky's history.

Chapter I. A Place Called Kentucke

Kentucky's remote past is studied in W.D. Funkhouser and W.S. Webb, *Ancient Life in Kentucky* (1928); David Pollack, Charles Hockensmith, and Thomas Sanders, *Late Prehistoric Research in Kentucky* (1984); Douglas W. Schwartz, *Conceptions of Kentucky Prehistory* (1967); and Brian M. Fagan, *Ancient North America* (1991). Bennett H. Young, *The Prehistoric Men of Kentucky* (1910); and Lucien Beckner, "Kentucky before Boone: The Siouan People," *Register* 46 (1948): 384-96, demonstrate a fascination with the Kentuckians of the pre-European era. A. Gwynn Henderson, "Dispelling the Myth: Seventeenth-and-Eighteenth Century Indian Life in Kentucky," *Register* 90 (Bicentennial issue, 1992): 1-25, corrects some of the many misconceptions. Lucien Beckner, "Eskippakithiki: The Last Indian Town in Kentucky," *FCHQ* 6 (1932): 355-82, describes the Indian town that had been abandoned before the white settlement of Kentucky began. John R. Swanton, *The Indians of the Southeastern United States* (1987); and Charles Hudson, *The Southeastern Indians* (1989), are good introductions to some of the tribes active in Kentucky. Two especially significant tribes are studied in Jerry E. Clark, *The Shawnee* (1977); and Theda Perdue, *The Cherokee* (1989).

Kentucky's wildlife has been carefully studied by Roger W. Barbour and several collaborators: see Roger W. Barbour, *Amphibians and Reptiles of Kentucky* (1971); Mary Wharton and Roger W. Barbour, *A Guide to the Wildflowers and Ferns of Kentucky* (1971); Roger W. Barbour et al., *Kentucky Birds: A Finding Guide* (1973); Mary Wharton and Roger W. Barbour, *Trees and Shrubs of Kentucky* (1973); and Roger W. Barbour and Wayne H. Davis, *Mammals of Kentucky* (1974). Wharton and Barbour also did a comprehensive survey of a region in *Bluegrass Land and Life: Land Character, Plants, and Animals of the Inner Bluegrass Region of Kentucky, Past, Present, and Future* (1991).

Jenny Wiley and Mary Draper Ingles have been the subjects of many brief articles. The best book-length accounts of Wiley's life are Harry M. Caudill, *Dark Hills to Westward: The Saga of Jennie Wiley* (1969); Arville Wheeler, *White Squaw: The True Story of Jennie Wiley* (1958); and Henry P. Scalf, *Jenny Wiley* (1964). William E. Connelley and E. Merton Coulter, *History of Kentucky,* edited by Charles Kerr, 5 vols. (1922), 1:75-93, has the best account of Mary Draper Ingles's ordeal. But see also Winfred Partin, "Mary Draper Ingles: The First White Woman in Kentucky," *Kentucky Images Magazine* 4 (1985): 9-12.

Much has been written about Daniel Boone, who for many personifies the eighteenth-century

American frontier. John Mack Faragher, *Daniel Boone: The Life and Legend of an American Pioneer* (1992); and Michael A. Lofaro, *The Life and Adventures of Daniel Boone* (1978), both examine the legend as well as the life. John E. Bakeless, *Daniel Boone* (1939), is more traditional but still useful. Charles G. Talbert's fine biography, *Benjamin Logan: Kentucky Frontiersman* (1962), is the best study of a pioneer leader whose career continued beyond statehood. Kathryn H. Mason, *James Harrod of Kentucky* (1951), is the standard life of a leader who simply disappeared, but see also Neal O. Hammon, "Captain Harrod's Company: A Reappraisal," *Register* 72 (1974): 243-61. Edna Kenton, *Simon Kenton: His Life and Period, 1750-1836* (1930), is the best account of a great woodsman. A fascinating pioneer is recalled in Anna M. Cartlidge, "Colonel John Floyd: Reluctant Adventurer," *Register* 66 (1968): 317-66.

Chapter 2. Exploring the Western Waters

Two good surveys of the westward movement are Thomas D. Clark, *Frontier America: The Story of the Westward Movement* (1959); and Ray Allen Billington, *Westward Expansion: A History of the American Frontier* (1974). Thomas Perkins Abernethy, *Three Virginia Frontiers* (1940), is a good brief introduction to the exploration of Kentucky, and Otis K. Rice, *Frontier Kentucky* (1975), reprinted in 1993, is an excellent summary of the frontier period in the state. Stephen Aron, "The Significance of the Kentucky Frontier," *Register* 91 (1993): 298-323; and Michael A. Flannery, "The Significance of the Frontier Thesis in Kentucky Culture: A Study in Historical Practice and Perception," *Register* 92 (1994): 239-266, are good summaries of the revisionist views of many modern historians of the West.

Willard Rouse Jillson, "The Discovery of Kentucky," *Register* 20 (1922): 117-29, discusses the first European contacts with the area. The journals of Dr. Thomas Walker and Christopher Gist are included in J. Stoddard Johnston, *First Explorations of Kentucky* (1898). Kenneth P. Bailey, *Christopher Gist: Colonial Frontiersman, Explorer, and Indian Agent* (1976), is a full biography. Lucien Beckner perhaps gave too much credit to Findley in "John Findley: The First Pathfinder of Kentucky," *FCHQ* 43 (1969): 206-15. A popular account of the early explorations is Dale Van Every, *Forth to the Wilderness: The First American Frontier, 1754-1774* (1961). George M. Chinn, *Kentucky: Settlement and Statehood, 1750-1800* (1975), covers the explorations in considerable detail. Brent Altsheler, "The Long Hunters and James Knox, Their Leader," *FCHQ* 5 (1931): 169-85, recalls the exploits of one of the less well-known Kentucky explorers.

Thomas Perkins Abernethy, *Western Lands and the American Revolution* (1937), is a good introduction to land acquisition in the West. The Ohio Company is examined in Kenneth P. Bailey, *The Ohio Company of Virginia and the Westward Movement, 1748-1792* (1939); and Alfred P. James, *The Ohio Company: Its Inner History* (1959). On the Indiana Company, see George E. Lewis, *The Indiana Company, 1763-1798* (1941). Archibald Henderson, *Dr. Thomas Walker and the Loyal Land Company of Virginia* (1931), reprinted from *American Antiquarian Society Proceedings,* n.s., 41 (1931), is a good survey of the Loyal Company. Lord Dunmore's War is treated in Randolph C. Downes, "Dunmore's War: An Interpretation," *MVHR* 21 (1934): 311-30; and Virgil A. Lewis, *History of the Battle of Point Pleasant* (1908).

In "Pioneers in Kentucky, 1773-1775," *FCHQ* 55 (1941): 268-83, Neal O. Hammon tries to ascertain who came to Kentucky during 1773-75.

Thomas D. Clark traces the establishment of Kentucky's boundaries in both *Historic Maps of Kentucky* (1979) and "The Jackson Purchase: A Dramatic Chapter in Southern Indian Policy and Relations," *FCHQ* 50 (1975): 302-20. But see also P.P. Karan and Cotton Mather, eds., *Atlas of Kentucky* (1977); and William Withington, *Kentucky in Maps* (1980). An example of the continuing boundary disputes is related in Eugene Oliver Porter, "The Kentucky-Ohio Boundary," *FCHQ* 17 (1943): 39-45. The state's geography is described in P.P. Karan, *Kentucky: A Regional Geography* (1973); Wilfrid Bladen, *A Geography of Kentucky* (1984); and Kentucky Geographic Alliance, *Kentucky: Geographic and Historical Perspective* (1989). Miscellaneous information about the state is contained in John Clements, *Kentucky Facts* (1990); and any good encyclopedia. Robert M. Rennick, *Kentucky Place Names* (1984), explains the origins of the names of many places in the state. Thomas P. Field ("The Indian Place Names of Kentucky," *FCHQ* 34 [1960]: 237-47) found few Indian-derived names.

Chapter 3. Settling a New Land

Many works cited for chapter 2 continue to be useful, as well as the general histories discussed previously. George W. Ranck, *Boonesborough, Its Founding, Pioneer Struggles, Indian Experiences. . . .* (1901), is still a good account of the settlement of Boonesborough. In addition to the works on Daniel Boone cited for chapter 1, the reader should note Charles W. Bryan Jr., "Richard Callaway, Kentucky Pioneer," *FCHQ* 9 (1935): 35-50; and R. Alexander Bate, "Colonel Richard Callaway, 1722-1780," *FCHQ* 29 (1955): 3-20, 166-78. Daniel's brother is credited with his own accomplishments in Willard Rouse Jillson, "Squire Boone," *FCHQ* 16 (1942): 141-71; and Ted Igleheart, "Squire Boone, the Forgotten Man," *FCHQ* 44 (1970): 356-66. The first journey to the site of Boonesborough is described in Neal O. Hammon, "The First Trip to Boonesborough," *FCHQ* 45 (1971): 249-63; and "The Journal of William Calk, Kentucky Pioneer," *MVHR* 7 (1921): 363-77. An interesting account of early settlement as it appeared to Elizabeth Thomas is Louise Phelps Kellogg, ed., "A Kentucky Pioneer Tells Her Story of Early Boonesborough and Harrodsburg," *FCHQ* 3 (1929): 223-36.

The roles of Richard Henderson and the Transylvania Company are described in Archibald Henderson, "Richard Henderson and the Occupation of Kentucky, 1775," *MVHR* 1 (1914): 341-63. This author usually favored his ancestor; a more objective work is William S. Lester, *The Transylvania Colony* (1935).

Accounts of some other early settlements include Charles R. Staples, *The History of Pioneer Lexington* (1939); Neal O. Hammon, "Early

Louisville and the Beargrass Stations," *FCHQ* 52 (1978): 147-65; and Ellen Eslinger, "Migration and Kinship on the Trans-Appalachian Frontier: Strode's Station, Kentucky," *FCHQ* 62 (1988): 52-66. Thomas Froncek, ed., *Voices from the Wilderness: The Frontiersman's Own Story* (1974), includes some Kentucky voices. Willard Rouse Jillson, *Pioneer Kentucky* (1934), locates most of the early stations and forts. Timothy Flint, *Indian Wars of the West* (1833); and John A. McClung, *Sketches of Western Adventures* (1847), are two of the many accounts of Indian warfare written from the perspective of the European pioneers. Thomas D. Clark, ed., *The Voice of the Frontier: John Bradford's Notes on Kentucky* (1993), contains several articles on the early settlements and their Indian problems.

Among the many interesting accounts of early pioneer life are Roseann R. Hogan, ed., "Buffaloes in the Corn: James Wade's Account of Pioneer Kentucky," *Register* 89 (1991): 1-31; Lucien Beckner, ed., "Reverend John D. Shane's Interview with Pioneer William Clinkenbeard," *FCHQ* 2 (1928): 95-128; Robert B. McAfee, "The Life and Times of Robert B. McAfee and His Family and Connections," *Register* 25 (1927): 5-37, 111-43, 215-37; Charles G. Talbert, "William Whitley, 1749-1813," *FCHQ* 25 (1951): 101-21, 210-16, 300-316; and Chester R. Young, ed., *Westward into Kentucky: The Narrative of Daniel Trabue* (1981). The Draper Collection at the State Historical Society of Wisconsin is rich in such personal accounts.

Richard Henderson's attempt to establish a government is discussed in the works on him and the Transylvania Company and in the studies of the pioneer leaders who opposed him. The important opposition of George Rogers Clark is traced in James Alton James, *The Life of George Rogers Clark* (1928); Temple Bodley, *George Rogers Clark, His Life and Public Service* (1926); John Bakeless, *Background to Glory* (1957); and Wilbur H. Siebert, "Kentucky's Struggle with Its Loyalist Proprietors," *MVHR* 7 (1920): 113-26. Robert Spencer Cotterill, *History of Pioneer Kentucky* (1917), is hostile toward Clark; William S. Lester, *The Transylvania Colony* (1935), is somewhat anti-Henderson.

Chapter 4. The Years of the American Revolution

Two good general accounts of the Revolution are John R. Alden, *The South in the American Revolution, 1763-1789* (1957); and Don Higginbotham, *The War of American Independence* (1971). Dale Van Every's popular account, *A Company of Heroes: The American Frontier, 1775-1783* (1962), and Jack M. Sosin, *The Revolutionary Frontier, 1763-1783* (1967), devote much attention to Kentucky. Clark's role is examined in Lowell H. Harrison, *George Rogers Clark and the War in the West* (1976); and John D. Barnhart, *Henry Hamilton and George Rogers Clark in the American Revolution* (1951). Charles G. Talbert has written a series of excellent articles on military expeditions during these years for the *Register*: "Kentucky Invades Ohio—1779," 51 (1953): 228-35; "Kentucky Invades Ohio—1780," 52 (1954): 291-300; "Kentucky Invades Ohio—1782," 53 (1955): 288-97; and "Kentucky Invades Ohio—1786," 54 (1956): 203-13. One should also read Talbert's "A Roof for Kentucky," *FCHQ* 29 (1955): 145-65; and Patricia Watlington's "Discontent in Frontier Kentucky," *Register* 65 (1967): 77-93. Thomas Boyd, *Simon Girty: The White Savage* (1928), is a biography of the man perhaps most hated by the Kentucky settlers.

The general histories and biographies previously cited all place emphasis on the critical war years. Among the many interesting accounts of specific episodes are Samuel M. Wilson, "Shawnee Warriors at the Blue Licks," *Register* 32 (1934): 160-68; Richard H. Collins, "The Siege of Bryan's Station," edited by Willard Rouse Jillson, *Register* 36 (1938): 15-25; Maude Ward Lafferty, "Destruction of Ruddle's and Martin's Forts in the Revolutionary War," *Register* 54 (1956): 297-338; Bessie Taul Conkright, "Estill's Defeat; or, The Battle of Little Mountain," *Register* 22 (1924): 311-22; and Neal O. Hammon and James Russell Harris, "'In a Dangerous Situation': Letters of Col. John Floyd, 1774-1783," *Register* 83 (1985): 202-36. The Treaty of Paris is discussed in detail in Samuel F. Bemis, *The Diplomacy of the American Revolution* (1935).

Chapter 5. The Road to Statehood

The famed Wilderness Road is best studied in William Allen Pusey, *The Wilderness Road to Kentucky* (1921); Robert L. Kincaid, *The Wilderness Road* (1947); and Thomas L. Connelly, "Gateway to Kentucky: The Wilderness Road, 1748-1792," *Register* 59 (1961): 109-32. Neal O. Hammon traces the exact route of this and other early roads in "Early Roads into Kentucky," *Register* 68 (1970): 91-131. The river passage to Kentucky is well described in Robert L. Reid, *Always a River: The Ohio River and the American Experience* (1991); and Michael Allen, *Western Rivermen, 1763-1861: Ohio and Mississippi Boatmen and the Myth of the Alligator Horse* (1990). Allen, however, goes too far in debunking what he calls the myth of the Mike Fink type of riverman. John G. Stuart, "A Journal Remarks; or, Observations in a Voyage Down the Kentucky, Ohio, and Mississippi Rivers, etc.," *Register* 50 (1952): 5-25, is based on an 1806 trip. Charles Henry Ambler, *A History of Transportation in the Ohio Valley* (1932), is a good overview of the transportation options.

Fredrika Johanna Teute, "Land, Liberty, and Labor in the Post-revolutionary Era: Kentucky As the Promised Land" (Ph.D. diss., Johns Hopkins University, 1988), explains the rush to obtain Kentucky lands. Two works compiled by Willard Rouse Jillson, *The Kentucky Land Grants* (1925) and *Old Kentucky Entries and Deeds* (1926), provide an index to these transactions, but see also Neal O. Hammon, *Early Kentucky Land Records, 1773-1800* (1992). The troublesome land problem is approached from fresh perspectives in Neal O. Hammon, "Land Acquisition on the Kentucky Frontier," *Register* 78 (1980): 297-321; idem, "Settlers, Land Jobbers, and Outlayers: A Quantitative Analysis of Land Acquisition on the Kentucky Frontier," *Register* 84 (1986): 241-62; and Stephen Aron, "Pioneers and Profiteers: Land Speculation and the Homestead Ethic in Frontier Kentucky," *Western Historical Quarterly* 22 (1992): 179-98. Marcia Brawner Smith, in "'To Embrace the Value of the Land': Land Survey Legislation in the Jackson Purchase, 1820," *Register* 91 (1993): 386-402, discusses land problems in the state's best-surveyed region. William W. Hening, comp., *The Statutes at Large: Being a Collection of All the Laws of Virginia, 1619-1792,* 13 vols. (1819-23), contains the Virginia land laws in effect before Kentucky's statehood.

The most recent study of Kentucky's separation from Virginia is Lowell H. Harrison, *Kentucky's Road to Statehood* (1992). Patricia Watlington's *The Partisan Spirit: Kentucky Politics, 1779-1792* (1972) is a meticulous study, although her assertion that political parties existed in Kentucky before the 1790s has been challenged. Joan Wells Coward, *Kentucky in the New Republic: The Process of Constitution Making* (1979), concentrates on the 1790s and is especially good on the 1799 constitution. *The Calendar of Virginia State Papers and Other Manuscripts,* 11 vols. (1875-93); and James R. Robertson, *Petitions of the Early Inhabitants of Kentucky* (1914), are indispensable for a study of the statehood movement. The extant journals of the conventions are in the Manuscript Division, Kentucky Historical Society. The first convention journal was published in Thomas Perkins Abernethy, ed., "Journal of the First Kentucky Convention, December 27, 1784-January 5, 1785," *JSH* 1 (1935): 67-78. Thomas D. Clark, ed., *The Voice of the Frontier: John Bradford's Notes on Kentucky* (1993), contains several articles on the statehood process. The *Kentucky Gazette* also printed some extracts from the convention journals.

For several years Danville was the political capital of Kentucky. The best histories of the town are Richard C. Brown, *A History of Danville and Boyle County, Kentucky, 1774-1992* (1992); and Calvin Morgan Fackler, *Early Days in Danville* (1941). Thomas Speed, *The Political Club, Danville, Kentucky, 1786-1790* (1894), should be supplemented by Ann Price Combs, "Notes on the Political Club of Danville and Its Members," *FCHQ* 35 (1961): 333-52.

The Spanish Conspiracy has received much attention, a great deal of it highly partisan. William Littell was employed by some gentlemen accused of being participants to prove their innocence. His effort is best used in Temple Bodley, ed., *Littell's Political Transactions in and concerning Kentucky and Letter of George Nicholas, also General Wilkinson's Memorial* (1926). Humphrey Marshall (*A History of Kentucky* [1812]) was convinced of the guilt of the accused; Mann Butler, in *A History of the Commonwealth of Kentucky* (1834), defended them. John Mason Brown, *The Political Beginnings of Kentucky* (1889), is a defense of the author's grandfather and his associates; Brown was answered by another partisan grandson in Thomas Marshall Green, *The Spanish Conspiracy* (1891). Among the many articles dealing with this alleged conspiracy are Lowell H. Harrison, "James Wilkinson: A Leader for Kentucky?" *FCHQ* 66 (1992): 334-68; W.A. Shepherd, "Wilkinson and the Beginnings of the Spanish Conspiracy," *American Historical Review* 9 (1904): 490-506; and Arthur P. Whitaker, "Harry Innes and the Spanish Intrigue, 1794-1795," *MVHR* 15 (1928): 236-48. Elizabeth Warren wrote three articles on this topic: "John Brown and His Influence on Kentucky Politics, 1784-1795," *Register* 36 (1938): 61-65; "Benjamin Sebastian and the Spanish Conspiracy in Kentucky," *FCHQ* 20 (1946): 107-30; and "Senator John Brown's Role in the Kentucky Spanish Conspiracy," *FCHQ* 36 (1962): 158-76. Warren found Sebastian guilty and Brown innocent. Patricia Watlington, in "John Brown and the Spanish Conspiracy," *Virginia Magazine of History and Biography* 75 (1967): 52-68, declared Brown guilty. Among the best studies of Wilkinson's devious career are Royal Ornan Shreve, *The Finished Scoundrel* (1933); James Ripley Jacobs, *Tarnished Warrior* (1938); and Thomas R. Hay and M.R. Werner, *The Admirable Trumpeter* (1941). A judicious evaluation is Thomas R. Hay, "Some Reflections on the Career of General James Wilkinson," *MVHR* 21 (1935): 471-94.

Huntley Dupre, in "The Political Ideas of George Nicholas," *Register* 39 (1941): 201-23, discusses the most important member of the 1792 constitutional convention, and Vernon P. Martin, in "Father Rice, the Preacher Who Followed the Frontier," *FCHQ* 29 (1955): 324-30, describes the Presbyterian who led the antislavery fight in the convention. Sylvia Wrobel and George Grider, *Isaac*

Shelby: Kentucky's First Governor and Hero of Three Wars (1974), is the best biography of a man who deserves a full study. The best sketch of Harry Innes is in Mary K. Bonsteel Tachau, *Federal Courts in the Early Republic: Kentucky, 1789-1816* (1978).

The 1792 constitution is printed in Lowell H. Harrison, *Kentucky's Road to Statehood* (1992), and in Bennett H. Young, *History and Texts of the Three Constitutions of Kentucky* (1890). It is analyzed in John D. Barnhart, "Frontiersmen and Planters in the Formation of Kentucky," *JSH* 7 (1941): 19-36; and E. Merton Coulter, "Early Frontier Democracy in the First Kentucky Constitution," *Political Science Quarterly* 39 (1924): 665-77. See also George L. Willis Sr., "History of Kentucky Constitutions and Constitutional Conventions," *Register* 28 (1930): 305-29.

Pratt Byrd, "The Kentucky Frontier in 1792," *FCHQ* 25 (1951): 181-203, 286-94; and John D. Barnhart, *Valley of Democracy: The Frontier versus the Plantation in the Ohio Valley, 1775-1818* (1953), place the statehood movement in its social and economic context. Elizabeth A. Perkins has made a major contribution to the knowledge of frontier life with both "Border Life: Experience and Perception in the Revolutionary Ohio Valley" (Ph.D. diss., Northwestern University, 1992); and "The Consumer Frontier: Household Consumption in Early Kentucky," *JAH* 78 (1991): 486-510.

Chapter 6. From Constitution to Constitution, 1792-1799

The Kentucky Department for Libraries and Archives and the Kentucky Historical Society hold the surviving state records. Vital for a study of the period are the Kentucky *House Journal* and *Senate Journal*, the papers of the governors, and the reports of the various agencies of the government. Lowell H. Harrison, ed., *Kentucky's Governors, 1792-1985* (1985), contains a sketch of each governor and his or her gubernatorial term, with references to other sources of information. Mabel Weaks has edited some of Isaac Shelby's official papers and published them in *FCHQ* 30 (1956): 203-31; and *Register* 27 (1929): 587-94 and 28

(1930): 1-24, 139-50, 203-13. Rhea A. Taylor, "The Selection of Kentucky's Permanent Capital Site," *FCHQ* 23 (1949): 267-77; and Carl E. Kramer, *Capital on the Kentucky: A Two Hundred Year History of Frankfort and Franklin County* (1986), explain Frankfort's selection. Sylvia Wrobel and George Grider, *Isaac Shelby: Kentucky's First Governor and Hero of Three Wars* (1974); and Lowell H. Harrison, *Kentucky's Road to Statehood* (1992), describe the start of Shelby's first administration. H.E. Everman, *Governor James Garrard* (1981), carries the second governor through his two terms. A major political figure from his arrival in Kentucky in 1793 until his death in 1806 is studied in Lowell H. Harrison, *John Breckinridge, Jeffersonian Republican* (1969). The important role of the counties has been described well in multiple works by Robert M. Ireland: *The County Courts in Antebellum Kentucky* (1972); *The County in Kentucky History* (1976); "The Place of the Justices of the Peace in the Legislative and Party System in Kentucky, 1792-1850," *American Journal of Legal History* 13 (1969): 202-22; and "Aristocrats All: The Politics of County Government in Antebellum Kentucky," *Review of Politics* 32 (1970): 365-83. James Lane Allen captured the flavor of a nineteenth-century institution in "County Court Day in Kentucky," *Harper's Magazine* 79 (1889): 383-97.

Stephen Aron has made a careful study of the state's land policy and its effects in "How the West Was Lost: The Transformation of Kentucky from Daniel Boone to Henry Clay" (Ph.D. diss., University of California, Berkeley, 1989), as well as his "Pioneers and Profiteers: Land Speculation and the Homestead Ethic in Frontier Kentucky," *Western Historical Quarterly* 22 (1992): 179-98. See also Fredrika Johanna Teute, "Land, Liberty, and Labor in the Post-revolutionary Era: Kentucky As the Promised Land" (Ph.D. diss., Johns Hopkins University, 1988).

In the 1790s Kentucky remained concerned with the Indian problem in the Northwest Territory. Paul David Nelson, "'Mad' Anthony Wayne and the Kentuckians of the 1790s," *Register* 84 (1986): 1-17; and idem, "General Charles Scott, the Kentucky Mounted Volunteers, and the North-west Indian Wars, 1784-1794," *Journal of the Early Republic* 6 (1986): 219-52, are good introductions to the problem. The often-neglected role of Scott is described in Harry M. Ward, *Charles Scott and the "Spirit of '76"* (1988). Milo M. Quaife, ed., "General Wilkinson's Narrative of the Northwestern Campaign of 1794," *MVHR* 16 (1929): 81-90; and William Clark, "William Clark's Journal of General Wayne's Campaign," *MVHR* 1 (1914): 418-44, are contemporary accounts of the decisive campaign.

Joan Wells Coward, *Kentucky in the New Republic: The Process of Constitution Making* (1979), is excellent on the push in the 1790s for another constitution. John Breckinridge participated in most of the important political events of the decade; his roles are examined in Lowell H. Harrison, *John Breckinridge, Jeffersonian Republican* (1969). Most Kentucky Democratic Republicans were pro-French, and the activities of Citizen Edmond-Charles Genet have attracted several historians. Archibald Henderson, "Isaac Shelby and the Genet Mission," *MVHR* 6 (1920): 451-69; Richard Lowitt, "Activities of Citizen Genet in Kentucky, 1793-1794," *FCHQ* 22 (1948): 252-67; J.W. Cooke, "Governor Shelby and Genet's Agents," *FCHQ* 37 (1963): 162-70; and Harry Ammon, "The Genet Mission and the Development of American Political Parties," *JAH* 52 (1966): 725-41, discuss aspects of the affair. E. Merton Coulter, "The Efforts of the Democratic Societies of the West to Open the Navigation of the Mississippi," *MVHR* 11 (1924): 376-89; and Thomas J. Farnham, "Kentucky and Washington's Mississippi Policy of Patience and Persuasion," *Register* 64 (1966): 14-28, examine the question in the state. Eugene P. Link, *Democratic-Republican Societies* (1942); and Philip S. Foner, ed., *The Democratic-Republican Societies, 1790-1800: A Documentary Sourcebook of Constitutions, Declarations, Addresses, Resolutions, and Toasts* (1976), examine the societies in more detail. Mary K. Bonsteel Tachau, "The Whiskey Rebellion in Kentucky: A Forgotten Episode of Civil Disobedience," *Journal of the Early Republic* 2 (1982): 239-60; and John W. Kuehl, "Southern Reaction to the XYZ Affair: An Incident

in the Emergence of American Nationalism," *Register* 70 (1972): 21-49, deal with two issues that created considerable excitement in the state.

The movement for the second constitution is admirably traced in Joan Wells Coward, *Kentucky in the New Republic: The Process of Constitution Making* (1979). The case of an opponent of the movement is presented in Lowell H. Harrison, "John Breckinridge and the Kentucky Constitution of 1799," *Register* 57 (1959): 209-33. The text of the new constitution is in Bennett H. Young, *History and Texts of the Three Constitutions of Kentucky* (1890). George L. Willis Sr., *Kentucky Constitutions and Constitutional Conventions, 1784-1932* (1930), should also be consulted.

Chapter 7. Kentucky in the New Nation, 1792-1815

Kentucky's political orientation is examined in Thomas D. Matijasic, "Antifederalism in Kentucky," *FCHQ* 66 (1992): 36-59. The state's most persistent Federalist has been inadequately studied in A.C. Quisenberry, *The Life and Times of Hon. Humphrey Marshall* (1892). James Morton Smith, "The Grass Roots Origins of the Kentucky Resolutions," *William and Mary Quarterly*, 3d ser., 27 (1970): 221-45; and Adrienne Koch and Harry Ammon, "The Virginia and Kentucky Resolutions: An Episode in Jefferson's and Madison's Defense of Civil Liberties," *William and Mary Quarterly*, 3d ser., 5 (1948): 145-76, provide background on the Kentucky Resolutions. The controversial legislation is discussed in John C. Miller, *Crisis in Freedom: The Alien and Sedition Acts* (1951); and James Morton Smith, *Freedom's Fetters: The Alien and Sedition Laws and American Civil Liberties* (1956). Ethelbert D. Warfield, *The Kentucky Resolutions of 1798* (1887), overemphasizes the role of John Breckinridge, whose contribution to the protests is evaluated more objectively in Lowell H. Harrison, *John Breckinridge, Jeffersonian Republican* (1969). Paul Knepper, "Thomas Jefferson, Criminal Code Reform, and the Founding of the Kentucky Penitentiary at Frankfort," *Register* 91 (1993): 129-49; and idem, "The Kentucky Penitentiary at Frankfort and the Origins of America's First Convict Lease System, 1798-1843," *FCHQ* 69 (1995): 41-66, are excellent descriptions of a state institution that Kentucky provided at an early date.

The purchase of Louisiana is discussed in all the general state histories and in such surveys of the westward movement as Ray Allen Billington, *Westward Expansion: A History of the American Frontier* (1974); and Thomas D. Clark, *Frontier America: The Story of the Westward Movement* (1959). Biographies of Thomas Jefferson, such as Dumas Malone, *Jefferson and His Time: Jefferson the President, First Term, 1801-1805* (1970), emphasize the transaction. Arthur P. Whitaker, *The Mississippi Question* (1934), is a good overall treatment of the issue. The Kentucky newspapers paid a great deal of attention to the question.

The Burr Conspiracy is discussed in all the standard state histories and in the biographies of Jefferson and comprehensive studies of his administration. Full-scale studies include Thomas Perkins Abernethy, *The Burr Conspiracy* (1954); Francis F. Beirne, *Shout Treason: The Trial of Aaron Burr* (1959); and Walter F. McCaleb, *The Aaron Burr Conspiracy* (1936). See also Milton Lomask, *The Conspiracy and Years of Exile, 1805-1836* (1982); and Samuel M. Wilson, "The Court Proceedings of 1806 in Kentucky against Aaron Burr and John Adair," *FCHQ* 10 (1936): 31-40. Henry Clay's involvement in the affair is discussed in Robert V. Remini, *Henry Clay: Statesman for the Union* (1991), as well as the older biographies: Bernard Mayo, *Henry Clay* (1937); and Glyndon G. Van Deusen, *The Life of Henry Clay* (1937). Also helpful are *The Papers of Henry Clay*, 11 vols. (1959-92). The first volume, which covers the Burr Conspiracy, was edited by James F. Hopkins; the associate editor was Mary W.M. Hargreaves.

Bradford Perkins, *Prologue to War* (1961); and Reginald Horsman, *The Causes of the War of 1812* (1962), are good on the background to the early nineteenth-century conflict. Robert B. McAfee, *History of the Late War in the Western Country* (1816), is an interesting contemporary account of

Kentucky's part in the war. General accounts include John K. Mahon, *The War of 1812* (1972); and Francis F. Beirne, *The War of 1812* (1949). James Wallace Hammack Jr., *Kentucky and the Second American Revolution: The War of 1812* (1976); and Alec R. Gilpin, *The War of 1812 in the Old Northwest* (1958), concentrate on Kentucky's participation. Richard G. Stone Jr., *A Brittle Sword: The Kentucky Militia, 1776-1912* (1977), discusses the role of the state militia. A.C. Quisenberry wrote a series of articles on the war for the *Register* in 1912-15; they form the basis for his book *Kentucky in the War of 1812* (1915). Federal Writers Project, *Military History of Kentucky* (1939), is dull but occasionally helpful. Samuel M. Wilson summarized the state's role in "Kentucky's Part in the War of 1812," *Register* 60 (1962): 1-8; James Russell Harris has added useful information in "Kentuckians in the War of 1812: A Note on Numbers, Losses, and Sources," *Register* 82 (1984): 277-86. The controversy over the Kentucky troops at New Orleans is covered in Robert V. Remini, *Andrew Jackson and the Course of American Empire, 1767-1821* (1977); Joseph G. Tregle Jr., "Andrew Jackson and the Continuing Battle of New Orleans," *Journal of the Early Republic* 1 (1981): 373-94; and John S. Gillig, "In the Pursuit of Truth and Honor: The Controversy between Andrew Jackson and John Adair in 1817," *FCHQ* 58 (1984): 177-201.

The *Register of the Kentucky Historical Society* and *The Filson Club History Quarterly*, as well as the manuscript collections at The Filson Club and the University of Kentucky, contain a number of firsthand accounts of the war.

Chapter 8. Kentucky after Fifty Years of Settlement

The nation's postwar surge of nationalism has been described in two books by George Dangerfield: *The Era of Good Feelings* (1952); and *The Awakening of American Nationalism, 1815-1828* (1965). As the Missouri Controversy indicated, bad feelings also existed. M.N. Rothbard, *The Panic of 1819* (1962), is a good account of the severe depression.

Thomas D. Clark, *A History of Kentucky* (1937); Richard H. Collins and Lewis Collins, *History of Kentucky*, 2 vols. (1874); and William E. Connelley and E. Merton Coulter, *History of Kentucky*, edited by Charles Kerr, 5 vols. (1922), all comment on aspects of the events in the postwar years.

Glover Moore, *The Missouri Controversy, 1819-1821* (1953), is a comprehensive account of the crisis. Henry Clay's role in finding a compromise was not as great as some admirers have claimed, but his biographies cited above, under chapter 7, should be examined.

Several studies have looked at the Kentuckians of the early nineteenth century. Thomas L. Purvis ("The Ethnic Descent of Kentucky's Early Population: A Statistical Investigation of European and American Sources of Emigration, 1790-1820," *Register* 80 [1982]: 253-66) found some interesting shifts during the three decades from 1790 to 1820. Samuel M. Wilson, "Pioneer Kentucky in Its Ethnological Aspect," *Register* 31 (1933): 283-95, is an early survey; Mellie Scott Hortin, "A History of the Scotch-Irish and Their Influence in Kentucky," *FCHQ* 34 (1960): 248-55, examines one important group. Henry P. Scalf, *Kentucky's Last Frontier* (1966); and Carol Crowe-Carraco, *The Big Sandy* (1979), describe the settlement of the area that most of the early pioneers passed by. South-central Kentuckians are studied in James A. Ramage, "The Green River Pioneers: Squatters, Soldiers, and Speculators," *Register* 75 (1977): 171-90; Cecil E. Goode, *Southern Kentuckians: Historical Sketches of Barren and Surrounding Counties in Kentucky* (1989); and idem, *Heart of the Barrens* (1986). A countertrend to the state's immigration patterns is observed in John D. Barnhart, "The Migration of Kentuckians across the Ohio River," *FCHQ* 25 (1951): 24-32.

Much has been written about pioneer life in the state and the changes that occurred in the first half of the nineteenth century. Three good general accounts are Jack Larkin, *The Reshaping of Everyday Life, 1790-1840* (1988); William E. Collins Sr., *Ways, Means, and Customs of Our Forefathers* (1976);

and Thomas D. Clark, *The Rampaging Frontier* (1939), but see also William E. Collins Sr., *Folkways and Customs of Old Kentucky* (1971). Two of the best accounts of life in Kentucky after the early pioneer days are Daniel Drake, *Pioneer Life in Kentucky, 1785-1800*, edited by Emmet F. Horine (1948), which was first published in 1870; and Mann Butler, "Details of Frontier Life," *Register* 62 (1964): 206-29. Butler's incomplete book *The Valley of the Ohio* was edited by G. Glenn Clift and published in 1971. The work of Nancy Disher Baird and Carol Crowe-Carraco, *Pioneer Life in South Central Kentucky* (1988), prepared as a teacher's guide, merits wider circulation. Louis B. Wright, *Culture on the Moving Frontier* (1955); and Arthur K. Moore, *The Frontier Mind* (1957), contain many references to Kentucky, some controversial. Michael A. Flannery, "Arthur K. Moore and Kentucky Culture," *FCHQ* 69 (1995): 25-40, is a needed critique of Moore's conclusions. Three of the many articles that depict aspects of frontier life are Martin L. Primack, "Land Clearing under Nineteenth Century Techniques," *Journal of Economic History* 22 (1962): 484-97; Lee Soltow, "Horse Owners in Kentucky in 1800," *Register* 79 (1981): 203-10; and Elizabeth A. Perkins, "The Consumer Frontier: Household Consumption in Early Kentucky," *JAH* 78 (1991): 486-510. Frank F. Mathias, ed., *Incidents and Experiences in the Life of Thomas W. Parsons* (1975), deals more with the mid–nineteenth century. For examples of articles dealing with specific aspects of Kentucky life, see Emmet V. Mittlebeeler, "The Decline of Imprisonment for Debt in Kentucky," *FCHQ* 49 (1975): 169-89; James I. Robertson Jr., "Revelry and Religion in Frontier Kentucky," *Register* 79 (1981): 354-68; Zachariah F. Smith, "Dueling and Some Noted Duels in Kentucky," *Register* 8 (1910): 77-87; and Robert M. Ireland, "The Problem of Concealed Weapons in Nineteenth Century Kentucky," *Register* 91 (1993): 370-85.

Although most Kentuckians lived in rural areas or small towns, urban growth is described in Allen J. Share, *Cities in the Commonwealth* (1982), which emphasizes Lexington and Louisville. Richard C. Wade, *The Urban Frontier: Pioneer Life in Early Pittsburgh, Cincinnati, Lexington, Louisville, and St. Louis* (1964), shows the rivalry among various cities. Early Lexington is described in George W. Ranck, *History of Lexington, Kentucky, Its Early Annals and Recent Progress* (1872); Charles R. Staples, *The History of Pioneer Lexington* (1939); and William A. Leavy, "A Memoir of Lexington and Its Vicinity," *Register* 40 (1942): 107-31, 253-67, 353-75; 41 (1943): 44-62, 107-37, 250-60, 310-46; 42 (1944): 26-53. John D. Wright Jr., *Lexington: Heart of the Bluegrass* (1982), brings the story into the modern era. H. Mc'Murtrie, *Sketches of Louisville and Its Environs* (1819), reprinted in 1969, contains a wealth of information about the early town and Ohio River. George H. Yater, *Two Hundred Years at the Falls of the Ohio: A History of Louisville and Jefferson County* (1987), is a good recent account. On the failure of some urban dreams, see Mariam S. Houchens, "Three Kentucky Towns That Never Were," *FCHQ* 40 (1966): 17-21.

Travelers who wrote accounts of their experiences often commented on Kentucky characteristics. Eugene L. Schwaab, ed., *Travels in the Old South*, 2 vols. (1973); and Raymond F. Betts, "'Sweet Meditation through This Pleasant Country': Foreign Appraisals of the Landscape of Kentucky in the Early Years of the Commonwealth," *Register* 90 (1992): 26-44, are good starting points. Among the many publications that attempt to characterize Kentucky and Kentuckians, the following have particular interest: Harry Toulmin, *A Description of Kentucky in North America to Which Are Prefixed Miscellaneous Observations Respecting the United States* (1792); idem, "Comments on America and Kentucky, 1793-1802," *Register* 47 (1949): 3-20, 97-115; Gilbert Imlay, *A Topographical Description of the Western Territory of North America* (1793); Thomas Ashe, *Travels in America Performed in 1806* (1808): James Walker, "Diary of the Wilderness Road in the Year 1816," *Register* 39 (1941): 224-29; Earl Gregg Swem, ed., *Letters on the Condition of Kentucky in 1825* (1916); Mrs. Frances Trollope, *Domestic Manners of the Americans* (1832); and Harriet Martineau, *Retrospect of Western Travel*, 3 vols.

(1838). George Robertson, *Scrap Book on Law and Politics, Men and Times* (1855), offers some pertinent observations.

Chapter 9. Politics and Politicians, 1820-1859

Arndt M. Stickles, *The Critical Court Struggle in Kentucky, 1819-1829* (1929), remains the best study of the New Court–Old Court Controversy. It can be supplemented with Arndt M. Stickles, ed., "Joseph R. Underwood's Fragmentary Journal of the New and Old Court Contest in Kentucky," *FCHQ* 13 (1939): 202-10; Edward H. Hilliard, "When Kentucky Had Two Courts of Appeal," *FCHQ* 34 (1960): 228-36; and Frank F. Mathias, "The Relief and Court Struggle: Half-way House to Populism," *Register* 71 (1973): 154-76. The key elections in the struggle are discussed in Paul E. Doutrich III, "A Pivotal Decision: The 1824 Gubernatorial Election in Kentucky," *FCHQ* 56 (1982): 14-29; Billie J. Hardin, "Amos Kendall and the 1824 Relief Controversy," *Register* 64 (1966): 196-208; and Leonard P. Curry, "Election Year—Kentucky, 1828," *Register* 55 (1957): 196-212.

Richard P. McCormick, *The Second American Party System: Party Formation in the Jacksonian Era* (1966); Frank F. Mathias, "The Turbulent Years of Kentucky Politics, 1820-1850" (Ph.D. diss., University of Kentucky, 1966); and Wallace B. Turner, "Kentucky in a Decade of Change, 1850-1860" (Ph.D. diss., University of Kentucky, 1954), are detailed studies of politics during the Jacksonian era. The two dissertations have been summarized in Frank F. Mathias, "The Turbulent Years of Kentucky Politics, 1820-1850," *Register* 72 (1974): 309-18; and Wallace B. Turner, "Kentucky State Politics in the Early 1850s," *Register* 56 (1958): 123-42. Among the best political studies of this period are Ralph A. Wooster, *Politicians, Planters, and Plain Folk: Courthouse and Statehouse in the Upper South, 1850-1860* (1975); Jasper B. Shannon and Ruth McQuown, comps., *Presidential Politics in Kentucky, 1824-1948* (1950); Frank F. Mathias and Jasper B. Shannon, "Gubernatorial Politics in Kentucky, 1820-1851," *Register* 88 (1990): 245-77; William C.

Richardson, *An Administrative History of Kentucky Courts to 1850* (1983); Robert M. Ireland, "Aristocrats All: The Politics of County Government in Ante-bellum Kentucky," *Review of Politics* 32 (1970): 365-83; and James W. Gordon, *Lawyers in Politics: Mid–Nineteenth Century Kentucky As a Case Study* (1990). In addition to such well-known politicians as Henry Clay and John J. Crittenden, a number of other antebellum politicians have attracted scholarly attention. Such works include George Baber, "Joseph Rogers Underwood: Jurist, Orator, and Statesman," *Register* 10 (1912): 49-54; Lucius P. Little, *Ben Hardin: His Times and Contemporaries* (1887); Leland Winfield Meyer, *The Life and Times of Richard M. Johnson of Kentucky* (1932); Orval W. Baylor, *John Pope, Kentuckian: His Life and Times, 1770-1845* (1953); William Stickney, ed., *Autobiography of Amos Kendall* (1872); Holman Hamilton, "Kentucky's Linn Boyd, and the Dramatic Days of 1850," *Register* 55 (1957): 185-95; John F. Dorman, "Gabriel Slaughter, 1767-1830," *FCHQ* 40 (1966): 338-56; Will D. Gilliam Jr., "Robert Perkins Letcher, Whig Governor of Kentucky," *FCHQ* 24 (1950): 6-27; George Baber, "James Guthrie: Lawyer, Financier, and Statesman," *Register* 10 (1912): 9-13; Robert Spencer Cotterill, "James Guthrie—Kentuckian, 1792-1869," *Register* 20 (1922): 290-96; John Wilson Townsend, *Richard Hickman Menefee* (1907); and Stephen W. Fackler, "John Rowan and the Demise of Jeffersonian Republicanism in Kentucky, 1819-1831," *Register* 78 (1980): 1-26.

Politicking in the antebellum years depended a great deal upon public speaking, and Kentucky had some masters of oratorical art. For a sampling, try Gifford Blyton and Randall Capps, *Speaking Out: Two Centuries of Kentucky Orators* (1977); and William C. Davis, "Taking the Stump: Campaigns in Old-Time Kentucky," *Register* 80 (1982): 367-91.

The Mexican War created great excitement in the state. A.H. Bill, *Rehearsal for Conflict: The War with Mexico, 1846-1848* (1947); and Jack Bauer, *The Mexican-American War, 1846-1848* (1974), provide good overviews. Aspects of Kentucky's participation are discussed in Damon R. Eubank, "A Time of Enthusiasm: The Response of Kentucky to the Call for Troops in the Mexican War," *Register* 90 (1992): 323-44; James A. Ramage, "John Hunt Morgan and the Kentucky Cavalry Volunteers in the Mexican War," *Register* 81 (1983): 343-65; and Richard V. Salisbury, "Kentuckians at the Battle of Buena Vista," *FCHQ* 61 (1987): 34-53. See also Holman Hamilton, *Zachary Taylor: Soldier of the Republic* (1946). Frank F. Mathias, "The Turbulent Years of Kentucky Politics, 1820-1850," *Register* 72 (1974): 309-18; George L. Willis Sr., "History of Kentucky Constitutions and Constitutional Conventions," *Register* 28 (1930): 305-29; and Carl R. Fields, "Making Kentucky's Third Constitution" (Ph.D. diss., University of Kentucky, 1951), provide an overview of constitution making at midcentury. Frank F. Mathias describes a conservative trend in "Kentucky's Third Constitution: A Restriction of Majority Rule," *Register* 75 (1977): 1-19. Unlike its predecessors, the third constitutional convention kept a detailed record of its proceedings: see the 1,129-page *Report of the Debates and Proceedings of the Convention for the Revision of the Constitution of the State of Kentucky, 1849* (1849).

Henry Clay was the state's favorite son for half a century and one of the nation's leading statesmen. Robert V. Remini, *Henry Clay: Statesman for the Union* (1991), is the best biography, but Glyndon G. Van Deusen, *The Life of Henry Clay* (1937); and Bernard Mayo, *Henry Clay* (1937), are still useful. Mayo's work examines Clay only to 1812. Clay's role as a party leader is explored in George R. Poage, *Henry Clay and the Whig Party* (1936); and Clement Eaton, *Henry Clay and the Art of American Politics* (1957). The charge that haunted Clay after 1824 is studied in William G. Morgan, "The 'Corrupt Bargain' Charge against Clay and Adams: An Historiographical Analysis," *FCHQ* 42 (1968): 132-49; and idem, "Henry Clay's Biographers and the 'Corrupt Bargain' Charge," *Register* 66 (1968): 242-58. Frank F. Mathias, "Henry Clay and His Kentucky Power Base," *Register* 78 (1980): 123-39; and Everett William Kindig, "Western Opposition to Jackson's 'Democracy': The Ohio Valley As a Case

Study, 1827-1836" (Ph.D. diss., Stanford University, 1974), help explain why Clay was able to remain in the political foreground so long. Some of the facets of Clay's long political career are discussed in Thomas B. Jones, "Henry Clay and Continental Expansion, 1820-1844," *Register* 73 (1975): 241-62; Robert Seager II, "Henry Clay and the Politics of Compromise and Non-compromise," *Register* 85 (1987): 1-28; and Peter B. Knupfer, "Henry Clay's Constitutional Unionism," *Register* 89 (1991): 32-60. Clay's last great effort at compromise is admirably described in Holman Hamilton, *Prologue to Conflict: The Crisis and Compromise of 1850.*

Wallace B. Turner, "Kentucky in a Decade of Change, 1850-1860" (Ph.D. diss., University of Kentucky, 1954), summarizes the political developments of the 1850s. David M. Potter, *The Impending Crisis, 1848-1861* (1976), presents an overview of the national problems; Michael F. Holt, *The Political Crisis of the 1850s* (1978), concentrates on the politics of the 1850s. Arthur C. Cole, *The Whig Party in the South* (1913), is still a sound study. Christopher R. Waldrep, "Who Were Kentucky's Whig Voters? A Note on Voting in Eddyville Precinct in August 1850," *Register* 79 (1981): 326-32; and E. Merton Coulter, "The Downfall of the Whig Party in Kentucky," *Register* 23 (1925): 162-74, attempt to answer two questions about the Whigs.

The nativism movement led to the formation of the American Party, or the Know-Nothings, which flourished briefly in the 1850s. The best accounts of the party in Kentucky are Agnes Geraldine McGann, *Nativism in Kentucky to 1860* (1944); and Wallace B. Turner, "The Know-Nothing Movement in Kentucky," *FCHQ* 28 (1954): 266-83. Louisville's violent riot has been described in Charles E. Deusner, "The Know Nothing Riots in Louisville," *Register* 61 (1962): 122-47; and Wallace S. Hutcheon Jr., "The Louisville Riots of August, 1850," *Register* 69 (1971): 150-72. On the disputed role played by the *Louisville Journal,* see Betty C. Congleton, "George D. Prentice and Bloody Monday: A Reappraisal," *Register* 63 (1965): 218-39; and William C. Mallalieu, "George D. Prentice: A Re-

appraisal Reappraised," *Register* 64 (1966): 44-50. Another view of the affair is offered in Philip Wayne Kennedy, "The Know-Nothing Movement in Kentucky: Role of M.J. Spalding, Catholic Bishop of Louisville," *FCHQ* 38 (1964): 17-35.

Allan Nevins, *The Ordeal of the Union,* 2 vols. (1947); and idem, *The Emergence of Lincoln,* 2 vols. (1950), give detailed accounts of the changes in political parties and politics between 1847 and 1861.

Chapter 10. Economic Development

Transportation has been a vital concern for Kentuckians since the first years of settlement. All of the general histories devote space to the topic, and newspapers and legislative records treat it frequently. Charles Henry Ambler, *A History of Transportation in the Ohio Valley* (1932), is a good introduction to the subject. Leland D. Baldwin, "Shipbuilding on the Western Waters, 1793-1817," *MVHR* 20 (1933): 29-44; and Stuart Seely Sprague, "Kentucky and the Navigation of the Mississippi: The Climatic Years, 1793-1795," *Register* 71 (1973): 364-92, indicate the importance of the steamboats. C.W. Hackensmith, "John Fitch: A Pioneer in the Development of the Steamboat," *Register* 65 (1967): 187-211, tells the story of an unlucky inventor. Navigation on the Kentucky River is described in Thomas D. Clark, *The Kentucky* (1942), revised in 1992; Mary Verhoeff, *The Kentucky River Navigation* (1917); and J. Winston Coleman Jr., "Kentucky River Steamboats," *Register* 63 (1965): 299-322. The Green River has been studied by Helen Bartter Crocker in several works: *The Green River of Kentucky* (1976); "Steamboats on Kentucky's Green River," *Antiques* 105 (1974): 570-75; and "Steamboats for Bowling Green: The River Politics of James Rumsey Skiles," *FCHQ* 46 (1972): 9-23. Agnes S. Harralson captured the flavor of riverboating in *Steamboats on the Green and the Colorful Men Who Operated Them* (1981). Arthur E. Hopkins, "Steamboats at Louisville and on the Ohio and Mississippi Rivers," *FCHQ* 17 (1943): 143-62, can be supplemented by Ben Cassedy, *History of Louisville* (1852), for an account of early steamboats at Louisville.

The Wilderness Road has received a great deal of attention. Robert L. Kincaid, *The Wilderness Road* (1947); and William Allen Pusey, *The Wilderness Road to Kentucky* (1921), are two of the best studies. Turner W. Allen, "The Turnpike System of Kentucky: A Review of State Road Policy in the Nineteenth Century," *FCHQ* 28 (1954): 239-59, is an excellent summary. S.G. Boyd, "The Louisville and Nashville Turnpike," *Register* 24 (1926): 163-74, tells the story of a major road. J. Winston Coleman Jr., *Stage-Coach Days in the Bluegrass* (1935), reprinted in 1995, tells much about the roads and their use in addition to the stagecoach operations.

The best introduction to state railroads is Robert Spencer Cotterill, "Early Railroading in Kentucky," *Register* 17 (1919): 55-62. Studies of individual lines include Thomas D. Clark, "The Lexington and Ohio Railroad—A Pioneer Venture," *Register* 31 (1933): 9-28; Stuart Seely Sprague, "Kentucky and the Cincinnati-Charleston Railroad, 1835-1839," *Register* 73 (1975): 122-35; Thomas D. Clark, *The Beginning of the L&N* (1933); Kincaid A. Herr, *The Louisville and Nashville Railroad, 1850-1942* (1943); and Maury Klein, *History of the Louisville and Nashville Railroad* (1972). Carl B. Boyd Jr., "Local Aid to Railroads in Central Kentucky, 1850-1891," *Register* 62 (1964): 4-23, 112-33, shows the importance of local aid in early construction. John E. Tilford Jr., "The Delicate Track: The L&N's Role in the Civil War," *FCHQ* 36 (1962): 209-21, explains how vital the L&N was to the Union armies.

Much writing about the antebellum years touches upon agriculture, the basic economic activity in the state. Lewis C. Gray, *History of Agriculture in the Southern United States to 1860*, 2 vols. (1933), devotes considerable attention to Kentucky. Richard L. Troutman, "Aspects of Agriculture in the Ante-bellum Bluegrass," *FCHQ* 45 (1971): 163-73, is an introduction to the Bluegrass region, while Thomas D. Clark, *Agrarian Kentucky* (1977); and James E. Wallace, "Let's Talk about the Weather: A Historiography of Antebellum Kentucky Agriculture," *Register* 89 (1991): 179-99, provide overviews for the state. Wallace's article is the best guide to the literature on agriculture. Richard L. Troutman, "Social and Economic Structure of Kentucky Agriculture, 1850-1860" (Ph.D. diss., University of Kentucky, 1958), is an important study of the decade of the 1850s. Thomas D. Clark, *Footloose in Jacksonian America: Robert W. Scott and His Agrarian World* (1989), describes Scott's association with agrarian reform. William F. Axton, *Tobacco and Kentucky* (1975), is the most complete study of tobacco in the state, but see also the Tobacco Institute, *Kentucky's Tobacco Heritage* (n.d.). Corn, the vital pioneer crop, is discussed in Allan Bogue, *From Prairie to Corn Belt* (1963); and John C. Hudson, *Making the Corn Belt: A Geographical History of Middle-Western Agriculture* (1994). James F. Hopkins, *A History of the Hemp Industry in Kentucky* (1951), describes all aspects of the production, manufacturing, and sale of hemp; Ann I. Ottesen, "A Reconstruction of the Activities and Outbuildings at Farmington, an Early Nineteenth Century Hemp Farm," *FCHQ* 59 (1985): 395-425, examines one farm. An unsuccessful experiment is examined in Spalding Trafton, "Silk Culture in Henderson County, Kentucky," *FCHQ* 4 (1930): 184-89. Kent Hollingsworth, *The Kentucky Thoroughbred* (1976); Sara S. Brown, "The Kentucky Thoroughbred," *FCHQ* 25 (1951): 3-23; and Ken McCarr, *The Kentucky Harness Horse* (1978), discuss the horse, which has been so important in the state's history. Kentucky has a prominent place in Paul C. Henlein, *The Cattle Kingdom in the Ohio Valley, 1783-1860* (1951). The North Kentucky Cattle Importing Company, "Introduction of Imported Cattle in Kentucky," *Register* 29 (1931): 400-15; 30 (1932): 37-60, relates the role of that company. Richard L. Troutman, "Stock Raising in the Antebellum Bluegrass," *Register* 55 (1957): 15-28, shows the progress made by 1860. See also Lucien Beckner, "Kentucky's Glamorous Shorthorn Age," *FCHQ* 26 (1952): 37-53; and Worth Estes, "Henry Clay As a Livestock Breeder," *FCHQ* 32 (1958): 350-55.

Isaac Lippincott, *History of Manufacturing in the Ohio Valley to the Year 1860* (1914), is a comprehensive survey; J.B. DeBow, *Industrial Resources of the Southern and Western States,* 3 vols. (1852-53), contains many references to Kentucky's industry. David L. Smiley, "Cassius M. Clay and Southern Industrialism," *FCHQ* 28 (1954): 315-27, examines Clay's advocacy of manufacturing. Julia Neal, "Shaker Industries in Kentucky," *Antiques* 105 (1974): 603-11, describes the manufacture and distribution of products at the two Shaker communities in the state. Iron manufacturing is examined in J. Winston Coleman Jr., "Old Kentucky Iron Furnaces," *FCHQ* 31 (1957): 227-42; Donald E. Rist, *Kentucky Iron Furnaces of the Hanging Rock Iron Region* (1974); and O.M. Mather, "Aetna Furnace, Hart County, Kentucky (1816-5-)," *Register* 39 (1941): 95-105. The story of bourbon is told in Henry G. Crowgey, *Kentucky Bourbon: The Early Years of Whiskey Making* (1971); and Gerald Carson, *The Social History of Bourbon* (1963). Davis W. Maurer, *Kentucky Moonshine* (1974), reports on a persistent industry in the state. Saltpeter mining and the manufacture of gunpowder have attracted considerable attention. Some representative articles are Angelo I. George, "Saltpeter and Gunpowder Manufacturing in Kentucky," *FCHQ* 60 (1986): 189-217; Carol Hill and Duane DePaepe, "Saltpeter Mining in Kentucky Caves," *Register* 77 (1979): 247-62; and Gary A. O'Dell, "Bluegrass Powdermen: A Sketch of the Industry," *Register* 87 (1989): 99-117. Mammoth Cave has received attention in Burton Faust, "The History of Saltpetre Mining in Mammoth Cave, Kentucky," *FCHQ* 41 (1967): 5-20, 127-40, 227-62, 323-32. A family enterprise is examined in Gary A. O'Dell, "The Trotter Family, Gunpowder, and Early Kentucky Entrepreneurship, 1784-1833," *Register* 88 (1990): 394-430. William Allen Pusey, "Grahamton and the Early Textile Mills of Kentucky," *FCHQ* 5 (1931): 123-35, describes another early state industry. Tyrel G. Moore, "Economic Development in Appalachian Kentucky, 1800-1860," in *Appalachian Frontiers: Settlement, Society, and Development in the Pre-industrial Era,* edited by Robert D. Mitchell (1991), discusses the limited industry in eastern Kentucky.

Thomas D. Clark, "Salt, a Factor in the Settlement of Kentucky," *FCHQ* 12 (1938): 42-52, explains the importance of that commodity. Two salt operations are described in William M. Talley, "Salt Lick Creek and Its Salt Works," *Register* 64 (1966): 85-109; and Robert E. McDowell, "Bullitt's Lick, the Related Saltworks and Settlements," *FCHQ* 30 (1956): 241-69. The early coal industry is discussed in Roy Carson, "Coal Industry in Kentucky," *FCHQ* 40 (1966): 29-42; and Willard Rouse Jillson, "A History of the Coal Industry in Kentucky," *Register* 20 (1922): 21-45. Jillson also wrote "Kentucky Petroleum: Its History and Present Status," *Register* 17 (1919): 47-49, but also see Mrs. C.M. McGee, "The Great American Oil Well, Burkesville, Kentucky," *FCHQ* 33 (1959): 318-26.

Aspects of Kentucky's commerce have been studied in several articles: see Elizabeth Parr, "Kentucky's Overland Trade with the Antebellum South," *FCHQ* 2 (1928): 71-81; Thomas D. Clark, "Live Stock Trade between Kentucky and the South, 1840-1860," *Register* 27 (1929): 569-81; idem, "The Ante-bellum Hemp Trade of Kentucky with the Cotton Belt," *Register* 27 (1929): 538-44; and Martha Kreipke, "The Falls of the Ohio and the Development of the Ohio River Trade, 1810-1860," *FCHQ* 54 (1980): 196-217. An important person in the state's commercial development is presented in James A. Ramage, *John Wesley Hunt: Pioneer Merchant, Manufacturer, and Financier* (1974). Robert Spencer Cotterill, "James Guthrie—Kentuckian, 1792-1869," *Register* 20 (1922): 290-96, is a brief account of a man who was active in many phases of the state's economic and political life.

The legislative journals and the statute law contain much information about the state's banks and tax laws. Basil W. Duke, best known for Civil War exploits, wrote *A History of the Bank of Kentucky* (1895), but also see Dale Royalty, "Banking and the Commonwealth Ideal in Kentucky, 1806-1822," *Register* 77 (1979): 91-107; idem, "James Prentiss and the Failure of the Kentucky Insurance Company, 1813-1818," *Register* 73 (1975): 1-16; and William C. Mallalieu and Sabri M. Akural, "Kentucky Banks in the Crisis Decade: 1834-1844," *Register* 65 (1967): 294-303. Nollie Olin Taff, *History of State Revenue and Taxation in Kentucky* (1931), is a valuable study of an often-neglected function of state government. Lee Soltow, "Kentucky Wealth at the End of the Eighteenth Century," *Journal of Economic History* 43 (1983): 617-33, describes some unexpected wealth. James C. Klotter, "Two Centuries of the Lottery in Kentucky," *Register* 87 (1989): 405-25, relates the use of a nontax source of income.

Paul Salstrom, *Appalachia's Path to Dependency: Rethinking a Region's Economic History, 1730-1940* (1994), discusses the origins of the economic problems in one of the state's most depressed areas.

Chapter 11. Social and Cultural Changes

Too little has been written about women in antebellum Kentucky, in large part because they were so restricted by law and custom that they had little opportunity to demonstrate their talents. Margaret Ripley Wolfe, *Daughters of Canaan: A Saga of Southern Women* (1995), provides an excellent overview. Helen Deiss Irvin, *Women in Kentucky* (1979); and Margaret Ripley Wolfe, "Fallen Leaves and Missing Pages: Women in Kentucky History," *Register* 90 (1992): 64-89, are the best guides to the status of women in the commonwealth. Nancy Disher Baird and Carol Crowe-Carraco, "A 'True Woman's Sphere': Motherhood in Late Antebellum Kentucky," *FCHQ* 66 (1992): 369-94, describes a woman's "proper" role. Carol Guethlein ("Women in Louisville: Moving toward Equal Rights," *FCHQ* 55 [1981]: 151-78) found that most progress came after the Civil War. A few studies of individuals have been done. Miriam Corcoran, "Catherine Spalding—Sister and Servant," *FCHQ* 62 (1988): 260-67; and Sister Mary Michael Creamer, "Mother Catherine Spalding—St. Catherine Street, Louisville, Kentucky," *FCHQ* 63 (1989): 191-223, tell of a woman who achieved a great deal on her own. Anna Cook Beauchamp gained fame because of her part in the Beauchamp-Sharp affair: see Willard Rouse Jillson, "The Beauchamp-Sharp

Tragedy in American Literature," *Register* 36 (1938): 54-60; and J.W. Cooke, "Portrait of a Murderess: Anna Cook(e) Beauchamp," *FCHQ* 65 (1991): 209-30. Carol DeLatte, *Lucy Audubon: A Biography* (1982), tells the story of the life of the wife of a famous man. Some knowledge of wives can be gleaned from the biographies of such Kentucky figures as Daniel Boone, John Breckinridge, and Henry Clay. James C. Klotter, *The Breckinridges of Kentucky, 1760-1981* (1986), has a great deal of information about some exceptional women, but the pre–Civil War women did not have the opportunities available to those who came later. Too few studies exist of individuals; see Willard Rouse Jillson, "A Sketch of the Life and Times of Rebecca Witten Graham, of Floyd County, Kentucky, 1775-1843," *Register* 37 (1939): 116-26.

Ellis Hartford, *The Little White Schoolhouse* (1977); and Edwin A. Doyle, Ruby Layson, and Anne Armstrong Thompson, eds., *From the Fort to the Future: Educating the Children of Kentucky* (1987), are two good general studies of the state's public schools. Others include Moses E. Ligon, *A History of Public Education in Kentucky* (1942); Frank L. McVey, *The Gates Open Slowly: A History of Education in Kentucky* (1949); and C.W. Hackensmith, *Out of Time and Tide: The Evolution of Education in Kentucky* (1970). A perceptive overview is Thomas D. Clark, "Kentucky Education through Two Centuries of Political and Social Change," *Register* 83 (1985): 173-201. Edsel T. Godby, "The Governors of Kentucky and Education, 1780-1852," *Bulletin of the Bureau of School Services* 32 (1960): 1-122; Frank F. Mathias, "Kentucky's Struggle for Common Schools, 1820-1850," *Register* 82 (1984): 214-34; and William Hutchinson Vaughan, *Robert Jefferson Breckinridge As an Educational Administrator* (1937), all address the antebellum years. Marion B. Lucas, *A History of Blacks in Kentucky: From Slavery to Segregation, 1760-1891* (1992); and Clarence L. Timberlake, "The Early Struggle for Education of the Blacks in the Commonwealth of Kentucky," *Register* 71 (1973): 225-52, show what little was achieved in education for blacks before the Civil War. Ella Wells

Drake, "Choctaw Academy: Richard M. Johnson and the Business of Indian Education," *Register* 91 (1993): 260-97, describes one of the state's most unusual schools.

Higher education fared better in antebellum Kentucky than did the public schools. Alvin F. Lewis, *A History of Higher Education in Kentucky* (1899), is still useful although dated. Earl Gregg Swem, "Kentuckians at William and Mary College before 1861 with a Sketch of the College before That Date," *FCHQ* 23 (1949): 173-98, describes one alternative to attending a college in the state. Most of the accounts of higher education focus on a particular school. John D. Wright Jr., *Transylvania: Tutor to the West* (1975), can be supplemented by James L. Miller Jr., "Transylvania University As the Nation Saw It, 1818-1828," *FCHQ* 34 (1960): 305-18; William J. McGlothin, "Rev. Horace Holley: Transylvania's Unitarian President, 1818-1827," *FCHQ* 51 (1977): 234-48; and Huntley Dupre, "Transylvania University and Rafinesque, 1819-1826," *FCHQ* 35 (1961): 110-21. James F. Hopkins, *The University of Kentucky: Origins and Early Years* (1951), clarifies the start of the University of Kentucky, while Dwayne Cox, "A History of the University of Louisville" (Ph.D. diss., University of Kentucky, 1984), does the same for the University of Louisville. Elisabeth S. Peck and Emily Ann Smith, *Berea's First 125 Years, 1855-1980* (1955), revised in 1982; Walter H. Rankins, *Augusta College* (1957); Hardin Craig, *Centre College of Kentucky: A Tradition and an Opportunity* (1967); Robert Snyder, *A History of Georgetown College* (1979); and Felix Newton Pitt, "Two Early Catholic Colleges in Kentucky: St. Thomas and Gethsemani," *FCHQ* 38 (1964): 133-48, tell the stories of other early colleges.

John B. Boles, *Religion in Antebellum Kentucky* (1976), is an excellent introduction to a topic about which much has been written. Boles's *The Great Revival, 1787-1805: The Origins of the Southern Evangelical Mind* (1972), is also a fine introduction to a particular religious phase. It should be supplemented by William L. Hiemstra, "Early Frontier Revivalism in Kentucky," *Register* 59 (1961): 133-49; Mariam S. Houchens, "The Great Revival of 1800," *Register* 69 (1971): 216-34; and Paul K. Conkin, *Cane Ridge: America's Pentecost* (1990). Some of the most interesting articles on religion are Charles R. Staples, "Pioneer Kentucky Preachers and Pulpits," *FCHQ* 9 (1935): 135-57; Walter B. Posey, "Baptist Watch-Care in Early Kentucky," *Register* 34 (1936): 311-17; Howard Elmo Short, "Some Early Church Experiences," *Register* 49 (1951): 269-79; and George W. Ranck, "'The Travelling Church': An Account of the Baptist Exodus from Virginia to Kentucky in 1781," *Register* 79 (1981): 240-65. Lee Shai Weissbach, *The Synagogues of Kentucky: Architecture and History* (1995), makes important contributions to both religious and architectural history. Some of the most interesting religious writing deals with ministers: W.P. Strickland, ed., *Autobiography of Peter Cartwright, the Backwoods Preacher* (1856); David R. Driscoll Jr., "Stephen Theodore Badin, Priest of Frontier Kentucky," *FCHQ* 31 (1957): 243-66; the Reverend Monsignor Charles C. Boldrick, "Martin John Spalding, 1810-1872: Second Bishop of Louisville, 1848-1864," *FCHQ* 33 (1959): 3-25; John R. Finger, "Witness to Expansion: Bishop Francis Asbury on the Trans-Appalachian Frontier," *Register* 82 (1984): 334-57; and Richard L. Troutman, ed., *"The Heavens Are Weeping": The Diaries of George Richard Browder, 1852-1886* (1987).

The Shakers have attracted more attention than any group of comparable size. A fine general study is Stephen J. Stein, *The Shaker Experience in America: A History of the United Society of Believers* (1992). Both Kentucky communities are studied in Julia Neal, *The Kentucky Shakers* (1982). Julia Neal, *By Their Fruits: The Story of Shakerism in South Union* (1947); and Julia Neal, ed., *The Journal of Eldress Nancy* (1963), tell the South Union story. On textile manufacturing by the South Union Shakers, see Jonathan Jeffrey and Donna Parker, "A Thread of Evidence: Shaker Textiles at South Union, Kentucky," *Register* 94 (1996): 33-58. Thomas D. Clark and Gerald F. Ham, *Pleasant Hill and Its Shakers* (1968); and Samuel W. Thomas and James C. Thomas, *The Simple Spirit: A Pictorial*

History of Pleasant Hill (1973), relate the story of the community at Pleasant Hill.

The limited antebellum literature that was produced in Kentucky is discussed in William Smith Ward, *A Literary History of Kentucky* (1988); and John Wilson Townsend, *Kentucky in American Letters,* 2 vols. (1913). Dorothy Townsend added a third volume of *Kentucky in American Letters* in 1976.

Herndon J. Evans, *The Newspaper Press in Kentucky* (1976); Donald B. Towels, *The Press of Kentucky, 1787-1994* (1994); and W.H. Perrin, *The Pioneer Press of Kentucky* (1888), are the best general surveys. George D. Prentice has been the subject of several studies, including Betty C. Congleton, "George D. Prentice: Nineteenth Century Southern Editor," *Register* 65 (1967): 94-119; and idem, "The Louisville Journal: Its Origin and Early Years," *Register* 62 (1964): 87-103. J. Winston Coleman Jr., "John Bradford and the *Kentucky Gazette,*" *FCHQ* 34 (1960): 24-34; and Thomas D. Clark, introduction to *The Voice of the Frontier: John Bradford's Notes on Kentucky,* edited by Thomas D. Clark (1993), provide sketches of Bradford. His role as a printer brought on a debate in the 1930s: see Willard Rouse Jillson, "A Sketch of Thomas Parvin—First Printer of Kentucky," *Register* 34 (1936): 395-99; and Samuel M. Wilson, "John Bradford, Not Thomas Parvin, First Printer in Kentucky," *FCHQ* 11 (1937): 145-51. Mary Verhoeff, "Louisville's First Newspaper—*The Farmers Library,*" *FCHQ* 21 (1947): 275-300; and Martin F. Schmidt, "The Early Printers of Louisville, 1800-1860," *FCHQ* 40 (1966): 307-34, discuss early journalism in the Falls City. Other newspapers and editors are discussed in Paul C. Pappas, "Stewart's *Kentucky Herald,* 1795-1803," *Register* 67 (1969): 335-49; James D. Daniels, "Amos Kendall: Kentucky Journalist, 1815-1829," *FCHQ* 52 (1978): 46-65; and Ronald Rayman, "Frontier Journalism in Kentucky: Joseph Montfort Street and the *Western World,* 1806-1809," *Register* 76 (1978): 98-111. Cherry Cartwright Parker, "*The Medley:* First Magazine of the New West," *FCHQ* 40 (1966): 167-78, discusses the start of magazines in Kentucky.

John H. Ellis, *Medicine in Kentucky* (1977), is a useful introduction to the subject. Emmet F. Horine, "A History of the Louisville Medical Institute and of the Establishment of the University of Louisville and Its School of Medicine, 1833-1846," *FCHQ* 7 (1933): 133-47, has been augmented by Dwayne Cox, "The Louisville Medical Institute: A Case History in American Medical Education," *FCHQ* 62 (1988): 197-219; and idem, "From Competition to Consolidation: Medical Education in Louisville, 1850-1889," *FCHQ* 66 (1992): 562-77. Among the articles dealing with aspects of Kentucky's medical history are Philip D. Jordan, "Milksickness in Kentucky and the Western Country," *FCHQ* 19 (1945): 29-40; Nancy Disher Baird, "Asiatic Cholera's First Visit to Kentucky: A Study in Panic and Fear," *FCHQ* 48 (1974): 228-40; idem, "Asiatic Cholera: Kentucky's First Public Health Instructor," *FCHQ* 48 (1974): 327-41; Lucien Beckner, "Groping for Health in the Mammoth Cave," *FCHQ* 20 (1946): 302-7; Aloma Williams Dew, "From Cramps to Consumption: Women's Health in Owensboro, Ky., during the Civil War," *Register* 74 (1976): 85-98; and Ronald F. White, "John Rowan Allen, M.D., and the Early Years of the Psychiatric Profession in Kentucky, 1844-1854," *FCHQ* 63 (1989): 5-23.

The state's most famous operation has been studied in August Schachner, *Ephraim McDowell: "Father of Ovariotomy" and Founder of Abdominal Surgery* (1921); and Laman A. Gray, "Ephraim McDowell: Father of Abdominal Surgery, Biographical Data," *FCHQ* 43 (1969): 216-29. The patient has received attention in Mrs. Arthur Thomas McCormack, "Our Pioneer Heroine of Surgery—Mrs. Jane Todd Crawford," *FCHQ* 6 (1932): 109-23.

Other physicians have received biographical attention: see J. Christian Bay, "Dr. Daniel Drake, 1785-1852," *FCHQ* 7 (1933): 1-17; P. Albert Davies, "Charles Wilkins Short, 1794-1863," *FCHQ* 19 (1945): 131-55, 208-49; Nancy Disher Baird, *David Wendel Yandell: Physician of Old Louisville* (1978); and idem, *Luke Pryor Blackburn: Physician, Governor, Reformer* (1979).

The theater provided entertainment for many Kentuckians from an early day. West T. Hill Jr., *The Theatre in Early Kentucky, 1790-1820* (1971), is a fine survey. John J. Weisert has written extensively on the Kentucky theater in such articles as "Beginnings of German Theatricals in Louisville," *FCHQ* 26 (1952): 347-59; "Beginnings of the Kentucky Theatre Circuit," *FCHQ* 34 (1960): 264-85; "The First Decade at Sam Drake's Louisville Theatre," *FCHQ* 39 (1965): 287-310; "Golden Days at Drake's City Theatre, 1830-1833," *FCHQ* 43 (1969): 255-70; and "An End and Several Beginnings: The Passing of Daniel Drake's City Theatre," *FCHQ* 50 (1976): 5-28. Music was also performed early in the state's history, as Joy Carden shows in *Music in Lexington before 1840* (1980). Burt Feintuck, *Kentucky Folkmusic* (1985); and Charles K. Wolfe, *Kentucky Country: Folk and Country Music of Kentucky* (1982), discuss the music most widely played in the state.

A favorite amusement for those who could afford it was a visit to one of the springs described by J. Winston Coleman Jr. in *The Springs of Kentucky* (1955) and "Old Kentucky Watering Places," *FCHQ* 16 (1942): 1-26. Three of the best-known springs have received particular attention in Mai Flournoy van Deren Van Arsdall, "The Springs at Harrodsburg," *Register* 61 (1963): 300-328; Martha Stephenson, "Old Graham Springs," *Register* 12 (1914): 27-35; and Audrea McDowell, "The Pursuit of Health and Happiness at the Paroquet Springs in Kentucky, 1838 to 1888," *FCHQ* 69 (1995): 390-420. The everyday amusements of nineteenth-century Kentuckians are mentioned in passing in many manuscripts and autobiographical writings of the period.

Useful overviews of Kentucky's architecture are provided in Clay Lancaster, *Antebellum Architecture of Kentucky* (1991); idem, "Kentucky's Architectural Firsts," *Antiques* 52 (1947): 331-43; Rexford Newcomb, *Old Kentucky Architecture* (1940); and idem, "Kentucky Architecture: Your Heritage—Its Meaning Today," *FCHQ* 26 (1952): 209-22. Among the best specialized studies are Julian C. Oberwarth and William B. Scott Jr., *A*

History of the Profession of Architecture in Kentucky (1987); Lois L. Olcott, "Public Architecture of Kentucky before 1870," *Antiques* 105 (1974): 830-39; J. Winston Coleman Jr., "Early Lexington Architects and Their Work," *FCHQ* 42 (1968): 222-34; James C. Thomas, "Shaker Architecture in Kentucky," *FCHQ* 53 (1979): 26-36; Rexford Newcomb, "Gideon Shryock—Pioneer Greek Revivalist of the Middle West," *Register* 26 (1928): 221-35; and Alfred J. Andrews, "Gideon Shryock, Kentucky Architect, and Greek Revival Architecture in Kentucky," *FCHQ* 18 (1944): 67-77. Richard S. DeCamp, *The Bluegrass of Kentucky: A Glimpse of the Charm of Central Kentucky Architecture* (1985), focuses on the Bluegrass region. William Lynwood Montell and Michael Lynn Morse, *Kentucky Folk Architecture* (1976), describes the most common architecture during the early days.

Kentucky artists of the antebellum years were most successful as portrait painters, before photography began to offer cheaper likenesses. J. Winston Coleman Jr., *Three Kentucky Artists: Hart, Price, Troye* (1974), can be supplemented with Gayle R. Carver, "Joel Tanner Hart: Kentucky's Poet-Sculptor," *Register* 38 (1940): 49-53; David B. Dearinger, "The Diary of Joel Tanner Hart, Kentucky Sculptor," *FCHQ* 64 (1990): 5-31; and William Barrow Floyd, "Edward Troye, Sporting Artist," *Antiques* 105 (1974): 799-817. The state's best-known portraitist is the subject of E.A. Jonas, *Matthew Harris Jouett: Kentucky Portrait Painter (1787-1827)* (1938). Two lesser-known artists are presented in Edna Talbott Whitley, "George Beck, an Eighteenth Century Painter," *Register* 67 (1969): 20-36; and Martin F. Schmidt, "The Artist and the Artisan: Two Men of Early Louisville," *FCHQ* 62 (1988): 32-51. Artist Thomas Campbell and artisan Colin R. Milne started lithographic printing in the Falls City. The most recent biography of John J. Audubon is Shirley Streshinsky, *Audubon: Life and Art in the American Wilderness* (1993). Clark Keating, *Audubon: The Kentucky Years* (1976); and J. David Book, "Audubon in Louisville, 1807-1810," *FCHQ* 45 (1971): 186-98, focus on the artist's time in Kentucky.

Silversmiths have received the most attention among the state's artisans. Good starting points for a study of their work are Marquis Boultinghouse, *Silversmiths, Jewelers, Clock and Watch Makers of Kentucky, 1785-1900* (1980); Noble W. Hiatt and Lucy F. Hiatt, *The Silversmiths of Kentucky, 1785-1850* (1954); Margaret M. Bridwell, "Kentucky's Silversmiths before 1850," *FCHQ* 16 (1942): 111-26; and idem, "Edward West: Silversmith and Inventor," *FCHQ* 21 (1947): 301-8. State glassmakers have been studied in Jane Keller Caldwell, "Early Kentucky Glass," *Antiques* 52 (1947): 368-69; and Henry Charles Edelen, "Nineteenth-Century Kentucky Glass," *Antiques* 105 (1974): 825-29. Mark Washington Clarke, *Kentucky Quilts and Their Makers* (1976), reprinted in 1993; and Lou Tate, "Kentucky's Coverlets," *Antiques* 105 (1974): 901-5, describe activities that have attracted many Kentucky women since pioneer days. Riflemakers have been considered in Thomas A. Strohfeldt, "The Kentucky Long Rifle," *Antiques* 105 (1974): 840-43; idem, "Jacob Rizer: A Bardstown Riflemaker," *FCHQ* 48 (1974): 5-15; and Shelby W. Gallien, "David Weller, an Early Kentucky Gunsmith," *FCHQ* 60 (1986): 5-36. For information on furniture makers, consult Mrs. Wade Hampton Whitley, *A Checklist of Kentucky Cabinetmakers from 1775-1859* (1970); and Lois L. Olcott, "Kentucky Federal Furniture," *Antiques* 105 (1974): 870-82. Kenneth Clarke and Ira Kohn, *Kentucky's Age of Wood* (1976), is an interesting discussion of woodworking during the nineteenth century. Frances L.S. Dugan and Jacqueline P. Bull, *Bluegrass Craftsman: Being the Reminiscences of Ebenezer Hiram Stedman, Papermaker, 1808-1885* (1959), tells a great deal about an interesting craftsman who had opinions on many issues.

Chapter 12. Slavery and Antislavery

Marion B. Lucas, *A History of Blacks in Kentucky: From Slavery to Segregation, 1760-1891* (1992), is now the standard study of blacks in Kentucky before 1891. Still useful are J. Winston Coleman Jr., *Slavery Times in Kentucky* (1940); Ivan E. McDougle, *Slavery in Kentucky, 1792-1865* (1918); Alice Alli-

son Dunnigan, *The Fascinating Story of Black Kentuckians: Their Heritage and Traditions* (1982); and Kentucky Commission on Human Rights, *Kentucky's Black Heritage* (1971). Lowell H. Harrison, "Memories of Slavery Days in Kentucky," *FCHQ* 47 (1973): 242-57, is based on the WPA slave narratives for the state. Wallace B. Turner, "Kentucky Slavery in the Last Ante Bellum Decade," *Register* 58 (1960): 291-307; and Frank F. Mathias, "Slavery, the Solvent of Kentucky Politics," *Register* 70 (1972): 1-16, examine the "peculiar institution" just before the Civil War. Jeffrey Brooke Allen, "The Origins of Proslavery Thought in Kentucky, 1792-1799," *Register* 77 (1979): 75-90; Edward M. Post, "Kentucky Law concerning Emancipation or Freedom of Slaves," *FCHQ* 59 (1985): 344-67; and Juliet E.K. Walker, "The Legal Status of Free Blacks in Early Kentucky, 1792-1825," *FCHQ* 57 (1983): 382-95, examine some interesting aspects of the lives of blacks during the era of slavery. Richard Sears, "Working Like a Slave: Views of Slavery and the Status of Women in Antebellum Kentucky," *Register* 87 (1989): 1-19, makes an unusual comparison. Boynton Merrill Jr., *Jefferson's Nephews: A Frontier Tragedy* (1976), recalls one of the state's most grisly crimes against a slave. W.B. Hartgrove, "The Story of Josiah Henson," *JNH* 3 (1918): 1-21; and Juliet E.K. Walker, *Free Frank: A Black Pioneer on the Antebellum Frontier* (1983), tell the stories of two exceptional men. Kentucky's controversial slave trade with the Lower South has been examined in J. Winston Coleman Jr., "Lexington's Slave Dealers and Their Southern Trade," *FCHQ* 12 (1938): 1-23; Thomas D. Clark, "The Slave Trade between Kentucky and the Cotton Kingdom," *MVHR* 21 (1934): 331-42; and William Calderhead, "How Extensive Was the Border Slave Trade?" *CWH* 18 (1972): 42-55, as well as in the general histories of the state.

Lowell H. Harrison, *The Antislavery Movement in Kentucky* (1978), carries the issue to legal freedom in 1865; Asa E. Martin, *The Antislavery Movement in Kentucky prior to 1850* (1918), stopped with the third constitutional convention. Kentucky's early antislavery efforts are placed in context in Gordon E. Finnie, "The Antislavery Movement in the Upper South before 1840," *JSH* 35 (1969): 317-42. On the colonization effort, see J. Winston Coleman Jr., "The Kentucky Colonization Society," *Register* 39 (1941): 1-9; Jean Keith, "Joseph Rogers Underwood, Friend of African Colonization," *FCHQ* 22 (1948): 117-32; and Jeffrey Brooke Allen, "Did Southern Colonizationists Oppose Slavery? Kentucky, 1816-1850, As a Test Case," *Register* 75 (1977): 92-111. Wallace B. Turner ("A Rising Social Consciousness in Kentucky during the 1850s," *FCHQ* 36 [1962]: 18-31) found the development of abolitionist thought; see Turner, "Abolitionism in Kentucky," *Register* 69 (1971): 319-38. Also helpful are Jeffrey Brooke Allen, "Means and Ends in Kentucky Abolitionism, 1792-1823," *FCHQ* 57 (1983): 365-81; and idem, "Were Southern White Critics of Slavery Racists? Kentucky and the Upper South, 1791-1824," *JSH* 44 (1978): 169-90. Stanley Harrold, in "Violence and Nonviolence in Kentucky Abolitionism," *JSH* (1991): 15-38, examines a difference of opinion that hurt the state's antislavery movement. Hambleton Tapp, in "The Slavery Controversy between Robert Wickliffe and Robert J. Breckinridge prior to the Civil War," *FCHQ* 19 (1945): 156-70, recalls an extensive pamphlet battle in Kentucky history. Hambleton Tapp, "Robert J. Breckinridge and the Year 1849," *FCHQ* 12 (1938): 125-50; James P. Gregory Jr., "The Question of Slavery in the Kentucky Constitutional Convention of 1849," *FCHQ* 23 (1949): 89-110; and Victor B. Howard, "Robert J. Breckinridge and the Slavery Controversy in Kentucky in 1849," *FCHQ* 53 (1979): 328-43, deal with slavery and constitutional revision.

Cassius Marcellus Clay's violent encounters obscured the mildness of his antislavery views but have attracted numerous writers to study his career. The best biographies are David L. Smiley, *Lion of White Hall: The Life of Cassius M. Clay* (1962); and H. Edward Richardson, *Cassius Marcellus Clay: Firebrand of Freedom* (1976). Clay's own *Life of Cassius Marcellus Clay: Memoirs, Writings, Speeches* (1886), is often inaccurate and exaggerated in his

favor. Among the many articles dealing with his antislavery stance are David L. Smiley, "Cassius M. Clay and Southern Abolitionism," *Register* 49 (1951): 331-36; idem, "Cassius M. Clay and John G. Fee: A Study in Southern Antislavery Thought," *JNH* 42 (1957): 201-13; Stanley Harrold, "The Intersectional Relationship between Cassius M. Clay and the Garrisonian Abolitionists," *CWH* 35 (1989): 101-19; and Lowell H. Harrison, "Cassius Marcellus Clay and the *True American*," *FCHQ* 22 (1948): 30-49. The unusual Clay-Fee relationship is examined in Richard Sears, *The Kentucky Abolitionists in the Midst of Slavery, 1854-1864: Exiles for Freedom* (1993).

Three other Kentucky abolitionists are described in Randolph Paul Runyon, *Delia Webster and the Underground Railroad* (1996); J. Winston Coleman Jr., "Delia Webster and Calvin Fairbank—Underground Railroad Agents," *FCHQ* 17 (1943): 129-42; and Will Frank Steely, "William Shreve Bailey: Kentucky Abolitionist," *FCHQ* 31 (1957): 274-81. Larry Ceplair, "Mattie Griffith Browne: A Kentucky Abolitionist," *FCHQ* 68 (1994): 219-31, tells the story of a woman who freed her slaves, then moved to the North to write against slavery.

Victor B. Howard, *Black Liberation in Kentucky: Emancipation and Freedom, 1862-1884* (1983), is a detailed account that goes beyond the final legal action. See also Marion B. Lucas, *A History of Blacks in Kentucky: From Slavery to Segregation, 1760-1891* (1992). President Lincoln's concerns regarding slavery are treated in Robert W. Johannsen, *Lincoln, the South, and Slavery: The Political Dimension* (1991); William H. Townsend, *Lincoln and the Bluegrass: Slavery and the Civil War in Kentucky* (1955); and Lowell H. Harrison, "Lincoln and Compensated Emancipation in Kentucky," *Lincoln Herald* 84 (1982): 11-17.

The plight of blacks at Camp Nelson during the Civil War has been studied in Richard D. Sears, *"A Practical Recognition of the Brotherhood of Man": John G. Fee and the Camp Nelson Experience* (1986); and Marion B. Lucas, "Camp Nelson, Kentucky, during the Civil War: Cradle of Liberty or Refugee Death Camp?" *FCHQ* 63 (1989): 439-52.

Chapter 13. The Road to War

Good overviews of the sectional controversies of the 1850s are David M. Potter, *The Impending Crisis, 1848-1861* (1976); Michael F. Holt, *The Political Crisis of the 1850s* (1978); Allan Nevins, *The Ordeal of the Union,* 2 vols. (1947); and idem, *The Emergence of Lincoln,* 2 vols. (1950). David M. Potter, *Lincoln and His Party in the Secession Crisis* (1942); and Kenneth Stampp, *And the War Came: The North and the Secession Crisis, 1860-1861* (1950), focus on the 1860 election and the subsequent secession movement.

E. Merton Coulter, *The Civil War and Readjustment in Kentucky* (1926), is still the most complete study of developments in the state during the secession crisis. James R. Robertson, "Sectionalism in Kentucky from 1855 to 1865," *MVHR* 4 (1917): 49-63; and Harry August Volz III, "Party, State, and Nation: Kentucky and the Coming of the American Civil War" (Ph.D. diss., University of Virginia, 1982), are good accounts of Kentucky's place in the sectional disputes and the secession movement. David L. Porter, "The Kentucky Press and the Election of 1860," *FCHQ* 46 (1972): 49-52, describes sharp differences within the state.

John J. Crittenden was a national leader in the futile efforts to find an acceptable compromise. Albert D. Kirwan, *John J. Crittenden: The Struggle for the Union* (1962), is a fine biography, but see also Donald W. Zacharias, "John J. Crittenden Crusades for the Union and Neutrality in Kentucky," *FCHQ* 38 (1964): 193-205; Jack Kelly, "John J. Crittenden and the Constitutional Union Party," *FCHQ* 48 (1974): 265-76; and Patsy S. Ledbetter, "John J. Crittenden and the Compromise Debacle," *FCHQ* 51 (1977): 125-42. Peter B. Knupfer, in *The Union As It Is: Constitutional Unionism and Sectional Compromise, 1787-1861* (1991), sees the 1860-61 efforts as part of an American political tradition. Christopher R. Waldrep, "Rank-and-File Voters and the Coming of the Civil War: Caldwell County, Kentucky, As a Test Case," *CWH* 35 (1989): 59-72, is an interesting study that needs to be repeated for a number of counties.

William T. McKinney, "The Defeat of the Secessionists in Kentucky in 1861," *JNH* 1 (1916): 377-91; Wallace B. Turner, "The Secession Movement in Kentucky," *Register* 66 (1968): 259-78; James E. Copeland, "Where Were the Kentucky Unionists and Secessionists?" *Register* 71 (1973): 344-63; and Lowell H. Harrison, "Governor Magoffin and the Secession Crisis," *Register* 72 (1974): 91-110, all examine the failure of the secession movement in the state. See also Lowell H. Harrison, *The Civil War in Kentucky* (1975), reprinted in 1988; and idem, "The Civil War in Kentucky: Some Persistent Questions," *Register* 76 (1978): 1-21. Kentucky's unusual neutrality is discussed in A.C. Quisenberry, "Kentucky's 'Neutrality' in 1861," *Register* 15 (1917): 9-21; Wilson Porter Shortridge, "Kentucky's Neutrality in 1861," *MVHR* 9 (1923): 283-301; and Steven E. Woodworth, "'The Indeterminate Quantities': Jefferson Davis, Leonidas Polk, and the End of Kentucky's Neutrality, September 1861," *CWH* 38 (1992): 289-97.

Much of the story of these troubled years can be found in the biographies of those who participated actively in the events. In addition to the biographies cited above for John J. Crittenden and Cassius M. Clay, the following sources are useful: Patrick Sowle, "Cassius Clay and the Crisis of the Union, 1860-1861," *Register* 65 (1967): 144-49; William C. Davis, *Breckinridge: Statesman, Soldier, Symbol* (1974); Frank H. Heck, *Proud Kentuckian: John C. Breckinridge* (1976); and Lowell H. Harrison, "John C. Breckinridge: Nationalist, Confederate, Kentuckian," *FCHQ* 47 (1973): 125-44. James C. Klotter, *The Breckinridges of Kentucky, 1760-1981* (1986), describes the roles of both Unionist Robert J. Breckinridge and his Confederate nephew, John C. Breckinridge, as well as some of the less well-known members of this family.

The Provisional Government of Confederate Kentucky is described in several articles by Lowell H. Harrison: "George W. Johnson and Richard

Hawes: The Governors of Confederate Kentucky," *Register* 79 (1981): 3-39; "Letters of George W. Johnson," *Register* 40 (1942): 337-52; and "Confederate Kentucky: The State That Almost Was," *Civil War Times Illustrated* 12 (1973): 12-21. *The War of the Rebellion: A Compilation of the Official Records of the Union and Confederate Armies,* 128 vols. (1880-1901), usually cited as *Official Records* or *OR,* is an incomparable collection of source materials for the Civil War period. Some thirty volumes contain information relating to Kentucky, including a number of documents dealing with the state's neutrality.

Chapter 14. The Civil War

In addition to the *Official Records,* other publications contain much information about Kentucky's part in the Civil War, including *Official Records of the Union and Confederate Navies in the War of the Rebellion,* 30 vols. (1894-1922); and Robert Underwood Johnson and Clarence Clough Buel, eds., *Battles and Leaders of the Civil War,* 4 vols. (1887-88). E. Merton Coulter, *The Civil War and Readjustment in Kentucky* (1926), is excellent on economic and political developments; it pays little attention to the military situation. Lowell H. Harrison, *The Civil War in Kentucky* (1975), reprinted in 1988, is limited by the format of the series of which it is a part, but it does devote more attention to military affairs in the state. The rosters and brief histories of the Kentucky units in both armies are found in *Report of the Adjutant General of the State of Kentucky: Union Troops, 1861-1866,* 2 vols. (1867); and *Report of the Adjutant General of the State of Kentucky: Confederate Kentucky Volunteers,* 2 vols. (1918). Thomas Speed, *The Union Cause in Kentucky, 1860-1865* (1907); and idem, *The Union Regiments of Kentucky* (1897), should be balanced by the equally partisan J. Stoddard Johnston, *Kentucky,* vol. 9 of *Confederate Mili-tary History,* edited by Clement A. Evans, 10 vols. (1899). Hambleton Tapp, ed., "The Civil War Annals of Kentucky," *FCHQ* 35 (1961): 205-322, is a reprint of the appropriate annals in Richard H. Collins and Lewis Collins, *History of Kentucky,* 2 vols. (1874). Richard G. Stone Jr., in *Kentucky Fighting Men, 1861-1945*

(1982), looks at the Kentuckians who fought on each side in the Civil War.

The most famous Confederate unit from Kentucky has been well studied in Ed Porter Thompson, *History of the Orphan Brigade* (1898); William C. Davis, *The Orphan Brigade: The Kentucky Confederates Who Couldn't Go Home* (1980); and in two excellent diaries from members of the brigade: William C. Davis, ed., *Diary of a Confederate Soldier: John S. Jackman of the Orphan Brigade* (1990); and Albert D. Kirwan, ed., *Johnny Green of the Orphan Brigade* (1956). Kentucky's most famous Federal unit has been studied in Sergeant E. Tarrent, *The Wild Riders of the First Kentucky Cavalry: A History of the Regiment, in the Great War of the Rebellion, 1861-1865* (1894); and Hambleton Tapp, "Incidents in the Life of Frank Wolford, Colonel of the First Kentucky Union Cavalry," *FCHQ* 10 (1936): 82-99. John Hunt Morgan has received more attention than any other state participant in the war. James A. Ramage, *Rebel Raider: The Life of General John Hunt Morgan* (1986), is a superior scholarly biography; most of the others are uncritical paeans of praise. Excellent accounts of Duke's command are Basil W. Duke, *History of Morgan's Cavalry* (1867); and idem, *Reminiscences of General Basil W. Duke, C.S.A.* (1911), but see also Lowell H. Harrison, "General Basil W. Duke, C.S.A.," *FCHQ* 54 (1980): 5-36. Edison H. Thomas, *John Hunt Morgan and His Raiders* (1975), is another modern study. Edwin C. Bearss did an intensive study of the Christmas Raid in "Morgan's Second Kentucky Raid, December, 1862," *Register* 70 (1972): 200-18; 71 (1973): 177-88, 426-38; 72 (1974): 20-37. Brief biographies of Kentucky's numerous generals can be found in Ezra J. Warner, *Generals in Blue* (1964); and William C. Davis, ed., *The Confederate General,* 6 vols. (1991). The role of Kentucky cavalrymen is well described in Kenneth A. Hafendorfer, *They Died by Twos and Threes* (1996).

The battle of Mill Springs has been studied in Raymond E. Myers, *The Zollie Tree* (1964); R. Gerald McMurtry, "Zollicoffer and the Battle of Mill Springs," *FCHQ* 29 (1955): 303-19; and C. David Dalton, "Zollicoffer, Crittenden, and the Mill Springs Campaign: Some Persistent Questions," *FCHQ* 60 (1986): 463-71. The disastrous Donelson campaign is considered in great detail in Benjamin Franklin Cooling, *Forts Henry and Donelson: The Key to the Confederate Heartland* (1987). The Confederate efforts to hold southern Kentucky are examined in Charles P. Roland, *Albert Sidney Johnston: Soldier of Three Republics* (1964); and William Preston Johnston, *The Life of General Albert Sidney Johnston* (1878). Steven E. Woodworth, *Jefferson Davis and His Generals: The Failure of Confederate Command in the West* (1990), is an excellent discussion of Confederate military leadership in the western theater. Thomas L. Connelly, *Army of the Heartland: The Army of Tennessee, 1861-1862* (1967); and Stanley F. Horn, *Army of Tennessee* (1953), provide good coverage of the periods when Confederates were in much of the state. The many specialized studies of aspects of the Civil War in eastern Kentucky include Henry P. Scalf, "The Battle of Ivy Mountain," *Register* 56 (1958): 11-26; Joseph D. Carr, "Garfield and Marshall in the Big Sandy Valley, 1861-1862," *FCHQ* 64 (1990): 247-63; and John David Preston, *The Civil War in the Big Sandy Valley of Kentucky* (1984).

The 1862 invasion of the state by Kirby Smith and Braxton Bragg is considered at length in Connelly's and Horn's histories of the Army of Tennessee and in James Lee McDonough, *War in Kentucky: From Shiloh to Perryville* (1994); Joseph H. Parks, *General E. Kirby Smith, C.S.A.* (1954); and Grady C. McWhiney, *Braxton Bragg and Confederate Defeat* (1969). Among the special studies of aspects of the campaign are Gary Donaldson, "'Into Africa': Kirby Smith and Braxton Bragg's Invasion of Kentucky," *FCHQ* 61 (1987): 444-65; Grady C. McWhiney, "Controversy in Kentucky: Braxton Bragg's Campaign of 1862," *CWH* 6 (1960): 5-42; Lowell H. Harrison, "Should I Surrender?—A Civil War Incident," *FCHQ* 40 (1966): 297-306; A.C. Quisenberry, "The Battles of Big Hill and Richmond, Kentucky, September 1862," *Register* 16 (1918): 9-25; and Roger C. Adams, "Panic on the Ohio: The Defense of Cincinnati, Covington, and

Newport, September, 1862," *Journal of Kentucky Studies* 9 (1992): 80-90.

The major engagement at Perryville has also attracted the efforts of a number of writers. The most complete study by far is Kenneth A. Hafendorfer, *Perryville: Battle for Kentucky* (1991); its maps are especially good. It can be supplemented with Hambleton Tapp, "The Battle of Perryville, 1862," *FCHQ* 9 (1935): 158-81; Ralph A. Wooster, "Confederate Success at Perryville," *Register* 59 (1961): 318-23; and Christen Ashby Cheek, ed., "Memoirs of Mrs. E.B. Patterson: A Perspective on Danville during the Civil War," *Register* 92 (1994): 347-399. Edwin C. Bearss has examined an important decision in "General Bragg Abandons Kentucky," *Register* 59 (1961): 217-44. Several of the generals involved in the campaign have been the subjects of biographies, which should be consulted for other perspectives.

Aided by the legend of the Lost Cause, Kentucky Confederates have received more attention than Unionists. These works help create a balance: Hambleton Tapp and James C. Klotter, eds., *The Union, the Civil War, and John W. Tuttle: A Kentucky Captain's Account* (1980); David G. Farrelly, "John Marshall Harlan and the Union Cause in Kentucky, 1861," *FCHQ* 37 (1963): 5-23; the Reverend Roger J. Bartman, "Joseph Holt and Kentucky in the Civil War," *FCHQ* 40 (1966): 105-22; Robert L. Kincaid, "Joshua Fry Speed: Lincoln's Confidential Agent in Kentucky," *Register* 52 (1954): 99-110; A.M. Ellis, "Major General William Nelson," *Register* 4 (1906): 56-64; and Will D. Gilliam Jr., "Robert J. Breckinridge: Kentucky Unionist," *Register* 69 (1971): 362-85.

Many studies exist for specialized aspects of the war and Kentucky's role in them. John David Smith has written two interesting articles about the Union recruits in the state: "The Recruitment of Negro Soldiers in Kentucky, 1863-1865," *Register* 72 (1974): 364-90; and "Kentucky Civil War Recruits: A Medical Profile," *Medical History* 24 (1980): 185-96. The plight of the pacifist Shakers is recorded in Thomas D. Clark, *Pleasant Hill in the Civil War* (1972); and Julia Neal, "South Union

Shakers during the War Years," *FCHQ* 39 (1965): 147-50. Richard L. Troutman, ed., *"The Heavens Are Weeping": The Diaries of George Richard Browder, 1852-1886* (1987), shows how the war affected a Methodist minister in south-central Kentucky. Paul G. Ashdown, "Samuel Ringgold: An Episcopal Clergyman in Kentucky and Tennessee during the Civil War," *FCHQ* 53 (1979): 231-38; and Frances L.S. Dugan, ed., "Journal of Mattie Wheeler: A Blue Grass Belle Reports on the Civil War," *FCHQ* 29 (1955): 118-44, show the war's effect on two other civilians. Palmer H. Boeger, "The Great Kentucky Hog Swindle of 1864," *JSH* 28 (1962): 59-70, describes the state's worst economic scandal of the war. Lon Carter Barton, "The Reign of Terror in Graves County," *Register* 46 (1948): 484-95; J.T. Dorris, "President Lincoln's Treatment of Kentuckians," *FCHQ* 28 (1954): 3-20; and Louis DeFalaise, "General Stephen Gano Burbridge's Command in Kentucky," *Register* 69 (1971): 101-27, help explain why most Kentuckians disliked the Lincoln administration despite its growing influence in the state. James Larry Hood explains this influence in "For the Union: Kentucky's Unconditional Unionist Congressmen and the Development of the Republican Party in Kentucky, 1863-1865," *Register* 76 (1978): 197-215.

James B. Martin, "Black Flag over the Bluegrass: Guerrilla Warfare in Kentucky, 1863-1865," *Register* 86 (1988): 352-75, is an excellent survey of a troublesome problem. Martin's article can be supplemented with Adam ("Stovepipe") Johnson, *The Partisan Rangers of the Confederate States Army* (1904); Albert Castel, "Quantrill's Missouri Bushwhackers in Kentucky," *FCHQ* 38 (1964): 125-32; Young E. Allison, "Sue Mundy: An Account of the Terrible Kentucky Guerrilla of Civil War Times," *Register* 57 (1959): 295-316; and L.L. Valentine, "Sue Mundy of Kentucky," *Register* 62 (1964): 175-205, 278-306.

Several authors have studied the impact of the war on a particular locality. The Louisville story has been told in Robert E. McDowell, *City of Conflict: Louisville in the Civil War, 1861-1865* (1962); Charles Messmer, "Louisville on the Eve of the Civil War," *FCHQ* 50 (1976): 249-89; idem, "Louisville and the Confederate Invasion of 1862," *Register* 55 (1957): 299-324; idem, "Louisville during the Civil War," *FCHQ* 52 (1978): 206-33; and William G. Eidson, "Louisville, Kentucky, during the First Year of the Civil War," *FCHQ* 38 (1964): 224-38. Other localities have received special study in James Barnett, "Munfordville in the Civil War," *Register* 69 (1971): 339-61; Aloma Williams Dew, "'Between the Hawk and the Buzzard': Owensboro during the Civil War," *Register* 77 (1979): 1-14; Eliza Calvert Hall, "Bowling Green and the Civil War," *FCHQ* 11 (1937): 241-51, which was written in 1894; Helen Bartter Crocker, "A War Divides Green River Country," *Register* 70 (1972): 295-311; and Glenn Hodges, *Fearful Times: A History of the Civil War Years in Hancock County, Kentucky* (1986).

Chapter 15. 1865 and After

The best sources for social history are various contemporary newspapers, the numerous county histories, the many personal printed recollections, the revealing letters and diaries, and, for later periods, the large body of collected interviews available in many repositories. Estate inventories and tax and census records are among the many other records that help re-create the life of a people. Still more work needs to be done on this aspect of Kentucky history.

Among the printed sources, John E. Kleber, editor in chief, *The Kentucky Encyclopedia* (1992), offers a wealth of information. P.P. Karan and Cotton Mather, eds., *The Atlas of Kentucky* (1977), is a helpful supplement. On the fifty years after the end of the Civil War, a half dozen works provide the Kentucky setting: E. Merton Coulter, *The Civil War and Readjustment in Kentucky* (1926); Ross A. Webb, *Kentucky in the Reconstruction Era* (1979); Thomas D. Clark, *Agrarian Kentucky* (1977); idem, *Kentucky: Land of Contrast* (1968); Hambleton Tapp and James C. Klotter, *Kentucky: Decades of Discord, 1865-1900* (1977); and James C. Klotter, *Kentucky: Portrait in Paradox, 1900-1950* (1996). The general histories mentioned at the beginning of this bibliography offer overviews as well.

Many works provide the national or regional perspective and details necessary to understand Kentucky. Among these are Charles Reagan Wilson and William Ferris, *Encyclopedia of Southern Culture* (1989); Edward L. Ayers, *The Promise of the New South* (1992); and Albert E. Cowdrey, *This Land, This South: An Environmental History,* rev. ed. (1996).

On specific Kentucky matters, Thomas D. Clark's *Pills, Petticoats, and Plows: The Southern Country Store* (1944), is one of his best works, while J. Winston Coleman Jr.'s evocative *Springs of Kentucky* (1955) re-creates a bygone era. Judith J. Phillips, "Enlightenment, Education, and Entertainment: A Study of the Chautauqua Movement in Kentucky" (M.A. thesis, University of Louisville, 1985); and Shelia E. Brown Heflin, "Owensboro's Chautauqua Years, 1902-1932," *Daviess County Historical Quarterly* 1 (1983): 3-14, highlight one aspect of state culture. Milton D. Feinstein, "History and Development of Football at the University of Kentucky, 1877-1920" (M.A. thesis, University of Kentucky, 1941), treats the formative era of organized sports. On the early urban setting, see Allen J. Share, *Cities in the Commonwealth* (1982); on Louisville specifically, see Gary P. Kocolowski, "Louisville at Large: Industrial-Urban Organization, Inter-City Migration, and Occupational Mobility . . . 1865-1906" (Ph.D. diss., University of Cincinnati, 1978); Charlene M. Cornell, "Louisville in Transition, 1870-1890" (M.A. thesis, University of Louisville, 1970); J. Stoddard Johnston, ed., *Memorial History of Louisville,* 2 vols. (1896); and George H. Yater, *Two Hundred Years at the Falls of the Ohio: A History of Louisville and Jefferson County* (1987). On northern Kentucky, see Paul A. Tenkotte, "Rival Cities to Suburbs: Covington and Newport, Kentucky, 1790-1890" (Ph.D. diss., University of Cincinnati, 1989).

There are many good city and county histories, too numerous to mention, and most provide the details needed to form wider generalizations. Among the best are John D. Wright Jr., *Lexington: Heart of the Bluegrass* (1982); Carl E. Kramer, *Capital on the Kentucky: A Two Hundred Year History of Frankfort and Franklin County* (1986); Lee A. Dew and Aloma Williams Dew, *Owensboro* (1988); John E.L. Robertson, *Paducah, 1830-1980* (1980); Carl B. Boyd Jr. and Hazel M. Boyd, *A History of Mt. Sterling, Kentucky, 1792-1918* (1984); Richard C. Brown, *A History of Danville and Boyle County, Kentucky, 1774-1992* (1992); William David Deskins, *Pike County* (1994); Lindsey Apple, Frederick A. Johnston, and Ann Bolton Bevins, eds., *Scott County, Kentucky: A History* (1993); and William E. Ellis, H.E. Everman, and Richard D. Sears, *Madison County* (1985). William Lynwood Montell has examined the Upper Cumberland region in a series of books that focus on race, religion, violence, and folklife.

Chapter 16. Reconstruction, Readjustment, and Race, 1865-1875

The national and regional literature on the Reconstruction era is extensive. The text and notes in James M. McPherson, *Ordeal by Fire* (1982); Michael Perman, *Reunion without Compromise* (1973); Allen W. Trelease, *White Terror* (1971); and Leon Litwack, *Been in the Storm so Long* (1979), all provide good guides. For Kentucky, county histories, newspapers, manuscript sources, and *The Kentucky Encyclopedia* all are important.

Studies that focus on the process of freedom and the lives of those experiencing it for the first time include Victor B. Howard, *Black Liberation in Kentucky: Emancipation and Freedom, 1862-1884* (1983); Marion B. Lucas, "Kentucky Blacks: The Transition from Slavery to Freedom," *Register* 91 (1993): 403-19; Paul J. Lammermeier, "The Urban Black Family of the Nineteenth Century: A Study of Black Family Structure in the Ohio Valley, 1850-1880," *Journal of Marriage and the Family* 35 (1973): 440-56; and Marion B. Lucas, *A History of Blacks in Kentucky: From Slavery to Segregation, 1760-1891* (1992). On the urban experience, see George C. Wright, *Life behind a Veil: Blacks in Louisville, Kentucky, 1865-1930* (1985), as well as three good articles on central Kentucky: Herbert A. Thomas, "Victims of Circumstance: Negroes in a Southern Town [Lexington], 1865-1880," *Register*

71 (1973): 253-71; John Kellogg, "Negro Urban Clusters in the Postbellum South," *Geographical Review* 67 (1977): 310-21; and idem, "The Formation of Black Residential Areas in Lexington, Kentucky, 1865-1887," *JSH* 48 (1982): 21-52. Zane Miller, "Urban Blacks in the South, 1865-1920," in *The New Urban History*, edited by Leo F. Schnore (1975), focuses in part on Louisville. More studies are needed of other areas of the commonwealth. Violence and the Freedmen's Bureau are examined in George C. Wright, *Racial Violence in Kentucky, 1865-1940* (1990); W.A. Low, "The Freedmen's Bureau in the Border States," in *Radicalism, Racism, and Party Alignment: The Border States during Reconstruction*, edited by Richard O. Curry (1969), 245-64; and Philip C. Kimball, "Freedom's Harvest: Freedmen's Schools in Kentucky after the Civil War," *FCHQ* 54 (1980): 272-88. Individuals leading the fight for black rights are highlighted in Kentucky Commission on Human Rights, *Kentucky's Black Heritage* (1971); Alice Allison Dunnigan, *The Fascinating Story of Black Kentuckians: Their Heritage and Traditions* (1982); and W.D. Johnson, *Biographical Sketches of Prominent Negro Men and Women of Kentucky* (1897).

The changing political world of the decade after the Civil War can be partially reconstructed from the Kentucky *Acts of the General Assembly*, as well as the Kentucky *House Journal* and *Senate Journal*. General overviews include, for the Republicans, E.A. Jonas, *A History of the Republican Party in Kentucky* (1929); and Thomas L. Owen, "The Formative Years of the Kentucky Republican Party, 1864-1871" (Ph.D. diss., University of Kentucky, 1981). On the Democrats, see Arthur J. Wormuth, "The Development of the Democratic Party in Fayette County, Kentucky, 1864-1868" (M.A. thesis, University of Kentucky, 1971); and George L. Willis Jr., *Kentucky Democracy*, 3 vols. (1935). Presidential election statistics, with analysis, can be found in Jasper B. Shannon and Ruth McQuown, comps., *Presidential Politics in Kentucky, 1824-1948* (1950).

In-depth examinations of the era come from several sources and various viewpoints. The older but still useful E. Merton Coulter, *The Civil War and Readjustment in Kentucky* (1926), set the standard for four decades, with its analysis that Kentucky turned pro-Confederate after the war's end. Thomas L. Connelly, "Neo-Confederatism or Power Vacuum: Post-war Kentucky Politics Reappraised," *Register* 64 (1966): 257-69, challenged that view, stressing instead the growth of regionalism and of various power blocs. In three studies, Ross A. Webb emphasized the commonwealth's antiadministration aspects rather than pro-Confederate elements: "Kentucky: 'Pariah among the Elect,'" in *Radicalism, Racism, and Party Alignment: The Border States during Reconstruction*, edited by Richard O. Curry (1969); *Kentucky in the Reconstruction Era* (1979); and "'The Past Is Never Dead, It's Not Even Past': Benjamin P. Runkle and the Freedmen's Bureau in Kentucky, 1866-1870," *Register* 84 (1986): 343-60. Taking a middle ground among the various views is Hambleton Tapp and James C. Klotter, *Kentucky: Decades of Discord, 1865-1900* (1977).

The connection between politics and economics is developed in Metta M. Sublett, "The Role of the Confederate Veteran in the Industrial Development of Kentucky" (M.Phil. diss., University of Wisconsin, 1945); James P. Sullivan, "Louisville and Her Southern Alliance, 1865-1890" (Ph.D. diss., University of Kentucky, 1965); and Leonard P. Curry, *Rail Routes South: Louisville's Fight for the Southern Market, 1865-1872* (1969). A good nineteenth-century source for brief treatments of year-by-year events is the *Annual Cyclopedia*.

Numerous biographical works exist. Among those dealing with Democratic leaders are Joseph F. Wall, *Henry Watterson* (1956); and Leonard N. Plummer, "The Political Leadership of Henry Watterson" (Ph.D. diss., University of Wisconsin, 1940). On W.C.P. Breckinridge, see James C. Klotter, *The Breckinridges of Kentucky, 1760-1981* (1986). On the Republican leadership, see Ross A. Webb, *Benjamin Helm Bristow* (1969); on Harlan, see Louis Hartz, "John M. Harlan in Kentucky, 1855-1877," *FCHQ* 14 (1940): 17-40; David G.

Farrelly, "Harlan's Formative Period," *Kentucky Law Journal* 46 (1958): 367-406; Thomas L. Owen, "The Pre-Court Career of John Marshall Harlan" (M.A. thesis, University of Louisville, 1970); Tinsley E. Yarbrough, *Judicial Enigma: The First Justice Harlan* (1975); and Loren P. Beth, *John Marshall Harlan: The Last Whig Justice* (1992). Sketches of the governors appear in Lowell H. Harrison, ed., *Kentucky's Governors, 1792-1985* (1985).

Chapter 17. Decades of Discord, 1875-1900

Robert M. Ireland has studied the question of violence in depth. His two articles "Homicide in Nineteenth Century Kentucky," *Register* 81 (1983): 134-53, and "Law and Disorder in Nineteenth Century Kentucky," *Vanderbilt Law Review* 32 (1979): 281-99, provide a good introduction. On individual instances of violence, see Ireland's "The Thompson-Davis Case and the Unwritten Law," *FCHQ* 62 (1988): 417-41; and L.F. Johnson, *Famous Kentucky Tragedies and Trials* (1916), reprinted in 1972. See also William Lynwood Montell, *Killings: Folk Justice in the Upper South* (1986).

Feud violence attracted much attention to Kentucky, but aside from one of the feuds, most "troubles" have not received in-depth scholarly attention. An underappreciated early general examination is Charles G. Mutzenberg's *Kentucky's Famous Feuds and Tragedies* (1897), revised in 1917; more recent ones are James C. Klotter, "Feuds in Appalachia: An Overview," *FCHQ* 56 (1982): 290-317; and John Ed Pearce, *Days of Darkness: The Feuds of Eastern Kentucky* (1994). Hambleton Tapp and James C. Klotter, *Kentucky: Decades of Discord, 1865-1900* (1977); and Otis K. Rice, *The Hatfields and the McCoys* (1978), provide briefer surveys. On specific feuds, see the lengthy *Majority and Minority Reports and Testimony Taken by the Rowan County Investigating Committee . . . March 16th, 1888* (1888); the strange E.L. Noble, *Bloody Breathitt's Feuds,* 4 vols. (1936-47); and the various Hatfield-McCoy studies, including Virgil C. Jones, *The Hatfields and the McCoys* (1948); and Altina L. Waller's fresh

Feud: Hatfields, McCoys, and Social Change in Appalachia, 1860-1900 (1988).

Such violence attracted more attention to Appalachia and helped fashion an image of the region. On that developing stereotype, see, for example, Henry D. Shapiro, *Appalachia on Our Mind* (1978); James C. Klotter, "The Black South and White Appalachia," *JAH* 66 (1980): 832-49; Tommy R. Thompson, "The Image of Appalachian Kentucky in American Popular Magazines," *Register* 91 (1993): 176-202; and Cratis D. Williams, "The Southern Mountaineer in Fact and Fiction," *Appalachian Journal* 3 (1975-76): 8-61, 100-162, 186-261, 334-92. Many late nineteenth- and early twentieth-century accounts of the region were written, but two of the most influential were William G. Frost, "Our Contemporary Ancestors in the Southern Mountains," *Atlantic Quarterly* 83 (1899): 311-19; and Horace Kephart, *Our Southern Highlanders* (1913). A whole scholarly subfield has developed in Appalachian studies, and the analysis of the area is extensive. Studies include Ronald D Eller, *Miners, Millhands, and Mountaineers: Industrialization of the Appalachian South, 1880-1930* (1982); Randall G. Lawrence, "Appalachian Metamorphosis: Industrializing Society on the Central Appalachian Plateau, 1860-1913" (Ph.D. diss., Duke University, 1983); Paul Salstrom, *Appalachia's Path to Dependency: Rethinking a Region's Economic History, 1730-1940* (1994); Mary Beth Pudup, Dwight B. Billings, and Altina L. Waller, eds., *Appalachia in the Making: The Mountain South in the Nineteenth Century* (1995); and Thomas A. Arcury and Julia D. Porter, "Household Composition in Appalachian Kentucky in 1900," *Journal of Family History* 10 (1985): 183-95.

The literature on late nineteenth-century politics and issues is quite sizable. Surveys of the political climate appear in Hambleton Tapp and James C. Klotter, *Kentucky: Decades of Discord, 1865-1900* (1977); Gordon B. McKinney, *Southern Mountain Republicans, 1865-1900* (1978); and Robert M. Ireland, *Little Kingdoms: The Counties of Kentucky, 1850-1891* (1977). Individual leaders are studied in Nancy Disher Baird, *Luke Pryor Blackburn: Physician, Governor, Reformer* (1979); Arndt M. Stickles, *Simon Bolivar Buckner* (1940); James A. Barnes, *John G. Carlisle* (1931); Maurice H. Thatcher, *Stories and Sketches of William O. Bradley* (1916); Lowell H. Harrison, ed., *Kentucky's Governors, 1792-1985* (1985); and John E. Kleber, editor in chief, *The Kentucky Encyclopedia* (1992). William Goebel's life and death have fostered many works, including the good, near-contemporary R.E. Hughes, F.W. Schaefer, and E.L. Williams, *That Kentucky Campaign* (1900). Also useful are Urey Woodson, *The First New Dealer* (1939); Thomas D. Clark, "The People, William Goebel, and the Kentucky Railroads," *JSH* 5 (1939): 34-48; and James C. Klotter, *William Goebel: The Politics of Wrath* (1977). Goebel's bitter enemy comes alive in Mary K. Bonsteel Tachau, "The Making of a Railroad President: Milton Hannibal Smith and the L&N," *FCHQ* 37 (1963): 117-36; and Edison H. Thomas, "Milton H. Smith Talks about the Goebel Affair," *Register* 78 (1980): 322-42.

The political unrest of the late nineteenth century is well covered in Edward F. Prichard Jr.'s sizable senior thesis at Princeton, "Popular Political Movements in Kentucky, 1875-1900" (1935), as well as a series of theses, dissertations, and articles, including Donald Schaefer, "Yeoman Farmers and Economic Democracy: A Study of Wealth and Economic Mobility in the Western Tobacco Region, 1850 to 1860," *Explorations in Economic History* 15 (1978): 421-37; Franklin T. Lambert, "The Kentucky Democracy in the 1890's" (M.A. thesis, University of Louisville, 1977); idem, "Free Silver and the Kentucky Democracy, 1891-1895," *FCHQ* 53 (1979): 145-77; Thomas J. Brown, "The Roots of Bluegrass Insurgency: An Analysis of the Populist Movement in Kentucky," *Register* 78 (1980): 219-42; and Gaye Keller Bland, "Populism in Kentucky, 1887-1896" (Ph.D. diss., University of Kentucky, 1979).

The fourth state constitution, reflecting some voter anger, has been analyzed in George L. Willis Sr., "History of Kentucky Constitutions and Constitutional Conventions," *Register* 29 (1931): 52-81;

Jesse S. Hunter, "The Kentucky Constitutional Convention of 1890" (M.A. thesis, University of Louisville, 1947); Rhea A. Taylor, "Conflicts in Kentucky As Shown in the Constitutional Convention of 1890-1891" (Ph.D. diss., University of Chicago, 1948); and Kentucky Legislative Research Commission, *A Citizens' Guide to the Kentucky Constitution*, rev. ed. (1993). The long-winded and tedious debates are printed in full in the four-volume *Official Report of the Proceedings and Debates in the Convention . . . to . . . Change the Constitution of the State of Kentucky* (1890).

The Tate affair is carefully covered in Emmet V. Mittlebeeler, "The Great Kentucky Absconsion," *FCHQ* 27 (1953): 335-52; the Tollgate Wars, in a part of J. Winston Coleman Jr., *Stage-Coach Days in the Bluegrass* (1935), reprinted in 1995; the railroad lobby, in the Joint Committee Report, in Kentucky *Senate Journal* (1887-88); and the 1895 election, in two articles by John Wiltz: "APA-ism in Kentucky," *Register* 56 (1958): 143-55; and "The 1895 Election," *FCHQ* 37 (1963): 117-36. The military (in feuds and the Spanish-American War) is addressed in Federal Writers Project, *Military History of Kentucky* (1939); Richard G. Stone Jr., *A Brittle Sword: The Kentucky Militia, 1776-1912* (1977); and idem, *Kentucky Fighting Men, 1861-1945* (1982). See also *Report of the Adjutant General of the State of Kentucky: Kentucky Volunteers, War with Spain, 1898-99* (1908). On state prisons, Robert G. Crawford's "A History of the Kentucky Penitentiary System, 1865-1937" (Ph.D. diss., University of Kentucky, 1955) is excellent and can be supplemented with Kyle Ellison, "Changing Faces, Common Walls: History of Corrections in Kentucky," typescript, 10th ed. (1985); and the various warden reports in *Kentucky Documents* (1839-1943). Medical care in the commonwealth is surveyed in John H. Ellis's *Medicine in Kentucky* (1977) and in the reports of the Board of Health; reform in the system is presented in *Report of the Kentucky Agricultural Experiment Station on the Enforcement of the Pure Food Laws* (1904) and in Margaret Ripley Wolfe, "The Agricultural Experiment Station and Food and Drug Control: Another Look at Kentucky

Progressivism, 1898-1916 *FCHQ* 49 (1975): 323-38. A superb study that gives the context in which to place Kentucky in national events is Morton Keller, *Affairs of State: Public Life in Late Nineteenth Century America* (1977). Manuscript and newspaper sources are rich for this period as well.

Chapter 18. Progressivism, Prohibition, and Politics, 1900-1920

No in-depth study examines the role of political bosses in Kentucky politics, and few works look at the individuals in much detail. James C. Klotter, *Kentucky: Portrait in Paradox, 1900-1950* (1996), provides an overview for the first half of the twentieth century, while Klotter and John W. Muir focus on one leader in "Boss Ben Johnson, the Highway Commission, and Kentucky Politics, 1927-1937," *Register* 84 (1986): 18-50. Johnson's son-in-law is perhaps overstudied in Orval W. Baylor, *J. Dan Talbott* (1942), while Johnson's important enemy Percy Haly has unfortunately not been the subject of much specific scholarly work. Nancy C. Graves, in a Transylvania University seminar paper, "William Frederick Klair" (1953); and James Duane Bolin, in "Bossism and Reform: Politics in Lexington, Kentucky, 1880-1940" (Ph.D. diss., University of Kentucky, 1988), look at the Lexington situation. John Erle Davis, "When the Whallens Were Kings," *Louisville* 30 (1979): 18-21; and Carolyn L. Denning, "The Louisville (Kentucky) Democratic Party: Political Times of 'Miss Lennie' McLaughlin" (M.A. thesis, University of Louisville, 1981), focus on the Falls City. Newspapers and oral histories remain the best sources for re-creating the hidden politics, but additional local studies are much needed.

Dewey W. Grantham, *Southern Progressivism* (1983); Jack Temple Kirby, *Darkness at the Dawning: Race and Reform in the Progressive South* (1972); and William A. Link, *The Paradox of Southern Progressivism, 1880-1930* (1992), provide the regional context for Kentucky. James Larry Hood, "The Collapse of Zion: Rural Progressivism in Nelson and Washington Counties, Kentucky" (Ph.D. diss., University of Kentucky, 1980); and idem, "March to Zion," *Register* 87 (1989): 144-61, give a good local

case study. A fine presentation of one aspect of progressivism is Thomas H. Appleton Jr., "'Like Banquo's Ghost': The Emergence of the Prohibition Issue in Kentucky Politics" (Ph.D. diss., University of Kentucky, 1981).

The Tobacco Wars, particularly in the Black Patch, have become one of the most studied, and best examined, aspects of Kentucky history. The field attracted much early study, starting with contemporary accounts, such as John L. Mathews, "The Farmers' Union and the Tobacco Pool," *Atlantic Monthly* 102 (1908): 482-91, then continuing in the 1930s with Marie Taylor, "Night Riders in the Black Patch" (M.A. thesis, University of Kentucky, 1934), which was published in part in the *Register* in 1963-64; John G. Miller, *The Black Patch War* (1936); and James O. Nall, *The Tobacco Night Riders of Kentucky and Tennessee, 1905-1909* (1939). After almost a scholarly hiatus for decades, broken chiefly by Dewey W. Grantham's "Black Patch War," *South Atlantic Quarterly* 59 (1960): 215-25, four good dissertations all appeared at nearly the same moment. Three came out as books in 1993 and 1994. See Rick S. Gregory, "Desperate Farmers: The Dark Tobacco District Planters' Protective Association of Kentucky and Tennessee, 1904-1914" (Ph.D. diss., Vanderbilt University, 1989); Tracy Campbell, *The Politics of Despair: Power and Resistance in the Tobacco Wars* (1993), particularly good on economics and the burley area; Christopher R. Waldrep, *Night Riders: Defending Community in the Black Patch, 1890-1915* (1993), which emphasizes community mores and legal issues; and Suzanne Marshall, *Violence in the Black Patch of Kentucky and Tennessee* (1994), which is strong on social matters. See also Bill Cunningham, *On Bended Knees: The Night Rider Story* (1983); and for the general context, William F. Axton, *Tobacco and Kentucky* (1975).

Kentucky politics in the first two decades of the twentieth century has been covered in some depth by several studies, including James C. Klotter, *Kentucky: Portrait in Paradox, 1900-1950* (1996); Thomas H. Appleton Jr., "'Like Banquo's Ghost': The Emergence of the Prohibition Issue in Kentucky Politics" (Ph.D. diss., University of Kentucky,

1981); and Nicholas C. Burckel, "Progressive Governors in the Border States: Reform Governors of Missouri, Kentucky, West Virginia, and Maryland, 1900-1918" (Ph.D. diss., University of Wisconsin, 1971). Parts of Burckel's dissertation appeared in two articles: "From Beckham to McCreary: The Progressive Record of Kentucky Governors," *Register* 76 (1978): 285-306; and "A.O. Stanley and Progressive Reform, 1902-1919," *Register* 79 (1981): 136-61. On other specific elections, see Jasper B. Shannon and Ruth McQuown, comps., *Presidential Politics in Kentucky, 1824-1948* (1950); Lowell H. Harrison, "Kentucky and the Presidential Elections, 1912-1948," *FCHQ* 26 (1952): 320-32; Glenn Finch, "The Election of United States Senators in Kentucky: The Beckham Period," *FCHQ* 44 (1970): 38-50; George P. Metcalf, "The Fusion Movement in Louisville, 1905-1907" (M.A. thesis, Murray State University, 1969); Percy N. Booth, "The Louisville Contested Election Cases," *Green Bag* 20 (1908): 81-90; and Thomas H. Appleton Jr., "Prohibition and Politics in Kentucky: The Gubernatorial Campaign and Election of 1915," *Register* 75 (1977): 28-54.

On individual political leaders, see the indispensable John E. Kleber, editor in chief, *The Kentucky Encyclopedia* (1992); and Lowell H. Harrison, ed., *Kentucky's Governors, 1792-1985* (1985). See also Robert K. Foster, "Augustus E. Willson and the Republican Party of Kentucky, 1895-1911" (M.A. thesis, University of Louisville, 1956); Joseph F. Wall, *Henry Watterson* (1956); Harry M. Caudill, "The Strange Career of John C.C. Mayo," *FCHQ* 56 (1982): 258-89; C.C. Turner and C.H. Traum, *John C.C. Mayo* (1983); Thomas W. Ramage, "Augustus Owsley Stanley" (Ph.D. diss., University of Kentucky, 1968); idem, "Augustus Owsley Stanley," in *Kentucky Profiles,* edited by James C. Klotter and Peter J. Sehlinger (1982); and Willard Rouse Jillson, *Edwin P. Morrow—Kentuckian* (1921). Ollie James has been the subject of many unpublished works, including Forest C. Pogue Jr., "The Life and Work of Senator Ollie Murray James" (M.A. thesis, University of Kentucky, 1932); Virginia M. McCalister, "The Political Career of Ollie M. James" (M.A.

thesis, Indiana University, 1933); and Thaddeus M. Smith, "Ollie Murray James" (M.A. thesis, Eastern Kentucky University, 1973). The Kentucky *House Journal* and *Senate Journal,* the *Acts of the General Assembly,* the newspapers of the period, and general Kentucky histories all provide needed information.

A definitive study of the women's rights movement in Kentucky has not appeared in print, but some very strong works have set the stage for that event. On the regional context, see Margaret Ripley Wolfe, *Daughters of Canaan: A Saga of Southern Women* (1985); on the national, see, among many good works, Sara M. Evans, *Born for Liberty: A History of Women in America* (1989). Margaret Ripley Wolfe, "Fallen Leaves and Missing Pages: Women in Kentucky History," *Register* 90 (1992): 64-89, is a well-crafted starting place for studying women in Kentucky. Helen Deiss Irvin, *Women in Kentucky* (1979), is a concise overview, and both Elizabeth Cady Stanton et al., eds., *The History of Woman Suffrage,* 6 vols. (1881-1922); and James C. Klotter, *Kentucky: Portrait in Paradox, 1900-1950* (1996), contain useful sections. A full study on suffrage is Claudia Knott, "The Woman Suffrage Movement in Kentucky, 1879-1920" (Ph.D. diss., University of Kentucky, 1989); a more specific look appears in Carol Guethlein, "Women in Louisville: Moving toward Equal Rights," *FCHQ* 55 (1981): 151-78.

The two key leaders of the women's movement in the commonwealth have received excellent historical scrutiny. Paul E. Fuller, in his *Laura Clay and the Woman's Rights Movement* (1975) and in his "Suffragist Vanquished: Laura Clay and the Nineteenth Amendment," *Register* 93 (1995): 4-24, gives his subject her due. "Madge" Breckinridge received early attention by her talented sister-in-law, Sophonisba Breckinridge, in *Madeline McDowell Breckinridge* (1921), while James C. Klotter, in his *Breckinridges of Kentucky, 1760-1981* (1986), looks at both those Breckinridge women plus progressive leader Desha Breckinridge, among others. But Madge Breckinridge found her biographer in Melba Porter Hay, in such works as "Madeline McDowell Breckinridge: Her Role in the Kentucky Woman Suffrage Movement, 1980-1920," *Register* 72 (1974): 342-63; "Madeline McDowell Breckinridge" (Ph.D. diss., University of Kentucky, 1980); and "Suffragist Trimphant: Madeline McDowell Breckinridge and the Nineteenth Amendment," *Register* 93 (1995): 25-42. On the child labor question, see Francis S. Jennings, "The History of Child Labor Legislation in Kentucky" (M.A. thesis, University of Kentucky, 1926); and Edward N. Clopper, *Child Welfare in Kentucky* (1919).

An early analysis concerning World War I was George Dan Hagan, "Kentucky's Part in the World War" (M.A. thesis, University of Kentucky, 1926). Federal Writers Project, *Military History of Kentucky* (1939); and Richard G. Stone Jr., *Kentucky Fighting Men, 1861-1945* (1982), cover the military side. See also Larry L. Arnett, *Call to Arms: A Collection of Fascinating Stories, Events, Personalities, and Facts about Kentucky's Military History* (1995). Aspects of the home front come alive in Clyde F. Crews, "Over Here: Louisville Faces World War I," *Louisville Magazine* (Aug. 1989): 13-15; John P. Meyer, "History and Neighborhood Analysis of Camp Taylor" (M.A. thesis, University of Louisville, 1981); and Ronald Alexander, "To Hell with the Hapsburgs and Hohenzollerns: Henry Watterson Looks at World War I," *Journal of the West Virginia Historical Association* 1 (1977): 15-25. The *Report of the Activities of the Kentucky Council of Defense to January 1, 1919* (1919) is the official summary. The influenza epidemic is covered well in Nancy Disher Baird, "The 'Spanish Lady' in Kentucky, 1918-1919," *FCHQ* 50 (1976): 290-301; and Gregory K. Culver, "The Impact of the 1918 Spanish Influenza Epidemic on the Jackson Purchase," *FCHQ* 65 (1991): 487-504. Culver's 1978 master's thesis at Murray State University has the same title as his article.

Chapter 19. Bourbon Barons, Tobacco Tycoons, and King Coal

Numerous studies place Kentucky agriculture in its regional context. They include Gilbert C. Fite, *Cotton Fields No More: Southern Agriculture, 1865-1980* (1984); Pete Daniel, *Breaking the Land: The Transformation of Cotton, Tobacco, and Rice Cultures since 1880* (1985); Howard W. Odum, *Southern Regions of the United States* (1936); Roger Biles, *The South and the New Deal* (1994); and Jack Temple Kirby, *Rural Worlds Lost: The American South, 1920-1960* (1987).

There is no comprehensive history of agriculture and its impact on Kentucky, though such a work is much needed. Thomas D. Clark's *Agrarian Kentucky* (1977) is a start, while other studies that provide some overviews are Hambleton Tapp and James C. Klotter, *Kentucky: Decades of Discord, 1865-1900* (1977); James C. Klotter, *Kentucky: Portrait in Paradox, 1900-1950* (1996); Judge Watson, "The Economic and Cultural Development of Eastern Kentucky from 1900 to the Present" (Ph.D. diss., Indiana University, 1963); John Clements, *Kentucky Facts* (1990); and *Kentucky's Historic Farms* (1994). Particularly rich are the early reports, with county breakdowns, of what was once called the Bureau of Agriculture, Labor, and Statistics. For more recent periods, *Kentucky Agricultural Statistics* provides figures, as does the U.S. Census.

Various crops have spawned historical studies. A classic one is James F. Hopkins, *A History of the Hemp Industry in Kentucky* (1951). On tobacco, see William F. Axton, *Tobacco and Kentucky* (1975); and Michael T. Childress, *The Future of Burley Tobacco* (1994). A large literature exists on the thoroughbred industry, but few studies treat other aspects of livestock raising. Introductions to the horse include Kent Hollingsworth, *The Kentucky Thoroughbred* (1976); and Bruce Denbo, ed., *The Horse World of the Bluegrass* (1980). Older works include Thomas A. Knight and Nancy L. Greene, *Country Estates of the Blue Grass* (1904), reprinted in 1973; and James Lane Allen, *The Blue-Grass Region of Kentucky* (1892). R. Gerald Alvey's *Kentucky Bluegrass Country* (1992) in a sense updates the Allen overview. Ken McCarr, *The Kentucky Harness Horse* (1978), presents the standardbred story. The *Blood-Horse* (1916-) and the *Thoroughbred Record* (1877-) give the year-by-year account of the industry. Statistics on foals and stakes winners come from the

Jockey Club, *The American Stud Book: Foals of 1992* (1993); and *Thoroughbred Times Statistical Review of 1994* (1995).

On the commercial side of Kentucky life, Charles B. Roberts, "The Building of Middlesborough," *FCHQ* 7 (1933): 18-33, tells a small part of the saga well, while the early lumber industry and the independent loggers who made it are treated in Burdine Webb, "Old Times in Eastern Kentucky," *Southern Lumberman* (Dec. 15, 1956), 178G-J; and Thomas D. Clark, "Kentucky Logmen," *Journal of Forest History* 25 (1981): 144-57. More general economic overviews are J.J. Hornback, "Economic Development in Kentucky since 1860" (Ph.D. diss., University of Michigan, 1932); and Joseph L. McConnell, "Growth of Manufacturing in Kentucky, 1904 to 1929" (M.A. thesis, University of Kentucky, 1932). A good picture of the conditions at a particular year emerges from Kentucky Bureau of Agriculture, *Kentucky: Natural Resources, Industrial Statistics, Industrial Directory, Description by Counties* (1930). The more recent situation has to be reconstructed from a series of sources, including the Kentucky Department of Economic Development, *Kentucky Locational Advantages for the Auto Parts Industry* (1984); the *1996 Kentucky Deskbook of Economic Statistics* (1996); and various periodicals, including *Reviews and Perspectives, Kentucky's Global Connections,* and the *Lane Report.* Sam Goldstein, "The History and Development of Kentucky Distilleries" (M.B.A. thesis, University of Louisville, 1958), studies the distilling industry.

While the one comprehensive history of the coalfields and those who worked there has yet to be written, many more specific studies exist. On the camps where workers lived, a good general overview (though thin on Kentucky) is Crandall A. Shifflett, *Coal Towns: Life, Work, and Culture in Company Towns of Southern Appalachia, 1880-1960* (1991). A fine case study is Thomas A. Keleman, "A History of Lynch, Kentucky, 1917-1930," *FCHQ* 48 (1974): 156-76. On the miners, see Bruce Crawford, "The Coal Miner," in *Culture in the South,* edited by W.T. Couch (1934); on children, women, and immigrants in the camps, see Mabel B. Ellis, "Children of the Kentucky Coal Fields," *American Child* 1 (1920): 285-405; Glenna H. Graves, "'In the Morning We Had Bulldog Gravy': Women in the Coal Camps of the Appalachian South, 1900-1940" (Ph.D. diss., University of Kentucky, 1993); Margaret Ripley Wolfe, "The Appalachian Reality: Ethnic and Class Diversity," *East Tennessee Historical Society Publications* 52-53 (1981-82): 40-60; and Doug Cantrell, "Immigrants and Community in Harlan County, 1910-1930," *Register* 86 (1988): 119-41. Oral histories of importance are available as well.

On coal mining itself, brief introductions come from Willard Rouse Jillson, "A History of the Coal Industry in Kentucky," *Register* 20 (1922): 21-45; idem, *The Coal Industry in Kentucky* (1924); and Henry C. Mayer, "A Brief History of the Kentucky Coal Industry," in *The Kentucky Underground Coal Mine Guidebook,* edited by Forrest Cameron (1985). On the often-ignored western Kentucky area, see Claude E. Pickard, "The Western Kentucky Coal Fields" (Ph.D. diss., University of Nebraska, 1969), and on one system of coal extraction, see the Kentucky Legislative Research Commission, *Strip Mining in Kentucky,* Research Publication no. 5, o.s. (1949). Indispensable are such primary sources as the *Report of the Inspector of Mines,* which began in 1884 and later evolved into the *Report of the Department of Mines and Minerals.* See also Curtis Seltzer, *Fire in the Hole: Miners and Managers in the American Coal Industry* (1985), and the numerous transcripts of congressional hearings through the years.

On the state's early oil industry, see the following works by Willard Rouse Jillson: "Kentucky Petroleum: Its History and Present Status," *Register* 17 (1919): 47-49; "The Re-born Oil Fields of Kentucky," *Register* 18 (1920): 35-43; "Oil and Gas in the Big Sandy Valley," *Register* 20 (1922): 21-45; and *New Oil Horizons in Kentucky* (1948). The development of one of the state's largest corporations is detailed in Joseph L. Massie, *Blazer and Ashland Oil* (1960); and Otto J. Scott, *The Exception: The Story of Ashland Oil* (1968). Kentucky Department of Economic Development, *Energy and Natural Resources in Kentucky* (1984) covers other minerals.

The state's transportation history for the period since the Civil War has been examined well for certain areas, imperfectly for others. On the rivers, see Thomas D. Clark, *The Kentucky* (1942), revised in 1992; Helen Bartter Crocker, *The Green River of Kentucky* (1976); Carol Crowe-Carraco, *The Big Sandy* (1979); Charles E. Parrish, "History of Navigation on the Kentucky River," *Army Engineer* 3 (1995): 17-20; Richard E. Banta, *The Ohio* (1949); Mary Verhoeff, *The Kentucky River Navigation* (1917); idem, *The Kentucky Mountains: Transportation and Commerce, 1750 to 1911* (1911); and Leland R. Johnson, *The Falls City Engineers: A History of the Louisville District, Corps of Engineers* (1975).

Railroads seem to have left a strong impression on those who rode them, and many have hastened to write on aspects of railroading history. Most scholars base part of their research on the *Report of the Railroad Commission of Kentucky*, which began in 1880. On early railroad mania, see Carl B. Boyd Jr., "Local Aid to Railroads in Central Kentucky, 1850-1891," *Register* 62 (1964): 4-23, 112-33; Sam W. Moore II, "The Early Railroads in Green County," *Green County Review* 6 (1982): 28-32; and Daniel W. Lynch, "The Development of State and Local Debt in Kentucky, 1890-1962" (Ph.D. diss., University of Kentucky, 1965). Kincaid A. Herr, *The Louisville and Nashville Railroad, 1850-1942* (1943); John L. Kerr, *The Story of a Southern Carrier: The Louisville & Nashville* (1933); and Maury Klein, *History of the Louisville & Nashville Railroad* (1972), study one important line in depth. Regulation of railroads is traced in detail in Maxwell Ferguson, *State Regulation of Railroads in the South* (1916); a local study is Lee A. Dew, "Henderson, Kentucky, and the Fight for Equitable Freight Rates, 1906-1918," *Register* 76 (1978): 34-44. Most county histories look at railroads in the local area, and some specific studies go into more detail: see, for a large city, Milo M. Meadows Jr., "Urban Transportation in Louisville from 1830-1910" (M.A. thesis, University of Louisville, 1967); and, for a small county, Lee A. Dew, *Shaping Our Society: Transportation and the Development of the Culture of Hancock County* (1989).

On highways, see the *Report of the Department of Public Roads,* which began in 1912 (and was later renamed). On early Kentucky-made automobiles, see Louis S. Schafer, "Early Engines," *Kentucky Living* 47 (1993): 14-15.

Chapter 20. Culture and Communications, 1865-1995

A full history of journalism in the commonwealth has not yet appeared. An episodic overview is Herndon J. Evans, *The Newspaper Press in Kentucky* (1976). In two larger-scope studies, Thomas D. Clark presents many Kentucky examples: see *The Rural Press and the New South* (1948) and *Southern Country Editor* (1948). State newspapers deserve more individual scholarly study than they have received. Perhaps the best-presented is the specialized press. See, for example, Stanley Ousley, "The Kentucky Irish American," *FCHQ* 53 (1979): 178-95; and Clyde F. Crews, ed., *Mike Barry and the Kentucky Irish American: An Anthology* (1995).

Among the editors, Desha Breckinridge is covered in James C. Klotter, *The Breckinridges of Kentucky, 1760-1981* (1986). One giant, however, dominates that literature—Henry Watterson. The best biography is Joseph F. Wall, *Henry Watterson* (1956), and other studies include Leonard N. Plummer, "The Political Leadership of Henry Watterson" (Ph.D. diss., University of Wisconsin, 1940); Lena C. Logan, "Henry Watterson, Border Nationalist, 1840-1877" (Ph.D. diss., Indiana University, 1942); and Robert K. Thorp, "'Marse Henry' and the Negro: A New Perspective," *Journalism Quarterly* 46 (1969): 467-74. From the pens of those who knew Watterson came Isaac F. Marcosson, *"Marse Henry": A Biography of Henry Watterson* (1951); and Arthur Krock, ed., *The Editorials of Henry Watterson* (1923). The editor wrote his recollections under the title *"Marse Henry,"* 2 vols. (1919), and published some lectures in *The Compromises of Life* (1903). See also a section on Watterson in Carl R. Osthaus, *Partisans of the Southern Press* (1994). On Watterson's successor, Robert W. Bingham, see chapter 21. On the next editor, Barry Bingham Sr., see Samuel W. Thomas, ed., *Barry Bingham: A Man of His Word* (1993); *Remembering Barry Bingham* (1990); and Susan E. Tifft and Alex S. Jones, *The Patriarch* (1991).

Writing on Kentucky authors and Kentucky literature is appropriately large. Numerous general overviews exist, almost all focusing on the lives of individuals. One of the earliest was John Wilson Townsend, *Kentucky in American Letters,* 2 vols. (1913); a third volume came much later (1976) from the pen of Dorothy Townsend. Similar in approach are Ish Ritchey, *Kentucky Literature, 1784-1963* (1963); and Mary C. Browning, *Kentucky Authors* (1968). On the story lines of various books, see Lawrence S. Thompson and Algernon Thompson, *The Kentucky Novel* (1953). For briefer overviews, see two pamphlets by R. Gerald Alvey, *Cultural Conflicts in Kentucky* (n.d.) and *Cultural Stereotypes in Kentucky Literature* (n.d.), both published by the University of Kentucky College of Agriculture Cooperative Extension Service; James C. Klotter, "Little Shepherds, Little Colonels, and Little Kingdoms: A Selective Review of Kentucky Writing, 1784-1950," *Journal of Kentucky Studies* 3 (1986): 61-72; and James C. Klotter, *Kentucky: Portrait in Paradox, 1900-1950* (1996). But by far the best study is William Smith Ward, *A Literary History of Kentucky* (1988).

Individual authors have generally attracted a good amount of attention. Among the most useful studies on the 1865-1915 period are William K. Bottorff, *James Lane Allen* (1964); Grant C. Knight, *James Lane Allen and the Genteel Tradition* (1935); Elizabeth Fox Moore, *John Fox, Jr., Personal and Family Letters and Papers* (1955); Warren I. Titus, *John Fox, Jr.* (1971); Thomas Nelson Page, "John Fox," *Scribner's Magazine* 66 (1919): 674-83; Sue Lynn McGuire, "The Little Colonel," *Register* 89 (1991): 121-46; Abby M. Roach, "The Authors Club of Louisville," *FCHQ* 31 (1957): 28-37; and Anne Gabbard Shelby, "Appalachian Literature and American Myth" (M.A. thesis, University of Kentucky, 1981). In the later period, two Kentucky authors in particular—Elizabeth Madox Roberts

and Robert Penn Warren—have generated considerable study. Among the works on Roberts are F. Lamar Janney, "Elizabeth Madox Roberts," *Sewanee Review* 45 (1937): 389-410; Andrew J. Beeler Jr., "Elizabeth Madox Roberts: Her Interpretation of Life" (M.A. thesis, University of Louisville, 1940); Woodridge Spears, "Elizabeth Madox Roberts" (Ph.D. diss., University of Kentucky, 1953); Harry M. Campbell and Ruel E. Foster, *Elizabeth Madox Roberts* (1956); and Earl H. Rovit, *Herald to Chaos: The Novels of Elizabeth Madox Roberts* (1960). The Warren literature includes Leonard Casper, *Robert Penn Warren* (1960); Victor H. Standberg, *The Poetic Vision of Robert Penn Warren* (1977); James H. Justus, *The Achievement of Robert Penn Warren* (1981); Randolph P. Runyan, *The Braided Dream: Robert Penn Warren's Late Poetry* (1990); and William B. Clark, *The American Vision of Robert Penn Warren* (1991). Both Roberts and Warren, as well as Jesse Stuart and Caroline Gordon, are covered in Joseph M. Flora and Robert Bain, eds., *Fifty Southern Writers after 1900* (1987).

Various other Kentucky authors have been examined in some depth. See, for example, Michael A. Flannery, "The Local Color of John Uri Lloyd," *Register* 91 (1993): 24-50; Anita Lawson, *Irvin S. Cobb* (1984); Ruel E. Foster, *Jesse Stuart* (1968); J.R. Lemaster, *Jesse Stuart* (1980); H. Edward Richardson, *Jesse: The Biography of an American Writer, Jesse Hilton Stuart* (1984); Dayton Kohler, "Jesse Stuart and James Still: Mountain Regionalists," *College English* 3 (1942): 523-33; Dean Cadle, "Man on Troublesome," *Yale Review* 87 (1968): 236-55; Wilton Eckley, *Harriette Arnow* (1974); Glenda K. Hobbs, "Harriette Arnow's Literary Journey" (Ph.D. diss., Harvard University, 1975); William E. Ellis, "Walter Tevis," *Journal of Kentucky Studies* 12 (1995): 73-77; Kay Johnson, "They had to get away to come home . . . ," *Kentucky Alumnus* (1986): 7-11 (on Hall, Norman, Mason, Berry, and McClanahan). The best sources on more recent authors are the interviews with them in Linda Beattie, ed., *Conversations with Kentucky Writers* (1996). See also entries in *The Dictionary of Literary Biography,*

The Kentucky Encyclopedia, and the appropriate sections in the textbooks cited above.

On Kentucky poetry, see the individual biographies mentioned above, as well as the general overviews cited earlier. In addition, see R.W. Thompson, "Negroes Who Are 'Doing Things,'" *Alexander's Magazine* 1 (Aug. 15, 1905): 25-26 (on Joseph S. Cotter); Otto A. Rothert, *The Story of a Poet: Madison Cawein* (1921); Lindsey Apple, *Never Excelled: Tradition and Modernity in an Early Twentieth Century Woman* (1996), focusing on Susan Clay Savitzky but offering more than just an examination of her literary life; and David Deskins, "Effie Waller Smith," *Kentucky Review* 8 (1988): 26-46.

Kentucky historians have probably not examined their profession or its leaders enough. The works on Richard Collins include James P. Gregory Jr., "Lewis and Richard H. Collins," *FCHQ* 21 (1947): 309-26; and Stuart Seely Sprague, "Richard H. Collins and His History of Kentucky," *Register* 70 (1972): 17-20. Studies of the writings of Thomas D. Clark include Bill Cunningham, *Kentucky's Clark* (1987); Frank Steely and H. Lew Wallace, "Thomas D. Clark: A Biographical Sketch," *FCHQ* 60 (1986): 293-318; and Holman Hamilton, introduction to *Three Kentucky Frontiers: Writings on Thomas D. Clark,* edited by Holman Hamilton (1968). For an overview of the status of the profession in the early 1980s, see James C. Klotter, "Clio in the Commonwealth: The Status of Kentucky History," *Register* 80 (1982): 65-88.

Nancy Disher Baird's "Enid Yandell," *FCHQ* 62 (1988): 5-32, is the best study of a Kentucky sculptor, and Robert C. May's *The Lexington Camera Club, 1936-1972* (1989), is the strongest work on photography. Other artists have been studied in more depth: see J. Winston Coleman Jr., *Three Kentucky Artists: Hart, Price, Troye* (1974); idem, *Robert Burns Wilson* (1956); Willard Rouse Jillson, *Paul Sawyier, American Artist* (1961); Arthur F. Jones, *The Art of Paul Sawyier* (1976); Justus Bier, "Carl C. Brenner," *American-German Review* 17 (1951): 20-29, 33; Royal Cortissoz, "The Field of Art—Frank Duveneck and His Munich Tradition," *Scribner's Magazine* 81 (1927): 216-20; and

Walter S. Siple, *Frank Duveneck* (1936). On architecture in the commonwealth, see Theodore M. Brown, *Introduction to Louisville Architecture* (1960); William Lynwood Montell and Michael Lynn Morse, *Kentucky Folk Architecture* (1976); Clay Lancaster, *Vestiges of the Venerable City: A Chronicle of Lexington, Kentucky, Its Architectural Development and Survey of Its Early Streets and Antiquities* (1978); and Julian C. Oberwarth and William B. Scott Jr., *A History of the Profession of Architecture in Kentucky* (1987). County histories are also useful. John A. Jakle, Robert W. Bastian, and Douglas K. Meyer, *Common Houses in America's Small Towns* (1989), compares a Kentucky example with national trends. See also various surveys of historic sites, often funded by the Kentucky Heritage Council.

The richness of the state's musical traditions is well presented in four studies in particular: Charles K. Wolfe, *Kentucky Country: Folk and Country Music of Kentucky* (1982); Bill C. Malone, *Southern Music, American Music* (1979); idem, "William S. Hays: The Bard of Kentucky," *Register* 93 (1995): 286-306; and William Lynwood Montell, *Singing the Glory Down: Amateur Gospel Music in South Central Kentucky, 1900-1990* (1991). Different kinds of musical presentation in one city are covered in Carol C. Birkhead, "The History of the Orchestra in Louisville" (M.A. thesis, University of Louisville, 1977); and Pen Bogert, "Louisville Blues in the 1950's," *Blues News* (Dec. 1993): 1-2, (Jan. 1994): 1-2.

J. Winston Coleman Jr. wrote of an early pioneer of radio in Kentucky in *Nathan B. Stubblefield: The Father of Radio* (1982), while Terry L. Birdwhistell broke new historiographical ground with his "WHAS Radio and the Development of Broadcasting in Kentucky, 1922-1942," *Register* 79 (1981): 333-53. See also Francis M. Nash, *Towers over Kentucky: A History of Radio and Television in the Bluegrass State* (1995). Early film history in one locale is covered in two Gregory B. Waller articles: "Introducing the 'Marvellous Invention' to the Provinces: Film Exhibitions in Lexington, Kentucky, 1896-1897," *Film History* 3 (1989): 223-34; and "Situating Motion Pictures in the Prenickelodeon Period: Lexington, Kentucky, 1897-1906," *Velvet Light Trap* 25 (1990): 12-27. Three excellent works allow the placement of films on Kentucky in a regional context: Edward D.C. Campbell, *The Celluloid South* (1981); Jack Temple Kirby, *Media-Made Dixie,* rev. ed. (1986); and J.W. Williamson, *Southern Mountaineers in Silent Films: Plot Synopses of Movies about Moonshining, Feuding, and Other Mountain Topics, 1904-1929* (1994). See also Jerry P. Perry, "Kentucky Educational Television Network" (Ph.D. diss., Syracuse University, 1977).

The literature on D.W. Griffith is vast. Examples are Robert M. Henderson, *D.W. Griffith: His Life and Work* (1972); Iris Barry, *D.W. Griffith: American Film Master* (1940); Raymond A. Cook, "The Man behind *The Birth of a Nation,*" *North Carolina Historical Review* 39 (1962): 519-41; and Richard Schickel, *D.W. Griffith: An American Life* (1984). The Louisville cultural scene is presented in "Culture's New Kentucky Home," *Life* (April 8, 1957): 125-30; William Manchester, "Louisville Cashes in on Culture," *Harper's Magazine* (Aug. 1955): 77-83; and Holly Hill, "Arts Supporting America: A Model City," *Contemporary Review* 241 (1982): 324-28.

Chapter 21. The Transitional Twenties

For overviews, national and regional, of the 1920s, the older but still interesting Frederick Lewis Allen, *Only Yesterday* (1931), has been superseded by such works as William E. Leuchtenburg, *Perils of Prosperity, 1914-1932* (1958); Loren Boritz, *The Culture of the Twenties* (1969); and George B. Tindall, *The Emergence of the New South, 1913-1945* (1967). Kentucky's specific demographics can be garnered from census reports; George A. Hillery Jr., "Population Growth in Kentucky, 1820-1960," *University of Kentucky Agricultural Experiment Station Bulletin 705* (1966); and Thomas R. Ford, *Health and Demography in Kentucky* (1964). James C. Klotter, *Kentucky: Portrait in Paradox, 1900-1950* (1996), gives an overview of the first half of the twentieth century, while one specific incident and its surroundings are colorfully captured in Robert K. Murray and Roger W. Brucker, *Trapped! The Story of*

the Struggle to Rescue Floyd Collins (1979). The state's sporting contribution can be garnered from Milton D. Feinstein, "History and Development of Football at the University of Kentucky, 1877-1920" (M.A. thesis, University of Kentucky, 1941); Mike Embry, "Kentuckians in the Halls of Fame," *Kentucky Living* 46 (1992): 12-16; and Henry C. Mayer, "Kentucky's All-Time All Stars," *Rural Kentuckian* 42 (1988): 28-30.

The antievolution fight generated considerable historical material, as well as contemporary passion. An early outcry was Alonzo W. Fortune, "The Kentucky Campaign against the Teaching of Evolution," *Journal of Religion* 2 (1922): 225-35. Later studies, generally all critical of the antievolution effort, include L. Beatrice Simms, "The Anti-evolution Conflict in the 1920's" (M.A. thesis, University of Kentucky, 1953); R. Halliburton Jr., "Kentucky's Anti-evolution Controversy," *Register* 66 (1968): 97-107; Milo M. Meadows Jr., "Fundamentalist Thought and Its Impact in Kentucky, 1900-1928" (Ph.D. diss., Syracuse University, 1972); and three works by William E. Ellis: "Frank LeRond McVey—His Defense of Academic Freedom," *Register* 67 (1969): 37-54; "The Fundamentalist-Moderate Schism over Evolution in the 1920's," *Register* 74 (1976): 112-23; and *"A Man of Books and A Man of the People": E.Y. Mullins and the Crisis of Moderate Southern Baptist Leadership* (1985). See also George E. Webb, *The Evolution Controversy in America* (1994). On Thomas Hunt Morgan, see Ian Shine and Sylvia Wrobel, *Thomas Hunt Morgan: Pioneer of Genetics* (1976); and James A. Ramage, "Thomas Hunt Morgan," *FCHQ* 53 (1979): 5-25.

On the general background to the life of blacks during the era, see George C. Wright, *Life behind a Veil: Blacks in Louisville, Kentucky, 1865-1930* (1985); and Marion B. Lucas and George C. Wright, *A History of Blacks in Kentucky,* 2 vols. (1992). Also helpful are contemporary magazines, such as the *Crisis,* as well as newspapers. The Will Lockett riot spawned three good studies: Joe Jordan, "Lynchers Don't Like Lead," *Atlantic Monthly* 177 (1946): 103-8; J. Winston Coleman Jr., *Death at the*

Court-House (1952); and John D. Wright Jr., "Lexington's Suppression of the 1920 Will Lockett Lynch Mob," *Register* 84 (1986): 263-79. Klan activities in Kentucky are covered in general terms in David M. Chalmers, *Hooded Americanism: The History of the Ku Klux Klan* (1965), and more specifically to the state in Thomas D. Matijasic, "The Ku Klux Klan in the Big Sandy Valley of Kentucky," *Journal of Kentucky Studies* 10 (1993): 75-80. E.H. Lougher's *The Kall of the Klan in Kentucky* (1924) is a contemporary presentation.

The chaotic politics of the era have generated a full spectrum of studies, ranging from overviews, such as E.A. Jonas, *A History of the Republican Party in Kentucky* (1929); Walter A. Baker, "The GOP in Kentucky: A History of the Kentucky Republican Party, 1919-1956" (B.A. thesis, Harvard College, 1958); and George L. Willis Jr., *Kentucky Democracy*, 3 vols. (1935), to specific election accounts, including Malcolm E. Jewell, *Kentucky Votes*, 3 vols. (1963); and Francis S. Wagner, "The Kentucky Gubernatorial Election of 1927" (M.A. thesis, University of Louisville, 1969). The works on presidential elections cited above, under chapter 18, are also useful. On the pari-mutuel issue, see M.P. Hunt, *The Story of My Life* (1941); Ralph W. Clark, "The Legal Regulation of Organized Racing in Kentucky" (M.A. thesis, University of Kentucky, 1941); Joseph M. Porter, "The Kentucky Jockey Club" (M.A. thesis, Eastern Kentucky University, 1969); and Robert F. Sexton, "The Crusade against Pari-mutuel Gambling in Kentucky: A Study of Southern Progressivism in the 1920's," *FCHQ* 50 (1976): 47-57. Sexton's dissertation, "Kentucky Politics and Society, 1919-1932" (University of Washington, 1970), gives a good analysis of the era's political character.

For information on the government of the commonwealth, see Nollie Olin Taff, *History of State Revenue and Taxation in Kentucky* (1931); Vance Armentrout, *An Inventory of Kentucky* (1922); and *The Government of Kentucky: Report of the Efficiency Commission of Kentucky*, 2 vols. (1924). An annual series called *The Kentucky Directory* offers details about legislators and government departments.

Henry B. Simpson, in "The General Assembly of 1926" (M.A. thesis, University of Kentucky, 1926), gives a full analysis of his subject.

Individual studies of political leaders of the period range from full and extensive to sketchy and thin. On the Republican side, see Willard Rouse Jillson, *Edwin P. Morrow—Kentuckian* (1921); Bernard V. Burke, "Senator and Diplomat: The Public Career of Frederic M. Sackett," *FCHQ* 61 (1987): 185-216; James B. Skaggs, "The Rise and Fall of Flem D. Sampson" (M.A. thesis, Eastern Kentucky University, 1976); and the defensive autobiography of John W. Langley, *They Tried to Crucify Me* (1929). On the Democratic side, see George W. Robinson, "The Making of a Kentucky Senator: Alben W. Barkley and the Gubernatorial Primary of 1923," *FCHQ* 40 (1966): 123-35; James K. Libbey, *Dear Alben* (1979); and Barkley's autobiography, *That Reminds Me* (1954). Behind-the-scenes Democratic operative Jim Brown is discussed in George R. Leighton, *Five Cities* (1939). John E. Kleber, editor in chief, *The Kentucky Encyclopedia* (1992); and Lowell H. Harrison, ed., *Kentucky's Governors, 1792-1985* (1985), give sketches of politicians of both parties.

Books and articles on the Bingham family have appeared with regularity during the last decade, but the historical profession would have been better served had several of the studies never made it into print. Good scholarly accounts of Robert Worth Bingham appear in four William E. Ellis works: "The Bingham Family," *FCHQ* 61 (1987): 5-33; "Robert Worth Bingham and the Crisis of Cooperative Marketing in the Twenties," *Agricultural History* 56 (1982): 99-116; "Robert Worth Bingham and Louisville Progressivism, 1905-1910," *FCHQ* 54 (1980): 169-95; and *Robert Worth Bingham and the Southern Mystique* (1996). Family accounts usually focus on R.W. Bingham in some form, and they range from the solid—Marie Brenner, *House of Dreams* (1988)—to the angry—Sallie Bingham, *Passion and Prejudice* (1989)—to the weak—David L. Chandler and Mary V. Chandler, *The Binghams of Louisville* (1987). See also Markeeta Vincent Wood, "Robert Worth Bingham, American

Ambassador to the Court of St. James, 1933-1934: The Productive Years" (M.A. thesis, Western Kentucky University, 1978).

Two controversial issues of the era were prisons and water use. On the latter, see Tom Wallace, "Caught in the Power Net," *Survey* 62 (1929): 389-94; and the good study by George W. Robinson, "Conservation in Kentucky: The Fight to Save Cumberland Falls, 1926-1931," *Register* 81 (1983): 25-58. On the penitentiary question, the *Report of the Board of Prison Commissioners* (from the agency that was later called the Department of Corrections) and various investigating committee reports in the Kentucky *House Journal* and *Senate Journal* are starting places. Joseph P. Byers, in "Parole in Kentucky," *Journal of Social Forces* 1 (1923): 135-36, presented the situation at the time, while later surveys usually have focused more on events than on the politics of prisons. See Robert G. Crawford, "A History of the Kentucky Penitentiary System, 1865-1937" (Ph.D. diss., University of Kentucky, 1955); Kyle Ellison, "Changing Faces, Common Walls: History of Corrections in Kentucky," typescript, 10th ed. (1985); and Bill Cunningham, *Castle: The Story of a Kentucky Prison* (1994).

Chapter 22. Old Problems and a New Deal

On conditions during the Great Depression and in wartime, important sources include newspapers, interviews, and county histories. On the hardship of the 1930s, Elizabeth Woodruff, in *As Rare As Rain: Federal Relief in the Great Southern Drought of 1930-31* (1985), notes nature's role and government's response; the state reply to economic want is presented in Arthur H. Estabrook, "Poor Relief in Kentucky," *Social Science Review* 3 (1929): 224-42. Further discussion of the people's needs and the early situation can be found in Mary Breckinridge, "The Corn-Bread Line," *Survey* 64 (Aug. 15, 1930): 423; James C. Klotter, *Kentucky: Portrait in Paradox, 1900-1950* (1996); and Donald W. Whisenhunt, "The Great Depression in Kentucky: The Early Years," *Register* 67 (1969): 37-54. The effect on the banking industry can be observed through the

annual *Report of the Banking Commissioner of the State of Kentucky* and in several bank histories, such as Thomas D. Clark, *A Century of Banking History in the Bluegrass* (1983); and John E.L. Robertson, *The History of Citizens Bank and Trust Company of Paducah, Kentucky* (1988). The failure of the South's largest bank is well presented in Robert Fugate, "The BancoKentucky Story," *FCHQ* 50 (1976): 29-46.

The story of the "Roosevelt revolution" in the commonwealth fortunately has been told well in George T. Blakey's *Hard Times and New Deal in Kentucky, 1929-1939* (1986), and with a more limited scope in Mary C. Erwin, "The Vicious Circle: A Study of the Effects of the Depression and New Deal Relief Programs in Eastern Kentucky" (M.A. thesis, University of Louisville, 1968); James Duane Bolin, "The Human Side: Politics, the Great Depression, and the New Deal in Lexington, Kentucky, 1929-35," *Register* 90 (1992): 256-83; and Joseph E. Brent, "The Civil Works Administration in Western Kentucky," *FCHQ* 67 (1993): 259-76.

The struggle over labor rights during the New Deal erupted in violence in eastern Kentucky. For the general background on labor before 1930, see such varied sources as Herbert Finch, "Organized Labor in Louisville, Kentucky, 1880-1914" (Ph.D. diss., University of Kentucky, 1965); James H. Horan, "The Trade Union Movement in Kentucky to 1900" (M.A. thesis, University of Louisville, 1964); and *Labor History in Kentucky: A Teaching Supplement* (1986). On mining specifically, see Henry C. Mayer, "Glimpses of Union Activity among Coal Miners in Nineteenth Century Eastern Kentucky," *Register* 86 (1988): 216-29, as well as the *Reports* of the Labor Inspector and the Adjutant General. Two good case studies—all too rare, unfortunately—are Bill L. Weaver, "Louisville's Labor Disturbances, July, 1877," *FCHQ* 48 (1974): 177-86; and Nancy S. Dye, "The Louisville Woolen Mills Strike of 1887," *Register* 82 (1984): 236-50. A full history of the labor movement would be welcome.

The background to the Harlan County Coal Wars is covered in Doug Cantrill, "Immigrants and

Community in Harlan County, 1910-1930," *Register* 86 (1988): 119-41; and Paul F. Cressey, "Social Disorganization and Reorganization in Harlan County, Kentucky," *American Sociological Review* 14 (1949): 389-94. Several good studies examine the conflicts in some depth. These range from article-length accounts, such as Stuart Seely Sprague, "Hard Times in Bell and Harlan," *Mountain Review* 2 (1976): 19-22, 42-48, to book-length treatments, such as Paul F. Taylor, *Bloody Harlan: The United Mine Workers of America in Harlan County, Kentucky, 1931-1941* (1990); and the fine John W. Hevener, *Which Side Are You On?* (1978). Federal hearings on the issue appeared in print: U.S. Senate, *Violation of Free Speech and Rights of Labor Hearing,* 75th Cong., 1st sess. (1937). Considerably more material, often reflecting the viewpoint of one side or the other, also exists.

Politics permeated most issues of the 1930s and 1940s, whether relief economics or labor questions were in dispute. For the general and statistical background, see Lawrence A. Burdon, "A Statistical Study of Kentucky Elections, 1920-1948" (M.A. thesis, University of Louisville, 1950); Jasper B. Shannon and Ruth McQuown, comps., *Presidential Politics in Kentucky, 1824-1948* (1950); Lowell H. Harrison, "Kentucky and the Presidential Election, 1912-1948," *FCHQ* 26 (1952): 320-32; Malcolm E. Jewell, *Kentucky Votes,* 3 vols. (1963); Ernest Collins, "The Political Behavior of the Negroes in Cincinnati, Ohio, and Louisville, Kentucky" (Ph.D. diss., University of Kentucky, 1950); John H. Fenton, *Politics in the Border States* (1957); James C. Klotter, *Kentucky: Portrait in Paradox, 1900-1950* (1996); and John Ed Pearce, *Divide and Dissent: Kentucky Politics, 1930-1963* (1987).

Political leaders have been studied in varying degrees of depth. On Alben Barkley, see the citations under chapter 21, as well as John Henry Hatcher, "Alben Barkley, Politics in Relief and the Hatch Act," *FCHQ* 40 (1966): 249-64; Walter L. Hixson, "The 1938 Kentucky Senate Election," *Register* 80 (1982): 309-29; and Donald A. Ritchie, "Alben W. Barkley: The President's Man," in *First among Equals: Outstanding Senate Leaders of the Twentieth Century,* edited by Richard A. Baker and Roger H. Davidson (1991). Similarly well examined is A.B. Chandler, though a comprehensive biography is lacking. See Happy's autobiography, *Heroes, Plain Folks, and Skunks: The Life and Times of Happy Chandler* (1989), which should be used with care, as well as Charles P. Roland, "Happy Chandler," *Register* 85 (1987): 138-61; Stephen D. Boyd, "The Campaign Speaking of A.B. Chandler," *Register* 79 (1981): 227-39; and Terry L. Birdwhistell, "A.B. 'Happy' Chandler," in *Kentucky: Its History and Heritage,* edited by Fred J. Hood (1978). Numerous contemporary works are also useful, such as Jasper B. Shannon, "Happy Chandler: A Kentucky Epic," in *The American Politician,* edited by J.T. Salter (1938); and Walter Davenport, "Happy Couldn't Wait," *Colliers* (July 16, 1938): 12-13, 49-51. The governors before and after Chandler have been covered in Vernon Gipson, *Ruby Laffoon* (1978); Frederic D. Ogden, ed., *The Public Papers of Keen Johnson, 1939-1943* (1982); James C. Klotter, ed., *The Public Papers of Simeon Willis, 1943-1947* (1988); and Phillip H. Losey, "The Election and Administration of Governor Simeon Willis, 1943-1947" (M.A. thesis, Eastern Kentucky University, 1978), as well as Lowell H. Harrison, ed., *Kentucky's Governors, 1792-1985* (1985); and John E. Kleber, editor in chief, *The Kentucky Encyclopedia* (1992). On specific elections, see Olivia M. Frederick, "Kentucky's 1935 Gubernatorial Election" (M.A. thesis, University of Louisville, 1967); Robert J. Leupold, "The Kentucky WPA: Relief and Politics, May-November, 1935," *FCHQ* 49 (1975): 152-68; William Clark Spragens, "The 1947 Kentucky Gubernatorial Election" (M.A. thesis, University of Kentucky, 1952); and Glenn Finch, "The Election of United States Senators in Kentucky: The Barkley Period," *FCHQ* 45 (1971): 286-304.

The political actions regarding foreign affairs are presented in Heinz H. Seelbach, "The Attitude of Kentucky Congressmen toward Foreign Relations from 1935 to Pearl Harbor" (M.A. thesis, University of Kentucky, 1943), but a full history of the state's role in what followed is needed. The best short comprehensive overview is Kentucky Historical Society, *"Praise the Lord and Pass the Ammunition!": Kentuckians in World War II* (1994). On the military side, see Richard G. Stone Jr., *Kentucky Fighting Men, 1861-1945* (1982), for broad coverage; for an excellent and poignant case study, see James Russell Harris, "The Harrodsburg Tankers: Bataan, Prison, and the Bonds of Community," *Register* 86 (1988): 230-77. Among the several memoirs and collected letters, good sources include Nancy Disher Baird, "'To Lend You My Eyes': The World War II Letters of Special Services Officer Harry Jackson," *Register* 88 (1990): 287-317; Philip Ardery, *Bomber Pilot* (1978); and Frank F. Mathias, *G.I. Jive: An Army Bandsman in World War II* (1982). The costs of conflict can be found in *World War II Honor List of Dead and Missing: State of Kentucky* (1946).

A brief look at the commonwealth's wartime role appears in Mary Jean Kinsman, "The Kentucky Home Front: World War II," *FCHQ* 68 (1994): 365-78, while more specific topics are treated in James D. Cockrum, "Owensboro Goes to War," *Daviess County Historical Quarterly* 2 (1984): 2-9; and Charles E. Parrish, "The Louisville Engineer District," in *Builders and Fighters: U.S. Army Engineers in World War II,* edited by Barry W. Fowle (1992). The out-migration process is examined well in Olaf F. Larson, "Wartime Migration and the Manpower Reserve on Farms in Eastern Kentucky," *Rural Sociology* 8 (1943): 148-60; and Wayne T. Gray, "Population Movements in the Kentucky Mountains," *Rural Sociology* 10 (1945): 380-86. A full study of the Kentucky home front remains much needed.

Chapter 23. Education and Equality, 1865-1995

The starting places for any history of education in Kentucky are the *Reports* of the superintendent of public instruction, which contain a wealth of primary material. Using those as the core, several general studies have been written, and in contrast to many areas of the commonwealth's history, the field boasts a good secondary literature. Barksdale Ham-

lett, in *History of Education in Kentucky* (1914), summarized those reports, while the Kentucky Education Commission's *Public Education in Kentucky* (1921) and the chapter on schools in the National Child Labor Committee's *Child Welfare in Kentucky* (1919) gave good summaries of the situation at the time they were published. The Kentucky Department of Education updated Hamlett's work under the title *History of Education in Kentucky, 1915-1940* (1940). Then two more descriptive and analytic works followed in the 1940s: Moses E. Ligon, *A History of Public Education in Kentucky* (1942); and Frank L. McVey, *The Gates Open Slowly: A History of Education in Kentucky* (1949). C.W. Hackensmith's *Out of Time and Tide: The Evolution of Education in Kentucky* followed in 1970. On the dynamics of the schoolroom, see Ellis Hartford, *The Little White Schoolhouse* (1977), and for a collection of articles on education, see Edwin A. Doyle, Ruby Layson, and Anne Armstrong Thompson, eds., *From the Fort to the Future: Educating the Children of Kentucky* (1987). A good brief introduction to the whole issue is Thomas D. Clark's "Kentucky Education through Two Centuries of Political and Social Change," *Register* 83 (1985): 173-201.

More narrowly based studies, both by chronology and by subject, include chapters in Hambleton Tapp and James C. Klotter, *Kentucky: Decades of Discord, 1865-1900* (1977); and James C. Klotter, *Kentucky: Portrait in Paradox, 1900-1950* (1996). Also helpful are Fred A. Engle Jr., "The Superintendents and the Issues: A Study of the Superintendents of Public Instruction in Kentucky, 1891-1943" (Ed.D. diss., University of Kentucky, 1966); Louise Combs and Kern Alexander, "The Development of the Kentucky State Department of Education" (unpublished manuscript); and Terry L. Birdwhistell, "Divided We Fall: State College and the Normal School Movement in Kentucky, 1880-1910," *Register* 88 (1990): 431-56. On the 1990 Education Reform Act specifically, see the Kentucky Legislative Research Commission, *A Guide to the Kentucky Reform Act of 1990* (1990); Paul D.

Blanchard, "Education Reform and Executive-Legislative Relations in Kentucky," *Journal of Kentucky Studies* 10 (1993): 66-74; and Angela Jones, "KERA," *Odyssey* 13 (1995): 12-16.

The moonlight schools of Cora Wilson Stewart have attracted much scholarly interest. Examinations of Stewart's work include Willie E. Nelms Jr., "Cora Wilson Stewart and the Crusade against Illiteracy in Kentucky," *Register* 74 (1976): 10-29; 82 (1984): 151-69; and Florence Estes, "Cora Wilson Stewart and the Moonlight Schools of Kentucky, 1911-1920: A Case Study in the Rhetorical Uses of Literacy" (Ed.D. diss., University of Kentucky, 1988). Another form of education, the settlement schools—particularly in eastern Kentucky—have generated some scholarly debate as well as a fair amount of study. An early examination came in Ellen C. Semple, "A New Departure in Social Settlements," *Annals of the American Academy of Political and Social Science* 15 (1900): 157-60. Various limited works followed over the years. The arguments took new form with the critical focus on Hindman in David E. Whisnant, *All That Is Native and Fine: The Politics of Culture in an American Region* (1983). Several writers took issue with Whisnant's generalizations and challenged him: see Nancy K. Forderhase, "Eve Returns to the Garden: Women Reformers in Appalachian Kentucky in the Early Twentieth Century," *Register* 85 (1987): 237-61; and P. David Searles, *A College for Appalachia: Alice Lloyd on Caney Creek* (1995). It would be welcome for such debate to occur in the study of education of women in the state, but the literature on that subject is brief. Jo Della Alband's "A History of the Education of Women in Kentucky" (M.A. thesis, University of Kentucky, 1934), basically describes the various institutions. A start on the kind of studies needed is Terry L. Birdwhistell, "An Educated Difference: Women at the University of Kentucky through the Second World War" (Ed.D. diss., University of Kentucky, 1994).

Blacks often appeared almost as an afterthought in the early histories of Kentucky education, but slowly studies began to look at the so-called separate but equal system. The U.S. Department of the Interior's *Negro Education,* 2 vols. (1917), gave a county-by-county breakdown, but more analysis came in Myrtle R. Phillips, "The Origin, Development, and Present Status of Public Secondary Education for Negroes in Kentucky," *Journal of Negro Education* 1 (1932): 414-23; Leonard E. Meece, "Negro Education in Kentucky," *Bulletin of the Bureau of School Service* (University of Kentucky) 10 (1938): 1-180; Howard W. Beers and Catherine P. Heflin, "The Negro Population of Kentucky," *Kentucky Agricultural Experiment Station Bulletin 481* (1946); Thomas C. Venable, "A History of Negro Education in Kentucky" (Ph.D. diss., George Peabody College, 1953); and Truman M. Pierce et al., *White and Negro Schools in the South* (1955). An overview by Clarence L. Timberlake ("The Early Struggle for Education of the Blacks of the Commonwealth of Kentucky," *Register* 71 [1973]: 225-52) set the stage for the fine in-depth study presented in Marion B. Lucas and George C. Wright, *A History of Blacks in Kentucky,* 2 vols. (1992). Good studies of more limited focus include William H. Fouse, "Educational History of the Negroes of Lexington, Kentucky" (M.A. thesis, University of Cincinnati, 1937); Lee A. Dew, "*Claybrook v. Owensboro:* An Early Victory for Equal Education in Kentucky," *Daviess County Historical Quarterly* 8 (1990): 3-15; George C. Wright, "The Founding of Lincoln Institute," *FCHQ* 49 (1975): 57-70; J. Morgan Kousser, "Making Separate Equal: The Integration of Black and White School Funds in Kentucky, 1882," *Journal of Interdisciplinary History* 20 (1980): 399-428; and James Blaine Hudson III, "The History of Louisville Municipal College" (Ed.D. diss., University of Kentucky, 1981). Placing the Kentucky story in context can be done through use of James D. Anderson, *The Education of Blacks in the South, 1860-1935* (1988).

Integration came to Kentucky schools again in the 1950s, but the struggle for equal rights had been going on for many decades before that. Successful efforts were noted, for instance, in Marjorie Norris, "An Early Instance of Nonviolence: The

Louisville Demonstrations of 1870-71," *JSH* 32 (1966): 487-504; Patrick S. McElhone, "The Civil Rights Activities of the Louisville Branch of the National Association for the Advancement of Colored People, 1914-1960" (M.A. thesis, University of Louisville, 1976); George C. Wright, "The NAACP and Residential Segregation in Louisville, Kentucky, 1914-1917," *Register* 78 (1980): 39-54; and idem, "Desegregation of Public Accommodations in Louisville," in *Southern Businessmen and Desegregation*, edited by Elizabeth Jacoway and David R. Colburn (1982). The story of Kentuckians' roles in the integration of baseball can be followed in Roger Kahn, *The Boys of Summer* (1972); Jules Tygiel, *Baseball's Great Experiment* (1983); and William J. Marshall, "A.B. Chandler As Baseball Commissioner, 1945-51: An Overview," *Register* 82 (1984): 358-88.

Integration took different forms across the state. The often-nonreported situation regarding integration in Lexington can be followed, for example, in Gerald L. Smith's "Blacks in Lexington, Kentucky: The Struggle for Civil Rights, 1945-1980" (M.A. thesis, University of Kentucky, 1983); while the Louisville response can be garnered from Myrtle B. Crawford, "Some Aspects of Preparation for Desegregation in the Public Schools of Louisville," *Negro History Bulletin* 20 (1957): 79-82; Omer Carmichael, "A Workable Integration Plan," *Saturday Review of Literature* (May 23, 1959): 17; and idem, *The Louisville Story* (1957). An excellent study of the instance when troops were needed to keep the peace is Bonnie J. Burns, "The Sturgis Incident— Desegregation of Public Schools in Union County, Kentucky" (M.A. thesis, Murray State University, 1969), while a more peaceful western Kentucky integration is outlined in Lisa Bell, "Achieving Equality: Desegregation of the Owensboro Schools, 1955-1969," *Daviess County Historical Quarterly* 7 (1989): 26-33. The later racial problems in Louisville are covered in John M. Thompson, "School Desegregation in Jefferson County, Kentucky, 1954-1975" (Ed.D. diss., University of Kentucky, 1976); and Kenneth H. Williams, "'Oh Baby . . . It's Really Happening': The Louisville Race Riot of 1968," *Kentucky History Journal* 3 (1988): 48-64. Advances and continuing problems were presented every year after 1961 in the very useful *Report of the Kentucky Commission on Human Rights.*

Individuals played key roles in bringing about civil rights. Chief Justice Frederick Vinson has been studied in some detail, although more work on his non-Court career would be welcome. See John Henry Hatcher, "Fred Vinson, Congressman from Kentucky: A Political Biography, 1890-1938" (Ph.D. diss., University of Cincinnati, 1967); John P. Frank, "Fred Vinson and the Chief Justiceship," *University of Chicago Law Review* 21 (1954): 212-46; James Bolner, "Fred M. Vinson, 1890-1938," *Register* 63 (1968): 3-23; idem, "Mr. Chief Justice Fred M. Vinson and Racial Discrimination," *Register* 64 (1966): 29-43; W.B. Johnson, "The Vinson Court and Racial Segregation, 1946-1953," *JNH* 63 (1978): 220-30; and Richard Kirkendall, "Fred M. Vinson," in *The Justices of the United States Supreme Court, 1789-1969*, edited by Leon Friedman and Fred L. Israel, 4 vols. (1969). On the black leadership, see such autobiographical-style works as Wade Hall, *The Rest of the Dream: The Black Odyssey of Lyman Johnson* (1988), and Georgia Davis Powers, *I Shared the Dream* (1995); biographical studies such as Nancy J. Weiss, *Whitney M. Young, Jr., and the Struggle for Civil Rights* (1990), and Gerald L. Smith, *A Black Educator in the Segregated South: Kentucky's Rufus B. Atwood* (1994); and broader works such as Alice Allison Dunnigan, *The Fascinating Story of Black Kentuckians: Their Heritage and Traditions* (1982), and Kentucky Commission on Human Rights, *Kentucky's Black Heritage* (1971).

A full history of higher education in the commonwealth and the institutions that constitute it is needed, but fortunately, many fine college and university histories have been written. See, for example, James F. Hopkins, *The University of Kentucky: Origins and Early Years* (1951); Charles G. Talbert, *The University of Kentucky: The Maturing Years* (1965); Dwayne Cox, "A History of the University of Louisville" (Ph.D. diss., University of Kentucky, 1984); Lowell H. Harrison, *Western Kentucky Uni-*

versity (1987); John A. Hardin, *Onward and Upward: A Centennial History of Kentucky State University, 1886-1986* (1987); Harry E. Rose, "The Historical Development of a State College: Morehead Kentucky State College, 1887-1964" (Ed.D. diss., University of Cincinnati, 1965); J.T. Dorris, ed., *Five Decades of Progress: Eastern Kentucky State College, 1906-1956* (1957); and *Eastern Kentucky University Then and Now* (1992). There are many good studies of private schools as well, including but not limited to the following: Elisabeth S. Peck and Emily Ann Smith, *Berea's First 125 Years, 1855-1980* (1955), revised in 1982; John D. Wright Jr., *Transylvania: Tutor to the West* (1975); Lee A. Dew and Richard A. Weiss, *In Pursuit of the Dream: A History of Kentucky Wesleyan College* (1992); Robert Snyder, *A History of Georgetown College* (1979); and Hardin Craig, *Centre College of Kentucky: A Tradition and an Opportunity* (1967). See also individual entries in John E. Kleber, editor in chief, *The Kentucky Encyclopedia* (1992). For an early survey of the state's schools, see Alvin F. Lewis, *A History of Higher Education in Kentucky* (1899), and for the status at the mid–twentieth century, see Kentucky Legislative Research Commission, *Public Higher Education in Kentucky*, Research Publication no. 25, o.s. (1951).

Chapter 24. A Half Century of Kentucky Politics

A comprehensive study of the Kentucky political world of the half century after World War II has not yet been written. As a result, often the best sources remain the state newspapers, the national magazines, collected interviews, and the Kentucky *Acts of the General Assembly*. Most of the studies covering the 1940s and 1950s focus on individuals, with some broader scope provided by John Ed Pearce, *Divide and Dissent: Kentucky Politics, 1930-1963* (1987); and Lowell H. Harrison, ed., *Kentucky's Governors, 1792-1985* (1985). On the individual administrations, see Thomas H. Syvertsen, "Earle Chester Clements and the Democratic Party, 1920-1950" (Ph.D. diss., University of Kentucky, 1982); John E. Kleber, ed., *The Papers of Governor Lawrence W. Wetherby, 1950-1955* (1983); John E. Kleber, "As

Luck Would Have It: An Overview of Lawrence W. Wetherby As Governor, 1950-1955," *Register* 84 (1986): 397-421; George W. Robinson, ed., *The Public Papers of Governor Bert Combs, 1959-1963* (1979); and idem, ed., *Bert Combs, the Politician: An Oral History* (1991). The 1948 election is covered in Robert Bendiner, "Tour of the Border States: Kentucky," *Nation* (Oct. 16, 1948): 424-25; and Philip A. Grant Jr., "The Presidential Election of 1948 in Kentucky," *Journal of Kentucky Studies* 6 (1989): 86-91. Jasper B. Shannon analyzes the situation four years later in *Presidential Politics in Kentucky, 1952* (1954) and examines the overall picture in "The Political Process in Kentucky," *Kentucky Law Journal* 45 (1957): 395-447. Wilson W. Wyatt Sr. told his story in his autobiography, *Whistle Stops: Adventures in Public Life* (1985). On Chandler, see the sources cited under chapter 22, plus Robert L. Riggs, "Happy Chandler Rides Again," *Saturday Evening Post* (Oct. 15, 1955): 19-21, 155-58; "Happy Paws the Public," *Life* (Aug. 8, 1955): 36-37; and Gladys M. Kammerer, "Kentucky's All Pervasive Spoils Politics," *Good Government* 75 (1958): 32-37. Louis C. Kesselman's "Negro Voting in a Border Community: Louisville, Kentucky," *JNH* 26 (1957): 273-80, is one of the few studies of changing voter patterns in the era, while Phyllis C. Soloman, "The 1960 Presidential Election in Kentucky" (M.A. thesis, University of Louisville, 1968), is a good case study of one election. For a comprehensive regional study, see Numan V. Bartley, *The New South, 1945-1980* (1995).

On the Republican side, an overview is provided in Walter A. Baker's "The GOP in Kentucky: A History of the Kentucky Republican Party, 1919-1956" (B.A. thesis, Harvard College, 1958); and, on Senate races, in Glenn Finch, "The Election of United States Senators in Kentucky: The Cooper Period," *FCHQ* 46 (1972): 161-78. The two leaders of the party's successes have been studied in some depth, but more work is still needed. An excellent introduction to one of those key leaders is Bill Cooper, "John Sherman Cooper: A Senator and His Constituents," *Register* 84 (1986): 192-210. Other good works include Robert Schulman, *John*

Sherman Cooper: The Global Kentuckian (1976); Richard C. Smoot, "John Sherman Cooper: The Paradox of a Liberal Republican in Kentucky Politics" (Ph.D. diss., University of Kentucky, 1988); and idem, "John Sherman Cooper: The Early Years, 1901-27," *Register* 93 (1995): 133-58. On Cooper's fellow senator, see Sara J. Smiley, "The Political Career of Thruston B. Morton" (Ph.D. diss., University of Kentucky, 1975); and Byron Hulsey, "Partisanship and the National Interest: Thruston Morton, Lyndon Johnson, and the Vietnam War," *Woodberry Forest Magazine and Journal* 34 (1994): 28-30.

The 1960s saw the War on Poverty and the Vietnam War both break out in full force. The state's role in the overseas conflict has not been examined in depth, but a fine case study of tragedy is Anthony B. McIntire, "The Kentucky National Guard in Vietnam: The Story of Bardstown's Battery C at War," *Register* 90 (1992): 140-64. See also Kentucky's *Report of the Adjutant General;* and Jim Wilson, *The Sons of Bardstown: 25 Years of Vietnam in an American Town* (1994). On the migration patterns resulting from the problems of poverty, see George E. Harris, "The Drain of Talent Out of Ohio and Kentucky" (M.A. thesis, Kent State University, 1956); Harry K. Schwarzweller, James S. Brown, and J.J. Mangalam, *Mountain Families in Transition* (1971); William W. Philliber and Clyde B. McCoy, eds., *The Invisible Minority: Urban Appalachians* (1981); and Stephen E. White, "America's Soweto: Population Distribution in Appalachian Kentucky, 1940-1986," *Appalachian Journal* 16 (1989): 350-60. The situation in the region itself is discussed in John C. Wells Jr., "Poverty amidst Riches: Why People Are Poor in Appalachia" (Ph.D. diss., Rutgers University, 1977); "Appalachia As a Developing Nation," *Business Week* (July 18, 1970): 46-54; and Appalachian Land Ownership Task Force, *Who Owns Appalachia?* (1983). Federal efforts to address the situation are well surveyed in John M. Glen, "The War on Poverty in Appalachia," *Register* 87 (1989): 40-57. See also David E. Whisnant, *Modernizing the Mountaineer: People, Power, and Planning in Appalachia* (1980).

Not a great deal of historical analysis has appeared in books and articles on Kentucky politics covering the period since the mid-1960s. Most work has come from political scientists, and their efforts provide a good framework for further study: Malcolm E. Jewell and E.W. Cunningham, *Kentucky Politics* (1968); Joel Goldstein, ed., *Kentucky Government and Politics* (1984); Paul D. Blanchard, *Kentucky State and Local Government* (1987); Malcolm E. Jewell and Penny M. Miller, *The Kentucky Legislature: Two Decades of Change* (1988); Penny M. Miller and Malcolm E. Jewell, *Political Parties and Primaries in Kentucky* (1990); and the broad-based study Penny M. Miller, *Kentucky Politics and Government* (1994). See also the survey of a journalist: Neal R. Pierce, *The Border South States* (1975).

On specific administrations, good starting points are Kenneth E. Harrell, ed., *The Public Papers of Edward T. Breathitt, 1963-1967* (1984); Robert F. Sexton, ed., *The Public Papers of Louie B. Nunn, 1967-1971* (1975); W. Landis Jones, ed., *The Public Papers of Wendell H. Ford, 1971-1974* (1978); and Wallace G. Wilkinson's autobiographical *You Can't Do That, Governor!* (1995). On factors leading to Martha Layne Collins's win, see Liz Demoran, "We Made History, Kentucky," *Kentucky Alumnus* 53 (1983-84): 7. On the state legislature, see Kwang S. Shin and John S. Jackson III, "Membership Turnover in the U.S. State Legislatures: 1931-1976," *Legislative Studies Quarterly* 4 (1979): 95-104; Malcolm E. Jewell and Penny M. Miller, *The Kentucky Legislature: Two Decades of Change* (1988); A Kentucky Legislator, "How an Election Was Bought and Sold," *Harper's Magazine* (1960): 33-38. Also consult the *Legislative Record* and the Kentucky *House Journal* and *Senate Journal.* A study of the state judiciary remains much needed.

Chapter 25. New Challenges, Old Traditions

A variety of sources were used in preparing this chapter, including newspapers, collected interviews, printed recollections, manuscript collections, and a wide range of official reports. Feature writers and columnists of the *Louisville Courier-Journal,* particularly when it published its own *Sunday Magazine,* provided key items, as did writers in the *Lexington Herald-Leader.* Other, smaller papers have been useful as well.

Two of the most recognizable Kentuckians are two of the most different: Harland Sanders and Muhammad Ali. On Sanders, see John Ed Pearce, *The Colonel* (1982); on Ali, see, for example, his autobiography, *The Greatest* (1975); Robert Hoskins, *Muhammad Ali* (1980); and John Egerton, "Heritage of a Heavyweight: The Ancestry of Muhammad Ali," in *Shades of Gray: Dispatches from the Modern South* (1991). On another of the state's images—basketball—the literature is voluminous and ranges from the truly awful to the awfully good. Catching the flavor of the high school sport is Dave Kindred, *Basketball: The Dream Game in Kentucky* (1976), while Mike Embry, in "Kentuckians in the Halls of Fame," *Kentucky Living* 46 (1992): 12-16, looks at those who gained national acclaim. Virtually every year another work appears on University of Kentucky basketball, but three good introductions to the pre-1980 era are Bert Nelli, *The Winning Tradition* (1984); Harry Lancaster, *Adolph Rupp As I Knew Him* (1979); and Russell Rice, *Adolph Rupp* (1994). On Diddle, see C. Harvey Gardiner, *Coach Diddle, Mister Diddle: Motivator of Men* (1984).

On demographics, see Thomas R. Ford, *Health and Demography in Kentucky* (1964), plus the long-term studies noted below. On the role of women, see "The Legal Status of Women in the United States of America, January 1, 1938, Report for Kentucky," *Bulletin of the Women's Bureau* (1938); U.S. Department of Labor, *Women Workers in Kentucky, 1960* (1960); Annie Harrison, comp., *Women in Kentucky State Government, 1940-1980* (1981); and Margaret Ripley Wolfe, "Fallen Leaves and Missing Pages: Women in Kentucky History," *Register* 90 (1992): 64-89. An autobiography of one woman leader is Emma Guy Cromwell, *Woman in Politics* (1939). The statistics on violence given in the text come from the FBI *Uniform Crime Reports* and the *Bulletin of the State Board of Health in Kentucky* (later *Kentucky Vital Statistics Report*), and a good discussion of the issue appears in Raymond D. Gastil, "Homicide and a Regional Culture of Violence," *American Sociological Review* 36 (1971): 412-26. The environmental situation is outlined in Environmental Quality Commission, *State of Kentucky's Environment: 1994* (1995), while the issue of suburbanization at the national level is discussed in Kenneth T. Jackson, *Crabgrass Frontier: The Suburbanization of the United States* (1985).

Studies of Kentucky's present status and future need have appeared periodically. Generally they have provided much information on current affairs, with more limited success as guideposts to development. Earlier works include *The Government of Kentucky: Report of the Efficiency Commission of Kentucky,* 2 vols. (1924); Howard W. Beers, ed., *Kentucky: Designs for Her Future* (1945); Postwar Planning Commission of Kentucky, *Final Report* (1945); Committee for Kentucky, *Reports* (1943-50); and Harry W. Schecter, *Kentucky on the March* (1949). A more systematic recent approach has been the creation of the Kentucky Long-Term Policy Research Center, which publishes the newsletter *Foresight,* as well as book-length works, including the very useful *The Context of Change: Trends, Innovations, and Forces Affecting Kentucky's Future* (1994).

Continuity and a sense of place play roles as important in Kentucky as change. A good article on those themes is Arthur P. Dudden, "Nostalgia and the Americans," *Journal of the History of Ideas* 22 (1961): 515-30, while a fine case study is John Egerton, *Generations: An American Family* (1983). But more important are the voices of the people themselves, as presented in letters, memories, memoirs, and interviews. They best tell what Kentucky is and what it means to them.

Acknowledgments

All who should be thanked cannot be. Space, or even memory, does not allow that. The authors, for instance, owe a great debt to all those who have written earlier on the state's history, for they made our tasks—and our understanding—much easier. Inclusion of our predecessors' works in the Selected Bibliography constitutes only a partial recognition, and even then, much is omitted. There are many thanks to be given.

Restricting ourselves to this book alone, while recognizing that those with whom we have worked all our lives have had an important influence on what is written herein, we wish to offer some particular thanks.

Lowell H. Harrison, Chapters 1-14

Since I have devoted most of my adult years to researching and writing Kentucky history, I owe long-term debts of gratitude and thanks to many historical organizations and to innumerable individuals who have assisted me along the way. Acknowledgments have been made in previous publications, but I want to repeat my sincere thanks here. During the research for this book, I revisited many of the historical organizations. While the personnel have changed with the passage of time, the willingness and desire to help researchers have remained. My special thanks go to the Kentucky Library at Western Kentucky University and its staff. Nancy Disher Baird, Jonathan D. Jeffrey, and Constance A. Mills provided me with a work area and gave me the benefit of their extensive knowledge of Kentucky sources and their critical reading of the manuscript. I am also grateful for the helpful comments and suggestions of Carol Crowe-Carraco and the two anonymous readers of The University Press of Kentucky. Special thanks go to Neal O. Hammon, who loves maps. Graduate students John Clay and Beth Gipson provided welcome research assistance. Elizabeth Jensen always knew the right key to strike as she transferred my typescript to the computer. The Department of History, Western Kentucky University, has been generous in its support of a former member.

James C. Klotter, Chapters 15-25

I wish to acknowledge the invaluable support provided over the years by the staff of the Kentucky Historical Society Library, in particular Anne J. McDonnell, Ron D. Bryant, and Mary Winter, and by Kim Lady Smith and the Kentucky Oral History Commission. Research aid was provided by Cheryl Conover, Dave Withers, and Paul Newman. Additional support was given by Helen Prewitt. At Special Collections, University of Kentucky Library, William C. Marshall's staff has been especially supportive, as have, indeed, those working with the public at virtually all the research institutions across the state, notably those aiding William J. Morison at the University of Louisville, Mark Wetherington at The Filson Club Historical Society, Charles C. Hay III at Eastern Kentucky University, Gerald F. Roberts at Berea College, Riley Handy at the Kentucky Library at Western Kentucky University, and Keith Heim at Murray State University. Aiding in the procurement of photographs were Mary Jean Kinsman of the Filson Club, B.J. Gooch of Transylvania University, Nancy Baird of Western Kentucky University, Bill Carner of the University of Louisville, Wade Hall of Bellarmine University, Pam Porter of the University of Kentucky, Holly Skaggs of the Louisville AAA Club, James Seacat of Actors Theatre of Louisville, Christopher Waldrep of Eastern Illinois University, and Nathan Pritchard of the Kentucky Historical Society. I am also grateful to the personnel at the Louisville Free Public Library, the Lexington Library, the Kenton County Public Library, the Owensboro Public Library, the Keeneland Library, as well as the Library of Congress, the National Archives, the University of Virginia, the Virginia Historical Society, the University of North Carolina at Chapel Hill, Duke University, West Virginia University, the University of Chicago, and the State Historical Society of Wisconsin.

Special recognition must be given to those who read my early drafts and whose comments made the final version much better. Thomas H. Appleton Jr., Walter Baker, Melba Porter Hay, Art Jester, John David Smith, and two good evaluators for The University Press of Kentucky read all or part of my manuscript carefully and critically. As one of the last authors who still write manuscripts by hand, I wish also to thank the courageous Glenda Harned for taking my prose and putting it into meaningful form.

Both authors wish to note what a special debt we owe to Thomas D. Clark, for he has done more to advance the cause of history in Kentucky than any other person. His work has made the study of the state's past more accessible and much more enjoyable to all who wish to examine it. Our dedication of this book to him expresses only a part of our gratitude for all he has done so well for so long.

Finally, we owe a particular recognition to our wives, Elaine M. Harrison and Freda Campbell Klotter, for they are vitally involved in all we do. Without them this would be a poorer book, and we poorer people. To them and to all who were a part of this project we offer our heartfelt thanks, for everything.

Index

119-21; and railroads, 132; on slavery, 76;
statesmanship of, 96-97; Union sentiments
of, 181-82; as war hawk, 89-90; and War of
1812, 91, 92-93
Clay, James B., 137
Clay, Laura, 287-88
Clay, Lucretia Hart, 89-90
Clay, Mary, 288
Clay, Mary Jane Warfield, 288
Clay, Sallie, 288
Clay, Thomas, 79
Clay County, 139, 254
Clements, Earle C., 385, 400-402, 404,
405, 407, 408-9
Cleveland, Grover, 262, 267
Clifty area, 23
Clinch River, 17
Clinch Valley, 28
Clinkenbeard, William, 34
Clinton, Bill, 423
Clooney, Rosemary, 341, 441
clothing, 229, 371
Clugston, W.G., 349
Cluke, Roy S., 204
coal. *See also* strip mining; deaths in mines, 309t;
discovery of, 16; and employment (1950-
1965), 367t; mining mechanization,
367, 409; and organized labor, 365-67;
production of, 142, 307-11; severance tax
on, 415; stagnation of mining, 409-10;
tons mined (1870-1990), 311t
Coal Wars, 365-67
Cobb, Alfred Leland, 329
Cobb, Irvin S., 345, 426
Cobb, Ty, 345
Cocke, William, 27, 31
Cockrell, Jim, 255
Cockrell, Tom, 255
Code of Fair Practices, 390
code of honor, 255-56
Coke, F. Van Deren, 336
Coleman, J. Winston "Squire," Jr., 332
Coleman, Richard, 251
colleges and universities, 151-53, 393-99
Collins, Floyd, 345-46

Collins, Lewis, 158
Collins, Martha Layne, 392, 417,
418-20, 423, 433
Collins, Richard H., 158, 332
colonization, of freed slaves, 120, 176
Colored Teachers State Association, 380
Columbus (Ky.) Dispatch, 293
Combs, Bert T.: and Breathitt, 411; and Clements,
409; death of, 442; on education, 392; as
governor, 390; gubernatorial races of,
403, 407
Combs, Earle B., 345
Combs, Leslie, 184
Combs, Sara, 423, 433
commerce, 142-43, 207-8, 300-302
Commonwealth of Kentucky, naming of, 63
communications, mass, 345-46
community colleges, 396. *See also* colleges and
universities; junior colleges
Compromise of 1850, 171, 182
Confederate Kentucky, 192-94, 201,
209, 210
Confederate States of America, 193, 201, 203,
205-6, 207, 210
Conn, Notley, 59
Connelley, William E., 332
Connolly, John, 19, 100-101
Conrad, William, 341
conservatism, 220
Conservative Party, 239. *See also* Democratic Party
Conservative Union Party, 240. *See also*
Democratic Party
Conspiracy. *See* Burr Conspiracy, Spanish
conspiracy
Constitution, of Kentucky: amendments to,
119, 264-65; Bill of Rights, 265;
delegates to convention, 77; disputes
over, 75-77; drafting of, 61-63;
on education, 64, 118; government
organization by, 265; models for, 63;
provisions of, 63-64; revision of 1799,
77-79; revision of 1850, 117-19;
revision
Constitution, of Kentucky of 1889, 264-65; on
slavery, 64, 77, 117-18

517

on Kentucky Resolutions, 81; on land laws, 69; on slavery, 64

Nicholas, S.S., 188

Nicholas, Wilson Cary, 82

Nichols, Bobby, 431

Night Riders, 280-81

Niles, John Jacob, 337

Nixon, Richard M., 409, 414, 415

Noe, James T. Cotton, 334

Nonimportation Act of 1833, 98, 118, 177

Non-Intercourse Act of 1809, 89

normal schools, 382

Norman, Gurney, 330

Norman, Marsha, 340

North Carolina, border resolutions with, 32

Northern Kentucky University, 396, 414

Northington, Nat, 390

Northwest Territory, 20, 70-71

Nunn, Lee, 411

Nunn, Louie B., 397, 400, 411, 413-14, 417

Oates, Warren, 341

Obenchain, Eliza Calvert, 287, 324

Oconostota (Cherokee chief), 6, 26

Ogden, Benjamin, 154

O'Hara, Theodore, 116, 158

Ohio, border resolution with, 21

Ohio Falls Express, 247

Ohio Land Company, 16-17

Ohio River: as boundary, 21; as immigration route, 51; legal use of, 61; steamboats on, 129-30; Warrior's Path to, 125

oil production, 142, 311

Old Court-New Court controversy, 111, 266

Olmsted, Frederick Law, 303

Order of Good Templars, 278-79

O'Rear, Edward C., 284, 285

organized labor, 258, 266, 365-67

Otey, J.A., 209

Ottawa Indians, 18

Otter Creek, 27

outlaws, raids on travelers, 52

Owen, David Dale, 122, 142

Owensboro, 236, 302, 434

Owensboro Messenger and Inquirer, 321

Owsley, William, 110, 111, 114-15, 116, 147

Paducah, 192; black migration to, 236; in Civil War, 203; crime rate in, 434; disease in 1900, 259; growth of, 302

Paducah Sun-Democrat, 320

Page, Greg, 431

Paine, E.A., 206-7

Paine, Thomas, 56, 155

Pakenham, Edward, 94

Paleo-Indian period, 6

Palmer, John M., 205, 206, 235, 268

Palmer passes, 235

Panic of 1819, 97, 109, 126

Panic of 1837, 114, 127, 131-32

paper industry, 140-41

pari-mutuel wagering, 353-54, 356

Paris, Kentucky, 103

Paris True Kentuckian, 244

Parker, Alton B., 277

park system, 423

Parrish, Charles H., Sr., 395

patent medicines, 259

Patrick, John (Groggan), 340

patronage, political, 250, 276, 354

Patrons of Husbandry, 257. *See also* Grange

Patterson, James K., 395

Patterson, Robert, 99

Patton, B.W., 111

Patton, Matthew, 135

Patton, Paul E., 424

Peace Convention, 185-86

Pearce, John Ed, 320, 404, 442

Peden, Katherine, 414

Peers, Benjamin O., 149

penal codes, 83

penal reform, 259-61, 354

penitentiaries, 83, 123, 260-61, 369. *See also* prisons

Penn, Shadrach, 159

Pennick, Mary Frances, 338

Pennyroyal region, 23

Perkins, Carl D., 390, 410, 419

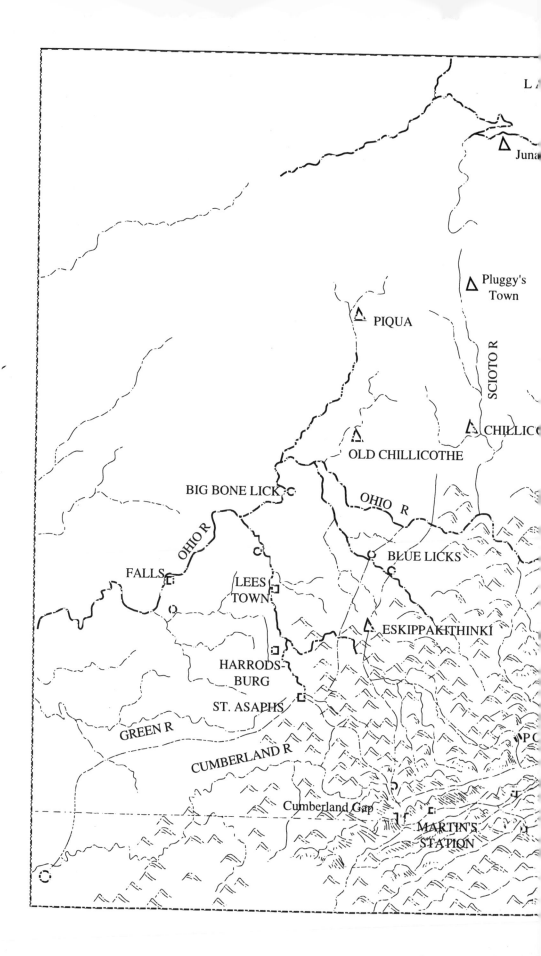